Fodor's Third Edition

India

WATERFORD CITY LIBRARY
2366592
L B C 929544
E24.47

The complete guide, thoroughly up-to-date

Packed with details that will make your trip

The must-see sights, off and on the beaten path

What to see, what to skip

Mix-and-match vacation itineraries

City strolls, countryside adventures

Smart lodging and dining options

Essential local dos and taboos

Transportation tips, distances and directions

Key contacts, savvy travel tips

When to go, what to pack

Clear, accurate, easy-to-use maps

Fodor's India

EDITOR: Christine Cipriani

Editorial Contributors: Michael W. Bollom, Vaihayasi Pande Daniel, Manish Jain, Vidhi Jain, Jayanth Kodkani, John Larson, Andy McCord, Shanti Menon, David Quegg, Modhurima Sinha, R. Edwin Sudhir
Editorial Production: Brian Vitunic
Maps: David Lindroth, *cartographer;* Rebecca Baer, Robert Blake, *map editors*
Design: Fabrizio La Rocca, *creative director;* Guido Caroti, *art director;* Jolie Novak, *photo editor*
Cover Design: Pentagram
Production/Manufacturing: Bob Shields
Cover Photograph: Lindsay Hebberd/Woodfin Camp

Copyright

Copyright © 2000 by Fodor's Travel Publications

Fodor's is a registered trademark of Random House, Inc.

All rights reserved under International and Pan-American Copyright Conventions. Published in the United States by Fodor's Travel Publications, a division of Random House, Inc., New York, and simultaneously in Canada by Random House of Canada Limited, Toronto. Distributed by Random House, Inc., New York.

No maps, illustrations, or other portions of this book may be reproduced in any form without written permission from the publisher.

Third Edition

ISBN 0-679-00410-6

ISSN 1079-6444

Special Sales

Fodor's Travel Publications are available at special discounts for bulk purchases for sales promotions or premiums. Special editions, including personalized covers, excerpts of existing guides, and corporate imprints, can be created in large quantities for special needs. For more information, contact your local bookseller or write to Special Markets, Fodor's Travel Publications, 201 East 50th Street, New York, NY 10022. Inquiries from Canada should be directed to your local Canadian bookseller or sent to Random House of Canada, Ltd., Marketing Department, 2775 Matheson Boulevard East, Mississauga, Ontario L4W 4P7. Inquiries from the United Kingdom should be sent to Fodor's Travel Publications, 20 Vauxhall Bridge Road, London SW1V 2SA, England.

PRINTED IN THE UNITED STATES OF AMERICA

10 9 8 7 6 5 4 3 2 1

Important Tip

Although all prices, opening times, and other details in this book are based on information supplied to us at press time, changes occur all the time in the travel world, and Fodor's cannot accept responsibility for facts that become outdated or for inadvertent errors or omissions. So **always confirm information when it matters,** especially if you're making a detour to visit a specific place.

CONTENTS

On the Road with Fodor's *vi*

Don't Forget to Write *vii*

Smart Travel Tips A to Z *x*

1 Destination: India *1*

Cosmic Chaos *2*
New and Noteworth *4*
What's Where *5*
Pleasures and Pastimes *7*
Great Itineraries *10*
Fodor's Choice *11*
Festivals and Seasonal Events *13*

2 The Himalayas *15*

3 Delhi *59*

4 North Central India *98*

5 Rajasthan *142*

6 Gujarat *189*

7 Bombay and the Ajanta and Ellora Caves *213*

8 Goa *257*

9 Karnataka *270*

10 Kerala *299*

11 Tamil Nadu *315*

12 Hyderabad *346*

13 Bhubaneswar *355*

14 Calcutta 369

15 Portraits of India 393

"The Religions of India," by Kathleen Cox and Andy McCord *394*
Books and Films *401*
Vocabulary *403*
Dining Glossary *403*

Index 405

Maps

India *viii–ix*
Northwest Indian Himalayas *21*
Sikkim *51*
Delhi *66–67*
Delhi Dining and Lodging *78–79*
North Central India *103*
Agra *105*
Khajuraho *119*
Varanasi *126*
Rajasthan *147*
Jaipur *150*
Gujarat *193*
Bombay *218–219*
Greater Bombay Dining and Lodging *226*
Downtown Bombay Dining and Lodging *227*
Ajanta Caves *247*
Ellora Caves *249*
Maharashtra Beaches *253*
Goa Beaches *261*
Bangalore *276*
Mysore *285*
Kerala *303*
Tamil Nadu *319*
Madras *322*
Mamallapuram *333*
Hyderabad *351*
Bhubaneswar and Environs *359*
Calcutta *374–375*

ON THE ROAD WITH FODOR'S

THE TRIPS YOU TAKE this year and next are going to be significant trips, if only because they'll be your first in the new millennium. Acutely aware of that fact, we've pulled out all stops in preparing *Fodor's India.* To guide you in putting together your India experience, we've created multiday itineraries and neighborhood walks. And to direct you to the places that are truly worth your time and money in these important years, we've rallied the team of endearingly picky know-it-alls we're pleased to call our writers. Having seen all corners of the regions they cover for us, they're real experts. If you knew them, you'd poll them for tips yourself.

Michael W. Bollom has six years of experience traveling, living, and working in India. Having studied Hindi literature, researched Indian political economy, and worked in development, he now teaches history and writing at the American Embassy School in New Delhi, where he indulges his passion for eating out.

A granddaughter of Estonian and Indian freedom-fighters, **Vaihayasi Pande Daniel** was born in Montréal, grew up in Baltimore, married a Tamil Christian, and has lived in India since 1976. Peripatetic tendencies draw her (and her two young children) all over India and elsewhere, but she prefers Bombay to any other place in the world. The travel editor at rediff.com, she writes on both travel and current affairs for this popular Indian news service.

Husband-and-wife team **Manish and Vidhi Jain** are based in Udaipur, where they work as coordinator and learning activist at Shikshantar: The Peoples' Institute for Rethinking Education and Development. Both were born in Rajasthan. Manish spent two years as an architect of the UNESCO initiative "Learning Without Frontiers"; prior to that, he consulted in several countries for UNICEF, the World Bank, and USAID. Vidhi recently designed and ran a grass-roots program aimed at inclusive schooling for children with special needs in rural Rajasthani villages.

Jayanth Kodkani, assistant editor of the *Times of India*–Bangalore, has lived in Bangalore all his life, watching it grow from a lazy garrison town to a booming metropolis. He itches for more time to roam the beaches of Goa and Karnataka. Writing for Fodor's, he says, gave new life to his inner tourist, helping him appreciate nooks and crannies he hadn't otherwise stopped to contemplate.

New York–based poet and writer **John Larson** has spent some two years traveling and writing in India. His interest in Tibetan Buddhism brings him repeatedly back to Sikkim and the eastern Himalayas.

Andy McCord first went to India in 1971, to live in a Punjabi village where his father was practicing medicine. As a Harvard undergraduate he took a two-year leave to study Indian languages and culture at Banaras Hindu University. Since then he has returned to India as a journalist, documentary-film scriptwriter, and Fulbright scholar. A book of his poems and translations is forthcoming from Ravi Dayal Publishers, New Delhi.

Shanti Menon is a frequent visitor to Kerala, her ancestral homeland, where she enjoys the privileges of both a native and a tourist. A former reporter for *Discover* Magazine in New York, she now gets a daily dose of the tropics in Singapore, where she writes for the lifestyle magazine *The Peak.*

David Quegg is elementary-science coordinator at the American Embassy School in New Delhi. He spends his vacation time in the hill stations of North India in search of the British legacy—golf courses and the wily brown trout.

Journalist **Modhurima Sinha** was born, raised, and educated (at Presidency College) in Calcutta. Formerly the Calcutta bureau chief of *Travel Scene Asia,* she has traveled widely and contributed travel articles, interviews, and features to several leading publications. Calcutta remains her home and her favorite city in the world; she knows this vibrant metropolis in all its myriad moods.

R. Edwin Sudhir, a journalist with the *Times of India,* has settled in his native Bangalore after living for several years in Maharashtra. For Fodor's he toured temples and heritage sites all over South and East India in addition to braving urban sprawls, and was reminded that no matter how much you see in this country, there's always more to be seen.

For their kind assistance in preparing this edition, we'd also like to thank the Government of India Tourist Office, particularly Gobind Bhuyan in New York and Ram Chopra and Neela Lad in Bombay; Nosh Nalavala, editor and publisher of *Traveler's India;* and the Taj Group of Hotels, particularly Pankaj Baliga and Sunita Nair in Bombay, Deepak Khullar and Aashish Vyas at the Taj Rambagh Palace, Jaipur, and V. V. Singh and Monica Lakhmana at the Taj Bengal, Calcutta.

Don't Forget to Write

Keeping a travel guide fresh and up-to-date is a big job. So we love your feedback—positive and negative—and follow up on all suggestions. Contact the India editor at editors@fodors.com or c/o Fodor's, 201 East 50th Street, New York, New York 10022. And have a wonderful trip!

Karen Cure
Editorial Director

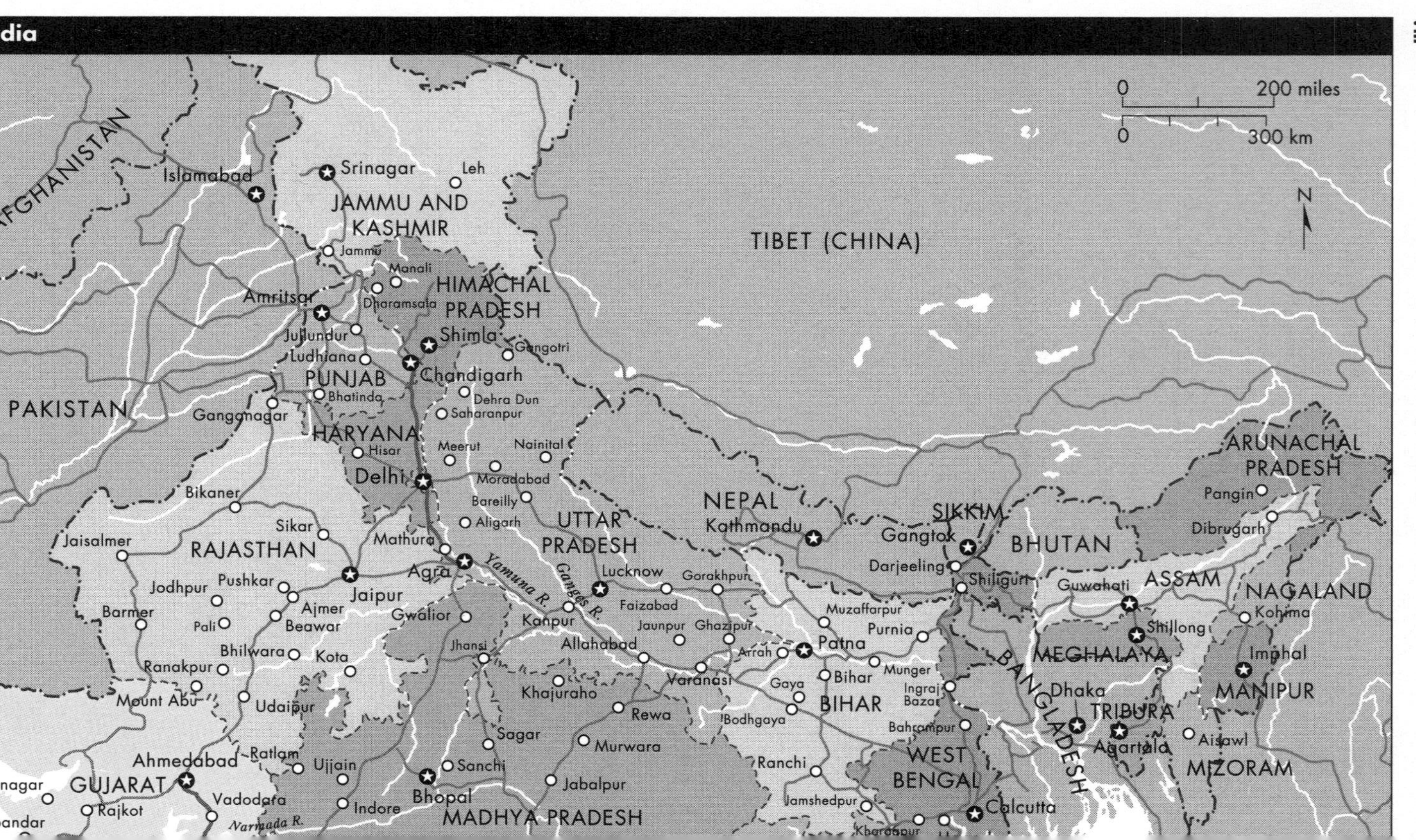
India
TIBET (CHINA)
AFGHANISTAN
PAKISTAN
NEPAL
BHUTAN
BANGLADESH
JAMMU AND KASHMIR
HIMACHAL PRADESH
PUNJAB
HARYANA
UTTAR PRADESH
RAJASTHAN
GUJARAT
MADHYA PRADESH
BIHAR
WEST BENGAL
SIKKIM
ASSAM
ARUNACHAL PRADESH
NAGALAND
MANIPUR
MIZORAM
TRIPURA
MEGHALAYA
0 200 miles
0 300 km
N
Islamabad
Srinagar
Leh
Jammu
Manali
Dharamsala
Amritsar
Jullundur
Ludhiana
Bhatinda
Shimla
Chandigarh
Gangotri
Dehra Dun
Saharanpur
Meerut
Nainital
Moradabad
Bareilly
Aligarh
Delhi
Hisar
Ganganagar
Bikaner
Sikar
Jaisalmer
Mathura
Agra
Yamuna R.
Ganges R.
Jaipur
Jodhpur
Pushkar
Ajmer
Beawar
Barmer
Pali
Gwalior
Bhilwara
Kota
Ranakpur
Mount Abu
Udaipur
Jhansi
Kanpur
Lucknow
Faizabad
Gorakhpur
Jaunpur
Ghazipur
Allahabad
Khajuraho
Varanasi
Kathmandu
Rewa
Sagar
Murwara
Jabalpur
Sanchi
Bhopal
Indore
Ujjain
Ratlam
Ahmedabad
Vadodara
Narmada R.
Jamnagar
Rajkot
Porbandar
Arrah
Patna
Muzaffarpur
Purnia
Munger
Gaya
Bihar
Bodhgaya
Ingraj Bazar
Bahrampur
Ranchi
Jamshedpur
Kharagpur
Calcutta
Darjeeling
Gangtok
Shiliguri
Guwahati
Shillong
Dhaka
Agartala
Aizawl
Imphal
Kohima
Dibrugarh
Pangin

Veraval
Diu
Gulf of Khambat
Surat
Navsari
Dhule
Bhusawal
Amravati
Akola
Nagpur
Raipur
Sambalpur
Cuttack
Bhubaneswar
Konark
Puri
ORISSA
Gopalpur-on-Sea
MYANMAR (BURMA)
Nasik
MAHARASHTRA
Aurangabad
Nanded
Bombay (Mumbai)
Ahmadnagar
Godavari R.
Pune
Nizamabad
Warangal
Vizianagaram
Vishakapatnam
Solapur
Hyderabad
Bhima R.
Miraj
Rajahmundry
Bijapur
Krishna R.
Vijayawada
Guntur
Belgaum
Kurnool
Goa
Hospet
Arabian Sea
GOA
Hubli
Guntakal
Penneru R.
ANDHRA PRADESH
Bay of Bengal
Davangere
Shimoga
Tirupati
KARNATAKA
Madras (Chennai)
Tumkur
Andaman Islands
Mangalore
Bangalore
Kanchipuram
TAMIL NADU
Mysore
Pondicherry
Cannanore
Salem
Cuddalore
Port Blair
Calicut
Coimbatore
Lakshadweep
KERALA
Cauvery R.
Karaikal
Trichur
Tiruchirappalli
Thanjavur
Amindivi Islands
Cannanore Islands
Madurai
Andaman Sea
Cochin
Islands
Tirunelveli
Gulf of Mannar
Quilon
Trivandrum
SRI LANKA
Cape Comorin
Kanyakumari
Nicobar Islands
Colombo

SMART TRAVEL TIPS A TO Z

Basic Information on Traveling in India, Savvy Tips to Make Your Trip a Breeze, and Companies and Organizations to Contact

AIR TRAVEL

AIRLINES

➤ FROM NORTH AMERICA: **Air Canada** (☎ 800/776–3000). **Air-India** (☎ 212/751–6200). **Delta** (☎ 800/241–4141). **Northwest** (☎ 800/447–4747). **Tower** (☎ 800/344–8693 or ☎ 718/553–8500). **United** (☎ 800/328–6877).

➤ FROM THE U.K.: **Air Canada** (☎ 0990/247–226). **Air-India** (☎ 01753/684–828). **British Airways** (☎ 0345/222–111). **United** (☎ 0800/888–555).

➤ FROM AUSTRALIA: **Qantas** (13–1313).

BOOKING YOUR FLIGHT

Look for nonstop flights. "Direct" flights stop at least once. Try to avoid connecting flights, which require a change of plane. **Check different routings,** and look into different airports. Note that on your way *back* from India, a departure tax of Rs. 450 may be payable in cash upon check-in for your international flight.

CHECK-IN & BOARDING

Bring a government-issued photo I.D. to the airport, as it may be required for check-in.

CUTTING COSTS

Consolidators buy tickets for scheduled international flights from the airlines at reduced rates, then sell them at prices that beat the best fares available directly from the airlines. Sometimes you can even get your money back if you need to return the ticket. Read the fine print detailing penalties for changes and cancellations, and **confirm your consolidator reservation with the airline.**

➤ CONSOLIDATORS: **Cheap Tickets** (☎ 800/377–1000). **Up & Away Travel** (☎ 212/889–2345). **Discount Airline Ticket Service** (☎ 800/576–1600). **Unitravel** (☎ 800/325–2222). **World Travel Network** (☎ 800/409–6753).

FLYING TIMES

Flying time to either Delhi or Bombay is 16 hours from New York, 18 hours from Chicago, 20 hours from Los Angeles, 8 hours from London or Amsterdam, and 14 hours from Sydney.

WITHIN INDIA

The entry of privately owned domestic carriers into the market has forced **Indian Airlines** (☎ 141 or 11/566–5121), the national domestic carrier, to improve its service. Flights are still subject to delays, however, and some are canceled without explanation. More reliable are two new private carriers, **Jet Airways** and **Sahara Airlines.** All flights cost about 40% to 50% higher than first-class air-conditioned train tickets on the same routes, but travel by air is much more comfortable and, obviously, faster.

If possible, **buy your tickets for domestic flights when you buy your international ticket to the subcontinent.** (Some carriers do not sell their tickets outside India.) **Don't schedule back-to-back flights;** allow enough time for unexpected delays.

Important: Because airlines often overbook flights to popular destinations, **you must reconfirm all domestic flights at least 72 hours before departure.** Ticket or no ticket, you may lose your seat if you don't reconfirm. **Check in 60 minutes before flight time** to allow for security procedures, and expect tight security at all airports. Do not pack a pocket knife in your hand luggage; even golf clubs are not allowed in the cabin. If you hand-carry a computer, you could be asked to turn it on during the security check. Many flights required you to identify your checked luggage on the tarmac before boarding.

Private airlines cannot give discounts to foreigners, but Indian Airlines has some concessional packages: "Discover India" buys you 21 days of unlimited travel within India for U.S.$720, and "India Wonderfare" offers a week of unlimited travel within either the north, south, east, or west of India for U.S.$300. (On the southern route, there's a surcharge of $100 for Port Blair, in the Andaman Islands.) You must pay in foreign currency.

Children under 12 and students ages 12 to 26 (with valid I.D.) qualify for discounts on most Indian airlines.

AIRPORTS

India's major international gateways are Delhi (Indira Gandhi International Airport) and Bombay.

➤ AIRPORT INFORMATION: **Indira Gandhi International Airport** (☎ 11/565–2011). **Mumbai (Bombay) International Airport** (☎ 22/836–6700).

BEGGING

Many Western travelers to India are upset by the number of beggars who beseech them for spare rupees, motioning from hand to mouth to indicate that they have nothing to eat. The grimy faces of tiny waifs in particular will pull on your heartstrings. If you give a beggar money, a dozen will immediately spring from nowhere, and you will be forced to provide for all; and it can be extremely difficult to get the first beggar off your tail. Moreover, beggars are not usually as destitute as they look—your contribution may well support a drug habit or prolong the abuse of a child. If you want to contribute, **donate to a legal charity**—India has plenty of anti-poverty organizations that will greatly appreciate your help.

BUS TRAVEL

Bus travel is not highly recommended within India, especially at night. If you do take buses, try to travel on privately run air-conditioned coaches and stick to popular routes.

BUSINESS HOURS

India has numerous national and religious holidays that shut the commercial world down.

BANKS & OFFICES

Most government and private banks are open weekdays 10 to 2 and Saturday 10 to noon, and closed on government holidays. Post offices are generally open Monday through Saturday 10 to 5 and closed on government holidays. International airports and some top hotels have 24-hour currency-exchange facilities, and the major American Express branches have extended hours for check-cashing.

MUSEUMS & SIGHTS

Most museums are closed on Monday and government holidays. Site museums (adjoining archaeological monuments) are normally closed on Friday. The Taj Mahal is closed on Monday.

SHOPS

Outside the four major metropolitan areas (Bombay, Delhi, Calcutta, and Madras), many shopkeepers close their establishments for an afternoon siesta.

CAMERAS & PHOTOGRAPHY

Photography is not permitted in airports, on airplanes, at some government buildings, at sensitive military sites (including some bridges), and at some religious sites and events.

Carry a bit of change for people who demand money for the privilege of taking their picture. If someone asks you to send a copy of the photo, don't say yes unless you intend to keep the promise. Most Indians are good-natured about posing for pictures, but some women and tribal people may object, so **ask before you snap.** Dust can be troublesome for sensitive electronic equipment; keep delicate items under wraps when they're not in use.

Always **keep film and tape out of the sun.** Carry an extra supply of batteries in case they're hard to find on the road. At airports, **be prepared to turn on your camera or camcorder** to prove to security personnel that the device is real.

CAR RENTAL

You can rent a car from a reliable firm in India's major cities, but this is not recommended—the rules of these roads are like nothing you've ever seen. Hiring a car and driver or a taxi for the day is a better alternative (☞ Driving, *below*). If you must get behind the wheel: Rates in New Delhi begin at $37 a day and $252 a week for an economy car with unlimited mileage.

REQUIREMENTS & RESTRICTIONS

Your own driver's license is not acceptable in India—you need an International Driver's Permit. In North America you can get one of these from the American or Canadian automobile association; in the United Kingdom, contact the Automobile Association or Royal Automobile Club.

CHILDREN

Taking your kids to India can be daunting prospect, but children love it here: India is like a giant circus, with color, chaos, and a side show every minute. In return, children are warmly welcome in India; you're free to bring them to virtually any restaurant (except the stuffiest one or two) and anywhere else you'll want to go. Most Indians will bend over backward to help you with a child-related need, and in fact, so much affection is lavished on children here—everyone wants to pick your toddlers up, pinch their cheeks, talk to them, take them for walks—that your little ones may even get perturbed.

Involve your youngsters as you plan your trip: Remember to schedule some sightseeing activities of particular interest to the little ones.

FLYING

If your kids are two or older, **ask about children's airfares.** As a general rule, infants under two who do not occupy a separate seat fly at greatly reduced fares, or even free. **Confirm your carry-on allowance in advance** if you're traveling with an infant; in general, for babies charged 10% of the adult fare, you're allowed one carry-on bag and a collapsible stroller. If the flight is full, the stroller may have to be checked or you may be limited to less.

Experts agree that it's a good idea to use safety seats aloft for children weighing less than 40 pounds. Airlines set their own policies: U.S. carriers usually require that the child be ticketed, even if he or she is young enough to ride free, since the seats must be strapped into regular seats. Since safety seats are not allowed everywhere in the plane, get your seat assignments early, and **check your airline's policy on using safety seats during takeoff and landing.**

When you reserve, **request children's meals or a freestanding bassinet** if you need them; just note that bulkhead seats, where you must sit to use the bassinet, may lack an overhead bin or storage space on the floor.

LODGING

Most hotels in India allow children under a certain age to stay in their parents' room at no extra charge, but others charge for them as extra adults. **Confirm the cutoff age for children's discounts.**

PACKING

Bring a bag of amusements to keep kids busy on the long international flight and on trips within India—books, coloring books, crayons, and other quiet toys.

Indian cities don't have much sidewalk space for strollers, but a stroller still makes a clean, safe, comfortable place to park your toddler in train stations, airports, shops, and thick crowds if he or she suddenly wants to sit down. **Bring all medicines, rash cream, zinc oxide, sunscreen, diapers, and diaper wipes.** Moist towelettes can be useful for wiping dirty little hands where no water is available. The major brands of disposable diapers are now available in major cities but can be hard to find. Clean bathrooms are also hard to come by in both cities and the countryside, so **carry a roll of toilet paper wherever you go.**

Milk powder from major brands like Amul and Nestle is easily available and ideal for carrying around. Nestle makes a few instant baby cereals, also available in big cities. Packed, hygienic snack foods, such as potato chips, cookies, fruit juices, chocolate bars, and soft drinks, are sold in stores throughout India; **try to buy well-known brands from larger stores.** Though not optimally nutritious, packaged snacks are often preferable to cooked food that may be spicy or not entirely safe. Keep a bottle of mineral water handy at all times. If you buy fresh produce, **wash and peel fruit yourself.** If you're heading out for a day of sightseeing, ask your hotel if they can pack a lunch for your child. A small hot pot or kettle can be useful for making soup or instant noodles; soup packets and noodles are available in stores in major cities.

Pack cool, loose, easy-to-wash clothes. If you'll be taking any air-conditioned trains, bring a few pieces of warm clothing, as the cars get cold. Leggings help protect against mosquitoes in the evening; hats shade youthful faces from the sun; and rubber slippers or sandals are always practical.

If you rent a car, don't forget to **arrange for a car seat** when you reserve.

COMPUTERS ON THE ROAD

If you plan to bring a laptop to India, **consider carrying a spare battery and spare adapter.** New batteries and replacement adapters are expensive and can be hard to find. Never plug your computer into any socket before asking about surge protection—some hotels do not have built-in current stabilizers, and the country's extreme electrical fluctuations and surges can short your adapter or even destroy your computer. IBM sells a pen-size modem tester that plugs into a phone jack and tells you whether or not the line is safe to use; this gadget is invaluable in India, where phone lines are not always reliable and can harm your modem.

CUSTOMS & DUTIES

Keep receipts for all purchases, and **be ready to show customs officials what you've bought** upon reentering your home country. If you feel a duty is incorrect or object to the way your clearance was handled, note the inspector's badge number and ask to see a supervisor. If the problem isn't resolved, write to the appropriate authorities, beginning with the port director at your point of entry.

ENTERING INDIA

If you're bringing dutiable or valuable articles into India, you must stop at Customs and mention this; they may ask you to fill in a Tourist Baggage Re-Export Form (TBRE). These articles must be re-exported at the time of departure. Failure to re-export anything listed on the TBRE means you'll have to pay a duty on each missing item. Depending on the attitude of the customs official, you may have to enter your laptop computer on a TBRE form.

You may bring the following into India duty-free: personal effects (clothing and jewelry); cameras and up to five rolls of film; binoculars; a portable musical instrument; a radio or portable tape recorder; a tent and camping equipment; sports equipment (fishing rod, a pair of skis, two tennis rackets); 200 cigarettes or 50 cigars;.95 liters of liquor; and gifts not exceeding a value of Rs. 600 (about U.S.$14). (In practice, customs are relaxed enough not to trouble tourists about bringing in, say, 100 cigars instead of 50.) You may *not* bring in dangerous or addictive drugs, firearms, gold coins, gold and silver bullion or silver coins not in use, Indian currency, or live plants.

LEAVING INDIA

Rupees are not allowed out of India; you must exchange them before you depart. Foreign-exchange facilities are usually in the same airport hall as the check-in counters—note that you'll have no access to these facilities once you pass through immigration.

All animal products, souvenirs, and trophies are subject to the Wildlife (Protection) Act, 1972. The export of skins made from protected species is not allowed, and enforcement of this rule is getting increasingly rigorous. (Such items cannot be imported into many other countries anyway, including the United States.) As a general rule, avoid any souvenir made of wild animal skins, barring crocodile-leather goods. Ivory is widely available for purchase in India, but unless you can prove that it's antique, you can't bring it into the United States. Forgo ivory products and you'll help stop the poaching that is reducing elephant herds.

Generally, items more than 100 years old cannot be exported without a permit from the Archaeological Survey, which has offices in many cities including Delhi, Bombay, Calcutta, Bhubaneswar, Madras, and Bangalore. Reputable shops will provide you with the necessary permit or help you procure it. Items without permits will be detained by Indian Customs if they are believed to be more than 100 years old.

ENTERING AUSTRALIA

Australian residents 18 or older may bring home $A400 worth of souvenirs and gifts (including jewelry), 250 cigarettes or 250 grams of tobacco, and 1,125 ml of alcohol (including wine, beer, and spirits). Residents under 18 may bring back $A200 worth of goods. Seeds, plants, and fruits need to be declared upon arrival. Prohibited items include meat products.

➤ INFORMATION: **Australian Customs Service** (Regional Director, ✉ Box 8, Sydney, NSW 2001, ☎ 02/9213–2000, FAX 02/9213–4000).

ENTERING CANADA

Canadian residents who have been out of the country for at least 7 days may bring home C$500 worth of goods duty-free. If you've been away less than 7 days but more than 48 hours, the duty-free allowance drops to C$200; if your trip lasts 24–48 hours, the allowance is C$50. You may not pool allowances with family members. Goods claimed under the C$500 exemption may follow you by mail; those claimed under the lesser exemptions must accompany you. Alcohol and tobacco products may be included in the 7-day and 48-hour exemptions but not in the 24-hour exemption. If you meet the age requirements of the province or territory through which you reenter Canada, you may bring in, duty-free, 1.14 liters (40 imperial ounces) of wine or liquor *or* 24 12-ounce cans or bottles of beer or ale. If you are 16 or older you may bring in 200 cigarettes and 50 cigars. Check ahead of time with Revenue Canada or the Department of Agriculture for policies regarding meat products, seeds, plants, and fruits.

You may send an unlimited number of gifts worth up to C$60 each to Canada duty-free; label the package UNSOLICITED GIFT—VALUE UNDER $60. Alcohol and tobacco are excluded.

➤ INFORMATION: **Revenue Canada** (✉ 2265 St. Laurent Blvd. S, Ottawa, Ontario K1G 4K3, ☎ 613/993–0534; 800/461–9999 in Canada).

ENTERING NEW ZEALAND

Homeward-bound residents 17 or older may bring back $700 worth of souvenirs and gifts, including 4.5 liters of wine or beer; one 1,125-ml bottle of spirits; and either 200 cigarettes, 250 grams of tobacco, 50 cigars, or a combination of the three up to 250 grams. Prohibited items include meat products, seeds, plants, and fruits.

➤ INFORMATION: **New Zealand Customs** (Custom House, ✉ 50 Anzac Ave., Box 29, Auckland, New Zealand, ☎ 09/359–6655, FAX 09/359–6732).

ENTERING THE U.K.

From countries outside the EU you may bring home, duty-free, 200 cigarettes or 50 cigars; 1 liter of spirits or 2 liters of fortified or sparkling wine or liqueurs; 2 liters of still table wine; 60 ml of perfume; 250 ml of toilet water; plus £136 worth of other goods, including gifts and souvenirs. Prohibited items include meat products, seeds, plants, and fruits.

➤ INFORMATION: **HM Customs and Excise** (✉ Dorset House, Stamford St., Bromley Kent BR1 1XX, ☎ 020/7202–4227).

ENTERING THE U.S.

U.S. residents who have been out of the country for at least 48 hours (and who have not used the $400 allowance or any part of it in the past 30 days) may bring home $400 worth of foreign goods duty-free.

Within that allowance, U.S. residents 21 and older may bring back 1 liter of alcohol duty-free. Residents of any age are allowed 200 cigarettes and 100 non-Cuban cigars. Antiques, which the U.S. Customs Service defines as objects more than 100 years old, enter duty-free, as do original works of art done entirely by hand, including paintings, drawings, and sculptures.

You may also send packages home duty-free: up to $200 worth of goods for personal use, with a limit of one parcel per addressee per day (and no alcohol or tobacco products or perfume worth more than $5). Label the package PERSONAL USE and attach a list of its contents and their retail value. Do not label the package UNSOLICITED GIFT or your duty-free exemption will drop to $100. Mailed items do not affect your duty-free allowance upon your return.

➤ INFORMATION: **U.S. Customs Service** (inquiries, ✉ 1300 Pennsylvania Ave. NW, Washington, DC 20229, ☎ 202/927–6724; complaints, ✉ Office of Regulations and Rulings, 1300 Pennsylvania Ave. NW, Washington, DC 20229; registration of equipment, ✉ Registration Information, 1300 Pennsylvania Ave. NW, Washington, DC 20229; ☎ 202/927–0540).

DINING

The restaurants we list are the cream of the crop in each price category. An ✕🏨 icon indicates a hotel whose restaurant warrants a trip of its own.

Delhi and Bombay are in a financial league of their own, so we categorize their dining prices in the chapters themselves. For the rest of India, dining categories are as follows. The major cities are Agra, Bangalore, Calcutta, Jaipur, Madras, and Varanasi.

CATEGORY*	MAJOR CITIES	OTHER AREAS
$$$$	over Rs. 500	over Rs. 350
$$$	Rs. 350–500	Rs. 250–350
$$	Rs. 150–350	Rs. 100–250
$	under Rs. 150	under Rs. 100

**per person for a three-course meal, excluding drinks, service, and sales tax*

MEALTIMES

Restaurants in cities normally stay open until 11 PM or midnight. In other areas, expect an earlier dinner unless you're staying in a luxury hotel.

RESERVATIONS

Reservations are always a good idea, but we mention them only when they're essential. Reserve as far ahead as you can, and reconfirm as soon as you arrive in that city.

WINE, BEER & SPIRITS

Dry days—when alcohol is not available anywhere in the country—are observed on January 26, August 15, October 2, and some festivals. Some states observe additional dry days, while others prohibit everything but beer. Gujarat is always dry; Andhra Pradesh allows liquor but not bars or pubs. Out-of-state visitors can buy a drinking permit through their hotel for about Rs. 100 per day. As a foreign traveler you may apply to the Gujarat Tourism Development Corporation for a permit that allows you to buy alcohol in the state; the Government of India Tourist Office abroad can also issue a three-month liquor permit allowing you to carry liquor into Gujarat.

DISABILITIES & ACCESSIBILITY

India has a large population of people with disabilities, but in a country with so many fundamental problems, the needs of these people are not a high priority. Luxury hotels have ramps for those using wheelchairs or walkers, but few bathrooms are designed for use by people with disabilities. Also, except for a few international airports, disembarkation from planes is via staircase. There are very few sidewalks in India, and no such thing as the pedestrian right of way: Any pedestrian crossing the street is considered fair game.

DRIVING

Driving in India is not for the faint of heart. Traffic is incredibly multifarious: Slow-moving cyclists, bullock carts, and occasional cows (sacred to Hindus) or, in Rajasthan, camels or even elephants share the road with zipping motorcyclists and daredevil long-distance trucks and buses. Speeds vary according to road conditions, but the 30-MPH urban limit is widely ignored. Drivers liberally use their horns to warn others that they'll be passing and to get pedestrians out of the way. Moreover, outside the cities, two-way roads are often only one lane wide, creating a hair-raising game in which (if you've hired a driver) your speeding, horn-blowing vehicle dodges oncoming traffic for hours on end.

Barring a few principal "trunk" roads, Indian roads can be a mess, especially during monsoons. In rural areas, some roads also serve as innovative extensions to farms, with grain laid out to dry on the pavement, necessitating a dodge, or sisal rope strung over the road so that passing vehicles tamp the grain down. Drivers generally brake for animals, be they dogs, goats, or scatterbrained chickens. British-style left-side driving creates one more challenge to American and Canadian motorists. When there are road signs, they're usually in Hindi or the local language. Bottom line: **Hire a car and driver or a taxi rather than take to the road yourself.**

HIRED CARS WITH DRIVERS

Hiring a car and driver is the best way to get around India if you plan to concentrate on one or two states or regions. Hiring this kind of chauffeur is reasonably priced by Western standards. The cost varies from state to state but generally allows for a certain number of hours and kilometers, after which you pay extra; add to that a halt charge of Rs. 100 to Rs. 200 per night for overnight trips. **Establish the rate and the surcharge in advance.** We estimate rates in the "A to Z" sections of individual chapters in this book; generally speaking, figure Rs. 8 to Rs. 10 per kilometer for a non-air-conditioned Ambassador, a hefty, roomy car designed by the British in the 1950s. In some locations, a higher rate buys you a ride in an air-conditioned Cielo, Contessa, or Audi, and yet more cash gets you a Toyota, minivan, or Mercedes-Benz. Roads in some areas, such as wildlife sanctuaries, require a jeep. **Arrange a car and driver only through a licensed, government-approved operator** (☞ Travel Agencies *at the end of each chapter*) or, for a bit more money, through your hotel.

ELECTRICITY

To use electric equipment from the U.S., **bring a converter and adapter.** The electrical current in India is 220 volts, 50 cycles alternating current (AC); wall outlets take plugs with two round prongs.

If your appliances are dual-voltage (as are most laptop computers) or British in origin, you'll need only an adapter. Don't use 110-volt outlets marked FOR SHAVERS ONLY for high-wattage appliances such as hair dryers.

EMBASSIES

All foreign embassies are in Chanakyapuri, New Delhi.

➤ AUSTRALIA: The **Australian High Commission** (✉ 1/50G Shanti Path, ☎ 11/688–8223) is open weekdays from 8:30 to 1 and 2 to 4:30 for consular services.

➤ CANADA: The **Canadian High Commission** (✉ 7/8 Shanti Path, ☎ 11/687–6500) is open Monday through Thursday 8:30 to 12:45 and 1:30 to 5:30 and Friday 8:30 to 1 for consular services.

➤ NEW ZEALAND: The **New Zealand High Commission** (✉ 50N Nyaya Marg, ☎ 11/688–3170) is open Monday through Thursday from 8:30 to 5:15 and Friday from 8:30 to 1 for consular services.

➤ UNITED KINGDOM: The **British High Commission** (✉ Shanti Path, ☎ 11/687–2161) is open weekdays 9 to 1 and 2 to 5 for consular services.

➤ UNITED STATES: The **United States Embassy** (✉ Shanti Path, ☎ 11/419–8000) is open weekdays 8:30 to 1 and 2 to 4 for consular services.

EMERGENCIES

Delhi's 24-hour **East-West Medical Center** has a referral list of doctors, dentists, opticians, pharmacists, and lawyers throughout India. At the moment, it's the only clinic in India recognized by most international insurance companies. If you run into medical trouble, you pay for services here (credit cards accepted) and get reimbursed by your insurance company later, or you arrange for payment through International SOS (☞ Health, *below*). East-West also sends emergency medical services (including medevac) all over India.

Meera Rescue, based in Delhi with branches in Bombay and Goa, is an extremely professional evacuation service recognized by international insurance companies. Meera evacuates from anywhere in the country to hospitals in major cities, as well as overseas if necessary.

➤ CONTACTS: **East-West Medical Center** (✉ 38 Golf Links, New Delhi 110003, ☎ 11/462–3738, 11/469–9229, 11/469–0955 11/469–0429, or 11/469–8865; FAX 11/469–0428 or 11/463–2382). **Meera Rescue** (✉ 112 Jor Bagh, New Delhi 110003, ☎ 11/469–3508 or 11/465–3170, FAX 11/461–8286).

ETIQUETTE AND BEHAVIOR

If you are invited to a traditional Indian home, **observe the prevailing rules governing seating.** Often men sit separate from women. Sometimes, when the menfolk entertain a foreign visitor (even a woman), the women of the house shy away or do not emerge; they may not speak English, or may be mildly xenophobic. If in doubt, ask. In some homes, shoes are taken off before entering; here too, inquire, or watch what the family does. Numerous other customs govern food and the partaking of meals. In many households, you arrive, sit and talk for a while, and then have your meal; after you eat the evening is over. Don't be surprised if the woman of the house serves her guests but doesn't join the gathering. Don't protest, and don't follow her into the kitchen (in orthodox Hindu homes the kitchen is frequently off-limits)—just accept her behavior as the tradition of this particular home. When you eat in villages or remote areas, you may not be given utensils; **eat only with your right hand,** as the left is considered unclean. If you want a second helping or are buying openly displayed food, don't help yourself with your hands, especially in a Hindu area; this act pollutes the food. **Let your host or vendor serve you.**

GAY & LESBIAN TRAVEL

Although India is a sexually conservative society, there is a growing awareness and acceptance of homosexuality and lesbianism in major cities. Still, gay and lesbian travelers should keep their sexual preference to themselves in India. No hotel will object to two people of the same sex sharing a bedroom, but **don't display your affection in public.** Note that Indian men and boys commonly walk hand in hand as a sign of friendship.

HEALTH

No vaccination certificate or inoculations are required to enter India from the United States, Canada, or the United Kingdom. Immigration officials don't normally ask to see an International Health Certificate, but it's smart to have one in case you need medical attention. See your doctor about obtaining the certificate, and **talk to your doctor about vaccinations three months before departure** in any case. The Centers for Disease Control and Prevention posts a helpful list of recommended vaccinations for the Indian subcontinent on its Web site; these include hepatitis and typhoid fever.

In areas where malaria and dengue—both carried by mosquitoes—are prevalent, use mosquito nets, wear clothing that covers the body, apply repellent containing DEET, and use spray for flying insects in living and sleeping areas. **Consider taking antimalaria pills,** as malaria is common even in the big cities. There is no vaccine to combat dengue.

Depending on where in India you'll be traveling, **bring a medical kit** containing aspirin or its equivalent, diarrhea medication, moist towelettes, antibacterial skin cleanser, adhesive bandages, antibiotics, mosquito repellent with at least 95% DEET (N. diethyl toluamide), water-purification kit, and a plastic strip thermometer.

➤ HEALTH ADVISORIES: **Centers for Disease Control** (CDC, National Center for Infectious Diseases, Division of Quarantine, Traveler's Health

Section, ✉ 1600 Clifton Rd. NE, M/S E-03, Atlanta, GA 30333, ☎ 888/232–3228, FAX 888/232–3299, www.cdc.gov/travel).

ALTITUDE SICKNESS

An adverse reaction to low oxygen pressure, altitude sickness can be deadly. If your urine turns bright yellow, you're not drinking enough water. **To minimize high-altitude misery, drink lots of water, eat foods high in carbohydrates, and cut back on salt.** Stop and rest immediately if you develop any of the following symptoms: nausea, loss of appetite, extreme headache or lightheadedness, unsteady feet, sleeplessness. If resting doesn't help, head for lower ground immediately.

THE BATHROOM

Bring some toilet paper. Nicer hotels and restaurants provide it, but you can't depend on this, as most Indians do not use the stuff. **Never throw anything in a toilet** in India, as the septic systems can't handle it—in many bathrooms you'll find sanitary bags, which you can use, close, and place in the trash bin. In place of toilet paper many Indians use their left hand, which is why it's considered unclean—**never pick up food with your left hand.** Left-handers can use utensils; left-handedness in general is considered curious. Traditional Indian toilets are covered holes in the ground. In many Indian bathrooms you'll see a faucet, a small hand-held shower head, and/or a bucket with a beaker or other small vessel; Indians use these to rinse, bidet-style, after using the toilet. Hands are always washed elsewhere.

FOOD & DRINK

In India, drinking water, fresh fruit, and vegetables are often contaminated by fecal matter, which causes traveler's diarrhea. **Watch what you eat**—stay away from uncooked or cold food and unpasteurized milk and milk products. **Drink only water that has been bottled or boiled** for at least 20 minutes; avoid tap water, ice, fruit juices, or drinks to which water has been added. **Turn down offers of "filtered" or "aquaguard" water;** it may have been filtered to take out particles, but that doesn't mean it was purified to kill off parasites. Buy bottled water from a reputable hotel or shop (Bisleri is a good brand) and **check the cap to make sure it hasn't been tampered with.** Bottles are sometimes refilled with tap water.

Always **keep at least one bottle of water in your hotel room** for brushing your teeth and for a late-night drink. India's heat can dehydrate you, and dust can irritate your throat, so **drink liquids** regularly. Dehydration will make you weak and more susceptible to other health problems.

In restaurants, **avoid raw vegetables and fruit** that have been peeled. Many buffets and salad bars serve vegetables that have been presoaked in an iodine preparation to kill parasites; but ask the waiter before you indulge. Fruit and salads at luxury hotels are mostly hygienic, but it's always safest to give raw produce a miss. If you're dying for some fresh fruit or vegetables, cut and peel your own, choosing varieties with thick skins. Pork products should be avoided outside luxury hotels; make sure that other meats are thoroughly cooked. It's not necessary to go vegetarian, and to do so would mean missing out on some delicious dishes; just choose restaurants with care and eat hot foods while they're hot.

When choosing where to dine, know that locally popular restaurants that look worn around the edges often serve the safest food. A small restaurant that can't afford refrigeration cooks food acquired that day—not always the case with the upscale hotels. Because some hotel chefs buy in bulk and electricity can be temperamental, a hotel's refrigerator can preserve more than just foodstuffs. Remember, however, that stomach upsets often are due as much to the richness and spice of Indian cuisine as to the lack of hygiene. Many hotel restaurants in particular tend to cook Indian dishes with quite a bit of oil, which can trigger Delhi Belly. **If you have a sensitive stomach, ask the chef to use less oil.** Fried foods from street vendors often look delicious, but inspect the oil: If it looks as old as the pot, it could be rancid and lead to trouble. It's safest to resist the temptation.

If you travel by train, **never accept food or beverage from a fellow passenger.** Foreigners who accept such generosity sometimes ingest drug-laced refreshment and are robbed once the drug takes effect.

Mild cases of intestinal distress may respond to Immodium A-D (known generically as loperamide) or Pepto-Bismol (a little weaker), both available over the counter. Paregoric, another antidiarrheal agent, requires a doctor's prescription in India. Drink plenty of purified water or tea—chamomile is a good folk remedy for diarrhea. In severe cases, rehydrate yourself with a salt-sugar solution (½ tsp. salt and 4 tbsp. sugar per quart/liter of water).

A little bit of personal hygiene can also go a long way in preventing stomach upsets. **Wash your hands before you eat anything, and carry moist towelettes** (readily available throughout India) for times when soap and water are not available.

MEDICAL PLANS

No one plans to get sick while traveling, but it happens, so **consider signing up with a medical-assistance company.** Members get doctor referrals, emergency evacuation or repatriation, hotlines for medical consultation, cash for emergencies, and other assistance.

➤ MEDICAL-ASSISTANCE COMPANIES: **AEA International SOS** (✉ 8 Neshaminy Interplex, Suite 207, Trevose, PA 19053, ☎ 215/245–4707 or 800/523–6586, FAX 215/244–9617; ✉ 12 Chemin Riantbosson, 1217 Meyrin 1, Geneva, Switzerland, ☎ 4122/785–6464, FAX 4122/785–6424; ✉ 331 N. Bridge Rd., 17-00, Odeon Towers, Singapore 188720, ☎ 65/338–7800, FAX 65/338–7611).

PESTS & OTHER HAZARDS

All Indian cities are heavily polluted. Pollution-control regulations and devices were introduced in 1995, but most vehicles still use leaded gas or diesel fuel. People with breathing problems, especially asthma, should **carry the appropriate respiratory remedies.**

If you travel into forested areas during or right after the monsoon, **protect yourself against leeches** by covering your legs and carrying salt. Do not wear sandals. If a leech clings to your clothing or skin, dab it with a pinch of salt and it will fall off. If itching persists, apply an antiseptic; infection is rare.

For bedbugs, buy a bar of Dettol soap (available throughout India) and use it when you bathe to relieve itching and discomfort. If you're staying in an unknown, perhaps dubious hotel, **check under the mattress** for bedbugs, cockroaches and other unwanted bedfellows. Flit, Finit and other readily available anti-insect sprays can be useful for spraying down suspicious-looking furniture and mosquito-infested rooms. Tortoise coils, or *kachua,* and Good Knight are fairly effective at "smoking" mosquitoes away; these need to be plugged into the wall or lit with a match and placed under a bed or table, and will then burn for several hours. On the road, **treat scratches, cuts, or blisters at once.** If you're trekking, save the bottle and cap from your first bottled water so you can refill it with water that you purify yourself.

Send your clothes to be laundered only through decent hotels. *Dhobi,* or washerman's itch—that is, scabies—can be picked up from poorly washed clothes. It's better to **wash your clothes yourself** and send them out for ironing, or give them directly to a reliable dry-cleaner.

SUN EXPOSURE

The sun can be intense in India: Beware of overexposure even on overcast days. To avoid sunburn, **use a sunscreen** with a sun-protection factor of at least 24. To play it extra-safe, **wear a wide-brimmed hat.** If you plan to travel above 10,000 feet, use zinc oxide, lip balm with sunblock, and sunglasses that block ultraviolet rays. When you're on snowy terrain, remember that UV rays reflect from below.

HOLIDAYS

India's fixed national holidays are January 26 (Republic Day), August 15 (Independence Day), October 2 (Gandhi's birthday), and December 25 (Christmas). Endless festivals enliven—and shut down—different parts of the country throughout the year; ☞ Festivals and Seasonal Events *in* Chapter 1.

INSURANCE

The best travel insurance is a comprehensive policy that includes coverage for trip cancellation and interruption, default, trip delay, and medical expenses (with a waiver for pre-existing conditions).

Without insurance, you will lose all or most of your money if you cancel your trip, regardless of the reason. Default insurance covers you if your tour operator or airline goes out of business. Trip-delay insurance covers expenses that arise because of bad weather or mechanical delays. **Study the fine print** when comparing policies.

A key component of travel insurance for international trips is coverage of medical bills incurred on the road, as such expenses are not generally covered by Medicare or private policies. U.K. residents can buy a travel-insurance policy valid for most vacations taken the year it's purchased; just check coverage for pre-existing conditions. British and Australian citizens need extra medical coverage when traveling overseas.

Always **buy a travel policy directly from the insurance company.** If you buy it from a tour operator or airline and that company goes out of business, you probably will not be covered for the agency or operator's default, a major risk. Finally, before you make a purchase **review your existing health and homeowner's policies** to find what they cover away from home.

➤ TRAVEL INSURERS: In the U.S.: **Access America** (✉ 6600 W. Broad St., Richmond, VA 23230, ☎ 804/285–3300 or 800/284–8300), **Travel Guard International** (✉ 1145 Clark St., Stevens Point, WI 54481, ☎ 715/345–0505 or 800/826–1300). In Canada: **Voyager Insurance** (✉ 44 Peel Center Dr., Brampton, Ontario L6T 4M8, ☎ 905/791–8700; in Canada, 800/668–4342).

➤ INSURANCE INFORMATION: In the U.K.: **Association of British Insurers** (✉ 51–55 Gresham St., London EC2V 7HQ, ☎ 020/7600–3333, FAX 020/7696–8999). In Australia: **Insurance Council of Australia** (☎ 03/9614–1077, FAX 03/9614–7924).

LANGUAGE

Hindi is the national language, but India is not truly unified linguistically; most states and countless smaller areas have their own mother tongues. The country functions in English alongside Hindi, however, so barring rural areas you aren't likely to experience a language barrier.

LODGING

India has many and varied room classifications. We review hotels based on standard double rooms, but many luxury hotels in major cities offer a mind-boggling range of options. Some hotels call their least expensive rooms "superior," with "deluxe" rooms more expensive; at others, "superior" is the top category. Many top hotels also have yet other categories of rooms on exclusive club floors. When you reserve rooms in India, **ask for a complete description of the room's classification** to be certain you get what you want. Remember that the cheapest rooms in any hotel, from deluxe properties down to rustic lodges, are usually the worst and sometimes downright substandard, while the next class up might be perfectly delightful. (The cheap ones might be overdue for renovation, or lack bathtubs or views.) Unlike hotels elsewhere, Indian hotels tend to skimp on their economy rooms.

India's Tourism Department also approves and classifies hotels based on a rating system ranging from five stars (the fanciest) to no stars (no frills). Some perfectly excellent hotels and inns that prefer to maintain an Old World ambience are not classified at all, as the ratings are based solely on number of facilities and on hotel and bedroom size. Hotels without pools or those that serve only vegetarian food—including some highly historic, charming, comfortable properties—do not qualify for five-star status but are often just as luxurious as those that do. The rating system also fails to account for service and other important intangibles that can add up to a pleasant stay.

Because the star ratings can be misleading and exclude viable options, we don't cite them. Many tour operators do, however, so it's handy to **know what the stars represent.** A five-star hotel has a large lobby and large bedrooms, numerous restaurants, and a full range of facilities from swimming pool to shopping arcade. A four-star hotel usually has the same size bedrooms as a five-star hotel, but a smaller lobby, perhaps only two restaurants, and normally fewer shops; it will have a swimming pool. A three-star hotel isn't required to have a swimming pool or extensive shops, and its bedrooms are smaller and less luxurious. Two-star hotels and below are very simple by Western standards, with limited facilities. Heritage Hotels (☞ *below*) have their own classification.

The prudent traveler will **secure all room reservations before arrival,** especially during peak season (September to March) and in the major cities and popular tourist destinations like Agra, Kerala, and Goa. Note that school holidays have Indians vacationing for a few days in October or November (for Diwali or, in eastern India, Durga Puja) and for ten days between Christmas and the New Year—reservations are extra-difficult then. Urban hotels rarely have off-season discounts, though some international chains have incentive programs for frequent guests.

Room rates are skyrocketing in business-oriented cities such as Bangalore, Bombay, Calcutta, Delhi, and Madras. In other areas, hotels may even be seeking guests, and you may be able to negotiate your price. When you reserve, **ask about additional taxes** and service charges, which increase the quoted room price (☞ Taxes, *below*).

In smaller towns where hotels are few, opt for the best room in the best hotel. If the room or bathroom still looks doubtful, tip the bellboy to have it re-cleaned in front of you.

The lodgings we review are the cream of the crop in each price category. Unless otherwise noted, rooms in all hotels reviewed in this book have private bathrooms. We always list facilities, but we don't specify whether they cost extra: When pricing rooms, always **ask what's included and what costs extra.** An ✕☒ icon indicates a hotel whose restaurant warrants a trip of its own. Assume that hotels operate on the European Plan (no meals) unless we specify that breakfast and/or other meals are included.

Delhi and Bombay are in a financial league of their own, so we categorize their lodging prices in the chapters themselves. For the rest of India, lodging categories are as follows. The major cities are Agra, Bangalore, Calcutta, Jaipur, Madras, and Varanasi.

CATEGORY*	MAJOR CITIES	OTHER AREAS
$$$$	over Rs. 8,000	over Rs. 4,000
$$$	Rs. 5,000–8,000	Rs. 2,500–4,000
$$	Rs. 2,000–5,000	Rs. 1,500–2,500
$	under Rs. 2,000	under Rs. 1,500

**All prices are for a standard double room, excluding taxes and service charge.*

GOVERNMENT LODGING

The Government of India, individual state governments, Public Works Department (PWD), and Forestry Department provide inexpensive accommodation throughout India. The bulk of these facilities are poorly maintained, and government employees and officials receive priority booking, which means you can be thrown out upon the unexpected arrival of a VIP even if you have a reservation. Some states, however—particularly Madhya Pradesh, Maharashtra, and Kerala—run fairly competent hotels and often provide the best lodgings in remote destinations.

HERITAGE HOTELS

The Indian government has an excellent, relatively new incentive program that encourages owners of traditional *havelis* (mansions), forts, and palaces to convert their properties into hotels or bring existing historic hotels up to government standards. These properties are designated Heritage Hotels, and their architecture and the interiors are authentically Indian, not Western. If such lodgings appeal to you (they're generally well outside large cities), **contact your nearest Government of India Tourist Office for a list of Heritage Hotels.** We also note the designation in our reviews of Heritage Hotels.

HOSTELS

No matter what your age, you can **save on lodging costs by staying at hostels.** In some 5,000 locations in more than 70 countries around the world, Hostelling International (HI), the umbrella group for a number of national youth-hostel associations, offers single-sex, dorm-style beds and, at many hostels, couples' rooms and family accommodations. Membership in any national hostel association, open to travelers of all ages, allows you to stay in HI-affiliated hostels at member rates (one-year membership is about $25 for adults; hostels run about $10–$25 per night). Members also have priority if the hostel is full and are eligible for discounts around the world, even on rail and bus travel in some countries.

➤ ORGANIZATIONS: **Australian Youth Hostel Association** (✉ 10 Mallett St., Camperdown, NSW 2050, ☎ 02/9565–1699, FAX 02/9565–1325). **Hostelling International—American Youth Hostels** (✉ 733 15th St. NW, Suite 840, Washington, DC 20005, ☎ 202/783–6161, FAX 202/783–6171). **Hostelling International—Canada** (✉ 400–205 Catherine St., Ottawa, Ontario K2P 1C3, ☎ 613/237–7884, FAX 613/237–7868). **Youth Hostel Association of England and Wales** (✉ Trevelyan House, 8 St. Stephen's Hill, St. Albans, Hertfordshire AL1 2DY, ☎ 01727/855215 or 01727/845047, FAX 01727/844126). **Youth Hostels Association of New Zealand** (✉ Box 436, Christchurch, New Zealand, ☎ 03/379–9970, FAX 03/365–4476). Membership in the U.S. $25, in Canada C$26.75, in the U.K. £9.30, in Australia $44, in New Zealand $24.

HOTELS

➤ INDIAN HOTEL CHAINS: **Ashok Hotels** (reserve through a travel agent or Ashok Sales Office, ✉ Jeevan Vihar, 3rd floor, 3 Sansad Marg, New Delhi 110001, ☎ 11/353557). **Clarks** (✉ U.P. Hotels, 1101 Surya Kiran, 19 Kasturba Gandhi Marg, New Delhi 110001, ☎ 11/331–2367 or 11/372–2596). **Oberoi Hotels** (☎ 800/562–3764 in the U.S.; ☎ 800/515517 in the U.K.). **Taj Group** (☎ 800/458–8825 or 212/972–6830 in the U.S., ☎ 800/282699 or 020/7828–5909 in the U.K.). **Welcomgroup** (✉ New Delhi, ☎ 11/614–3199, –0925, or –5352).

MAIL & SHIPPING

POSTAL RATES

The cost of an airmail letter (weighing 10 grams) to the United States, Canada, or Europe is Rs. 11.50. Aerograms cost Rs. 6.50. Airmail postcards are Rs. 6.

RECEIVING MAIL

To receive mail in India, **have letters or packages sent to an American Express office.** Mail is held at these offices for 30 days before it's returned to the sender; it can also be forwarded for a nominal charge. To retrieve your mail, show your American Express card or American Express Travelers Checks plus one piece of identification, preferably a passport. This service is free to AmEx cardmembers and traveler's-check holders; others pay a fee.

MONEY

India is still cheaper than most destinations when it comes to shopping, eating at independent restaurants, and staying in comfortable lodgings. It's no longer a total bargain, however, as the increasing cost of gasoline has led to fare hikes of about 50% for planes, trains, hired cars with drivers, taxis, and auto-rickshaws. Moreover, both business and leisure travel are on the rise here, with the result that room prices at deluxe hotels in major cities are comparable to those anywhere else in the world, and resorts in Goa (popular with Westerners) are the most expensive in the country. Many top hotels and some airlines charge foreigners U.S.-dollar prices that are substantially higher than the rupee prices paid by Indian citizens.

A cup of tea from a stall costs about U.S. 10 cents, but in a top hotels it can cost more than $1. A 650-ml bottle of beer costs about U.S.$1 in a shop, $4 without taxes in a top hotel. A 5-km (3-mi) taxi ride in Delhi is supposed to cost about U.S.$1.50 (though it rarely does).

Throughout this book, we quote admission fees for adults, which are usually the same as those for children. For information on taxes, *see* Taxes, *below.*

ATMS

There are very few cash machines in India. If you expect to want cash advances from your credit-card account, **make sure that your credit cards are programmed for ATM use in India** before you leave home. Note that American Express is not widely accepted in India, and Discover is not even worth bringing. Local bank cards often do not work overseas, or may access only your checking account; **ask your bank about a MasterCard/Cirrus or Visa debit card,** which can be used at any ATM displaying a MasterCard/Cirrus or Visa logo. These cards, too, may tap only your checking account—ask your bank.

CREDIT CARDS

American Express is not widely accepted in India. In this book we use the following abbreviations: AE, American Express; DC, Diner's Club; MC, MasterCard; V, Visa.

CURRENCY

The units of Indian currency are the *rupee* and the *paisa*—100 paise equal one rupee. Paper money comes in denominations of 2, 5, 10, 20, 50, 100, and 500 rupees. Coins are worth 5, 10, 20, 25, and 50 paise, one rupee, two rupees, and five rupees. The rate of exchange, which fluctuates, is approximately U.S.$1 = Rs. 43; £1 = Rs. 68.50; C$1 = Rs. 27; Aus$1 = Rs. 28.5; NZ$1 = Rs. 22.4.

CURRENCY EXCHANGE

India has strict rules against importing or exporting its currency. The currency-exchange booths at the international airports are always open for arriving and departing overseas flights. When you change money, remember to get a certain amount in small denominations to pay taxi drivers and such. **Reject torn bills,** as many merchants, hotels, and restaurants won't accept them, and it's a hassle to find a bank to get them exchanged.

Always **change money from an authorized money-changer and insist on receiving an encashment slip.** Some banks now charge a nominal fee for this slip, which you'll need if you want to pay hotel bills or travel expenses in rupees, and again if you want to reconvert rupees into your own currency upon departure from India. Do not be lured by illegal street hawkers who offer you a higher exchange rate.

For the most favorable rates, **change money at banks.** Although ATM transaction fees may be higher abroad than at home, ATM rates are excellent because they're based on wholesale rates offered only by major banks. India's state-run banks can take forever to cash traveler's checks; if possible, save time and use an American Express office or the foreign-exchange service at your hotel. Rates will be slightly lower, but you'll save irritation and time. Rates are also unfavorable in airports, at train and bus stations, in restaurants, and in stores.

TRAVELER'S CHECKS

Traveler's checks are best exchanged in major cities as soon as you need more cash. Most merchants, whether urban or rural, do not accept them. Lost or stolen checks can usually be replaced within 24 hours. To ensure a speedy refund, buy your own traveler's checks—don't let someone else pay for them. The person who bought the checks should also make the call to request a refund.

PACKING

Delicate fabrics do not stand up well to Indian laundering facilities except at deluxe hotels. Although dry-cleaning is available at all top hotels in major cities, the cleaning fluid can be harsh; if you bring clothing that requires dry-cleaning, you may want to wait and have it cleaned back home. Plain cottons and cotton/synthetic blends are coolest in summer and easiest to wash; in general, **avoid synthetic fabrics that don't breathe.**

Most important, **dress modestly. Remember that what is appropriate in the West is not necessarily appropriate in the East.** Only children can get away with short shorts. Men should wear comfortable jeans or longer shorts. T-shirts are fine, but the male topless look should be left to wandering *sadhus* (Hindu ascetics). Women should **stick to long skirts or lightweight slacks regardless of the weather,** as bare legs, even under a conservative pair of shorts, may attract undesired attention. Possible exceptions to this rule are Goa, Bombay, and New Delhi; but even in the major cities shorts are rare. You're bound to feel more comfortable, and command more respect, if you're covered up. Women should also avoid tight tops and sloppy T-shirts, not to mention plunging necklines, which may attract wandering eyes and unflattering remarks. To visit any sacred site, women should wear a below-the-knee skirt or dress or neat pants. Travel in a Muslim community calls for even more discretion: Women should consider wearing a *salwar kameez,* the popular Indian outfit of a long tunic over loose pants gathered at the ankle. (A cotton salwar kameez is inexpensive, comfortable, and flattering.) Bathing suits should be conservative.

All that said, India is not a dressy society. If you attend an upscale function (barring weddings), men can wear a standard business suit; women can wear a dress or skirt and blouse with flats or low heels.

Along with your clothes, bring basic medical and hygienic supplies (☞ Health, *above*), a sewing kit, a lock and key for each piece of luggage, high-power impact-resistant flashlight, a pocket knife, and spare batteries (unless they're a popular size). Good sanitary napkins are sold in India, but tampons are substandard. Sports enthusiasts should bring their own tennis or golf balls, as they're expensive in India.

Bring an extra pair of eyeglasses or contact lenses in your carry-on luggage, and if you have a health problem **pack enough medication** to last the entire trip, or have your doctor write you a prescription using the drug's generic name—brand names vary from country to country. **Don't put prescription drugs or valuables in luggage to be checked:** It might go astray. To avoid problems with customs officials, carry medications in their original packaging.

If you come during the monsoon season, bring a collapsible umbrella. In winter, bring a sweater or a light jacket for cool evenings, and **if you plan to spend time in the Himalayas, bring a warm wardrobe,** as it can be downright cold by day as well as by night, and many accommodations don't have central heating. The trick to assembling your alpine arsenal is triple layering. The layer next to your skin (long johns) should be made of synthetic fabrics or silk that carry moisture away from the skin to the garment's outer surface. (Cotton soaks up perspiration and will keep you wet.) For the second layer, wool, fleece, or a synthetic fabric knitted into thick pile, like Polar Plus, is best. Bring a down vest if you anticipate extremely cold weather; on the bottom half, lightweight Polar Plus trousers are a good choice. For the third layer, bring a well-made, generously sized windbreaker or lightweight parka insulated with a small amount of down and made of Gore-Tex (or an equivalent fiber like Zepel or VersaTech), which not only allows moisture to escape but is waterproof, not merely water-repellent. Bulky down parkas are advisable only for winter excursions or a climb into higher altitudes. A pair of lined Gore-Tex over-pants is indispensable in the rain and cold or when you're thrashing through wet underbrush.

Most adventure-travel firms supply sleeping bags for their clients. If you're roughing it on your own and need a sleeping bag, choose one with an outer shell that will keep you dry, and try to keep it lightweight—you don't need a bag designed for an assault on a mountain peak unless that's the trip you've planned. A down bag guaranteed to keep you warm at 15°F (a fairly low temperature in the Himalayan trekking season) is adequate. If you plan to take overnight trains, consider a sleeping-bag liner.

On any outdoor adventure, long or short, **assemble a day pack for your sweater, camera, and plastic water bottle.** For bird-watching or wildlife-spotting trips, try to bring a good pair of binoculars. Trekkers should also pack out their nonbiodegradable garbage and bury biodegradable refuse away from water sources. Use a trekking agency that carries kerosene for cooking.

PASSPORTS & VISAS

Make two photocopies of your passport's data page, one for someone at home and another for you to carry separately from your passport. If you lose your passport, promptly call your nearest embassy or consulate and the local police.

ENTERING INDIA

Obtain your tourist visas from the Indian embassy or consulate in your home country, or through your travel agent or tour operator. You must **arrive in India within six months of the date your visa is issued.** If you need to extend your visa, go to the Foreigners' Regional Registration Office in one of the major cities or any of the Offices of the Superintendent of Police in the District Headquarters.

Travelers to certain parts of the Himalayas need special permits; ☞ Chapter 2.

PASSPORT OFFICES

The best time to apply for a passport, or to renew the one you have, is during fall or winter. Before any trip, check your passport's expiration date, and renew it as soon as possible if necessary.

➤ AUSTRALIAN CITIZENS: **Australian Passport Office** (☎ 131–232).

➤ CANADIAN CITIZENS: **Passport Office** (☎ 819/994–3500 or 800/567–6868).

➤ NEW ZEALAND CITIZENS: **New Zealand Passport Office** (☎ 04/494–0700 for information on how to apply; 04/474–8000 or 0800/22–5050 for a status report on an application already submitted).

➤ U.K. CITIZENS: The **London Passport Office** (☎ 0990/210–410) can advise you on fees and documentation requirements and facilitate emergency passports.

➤ U.S. CITIZENS: **National Passport Information Center** (☎ 900/225–5674; calls are 35¢ per minute for automated service, $1.05 per minute for operator service).

RELIGION

SACRED SITES

Religious monuments demand respect. With all of India's faiths, you must **remove your shoes before entering a shrine,** even if it appears to be in ruins. All religions ask that you **do not smoke, drink alcohol, or raise your voice** on the premises. Some temples and mosques are off-limits to travelers who don't practice the faith; **don't try to bribe your way inside.** Women visiting sacred places should dress modestly (☞ Packing, *above*) and should cover their heads before entering a Sikh temple or a mosque. Cameras and video cameras are sometimes prohibited inside houses of worship.

Some Hindu and Jain temples do not allow any leather products inside their shrines, including wallets, purses, shoes, belts, and camera cases. Many temples also expect you to purify yourself by washing your hands and feet in a nearby tap or tank before you enter. In Sikh temples, do not point your feet toward the Holy Book or step over anyone sitting in prayer or meditation. Play it safe in both Hindu and Sikh temples: **if you decide to sit on the floor, sit cross-legged or with your feet tucked beneath you.** In some religious shrines, the sexes are separated; look around (or follow instructions) and let the situation govern what you do. When you enter a mosque, you're supposed to step into the courtyard with your right foot first.

Many well-meaning travelers commit an unforgivable sacrilege when they visit a Buddhist monastery. You're welcome to spin any prayer wheel, but just as you must circumambulate the interior and exterior of a monastery, *stupa*, or *mani* wall in a clockwise direction, you must **spin prayer wheels clockwise only.** Inside the monastery, interior cushions and chairs are reserved for lamas (monks), so sit on the steps outside or on the floor. If you have the opportunity to meet a *rimpoche* (head lama) or a respected monk, it's polite not to turn your back on him when you leave. You should also **remove your hat and lower your umbrella** within the confines of a monastery and in the presence of a lama.

ANIMAL SACRIFICE

On relatively rare occasion, a Hindu or Muslim festival involves animal sacrifice, which may upset you or your child (☞ Festivals and Seasonal Events *in* Chapter 1).

SAFETY

Avoid leaving an unlocked suitcase in a hotel room, and unless you have a personal safe, **never leave money, traveler's checks, passports, or jewelry in a hotel room.** Don't even leave your personal effects strewn about; your cosmetics, perfume, and aftershave might vanish. As anywhere, never leave suitcases unattended in airports or train stations. India has no tourist police; the most visible policemen are traffic cops, clad in white and khakhi; they can usually help out, even with a non-traffic problem (though taxis are in their jurisdiction). Otherwise, look for a regular policeman, clad in khakhi.

LOCAL SCAMS

Avoid strangers who offer their services as guides or money-changers. Both functions have legal designates who will not hassle you. In crowds, **be alert for pickpockets**—wear a money belt, and/or keep your purse close to your body and securely closed. Be careful, too, when you use credit cards; when dining out, you can ask that the machine be brought to your table to make sure the card isn't used to make an impression on more than one form. Many restaurants will return your card only after they compare your signature to that on the card. In train stations, **ignore touts who tell you that your hotel of choice is full or has closed;** they are hoping to settle you into a place where they get a kickback for bringing in business.

WOMEN TRAVELERS

Women traveling alone should never get into a taxi or auto-rickshaw if a second man accompanies the driver. Women should also avoid traveling late at night, except perhaps in Bombay. If you find yourself in a tricky situation—a taxi driver demanding a king's ransom, a hawker plaguing you, a stranger following you—head straight for a policeman or at least threaten to do so, which often works just as well. Solo women (everyone, really) should also chain-lock the door to their hotel room, as the staff often knock quickly and come right in.

SENIOR-CITIZEN TRAVEL

To qualify for age-related discounts from Western chain hotels, **mention your senior-citizen status when you reserve,** not when you check out.

SHOPPING

Before you buy anything in India, check your selection for damage, defects, or tears. Don't buy the first item you see in the first shop you visit; shop around. Prices for tourists vary tremendously. Your best line of defense is to learn the going price of an item or class of goods at a fixed-price government emporium, then hit the rest of the retail trail. Note that government-approved shops are not the same as government-run shops; the quality of goods is usually assured in government-approved shops, but prices are not fixed.

WATCH OUT

Be extra-careful when buying jewelery, beads, and anything made of silver, as you have no guarantee that the item is the real thing. Fakes abound: A string of pearls might be made of plastic, a silver necklace of white metal. Gold earrings might be merely gold-plated. A leather bag may not be genuine. Artificial silk is sold as real silk. Bargaining is expected in bazaars. **Offer one-third the stated price,** then settle for about 60%.

In popular shopping areas like Rajasthan, **beware of drivers or touts who want to take you to a certain store,** particularly an alleged friend's or relative's store. This huckster gets a commission on each purchase he brings in. You will feel pressure to buy from the moment you arrive, and will pay a higher price (to cover the commission) if you do.

Buying wild animal skins or ivory is illegal. These items are sold, however, and the poaching that produces them is decimating India's wildlife. Before you purchase any item that a shopkeeper claims is 100 years old, **ask for an export permit.** A reputable shopkeeper will have the permit or help you procure it. If he refuses, the item is a fake or, if it's old, has not been approved by the government for export. Inspect your goods after you pay, and **count your change.**

TAXES

AIRPORT

You may have to pay an airport departure tax when you leave India (increasingly, this tax is included in the price of your airline ticket). If you're moving on to Bhutan, Nepal, Pakistan, Sri Lanka, Bangladesh, Myanmar (Burma), or the Maldives, the tax is Rs. 150; otherwise, it's Rs. 450.

HOTEL

At press time, India levies a 10% expenditure tax on any room costing more than Rs. 1,200 (about U.S.$32). Some states also levy luxury and sales taxes, including a tax on food and beverage bills. The hotel industry is lobbying to reduce these deterrents, but currently taxes on a hotel room can easily increase the cost by 30%. You should also expect an additional sales tax on food and beverages; the percentage varies from state to state.

TELEPHONES

Note that **many Indian businesses have a series of phone numbers** instead of just one, as they don't all consistently work and networks can get congested. If a number reads ☎ 562/331701 (–708), for example, you can reach the establishment using any number between 331701 and 331708—including 331702, 331703, and so forth.

CELLULAR PHONES AND PAGERS

Cell phones in India work on the GSM standard, so phones designed for the American standard will not work in India. Cellular service is available in more and more parts of the country and is active in most major cities; in many cities you can rent a cell phone on a daily or weekly basis from a luxury hotel or the airport. Luxury hotels can also provide you with a pager. Since standard phones are erratic, cellular phones are extremely useful for technical reasons alone.

COUNTRY & AREA CODES

The country code for India is 91. Area codes begin with a 0 within India, but not when calling from overseas. **In India, when dialing a long-distance number listed in this book, add 0 before the area code.** Calling home: The country code is 1 for the U.S. and Canada, 61 for Australia, 64 for New Zealand, and 44 for the U.K.

DIRECTORY & OPERATOR INFORMATION

For local phone numbers, dial 197. For long-distance numbers within India, dial 183. Speak slowly, but don't be surprised if the operator just hangs up on you; India is modernizing its phone system, and the operator may not even have the latest number. Remember that the number of digits in Indian phone numbers varies, even within cities.

If you're not calling from an ISD facility (☞ *below*), dial 186 to reach an international operator.

INTERNATIONAL CALLS

International telecommunications can be subject to long delays outside major cities, but most hotels, airports, and post offices are connected to the computerized International Subscriber Dialing (ISD) system, which eliminates the need for an operator. With ISD, you just dial 00, followed by the country code, the area code, and the number. Remember that **hotels, especially luxury hotels, add an enormous surcharge to international calls and faxes, including those made on your calling card.** If you're at all concerned about costs, ask what they charge before you dial. To avoid the surcharge, make your calls at an ISD/STD offices (even then, the price will be around U.S. $3 a minute to most places in the world). There are no reduced-rate calling hours for international calls.

LOCAL CALLS

A local call normally costs between Rs. 1 and Rs. 5. Some deluxe hotels have coin-operated public phones that take Rs.-1 coins or special tokens available at the reception desk.

LONG-DISTANCE CALLS

Domestic long-distance calls are expensive. You can make them quickly through a computer system called Subscriber Trunk Dialing (STD), which is available in most hotels, at specially designated public phones, and at private ISD/STD offices, easily spotted by their bright-yellow signs. The system carries no surcharge, but most hotels will add their own, which can be extremely high. Ask before you dial.

LONG-DISTANCE SERVICES

AT&T, MCI, and Sprint access codes make phoning home fairly convenient, but you may find the local access number blocked in many hotels. If this happens, ask the hotel operator to connect you; if for some reason he or she can't comply, ask for an international operator, or dial the international operator yourself. One way to improve your odds of reaching your long-distance carrier is to travel with more than one company's calling card (a hotel may block Sprint, for example, but not MCI). If all else fails, call from a pay phone.

➤ ACCESS CODES: **AT&T USADirect** (☎ 000116 or 000117). **MCI Call USA** (☎ 000126 or 000127). **Sprint Express** (☎ 000136 or 000137).

PUBLIC PHONES

To use a public phone, dial the number, then deposit the required coin once the connection is made. The time limit is three minutes, and can be extended to six. The dial tone sounds, but often after you dial the number you'll hear a pulsing tone for a few seconds before the ring cuts in. If you use an International Subscriber Dialing/Subscriber Trunk Dialing (ISD/STD) facility, there is no time limit—a meter records the duration of your chat, and you pay the proprietor the required amount.

When using an STD booth, **check the meter reading before you pay** to see that the time on the slip matches the actual time used on the phone, and that the number recorded on the slip matches the number you dialed. Rates for domestic calls decrease by 50% after 7 PM and 75% after 10:30 PM.

TIME

India is 5½ hours ahead of Greenwich Mean Time, 10½ hours ahead of Eastern Standard Time, 13½ hours ahead of Pacific Standard Time, 4½ hours behind Sydney time, and 7½ hours behind Auckland time.

TIPPING

Some major hotels include in their bills a service charge of 10%, which is also an appropriate amount to leave the waiter in any restaurant. Waiters, room-service attendants, housekeepers, porters, and doormen all expect to be tipped. You won't go wrong if you tip your room valet Rs. 20 per night. Bellboys and bell captains should be paid Rs. 10 per bag. For room service, tip 10% of the bill. Tip the concierge about Rs. 5 if he gets you a taxi. Train-station and airport porters should be paid Rs. 5–Rs. 10 per bag, depending on the weight; set the rate before you let him take your bags. Taxi drivers don't expect tips unless they go through a great deal of trouble to reach your destination; but if you hire a car and driver, tip the driver about Rs. 50–Rs. 100 per day, depending on the distance traveled. If you hire a local guide, tip him or her Rs. 40 for four hours, Rs. 80 for a full day.

TOURS & PACKAGES

On a prepackaged tour (or independent vacation) everything is prearranged, so you'll spend less time planning your trip and avoid budget shocks. Don't confuse packages and guided tours: When you buy a package, you travel on your own, just as though you had planned the trip yourself. Fly/drive packages, which combine airfare and car rental, are often a good deal.

BOOKING WITH AN AGENT

Travel agents are excellent resources. Collect brochures from several, however, as some agents' suggestions may be influenced by relationships with tour and package firms that reward them for volume sales. If you have a special interest, **find an agent with expertise in that area.** ASTA (☞ Travel Agencies, *below*) has a database of specialists worldwide.

Make sure your travel agent is familiar with the rooms and other facilities in any hotel they recommend. Ask about location, room size, beds, and whatever amenities are particularly important to you. Has your agent been there in person, or sent others you can contact?

Do some homework on your own, too: Local tourist boards sometimes have information on lesser-known and niche operators, some of which may sell only direct.

BUYER BEWARE

Every year consumers are stranded or lose their money when tour operators—even large ones with excellent reputations—go out of business. **Check out the operator**—ask several travel agents about its reputation, and try to **go with a company that has a consumer-protection program.** (Look for this information in the company's brochure.) In the United States, members of the National Tour Association and United States Tour Operators Association are required to set aside funds to cover your payments and travel arrangements in case the company defaults. It's also a good idea to choose a company that participates in the American Society of Travel Agent's Tour Operator Program (TOP); ASTA will act as mediator in any disputes between you and your tour operator.

Remember that the more your package or tour includes, the better you can predict the ultimate cost of your vacation. **Beware of hidden costs.** Are taxes, tips, and transfers included? Entertainment and excursions? These can add up.

➤ TOUR-OPERATOR RECOMMENDATIONS: **American Society of Travel Agents** (☞ Travel Agencies, *below*). **National Tour Association** (NTA, ✉ 546 E. Main St., Lexington, KY 40508, ☎ 606/226–4444 or 800/682–8886). **United States Tour Operators Association** (USTOA, ✉ 342 Madison Ave., Suite 1522, New York, NY 10173, ☎ 212/599–6599 or 800/468–7862, FAX 212/599–6744).

TRAIN TRAVEL

Many new trains designated "Superfast," such as the *Shatabdi* and *Rajdhani* expresses, have "air-conditioned chair cars" with seats that recline. These trains link more and more important destinations, and should be your choice if time is a factor.

The next-fastest trains are called "Mail" trains. "Passenger" trains, which usually offer only second-class accommodations, make numerous stops, and are crowded. Trains that run on broad-gauge tracks are much faster than those on meter-gauge or narrow-gauge tracks. Even on the best trains in this group, lavatories are less than pleasant and seats can be well worn.

The *Shatabdi Express* and *Taj Express* travel between Delhi and Agra. Both leave early in the morning from Delhi; the *Shatabdi* takes about two hours, the *Taj* 2½. Each allows for a full day of sightseeing before returning to Delhi. The *Pink Express,* which links Delhi and Jaipur, takes six hours and allows for about five hours of sightseeing before returning to Delhi. Another convenient *Shatabdi Express* runs overnight between Bombay and Delhi; and the overnight *Rajdhani Express* connects Delhi and Calcutta.

Trains offer two kinds of lavatories, the Western-style commode lavatory and the Indian-style toilet (essentially a hole in the ground over which you squat). Although it can be hard to get used to Indian-style facilities, these are actually safer in the sense that there is no contact: Toilet seats in trains are notorious conductors of urinary infections.

For long train rides, **consider buying a yard-long chain with loops and a padlock to secure your luggage.** (You might find a vendor on the platform at a large train station.) After you have *locked* your bag and stowed it in its place, loop the chain through its handle and attach it to a bar or post below the seat. Lock it once more and you won't have to mind your luggage—which does need minding from India's shrewd rail thieves. You can even step off the train to stretch your legs at interim stations, knowing your possessions are safe.

CLASSES

Indian trains have numerous classes of accommodation: first-class air-conditioned (private compartments with two or four sleeping berths), ordinary first-class (non-air-conditioned private compartments with two or four sleeping berths), second-class air-conditioned sleeper (only available on some trains), second-class two-tier sleeper (padded berths), and ordinary second class (always crowded and never comfortable).

RESERVATIONS

Many travelers assume that rail passes guarantee them seats on the trains they wish to ride—not so. You need to **reserve seats in advance,** even if you're using a rail pass. You also need to reserve a sleeping berth if you purchase sleeping accommodations on an overnight train.

If your plans are flexible, you can try to get reservations once you arrive in India. **To save time, use a local travel agent** (who may need to borrow your passport); otherwise, head to the train station and prepare for lines and long waits to make the arrangements yourself. Train stations in big cities have a special tourist counter for foreigners; you can buy "tourist quota" tickets here. (Every train reserves a few seats for tourists who have not made advance reservations.) If you arrive early enough in the morning—around 8—this process should not take you more than half an hour, but in the high season tourist quotas fill quickly, and you may have to change your dates altogether. When it's time to travel, **arrive at the station with enough time to find your seat.** Sleeper and seat numbers are displayed on the platform and on each carriage, along with a list of passengers' names and seat assignments.

LUXURY TRAINS

India's two luxury trains are destinations in themselves, offering sumptuous meals and quarters as well as fine itineraries: Rajasthan's ***Palace on Wheels*** (✉ Rajasthan Tourism Development Corporation, Palace on Wheels Division, Rajasthan Tourism, Bikaner House, Pandara Rd., near India Gate, New Delhi 110011, ☎ 11/338–1884) and Gujarat's ***Royal Orient*** (✉ Gujarat State Tourism Development Corporation, A/6 State Emporia, Baba Kharak Singh Marg, New Delhi 110008, ☎ 11/373–4015), which includes parts of Rajasthan.

DISCOUNT PASSES

Indian Railways offers the Indrail Pass on accommodations ranging from second class to air-conditioned first class. The fares are: one-day pass, U.S.$19–$95; seven-day pass, $80–$270; 15-day pass, $90–$370; 21-day pass, $100–$440; 30-day pass, $125–$550; 60-day pass, $185–$800; 90-day pass, $235–$1,060. Children between 5 and 11 pay half. Try to **buy the rail pass at least two months before your trip.** Provide your agent with your complete rail itinerary to ensure seat confirmation. Every Government of India Tourist Office overseas should have copies of the Tourist Railway Timetable; otherwise, consult Thomas Cook's International Railway Timetable. In India, *Travel Links* and *Travel Hour* list plane and some train schedules. Be aware that if you don't plan to cover terribly many miles, a rail pass may cost more than individual tickets.

To buy the Indrail Pass outside India, contact your travel agent, the Government of India Tourist Office

(☞ Visitor Information, *below*), or one of the designated sales agents listed below. In India, you can buy the pass at railway offices in major cities, international airports, and government-recognized travel agents in Bombay, Calcutta, Delhi, and Madras. You must pay in U.S. dollars, U.S.-dollar traveler's checks, or pounds sterling.

➤ INDRAIL PASS AGENTS ABROAD: **Australia** (✉ Adventure World, P.O. Box 480, North Sydney, New-2059, ☎ 02/9958–7766, FAX 02/9956–7707). **Canada** (✉ Hari World Travel Inc., 1 Financial Place, 1 Adelaide Street East, Concourse Level, Toronto M-SC2V8, ☎ 416/366–2000, FAX 416/366–6020). **United Kingdom** (✉ S D Enterprise, 103 Wembley Park Dr., Middlesex, ☎ 0208/903–3411, FAX 0208/903–0392). **United States** (✉ Hari World Travel Inc., 30 Rockefeller Plaza, North Mezzanine, Shop 21, New York, NY 10112, ☎ 212/957–3000, FAX 212/997–3320).

TRAVEL AGENCIES

A good travel agent puts your needs first. Look for an agency that has been in business at least five years, emphasizes customer service, and has someone on staff who specializes in your destination. In addition, **make sure the agency belongs to a professional trade organization.** The American Society of Travel Agents (ASTA), with 27,000 agents in some 170 countries, is the largest and most influential in the field; under the motto "Integrity in Travel," it maintains and enforces a strict code of ethics and will step in to help mediate agent-client disputes if necessary. ASTA's Web site includes a directory of agents. If your travel agency is also your tour operator, *see* Buyer Beware *in* Tours & Packages, *above*.

➤ LOCAL AGENT REFERRALS: **American Society of Travel Agents** (ASTA, ☎ 800/965–2782 24-hr hot line, FAX 703/684–8319, www.astanet.com). **Association of British Travel Agents** (✉ 68–271 Newman St., London W1P 4AH, ☎ 020/7637–2444, FAX 020/7637–0713). **Association of Canadian Travel Agents** (✉ 1729 Bank St., Suite 201, Ottawa, Ontario K1V 7Z5, ☎ 613/521–0474, FAX 613/521–0805). **Australian Federation of Travel Agents** (✉ Level 3, 309 Pitt St., Sydney 2000, ☎ 02/9264–3299, FAX 02/9264–1085). **Travel Agents' Association of New Zealand** (✉ Box 1888, Wellington 10033, ☎ 04/499–0104, FAX 04/499–0786).

VISITOR INFORMATION

For general information and brochures on India before you leave home, contact the nearest tourist office.

➤ GOVERNMENT OF INDIA TOURIST OFFICE: **New York** (✉ 30 Rockefeller Plaza, Room 15, North Mezzanine, New York, NY 10112, ☎ 800/953–9399, FAX 212/582–3274); **Los Angeles** (✉ 3550 Wilshire Blvd., Suite 204, Los Angeles, CA 90010, ☎ 213/380–8855, FAX 213/380–6111); **Toronto** (✉ 60 Bloor St. W, Suite 1003, Toronto, Ontario M4W 3B8, ☎ 416/962–3787, FAX 416/962–6279); **London** (✉ 7 Cork St., London W1X 2AB, ☎ 020/7437–3677, FAX 020/7494–1048). **Sydney** (✉ Level 2 Piccadilly, 210 Pitt St., New South Wales 200, ☎ 02/9264–4855, FAX 02/9264–4860).

➤ U.S. GOVERNMENT ADVISORIES: **U.S. Department of State** (✉ Overseas Citizens Services Office, Room 4811 N.S., 2201 C St. NW, Washington, DC 20520; ☎ 202/647–5225 for interactive hot line; 301/946–4400 for computer bulletin board; FAX 202/647–3000 for interactive hotline). If you write, enclose a stamped, self-addressed, business-size envelope.

WEB SITES

India is extraordinarily well represented on the World Wide Web, so **use the Web to help plan your trip** if at all possible. You'll find everything from splendid photos of Heritage Hotels to close-ups of temple carving to testaments from former travelers. Fodor's own Web site, www.fodors.com, is a great place to start your online journey. For more information specifically on India, visit www.rediff.com/travel/travhom1.htm, www.indiaserver.com/travel, www.indiamart.com/travel, and www.123india.com/travel_and_tourism.

WHEN TO GO

India's peak tourist season for the plains and the South (which encompass most of the major sights) is fall and winter: mid-September through March. Crowds may pack popular destinations during this time, so **make all reservations well in advance**—especially for trips to Rajasthan, Kerala, and Goa.

By May and June, only the Himalayas are still comfortable; the rest of India is unbearably hot. Himachal Pradesh and Ladakh, where the mountains usually hold back the monsoons, make great escapes from the torrential July and August rains that inundate most of the rest of North India; and summer is often the only time to visit these otherwise snowbound places. If you head for the hills in summer, reserve in advance.

India's monsoons can disrupt plane schedules and the phone and electrical systems; heavy rains can also wash away roads, or bury them in landslides. That said, the monsoons can be a pleasant time to see places that are hot the rest of the year: most of the South (except Kerala), central Gujarat, the Deccan Plateau (Madhya Pradesh and parts of Maharashtra). Rajasthan is also pretty and green in the rain, and Goa's resorts are nice and cheap then, too, if you don't mind having your swimming and sunbathing curtailed.

CLIMATE

India's climate is monsoon-tropical, with local variations. Temperate weather, which includes cool evenings, lasts from October to the end of February. Seriously hot and muggy weather hits South India from the beginning of April to the beginning of June, at which point the monsoon brings rain-laden clouds that then move north, watering nearly every part of India until September. The Himalayas can be extremely cold in winter, and deep snow renders many mountain passes and valleys impassable.

Below are average daily maximum and minimum temperatures for key Indian cities.

➤ FORECASTS: **Weather Channel Connection** (☎ 900/932–8437), 95¢ per minute from a Touch-Tone phone.

BOMBAY

Jan.	88F	31C	May	92F	33C	Sept.	86F	30C
	61	16		79	26		76	24
Feb.	90F	32C	June	90F	32C	Oct.	90F	32C
	63	17		79	26		74	23
Mar.	92F	33C	July	86F	30C	Nov.	92F	33C
	68	20		77	25		68	20
Apr.	92F	33C	Aug.	85F	29C	Dec.	90F	32C
	76	24		76	24		65	18

CALCUTTA

Jan.	79F	26C	May	97F	36C	Sept.	90F	32C
	54	12		79	26		79	26
Feb.	85F	29C	June	94F	34C	Oct.	88F	31C
	59	15		79	26		75	24
Mar.	94F	34C	July	90F	32C	Nov.	85F	29C
	68	20		79	26		64	18
Apr.	97F	36C	Aug.	90F	32C	Dec.	81F	27C
	76	24		79	26		55	13

DELHI

Jan.	70F	21C	May	106F	41C	Sept.	93F	34C
	45	7		81	27		77	25
Feb.	93F	34C	June	104F	40C	Oct.	95F	35C
	50	10		84	29		66	19
Mar.	86F	30C	July	95F	35C	Nov.	84F	29C
	59	15		81	27		54	12
Apr.	97F	36C	Aug.	93F	34C	Dec.	73F	23C
	70	21		79	26		46	8

GANGTOK

Jan.	57F	14C	May	72F	22C	Sept.	73F	23C
	39	4		57	14		61	16
Feb.	59F	15C	June	73F	23C	Oct.	72F	22C
	41	5		61	16		54	12
Mar.	66F	19C	July	73F	23C	Nov.	66F	19C
	48	9		63	17		48	9
Apr.	72F	22C	Aug.	73F	23C	Dec.	59F	15C
	54	12		63	17		43	6

MADRAS

Jan.	84C	29C	May	100F	38C	Sept.	93F	34C
	68	20		82	28		77	25
Feb.	88F	31C	June	99F	37C	Oct.	90F	32C
	70	21		82	28		75	24
Mar.	91F	33C	July	95F	35C	Nov.	84F	29C
	73	23		79	26		73	23
Apr.	95F	35C	Aug.	95F	35C	Dec.	82F	28C
	79	26		79	26		70	21

SHIMLA

Jan.	48F	9C	May	73F	23C	Sept.	68F	20C
	36	2		59	15		57	14
Feb.	50F	10C	June	75F	24C	Oct.	64F	18C
	37	3		61	16		50	10
Mar.	57F	14C	July	70F	21C	Nov.	59F	15C
	45	7		61	16		45	7
Apr.	66F	19C	Aug.	68F	20C	Dec.	52F	11C
	52	11		59	15		39	4

TRIVANDRUM

Jan.	88F	31C	May	88F	31C	Sept.	86F	30C
	72	22		77	25		73	23
Feb.	90F	32C	June	84F	29C	Oct.	86F	30C
	73	23		75	24		73	23
Mar.	91F	33C	July	84F	29C	Nov.	86F	30C
	75	24		73	23		73	23
Apr.	90F	32C	Aug.	84F	29C	Dec.	88F	31C
	77	25		72	22		73	23

1 DESTINATION: INDIA

COSMIC CHAOS

STEP INTO INDIA and you are stepping into the most democratic and the most feudal country in the world.

The marriage of feudalism to freedom is the grandest of India's many paradoxes, and part of its magic and charm. India's people are utterly free, yet the situations of many are fixed in time, at roughly 100 years ago. Contradictions in everyday Indian life may leave you nonplussed on your first trip here. No matter how quickly it charges onto the information superhighway, India remains an enigma, a perplexity, a puzzle you simply can't solve. And every time you think you know the place, something happens to jolt you out of your complacency.

The essence of contemporary Indian life is that people carry on with whatever activity pleases them, even if it's contrary to the law or the comfort of their neighbors—and neither the authorities or the bemused neighbors bat an eye. Parades of disgruntled workers with blaring microphones obstruct a city thoroughfare for 12 hours, and life goes on around them. Villagers use a highway running through their hamlet as a place to dry that season's rice crop, and truck drivers simply drop to the shoulder of the road, navigating carefully for miles—even if it means landing in a ditch—to protect the grain. Your toddler irrigates the second-class train compartment you share with six other people, and your fellow passengers smile benignly and keep their feet up.

Any religious activity in India has society's full sanction. Half the populace occupies the main road in prayer; a whole town blushes orange with religious banners. Festivals turn whole communities upside-down with noise, color, and commotion, but a *tamasha* (spectacle, or happy confusion) is enjoyed by all.

Lunatics stand at crossroads directing imaginary traffic. Cows may even amble into your house. *Dacoits* (highway robbers) are welcomed home, forgiven for a string of crimes, and asked to go into politics. *Sadhus* (ascetic holy men) arrive at your door looking for money. Husbands vanish for years on religious pilgrimages. Your employee takes two months off without leave for his uncle's wife's father's brother's funeral. Indians live as they please.

The flip side of this day-to-day liberty is that many Indians' fates are engraved in stone. The poor seldom become rich. The rich seldom become poor. Carpenters seldom become doctors. Widows seldom remarry. Wives seldom divorce alcoholic, do-nothing husbands. Untouchables never, technically at least, become touchable. Castes cannot be changed or ignored. Social mobility, while gaining momentum, is slow.

The people of India will warm your heart. Democratic or feudal, Indians can be touching in their respect, affection, and concern for you, a guest; their families; and their gods. Where else can you see thousands of people trudging barefoot through the night to pay their respects to a deity in a temple?

Indeed, religion in India is no one-day-a-week affair: It's a way of life, the force that moves the country. Faith governs the mind, defines most behavior, and sets much of the country's agenda and calendar. It becomes a personal lullaby or alarm clock for all, with Hindu temple bells tinkling intermittently and a muezzin calling the Muslim faithful to prayer five times a day. So many gods and goddesses are worshiped here that Mark Twain may have understated the case when he wrote in *Following the Equator* that "in religion all other countries are paupers, India is the only millionaire." Hinduism alone accounts for thousands of deities. Wherever you travel in this spiritual land, you'll find monuments with a sacred element: the Taj Mahal, with its carefully inlaid Koranic verses; Khajuraho's Hindu temples, with their astonishing erotic sculptures; the Ajanta Caves, with their serene murals of the Buddha; Catholic churches in Goa, with their Hindu-esque images of Jesus; Jain temples with their *tirthankaras* (perfect souls), whose poses and features resemble those of the Buddha; and even a handful of historic synagogues.

The earliest remnants of an Indian civilization date from at least 3200 BC, and since then the subcontinent's culture and heritage have endured repeated invasions. Some say India's ability to adapt is the very source of her strength and resilience. Persian-influenced Mogul tombs add delicacy to urban skylines. British bungalows anchor Himalayan hill stations and line major avenues. Cuisines, languages, dance and music styles, and artwork and handicrafts vary widely from state to state. There's no American-style homogeneity in India; each region is intensely proud of its own culture.

To be sure, many aspects of this country can be hard for the Westerner to understand. Why, for instance, do India's urban cows prefer to chew on newspaper rather than on rotting garbage (in plentiful supply) or on random patches of grass in a field? India can also be exasperating and exhausting—a difficult place for those accustomed to efficiency and a Western work ethic. To enjoy your stay in India, surrender, take it slow, and don't try to squeeze too much into a short trip. Prepare to give in to the laissez-faire attitude that seems a natural extension of India's fatalistic tendency. The favorite saying is, "Shall we adjust? We will adjust." In Hindi: "*Adjust karlenge.*" Accept that what happens is meant to be, or is the will of a supreme authority (frequent Indian explanations). If your flight is canceled, the phone doesn't work, or the fax won't go through, don't fly into a rage. When the slow-motion pace of workers in a government bank or post office is about to drive you crazy, remember that this lack of value for time will have an appealing effect when you venture into rural areas and start wondering why, exactly, you spend so much time in your office back home. Here, time's insignificance induces a dreamlike state. You can sit for hours and watch the simplest routines: village women drawing water from a well, or a man tilling the soil with a crude wooden plow. Walking around a deserted ancient city such as Fatehpur Sikri, or watching orthodox Hindus in Varanasi go through their purification or cremation rituals, you'll begin to understand why the art of meditation evolved here. Arrive with the determination to experience India, and make every attempt to adapt; otherwise, this country—which travelers tend to love or hate—might rub you the wrong way.

It helps to be forgiving about some elements of India's inefficiency and overstretched infrastructure. When this country gained independence in 1947, the new democracy chose nonalignment, set up a large national government, and legislated protectionist policies that kept out most foreign products and led almost to economic isolation. The first prime minister, Jawaharlal Nehru, believed protectionism would make India self-reliant and ultimately improve the standard of living, especially for the impoverished. India did move toward self-reliance, but lack of competition stifled the country's own development, with its captive market forced to accept indigenous products that were often substandard or old-fashioned. Until recently, the dominant car on India's roads was a copy of the Ambassador, a British design from the early 1950s with a curvaceous yet bulky chassis: a nostalgic gas-guzzler.

Then, in 1991, a severe debt crisis and a shortage of foreign exchange forced the government to initiate economic reforms whose results have been nothing short of astonishing. Having studiously fended off foreign corporations for decades, India is suddenly encouraging them to invest. Coke and Pepsi are staging their old war on new turf, and software companies are helping turn Bangalore and Hyderabad into 21st-century boom towns.

INDIA'S STIRRING has profound implications, and has already affected her once-rigid lifestyle. Cable TV is changing India, as British, American, French, Pakistani, and Chinese commentators relay their own views of the news on satellite channels. Teenagers now dance to MTV India, a frenetic mixture of Indian and Western pop. American cartoons capture the attention of every Indian child with access to the Cartoon Network. Reruns of *The Bold and the Beautiful* show steamy scenes to a people whose own "Bollywood" movies (made in Bombay) were not allowed to include a kiss until a few years ago. While most Indian women still wear saris or casual, two-piece *salwar-kameez,* some now rush off to their corporate jobs in the latest Western fashions, and many men have become equally label-conscious about everything from the shirts they wear to the foreign liquor they drink. An increasing number of people working in the private sector complain of a new work-related problem: stress.

Yet India still teems with pavement dwellers, otherwise known as the homeless. The poor are not shy about approaching strangers, and the Western traveler with a pocketful of rupees might find it hard to resist a plea, especially from a child. Faced with begging, you are encouraged to visit a local school or medical clinic and make a contribution through a responsible adult.

So, again, if you get frustrated here, remember that everyone from villagers to wealthy urbanites is equally annoyed by lousy services, and impatient for the kind of infrastructure that most Westerners take for granted. And along with this impatience comes a sense of concern: Many Indians lament the arrival of foreign competitors to solve their problems. They worry about the increasing disparity between the haves and have-nots as a result of reforms that have raised inflation. They wonder whether the benefits will really trickle down to the masses. Others wonder if India will succumb to a cultural imperialism that will rob them of their identity. And yet increased exposure to the Western world is unlikely to overturn Indian culture. Most imports will be examined, Indianized, and absorbed, the way Coca-Cola is drunk in western Uttar Pradesh: with salt, red pepper, and *chaat masala.*

All of these issues add dimension to any trip to India, as you are witnessing a country in profound transition. Today's India is more than its thousands of monuments; more than its hundreds of ethnic groups; more than its colorful fairs and festivals; more than the birthplace of Hinduism, Buddhism, Jainism, and Sikhism; more than the sum of its parts. India has taken its first steps toward becoming an economic giant. With a population of 1 billion as of 1999, it is a country that can't be ignored.

—Kathleen Cox and Vaihayasi Pande Daniel

NEW AND NOTEWORTHY

Microsoft has joined IBM, Oracle, Hewlett-Packard, Motorola, Sun Microsystems, and other technology firms in setting up development centers here, mostly in Bangalore and Hyderabad. **Software development** is one of India's fastest-growing industries; in fact, about 10% of Microsoft's employees worldwide are of Indian origin.

As newly arrived multinationals and expanding domestic firms demand more electrical power, phone connections, and water, India's **infrastructure** will remain stretched beyond capacity for years to come. City traffic is hideous during work hours, and pollution is breathtakingly awful—most cars are not fitted with catalytic converters. And while India introduced unleaded gas in 1995 in Delhi, Bombay, Calcutta, and Madras, cars that required unleaded gas may have trouble finding it on long-distance trips through the countryside.

India's **hotel** sector suffers from a shortage of government-approved rooms, especially in the moderate price range. In cities where business travelers outnumber vacationers, room prices at upscale properties have increased significantly. Major international chains are racing into the country to fill the room gap, and India's own chains are also building new properties, most aimed at moderate budgets. Unfortunately, state and federal room taxes can burst travelers' budgets; hoteliers are campaigning against these.

Economic liberalization has opened India's skies to **private domestic airlines,** which have proved that competition can lead to better service (including that of the national domestic carrier, Indian Airlines). The speed with which these new airlines start up, expand, and dissolve makes it impossible for us to document their available flights and schedules. Foreign partnerships, however, were blocked in 1997: The government decided not to open its domestic skies to investment by foreign carriers, who could bring in newer aircraft and higher standards of maintenance. This policy is still fiercely debated.

Finally, disturbances continue to beset the lovely but disputed state of **Jammu and**

Kashmir. Ladakh is open to travelers, but if you want to see any part of Jammu and Kashmir consult your state department and the Government of India Tourist Office in your home country before making plans.

WHAT'S WHERE

India lies in the Northern Hemisphere, bisected laterally by the Tropic of Cancer (which also bisects Mexico). With a total land area of 3,287,000 square km (1,261,000 square mi) and a coastline 6,100 km (3,535 mi) long, it's the world's seventh-largest country. To the north, the Himalayas separate India from Nepal and China. To the east is Bhutan, still closely connected to India by a special treaty. More mountains separate India from Myanmar (formerly Burma) on the eastern border. Also to the east lies Bangladesh, wedged between the Indian states of Assam, Meghalaya, Tripura, and West Bengal. Pakistan borders India's northwest. Just off the subcontinent's southeastern tip lies the island nation of Sri Lanka, separated from the mainland by 50 km (31 mi) of water, the Palk Straits. Conversely, the Lakshadweep Islands in the Arabian Sea and the Andaman and Nicobar islands in the Bay of Bengal, much farther away, are part of the Indian Union.

The Himalayas (*hima* means snow; *laya,* abode), the wall of mountains sweeping 3,200 km (1,984 mi) across north India, are divided into distinct ranges. Among them are the Greater Himalayas, or Trans-Himalayas, a crescendo of peaks that includes some of the world's highest massifs—many above 20,000 feet. In Ladakh, the lunar Karakorams merge into the northwestern edge of the Greater Himalayas. In both ranges, massive glaciers cling to towering peaks; rivers rage through deep gorges, chilled with melting snow and ice; and wild blue sheep traverse craggy cliffs.

Stretching south of the Himalayas is the densely populated Indo-Gangetic Plain. Mountains and hills separate numerous plateaus, and the basins of the Ganga (Ganges) and Brahmaputra rivers make the land rich and productive. This is particularly true in the Punjab, India's breadbasket. The enormous plain also includes the Thar Desert, which extends across western Rajasthan. Except when the vegetation from irrigated fields grows lush after the monsoon, most of its terrain is marked by scrub, cactus, and low rocky hills. The unusual Rann of Kutch, a wide salt flat, is southwest of Rajasthan in the state of Gujarat. Just a few feet above sea level, this strange land mass, which floods during the monsoon, is home to former nomads dependent on camels and what meager income they receive from their exquisite handicrafts.

More mountains cut through India's peninsula and follow its contour. The Eastern Ghats mark off a broad coastal strip on the Bay of Bengal; the Western Ghats define a narrower coast on the Arabian Sea. These low ranges merge in the Nilgiri Hills, near India's southern tip. In the more remote areas of these mountains and plateaus, as in the states of Madhya Pradesh and Orissa, numerous tribes continue to share forested land with wild animals.

South India is tropical, with rice paddies, coffee plantations, and forests that shade spice crops. In the southwestern state of Kerala and part of neighboring Karnataka, exquisite waterways thread inland from the Arabian Sea through a natural network of canals connecting palm-fringed fishing villages.

The Himalayas

Like the teeth of a giant ripsaw, the snow-capped Himalayas cut a border between India and China, passing through four Indian states: Jammu and Kashmir, Himachal Pradesh, Uttar Pradesh, and Sikkim. They inspire awe like no other mountain range in the world. A few hours north of Delhi you can escape the heat of the plains in a Raj-era hill station, hike through terraced fields and alpine passes on an exhilarating treks, or absorb religious teachings in a Hindu temple or Buddhist monastery.

Delhi

India's capital city is huge. Within Delhi, a succession of imperial capitals has left hundreds of monuments reflecting various influences, from Hinduism to Islam to the British Raj to secular independent India. If you want the crush of crowds, get lost in Chandni Chowk; to see Old Delhi without the masses, find Hazrat Nizamuddin Darga, a Sufi tomb in an old-world Muslim district. In New Delhi, wander museums that bring 3,000 years of Indian history to life, then browse contemporary art galleries to see what India's vibrant, modern-day culture is creating. Go shopping: Delhi is one big emporium for all of India's handicrafts. Feast on sumptuous meals and unwind among historic tombs in the verdant Lodi Gardens.

North Central India

Anchored by Agra, Khajuraho, and Varanasi, this section of the traveler's trail heads southeast of Delhi into the state of Uttar Pradesh, detouring into Madhya Pradesh and Bihar. The history of these lands is ancient and vast, with a religious heritage spanning Hinduism, Islam, Buddhism, and even, in Lucknow, Christianity. The spectacular architecture includes Agra's incomparable Taj Mahal and Khajuraho's exciting Hindu temples. Varanasi is the holiest city in Hinduism, drawing a constant stream of pilgrims to bathe in the Ganges River.

Rajasthan

Steeped in tales of chivalry, romance, and revelry, Rajasthan has a timeless spirit and haunting magic that draw travelers by the thousand. From its legendary cities of Jaipur, Jodhpur, Udaipur, and Jaisalmer, built by the mighty Rajputs, to its indigenous tribal and artisan communities, Rajasthan is veritably stuffed with awe-inspiring forts, sparkling palaces, soothing lakes and gardens, exquisite temples and shrines, and world-renowned handicrafts and folk arts.

Gujarat

High art, ancient civilizations, wildlife, and folk crafts all prosper in this northwestern coastal state. Le Corbusier built more buildings in Ahmedabad than he did in all of the United States; lions roam about the Gir Wildlife Sanctuary; Dhola Vira has the remains of a 4,000-year-old city; and crafts villages around Bhuj are known for their hand-woven textiles.

Bombay

Bombay is urbane, stylish, and as hip as India gets. Curving dramatically around the Arabic Sea, this giant metropolis crackles with local color, international commerce, and the glamour of its enormous film industry. But behind its East-West exterior, Bombay remains exuberantly Indian, its streets packed with traffic of every kind. Northwest of the city, the spectacular 2,000-year-old cave temples of Ajanta and Ellora span three religions: Buddhism, Hinduism, and Jainism.

Goa

The former Portuguese colony of Goa is India's most famous beach destination. Silvery strips of sand are never more than a short walk from charming villages here, and the towns—among the cleanest in India—are a pleasing blend of Portuguese and Indian culture and architecture, including a number of historic churches.

Karnataka

Outside Bangalore, Karnataka's high-tech tropical capital, village life transports you to an earlier time. Mysore is a city of palaces—the former maharaja's palace is an architectural tour de force. Near Mysore, the villages of Belur and Halebid have meticulously wrought 12th-century temples. The medieval city of Hampi is a hodgepodge of gorgeous ruins.

Kerala

Sea breezes brush coconut palms on India's southwestern shores, and ancient waterways wend their way inland toward traditional fishing villages. Ayurvedic health programs invite you to unwind completely. The age-old spice-trading city of Cochin has absorbed elements of both East and West, making it a pungent center of commerce and cosmopolitanism; and Kerala's elaborate dance form, the Kathakali dance-drama, is one of India's most colorful performing arts. Between its laid-back towns and the creatures in Lake Periyar Wildlife Sanctuary, Kerala might be called elemental India.

Tamil Nadu

Madras, the capital of Tamil Nadu, encapsulates the spirit and culture of India's southernmost state. From the Bay of Bengal to the Nilgiri Hills, Tamil Nadu resonates with the powerful Hinduism of the ancient Dravidians. The soaring, brilliantly carved, sometimes painted towers of magnificent South Indian temples dominate the landscape, just as faith permeates Tamil life.

Hyderabad

Capital of the southeastern state of Andhra Pradesh, Hyderabad is relatively undiscovered as a cultural destination, but its rich Muslim heritage combines intriguingly with its dynamic software industry. The city is known for its fiery cuisine, its shopping—especially for pearls—and, increasingly, its success in the global business of information technology.

Bhubaneswar

Bhubaneswar, capital of the eastern coastal state of Orissa, is an easy-going temple city with 500 ancient shrines. Small and reasonably peaceful, it's also a town of artisans, as are the villages of Raghurajpur and Pipli. Closer to the water, Konark is famous for its half-ruined Sun Temple—once a complete 225-ft-tall horse-drawn chariot in stone—while Puri still draws intense crowds of pilgrims to its towering Jagganath Temple.

Calcutta

Calcutta is India's best city for walkers, with streets that tell stories. Old mansions dripping with moss and spotted with mildew recall a rich mixture of foreign influence, particularly that of the founding British, and local affluence. Known at once for its Bengali heritage and cosmopolitan outlook, Calcutta is the creative capital of India, promoting art, music, and drama and drawing the best from both performers and their fans. More than its louder urban counterparts, Calcutta will surprise you with its warmth and hospitality.

PLEASURES AND PASTIMES

Beaches

Between October and March you can spend a few days or an entire vacation at a deluxe resort, a beach cottage, or even a safari-style tent on a luscious Indian beach. Goa is perennially popular with Westerners; far less trafficked are the picture-perfect Lakshadweep islands, off Kerala, where you can snorkel around coral reefs. On Kerala's own coast, the sandy beaches at Kovalam are lined with palm-fringed lagoons and rocky coves. At Mamallapuram, south of Madras, the beaches are steps from some of India's finest temple ruins. Gujarat hides an incredibly pristine beach at Mandvi, in Kutch, with clear water and calm surf.

Dining

Indian cuisine varies widely from region to region, but taken together it's a fine art. Meat, seafood, vegetables, lentils, and grains proliferate in splendid combinations—subtle and enticing. The word "curry" is a British corruption of the Hindi word *kari,* the aromatic leaf of the kari plant; typical "curries" are dishes cooked in *masala* (a spicy gravy). Over the centuries, each invading force brought new techniques, ingredients, and dishes; the Moguls, above all, revolutionized Indian cooking, especially in the north, introducing *birianis* (rice dishes), *kormas* (braised meat or vegetable dishes), kebabs, *kofta* (meat or vegetable balls), *dum pukht* (aromatic dishes that are sealed and slow-cooked), and tandoori cooking (which requires a tandoor, a cylindrical clay oven). The British introduced simple puddings and custards. Tibetan immigrants brought *momos* (steamed dumplings), *kothay* (fried dumplings), and hearty noodle soups called *thukpa.* In the northeast, the Bengalis and Assamese took advantage of the nearby waters to emphasize fish and seafood. Gujaratis, Rajasthanis, and South Indian Hindus, all of whom tend to shun meat, developed India's vegetarian cuisine.

Tea is a staple in India, customarily brewed with milk and sugar. In Buddhist areas, you'll find yak-butter tea, made with milk and salt; the butter keeps your lips from cracking in the dry Himalayan air. South Indian filter coffee has a caramel tang, something like café au lait; elsewhere you'll find little but instant coffee. India produces excellent beer, and its Riviera wine is reasonably good. Luxury hotels also import Western spirits, and sell them at luxury prices. Sikkim produces good rum, brandies, and *paan* liqueur. *Chang,* a local brew made from fermented barley, is available in many mountain areas. Goa makes tasty sweet wines and *feni,* a potent liquor made from cashew nuts.

Plenty of Indian restaurants serve delicious meals in appealing traditional or, occasionally, contemporary settings. Street stalls cook up simple specialties to satisfy cravings at next to no cost. In many cities, dining in a popular local restaurant can be a real culinary adventure—don't be afraid to ask your hotel for the name of a place that currently draws a crowd.

For a handy list of menu items, *see* the Dining Glossary *in* Chapter 15.

Performing Arts

India's folk dances derive from various sources, but Indian **classical dance** originates in the temple. The four main dance forms are Bharata Natyam in the south, particularly in Tamil Nadu; Kathakali in Kerala; Manipur in the northeast; and Kathak in the north.

Bharata Natyam is a dynamic, precise style in which the dancer wears anklets of bells to emphasize the rhythm. Many figures in South Indian temple sculptures strike Bharata Natyam dance poses. **Kathakali,** developed over the 16th and 17th centuries, was inspired by the heroic myths and legends of Hindu Vedas (sacred writings) and involves phenomenal body control, right down to synchronized movements of the eyeballs. Boys between the ages of 12 and 20 study this dance form for six years. Kathakali makeup is a particularly elaborate process, with characters classified into distinct types according to the colors of their makeup and costumes. **Manipur** dances revolve around episodes in the life of Vishnu. They are vigorous when performed by men, lyrical when performed by young women. The women's costumes are richly embroidered. **Kathak** is exciting and entertaining—the most secular of the classical dances. The footwork is fast, clever, expressive, and accentuated by bands of bells around the dancers' ankles. The great masters of each of these dance forms command great respect in India. They have studied for years to perfect their artistry, and their age becomes a factor only when they decide to put away their costumes.

Buddhist dances are as stylized as classical Hindu dance forms, except that the movements of the masked and costumed monks are more ritualized, usually working from a slow pace up to a whirl in which flowing skirts become a blur of color. The accompanying music, usually dominated by long horns and cymbals, adds an eerie counterpoint to the monks' deliberate footwork. The dances are usually enactments of important Buddhist legends, or are performed to ward off demons.

As with classical dance, the beginnings of **classical Indian music** can be traced to the Hindu Vedas. Over time, this music—an adjunct to worship—developed definite laws of theory and practice. It also evolved into two broadly divided forms, Carnatic in South India and Hindustani in the north. North Indian music uses a wide range of beautiful instruments such as the sitar and the flute; in the south, musical forms are stricter, with less improvisation. In both schools, the fundamental form is a **raga,** a song based on a twelve-tone system unusual, at first, to the Western ear. At a concert of ragas or **bhajans** (Hindu devotional songs with lyrics), the audience will participate with comments or gestures, expressing enthusiasm for the singer's technical skill and artistic power.

The arrival of the Moguls in the 12th century led to a new form of northern music incorporating the Persian **ghazal,** an Urdu rhyming couplet expressing love. In the ghazal, however, the object of devotion can be a woman or the divine or even the singer's home state. Part of the joy in hearing ghazals, at least for those who understand Urdu, comes from deciphering oblique references that give layers of meanings to a single line and are attributed to the skill of the poet and even the singer. Audiences at ghazal performance show appreciation by mirroring a hand motion of the musician or singer, or by praising a turn of phrase.

As with dancers, years of concentrated study lead to revered status for musicians. India's finest singers and instrumentalists are well over the age of 30 and frequently in their 60s.

Shopping

Each part of India specializes in different products. There are still plenty of villages where the majority of residents are weavers, painters, or sculptors, and similar artisan districts are clustered in the old bazaars of large cities.

India has the world's largest **rug** industry. Tibetan refugees and the Sikkimese make superb carpets with Buddhist themes. Dhurries, in wool or cotton, have charming folk or tribal motifs; some of the finest dhurries come from Rajasthan and Madhya Pradesh.

Delhi, Rajasthan, and Karnataka have wonderful **silver** work, including old ethnic and tribal jewelry. (Buyer beware: The silver is not always pure.) **Gold** jewelry is a smart purchase, and in many cities (Bombay, Calcutta, Delhi, Jaipur, and Madras in particular) you'll find jewelers who can quickly design to order. The price per gram is determined by the world rate, but the cost for the workmanship is a bargain. **Precious and semiprecious stones,** beautifully cut and highly polished, are another great buy here—Jaipur has wonderful gems that you can buy separately or have fashioned into exquisite jewelry. Jaipur also sells intricately worked **enamelware,** as does Madhya Pradesh. In Hyderabad, the center of India's pearl trade, **pearls** of every shape and hue are polished and sold according to sheen, smoothness, and roundness.

Intricate Mogul- and Rajput-style **miniature paintings** and cloth **batik** wall hangings are specialties of Rajasthan. Orissa is known for ***dhokra*** (animal and human figures in twisted brass wires), ***pata chitra*** (finely wrought temple paintings), and ***tala patra*** (palm-leaf art). Weavers throughout India work **textile designs** into cotton or silk, the latter sometimes threaded with real gold or silver. Beautiful brocades and crepe silk come from Varanasi; the finest heavy silks, many in brilliant jewel tones, are made in Kanchipuram, near Madras. Bangalore and Mysore are also important weaving centers. *Himru* (cotton and silk brocade) is woven in Aurangabad. *Jamdani* weaving, a cotton brocade with *zari* (silver) thread, comes from West Bengal. Orissa is known for *ikat,* a weave that creates a brushstroke effect to color borders on silk or cotton. Gujarat and Rajasthan create marvelous tie-dye and embroidered fabrics. To scan a good selection of all these products, stop into one of the fixed-price Central Cottage Industries Emporiums in Bangalore, Bombay, Calcutta, Delhi, Hyderabad, or Madras.

Beautiful **brass and copper** work are sold everywhere, but Tamil Nadu has especially fine sculptures and temple ornaments. Tribal areas in Orissa and Madhya Pradesh specialize in **metal figurines.** Hyderabad and Aurangabad produce jet and silver ***bidriware,*** especially boxes and bangles. Sculptors chisel delightful **stone statues** in Orissa, Tamil Nadu, and Rajasthan. Artisans in Agra create exquisite **marble inlay** work, carrying on a Mogul tradition: Jewels are sliced petal-thin and embedded in marble with such precision that the joints are imperceptible even with a magnifying glass.

Wherever people live in wooden dwellings, you find hand-crafted **teak, ebony, cedar, sandalwood,** or **walnut.** Rajasthan is known for objects covered with enchanting thematic paintings, from small boxes to furniture and doors. Artisans in Orissa and Andhra Pradesh create charming painted toys. ***Lac*** turnery is an Indian art form in which layers of color are added to wood and then polished; the best lac products—bangles, toys, boxes—come from Jaipur and Gujarat. Kashmir specializes in carved walnut items: boxes, tables, gorgeous screens. Kerala and Karnataka are known for finely wrought carvings in sandalwood.

Wildlife Sanctuaries

India has 59 national parks and more than 250 sanctuaries, home to more than 350 different mammals and 1,200 birds. Many of these creatures are unique to the subcontinent, such as the white tiger, royal Bengal tiger, Asian lion, lion-tailed macaque, Andaman teal, great Indian bustard, and monal pheasant.

Before 1947 India did not protect its wildlife. By 1952, 13 species had been declared endangered, and today the list has multiplied to 70 species of mammals, 16 species of reptiles, and 36 species of birds. Tigers, the symbolic mascot of India, were killed so frequently that by 1970, only 1,500 remained. In 1972, the Indian government finally passed the Wildlife Act, which designates natural parks and sanctuaries and provides for the protection of wild animals, particularly endangered species. Three years later, Corbett National Park became India's first tiger reserve, part of Project Tiger—a large-scale enterprise cosponsored by India's Department of Wildlife and the World Wildlife Fund to ban killing and set up 10 reserves. The total number of tigers has risen to over 4,000, but poachers may yet finish off this rare animal.

India is also attempting to re-cover a third of its land with forests—a daunting task that requires more than saplings. The rural poor must find viable fuel sources to replace wood, and a humane initiative is needed to control the movement of foraging livestock, including the sacrosanct cow.

Still, many of India's parks and sanctuaries are enchanting. If you have a safari in mind, remember that many of India's animals are elusive, moving in small packs at daybreak and twilight or at night. Count yourself lucky if you spot a tiger, an Asian lion, or a leopard. Come with the proper expectations and you *will* see many animals: numerous species of deer, wild boar, langur of all descriptions, and spectacular birds. Keep your camera and binoculars ready. Shooting, of course, is prohibited, but the hunter's loss is the photographer's gain. Wear neutral clothes to better blend into the forest. If you want to stay overnight *inside* a sanctuary, arrange to arrive before it closes at sunset.

GREAT ITINERARIES

Classic India

This tour is a broader version of the well-trod Golden Triangle, which concentrates on **Delhi, Jaipur, and Agra.** For a more comprehensive and exciting experience, start in **Bombay** and include **Khajuraho** and **Varanasi.** You can fly any or all of these legs, but touring with a hired car and driver gives you a better look at the countryside and allows for impromptu stops along the way.

DURATION➢ 17 days

TRANSPORTATION➢ Fly to Delhi, drive from Delhi to Khajuraho, fly to Varanasi, and fly back to Delhi.

THE ROUTE➢ **Two days: Bombay.** Dive into this heady metropolis for a crash course in all things Indian. Explore the historic Fort district, navigate some bazaars, and stroll around lovely Malabar Hill, saving time to wander from Chowpatty Beach down Marine Drive along the Arabian Sea.

Three days: Delhi to Jaipur. Fly to Delhi. After touring Delhi, drive from Delhi to Rajasthan's Neemrana Fort Palace, just off the main highway between Delhi and Jaipur. Set high on a bluff, this restored fort has amazing views and invites complete relaxation or scenic afternoon walks. The next day, drive about three hours to Jaipur, where you can stay at a converted palace or Heritage Hotel while you explore Jaipur's unforgettable bazaars and monuments.

Three days: Fatehpur Sikri and Agra. En route from Jaipur to Agra, tour the splendid buildings of the ancient and deserted Mogul capital Fatehpur Sikri. In Agra you'll encounter the world-famous Taj Mahal and the much less famous but almost equally beautiful tomb of Itmad-ud-Daulah.

Two days: Gwalior and Orchha. Drive from Agra to Gwalior to see its spectacular pre-Mogul Hindu fort and palace built into a high escarpment. An optional excursion brings you to Orchha, another seat of Hindu rajas that mixes palaces, temples, and monuments on a small, picturesque river.

Two days: Khajuraho. Drive on to Khajuraho and spend two days absorbing the exuberantly carved 10th- and 11th-century temples and the surrounding villages, which cling strongly to an agrarian lifestyle.

Two days: Varanasi. Fly from Khajuraho to Varanasi. Take a peaceful morning cruise on the Ganges River to witness Hindu rituals on the steps of the sacred waters. Wander among Varanasi's temples and silk or carpet emporiums and drive out to nearby Sarnath, imbued with Buddhist significance.

Three days: Delhi. Fly to Delhi to explore the old and new capitals. Old Delhi has Mogul remnants, such as the Red Fort, Jama Masjid, and Chandni Chowk, now a hodgepodge market; New Delhi has the Mogul Humayun's tomb and also the seat of the former British Raj and the lovely Lodi Gardens. Have a look at the Crafts Museum and save time for last-minute shopping.

Southern Idyll

Experience the tropical south beginning in **Tamil Nadu** with historic towns and massive temples. Relax at seaside resorts and on indigenous boats as you cruise through the lush backwaters of **Kerala.** Search for wildlife at Kerala's excellent **Lake Periyar Wildlife Sanctuary.** Add one more cultural dimension—say, a Kathakali dance performance—and, as a personal indulgence, a soothing ayurvedic massage to chase away any lingering stress.

DURATION➢ 13–14 days

TRANSPORTATION➤ Hire a car and driver for excursions from Madras, then fly from Madras to Madurai. Hire another car and driver for the trip west to Lake Periyar; continue to Cochin and then pause for a slow cruise on the backwaters near Alleppey. Drive on to Kovalam and wind up at Trivandrum, where you can catch flights to other major cities.

THE ROUTE➤ **Four days: Madras and Mamallapuram.** Spend two days in Madras, originally developed by the Portuguese and British but now decidedly South Indian, with bazaars, bustling Hindu temples, and a thriving film industry. Take a leisurely two-day excursion to Mamallapuram via Kanchipuram, a silk-weaving center and the site of more than 200 temples. At Mamallapuram, on the Bay of Bengal, see the exquisite cave sculptures and shore temple left behind by the Pallava dynasty (4th–8th centuries). Catch some sun and surf at a relaxing resort, and return to Madras.

Two days: Madurai. Fly from Madras to Madurai and spend two days exploring the city and its astonishing Meenakshi Temple, whose marvelous architecture includes soaring *gopurams* (entrance towers) and prominent displays of ritual. Comb through the bazaars surrounding the temple complex.

Two days: Lake Periyar Wildlife Sanctuary. Drive west from Madurai across the Western Ghats to Kerala's Lake Periyar, where boat rides provide the leisurely means for a safari: Wild elephants and other animals roam the banks of this lovely preserve.

Two days: Cochin. Proceed northwest by car to Cochin, and take two days to see this ancient port city, with its historic synagogue, curio shops, and Portuguese fort. At night, try to attend a Kathakali dance performance, where you can see how the dancers apply their complicated makeup before they mesmerize you with their hard-honed talent.

One or two days: Backwater Cruise. Drive to Alleppey early in the morning and cruise through some of Kerala's backwaters, past palm trees, shaded villages, and bright-green paddy fields. If you get hooked, take an overnight houseboat cruise. Back in the car, repair to a special beach resort just south of Kovalam.

Two days: Kovalam. Spend two nights at the Surya Samudra Beach Garden, tucked away in a cove on the Arabian Sea. Swim, have an ayurvedic massage, and loll about; you can even study yoga and meditation here. Fly out from nearby Trivandrum.

FODOR'S CHOICE

No two people agree on what makes a perfect vacation, but it's nice to know what others have experienced. For more details on each suggestion, see the appropriate regional chapter.

Ancient Wonders

★ **Cave temples, Ajanta and Ellora.** Dating back more than 2,000 years, these monolithic temples rank among the wonders of the ancient world. Monks and artisans carved whole cities of them into solid rock, decorating some with lavish frescoes and profusely carved statues.

★ **Hampi, Karnataka.** This ruined city was the center of the largest Hindu empire in South India prior to the 16th century. A jumble of vast stone temples, elephant stables, barracks, and palaces, it's an awesome spectacle.

★ **Sun Temple, Konark.** The Sun Temple was built in the form of the sun god Surya's chariot, its 24 giant wheels pulled by seven horses. Every inch is carved with some of the most fantastic sculptures in India: mythical animals, erotic couplings, and whimsical scenes from daily life.

★ **Taj Mahal, Agra.** Resplendent in soft white marble and resonant with a bittersweet love story, the Taj lives up to its reputation. Both the photogenic exterior and the quiet, exquisitely decorated interior leave a lingering sense of peace and wonder.

★ **Temples, Khajuraho.** Hinduism under the Chandelas drew no strict boundary between sacred and profane. Khajuraho's 9th- to 12th-century temples have some of the best sculptures in India: sinuous, twisting forms of virile men and voluptuous women, throbbing with life, tension, and conflict.

Unforgettable Scenes

★ **Backwaters, Kerala.** To see life in Kerala at a Keralite pace, float slowly through its inland waterways. Gliding past graceful coconut palms and blindingly green paddy fields, you'll see tile-roof houses with canoes moored outside, tiny waterfront churches, and people washing themselves and their clothes in the river.

★ **Chowpatty Beach and Marine Drive, Bombay.** Bombay's setting is part of what makes it so intoxicating. Chowpatty Beach is a taste of the Bombay carnival, with vendors, food stalls, and rides. Walk east along perfectly curved Marine Drive for a lingering encounter with the incredible geography and with locals of every stripe.

★ **Ganges River at dawn, Varanasi.** The rising sun casts a dark-gold glow on the city devout Hindus hold most dear. Pilgrims and devotees perform ablutions on the riverbank, and temples begin to whirr into action. Climb to the roof of the Alamgir Mosque for a sweeping view of the city along the river's languid curve.

★ **Jaisalmer.** Soaring out of Rajasthan's Thar Desert like a giant sand castle, Jaisalmer is resplendent in golden sandstone. The way light plays against this ancient city is magical. Approach slowly to savor the view of carved spires and palaces jutting above the fortress wall.

★ **North Calcutta.** History is palpable in the comparatively new city of Calcutta, founded by the British in 1690. Wander the charming, European-tinged streets of this old section for an immersion in the city's mixture of Western, Bengali, and Muslim elements, from mansions to bookstalls to pungent bazaars.

Flavors

★ **Fort Cochin, Cochin.** Bamboo and traditional furnishings give this outdoor restaurant the feel of a Keralite cottage. The day's catch is wheeled before you in a wooden cart, and your choice is cooked specially for you—simply grilled or exquisitely curried. *$$*

★ **Khyber, Bombay.** A maze of rooms on three floors, Khyber is designed in a cozy Himalayan style and superbly decorated with murals by local artists. The kitchen serves pungent, delectable Northwest Frontier food that you won't forget in a hurry. *$$$$*

★ **La Rochelle and Wine Bar, Delhi.** The chef in this elegant restaurant lives up to his nickname, Picasso: His East-West cuisine is so beautiful that it's almost painful to disturb your food, but natural ingredients and creative light preparations push you over the edge. *$$$$*

★ **Park Baluchi, Delhi.** North Indian barbecue inspires new superlatives at this wooded restaurant in the village of Hauz Khas. Incredibly delicate kebabs are followed by traditional and creative Baluchi dishes. *$$*

★ **Vishalla, Ahmedabad.** Snake charmers, folk musicians, and flickering lantern shadows cast an aura of magic at this outdoor restaurant, a re-created Gujarati village where you sit on straw mats and feast on superb local fare served on banana leaves. *$$$$*

Comforts

★ **Castle Mandawa, Shekhavati.** Towering high above its town, this rugged 15th-century fort offers large, airy rooms with period furniture. After a candlelight dinner in the breeze, sip tea on the terrace and behold the town and Rajasthan desert spreading out below. *$$*

★ **Lake Palace, Udaipur.** This 250-year-old palace floats like a vision of white marble in the middle of Lake Pichola, oozing history and romance. The suites are colorfully opulent, and most rooms have lake views. *$$$$*

★ **Neemrana Fort Palace, near Shekhavati.** Rooms in this 15th-century fort are furnished with antiques and decorated with Rajput handicrafts. Wooden latticework screens, cusped arches, niches, and gleaming pillars abound. Forget phones and TVs—relax and watch peacocks and parrots from the balconies and courtyards. *$$–$$$$*

★ **Surya Samudra, Kovalam.** This rambling, secluded resort overlooks the Arabian Sea and offers a full range of ayurvedic treatments. Most rooms are in stunningly restored wooden homes, each with a carved facade and spacious open-air bathroom. *$$–$$$*

★ **Taj Mahal, Bombay.** India's most famous hotel, this Victorian Gothic extravaganza looks past the Gateway of India to the Arabian Sea. Built in 1903, its stunning brownstone exterior, with rows of jutting white balconies, has made it a Bombay landmark in its own right. *$$$$*

FESTIVALS AND SEASONAL EVENTS

India holds religious celebrations year-round, along with numerous fairs and cultural festivals. Dates of some celebrations are determined by the lunar calendar, so check with the Government of India Tourist Office for details.

WINTER

DEC.➢ The **Shekhavati Festival** celebrates the frescoes on the local havelis (mansions), as well as other local arts, traditional music and dance, and cuisine from this Rajasthan region. At the **Shilp Darshan Mela** near Udaipur, master craftsmen show how they create award-winning handicrafts, and dancers and musicians perform.

JAN.➢ **Republic Day,** the 26th, commemorates the adoption of India's constitution with a big parade in Delhi and celebrations elsewhere. Kerala's four-day **Great Elephant March** features caparisoned elephants, snake-boat races, and cultural events in various locales. The two-day **Camel Festival** in Bikaner (Rajasthan) celebrates the ship of the desert with parades, races, and dancing. **Makar Sankranti** has people engaging in kite duels from rooftops in Ahmedabad. In Tamil Nadu, **Pongal,** a colorful three-day festival at the close of the harvest season gives thanks to the rain god, the sun god, and the cow with bonfires, games, dancing, and cows bedecked with garlands.

JAN.–FEB.➢ During **Gangasagar Mela,** the festival of the Ganges River, pilgrims from all over India celebrate the most important natural element in their mythology. Nagaur (Rajasthan) holds an enormous **cattle fair** complete with camel races and cultural programs. The five-day **Desert Fair,** Jaisalmer's gala, includes traditional Rajasthani music and dance, handicrafts, camel caravans, camel races, and turban-tying events.

FEB.➢ For the three-day **Elephanta Festival of Music and Dance,** artists perform nightly on a platform near these Maharashtra caves. The **Surajkund Crafts Mela** draws crowds to a village near Delhi to watch traditional dances, puppeteers, magicians, and acrobats and to shop for crafts made by artisans from every state. On **Losar,** the Buddhist New Year, costumed *lamas* (monks) perform dances at monasteries in Sikkim.

FEB.–MAR.➢ On the eve of **Holi,** the festival of spring, Hindus nationwide light a bonfire and send a female demon up in flames, demonstrating the destruction of evil; the next day, children throw colored water on each other and you. On **Id-ul-Fitr,** the Muslim holiday that concludes the month-long Ramadan fast, the devout give alms to the poor, offer prayers, and feast and rejoice. The **Kumbh Mela,** a celebration of immortality, is India's largest religious festival and a stunning spectacle of bathers in the Ganges. Held every three years in Allahabad, Haridwar, Nasik, or Ujjain, it comes to Allahabad in February 2001. The two-week **Taj Mahotsav** spotlights Agra's heritage through handicrafts and cultural events.

SPRING

MAR.➢ India's best performers entertain in the moonlight, with historic Kailasa Temple as a backdrop, for the three-day **Ellora Festival of Classical Music and Dance.** India's best dancers present classical works at the **Khajuraho Dance Festival,** held in part on an outdoor stage against the temples. Pachyderms have their day in Jaipur when the **Elephant Festival** sets off processions, races, and even elephant polo.

MAR.–APR.➢ **Carnival**—the Mardi Gras held just before Lent—hits Goa as a big party with masked dancers, floats, and good eating. The **Gangaur Festival** of Jaipur and Udaipur honors the goddess Parvati with processions of young girls and images of the goddess and, in Udaipur, fireworks, dancing, and a procession of boats on Lake Pichola.

APR.➢ Honoring Lord Jagannath, Bhubaneswar's 21-day **Chandan Yatra** features processions in which images of deities are carried to sacred tanks and rowed around in decorated boats.

APR.–MAY➢ At **Puram,** a major temple festival in Trichur (Kerala), elephants sporting gold-plated mail carry Brahmins with ceremonial umbrellas and the temple deity, Vadakkunathan (Shiva), in a procession to the beat of temple drums. The spectacular 10-day **Chitra Festival** celebrates the marriage of goddess Meenakshi to Lord Shiva at Madurai's Meenakshi Temple.

MAY➢ Buddhists celebrate **Buddha Jayanti**—the birthday, enlightenment, and death of Sakyamunni (Historic Buddha)—with rituals and chants at monasteries. Special celebrations are held in Sikkim and other major pilgrimage centers, such as Sarnath and Bodhgaya. On **Muharram,** Shiite Muslims commemorate the martyrdom of the Prophet Mohammed's grandson Hussain, who died in the battle of Karbala. Participants' intense self-flagellation may disturb the squeamish. On **Bakrid** or **Id-ul-Zuha,** celebrating the sacrifice of Harrat Ibrahim (Abraham), Muslims solemnly sacrifice one animal per family (or group of families) and conclude with a feast and joyous celebration.

SUMMER

JUNE–JULY➢ Puri's seven-day **Rath Yatra,** honoring Lord Krishna, is Orissa's most sacred festival and draws big crowds. The two-day **Hemis Festival** at Ladakh's largest monastery commemorates the birthday of Guru Padmasambhava with masked lamas performing ritual *chaams* (dances) and haunting music.

JULY–AUG.➢ In Jaipur, women and girls observe **Teej,** the arrival of the monsoon, dedicating their festivities to the goddess Parvati.

AUG.➢ **Independence Day,** on the 15th, commemorates India's independence from British rule in 1947.

AUG.–SEPT.➢ **Ganesha Chaturthi,** a 10-day festival celebrated in Bombay and Pune, marks the birthday of the Hindus' elephant-headed god; clay images of Ganesh are paraded through streets and installed on platforms. **Onam** celebrates Kerala's harvest season with dancing, singing, and exotic snake-boat races in Alleppey, Aranmula, and Kottayam. **Pang Lhabsol** offers thanks to Mt. Kanchenjunga, Sikkim's guardian deity, and honors Yabdu, the great warrior who protects the mountain.

AUTUMN

SEPT.–OCT.➢ Calcutta turns into one big party for **Dussehra,** or **Durga Puja,** a 10-day festival honoring the Hindu goddesses Durga, Lakshmi, and Sarasvati. Farther south, Mysore hosts concerts and cultural events in Durbar Hall, and the the maharaja himself comes out in full regalia, complete with some palace treasures, for the traditional procession.

OCT.➢ On **Gandhi Jayanti,** Mahatma Gandhi's birthday (the 2nd), pilgrims visit the Raj Ghat, where Gandhi was cremated. Jaipur's **Marwar Festival** brings to life myth and folklore in Marwari culture, music, and dance.

OCT.–NOV.➢ **Diwali,** the festival of lights, is India's most important Hindu festival, celebrating the day the Hindu God Rama (Vishnu) ended a 14-year exile, as well as the start of the New Year. Hindus worship Lakshmi, the goddess of prosperity; oil lamps flicker in most homes symbolizing the victory of truth (light) over ignorance (darkness); cities crackle with the explosion of fireworks; and Bengalis worship Kali, the black goddess of destruction.

NOV.➢ For the five-day **Konark Dance Festival,** Odissi (classical Orissan dances) are performed at the Sun Temple and a craft fair is held. Nomads assemble with their camels and gaily festooned cattle for Rajasthan's carnivalesque **Pushkar Festival.**

NOV.–DEC.➢ The **International Seafood Festival** at Miramar Beach, near Panaji (Goa), offers three to five days of good food, music, and Indian, Western, and local folk dances.

2 THE HIMALAYAS

Like the teeth of a giant ripsaw, the snowcapped Himalayas cut a border between India and China, passing through four Indian states: Jammu and Kashmir, Himachal Pradesh, Uttar Pradesh, and Sikkim. They strike awe like no other mountain range in the world. A few hours north of Delhi you can escape the heat of the plains in a Raj-era hill station, hike through terraced fields and alpine passes on exhilarating treks, or absorb religious teachings in a Hindu temple or Buddhist monastery.

By Michael Bollom, Andy McCord, Kathleen Cox, David Quegg, Modhurima Sinha, and John Larson

THE REGIONS OF THE INDIAN HIMALAYAS are united only by their proximity to the same mountain range. Culturally, and even physically, they're quite different. The people of Sikkim look more East Asian and practice Tibetan Buddhism, while Kumaonis from Uttar Pradesh are Hindus with distinctly Aryan features and darker skin. The people of Leh speak Tibetan and eat *momos* (stuffed dumplings), while just several hundred miles away Kashmiris converse in Urdu over meals of kebabs. Geographically, the moonscapes of Ladhakh stand in sharp contrast to the lush tea gardens of the Kangra Valley, and Manali's pine forests are a world apart from the rhododendron jungles around Gangtok. Because transportation between these regions is limited, few travelers have the time and energy to experience more than one or two, so choose your destination carefully.

If you're headed for the mountains of Himachal Pradesh, you may find Amritsar a worthwhile cultural detour. The largest city in the affluent, predominantly Sikh state of Punjab, Amritsar is the holiest city to the Sikh religion, its massive Golden Temple an inspiring destination in its own right. History buffs may also want to visit the site of the infamous Amritsar Massacre, a turning point in the fight for Indian Independence. Farther east—on the other side of Nepal—if you're Sikkim-bound, or just want a pastoral break from Calcutta, the historic hill station of Darjeeling invites exploration and easy alpine walks.

Whatever your interest, contact the recommended tour operators for details (☞ The Himalayas A to Z, *below*). Most will design a special trip just for you, whatever your budget or age. Try to make arrangements at least two months in advance. If you're planning a trek, contact a tour operator who is familiar with the specific area you have in mind. Play it safe: don't embark on any route without a guide. Travelers in high-altitude areas should heed all warnings about sun exposure and high-altitude sickness (☞ Health *in* Smart Travel Tips A to Z): Even if you'll be ensconced in a jeep, bring powerful UVA/UVB sunblock, a wide-brim hat, and sunglasses that block ultraviolet rays. Allow three days for full acclimatization. For travel to remote areas, bring a means of water purification, a quart-size canteen, and energy-producing snacks.

Foreigners must obtain an Inner Line Permit and travel with at least three other foreigners *and* a government-recognized tour operator to visit the Spiti Valley in Himachal Pradesh and the Khaltse (Drokhpa area), Nubra, and Nyoma subdivisions in Ladakh. Trekking in Sikkim requires a Restricted-Area Permit. Most tour operators can help you secure permits (☞ Permits *in* The Himalayas A to Z, *below*).

Numbers in the margin correspond to points of interest on the Northwest Indian Himalayas and Sikkim maps.

AMRITSAR

1 Because of its proximity to the Pakistani border (Lahore is only 40 mi away), Amritsar has not seen the development, and attendant sprawl, that other North Indian towns have endured. The city is an important commercial hub: much of the aromatic Basmati rice that's now an international staple is exported by Amritsar dealers, and dried fruits and woolens from hill regions as far away as Afghanistan are handled by wholesalers here. The robust rural culture of Punjab's farmlands permeates Amritsar, with tractors plying the city roads and peasants making their way through the market centers as well as the famous Sikh

temple. Traffic and tumult are muted, so you can get around easily by cycle- or auto-rickshaw.

The Golden Temple of the Sikhs is reason enough to come to Amritsar, and even if you think you've had enough of India's overwhelming religious pageantry you should not miss it. It resembles more a Mogul palace than a typical Indian temple, and its layout and ambience are a living lesson in the teachings of the Sikh religion, a syncretic movement combining Hinduism's *bhakti* (devotion to a personalized god) with Islam's monotheism and egalitarianism. Sikhism was founded by Guru Nanak around the turn of the 16th century, and developed under the gurus who succeeded him into a distinct new religion. Amritsar ("Pool of Nectar" in Punjabi and Sanskrit) takes its name from an ancient sacred pool that Nanak is said to have preferred for his meditation and teaching. The site was granted to the fourth guru, Ramdas, in 1577 by the great Mogul emperor Akbar, and gradually developed as a pilgrimage center. As the 1500s came to a close, songs by the Sikh gurus and selections from Hindu and Muslim poet-saints were canonized as the *Adi Granth* ("First Book") by the fifth guru, Arjan, at the same time as the great *gurdwara* (temple; "door to the guru") was being constructed here. In succeeding years, the temple and the sacred book together gained increasing importance in the Sikh faith. In 1699 the 10th guru, Gobind Singh, further consolidated the faith, establishing a distinctive physical appearance for his followers—most notably long hair kept in a turban for men, and braids for women. Singh marked this turning point by leading his followers to Amritsar from the Sikh gurdwara at Anandpur Sahib in the Punjab Hills. Upon his death in 1708, Singh's closest disciples announced his instruction that leadership of the Sikhs would henceforth be centered on the teachings of the sacred book (now called the *Guru Granth Sahib*) rather than a human guru. To this day, the life of the Golden Temple, as in all gurdwaras, revolves around the *Guru Granth Sahib,* beginning before dawn, when the book is taken out of a building called the Akal Takht and carried processionally across the huge, white marble compound—across a causeway on a square artificial pond—to Harmandir Sahib, the central temple whose gilded copper plating gives the complex its most commonly recognized name. The temple's day ends late in the evening, when the book is brought back to its resting place.

During the time of the gurus, the Sikhs' development as a separate community often brought them into conflict with other forces in Mogul India. In 1761, as the Mogul empire declined, the temple was sacked by the Afghan raider Ahmad Shah Durrani. (It was rebuilt three years later.) In 1802 the temple was covered in gilt copper by Maharaja Ranjit Singh (1780–1839), whose rule extended as far as Kabul and Kashmir and marked the height of Sikh power. In 1984, the Indian Army's "Operation Bluestar" brought tanks into the complex in a disastrous four-day firefight with heavily armed Sikh separatists who had virtually taken over the complex. India's Prime Minister Indira Gandhi was assassinated about five months later by two of her Sikh bodyguards, in what was widely believed to be retribution for the Army attack on the temple. Amazingly, the temple now shows few signs of this tragic event, or of the decade of separatist violence and state repression that plagued Punjab afterwards. The grievances of the Sikh community have perhaps not all been resolved, but the horrible tenor of the dispute is a thing of the past, and Amritsar and Punjab are generally safe places to travel. Harmandir Sahib was not badly damaged in 1984, and the outlying buildings that were harmed have been restored. All day long, while a select group of singers, or *ragis,* broadcast hymns from the *Guru Granth Sahib* throughout the complex, pilgrims from rustic Punjabi towns and villages—India's hugely productive breadbasket—make their way around it, some performing *seva* (voluntary service) by cleaning the marble or completing other tasks. These worshipers are very welcoming to strangers, proud to show off the most sacred place in the Sikh religion. The dignity that pilgrims invest in the site, and the grandeur of its design, transcend the turmoil of its past.

Most hotels and the train station are near the British-era cantonment, and the **Golden Temple** is about a 15-minute ride away. You approach the temple through the Hall Bazaar, which leads to the **clock tower** gate. To symbolize the religion's egalitarian welcome to all castes, all Sikh gurdwaras have four entrances, but this is the main one. To the left of the stairway leading into the complex is a counter where visitors leave their shoes (many of the attendants here are volunteers, and their handling of others' shoes is another illustration of the Sikh doctrine of caste equality.) If you smoke, leave all tobacco products behind, as they're forbidden here. Pilgrims wash their feet at a spigot by the gate before entering the temple complex. Sikhs will already have their heads covered, with turbans for males and the *chunni* scarves worn by women; if you haven't brought a head covering, make use of the bin of colorful scarves by the stairs.

From the top of the gateway stairs, you look across a wide pool of water—known as the ***sarovar,*** or "sea"—at the golden roof of Harmandir Sahib. Go down the steps on the other side and you'll reach the white marble walkway 24 ft wide, known as the ***parikrama*** (circumambulatory path), that surrounds the pool. Each side of the pool is 510 ft long, and pilgrims normally make a complete circuit before they approach the Harmandir Sahib. Doing so gives a good sense of the scale of the place, as well as providing a series of angles from which to gaze at the Golden Temple. (You can take pictures from a distance, but put your camera away before you leave the causeway for the central sanctum.) Various points around the parikrama are considered auspicious places to bathe; the bathing steps along the east length of the walkway are said to mark a spot that equals the purifying power of Hinduism's 68 most holy *tirthas* (holy places). Just behind this is the entrance to a small garden that adjoins an assembly hall on the right and two large pilgrims' hostels to the rear. On the left, under two tall minarets that have yet to be fully restored from the damage they suffered in the 1980s, is the **Guru Ram Das Langar**—named after the fourth Sikh guru, this is the temple's communal dining hall. All gurdwaras have such a *langar* (the name of the place as well as the free meal served here), as eating together and serving a meal to others is perhaps the most fondly practiced of all Sikh rituals. Don't hesitate to join in; meals are served daily from 11 to 3 and 7 to 11, and the food (usually a few thick *chapatis* and some *dal*) is simple and robust. In another kitchen at the southwest corner of the parikrama, pilgrims make a donation in return for a packet of *halvah,* made from cream of wheat, which is then taken to Harmandir Sahib and presented as an offering, with a portion given back to worshipers as *prasad* (which some translate as the "edible form of God's grace").

Halfway across the east side of the parikrama, the causeway out to Harmandir Sahib is on your right, and to the left is the five-story **Akal Takht,** topped by a gilt dome. This building, whose name means "Timeless Throne," represents Sikh temporal authority—day-to-day administration—as opposed to the spiritual authority of Harmandir Sahib. It was here that much of the heavy fire that met the Indian Army during Operation Bluestar originated; the original building was largely destroyed during the fighting, but it has now been fully restored.

To reach **Harmandir Sahib** you go under an archway known as the **Darshani Deorhi** ("Gateway of Vision") and cross a 204-ft long causeway, which has brass guide rails to separate arriving pilgrims from departing ones, as well as a central passageway for temple functionaries. Take the left passageway. (Note that sometimes, particularly right at dusk, pilgrims arrive in great numbers for particular ceremonies. Access to the Harmandir Sahib is controlled at such times and pilgrims can back up on the causeway, making a visit to the sanctum a lengthy undertaking.) Pilgrims typically bow down at the doorway after traversing the causeway, then circumambulate the central temple around a small exterior parikrama. Some stop to bathe on the east side. The exterior walls are decorated in beautiful *pietra dura* (marble inlaid with semiprecious stones) said to have been brought by Maharaja Ranjit Singh from Mogul monuments in Lahore.

On the temple's ground level, the *Guru Granth Sahib* sits on a special throne. Attendants wave whisks over it constantly to keep flies away, and a *granthi* (lay specialist in recitation) sits reciting the text with harmonium players and other musicians off to one side. Feel free to enter the temple and listen to the recitation of the holy book, or witness the continuous recitation (*akhand path*) of the second and third stories; just remember to keep your head covered and refrain from taking pictures. As you go back through the Darshani Deorhi (Gateway of Vision), a temple priest or volunteer will usually be stationed under a small tree handing out servings of the halvah that previous pilgrims have offered to the temple. The ritual of receiving prasad is one that Sikhs share with Hindus. Just around the northwest corner of the parikrama stands an old jujube tree that is said to have healing powers.

The **Central Sikh Museum,** upstairs in the clock-tower entrance, contains graphic paintings depicting the tumultuous history of the Sikh gurus and their followers. Included are scenes from the British period and Operation Bluestar. ⏲ *Daily, usually 5 AM–10 PM.* 🎫 *Free.*

Outside the temple's clock-tower entrance, about 500 yards north, a small plaque and narrow gateway mark the entrance to **Jallianwala Bagh.** Here, on April 13, 1919, occurred one of the defining moments in India's struggle for independence. The day was Baisakhi, celebrated by Sikhs as both the first day of the new year and the day that Guru Gobind Singh consolidated the faith under the leadership of the Khalsa ("God's own"; a fraternity of the pious) in 1699. The city was under curfew after reported attacks on some British residents, yet some 20,000 people had gathered here to protest the arrest of Indian nationalist leaders under the Rowlatt Act, a British legislation that allowed for detention without trial. Seeing this crowd, British Brigadier General Reginald E. H. Dyer positioned his troops just inside the narrow entrance to the small garden (which is surrounded on all sides by residential buildings) and ordered them to open fire. Some 1,200 people were wounded, and several hundred died. This event, which is chillingly reenacted in Richard Attenborough's film *Gandhi,* caused widespread outrage and contributed to the launch of Mahatma Gandhi's noncooperation movement. The British attempted to suppress news of the incident, and when an inquiry was finally held, such comments as "It was no longer a question of merely dispersing the crowd, but one of producing a sufficient moral effect" (Dyer) did nothing to assuage a worldwide response. Nobel Laureate poet Rabindranath Tagore renounced his English knighthood, and even Winston Churchill, himself no enemy of the empire, raised an uproar in Parliament (though a majority in the House of Lords approved of Dyer's actions). Jallianwala Bagh was subsequently purchased by Indian nationalists to prevent its being turned into a covered market, and it remains one of the most moving monuments to India's 20th-century history. Queen Elizabeth visited in 1997, after much negotiation over whether or not she should make a formal apology (she didn't, but she and Prince Philip removed their shoes before entering the grounds). Today the garden is planted with a few rosebushes, and the bullet holes from the British fusillade remain. The well, into which some dove in a vain attempt to save themselves, is on the north side. A modern memorial occupies the east end, and a small display to the left as you enter the garden features contemporary newspaper accounts of the incident. ⏲ *Dawn to dusk.* 🎟 *Free.*

Other sights in Amritsar include the 16th-century **Durgiana Temple** (opposite Gole Bagh, south of the train station), a Hindu shrine to the goddess Durga which in its design replicates its more famous Sikh neighbor. The **Ram Bagh** gardens, northeast of the train station (enter on Mall Rd.), date from the period of Maharaja Ranjit Singh (1780–1839). At the center of the garden, the **Punjab Government Museum** displays weapons and portraits from the maharaja's era in a period building; it's open Tuesday through Sunday 10–7, and admission is Rs. 5.

Dining and Lodging

$ ✕ **Bharawan Dhaba.** Amritsar is famous for its cheap *dhabas,* restaurants where the Punjabi love of good country cooking is emphasized over decor. Try this one or Surjit's Chicken House on Lawrence Road. River fish are a special attraction, as is chicken, cooked dry in a tandoor oven or with a spicy sauce. In winter, ask for *sarson ka saag*—mustard greens stewed in ginger with a dollop of *ghee* (clarified butter) and served on *makhai ki roti* (cornmeal chapatis). ✉ *Opposite Town Hall on the way to the Golden Temple. No credit cards.*

$$ 🏨 **Mohan International.** Though several new ones are going up in Amritsar, this remains the city's best-run modern hotel. The rooms are spacious, clean, and air-conditioned, and the restaurant is a popular place for Amritsar families to enjoy a fancy night out. ✉ *Albert Rd., 143001 Punjab,* ☎ *183/227801 (–9),* FAX *183/226520. 51 rooms. Restaurant, coffee shop, bar, pool, laundry service, travel services. AE, DC, MC, V.*

$ ★ 🏨 **Bhandari's Guesthouse.** This sprawling set of bungalows in the cantonment harkens back to an earlier era of travel in India. If you like "character" in your lodgings this is definitely the place to stay. The rooms, some of which have wall air-conditioners, are huge and well maintained, with high ceilings and an abundance of polished wood furnishings. Each opens onto a well-maintained lawn. Mildly spiced Anglo-Indian meals are served in your room or in a mess area known as the "Commando Bridge" (Mrs. Bhandari, the aged proprietor, is an Indian Army widow). ✉ *10 Cantonment Rd., 143001 Punjab,* ☎ *183/228509 or 183/225714,* FAX *183/222390. 16 rooms. Restaurant, travel services. No credit cards.*

HIMACHAL PRADESH

Spread five Himalayan mountain ranges across the northwestern state of Himachal Pradesh like fingers on an open hand (the Siwalik, Dhauladhar, Pir Panjal, Great Himalayas, and Zanskar), thread them with rivers, and dot them with lakes: This is Himachal Pradesh. Except for the capital, Shimla, and the overpopulated destinations of Dharamsala in the district of Kangra and Manali in the district of Kullu, Himachal is a state of villages. It's also the so-called Land of the Gods, with thousands of mainly Hindu and Buddhist temples and monasteries.

WATERFORD
NO
MUNICIPAL LIBRARY

Various cultures inhabit this alpine region, including two distinct seminomadic tribes, the Gaddi and Gujjar, who still follow many of their most ancient traditions. The Gaddi, who travel with sheep, goats, and cattle, are Hindu and believe in evil spirits that are appeased by animal sacrifices and animist rituals. Gaddi men wear a *chola* (a white thigh-length woolen coat) over *sutthan* (tight woolen trousers), held in place by a *dora* (a black rope of sheep's wool) coiled around the waist. Women wear a *luanchari* (a long, colorful dress) with a woven dora tied around the waist and lots of jewelry, both for good luck and to indicate wealth.

The Muslim Gujjar travel with buffalo and make their living by selling fresh milk and ghee. Normally bearded, the men wear turbans and long robes. Women wear the traditional Indian Muslim *salwar-kameez,* a long tunic over loose pants tapered at the ankle. Often somber in color, this outfit is accentuated by paisley scarves and chunky silver necklaces, bracelets, and dangling earrings.

The peak tourist season in Himachal Pradesh runs from May though September. In April and November, while the nights may hover around 40°F in Shimla, the days can be sunny and suitable for short sleeves—and "shoulder-season" hotel prices approximate winter rates, half of what they escalate to in summer. June and September are the most comfortable months: dry and warm. July and August have the monsoon rains. Winter is chilly, with temperatures not much above freezing. Although some hotels do close from December through February, many stay open, and some even charge a premium for Christmas and New Year's Eve stays. Note that only a few hotels have central heating—if you come in winter, expect to sleep in your long johns.

If you hire a driver to tour Himachal Pradesh, consider combining the potentially hair-raising road trip with an Indian rail journey: Send the driver ahead to **Chandigarh** and arrange for him to meet you as you arrive on the *Shatabdi Express* from Delhi, which departs at 7:30 AM and arrives at 10:30 AM. You'll arrive safe and rested. The capital of two states, Haryana and Punjab, Chandigarh was built in the 1950s from a plan designed by the French architect Le Corbusier. If you linger here, visit the innovative Rock Garden built by Nek Chand, a visionary Outsider artist—it's a 6-acre maze of waterfalls and walkways through sculptures and figures made from discarded materials and oddly shaped stones. In Pinjore, 20 km (12 mi) northeast of Chandigarh, the 17th-century Mogul-style Yadvindra Gardens are laid out on a gentle slope, with seven terraces of pools and fountains.

Shimla

❷ *360 km (225 mi) north of Delhi*

Shimla is the capital of Himachal Pradesh and is perhaps best perceived as a gateway to the newly opened district of Kinnaur. The charms of Rudyard Kipling's city have faded: paint peels on Victorian structures, and mortar is left to crumble. Shimla is generally packed with Indian families on holiday, and attracts a number of British travelers who have family history in India.

Lodging

$$$$ **Chapslee.** When you walk onto Chapslee's small lawn, golden retrievers greet you and a gray parrot jabbers, "Coochy-coo." But step inside this ivy-covered old manor house, now a Heritage Hotel, and faded opulence surrounds you: Gobelin tapestries, European wallpaper, rare textiles and furnishings from the Doge's Palace in Venice, Persian carpets, blue pottery from around the subcontinent. The formal dining room, which seats about 12, has exquisite imported wallpaper and furnishings. Expect a hot-water bottle slipped into your bed at night, afternoon tea, and sumptuous fixed-menu Indian lunches and Continental dinners. Meals are included; nonguests may dine here by reservation only. ✉ *Lakkar Bazar, 171001,* ☎ *177/258663,* FAX *177/258663. 6 rooms. Restaurant, travel services. DC, MC, V.*

$$$$ **Oberoi Cecil.** The towering Oberoi is on a ridge overlooking the valley, a good 25-minute walk from the town center. Afternoon tea and evening cocktails are served in the four-story wood-paneled atrium lounge. Guest rooms have hardwood floors and smart, if rather stiff, furnishings. The is the only hotel in Shimla with the most up-to-date creature comforts, and you can expect Oberoi quality and efficiency. Business seminars are often held here, however, so the place can feel crowded and impersonal. ✉ *The Mall, 171004,* ☎ *177/204848,* FAX *177/211024. 71 rooms, 8 suites. Restaurant, spa, meeting room, travel services. AE, DC, MC, V.*

En Route North of Shimla, the highway north from Kullu town to Manali runs along the Beas River, and during the monsoon season (July–August), magnificent waterfalls drop from the peaks high above you. This road was built largely with the labor of Tibetan refugees after their exodus in 1959; they were employed by the Indian government to pave the way north for army convoys. Many died during construction from tuberculosis as well as accidents.

A lunch stop at the medieval **Hotel Castle** in Nagar (01902/47816), on the eastern side of the Beas (5 km, or 3 mi, beyond Patlikuhl) will give you a spectacular view of the Kullu Valley. Built by Raja Sidh Singh in 1460, the castle is a fine example of authentic Himalayan architecture, complete with timbered mesh. In addition to a restaurant, the castle has a small museum and some rooms for overnight stays; nearby there's a gallery featuring the Russian artist Nicholas Roerich.

Manali

❸ *280 km (174 mi) north of Shimla.*

Until about 10 years ago, Manali was a small, relaxed place toward the top of the Kullu Valley. On one side of town was a settlement of Tibetan refugees, while on the other side, near the bus stop, backpackers smoked dope and swapped trekking stories in hippie restaurants serving apple pie and peanut butter. Then, in 1989, Kashmir descended into chaos following the kidnapping of the Indian Home Minister's daughter by militants. Most of the Indian and foreign travelers who would have otherwise headed to Kashmir detoured to the fast-growing village of Manali. The subsequent explosion of development has ruined the former pristine tranquility of this place; concrete hotels have come up cheek-by-jowl along narrow alleys now choked with garbage and motor vehicles, their horns blaring away.

All that said, Manali is still recommended for its location, deep in the stunningly beautiful and culturally rich Kullu Valley. The friendly people of this Himalayan strand are famous for their unique style of dress, including men's pill-box caps with a colorful style of geometric embroidery that's repeated on woolen shawls. In fall, when the valley's many apple trees bear fruit, the famous Perahera Festival (a local variation on the Hindu festival Dussehra, celebrated all over North India in October) is held: Ten days after the new moon, villagers bring their local temple deities—over 200 in all—down to Kullu town, at the head of the valley. Dragged by hand on palanquins or wheeled carts known as *raths,* the idols are brought to pay respect to Raghunathji, Kullu's patron god. For three nights people from all over the valley, including the descendants of local royalty, mill around a temporary market on the dusty fairgrounds next to the Beas River. Singing and dancing complete the festive atmosphere.

The Kullu Valley is also a place of great natural beauty. At the high end of the valley, near Manali, and farther up toward the Rohtang Pass, 20,000-ft peaks loom on three sides. Day hikers will find endless exhilarating paths to hike, often alongside Gujjar shepherds with their flocks of goats. Manali is also the origin and endpoint for many more-serious adventures into the Himalayan wilderness. From here you can launch trekking, driving, and rafting trips into the Lahaul, Spiti, and Kinnaur valleys. Heading west, more treks can take you toward the Kangra and Chamba valleys. Finally, the road through Manali and up over the Rohtang Pass is currently the only one on which travelers can drive to Ladakh. Manali now also has a short skiing season.

Dining and Lodging

$ ✕ **Mount View Restaurant.** Booths and tables are crammed into this narrow space, and the walls display photos of the Dalai Lama and Lhasa. The Tibetan chef creates Chinese, Tibetan, and Japanese dishes; try the momos, soups with homemade noodles, or spicy Szechuan fare. ☒ *The Mall, opposite taxi stand,* ☎ *no phone. No credit cards.*

$$ **Usha Sriram Snowcrest Manor.** High on a hill above Manali town, this large, modern hotel has truly spectacular views of the Rohtang Pass and Kullu Valley. The deck is an especially nice place for a meal on a sunny day. In season (summer and the fall festivals), you'll meet up with lots of Indian honeymooners and vacationing families. Skiing, river rafting, and paragliding can easily be arranged. Traveler's checks are not accepted. ☒ *Beyond Log Huts, 175131,* ☎ *1902/53351,* FAX *1902/53188; or reserve through Delhi,* ☎ *11/551–2501,* FAX *11/550–3827. 32 rooms. Restaurant, health club. AE, DC, MC, V.*

$ **John Bannon's Guest House.** It isn't Manali's most beautiful lodge, but it has a garden and an orchard, and John Bannon is a delightful host. The upstairs rooms in this inn, built in 1934 and extended in the 1980s, have good orchard and mountain views. The old section has the advantage of sweeping verandas on both floors. All the rooms have fireplaces; clean, simple furnishings; and showers. Meals are included. ☒ *Manali Orchards, Manali 175131,* ☎ *1901/2335 or 1901/3077,* FAX *1901/2392. 10 rooms. Restaurant, travel services. No credit cards.*

$ **Johnson's Lodge.** Set in an old family home with a large addition in the rear, these apartments are spacious and clean, perfect for families or groups of four. Across the garden is the popular restaurant, serving various Continental and Indian dishes. You can also stay in a lodge in the family's apple orchard 13 km (8 mi) south of Manali, in Raison, where the rooms are large but sparsely furnished. ☒ *Raison, Kullu (drive to top of Mall Rd., turn left at Nehru Park, and look for sign to Johnson's Restaurant),* ☎ *1902/45292,* FAX *1902/45123. 2 apartments. Restaurant. No credit cards.*

Kangra Valley

References to the Kangra Valley date back 3,500 years to the age of the Hindu *Vedas*. Densely populated, the valley climbs gently into Himachal Pradesh from the plains of Punjab; to the north is the pine-covered Dhauladhar Range, a Himalayan spur jutting out to the west. This upper part of the valley gave birth to the famous Kangra-style paintings: scenes from the life of Lord Krishna, often highly romantic, in a style heavily influenced by Mogul miniatures. A narrow-gauge train sometimes plies the tracks that wind slowly up the valley.

Today, with its tropical and alpine terrain backed by snow-topped mountains and intersected by rivers, the Kangra Valley is a popular destination for trekking, fishing, and horseback riding. Yet the valley is not wild; most of the land here is dedicated to agriculture. While local farmers grow mostly such "winter" crops as wheat and fruit, the plantations in Palampur contain the only tea gardens in this part of India. Take home a box of "Kangra Green Gold" to sip while remembering this gentle valley.

Up the road from Palampur is Baijnath, home of the **Vaidyanath Temple.** Dedicated to Lord Shiva, this 9th-century temple is really worth a visit—intricate stone carvings of lesser-known gods such as Surya (the sun god) and the Garuda (a birdlike creature) adorn the walls both inside and out. Aside from this, the valley has no sights per se; it's just a pleasant place to wander around and discover little bits of India. It's also home to two lovely Heritage Hotels that can enhance your experience. Given the valley's relatively low elevation and the lack of air-conditioning at any of its lodgings, try to come here before mid-April or after mid-September.

Dining and Lodging

$$ **Judges Court.** Standing in an 8-acre orchard of mango, lychee, plum, persimmon, clove, and cardamom trees, this 300-year-old ancestral home of the Kuthiala Sood family has been beautifully restored using original techniques. The hotel comprises three buildings, including the family's historic cottage and a country manor built in 1918 by Justice Sir Jai Lal. In spring and fall you can sit on a shady veranda and smell the trees in the garden; in winter, a fire can be arranged in the sitting room. When you're done gazing out over the distant Dhauladhar Range, stroll through the medieval Kangra hamlet of Pragpur, with its cobbled streets, ornamental village reservoir, and mud-plastered, slate-roof houses—the entire village has been declared a "Heritage Zone" by the Himachal Pradesh state government. All meals are included in the room rate, and served to guests only. ✉ *Jai Bhawan, Pragpur, 177107,* ☎ *1970/5035; or reserve through 3/44 Shanti Niketan, New Delhi, 110021,* ☎ *11/467–4135,* FAX *11/688–5970. 10 rooms, 2 suites. Restaurant, pool. AE, MC, V.*

$$ **Taragarh Palace Hotel and Jungle Camp.** This 1930s summer resort and its 15-acre forested estate now comprise a Heritage Hotel owned by a member of the Kashmir Hindu royalty. Take a dip in the pool, then relax in the Art Deco lounge. The teak-paneled dining room has an exquisite fireplace and smoked-glass windows; the fixed menu is Indian. The rooms, which are not opulent, contain eclectic furnishings from the family's estate; those in the back are more spacious. You can also stay at the adjoining Jungle Camp between October and June, in a fruit grove—here, electrified safari-style tents have hand-blocked interior walls, mat floors, and attached bathrooms with hot water by the bucket. Treks, safaris, and general touring can easily be arranged. Note that, while the hotel is only 20 km (12 mi) southeast of Dharamsala (between Palampur and Baijnath), the drive takes an hour. ✉ *P.O. Taragarh, Kangra Valley, 176081,* ☎ *1894/63034; or reserve through Delhi,* ☎ *11/464–3046,* FAX *11/469–2317. 22 rooms, 3 suites, 6 tents. Restaurant, pool, tennis court, horseback riding, travel services. No credit cards.*

Dharamsala

❹ *253 km (157 mi) west of Manali.*

Perched high above the floor of the Kangra Valley, Dharamsala is an old British hill station, but its main attractions now are the Tibetan arts community; the Tibetan Government in Exile; and the home of the Dalai Lama, Tenzin Gyatso, who fled Tibet in 1959. Devastated by an earthquake in 1905, Dharamsala now suffers from an infusion of ugly hotels and too many travelers, who disturb the tranquility that should surround the home of His Holiness.

Thousands of Buddhists live here and in the remote, high-altitude districts of Lahaul, Spiti, and Kinnaur. Most practice a Tibetan form of tantric Buddhism. The women twist their hair into numerous long pigtails held in place by a silver ornament; many men wear a long overcoat, usually of maroon or brown. As with most Buddhist communities, men and women share all tasks, from raising a family to working in the fields, where they grow crops of barley, buckwheat, and potatoes.

The tourist office is in lower Dharamsala while many hotels and the Dalai Lama's residence are in the upper part of town, called McLeod Ganj, 10 km (6 mi) by road through the Indian Army cantonment (1,500 ft uphill as the crow flies). Just before you reach the bus and taxi stands, you'll see **St. John's Church in the Wilderness,** one of the few structures remaining from the British colonial days. The headstones in the churchyard are evidence of the difficulties and disease the British suffered; included is the grave of Lord Elgin, Viceroy of India, who died in 1862.

McLeod Ganj is at the center of Tibetan efforts to preserve and maintain their culture during their exile. Several sites devoted to this effort are worth visiting. The **Tibetan Institute of Performing Arts (TIPA)** is on the road to Dharamkot, and a query at your hotel about performance schedules might result in a wonderful evening of dance and music. TIPA also organizes the International Himalayan Festival every December. The **Norbulingka Institute for Tibetan Culture,** 15 km (9 mi) below McLeod Ganj in Sidhpur, and registered as a trust under the Dalai Lama, is committed to preserving Tibetan art and craft skills. Master artists train young apprentices in *thangka* (Tibetan scroll painting depicting meditational deities), metal work, appliqué, embroidery, and woodcarving. You can visit the artists in their studios, pick up a souvenir in the gift shop, and pop into the **Losel Doll Museum** to see a wonderful collection of traditional Tibetan costumes in authentic settings.

The **Dalai Lama's private residence** and **Thekchen Choling temple** complex are on the east end of Temple Road. The view across the valley from the temple balcony is magnificent, and the complex includes a bookstore and restaurant. The Dalai Lama gives public audiences several times a year, so inquire at your hotel and then apply for clearance at the security office on Bhangsu Road just beyond the Hotel India House (bring your passport). July 6, the Dalai Lama's birthday, is a festive occasion, especially for the performances by students at the TCV school (☞ *below*).

For educators and students, a trip to the **Tibetan Children's Village** (TCV), on the road north to Naddi, is a memorable experience. Established in 1960, the TCV's boarding school is home to 2,400 Tibetan orphans and refugees supported by individual and agency donors from all over the world, primarily the SOS Kinderdorf International in Vienna. In all, the organization has over 11,000 children under its care in branches extending from Ladakh down to Bylakuppe, near Mysore. The pleasant 30-minute walk to the school takes you through deodar cedars (follow the water pipe). The **Handicraft Centre** (☎ 1892/21266) below the school has good crafts at reasonable prices.

Dining and Lodging

$ ✕ **Nick's Italian Kitchen.** If you need a break from tandoori chicken, try this restaurant in the Kunga Guest House. Quiches, pizza, and good pasta dishes are cooked by a Tibetan family whose kitchen skills were inspired by a benefit organized by a traveling Italian-American from New York. ✉ *Bhagsunag Rd.* ☎ *1892/21180. No credit cards.*

$ ✕ **Yak.** Stop in for a snack and watch the cook at work: These are the best momos and Tibetan noodle soups in town. The former are cheesy, and latter tend to be hearty. Don't be put off by the dark doorway, the tiny seating area, or the grease-stained walls—this place is full of local Tibetans for a reason. ✉ *Jogibara Rd. (opposite Aroma and Ashoka restaurants),* ☎ *no phone. No credit cards.*

$ ✕ **Hotel Tibet Restaurant.** McLeod Ganj's one fine-dining venue is attached to a good, low-end hotel. Run by the Tibetan Administration Welfare Society, the restaurant has a parquet floor and simple modern decor. Unfortunately, its windows overlook garbage and slum dwellings; concentrate on the distant Himalayas, the old, black-and-white Tibetan photos on the walls, or the food: Japanese, Chinese, Continental (including grilled meats), and authentic Tibetan. The guest rooms are basic but carpeted. ✉ *Bagsunagh Rd., McLeod Ganj,* ☎ *1892/2587. 20 rooms. Restaurant, bar. No credit cards.*

$ ✕ **India House.** Trying hard to raise the level of McLeod Ganj accommodations, this new hotel has an excellent restaurant with an ambitious menu. You'll know for certain you've arrived when you see the Astroturf in the entryway. The rooms have small balconies with pleasant views; furnishings are a bit heavy on velour, but the staff is attentive and the prices are reasonable. ✉ *Bhagsunag Rd. (just beyond Tibet House),* ☎ *1892/21457,* FAX *1892/21144. Restaurant. No credit cards.*

$$ ★ **Chonor House.** Built and run by the Norbulingka Institute, this is the best place to stay in McLeod Ganj. Each room is furnished with handmade furniture, carpets, and linens made by institute artists, and most have balconies. But the special touch is the murals, painted in each guest room on the Tibetan themes of myth, religion, and ecology. The "Cyber-Yak Room" has Internet connections, and the spacious reading room is available for meetings. The excellent restaurant serves traditional Tibetan cuisine, which you can take outdoors on a large balcony in season. Rooms are heated in winter. The local Lhasa Apso dogs, which often set up a chain reaction of midnight yelping, are unfortunately beyond the staff's control. ✉ *Temple Rd.* ☎ FAX *1892/21006. 11 rooms. Restaurant, meeting room. MC, V.*

$$ ★ **Glenmoor Cottages.** Twenty minutes' walk from McLeod Ganj, the Indian owners of this secluded hideaway live in a British bungalow that's been in their family since the 1940s. Four simple suites are available in the bungalow, two of which share a bath; separate cottages offer more privacy and spectacular mountain and valley views. An absence of TVs helps keep the atmosphere homey. The cottages' modest concrete-and-wood exteriors conceal charming interiors where crisp white walls set off modern spruce and pine furnishings; all have modern bathrooms with showers, and some have kitchenettes. Breakfast is included, and the (uninspired) fixed Indian and Continental dinners are served to guests only. ✉ *McLeod Ganj, 176219,* ☎ *1892/25010 or 1892/23355,* FAX *1892/21355. 7 rooms, 4 suites, 6 cottages. Restaurant, travel services. No credit cards.*

$ **Norling Guest House.** Comfortable, carpeted rooms and a garden restaurant are set along a small stream with pleasant waterfalls. At the top of the central stairway is a temple with a 14-ft Shakyumani Buddha. ✉ *From McLeod Ganj, go through Kotwali Bazaar and take the road through Khanyara (14 km/9 mi); reserve through Norbulingka Institute, P.O. Sidhpur 176057,* ☎ *1892/22664 or 1892/23522,* FAX *18922/24982. 8 rooms, 2 suites. Restaurant.*

Dalhousie

5 *130 km (81 mi) northwest of Dharamsala*

Dalhousie was a hill station fashionable with British colonialists from Lahore. It was established by the Marquess of Dalhousie, who, as India's governor general in the 1850s, founded the Indian rail system. Today Dalhousie is a crowded destination for Indian tourists during the summer months, so try to see it between March and May or September and November. The setting that drew the British is still spectacular, with forested slopes, green valleys, and the Dhauladhar Range in the distance. Evidence of the British colonial days is mostly gone, barring the two Christian churches at each *chowk* (crossroads or marketplace); **St. Francis Church,** on Subhash Chowk, was built in 1894. The town has vehicle-restricted walkways between Gandhi Chowk and Subhash Chowk, and along Potryn Road. Dalhousie was for a short time the assigned residence for Tibetan exiles, before they were directed to Dharamsala; a visit to the **Tibetan Handicraft Center** in Upper Bakrota is a must if you like hand-knotted Tibetan carpets.

Dining and Lodging

For quick bite, try the restaurant **Davat** (☎ 1899/42120 or 1899/40610), in the Hotel Mount View. The noise from the nearby bus stand detracts somewhat from the experience, but the food is reliable.

$–$$ 🏨 **Guncha Siddhartha.** Each room in this new building has a terrace overlooking the owner's orchard and residence below, with a scenic view of the valley and mountains beyond. Rooms are tiered down the hillside, with a restaurant planned for the roof. (For now, the staff brings vegetarian meals to your room.) Heating pads are provided in winter, and rates are discounted 50% to boot. ✉ *Church Baloon Rd.,* ☎ *1899/42709 or 1899/40620,* FAX *1899/40818. 9 rooms, 5 suites. Refrigerators, laundry service, travel services. No credit cards.*

$ 🏨 **Aroma-n-Claire.** Virtually unchanged since 1959, this family-run hotel is a furnishings flashback with an eclectic twist. The charm of the hosts, the view from the balcony, and the home cooking offset the worn carpets and fading art in the public sitting room. Heating costs extra. ✉ *Court Rd., 176304* ☎ *1899/42199,* FAX *1899/42639. 16 rooms. Restaurant, refrigerators, laundry service. MC, V.*

$ 🏨 **Princess.** These basic rooms are clean, well kept, and equipped with phones and, in the winter, with heat. The building has nice views over the valley. ✉ *Thandi Sarak (Mall walkway),* ☎ *1899/42154 or 1899/42545,* FAX *1899/40057. 12 rooms. Restaurant. No credit cards.*

$ 🏨 **Silverton Estate Guest House.** Built in 1939, this small and gracious home has both charm and location. The host, Vickram Singh, runs the estate—which includes a terraced garden—with an eye for hospitable detail. The cuisine is vegetarian Indian. ✉ *Top of Moti Tibba, above Circuit House (off Mall Rd.),* ☎ FAX *1899/40674. 5 rooms. Restaurant, putting green, badminton, croquet, nursery. No credit cards.*

En Route The road from Dalhousie to Chamba has two delightful stops for nature lovers. The first is **Kalatope Wildlife Sanctuary,** a forest preserve with beautiful mountain views. Leave your car at the entrance (unless you have a permit from the Forest Officer in Chamba) and stroll to the end of the 3-km (2-mi) paved road, which continues through mature deodar cedars and yews. Halfway to Chamba is **Khajiar.** Ambitiously known as the mini-Switzerland of India, this is a spacious glade encircled by virgin forest and centered on a pond with a grassy island that seems to float. Some literature says there's a golf course here, but all that seems to remain are eight wire circles guarding the greens against grazing sheep and cattle.

Chamba

6 *50 km (31 mi) east of Dalhousie*

The road into Chamba is not for the faint of heart, and you won't find the tourist crowd in this Indian town. Isolated for centuries, Chamba offers a fabulous chance to see an India unaffected by tourism. Chamba Valley lies between the Pir Panjal and Dhauladhar ranges, and the town itself sits on a bluff overlooking the swift Ravi River. The business district surrounds a large green, the Chaugan, site of the midsummer Minjar Festival. The **Bhuri Singh Museum** (⊠ Museum Rd.), open Tuesday through Sunday from 10 to 5, has an interesting collection, including a variety of miniature paintings in the Basholi and Kangra styles. The distinctive spires of the **Lakshmi Narayan** temple complex, dedicated to Shiva and Vishnu, rise above the surrounding skyline. Up the hill is the **Himachal Emporium,** housed in an old palace: The Chamba Valley is well known for *rumals,* pictures sewn in a reversible stitch that shows no knots. Above the showroom is a workshop where fine shawls are woven on looms.

A few doors from the Lakshmi Narayan temple is the office of **Mani Mahesh Travels** (⊠ Lakshmi Narayan Temple La., 176310, ☎ 1899/22507 or -607, FAX 1899/25333), operators of the Himalayan Orchard Hut, a tented camp and farmhouse 12 km (7 mi) north of Chamba in Kut-Chadiara, near the River Saal. The staff lead well-organized tours and treks in the Chamba Valley and direct studies of flora, fauna, Gaddi-Gujjar mountain-village life, and spiritual meditation.

Dining and Lodging

$ **Aravati.** This government-owned hotel is clean and inexpensive. The restaurant serves reliable South Indian food. ⊠ *South end of village green (near tourist office),* ☎ *1899/22671,* FAX *1899/22565. 19 rooms. Restaurant. No credit cards.*

Lahaul, Spiti, and Kinnaur

Beginning 51 km (32 mi) north of Manali on the far side of the Rohtang Pass, **Lahaul** offers good treks and jeep safaris. Though it's much smaller than Ladakh and has fewer and simpler *gompas* (monasteries), the two share a general mingling of religion and nature. Mountains bear in from all directions, and windswept passes throw preconceived notions of beauty into disarray. Glaciers look icy and somber, and an occasional lake sparkles under the hot sun. Prayer flags or a rare green valley beckon with unexpected displays of color, as do the gompas. But Lahaul is experiencing an influx of trekkers: Work with your tour operator to choose a route that avoids crowds.

You can raft, day-hike, trek, and tool around by jeep in the **Spiti Valley,** a sensitive border area on the far side of the Kunzum Pass (15,055 ft) southeast of Lahaul. Spiti's landscape is more arid than Lahaul's; its mountains, split by the raging Spiti River, are steeper; and it's more thoroughly Buddhist. Here you'll find the 11th-century **Tabo Gompa,** one of the holiest monasteries for Tibetan Buddhists.

Kinnaur, south of Spiti, is more fertile. Newly opened to travelers, this district beckons with great day hikes, treks, and jeep excursions. Sliced by the Sutlej River, it nestles in the towering Kinnaur Kailas Range, and, like Spiti, it hides wonderful old Buddhist monasteries.

Foreigners need an Inner Line Permit to visit Spiti (☞ Permits *in* The Himalayas A to Z, *below*), though formalities are getting looser over time.

Dining and Lodging

Facilities in Lahaul, Spiti, and Kinnaur are generally open to travelers between April and October.

$$ 🏨 **Banjara Camp.** Located in the Sangla Valley, one of loveliest valleys in Kinnaur, Banjara Camp is just 30 km (19 mi) from Tibet. The accommodations are Swiss-style deluxe tents with full-size beds and attached "loos" with running water. At 8,850 ft, the camp sits on the Baspa River, where brown trout live in the chilly runoff water. The room price includes all meals. Banjara has other camps in Tabo (Spiti), well into the high, arid plateau of eastern Himachal Pradesh; and Chail, 45 km (28 mi) from Shimla, set in deodar cedars near the world's highest cricket pitch. ✉ *Reserve through 1A Hauz Khas Village, New Delhi 110016* ☎ *11/685–5153,* FAX *11/685–1397. 18 tents. Restaurant. AE, MC, V.*

$ 🏨 **Timberline Camps.** In addition to organizing treks and jeep safaris, Timberline operates a hotel and camp in Kalpa (Kinnaur), overlooking Kinnaur Kailas—winter abode of Lord Shiva. The deluxe tents are quite comfortable, with wood floors, tables and chairs, and attached chemical toilets. You dine in the main hotel. ✉ *Reserve through Timberline Trekking Camps Ltd., 206 Allied House, 1 Local Shopping Centre, Madangir, New Delhi 110062,* ☎ *11/698–2903, –4037, –4049, or –8408,* FAX *11/698–0746. Restaurant.*

Adventures

Fishing

Fish for trout in the Pabar River near Rohru, a two-day trip from Shimla, or in the Larji River, at its confluence with the Tirthan River over the Jalori Pass. You can also catch trout in the Uhl River, near Barot, and in the Sangla. Try for *mahaseer* (a Himalayan river fish) in the Beas, near Dharamsala. Aquaterra Adventures (☞ Tour Operators *in* The Himalayas A to Z, *below*) can help you get the appropriate license and take you to good fishing spots in each district. There is no bag limit for mahseer, but conservation efforts dictate that you keep only as much trout as you can eat. The fishing season is March to October. You can rent poles here, but serious anglers should bring their own equipment.

TIRTHAN RIVER

The **Goshiani Guest House** (✉ Village and P.O. Goshiani, via Banjar, Kullu Hills, 175123, ☎ 1903/76808), on the road past Larji, is a rare find, a cedar guest house set in a garden and orchard (which helps supply superb meals) on the Tirthan River. Owner Ranjiv Bharti is also a fishing guide who knows where those wily browns live. The house is a few miles past the trout hatchery on the opposite side of the river; you ride in a basket across the roaring stream—a sound that later fills your room as you fall asleep thinking of tomorrow's catch. Buy your fishing license in Larji before you head up the valley. Rooms and meals total about Rs. 500.

Jeep Safaris

MANALI–LEH

Many companies offer jeep trips from Manali to Leh, so the route can be crowded with vehicles. Take three days to enjoy the show-shopping vistas as you scale four passes, cross high-altitude plains, and wend your way through valleys.

SHIMLA–KULLU

This two- to three-day drive follows a newly opened road along the old colonial route from Shimla to Kullu over the Jalori Pass (11,230 ft). You'll get plenty of ups and downs as you drive through mountain forests, across alpine valleys, and past enchanting Gaddi villages, where you get a nice glimpse of Gaddi culture. The route climbs past lakes bordered by modest wooden temples, and you cross the pass with views of Spiti and Kinnaur peaks. Camp near the pass by an old British Public Works Department bungalow—its garden is open mid-April to June and September to October. Contact Aquaterra Adventures (☞ Tour Operators *in* The Himalayas A to Z, *below*) for details.

Mountain Biking

MANALI-LEH HIGHWAY

This spectacular ride can be completed by avid bikers in eight days. More time is recommended, however, as there is plenty to see along the way, including spectacular scenery and views from 16,000-ft passes. The terminus, Leh, offers well-deserved rest and some monastery visits. A white-water rafting trip on the Indus River caps off this exciting tour, making it a kaleidoscope of activities. While this is the only road to Leh, traffic is not bad, and mountain drivers tend to be much more considerate than their counterparts on the plains. You must bring your own bike, but a support vehicle accompanies the group. The trip is only feasible from July through September; contact Aquaterra Adventures (☞ Tour Operators *in* The Himalayas A to Z, *below*) for details.

Pony Treks

KANGRA VALLEY

We highly recommend a Kangra Valley pony trek for experienced riders, who can enjoy lovely Himalayan views from high-spirited polo ponies owned by the family of the former maharaja of Kashmir. Wandering through meadows and forests, you visit Kangra villages and a Tibetan monastery, and spend each night in a tent at various idyllic campsites. One five-day trip is usually scheduled in May, but customized trips can be arranged from April through June and mid-September through October. Contact the Taragarh Palace Hotel (☞ Kangra Valley, *above*).

KINNAUR TO SPITI

This five-day trek starts at Kafnoo, in Kinnaur (a little beyond Wangtu), and climbs over the 16,000-ft Babha Pass to reach the village of Muth in the Pin Valley, a land of ibexes and snow leopards. The trip combines the greens of Kinnaur with the stark desolation of Spiti. Return to Delhi via Manali or Shimla. The total round trip from Delhi is about a week and a half, but you can extend it to as long as three weeks to include visits to the various monasteries and high-altitude villages and even fossil-hunting, usually in Spiti. Contact Aquaterra Adventures (☞ Tour Operators *in* The Himalayas A to Z, *below*) for details.

Rafting

SPITI RIVER

Offered July through August only, this wonderful 12-day adventure from Manali to Shimla includes a three-day run on the scenic Spiti River, surrounded by mountains, and sightseeing drives and day hikes to historic monasteries and villages. This trip is not for hard-core rafters—its cultural aspects are as important as its physical adventure. No experience is required, but you must be fit for the high altitude. Contact Himalayan River Runners (☞ Tour Operators *in* The Himalayas A to Z, *below*).

Skiing

MANALI

For those with a penchant for danger and a wallet full of cash, Manali now has a heliskiing outfit. In the midst of 20,000-ft peaks, the skiing can begin as high as 16,000 ft! The powder is said to be exceptional and the snow-pack, deep. Breathing can be difficult and avalanches are the rule, but Himachal Helicopter Skiing is a wholly professional operation, with Kiwi guides, a Canadian pilot, and a Swiss helicopter. All packages include 100,000 ft of vertical skiing; six days of guide service, skiing equipment, and the use of an avalanche transceiver; seven nights' lodging at Manali and all meals; escorted transfers from Delhi to Manali and back; and local taxes. The season is short (mid-January to early April), and the local hotel is not up to jet-setter ski-bum standards. One week of skiing runs U.S.$5,000–$7,000. Contact **HHS** (✉ G.P.O. Box 2489 V, Melbourne 3001, Australia, ☎ [61] 3/9593–9853 or [61] 3/9525–3405).

Trekking

DHAULADHAR

Starting at McLeod Ganj (Upper Dharamsala), in the Kangra Valley, at about 6,000 ft and passing over the mighty snowbound Dhauladhar Range, this trail ends at Machhetar, in the Ravi Valley. You follow the traditional migratory and grazing route of the Gaddis, who tend their flocks throughout the summer on the high alpine meadows adjoining the Dhauladhar and Pir Panjal ranges. Moving through forests of pine, oak, fir, and ash, the trail passes through open grazing areas and flowering meadows above the timberline. Wildlife such as black and brown bears, red foxes, and leopards, though hard to spot, inhabit these upper regions. An 18-day round trip from Delhi, this trek is best undertaken in early June or September–October. A shorter, six day trek goes over the range from Dharamsala to Bharmaur.

LAHAUL-SPITI-KINNAUR

Many tour operators lead this popular moderate (but high-altitude) 17-day trip, with a 13-day trek that starts when you drive from Manali across the Rohtang Pass (13,048 ft) into Lahaul to Patseo village. From there you head over Baralacha Pass (16,016 ft), with its astonishing mountain panorama, cross Kunzum Pass (15,055 ft), and enter Spiti, where you follow the Spiti River to the villages of Losar and Hansa. You visit La-Darcha, the site of a popular trade fair attended by Tibetans and Ladakhis, and then head to Kibber village (13,546 ft), the highest Asian village accessible by road. Following a mountain ridge, you'll visit some Buddhist monasteries, then drive through the Pinn Valley and see some more key villages and monasteries, including Tabo, before continuing to Kinnaur and then Shimla. The trip is offered May through mid-October.

MANALI–BIR

This fantastic, moderate-to-strenuous two-week trek takes you from the Kullu into the Kangra Valley along a lesser-known high-altitude route. From Manali, you enter evergreen forests that lead to the Manaslu Valley, where you follow icy streams, cross alpine meadows, and catch great views of the Kullu Valley en route. Crossing the Kaliheyni Pass (15,500 ft), where the landscape changes to patches of snow and glacial moraines, you see distant views of Buddhist Lahaul. You traverse a glacier and enter the Sunni River valley, with its meadows and gorges. A snow bridge leads to forests and Barabangal village, an isolated valley home of some Gaddi shepherds. Your next stop is the base of Thamser Pass (15,750 ft); from here, you travel through meadows and by lakes and waterfalls until you enter the Kangra Valley and the Tibetan settlement in Bir. This trek is offered in June and September only.

MANALI-LEH

This strenuous, extremely popular 10- or 20-day trek starts after a drive across the Rohtang Pass and the descent into Lahaul. Expect to ford snow-fed streams, cross a high-altitude pass into Ladakh's Zanskar district, visit ancient monasteries and typical Buddhist villages, and experience a panoramic lunar landscape. You can take a jeep from Padam, the district headquarters in Zanskar, or continue trekking to Leh, the capital of Ladakh. The most rigorous route includes four more passes. Each version is rugged but stunning, with multihue mountains, jagged glaciers, and green village oases. You're apt to see traders leading horses laden with goods, and many, many foreign trekkers. The route is available mid-July to mid-September.

SANGLA

We recommend this moderate, 11-day Kinnaur trek, which starts after a drive from Shimla to Sarahan and gives you a chance to see the Kinnauri culture. Between May and October you can walk through forests, cross streams and old bridges, follow a mountain ridge with great views, and see ancient temples steeped in Kinnauri Buddhist mythology. Count on plenty of up- and downhill walking and a steep climb over the Shibaling Pass. You can also expect forest or meadow campsites near streams, and visits to typical villages such as Sangla and Chitkul (the highest village in the valley), where many residents create exquisite Kinnauri wool shawls on hand looms.

LADAKH

Tucked between the two highest mountain ranges in the world—the Karakoram and the Greater Himalayas—Ladakh offers an adventure in the world of Mahayana Buddhism. Sometimes called Little Tibet, Ladakh is now more culturally pure than its namesake. Tourists in Leh, the capital, are diluting the Buddhist culture, but Ladakh's gompas are still splendid, with beautiful interior frescoes and statues as breathtaking as the ethereal landscape. With gray barren crags, an occasional green valley, jewel-like waterways, and mountains of different hues deepened by the sharp sun, this high-altitude desert is punctuated by colorful prayer flags and scattered *chortens*—memorial stupas or shrines for relics.

Outside the town of Leh, you can travel up and down Ladakh's windswept terrain and encounter little human life. The 150,000 residents in this part of the disputed region of Kashmir appear in the most surprising places, generally alongside the reminders of Buddhist culture that sprinkle the countryside. On the most deserted stretch of road you will find stones stacked into little chortenlike piles and *mani* (walls of beautifully engraved stones) that the inhabitants have erected to protect the land from demons and evil spirits. The walls are enticing, but don't touch or remove the stones because they are sacred to the people who put them there.

The Government of India oversees a number of specified tour circuits in this region. Foreign tourists in groups of four, sponsored by recognized tour operators, are allowed to visit the Khaltse (Drokhpa area), Nubra, and Nyoma subdivisions after obtaining a permit from the District Directorate in Leh. If you're planning a trip here, take all precautions against high-altitude sickness (☞ Health *in* Smart Travel Tips A to Z) and try to bring a flashlight for viewing poorly lit gompas. Ladakh gets crowded in July and August, but June and September are excellent months for touring this mountain state. The trekking season lasts from late May, after most of the snow has melted, until mid-October; rafting is best from early July to mid-September. Winter, when many accommodations are closed, will probably confine you to Leh and its vicinity.

Leh

7 *473 km (295 mi) north of Manali, 434 km (271 mi) east of Srinagar, 230 km (143 mi) east of Kargil.*

The two-day overland route from Manali to Leh has reached mythical status as an automotive ordeal. This mode of arrival is incredibly scenic, and a good way to acclimatize yourself to the altitude, but the ride can be lengthy and uncomfortable. The army convoys on the road increase the danger *and* the time involved, as they have immediate right-of-way over all traffic. The prudent and the humble take Indian Airlines: The flight leaves Delhi early in the morning, with the sun beginning to rise as you cross the great Indian plain and enter the Shivalik Hills. As the first snow-capped mountains rise up, the plane seems to skim over the summits, and the ice fields stretch to the horizon before you reach the barren moonscape of the high Tibetan plateau. The flight attendant may instruct you to lower your window blind as you approach Leh, your first hint of the military security here—you are to take no photos from the plane. Pack your Swiss Army knife in your checked luggage. If you arrive before the plows have opened the Manali road (early to mid-June), you'll have your pick of lodgings.

Take strong sunblock, aspirin, and a thick novel to Ladakh: The altitude change and intense sunshine will require you to spend a few days just relaxing and taking slow walks. Drink water and avoid alcohol. A visit to Leh's **Ecology Centre** one afternoon will distract you while you acclimatize; in addition to various exhibits, its excellent video, *Ancient Futures,* illustrates how Ladakhi culture is threatened by a rapidly changing world. For as long as you're here, initiate greetings of "*Jule*" (ju-*lay*) and you'll be pleased with the smiles and kindness you receive in return.

Leh is built into the base of the snow-covered Karakoram Range at over 11,500 ft. An important Buddhist center since the 3rd century BC, Leh has also been a major commercial hub on the Silk Road in central Asia. The 20th century has turned Leh into an important Indian military base and tourist boomtown. The **palace** and, above it, the **Temple of the Guardian Deities** are both in disrepair; still, Leh lends itself to exploration. The narrow lanes behind the main bazaar have tempting little shops, though everything here is overpriced. Find **Alisha,** the photo shop owned by Syed Ali Shah, beyond the Sunni mosque near the Sankar gompa. Shah sells a lifetime's worth of Ladakh photography, and his son will show you some treasures, especially the old black-and-white images. Taxi to the **Shanti Stupa,** in the village of Changspa, for a magnificent view of the valley—then walk down the 500-plus steps leading up to it. On your way south out of town, stop at the **Tibetan Refugee Handicraft Center** in the village of Choglamsar, open weekdays from 9 to 5. The beautiful crafts here include hand-woven rugs and thick woolens.

Before you leave town, arrange trips to area monasteries and get a festival schedule from the tourist office (dates vary from year to year according to the Tibetan lunar calendar). Gompas are the center of Ladakhi religion and culture. Driving south you can explore the Shey, Thiksay, Matho, and Hemis gompas; northwest are Spituk, Phyang, Likir, and **Alchi Choskor**—the jewel of Ladakh's religious sites. Plan an overnight stay in Alchi and travel onward and upward to the gompa at Lamayuru. The taxi union has reasonable fixed charges, but the roads are bumpy, so request a Tata Sumo to minimize bouncing. For a knowledgeable, English-speaking guide, contact Tondup Rahul at ☎ 53476. Respect religious customs when visiting gompas: Wear appropriate clothing, remove your shoes, do not smoke, circle all chortens or spin prayer wheels clockwise, leave a small donation, and never take a mani stone. Most monasteries do not allow flash photography.

Dining and Lodging

All of Leh's restaurants are small and informal. Try the standards: momos and *thukpa* (noodle soup). A *dzo* is a cross between a yak and a cow. Strange beast. You may also have a chance to try *chang* (a local brew made from fermented barley) or, more likely, some *gur-gur cha,* yak-butter tea mixed with milk and salt.

Leh is well organized for travelers, and hotels are divided into uniformly priced categories. The tourist office hands out a list of lodgings at the airport and in its main office; the most expensive ("A Class") cost around U.S. $50 a night including meals; the cheapest are the economy-class guest houses—over 100 in number—which can be as low as U.S. $2 or $3 per night. During slow periods, you may be able to negotiate. For extended stays, reserve a room for the first night or two, then spend a day checking out the places on the tourist-office list: You might end up in a lovely venue with a sun-filled room, terrace with view, and clean bathroom, which you'll most likely share. Begin your search in Changspa, near the Shanti Stupa, away from traffic noise.

$ ✕ **Summer Harvest Restaurant.** This second-floor restaurant features good Kashmiri cuisine. A local crowd attests to the quality of the cooking. ✉ *Down Fort Rd. from the taxi stand,* ☎ *1982/52336. No credit cards.*

$ ✕ **Tibetan Kitchen.** Locals agree that this joint serves the most authentic Tibetan food in Leh. ✉ *Hotel Tsokar, Fort Rd.,* ☎ *no phone. No credit cards.*

$$ 🏨 **Highland.** Up the road from the Ladakh Sarai (near the Stok Gompa), this two-story hotel has a Ladakhi-style exterior (white with black-and-red trim), a lovely back lawn, and modern, comfortably furnished rooms. Cultural performances are arranged on request. Fixed-menu meals with some Ladakhi dishes, airport transfer, and mountain bikes are included in the price. ✉ *Stok; reserve through* ✉ *Great Himalaya Adventure, Leh 194101,* ☎ *1982/53683. 12 rooms. Restaurant, bar, airport shuttle, travel services. AE, DC, MC, V. Closed Dec.–May.*

$$ 🏨 **Ladakh Sarai.** Here you stay in a yurt (large circular tent) in a willow grove with a view west across the valley to the Indus River and the majestic Stok Kangi Range. Each yurt has twin beds and a sitting area with a Western-style toilet attached in the rear. You dine in a hexagonal hall tastefully decorated with Ladakhi artifacts. All meals are included. The camp is in the village of Sabu, 6 km (4 mi) south of Leh. Jeep tours with both driver and guide can take you to the monasteries; you can also opt for a five-day Stok-Martselang trek and an eight-day Markha Valley trek. The camp is open April–October. ✉ *Reserve through Tiger Tops/Mountain Travel India, 1/1 Rani Jhansi Rd., New Delhi 110055,* ☎ *11/777–1055 or –35,* FAX *11/777–7483. 14 tents. Restaurant, travel services.*

$$ ★ 🏨 **Lha-Ri-Mo.** A short walk from the markets and nestled behind an attractive garden, this is the loveliest hotel in Leh. The Ladakhi look of the exterior is continued in the lobby and the restaurant, which also has intricately hand-painted beams. Rooms are simple, with Western toilets and hot and cold showers, and the meals are buffet-style Indian. ✉ *Leh, Ladakh 194101, Jammu and Kashmir,* ☎ *1982/52101,* FAX *1982/53345; or reserve through 1542 Sector 29, Noida, Delhi,* ☎ *11/554870. 30 rooms. Restaurant, travel services. AE. Closed Nov.–Apr.*

$$ 🏨 **Shambha-La.** Located between Leh and its airport (and offering a free shuttle into town), the Shambha-La is essentially a two-tier motel

centered on a shaded courtyard. Built in 1978 and run by the Oberoi group for several years, it is now locally owned. Comforts include a buffet restaurant with three cooks, a rooftop deck, a VCR and video library, and—in half the rooms—heat in May and October. ✉ *Just south of Leh,* ☎ *1982/52607,* FAX *1982/52067; or reserve through K-40 Hauz Khas, 1st floor, New Delhi 110016,* ☎ FAX *11/686–7785. 25 rooms. Restaurant, laundry service. AE. Closed Nov.–Apr.*

$–$$ **Khanghri.** Like all hotels in Leh, the Khangri has great views, but it goes one step farther in being the only place open year-round. Rooms are heated in winter (for a small fee), though the plumbing is not so luxurious. ✉ *Leh, Ladakh 194101, Jammu and Kashmir,* ☎ *1982/52762,* FAX *1982/52051; or reserve through* ☎ *11/646–1271. 40 rooms (4–5 in winter). Restaurant, laundry service, travel services. AE.*

$–$$ **Omasila.** Owned and operated by a Tibetan family since 1980, this hotel below the Shanti Stupa is popular with European tour groups. Its scenery, cleanliness, quiet privacy, and skillful kitchen should put it first on your list. A spacious terrace looks south to a stunning view, the grounds are planted with flowers, and a stream runs along the edge of the property. Each room has a Gideonlike version of Buddhist reading material. There are no TVs or telephones, but the front desk has a cordless phone. Only six rooms are heated in winter: Ask for a room number in the 40s. The evening meal is a buffet. ✉ *Changspa, Leh, Ladakh, 194101* ☎ FAX *1982/52119. 32 rooms. Restaurant.*

Padam

8 *270 km (169 mi) southwest of Leh.*

Former capital of the Kingdom of Zanskar, Padam is in the vast, high-altitude Zanskar Valley, ringed by mountains, with the Karsha Gompa perched on a nearby cliff. The valley's sweeping panoramas end at soft-hue mountains, and the bases of barren slopes are barricaded by sand and shaped by the wind and the water into oversize ramparts. Parts of the district consist of rocky desert punctuated by bits of green, and the Zanskar River races along a deep gorge. Zanskar men in robes gallop by on their handsome ponies.

Within this sparsely populated district, the dominant sounds come from chattering birds or the wind, which grows intense by late afternoon, rustling the wheat, barley, and countless prayer flags. The arrival of tourists, especially trekkers, has begun to alter Zanskar's lifestyle; the men, who traditionally worked alongside the women in the fields and helped with the household chores and child rearing, now look for jobs as porters. The women sell crafts. A growing attraction to money and Western goods is altering a society accustomed to bartering, and Buddhist traditions are threatened.

Pangong and Moriri Lakes, Nubra Valley, and Drogpa Villages

Foreigners need an Inner Line Permit to visit any of these areas (☞ Permits *in* The Himalayas A to Z, *below*).

The brackish **Pangong Tso** and **Tso Moriri** (*tso* means "lake") in the eastern district of Changthang are astonishing alpine bodies of water. Pangong, at an elevation of 14,018 ft, is over 150 km (90 mi) long—and two thirds of it lie in China. Tso Moriri, 240 km (150 mi) southeast of Leh at an elevation of 15,000 ft, is a pearl-shape lake rich in mineral deposits, giving it a mysterious range of colors against the barren mountains. Both lakes are accessible by road from Leh between late May and October.

North of Leh, Ladakh's "Valley of Flowers," the **Nubra Valley,** is sublime: a heady mixture of cultivated fields set in an arid desert surrounded by the Karakoram Range and sliced by rivers. (*Nubra* means "garden.") Getting to this richly vegetated area around the Shayok and Siachen rivers requires a journey over Khardungla Pass—the world's highest drivable road, at 18,383 ft. From here you descend through the towering peaks to the villages of Nubra, which were important stops for rations along the Silk Road to Central Asia. The trekking routes here go through virtually unexplored territory. Camel safaris and river rafting are available, and hot springs warm weary travelers at Panamik village.

In the **Drogpa villages** west of Leh, the Dard people still inhabit the shimmering Indus Valley. Isolated from the modern world, they remain Buddhist farmers, eking a living from the rugged mountain sides. You can arrange an overnight stay in Khaltsi, where the main road forks off toward Kargil, and in new tourist bungalows in the Dard village of Biama.

Adventures

Jeep and Camel Safari

NUBRA ADVENTURE

This special five-day adventure explores the Nubra Valley, a high-altitude area north of Leh that is home to Buddhists, Muslims, and double-humped Bactrian camels (once used for transport on the Silk Road). From Leh, a jeep takes you across the Khardungla Pass, with its exquisite valley and mountain vistas. Once you enter Nubra, you proceed to Disket village, your camping base, and visit its 500-year-old monastery followed by nearby Hunder village and its monastery. Then you begin a four-day safari through the ethereal valley on an intrepid Bactrian camel, with overnight stays at Panamik village (where you can take a dip in the hot springs) and Samtanling village, which has another old monastery. Finish back in Leh. Ibex Expeditions (☞ Tour Operators *in* The Himalayas A to Z, *below*) runs this tour mid-July–mid-October.

Jeep Safaris

MANALI-LEH

See Jeep Safaris *in* Himachal Pradesh, *above.*

LADAKH TOUR

Opened to tourists only in 1994, the Nubra Valley, Tso Moriri, and Dha Hanu remain largely mysterious to the outside world. This approximately 14-day trip—which can be bisected for those with less time—includes a visit to the Nubra Valley via the Khardungla Pass. Surrounded by snowcapped mountains, the valley also boasts some of the best monasteries in Ladakh and has preserved some of the finest Buddhist artifacts and ways of life. Across the More Plains are the remote Rupshu Plains and the Tso Moriri, surrounded by mountains towering over 20,000 ft. The nomadic Changpas, who camp here in yak-skin tents, graze their yaks and Pashmina goats (source of the coveted *shatoosh* wool) in the rich pastures adjoining the lake. For a short time in summer, these pastures are carpeted with wildflowers, giving the Nubra Valley its nickname. Finally, you visit the Dha Hanu region in the lower Indus Valley, home of the Drogpas, a group of Aryan Buddhists. Contact Aquaterra Adventures (☞ Tour Operators *in* The Himalayas A to Z, *below*) for details; the tour is available July–September.

PANGONG LAKE

Due to an expanding army presence on the banks of the lake, this four-day trip is less commendable than it used to be. The trek begins in Leh and heads across the Chang Pass (17,604 ft) to Pangong Lake, which, surrounded by mountains, straddles the border of Ladakh and Tibet. One of the world's largest glacier-fed lakes, Pangong dazzles the eye with its vibrant blue and green hues. The lake has long been a summer nesting place for migratory waterbirds and a summer home for shepherds (and their Pashmina goats), who cultivate barley and peas in fields near their lakeside villages. Ibex Expeditions (☞ Tour Operators *in* The Himalayas A to Z, *below*) leads tours mid-July–mid-October.

Rafting

Only experienced rafters should attempt Ladakh's challenging rivers, which generally offer good runs in July and August. Make sure your outfitter has all the right equipment and expertise.

ZANSKAR–INDUS RIVER

A 15-day round-trip adventure from Leh can start with short hikes and drives to important monasteries and great vistas. On the eighth day, you raft from Padam to Saspul villages, beginning a six-day trip with five days of rafting and a spectacular day hike in the Markha Valley. For two days you're locked in a gorge—a rough, fantastic journey that rates classes II–IV. There are fixed departures between July and September, depending on the weather; book well in advance with Himalayan River Runners or Aquaterra Adventures (☞ Tour Operators *in* The Himalayas A to Z, *below*).

Trekking

SPITI–TSO MORIRI

This remote trail forms a challenging 20-day trek in some of Ladakh's more spectacular areas. Following the traditional trade route between the people of Spiti, Changthang, and Tibet, it begins in the high-altitude meadows of Kibber, breeding ground of the famous Spiti horses and home to the endangered snow leopard. After descending into the Kibber gorge, the trail climbs over the Parangla Pass (18,480 ft). A Pare River crossing is followed by an incredible change of scenery as you walk toward the Rupshu plains of Changthang, known for an abundance of kiang (Tibetan wild ass). The last two nights you camp at spectacular sites, one on the southern edge of Tso Moriri; from there, walk along Tso Moriri until you reach Karzog, a settlement of the Changpas (Changthang nomads) on the shores of the Tso Moriri. Contact Aquaterra Adventures (☞ Tour Operators *in* The Himalayas A to Z, *below*).

LAMAYURU–CHILLING

Starting at Lamayuru, an immense monastery built in the 11th century, this moderate-to-difficult trek covers rugged terrain on its way to a part of Ladakh famous for its copper work. Lamayuru hasn't lost its ancient aura, and the diligence of the monks here makes it one of Ladakh's most vibrant monasteries. From here, you walk down the valley and climb to the village of Sumdahchenmo, from which you can look toward the Zanskar River. Farther on, you can either follow the Zanskar route to Chilling (10 days) or head back toward the Indus River and Alchi Gompa (5 days), an exquisite, 11th-century Indus Valley gompa in one of Ladakh's pristine hidden villages. From Chilling you can trek up to Leh via Hemis.

MANALI–LEH

Starting your trek in Manali allows for safer acclimatization. *See* Trekking *in* Himachal Pradesh, *above*.

NUBRA VALLEY

This easy but high-altitude seven-day trek starts after a drive from Leh to the Nubra Valley village of Sabu, with its apple and apricot orchards and unexpected fertile spots. You hike up to Polu Digar, a summer grazing pasture for yaks and sheep, then climb over the Digar La Pass, at

18,040 ft, and descend to Digar village. The next day you follow a river to the village of Khungru, and from here, you visit another typical Buddhist village before retracing the route back to Sabu. After visiting Sabu's monastery, wind things up by driving back to Leh. This trip is available July through September.

UTTAR PRADESH

The Himalayan stretch of Uttar Pradesh, also called Uttarakhand, is locked in by Himachal Pradesh, Tibet, and Nepal. Figuring prominently in the Hindu epics, Uttarakhand is the mythological abode of the Hindu pantheon. Every year thousands of pilgrims make *yatras* (Hindu pilgrimages) to the Garhwal mountains and the sacred Char Dhams (Four Temples)—Yamunotri, Gangotri, Kedarnath, and Badrinath—the homes of the Hindu gods Vishnu and Shiva and source of the holy Yamuna and Ganges rivers.

With more than 100 peaks towering above 20,000 ft, Uttarakhand's Garhwal mountains (especially Mt. Nanda Devi, at 26,056 ft) inspire climbers from all over the world. Trekkers are drawn to its natural sanctuaries, such as Nanda Devi (surrounding the peak of the same name) and the Valley of Flowers, strewn with blossoms and surrounded by glaciers and white-capped mountains. Few foreigners, however, are aware of other good treks through equally sublime Himalayan vistas to mountain villages and the revered Char Dhams and other hallowed shrines. Rafters searching for serious white water will find that Uttarakhand's runs, ranked with Asia's best, are indeed swift, long, and away from the mainstream.

In the Garhwal foothills, next to the Nepali border, is Uttarakhand's second major region, the Kumaon. Like the Garhwal, this is a place of temples and mountain walks, but on a smaller scale—the topography is much gentler, the forests thicker. Far from the frenzy of Garhwal's Hindu pilgrims and Mussoorie's honeymooners, the Kumaon has a more relaxed atmosphere, and the animal-rich Corbett National Park makes it a world-class destination.

Mussoorie

9 *278 km (172 mi) northeast of Delhi*

As you approach Mussoorie you'll see scads of cars with young Indian couples and billboards advertising hotels, both tip-offs that Mussoorie is not the place for a peaceful mountain getaway. With an altitude of about 6,500 ft, this former British hill station (high-altitude retreat) in the Himalayan foothills of Uttar Pradesh is a good place to escape the heat of the North Indian summer. The back side of the town's hill offers spectacular views of the Himalayas, while the town itself looks out south over the plains.

Upper-middle-class Indian tourists strut their stuff on Mussoorie's pedestrian-only thoroughfare, the Mall. The bonhomie of the carnivalesque atmosphere seems infectious for all those escaping the dusty heat of Delhi. Founded in 1823 by a British Army captain, Mussoorie still has a few remnants of the Raj—an Anglican church, old British library, and a "Gun Hill" from which the noon cannon was fired—but they're less extensive than those in Shimla or Nainital. There are some quiet walks around town, especially heading up through Landour Bazaar, with its imperial clock tower, toward Sister's Bazaar; but they're not reason enough to come. Use Mussoorie as a place to relax after a strenuous adventure trip, or to wind down after an overdose of large Indian cities.

The most pleasant way to get to Mussoorie is to take the 5½-hour *Shatabdi Express* train from Delhi (departing 7:30 AM) to Dehra Dun, then take a one-hour taxi ride from that station to Mussoorie. You can also hire a car all the way from Delhi; the road trip takes about as long as the train journey, but the roads make for unpleasant travel. If you decide to drive, expect to pay about Rs. 3,000 and a halt charge of Rs. 200–Rs. 250 per night. Use a travel agency to make arrangements (☞ Delhi A to Z *in* Chapter 3).

Lodging

$$ **Claridges Nabha.** Once the property of the maharaja of Nabha, this summer bungalow is the one place in Mussoorie that consciously maintains the ambience of an old-fashioned hill station. About a mile away from the crowded, polluted, and noisy Mall, it offers a chance to unwind in peaceful and natural surroundings. The 1845 main bungalow, with a typical red-tin roof, has an enormous foyer. Guest rooms were created in the 1940s. The best rooms open onto a veranda and face a courtyard; inside, their elegance is studiously understated. Between cups of tea on the front lawn under a gigantic cypress (where you can watch the escapades of langurs jumping through trees), take a stroll through terraced gardens with lilies and tuberoses or a nature walk in the nearby woods. Reserve well in advance for stays between May 15 and July 15. Breakfast and either lunch or dinner are included. ✉ *Airfield, Barlowganj Rd., 248179,* ☏ *0135/632525,* FAX *0135/631425; or reserve through Claridges, New Delhi,* ☏ *11/301–0211,* FAX *11/301–0625. 22 rooms, 1 suite. Restaurant, bar, lobby lounge, tennis court, billiards, business services, travel services. AE, DC, MC, V.*

The Kumaon Circle

A relatively peaceful, underdeveloped corner of the country, the Kumaon (pronounced "koom-ah-oh") is a wonderful place to begin a love affair with India (or a love affair *in* India). Ceded by Nepal to British India in 1815, it remains a place of forests and farmland, temples and tigers. The mountains here are small, gentle, and soft.

The Uttar Pradesh route outlined here and below is designed to give a delicious and lingering taste of India, minus many of the extreme flavors that often numb a first-time visitor's taste buds. The Kumaon has ancient culture, but it's not such an epicenter of Indian civilization as Varanasi; it has urban life but not the human onslaught of Bombay; and it has plenty of natural beauty that can be enjoyed without the physical intensity of a full-blown trek.

You must hire a car or jeep for this trip (☞ Travel Agencies *in* Delhi A to Z, Chapter 3). All of the hotels listed have complimentary overnight facilities for drivers. You can trace the circle in either direction, beginning at any point, but the most practical way to do it is to start by driving from Delhi to Ramnagar, site of Corbett National Park. (This is a six-hour drive *if* you leave Delhi at about 5 AM; after that, traffic around Delhi will extend the trip by several hours.) When you've had your fill of Corbett, drive to Nainital for a taste of modern Indian culture with a Raj garnish. From Nainital move on to Ranikhet for golf or peaceful walks through the pine forests; from here you can make side trips to several important Hindu temples. Finish the loop back at the north end of Corbett, perhaps by fishing on the Ramganga River. The entire circle takes anywhere from seven days to two weeks, depending on how much time you want to linger over such activities as searching for tigers.

The drive back to Delhi takes about seven hours—if you leave the Corbett National Park area before 2 AM. Depart after that and the rush-hour traffic outside Delhi will add an hour or four to this final leg of your trip. An alternative is to leave Corbett at a reasonable hour and, after a four-hour drive, spend the next night at the lovely Mud Fort in Kuchesar, 80 km (50 mi) west of Delhi. If you leave Kuchesar by 7 the next morning, you'll be back in central Delhi in 90 minutes.

The appeal of the Kumaon loop shifts during the year, but March and December are probably the best times to do it. Corbett National Park is closed from June 15 until November 15 for the monsoon; Nainital and Raniket get snow in January; and Indians throng to the hills during their school holidays, which begin April 15.

Corbett National Park

★ ⑩ *Ramnagar is 250 km (155 mi) northeast of Delhi*

India's oldest wildlife sanctuary (founded 1936), Corbett National Park is named after Jim Corbett, the fearless hunter and author of *Man-Eaters of Kumaon* who later became a conservationist and photographer. Corbett grew up in these hills, and the local people—a number of whom he saved from tigers at the risk of his own life—revered him. Corbett hunted tigers, but later came to regret the sport as he saw the turn-of-the-20th-century population of up to 40,000 tigers drastically reduced. Upon his death in 1956, India honored Corbett by renaming Hailey National Park after this well-liked man.

The park, with elephant grass, forests, and the Ramganga River slicing through its entire length, covers 1,318 square km (527 square mi). You can explore the park on the back of an elephant as it sways quietly through the jungle brush; you can sit in an open jeep as it rolls along miles of tracks; or you can just peer into the vast vista from the top of a stationary watchtower and listen to the sounds of the park's inhabitants. This is a great park, worthy of Corbett's memory: Here you'll see many species of deer, monkeys, and birds and, if you're very lucky, wild elephants, tigers, leopards, black bears, wild boars, snakes (including pythons), and crocodiles.

Only 100 day-trippers are allowed into the park each day, and the park is closed from June 15 to November 15. If you won't be staying overnight, you must get an entry permit from the tourist office at Ramnagar Reception to enter by the Amdanda Gate, which allows you to enter the Bijrani area for morning and evening safaris. If you stay at a private lodge, the staff there will make your daily excursion arrangements. A guide, available at the park, must accompany each vehicle. Before leaving Corbett, you may want to stop in at the small **museum** at Dhangarhi Gate, which houses some stuffed wildcats. Outside the museum, animals such as black buck wander about looking for handouts. ✉ *Ramnagar, Nainital district; for information contact Uttar Pradesh Tourist Office, Chandralok Bldg., 36 Janpath, New Delhi 110001,* ☎ *11/332–2251.* 🎫 *Rs. 100; cameras Rs. 50, video cameras Rs. 500, cars Rs. 100, guides Rs. 100.*

Dining and Lodging

No trip to Corbett is complete without at least one overnight stay in the park itself. At the government-owned Forest Rest Houses, most of which were originally built as stopping points for British forest officers on their way to and from inspections deep inside the jungle, you can watch game until sunset, then fall to sleep amid a deep silence pierced only by the occasional cry of a wild animal. There are a total of 24 Forest Rest Houses in the park—some, like Dhikala, are quite large, with electricity and food service, but most have four to six beds (in two to three rooms), no electricity, bucket baths, and only seasonal access.

While you can make personal arrangements to stay in the rest houses, it's not advisable; their management is highly bureaucratic and not attuned to customer service. Instead, stay at one of the lodges listed below, inform them of your wish in advance, and for a fee they'll make all the necessary arrangements, as well as provide conveyance and housekeeping provisions. These resorts are very close to Amdanda Gate, the park's main entrance, and offer package stays (called "Jungle Plans") that include full board and jeep and elephant safaris, both with knowledgeable naturalists.

$$$$ ★ ✕🏨 **Claridges Corbett Hideaway.** This resort is on the banks of the Kosi River, yet it lacks the dramatic views of its counterpart, Tiger Tops. More than compensatory, however, are the professional management and the lush setting in a mango orchard. Pebble walkways lead to the ochre cottages, which have *chaprel* (baked-tile) roofs, stone-tile floors, woven bamboo-mat ceilings, and fireplaces. Rattan and jute furniture add some rural-Indian character. Each cottage has a sitting area, a modern bathroom with a shower, and a veranda from which to enjoy the peaceful surroundings. Tea and snacks are served next to the immaculate pool. Fixed-menu meals are served in the new lodge on the riverbank, and these are followed by bonfires on the lawn. The staff is happy to arrange hikes, mountain-biking excursions, and jeep, elephant, and (with advance notice) horseback safaris. Traveler's checks are not accepted. ✉ *Zero Garjia, Dhikuli, Ramnagar, Nainital district, 224715,* ☎ *05942/35105,* FAX *05942/35103; in Delhi contact Claridges at* ☎ *11/301–0211. 28 rooms. Restaurant, bar, pool, archery, Ping-Pong, meeting room. AE, DC, MC, V.*

$$$$ ✕🏨 **Tiger Tops Corbett Lodge.** Due to management problems of several years' standing, housekeeping is lax here, maintenance is wanting, and the service is amateur. This is a shame, as the facility and location are magnificent. The lodge's location on a high bank of the Kosi River lets you listen to the rush of the water while looking beyond toward the foothills of the Himalayas. Each spacious room has a large picture window, a rough stone wall, a bamboo-and-tile ceiling, a modern bathroom with a shower, and a large private balcony from which you can see the gorgeously set but dirty outdoor pool. Most impressive is the circular central lodge, with its vaulted timber dome, where you can eat, drink, and relax. Refreshments can also be taken on the deck outside, which practically hangs over the river. The very-expensive room rate includes all meals (delicious homestyle Indian food and some Continental) and such activities as jeep safaris and hiking. There's an elephant in residence for both safaris and leisurely rides. ✉ *Dhikuli, Ramnagar, Nainital district, 224715,* ☎ *05946/85279; in Delhi contact Khatau International, A-3 Geetanjali Enclave, New Delhi 110017,* ☎ *11/686–1209. 24 rooms. Restaurant, bar, pool, Ping-Pong, playground, meeting room, travel services. AE, DC, MC, V.*

En Route Several miles north of the park's Dhangarhi Gate, driving along the river, you'll find the first of many small temples on this loop. The people of the Kumaon are predominately Shivites—worshipers of Shiva, the destroyer and re-creator of the Hindu pantheon. The **Garjia Temple** in Dhikuli is dedicated to Garjia Ma, a local incarnation of the goddess Parvati, Shiva's consort. Located in a small gorge, the temple is perched about 160 ft up on a tall rock that becomes an island in the middle of the Kosi River during the monsoon. Drive down the access road through the wheat fields and banana trees, then walk from the parking area through the gauntlet of rickety shops selling Hindu paraphernalia. Several of these shops sell coconuts and flowers that can be used as offerings to the goddess. The temple is open from sunrise to sunset.

Nainital

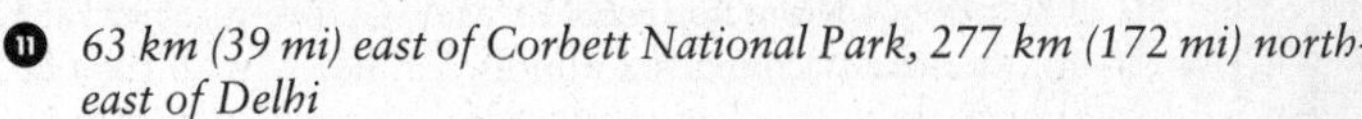

11 *63 km (39 mi) east of Corbett National Park, 277 km (172 mi) northeast of Delhi*

The drive from Corbett to Nainital is less than two hours long, but is memorable for both its solitude and its scenery. East of Ramnagar the road leads you on a tour of unspoiled agrarian India. Mud dwellings with grass roofs stand guard next to fields of sugarcane, wheat, and lentils; interspersed with the fields are small stands of teak and *sal* (tall trees that resemble black oak), with an occasional banana plantation thrown in. In the distance are glimpses of the Himalayan foothills that await you. Just before you turn up into the hills at Kaladungi, you'll pass Jim Corbett's old winter home, a small colonial bungalow whose museum offers a short break from the journey. The road uphill begins in a sal forest, which occasionally gives way to terraced fields. As the trees thin out, the road gets steep and starts to wind. Toward the top you might be held up by troops of langurs sunning themselves on the road or children on their way home from school in the city. Suddenly the road turns downhill, and the congestion of Nainital begins.

Nainital is one of India's most popular hill stations. This one, "discovered" by the British in the 1840s, was later made the official summer capital of Uttar Pradesh (then known as the United Provinces). Nainital clutches the steep slopes that surround a lake of the same name. It's easy to see why the British fell in love with this idyllic spot, yet seemingly uncontrolled development is beginning to take its toll in the form of congestion, pollution, and noise. Indian tourists, especially honeymooners, come to Nainital in all seasons to enjoy the cool air and mountain views. The school holidays, April 15–June 15, bring the real crowds and should be avoided if possible.

As a former colonial capital, Nainital packs quite a bit of history. Those interested in colonial architecture are in for a particular treat. There's another British building, generally with a high-gable tin roof, around every corner; check out the Clock Tower, the Boat Club, the Masonic Hall, the library, and the Church of St. John of the Wilderness. Most of these buildings are, however, slowly tumbling down. The north end of town is built up around the Flats, a large open field created by a landslide in the late 19th century. Facing the Municipal Office, this area is permeated by an air of perpetual carnival; magicians and acrobats perform as tourists munch away on snacks purchased from the many vendors. Sit and watch a cricket game, or take in a Hindi movie at the old Capital Cinema Hall on the Flats.

Elusive to the eye but unavoidable to the ear is the busy **Sri Ma Naini Temple** on the Flats. Open sunrise to sunset, this lakeside shrine is dedicated to many gods, including Shiva, but Naina Devi (an incarnation of Parvati) is its focus. Take off your shoes and wander around, watching the devout make offerings to the large black Shiva linga by the lake. If you're interested in the various Indian religions, take the time to also visit the **gurdwara** (Sikh temple) and **mosque** that face the Flats.

Two fabulous places to take in Nainital's famous Himalayan views are **Cheena Peak** and the outlook called **Snow View.** The former is the highest point near Nainital, at 8,566 ft, and was officially renamed Naini Peak after India's 1962 war with China. You can reach the peak on foot or on the back of one of the many horses for rent in town. Snow View can also be reached on foot or horseback, and there's a Tibetan monastery on the way. Tourists commonly take a gondola to Snow View from town (the "Ropeway"; Rs. 30 round trip), which runs roughly, not reliably, 9:30–1 and 2–5 daily.

Dining and Lodging

$$ **Claridges Naini Retreat.** In this elegant retreat not far from Nainital, the new is connected almost seamlessly with the old. The old is Hari Bhavan, built as a summer maharaja's residence in 1926; the new is a hotel run by Claridges of Delhi. Set around a red-tile garden patio, the bluestone buildings have classic Kumaoni red-tin roofs with latticework windows and high gables. Rooms are simple, with hardwood furniture and floors; some look down past wrought-iron railings to Nainital and across the lake to the development creeping up the hillsides. The duplexes, though a bit dark, are great for families. Meals—which can include traditional Kumaoni dishes—are served in a high-ceiling dining room, with breakfast and either lunch or dinner included in your room rate. Traveler's checks are not accepted, and the hotel does not exchange currency. ✉ *Ayarpatta Slopes, 263001,* ☏ *05942/35105,* FAX *05942/35103; in Delhi, contact Claridges at* ☏ *11/301–0625. 44 rooms. Restaurant, golf privileges, billiards (carom), Ping-Pong. AE, DC, MC, V.*

$$ **Mountain Quail Camp.** To avoid the congestion of Nainital, try this "camp" about half an hour's drive away. The deluxe tents have attached bathrooms and comfortable beds. At night you can sit around a communal fire and enjoy the peaceful, woodsy surroundings. The proprietor, "Sid" (Sidharth), is a true outdoorsman and naturalist of whom you should make use; if you have time, stay a few days and let him arrange some outdoor activities for you. Sid regularly organizes day hikes and short treks farther up into the hills, or down to his mother's small resort near Kaladhungi. Fishing, pony-trekking, bird watching, mountain biking, and rock climbing are other distractions. All meals are included in the room rate. Bring cash: credit cards are not accepted, nor are traveler's checks. ✉ *Pangot 263001; in Kaladhungi,* ☏ *5942/4227 or 5942/35493; in Delhi, 11/684–7759,* FAX *11/692–4671. Restaurant. No credit cards.*

Ranikhet

12 *55 km (34 mi) northwest of Nainital*

As with Nainital, the drive here takes less than two hours but is an event in itself. After leaving the crowded confines of Nainital on a road that hugs the mountainside, you'll quickly enter the town of **Bhiwali**—this grubby little place, with small shops and tea stalls, is the center of the local fruit industry. In season the roadside is crowded with men selling crates of apples, peaches, and plums to travelers and commercial dealers, and for the next hour of your drive the bottom of the river valley is filled with small orchards. After crossing another small river, you'll head back up to Ranikhet, at which point the forests give way to some spectacular sections of terraced farmland.

Ranikhet itself is ensconced in evergreen confines on a Himalayan hilltop. Of all the British hill stations in India, only Ranikhet retains some of its original sylvan tranquility. This may be because it's an army town, home of the Kumaon Regiment ever since the Raj, so development has been controlled. The spacious army cantonment stretches along the Mall, which winds along the top of hill, and many of the regiment's stone buildings, built well before Independence, are still smartly maintained specimens of colonial architecture. Walk on the **Upper Mall Road** to see the Parade Ground or Regimental Headquarters.

Ranikhet has at least six old colonial churches that can be explored. While each is unique, all are made of stone and have the high tin roofs typical of this area. Two of these churches, facing each other across a small athletic field in the center of the cantonment, have been deconsecrated and converted into the **Ranikhet Tweed and Shawl Factory,** a hand-loom production center of woolens. This operation is run by the Kumaon Regiment for soldiers injured in the line of duty and for army widows. Let the clattering draw you inside for a look at how hand looms work, or visit the little store down by the field, housed in the regiment's old bank. The factory and store are open Monday through Saturday from 9 to 5.

Heading uphill (south) from the Westview Hotel, take the **Lower Mall Road,** almost completely abandoned now, for a peaceful stroll through a mixed forest of pine and oak. About 2 km (1 mi) up the road, it merges once again with Upper Mall Road and you come upon the small, relatively new **Jhula Devi Temple,** open sunrise to sunset. The temple is bursting with brass bells small and large; Hindu temple bells are traditionally rung to alert the god to the devotee's need (which is why some temples are so clamorous). If you keep walking, a few more miles bring you to the **Chaubatia Orchards,** a huge (260-acre) fruit orchard run by the Uttar Pradesh state government. Feel free to stroll among the trees.

Dining and Lodging

$ ✕🏨 **Westview.** Perched on a small hill, the Westview's yellow-flagstone main building was designed as a home in the mid-19th century and is still the best place to enjoy Ranikhet's gentle ambience. Each room is unique; the Westview Suite and suite 28 are particularly large, bright, and quiet. In winter you can drift off in front of your own fireplace or wood-burning stove. Rooms are a little worn, but the dining room, with its 25-ft ceiling, calico wallpaper and linens, and high-back wooden chairs, is a treat, especially when a fire crackles in the hearth. Service is exceptional for such an unassuming place. The Continental food is, strangely, superior to the Indian: try the roast leg of lamb with mint sauce or fish munière, followed by crème caramel. There may be a different breakfast cook, for in the morning, the *aloo parantha* (pan-fried bread stuffed with potatoes) and *purie subzi* (deep-fried bread with spiced vegetables) are at once light and hearty. Order meals an hour in advance. ✉ *Mahatma Gandhi Rd., 263645,* ☎ *05966/200261,* FAX *05961/20396; or reserve through C-16 Greater Kailash 1, New Delhi 110048* ☎ *11/648–5981,* FAX *11/331–7582. 37 rooms. Restaurant, coffee shop, badminton, horseback riding. No credit cards.*

Hindu Temples

If you have an extra few days and don't mind more driving, take a side trip from Ranikhet to see several important temples dedicated to Lord Shiva. Many are quite old, dating from the Katyuri (8th–14th centuries) and Chand (15th–18th centuries) dynasties. The most significant temples northeast of Ranikhet are at **Baijanth, Bhageshwar,** and **Jageshwar.** Unlike temples on the plains, these are built from rough-hewn stone, and their alpine locations—such as the cedar forest in Jageshwar—give Hinduism an entirely different feel. The hill at **Binsar** has both a nature sanctuary and some ruins of the Chand dynasty's former capital. The views from on top are fabulous; tranquility abounds.

Dining and Lodging

$$$$ 🏨 **Binsar Valley Resort.** This small resort works as both a pleasant rest stop after a temple tour and a base for Himalayan adventures. Ideally located at the edge of the Binsar Sanctuary (which has exemplary birdwatching), it was built in 1934 as the summer home of Major B. P. Pande. The property is still held by the family, but the original home is now a guest house. Rooms are in three separate cottages; all have wood stoves and the public sitting room has an open fireplace, so winter stays are as enjoyable as summer visits. The staff can arrange plenty of adventures, including trekking, rafting, camping, and jeep safaris, but their crown offering is a stable full of trained Austrian mountain horses (Haflingers) for experienced riders and sturdy Tibetan mountain ponies for beginners and children. ✉ *Village Basoli, P.O. Bhainsori, Almora district, 263684,* ☎ *5962/53028; or reserve through F 8/1 Vasant Vihar, New Delhi 110057,* ☎ *11/615–2294* FAX *11/614–2623. 9 rooms. Dining room, horseback riding, travel services. AE.*

The Kumaon Circle: North Side

The three-hour drive from Ranikhet back down to Corbett National Park is breathtaking, both for its views of the Himalayas and for the sometimes frightening way the narrow road hugs the very steep mountainsides. Those subject to motion sickness might want to take their medication before beginning this drive; but the winding road is almost deserted, so the drive is peaceful. After passing through a very small town it meanders through dry hillsides and occasionally terraced farmlands. Toward the bottom it sinks into sal forests. Just before arriving at Corbett, turn right at the Mohan Forest Rest House and climb over the heavily forested ridge that separates the Kosi from the Ramganga river valleys. This brings you to the seldom-visited north side of the park, which offers anglers a unique fishing experience and all travelers a rest stop en route back to Delhi.

Lodging

$$$ **Corbett Ramganga Resort.** Landing a fierce-fighting mahaseer is a real test of a fisherman's acumen. While other resorts around Corbett allude to fishing facilities, this riverside resort specializes in helping the angler catch one, with a collection of well-maintained casting rods and a fishing guide whose successes are documented with photos in the reception room. Stay in a yellow-brick cottage (they're small, as are the beds, but clean and freshly painted) or a "safari tent" with attached brick bathroom. The grounds are laced with delightful flower beds, and the shallow pool sits in a spacious lawn next to the river. While Ramganga does arrange park safaris, it's too far from Amdanda Gate (an hour's drive) to make this convenient; fishing and hiking can occupy you here. Meals, served in a river-view dining lodge, are included in the room price. There is no foreign exchange. ✉ *Reserve through Surghi Adventures P. Ltd. F-40, NDSE-I, New Delhi 110049,* ☎ *11/461–8130,* FAX *11/462–5302. 10 cottages, 10 tents. Restaurant, pool. AE, DC, MC, V.*

Adventures

Coming to Uttar Pradesh in the summer allows you to avoid the crowd of foreigners that descends on Himachal Pradesh and Ladakh. Aside from a few routes frequented by Hindu and Sikh pilgrims, you'll be alone with the villagers and shepherds. Given the great rafting on the headwaters of the Ganges and its tributaries, tour companies recommend combination trips, which include trekking and rafting in addition to, say, fishing and mountain biking. The downside of Uttar Pradesh is the poor travel infrastructure; the lack of an airport deep in the mountains (as opposed to Kullu and Shimla) means more driving, and the roads are not as well maintained as those in Himachal Pradesh.

Fishing

RAMGANGA RIVER

The Ramganga River bisects Corbett National Park. Prior to entering the park it flows past the Corbett Ramganga Resort (☞ Lodging, *above*), which has made a specialty of pursuing the mahaseer. If you plan to stay here, alert them in advance of your inter care of your license (a one-day process) as well as pr ity poles and an expert guide. Leave everything to them away; then relax in the garden or by the pool in the evenin ing season runs from October 1 to June 30, peaking betwee ary and April.

Rafting

Whitewater rafting in Uttar Pradesh, especially on the Ganges Rive just upstream from Rishikesh, has become a major growth industry. At press time there were close to 10 separate rafting camps on the river in this area, set up by tour companies to provide Delhi's smart set with relaxing adventure vacations—people drive up for a weekend of rafting and horseplay on a sandy beach by the upper Ganges. This is a great time, highly recommended if you want to escape the city and do some rafting without committing to a long, strenuous adventure trip. The season runs from October to June; contact Aquaterra Adventures, Himalayan River Runners, or Outdoor Adventures India (☞ Tour Operators *in* The Himalayas A to Z, *below*) for information on their camps. The same companies can also arrange the longer trips listed below. Outdoor Adventures India—run by a charming couple, Ajay Maira and Pavanne Mann—stands out. Their camp on the upper Ganges is a favorite with American expats and their families; the focus is on safety, ecology, and good food, and Ajay knows the river well.

ALAKANANDA RIVER

Five-day runs (November–mid-December and February–April) follow the Alakananda from Rudraprayag to Rishikesh. Expect good rapids, historic temples, good Himalayan vistas, campsites on secluded beaches, and Class III and IV rapids.

BHAGIRATHI RIVER

This six-day Himalayan run (November–mid-December and February–April) goes from Tehri to Rishikesh. You move through at least two gorges and river valleys, and even maneuver a small waterfall.

GANGES RIVER

Enjoy an easy three-day rafting trip on the Ganges (October–mid-December and February–June). Float from Deoprayag to Rishikesh, both in the lower Himalayas.

KALI RIVER

Flowing past densely forested hillsides, this trip is a wilderness experience in a league of its own. The Kali River forms the international border between India and Nepal, flowing past the terraced farms of Kumaoni and Nepali villages, sandy beaches, thick tropical jungles, cliffsides of stalactite and stalagmite formations, riverside tea stops, and plantations. After the first few days of serene floating up to and past the confluence with the Saryu River at Pancheshwar (an ideal time to try landing a mahaseer), you hit some big rapids. The Kali makes its final descent to the plains on your last day on water, beginning with the mighty Chooka rapid. This 10-day round trip from Delhi is best undertaken between November and March. Aquaterra Adventures, recently featured leading this trip on an Indian adventure TV show, suggests that rafting be preceded by a jeep safari through the Kumaon, including Ranikhet, Binsar, and the temples of Mukteshwar and Bageshwar, indeed a most highly recommended trip that takes 12–15 days.

Trekking

GANGOTRI–GAUMUKH

This moderate, but high-altitude, nine-day trek is probably the most popular in Uttar Pradesh with foreign trekkers and Hindu pilgrims alike.

Best from April to June and September to October, it heads to the source of the sacred Ganges River, with a trailhead at Gangotri Temple in northern Uttar Pradesh. You first pass through forests and a valley, following the pilgrim route that climbs above the tree line to Bhijbasa and its solitary ashram. You cross flowering meadows backed by towering peaks and camp on the wide, sandy beach of the Gaumukh, where the holy Ganges emerges from the Gangotri Glacier. The trail weaves through moraine, cuts across the glacier, and climbs steeply up grassy slopes to Tapovan Valley, whose vast meadows brush against the base of Shivling Peak. Camping at Tapovan, you take day hikes to Kirti Bamak Glacier, the base of Kedarnath Dome and Kirti, and Meru Glacier and the base of Mt. Meru (believed by Hindus to be the center of the universe). From Tapovan, you make an excursion across the moraine-covered Gangotri Glacier to Nandanvan, at the confluence of the Chaturangi and Gangotri glaciers. After camping in a meadow against the Bhagirathi Massif, which is home to *bharal* (blue sheep), you follow a grassy ridge that runs parallel to the Chaturangi Glacier toward Vaski Tal (Lake) before retracing the route back to Nandanvan and Gangotri.

SAHASRATAL–BHILANGANA VALLEY

The likelihood that you'll see another trekker on this challenging route is remote. The Sahasratal group of lakes lie at an average altitude of 15,000 ft in the Uttarkashi district of Uttar Pradesh. These lakes are considered holy by the local people who take an annual pilgrimage carrying the *doli* (deity) on their shoulders. The route climbs through only one village, Sila, passing through high pastures. Depending on the season, you might meet only goatherds and Gujjars here. The trail winds its way through massive open meadows littered with wild daffodils and climbs over the 13,200-ft Kyarki Khal pass, offering brilliant views of all the mountain ranges in the area from Bandarpunch and Kala Nag to Jaonli. Each of the Sahasratal lakes—Lam Tal, Pari Tal, Narsingh Tal, Darshan Tal, Gaumukhi Tal, and many others—has a religious significance. Pilgrims from the Uttarkashi side return from the lake after making their offerings, but this route makes a steep descent through forested hillside to the Bhilangana Valley. The route now follows the river all the way to the roadhead at Ghuttu, starting point for the Khatling Glacier trek. The trip is accessible in June or September–October. Contact Aquaterra Adventurers (☞ Tour Operators *in* The Himalayas A to Z, *below*) for details.

DARJEELING

⑬ Anyone with a yen for hill stations must see the "Queen of the Hills" in the far northwestern corner of West Bengal. Built during the British Raj as a center for the lucrative tea trade, this colorful town quickly earned a reputation as a superb Himalayan resort. Most of the graceful old colonial buildings are a bit scruffy, but some still bear their regal stamp, and the town's Old World charm never ceases to enchant even jaded travelers. With a few days here you can soak up the majestic alpine ambience and scenery—dominated, in good weather, by far-off Mt. Kanchenjunga (28,208 ft)—bargain in a local market, and trek on a nearby hillside. Fog engulfs the town from below at unpredictable intervals, but when it clears and the sun sparkles on the exquisitely snowy Kanchenjunga, third-highest mountain in the world, the effect is dazzling.

The pride of Daj, as it's affectionately called, is its main promenade, **the Mall.** Stroll around, or hop on a pony, and drink in the general air of well-being. If you're hungry after a long train journey, stop in a roadside café for a plate of steamed Tibetan momos. From he Mall you can wander off into some of the town's hilly cobbled lanes.

Nature lovers have plenty to see right in town. The **Bengal Natural History Museum** (✉ Meadowbank Rd.) houses an exhaustive collection of alpine fauna and a splendid display of big-game trophies. Just north of the museum en route to the zoo is **Raj Bhavan,** former residence of the Maharaja of Burdwan, crowned by a lovely blue dome. **Padmaja Naidu Zoo** (✉ off Jawahar Rd. W) is famous for its rare snow leopards as well as shy red pandas and other alpine animals. The **Himalayan Mountaineering Institute** (✉ beyond the zoo), a training center with some public exhibits, was long directed by none other than Sherpa Tenzing Norgay, who accompanied Sir Edmund Hillary up Mt. Everest in 1953. Sacred sites also abound. South of the town center, **Dhirdham Temple** (✉ below the train station) was built along the lines of the Pashupatinath Temple in Kathmandu. Both Buddhists and Hindus revere **Observatory Hill** (✉ above Windamere Hotel), topped by an unusual shrine. There are several *gompas,* or Tibetan monasteries, nearby, beginning with **Aloobari** (✉ Tenzing Norgay Rd.). **Bhutia Busti** houses the original *Bhardo Thudol* (Tibetan *Book of The Dead*). Darjeeling's most celebrated house of worship is the **Yiga-Choling** monastery in Ghoom, ✉ 8 km/5 mi south of Darjeeling, which houses the extremely sacred Maitreya Buddha ("Coming Buddha") image.

To see how Darjeeling tea is processed, visit the **Happy Valley Tea Estate,** 3 km (2 mi) outside town, where tea is still made the orthodox way. An obliging employee can be an impromptu but effective guide. For such a small town, Darjeeling is a serious **shopping** center, with top-quality orange-pekoe tea, Tibetan artifacts, jewelry, thangka paintings, local woolen garments, hats, and carpets.

The weather up here is delightful year-round, barring only the monsoon season. You'll get the best views of Kanchenjunga between November and March. The town sometimes gets snow in December; bring heavy woolens in winter, light woolens in summer.

Dining and Lodging

Most of Darjeeling's good restaurants are in hotels, but the town has a few independent classics. Three are right on the Mall: **Glenary's** serves tandoori, Chinese, and Continental fare, including great sausage rolls, but is best known for its tea service and desserts, including cakes and pudding with a load of rum. Kev's, or **Keventer's,** a snack bar as old as the town itself, serves cakes, sausage rolls, and sandwiches. **Dekevas** is a hot favorite for big pizzas. Just east of the Mall, **Embassy** (✉ Hotel Valentino, Rockville Rd.) is Chinese food at its best—opt for fish.

$$$$ 🏨 **Windamere.** High tea at this grande dame of the Raj is an institution in itself. The atmosphere is at once formal and homey. The drawing room has a welcoming fireplace, sometimes enhanced by the live sounds of a Western string quarte, and the bar is wonderfully elegant. Guest rooms, decorated in soft colors, have heaters, hot-water bottles, and no TVs—at night, the silence of the hills is yours. All meals are included in the room rate. ✉ *Observatory Hill,* ☎ *354/54041. 41 rooms, 4 suites. Restaurant, bar, badminton, table tennis, laundry service, baby-sitting, travel services. AE, MC, V.*

$$$ 🏨 **New Elgin.** Rooms are elegant and decorative in this classic, comfortable option. Thick drapes and hot-water bottles add to the general coziness. The restaurant and bar are both solid. ✉ *32 H. D. Lama Rd.,* ☎ *354/54114. 22 rooms, 3 suites. Restaurant, bar, laundry service. AE, DC, MC, V.*

$$ 🏨 **Sinclairs.** Spacious and full of light, with polished wooden floors, this modern, centrally heated hotel commands excellent views (ask for a front room). Breakfast and either lunch or dinner are included in the already-reasonable room rate. ✉ *18/1 Gandhi Rd.,* ☎ *354/56431,* FAX *354/54355. 54 rooms, 2 suites. Restaurant, bar, recreation room, laundry service, meeting room, travel services. AE, DC, V.*

SIKKIM

Lepchas, or Rongkup (Children of Rong), the first known inhabitants of Sikkim, aptly called their mountain home paradise. The last *chogyal* (king), who ruled over Sikkim until it became India's 22nd state in 1975, was an avid conservationist who protected his Buddhist kingdom from development. Gangtok, the capital, is overbuilt and crowded, but once you escape its boundaries, you're surrounded by tropical forests rich with 600 species of orchids and 46 varieties of rhododendron. Waterfalls splash down mountains and power prayer wheels. Tidy hamlets with prayer flags flapping in the breeze and cultivated terraced fields occupy idyllic valleys. Sikkim's guardian deity, Mt. Kanchenjunga—the world's third-highest peak, at 28,208 ft; also spelled Khangchendzonga—is still revered by all who live in its shadow.

Three distinct ethnic groups live in Sikkim. The Lepchas originally lived in seclusion in north Sikkim, where they developed a harmonious relationship with the environment to ensure their survival. Although most Lepchas converted to Buddhism, many still worship aspects of their physical surroundings: rainbows, clouds, rivers, and trees. Village priests preside over elaborate rituals, including animal sacrifices, to appease their animist deities.

Bhutias from Tibet came into Sikkim with the first chogyal in the 17th century. Buddhism governs Bhutia life, with the monastery and the lama exerting tremendous influence over daily activities. Every village has its prayer flags and chortens, every home has an altar room, and most families have one relative in a monastery or convent. Buddhism even works its way into weavings, handwoven rugs, *thangka* (scroll) paintings, statues, and delicately carved *choktses* (tables). The Bhutias' culture, in turn, dominates Sikkim, right down to the women's national dress: the traditional *kho* or *bhoku,* the epitome of elegance, worn over a *wanju* (blouse), with the *pangden* (apron), the final colorful touch, restricted to married women and formal occasions.

Also sharing Sikkim are the Nepalese, who introduced terrace farming to the region. Although most Nepalese are Hindu, you'll see few Hindu temples in Sikkim, and their faith often incorporates Buddhist beliefs and practices (as it does in Nepal). The Nepalese are dominant in business, and theirs is the language most often heard in Sikkim.

June, July, and August bring monsoon rains and December and January have cold snows, so the times to visit Sikkim are March–May and September–mid-November. The peak period, when tourist services are taxed to the limit, is late September–early October: the Hindu festival Durga Puja.

Because of Sikkim's sensitive border location, foreigners need a Restricted-Area Permit (RAP) to visit (☞ Permits *in* The Himalayas A to Z, *below*).

Adventures

Yak safaris are available from Dzongri, and kayak trips on the Teesta or Rangeet rivers can be arranged for special groups (☞ Tour Operators *in* The Himalayas A to Z, *below*).

Sikkim

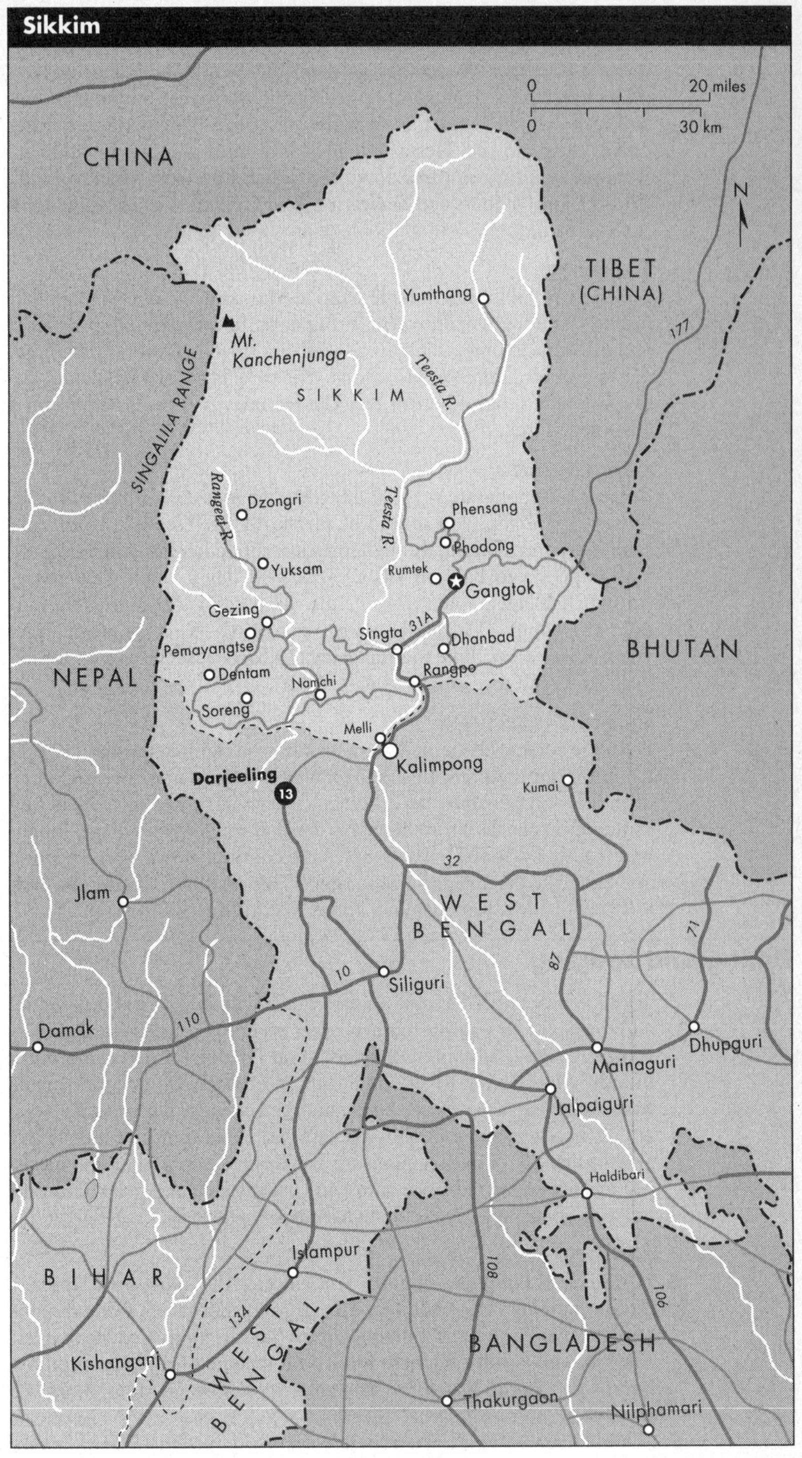
0
20 miles
0
30 km
N
CHINA
TIBET
(CHINA)
177
Yumthang
Mt.
Kanchenjunga
SIKKIM
Teesta R.
SINGALILA RANGE
Rangeet R.
Dzongri
Teesta R.
Phensang
Phodong
Yuksam
Rumtek
Gangtok
Gezing
Singta
31A
Dhanbad
Pemayangtse
BHUTAN
Dentam
Rangpo
NEPAL
Namchi
Soreng
Melli
Kalimpong
Darjeeling
13
Kumai
32
Jlam
WEST
BENGAL
71
87
10
Siliguri
110
Damak
Dhupguri
Mainaguri
Jalpaiguri
Haldibari
Islampur
108
BIHAR
106
134
WEST
BENGAL
BANGLADESH
Kishanganj
Thakurgaon
Nilphamari

Rafting

TEESTA AND RANGEET RIVERS

Rafting (October–November only) on the Teesta and Rangeet rivers offers everything from gentle rides through amazing mountain views and lush canyon vegetation to white water for the experienced rafter only. A trip on the Teesta will probably take you from Makha to Rongpo, while adventures down the Rangeet go from Sikip to Melli. Contact Tashila Tours and Travels (☞ Tour Operators *in* The Himalayas A to Z, *below*).

Trekking

Trekking in Sikkim (available March–May and October–December) means frigid nights and warm, tiring days. In the spring (April–May) you might face some nasty rain as well, but spring is best for such flowers as orchids and rhododendrons. Winter is best for Himalayan vistas. Contact a tour operator (☞ The Himalayas A to Z, *below*) for a customized trek.

KANCHENJUNGA

Because this moderate 7- to 10-day trek demands considerable up- and downhill walking, you should be physically fit. You hike from Yuksam, in western Sikkim, through forests of rhododendron, orchids, pine, and magnolia to Bakhim village. The next day's tough walk passes through a village populated by gentle yak-herding Tibetans to the outpost of Dzongri (13,218 ft), with views of Mt. Kanchenjunga. Here you can ride a yak, hike to Thangsing (12,890 ft), at the base of Jopino Peak, or climb to Zimathang (14,760 ft).

RHODODENDRON TREK

From the Soreng village in western Sikkim, you climb to Bershay (12,000 ft), in the forested Singalila Range, which is known as the rhododendron belt and has about 40 different varieties of flowering trees as well as numerous birds. From here you descend to Dentam village, inhabited mainly by Subba tribal people, and continue down to the historic and exquisite Pemayangtse Monastery. This easy, four- to five-day trek has views of Mt. Kanchenjung and is best in March, April, and May.

Dining and Lodging

Try Sikkimese sautéed ferns in season, sautéed bamboo shoots, nettle soup, and roast pork. If you like momos, order beef or vegetable—pork is risky if undercooked. Sikkim also makes good libations: Cherry and musk brandy, wine, Teesta River white rum, juniper gin, *paan* liquor (made from a mixture of leaves and betel nuts), and *chang* (Tibetan barley beer) are all worth trying, especially the last two. Note that new-moon days and the first day of the full moon are dry. For traditional Sikkimese meals, restaurants require advance notice and usually ask for parties of four or more. If you're solo, make some friends; it's worth it.

GANGTOK

$ ★ ✕ **House of Bamboo.** Popular with locals, this dark little upstairs restaurant is very informal, very Tibetan, and very cheap. Good momos (pork or beef only) and filling *gyathak* (noodle soup) are the staples. You can also opt for Chinese food. Aim for one of the three window booths so you can watch the street activity below. ✉ *M. G. Marg,* ☏ *no phone. No credit cards.*

$ ✕ **Tibet Kitchen.** This upstairs eatery near the Hotel Tashi Delek is simple, clean, authentic, friendly, and cheap, and it's open for breakfast. Highlights are the *then-tuk* (flat-noodle soup) and delicious Tibetan bread with honey. You can sample home-brewed chang at the small bar. ✉ *M. G. Marg,* ☏ *3592/26645. No credit cards.*

$$$$ ✕🏨 **Nor-Khill.** Now run by the Elgin group, Gangtok's oldest hotel sits on a quiet ridge below the city, just above the stadium. Once a royal guest house, it has lovely landscaped gardens and excellent views. Traditional Sikkimese architecture is emphasized throughout with colorful masks, etchings, and local paintings. Rooms are simple, comfortable, and decorated with discreet Buddhist and Sikkimese details such as traditional carpets and religious artwork. Service is excellent, meals are included in the price, and the ambience is relaxed. Reserve in advance, and ask for a room with a view. The small, elegant Shangrila Restaurant serves very good Sikkimese, Indian, Chinese, and Continental dishes. ✉ *Paljor Stadium Rd., 737101,* ☎ *3592/25637,* FAX *3592/25639. 32 rooms. Restaurant, bar, travel services. AE, DC, MC, V.*

$$$–$$$$ ★ ✕🏨 **Tashi Delek.** Don't be fooled by the drab facade: The public rooms are wonderfully bright, and decorated in a sort of Baroque Sikkimese style. Guest rooms are simple in comparison, but they're pleasant and well maintained, and the suites have sitting rooms with Sikkimese decor. Ask for a mountain view. There are two excellent restaurants: The menu at Dragon Hall's includes exotic seasonal greens such as ferns and stinging nettles, and the Blue Poppy serves Sikkimese, Indian, Chinese, and Continental food. The rooftop garden is the nicest place in town (in season) to enjoy an afternoon meal or drink. ✉ *M. G. Marg, 737101,* ☎ *3592/22991,* FAX *3592/22362. 40 rooms, 6 suites. Restaurant, bar, travel services. AE, DC, MC, V.*

$–$$ ★ ✕🏨 **Hotel Tibet.** Centrally located and run by the Dalai Lama Charitable Trust, this popular hotel has a peaceful Tibetan atmosphere, with thangkas, superbly colorful rugs, and other Buddhist artifacts. Rooms on the road side are the cheapest, and a little small; try for a mountain view. Not all bathrooms have tubs. A variety of meal plans are available, and the Snow Lion restaurant is one of the city's best. The menu mixes Tibetan, Japanese, Chinese, Continental, and Indian food; try the unusual *menyak polo* (slightly sweet, cheese-filled steamed dumplings). ✉ *Paljor Stadium Rd., 737101,* ☎ *3592/22523,* FAX *3592/22707. 40 rooms. Restaurant, bar, travel services. AE, DC, MC, V.*

PEMAYANGTSE

$ 🏨 **Mount Pandim.** This government-run hotel enjoys a fine hillside situation, with an attractive garden and good views of Kanchenjunga. Rooms are functional and reasonably sized, though some show signs of neglect. Ask for a view. The restaurant offers a few local dishes in addition to the usual Indian and Chinese food, but service can be tediously slow. ✉ *Pelling, 737113 West Sikkim,* ☎ *3593/50756. 25 rooms. Restaurant. No credit cards.*

THE HIMALAYAS A TO Z

Arriving and Departing

By Car or Bus

HIMACHAL PRADESH

Overnight **buses** connect Delhi with Shimla, Kuli, Manali, and Dharamsala, taking about 17 hours in all four cases. You may prefer to travel to Shimla by train, then take a bus to Dharamsala or Manali from there. Alternately, take a train from Delhi to Chandigarh and catch a Himachal Pradesh Tourism Development Corporation (HPTDC) bus up Highway 21 to Kullu, Manali, or Dharamşala (☞ Visitor Information, *below*).

LADAKH

In the winter there is no land access to Ladakh. In the summer two roads open up, crossing passes over 15,000 ft high. These are supposedly open from early June through September, but recently the weather has been severe, and not until mid-June at the earliest have buses made it through.

Even weather permitting, the road from Srinagar to Leh is not recommended unless you have kidnap insurance and an exaggerated sense of adventure. (Kashmiri separatists are wont to hold Westerners for ransom or behead them.) The other road, from Manali to Leh, is the world's second-highest drivable road. Once it's open (which often doesn't happen until as late as mid-July), the 530-km (330-mi) route is crowded with buses, trucks, jeeps, and motorcycles, all bouncing from rut to pothole to rut. The two-day journey first crosses Rohtang Pass (13,048 ft) to follow two Chenab tributaries, the Chandra and the Bhaga, before mounting the Baralacha Pass (15,899 ft) and Tanglang Pass (17,306 ft). The road then descends to Upshi before coasting the last 50 km (31 mi) into Leh. It's a trip to make once, but you may lose your ability to marvel at the scenery after a few hours in a crowded bus. The cost of the 20-hour, two-day bus ride is about Rs 1,700; a hired car and driver cost around Rs. 12,000.

UTTAR PRADESH

It's not advisable to take a bus to Uttar Pradesh; the vehicles are crowded and poorly maintained. Of course, so are the roads, but at least you can control the quality of car you hire. **RBS Travels** (✉ Shop G, Connaught Palace Hotel, 37 Shaheed Bhagat Singh Marg, Delhi, ☎ 11/373–3950 or 11/336–4603) maintains a large fleet of cars and offers good rates. Another option is to take a train to Dehra Dun or Kathgodam (☞ *below*) and either hire a car there or send your car ahead from Delhi (this allows you to avoid the traffic around Delhi, which is horrendous).

SIKKIM

Sikkim Nationalized Transport runs buses between Gangtok and Darjeeling (five hours), Kalimpong (four hours), Siliguri (five hours), all in West Bengal; and to district capitals in Sikkim. The Gangtok booking office is at the Sikkim Nationalized Transport Petrol Pump on Paljor Namgyal Stadium Road. Shared jeeps leave every 30 minutes from the private bus stand on National Highway 31A; these are more comfortable than the buses and take only 3½ hours to Siliguri, four hours to Darjeeling, and 2½ hours to Kalimpong. Shared jeeps to destinations in Sikkim leave from Children's Park and from the Lall Market.

By Plane

HIMACHAL PRADESH

Indian Airlines (☎ 11/462–0566) flies Monday, Wednesday, and Friday from Delhi to **Shimla**'s airstrip, Jubbarhatti Airport, a plateau created on top of a mountain 23 km (14 mi) south of Shimla. The flight costs U.S.$100 one way; taxis into Shimla cost Rs. 400. For U.S.$130 Indian Airlines will take you on to **Kullu,** whose airport is at Bhuntar, 9 km (5½ mi) from Kullu town and 50 km (30 mi) from Manali. Indian Airlines also flies to **Jammu** daily (U.S.$105 one way), from which it's a roughly four-hour drive to Dharamsala. You can also fly from Delhi to **Manali**.

Jagson Airlines (☎ 11/372–1593) flies to the Kullu Valley twice daily and once on Sunday, at a cost of U.S.$90. **Jet Airways** (☎ 11/685–3700) flies twice daily to Jammu for U.S.$108.

LADAKH

In the summer of 1999, **Indian Airlines** (☎ 11/462–0566) had daily flights from Delhi to Leh, as well as an extra flight on Monday, Tuesday, Wednesday, and Friday. The airline changes its schedule often, however, and flights are always fewer in the winter; moreover, the summer flights are very popular. With all this in mind, reserve tickets well in advance. The fare is U.S.$105 one way. Note that, because of Leh's high altitude and the Himalayas' capricious weather patterns, flights are often canceled.

UTTAR PRADESH

The only airport in the Himalayan part of Uttar Pradesh recently closed, so there is no air service here at present.

DARJEELING AND SIKKIM

The airport at **Bagdodra,** West Bengal, is about 90 km (56 mi) southeast of Darjeeling and 124 km (77 mi) south of Gangtok. **Indian Airlines** (☎ 3592/23099) runs scheduled flights from Calcutta and Delhi. For Darjeeling, hire a car to finish the trip with a two-hour drive, or taxi the 15 km (9 mi) to New Jalpaiguri to catch the Toy Train (☞ *below*). For Sikkim, hop on one of the shared jeeps that make the five-hour run to Gangtok.

By Train

AMRITSAR

The convenient and comfortable *Shatabdi Express* departs New Delhi Railway Station (☎ 11/373–4164) at 7:30 AM for the five-hour trip to Amritsar.

HIMACHAL PRADESH

The train is the best way to get to **Shimla.** A 95-km (62-mi) narrow-gauge track built in 1903 climbs from Kalka (2,131 ft) to Shimla (7,170 ft). Tiny trains known as the Shimla Toy Trains travel at speeds of 9–15 mph, passing through 102 tunnels and over 845 bridges to make the journey in five hours. First class on the toy train is extremely comfortable, with upholstered chairs to sink into as you marvel at the scenery. Second class is crowded with people pushing and shoving to sit on the wooden seats. The Toy Trains meet two trains from Delhi: The overnight train that departs Delhi at 10 PM arrives in Kalka at 6 AM, and the *Himalayan Queen,* which departs Delhi at 6 AM, arrives at Kalka at 11:40 AM.

The center of Shimla is pedestrian-only. From the train station it's a stiff uphill walk to the center, where most hotels are located. You may wish to hire a porter to carry your luggage; he'll expect Rs. 10–20. Porters also double as hotel touts, so don't let them steer you away from your lodging of choice.

The trip to the **Kangra Valley** and **Dharamsala** is also more pleasant by train than by car. The *Pathankot Express,* which leaves Delhi at 8 PM and arrives at Pathankot in the morning, has first-class compartments; after a good night's sleep you can hop in a car and enjoy the remaining three hours to Dharamsala.

The best train to Chandigarh, from which buses go to **Dharamsala, Kullu,** and **Manali,** is the fast, all-air-conditioned *Shatabdi Express,* which leaves Delhi at 7:30 AM and arrives in Chandigarh at 10:30 AM. Spend the night in Chandigarh and travel by car or bus the next day for the 12-hour trip to Kullu or the 14-hour trip to Manali.

UTTAR PRADESH

There is reasonably good train service to **Mussoorie** via Dehra Dun. If you're moving on to the Kumaon, the best train is to Kathgodam—the Delhi–Kathgodam–Ranikhet express leaves New Delhi at 11 PM and arrives in Kathgodam at 6 AM. From here, you must still drive 90 minutes to Ramnagar or an hour to Nainital. The night train from Delhi to Ramnagar (Corbett National Park) is only recommended for the adventurous, as it has no upper-class bogies.

DARJEELING

Overnight trains from Calcutta's Sealdah Station go to **New Jalpaiguri.** Here you can grab a taxi for the three- to four-hour drive to Darjeeling or board the famous **Toy Train** for a stunning eight-hour journey up a landscape of terraced fields and hairpin turns. The ride is extremely slow and leisurely—you can actually hop on and off the train as it moves along. This is the long but justly celebrated way to reach the famous hill station.

SIKKIM

Those coming from Delhi or Calcutta normally use the train station at Siliguri, in West Bengal. From here, shared jeeps and buses take you on to Gangtok, 114 km (71 mi) away, in four hours. In Gangtok, reserve your return trip at the Sikkim Nationalized Transport Petrol Pump on Paljor Namgyal Stadium Road.

Getting Around

HIMACHAL PRADESH

The road network through Himachal Pradesh is fairly extensive, even if the roads themselves are crowded and riddled with potholes. HPTDC tourist buses connect Shimla with Manali, Kullu, and Dharamsala, each of which trips takes about nine hours and costs just under Rs. 200. There is also an HPTDC bus between Manali and Dharamsala, and buses go from Manali to Leh between mid-July and September. A network of local buses covers the smaller villages.

UTTAR PRADESH

It's safest and most comfortable to stick with hired cars in Uttar Pradesh. Even so-called "luxury" buses generally turn out to be rattle traps with taped TV entertainment blaring up front.

Contacts and Resources

Currency Exchange

LADAKH

Cash traveler's checks at the **State Bank of India** (✉ Main Bazaar, Leh, ☎ 1982/52052).

Emergencies

LADAKH

Seek medical assistance at the **Casualty-District Hospital,** Leh, ☎ 1982/52360. For the **police,** dial ☎ 1982/52018.

Permits

SPITI VALLEY

Permits are required for the Spiti Valley, or for anyone wishing to traverse the Hindustan Tibet Road from Shimla to the Kullu Valley. Groups of four foreigners can obtain their own permits from the Himachal Pradesh Tourism Development Corporation in New Delhi (☞ Visitor Information, *below*), which technically offers next-day service; but given the Byzantine nature of Indian bureaucracy, this is not recommended. Let your tour operator handle your permit in advance.

LADAKH

A permit is required to travel outside Leh. Again, it's best to let your tour operator handle this concern; just bring extra passport photos.

SIKKIM

Foreigners need a permit to visit Sikkim. Good for 15 days, the general permit is easily obtainable within 24 hours from all Indian missions abroad and the following places in India: the **Foreigner's**

Registration Office in Delhi, Bombay, Calcutta, and Darjeeling, and the **Sikkim Tourist Information Centre** (✉ 14 Panchshal Marg, Chankyapuri, New Delhi 110021, ☎ 11/301–5346; ✉ 4C Poonam, 5/2 Russell St., Calcutta 700017, ☎ 33/297516; ✉ SNT Bus Compound, Tenzing Norgay Rd., Siliguri, ☎ 353/432646). Upon application, you must specify your date of entry into Sikkim. A 15-day extension is available in Gangtok from the Tashiling Secretariat (Home Department); one more 15-day extension brings you to the permitted total of 45 days. After that, you may not re-enter Sikkim within three months. No special permit is needed for Khecheopari Lake, Yuksom, Pelling (Pemayangtse), or Tashiling in Western Sikkim, but for points beyond these you need to travel with a government-recognized tour operator in a group of at least four people. The company will take care of the paperwork (☞ Tour Operators, *below*).

Tour Operators

GENERAL

Based in New Delhi, these firms run trips all over the Himalayas: **Aquaterra Adventures India** (J-1916, 2nd floor, Chittaranjan Park, 110019, ☎ 11/622–2588 FAX 11/628–7783). **Himalayan River Runners** F-5 Hauz Khas Enclave, 1st floor, 110017, ☎ 11/685–2602, FAX 11/686–5604). **Ibex Expeditions** (G-66 East of Kailash, 110065, ☎ 11/691–2641, FAX 11/684–6403). **Outdoor Adventures India** (S-234 Panchsheel Park, 2nd floor, 110017, ☎ 11/622–7485, FAX 11/621–4230).

LADAKH

Except for Above the Clouds, you can write to the tour operators below at simply "Leh, Ladakh 194101, Jammu and Kashmir, India."

Above the Clouds Trekking (✉ Box 398, Worcester, MA 01602, ☎ 508/799–4499 or 800/233–4499). **Adventure North Tours and Travels** (☎ 1982/53620). **Himalayan Trekking and Wilderness Expeditions** (✉ 1900 8th St., Berkeley, CA 94710, ☎ 510/540–8040 or 800/777–8735). **Gypsy's World Treks and Tours** (☎ 1982/52220, FAX 1932/52735). **Silk Route Travels** (☎ 1982/52303).

SIKKIM

Modern Tours and Travels (✉ opposite Sikkim Tourist Information Centre, Traffic Point, M. G. Marg, Gangtok 737101, ☎ 3592/27319), run by the knowledgeable and enthusiastic Karma Tse Ten, offers treks to Western Sikkim, including a six-day Dzongri trek and a 10-day Goechala trek that passes through Kanchenjunga Base Camp. There's also a four-day tour to the Yumthang Valley. Food and services are excellent. **Yak Tours and Travels** (✉ Yama House, M. G. Marg, Gangtok 737101, ☎ 3592/28060, FAX 3592/27968) leads tours to the Yumthang Valley. **Tashila Tours and Travels** (✉ 31-A National Hwy., P.B. No. 70, Gangtok 737101, ☎ 3592/22979, FAX 3592/22155) leads the way in river rafting on the beautiful Teesta and Rangeet rivers. **Kanchenjunga Treks and Tours** (✉ 1 D.B. Giri Rd., Darjeeling, West Bengal, ☎ 354/3058 or –3408) is run by Dhamey and Jamling Tenzing—the sons of Norgay Tenzing, who climbed Mt. Everest with Sir Edmund Hillary. They offer treks in Western Sikkim, including flora treks; vehicular tours in the north; and cultural tours to monasteries, as well as overnight stays in villages.

Visitor Information

HIMACHAL PRADESH

Tourist offices run by the **Himachal Pradesh Tourism Development Corporation** can tell you transportation schedules and recommend tour operators and hotels. **New Delhi:** ✉ Chandralok Building, 36 Janpath, ☎ 11/332–5320. **Shimla:** ✉ The Mall, 171001, ☎ 177/252561, FAX 177/252557. **Manali:** ✉ The Mall, 175131, ☎ 1902/53531, FAX 1902/

52325. **Dharamsala:** ✉ Kotwali Bazaar, 176215, ☎ 1892/24928, FAX 1892/24212.

LADAKH

The **Tourist Information Centre** (☎ 1982/52297) is a 3-km (2-mi) walk from Leh. Your best bet for government-supplied information before you go is at the **Jammu and Kashmir Tourism office** in New Delhi (✉ 201-203 Kanishka Shopping Plaza, 19 Ashok Rd., New Delhi 110001, ☎ 11/332–5373, FAX 11/371–6081). Mr. Sonom Dorjay, the tourist officer, comes from Leh and is extremely helpful.

SIKKIM

The **Sikkim Tourist Information Centre** (✉ M.G. Marg, Gangtok 737101, ☎ 3592/22064) is pleasantly helpful on trekking itineraries, tours, and accommodations.

UTTAR PRADESH

The **Uttar Pradesh Tourist Office** (✉ Chandralok Bldg., 36 Janpath, ☎ 11/332–2251) has information about the Garhwal and Kumaon regions. Local tourist offices are not helpful, when they exist at all.

3 DELHI

If you want the crush of crowds, get lost in Old Delhi's Chandni Chowk. To see the Old World without the masses, find Hazrat Nizamuddin Darga, a Sufi tomb in a timeless Muslim district. Museums in New Delhi bring 3,000 years of Indian history to life; contemporary art galleries show you what today's Indian artists are up to. Hit the markets: Delhi is one big emporium for all of India's handicrafts. Feast on sumptuous meals and unwind among historic tombs in the verdant Lodi Gardens.

By Kathleen Cox and Michael W. Bollom

DELHI IS CHANGING AND EXPANDING FAST. Residential enclaves are cropping up everywhere, along with new commercial centers, and many locals are experiencing a new headache: the suburban commute. Yet this trip bears little resemblance to a morning drive into a Western city: More cows stand in Delhi's streets than traffic police, and the absence of discipline means the roads are utter chaos. Vehicles swerve between lanes, around cows, or play "chicken" with a speeding bus as it barrels down from the opposite direction.

Still, Delhi's expansion is part of the continuum of history. By the mid-1600s, Delhi was already flourishing in magnificent pomp, the 450-year-old capital of a string of empires. Each new power created its own new Delhi, with each successive capital (there were eight) pushing slightly farther north until the British shifted their center of power from Calcutta to Delhi in 1911. While the British were building their district, called the Civil Lines, on this northerly route, they hit marshy land prone to floods; they then reversed direction and put the bulk of their capital, the Imperial City, to the south.

The impetus for Delhi's most recent growth, however, is different. Villagers from rural areas have descended on the capital to seek their fortunes. They move into small open fields, narrow strips along the road, or unused neighborhood pockets and build shanties that turn into overcrowded slums. Sadly, the "fortunes" most villagers make are barely enough to survive. Foreign companies are arriving and setting up shop, land prices have skyrocketed, and the market gobbles up every available square foot. Land is so pricey that many homeowners find it cheaper to add extensions to their houses than to buy another plot. As a result, many lawns in Delhi are razor-thin patches of grass.

Another historical building trend still has an impact today. When the British switched to Delhi, they introduced Western architecture, specifically the bungalow. Over time, the bungalow became more elaborate and hierarchical: the more important the British resident, the more lavish the house and the larger the property. Concentrated in the Civil Lines and in Central Delhi, bungalows became a class symbol, and their interior amenities became the new definition of the preferred lifestyle, even to many upper-class Indians. When the British quit India, some of their bungalows were bought by Delhi's elite, but most were taken over by embassies and the Indian government for its ministers and senior bureaucrats. To this day, the old hierarchy remains—the more important the individual, the better the bungalow.

With Independence, Delhi's architecture changed again. Wealthy families, especially the newly wealthy, developed a preference for more ostentatious Western designs. In residential enclaves or right next door to an old bungalow, you can see Indianized European-style villas that make no attempt to conceal their owners' affluence. The Delhi Development Authority, meanwhile, has for decades poured money and cement into dreary public housing; its character-free apartment buildings, their facades musty with mildew, have cropped up like weeds all over the city.

This hodgepodge can overwhelm the first-time visitor. The harmonious lines of old structures and ruins, often in the midst of new neighborhoods, accentuate the inferiority of much of Delhi's post-Independence architecture. Still, the city has its rewards, such as more than 1,000 monuments and two old capitals that are first-class achievements—Mogul emperor Shah Jahan's architectural tour de force in Old Delhi and the present seat of the government designed by the British in New Delhi. The city also has a surprising number of lovely gardens and parks, such as the peaceful Lodi Gardens, with solemn gray tombs that connect the land to the past, and a golf course where Muslim monuments share the fairways with peacocks.

Some cultural aspects of Delhi also distinguish it from other Indian cities. It's the nation's capital, of course, but Delhi is an unusual capital. It has absorbed the land of former villages, yet village life still flourishes in every part of the city, along with a curious mixture of the East and the West. Cows and pigs forage in garbage heaps near upscale houses with satellite dishes. Turbaned shepherds lead goats and sheep through ravines in the remaining open fields and near the airports. Eunuchs sashay past shops that sell Western products on Connaught Place. Rajasthani women in bright saris and men in *lungis* (skirtlike wraps) work with outdated tools on construction sites while executives work out on computerized equipment in chic health clubs. By day, temples are packed with the devout, and by night, hotel discos are packed with the affluent. *Sadhus* (Hindu holy men) in simple garb walk along the streets, often carrying tridents, while young men zoom around on motorcycles with their heads concealed in Darth Vader–style helmets.

Even the world of politics has its own character here. When Parliament is in session, fierce discussions can turn proceedings into a circus. Members often lose control—flinging shoes at one another—and storm out of the august chamber. Many cynics refer to Parliament as a *tamasha,* which translates loosely as an outlandish party. Heavy security for political bigwigs or wannabe bigwigs often disrupts daily life; senior bureaucrats and politicians travel in a cavalcade of cars whose lead vehicle uses a blaring siren to force traffic to the side of the road or completely close off a boulevard. When the car with the official screeches to a halt, Sten-toting security forces scramble around the VIP, VVIP, or VVVIP as he or she moves through an open door. In this respect, Delhi hasn't changed a bit in its hundreds of years as a center of power. Political big shots dominate this place, and their decisions and behavior are the talk of the town.

Pleasures and Pastimes

Dining

Dining in Delhi is a joy. Partake of the local passion for food, and don't worry about the bill—it's often startlingly low. The selection of restaurants, offering Indian, East and Southeast Asian, and European cuisine, grows almost daily. Top hotel restaurants bring in chefs from all over the world to create their scrumptious signature dishes, and new independent restaurants are opening all over town, often much cheaper than the top tier but just as delicious. For the adventurous, *dhabas* (open-air roadside restaurants) still serve hearty fare. Delhi dining is marred only by the fact that you can't necessarily have a drink with your meal; government regulations make it hard for most independent restaurants to obtain liquor licenses, and you can't BYOB.

CATEGORY	COST*
$$$$	over Rs. 1000
$$$	Rs. 600–1000
$$	Rs. 300–600
$	under Rs. 300

**per person for a three-course meal, excluding drinks, service, and 20% sales tax*

Lodging

Delhi's hotels are modernizing along a Western line that's obliterating many aesthetic distinctions. (The main exceptions to this rule are Claridges and the Imperial, which cling to their Victorian heritage.) But modernization has its virtues. Western-style hotels have good facilities, such as health clubs and business services, and are islands of refuge from the city's chronic power shortages, telephone disruptions, and unending crowds and chaos. Unfortunately, a chronic shortage of rooms has driven up room rates here, and upmarket hotels must levy an additional 20% tax on your room rate and food-and-beverage bill.

Cost-conscious travelers will be disappointed by the accommodations in Delhi. Hotels tend to be either five-star or flophouse, with the middle ground almost empty. Fortunately, there are a number of "guest houses," such as the Jukaso Inn and the Maharani Guest House, in Delhi's various residential colonies; these small hotels are often converted bungalows. Guest-house quality is uneven, and services are limited, but prices are about a fifth of those at the big hotels.

CATEGORY	COST*
$$$$	over Rs.13,000
$$$	Rs. 8,500–13,000
$$	Rs. 4,000–8,500
$	under Rs. 4,000

**per person for a standard double room, excluding 20% sales tax*

Performing Arts

India is richly endowed with music and dance traditions in both folk and classical forms. Most evenings, there's a performance somewhere in the city; check the weekly *Delhi Diary* or ask your hotel to find out the day's events. From the intricate footwork of the Kathak dance to the emotive singing that accompanies a performance of Hindu *bhajans* or Muslim *qawwalis,* Delhi's arts scene is fascinating in both classical and contemporary genres, and ticket prices are a bargain.

Shopping

Shopping in Delhi is endless and fabulous. In Old Delhi's Chandni Chowk, you can poke through shops that specialize in brassware, curios, and silver jewelry; in New Delhi you can stroll along a central boulevard and hit the row of state emporiums that sell regional handicrafts, fabrics, and products at reasonable prices. Head to Sunder Nagar, with its fancier shops (and fancier prices) to peruse gorgeous gems, textiles, artwork, and terrific tribal and Hindu curios. For a more local experience, go to the INA wet market—bursting with the smells of spices, the colors of fresh produce, and the squawking of chickens—or to Lajpat Nagar for the whirling chaos of a middle-class bazaar.

EXPLORING DELHI

For the first-time visitor, Delhi is complicated, as the sights worth seeing (and there are many) are scattered around this enormous capital. Delhi is not a walker's city, except for Chandni Chowk in Old Delhi, where cars are too wide for the lanes; but even in this area, pedestrians must still watch out for fast-moving carts and overloaded humans who plow through whatever's in their way. The city has few sidewalks, and even these are subject to serious obstructions: open manholes, dangling electric wires, excrement, even dead animals. Beggars and touts have the uncanny ability to appear from nowhere. Pedestrians are also fair game in the eyes of drivers; hire a car, taxi, or auto-rickshaw to get from place to place. Avoid public buses, as they're filthy, dangerous, and crammed with passengers. Women who take buses might also be subjected to pinches, flashing, or verbal abuse.

The geographic center of Delhi is Connaught Place. South of Old Delhi, this was the commercial hub of the British Raj. Every attempt to spruce up this district seems to grind to a halt; the old buildings that ring the green traffic circle are getting a face-lift, but there's still plenty of trash and not a single trash basket. Connaught Place is also a haunt of beggars, unlicensed money changers, and others engaged in dubious pursuits. Street hawkers sell second-rate merchandise on the pavement, and touts try to lure you into their shops. The inner circle is a mess, dominated by auto-repair shops.

About 2 km (1 mi) south of Connaught Place is the Imperial City. Designed by the British architect Sir Edwin Lutyens, it includes Rashtrapati Bhavan (the Presidential Palace), the North and South Secretariats, and the Sansad Bhavan (Parliament House). Just southwest of here is the Diplomatic Enclave; to the east is India Gate, a monument to British Indian Army soldiers killed in World War I and the Afghan wars. Southeast of India Gate and not far from the Oberoi hotel are the Purana Qila (Old Fort) and Humayun's Tomb; almost due south of India Gate is Lodi Gardens. The entire area surrounding these landmarks is filled with tree-lined boulevards, lovely old bungalows, and affluent residential neighborhoods.

Be prepared to remove your shoes when visiting religious institutions, including the Charity Birds Hospital. Women should also bring a scarf to cover their heads. Shorts are not appropriate attire for adults of either sex.

Great Itineraries

Given Delhi's congestion and pollution, don't plan to do too much in any one day. Take your time or the city will overwhelm you.

Numbers in the text correspond to numbers in the margin and on the Delhi map.

IF YOU HAVE 3 DAYS

Spend your freshest, most energetic day in **Old Delhi.** See Lal Qila (Red Fort) early in the morning, then venture into Chandni Chowk. Explore **New Delhi** the next day. On day three, take a car to the Qutab Minar, then head back to town and check out some museums and galleries. That afternoon, shop at the state emporia or visit a local market.

IF YOU HAVE 5 DAYS

Follow the three-day itinerary above, and on day four make an overnight excursion to the Neemrana Fort Palace outside 🏨 **Shekhavati** (☞ Chapter 5) and unwind in Rajput splendor. On day five, make a leisurely return to Delhi.

IF YOU HAVE 8 DAYS

Follow the five-day itinerary above. On day six, drive six hours northwest to 🏨 **Corbett National Park** (☞ Uttar Pradesh *in* Chapter 2), one of India's most enjoyable wildlife sanctuaries, and devote day seven to a Jeep safari. Get an early-morning start back to Delhi on your last day. *Alternately:* If your next stop is Rajasthan, head southwest of Delhi to spend these two days in **Sariska National Park** (☞ Jaipur and Environs *in* Chapter 5) and move on from there.

When to Tour Delhi

It's best to visit Delhi between mid-October and late March. The heat is intense from April until the monsoon arrives in July; then rain and mosquitoes add to the misery. Most museums are closed on Monday, and the museum at Lal Qila is closed on Friday, which is a difficult day to visit Jama Masjid (Friday Mosque). Qawwali singers are most apt to perform at Hazrat Nizamuddin Darga on Thursday evening.

Old Delhi

Old Delhi, about 6 km (4 mi) north of the city center, is in a state of decay. The old *havelis* (mansions) that line the *galis* (side lanes) of Chandni Chowk, the main artery of this old district, are architecturally stunning but cry out for repair. The whole area is extremely crowded. Still, Old Delhi's monuments—Lal Qila and Jama Masjid—are magnificent, and Chandni Chowk is great fun to explore.

A Good Walk

Start in Old Delhi with a morning tour of **Lal Qila** ①, Emperor Shah Jahan's sprawling 17th-century capital. From here set your sights on a red, rectangular three-story building (look for a flock of pigeons flying overhead) on the opposite side of Nataji Subhash Marg, the busy street in front of the fort: This is the **Charity Birds Hospital** ②, a delightful hospital that is as much a respite for human visitors as for the nonhuman patients tended inside.

After leaving the hospital, return to Nataji Subhash Marg and walk a short distance north to the famous **Chandni Chowk** ③. Walk about four blocks down this crowded thoroughfare to the marble-faced **Sisganj Gurdwara** ④, a Sikh shrine. Continue east on Chandni Chowk and cross three more galis; then turn left on **Gali Parante Wali** ⑤, whose entrance is almost directly opposite a large Central Bank of India. Continue down Gali Parante Wali until you see a signboard for the Vaishali Sahai Center at a fork in the road. Turn left onto Motiwali, which leads directly into Kinari Bazaar, a bridal-trimming market where Hindu families buy every item required in their symbol-rich wedding ceremony: garlands, beads, colorful ribbons, attractive boxes for sweets and gifts, masks, and statues of gods.

The Bombay Beads Centre at 2030 Kinari Bazaar is your next landmark; directly across from this shop is one of Chandni Chowk's most beautiful lanes, Naughara Gali, where beautiful old havelis, home to a community of Jains, are done up in art-deco colors—aquas, pinks, yellows. At the end of this peaceful lane is the exquisite Jain **Sweitana Temple** ⑥, with a white-marble elephant head on the railing and gleaming brass doors. Even if the temple is closed, Naughara Gali is an oasis, an ideal temporary escape from Chandni Chowk's bustle.

Return to Kinari Bazaar and turn right. If it suits your fancy, stop in a shop called **Shivam Zari Palace** (⊠ 2178 Kinari Bazari) and spend an hour or two dressing a tiny bronze statue of Gopal (baby Krishna) in an outfit of your choice, including a headpiece, necklace, bangles, and a throne. The cost for your finished memento is less than Rs. 350, depending on the size of the statue you choose. This is a novel way to learn a bit about Hinduism, with the shop owner your charming guru.

Continue down Kinari Bazaar until it intersects with Dariba Kalan, the "Street of Silver." Visit the silver shops on your left (☞ Shopping, *below*) or turn right and head down Dariba Kalan, which is lined with tiny stores selling gold and silver jewelry and artifacts. At the end of Dariba Kalan, turn right onto a broad street that leads through the brass and copper district. At a small corner shop, Prem Fireworks, turn right and walk about 20 ft, then turn left and walk under an arch that says ESTATE HANDICRAFTS. Head up Chah Rahat, a typical narrow lane with old wooden balconies and verandas.

When Chah Rahat lane opens into a small courtyard, make a hairpin turn to the left. Follow the arrow on a sign that reads SINGH COPPER AND BRASS PALACE and head down Chah Rahat. After about 30 ft, a second sign directs you down an alley on the right. Singh's emporium is filthy—dress for the occasion. But every floor is a great place to poke around, filled with treasures both cheap and supremely expensive.

From Singh's, return to the courtyard and Chah Rahat and walk left down a short, narrow lane. At the end of the lane you'll see the splendid **Jama Masjid** ⑦, preceded by an unexpected bazaar of small shops selling tools of every conceivable design.

At the end of this long tour, take a cycle-rickshaw to either Karim's or Chor Bizarre (☞ Dining, *below*) for a typical Muslim meal in Old Delhi.

TIMING

Allow a full day for this tour, and make sure the day will not be obscenely hot. Avoid Friday, when the fort museum is closed and entrance to the mosque is tricky for non-Muslims. Most shops in Chandni Chowk are closed on Sunday.

Sights to See

★ ❸ **Chandni Chowk.** Chandni Chowk is Delhi's former imperial avenue, where the Mogul emperor Shah Jahan rode at the head of his lavish cavalcade. Today, bullock carts, taxis, private cars, dogs, cows, autorickshaws, bicycles, horse-drawn tongas, and pedestrians plow indiscriminately through the congestion. If you suffer from claustrophobia you're in trouble; if not, you're in for an adventure. As in the days of the Moguls, astrologers set up their charts on the pavement; shoemakers squat and repair sandals and other leather articles, blithely ignoring the human swirl around them; sidewalk photographers with old box cameras take pictures for a small fee; medicine booths conceal doctors attending to patients; and oversize teeth grin from the windows of dentists' offices. Peer through a portico and you might see men getting shaved, silver being weighed, or any other conceivable form of commerce, while outside a cow lies complacently on the street. ✉ *6 km/4 mi north of Connaught Pl. Most shops closed Sun.*

❷ **Charity Birds Hospital.** Across from Lal Qila is a delightful and unusual attraction: a hospital not for humans, but primarily for birds. Founded by Jains in 1956, the hospital is modest, but it shows how tender loving care can stretch limited funds. Vegetarian birds (and rabbits) are treated inside on three floors, and carnivorous birds and other needy animals are treated in the courtyard. There's even an intensive-care ward and a research laboratory. Bathed, fed, and given vitamins, the healthy birds refuse to leave, and that's how you can spot the building—flocks of birds swirl around its roof. ✉ *Nataji Subhash Marg, opposite Lal Qila.* 🎟 *Free; donations welcome.* ⏲ *Daily 8–8.*

❺ **Gali Parante Wali.** This congested, narrow lane is filled with shops selling exquisite saris, including the well-known Ram Chandra Krishan Chandra's, where you can peruse some of the finest fabrics in India. The lane is named for the fabulous *parathas* (flat fried breads) also sold here, in simple open-air eateries. Stuffed with a variety of fixings, such as radishes, cheese, and seasonal vegetables, they're a real treat (just bring Handi Wipes). ▦ *Intersected by Chandni Chowk.*

★ ❼ **Jama Masjid.** An exquisite Islamic statement in red sandstone and marble, India's largest mosque was completed in 1656 by 5,000 laborers after six years of work. It was the last monument commissioned by the Mogul emperor Shah Jahan. Three sets of broad steps lead to two-story gateways and a magnificent courtyard with a square ablution tank

Baba Bangla Sahib Gurdwara, **9**
Bahai Temple, **20**
Chandni Chowk, **3**
Charity Birds Hospital, **2**
Crafts Museum, **13**
Gali Parante Wali, **5**
Gandhi Smriti, **16**
Hauz Khas, **21**
Hazrat Nizamuddin Darga, **18**
Humayun's Tomb, **19**
Jama Masjid, **7**
Lal Qila (Red Fort), **1**
Lodi Gardens, **17**
Lutyens's Imperial City, **10**
National Gallery of Modern Art, **12**
National Museum, **11**
Nehru Memorial Museum, **15**
Purana Qila (Old Fort), **14**
Qutab Minar, **22**
Raj Ghat and National Gandhi Museum, **8**
Sisganj Gurdwara, **4**
Sweitana Temple, **6**

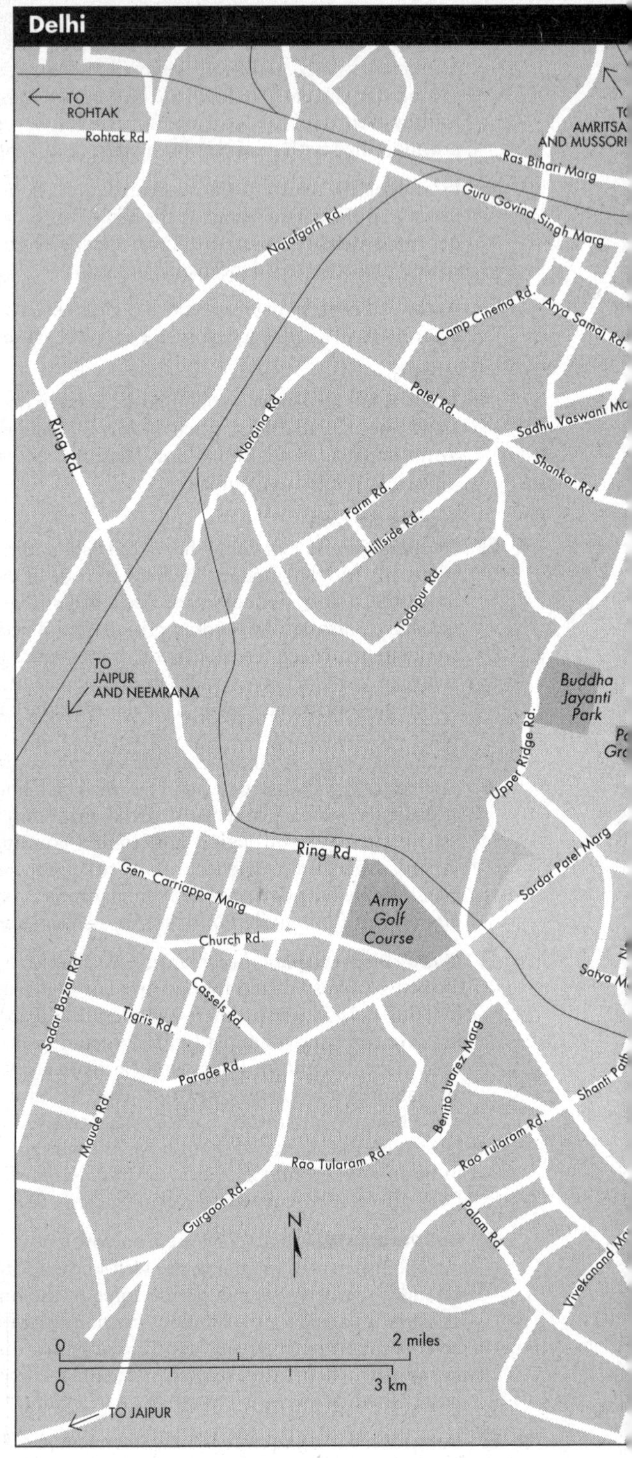

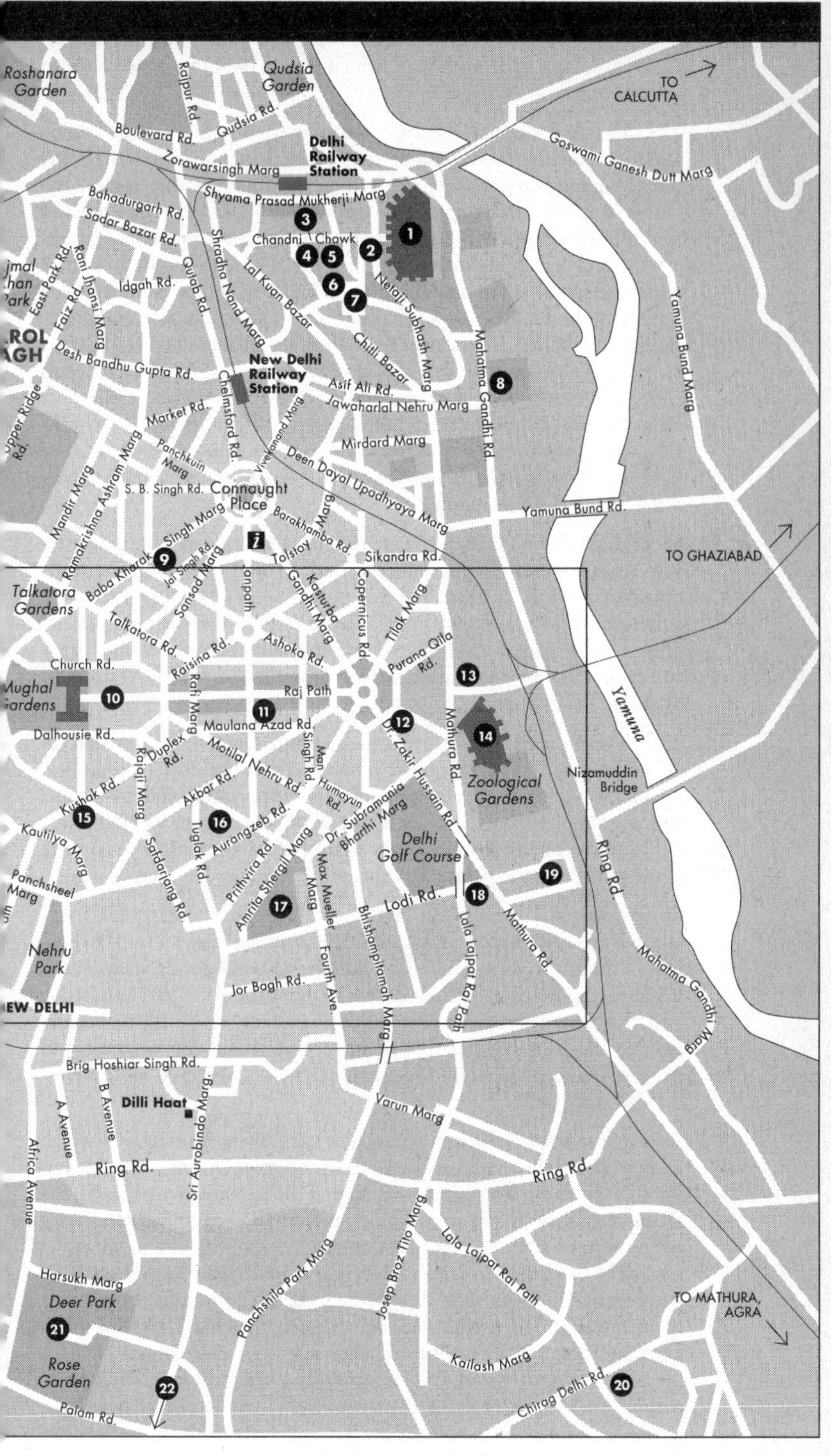

Roshanara Garden
Qudsia Garden
TO CALCUTTA
Rajpur Rd.
Qudsia Rd.
Boulevard Rd.
Delhi Railway Station
Zorawarsingh Marg
Goswami Ganesh Dutt Marg
Shyama Prasad Mukherji Marg
Bahadurgarh Rd.
Sadar Bazar Rd.
Chandni Chowk
Netaji Subhash Marg
Idgah Rd.
Qutab Rd.
Shradha Nand Marg
Lal Kuan Bazar
Rani Jhansi Marg
East Park Rd.
Faiz Rd.
Chitli Bazar
Mahatma Gandhi Rd.
Yamuna Bund Marg
Desh Bandhu Gupta Rd.
New Delhi Railway Station
Asif Ali Rd.
Jawaharlal Nehru Marg
Chelmsford Rd.
Market Rd.
Vivekanand Marg
Mirdard Marg
Upper Ridge Rd.
Panchkuin Marg
Deen Dayal Upadhyaya Marg
Mandir Marg
Ramakrishna Ashram Marg
S. B. Singh Rd.
Connaught Place
Yamuna Bund Rd.
Barakhamba Rd.
Singh Marg
Tolstoy Marg
Baba Kharak
Sikandra Rd.
TO GHAZIABAD
Talkatora Gardens
Sansad Marg
Janpath
Kasturba Gandhi Marg
Copernicus Rd.
Tilak Marg
Talkatora Rd.
Ashoka Rd.
Purana Qila Rd.
Raisina Rd.
Church Rd.
Mughal Gardens
Raj Path
Rafi Marg
Yamuna
Maulana Azad Rd.
Dalhousie Rd.
Dr. Zakir Hussain Rd.
Mathura Rd.
Zoological Gardens
Duplex Rd.
Motilal Nehru Rd.
Man Singh Rd.
Rajaji Marg
Nizamuddin Bridge
Akbar Rd.
Humayun Rd.
Kushak Rd.
Dr. Subramania Bharthi Marg
Tuglak Rd.
Aurangzeb Rd.
Kautilya Marg
Delhi Golf Course
Safdarjang Rd.
Prithvira Rd.
Amrita Shergil Marg
Max Mueller Marg
Ring Rd.
Panchsheel Marg
Lodi Rd.
Bhishampitamah Marg
Lala Lajpat Rai Path
Mathura Rd.
Nehru Park
Fourth Ave.
Mahatma Gandhi Marg
Jor Bagh Rd.
NEW DELHI
Brig Hoshiar Singh Rd.
Dilli Haat
Sri Aurobindo Marg
B Avenue
A Avenue
Varun Marg
Africa Avenue
Ring Rd.
Ring Rd.
Josep Broz Tito Marg
Lala Lajpat Rai Path
Harsukh Marg
Deer Park
Panchshila Park Marg
TO MATHURA, AGRA
Rose Garden
Kailash Marg
Chirag Delhi Rd.
Palam Rd.
1
2
3
4
5
6
7
8
9
10
11
12
13
14
15
16
17
18
19
20
21
22

in the center. The entire space is enclosed by pillared corridors with domed pavilions in each corner. Thousands gather to pray in this courtyard, especially on Friday, which is why the Jama Masjid is also called the Friday Mosque.

The mosque is characteristically Mogul, with an onion-shaped dome and tapering minarets. But Shah Jahan added an innovation: the novel stripes running up and down the well-proportioned marble domes. The whole structure breathes peace and tranquility—climb the open minaret to see how finely the mosque contrasts with the commercial streets around and beneath it. Inside the prayer hall (which you can only enter after a ritual purification at the ablution tank), the pulpit is carved from a single slab of marble. In one corner is a room where Shah Jahan installed the marble footprints of the Prophet Mohammed. ✉ *6 km/4 mi north of Connaught Pl., across from Lal Qila.* 🎫 *Free, Rs. 1 to climb minaret (women must be escorted by a "responsible" man).* ⏲ *Non-Muslims, Sat.–Thurs., 30 min after sunrise until 12:20 PM, 1:45 PM until 20 min before asar (afternoon prayer, roughly 3:30–4 PM), and 20 min after asar until 20 min before sunset; Fri., 30 min after sunrise until noon. Muslims, daily 7–5..*

★ ❶ **Lal Qila** (Red Fort). This is the greatest of Delhi's cities, outdoing even Lutyens's Imperial City in majesty. Built behind red sandstone walls that gave the fort its name, the Red Fort is Shah Jahan's 17th-century statement of Mogul power and elegance. Try to imagine imperial elephants swaying by with their *mahouts* (elephant drivers), a royal army of eunuchs, court ladies carried in palanquins, and other vestiges of Shah Jahan's pomp.

The view of the main entrance, called **Lahore Gate,** flanked with towers and facing Chandni Chowk, is blocked by a barbican (gatehouse), which the paranoid Aurangzeb added for his personal security—much to the grief of Shah Jahan, his father. From his prison, where he was held captive by his power-hungry son, Shah Jahan wrote, "You have made a bride of the palace and thrown a veil over her face."

Once you pass through the main gate, continue along the Chatta Chowk (Vaulted Arcade), originally the shopping district for the royal harem and now a bazaar selling rather less regal goods. The arcade leads to the Naubat Khana (Imperial Bandstand), a red sandstone structure where music was played five times daily. This is the main gateway to the fort; beyond this point, everyone but the emperor and princes had to proceed on foot, a rule that was observed until the Indian Mutiny of 1857.

An expansive lawn, once a courtyard serving as the boundary at which all but the nobility had to stop, leads to the great **Diwan-i-Am** (Hall of Public Audience). You have now entered the seventh city of Delhi, the Delhi of Shah Jahan, where marble dominates. Raised on a platform and open on three sides, the hall evokes past glories—like the moment described by François Bernier, a 17th-century French traveler overwhelmed by the hall's magnificence. According to Bernier, the emperor sat on a royal throne studded with decorative panels that sparkled with inlaid precious stones. (Stolen by British soldiers after the Indian Mutiny of 1857, the panels were restored 50 years later by Lord Curzon.) Watched by throngs of people from the courtyard below, the emperor heard the pleas of his subjects; the rest of the hall was reserved for rajas and foreign envoys, all standing with "their eyes bent downwards and their hands crossed." High above them, under a pearl-fringed canopy resting on golden shafts in the royal recess, "glittered the dazzling figure of the Grand Mogul, a figure to strike terror, for a frown meant death."

Behind the Diwan-i-Am, a row of palaces overlooks the distant Yamuna River. To the extreme south is the **Mumtaz Mahal,** now the Red Fort Museum of Archaeology, with relics from the Mogul period and numerous paintings and drawings. Next is the **Rang Mahal** (Painted Palace), once richly decorated with a silver ceiling that was dismantled to pay the bills when the treasury ran low. The Rang Mahal, which may have been for the royal ladies, contains a cooling water channel—called the Canal of Paradise—that runs from the marble basin in the center of the floor to the rest of the palace and to many of the others.

The third palace is the **Khas Mahal,** the exclusive palace of the emperor, divided into three sections: the sitting room, the so-called dream chamber (for sleeping), and the prayer chamber, all with lavishly decorated walls and painted ceilings still intact. The lovely marble screen is carved with the Scale of Justice—two swords and a scale that symbolize punishment and justice. From the attached octagonal tower the emperor Muthamman Burj would appear before his subjects each morning or watch elephant fights in the nearby fields.

The next palace is the **Diwan-i-Khas** (Hall of Private Audience), the most exclusive pavilion. Here Shah Jahan would sit on his Peacock Throne, made of solid gold and inlaid with hundreds of precious and semi-precious stones. (When Nadir Shah sacked Delhi in 1739, he hauled the throne to Persia.) A Persian couplet written in gold above an arch sums up Shah Jahan's sentiments about his city: "If there be a paradise on earth—It is this! It is this! It is this!"

Finally, you reach the **Royal Hammams,** exquisite Mogul baths with inlaid marble floors. The fountain supposedly had rose-scented water. A state-of-the-art steam bath, the hammam, was a sort of 17th-century health club.

From here, a short path leads to the **Moti Masjid** (Pearl Mosque), designed by Aurangzeb for his personal use and that of his harem. The prayer hall is inlaid with *musalla* (prayer rugs) outlined in black marble. Though the mosque has the purity of white marble, some critics say its excessively ornate style reflects the decadence that set in before the end of Shah Jahan's reign. ✉ *6 km (4 mi) north of Connaught Pl.,* ☎ *11/327–4580.* 🎫 *Sat.–Thurs. Rs. 2, free Fri.* ⏲ *Sat.–Thurs., sunrise–sunset; museum Sat.–Thurs. 10–5. Sound-and-light show (weather permitting): Rs. 25. Purchase tickets 30 min in advance. Show times: Feb.–Apr. and Sept.–Oct., daily 8:30–9:30; May–Aug., daily 9–10; Nov.–Jan., 7:30–8:30.*

❹ **Sisganj Gurdwara.** A Sikh shrine near the police station on Chandni Chowk, Sisganj Gurdwara is a restful place to take a break from the crowds. It marks the site where Aurangzeb beheaded Guru Teg Bahadur in 1675 when the guru refused to convert to Islam. Women must cover their heads. ✉ *Chandni Chowk.* ⏲ *Daily 24 hours.*

❻ **Sweitana Temple.** The interior of this splendid Jain temple is majestic, with painted murals and sacred idols. ✉ *End of Naughara Gali.* ⏲ *Apr.–Sept., daily 5:30 AM–12:30 PM and 7 PM–8 PM; Oct.–Mar., daily 6 AM–1 PM and 6 PM–7 PM.*

New Delhi

New Delhi, which begins in Connaught Place and extends up to 6 km (4 mi) south, is the city the British built when they moved their capital from Calcutta to Delhi in 1911. Its leafy colonial bungalows are slowly being replaced with office buildings, five-star hotels, and unsightly new residential quarters for government officials. New Delhi flows into South Delhi; the boundary is fluid. South Delhi also has its share of centuries-old monuments, such as the Qutab Minar, the village of Hauz Khas, and numerous Muslim tombs that lie abandoned in the center of a field or stand amid contemporary houses and apartments. Eastern South Delhi has the handsome new Bahai Temple.

A Good Tour

Hire a car or taxi and head to **Humayun's Tomb** ⑲ in the early morning. Created by the wife of the Mogul emperor, the 16th-century tomb is relatively peaceful at this time of day. Once the rush-hour traffic winds down, proceed north to **Purana Qila** ⑭ on your way to the **Crafts Museum** ⑬. Don't rush through the museum; give yourself ample time to appreciate the excellent displays and lovely creations. From here, head southeast to Dilli Haat and the INA Market, a wonderful shopping-and-eating complex. After a snack, drive up to **Baba Bangla Sahib Gurdwara** ⑨ to see Sikhism in action. On the trip back south, drive west along Raj Path to **Lutyens's Imperial City** ⑩, with its impressive architecture. Chill out for a bit in **Lodi Gardens** ⑰, where peace descends once again as you take an afternoon stroll to see the locals relax and examine the ancient tombs of the 15th- and 16th-century Lodi rulers. Around 5 PM, head to the nearby old Nizamuddin neighborhood and its wonderful, ethnically rich Muslim bazaar. Taped qawwalis (Sufi songs of ecstasy) set the mood as you walk down winding lanes to **Hazrat Nizamuddin Darga** ⑱, the tomb of a Sufi saint. Buy some flowers to place on the tomb when you arrive. Tomb administrators are descendants of the Sufi saint, and they can serve as useful guides to this little treasure, a perfect place to linger as the sun goes down. If you're lucky, the sun will set to the sound of qawwali singers performing their riveting songs live. Finally, take a ride to the lotus shaped **Bahai Temple** ⑳, which is open until 7 PM.

TIMING

This tour takes a full day if traffic slows you down, and it probably will. If you have time, you might want to divide the itinerary into two days and relax the first afternoon, then start a bit later the second day. Between April and October, when the sun is intense, consider splitting the tour in half just to prevent dehydration or sunstroke. Try not to plan this tour for a Monday, when the Crafts Museum is closed.

Sights to See

❾ **Baba Bangla Sahib Gurdwara.** Less than a mile (2 km) from Connaught Place, this *gurdwara* (Sikh temple) is always full of activity—no surprise given Delhi's huge Sikh population, most of whom came here as refugees from Pakistan in 1947. Today the Sikhs are a prosperous group, many arriving for prayers by car or motorcycle. If you can't make it to Amritsar to see the Golden Temple, by all means come to Bangla Sahib to see Sikhs worship and to admire the distinctively ostentatious style of their temples. Like Sikhism itself, gurdwaras reflect both the symmetry of Mogul mosques and the chaos of Hindu temples. Bangla Sahib is built of blinding white marble with a shiny, gold onion dome on top. There is a large tank of water off to the right, surrounded by a deep marble veranda that offers relief from the sun on hot days.

The gurdwara stands on the site where Guru Hari Krishan, the eighth of 10 Sikh gurus who lived between 1469 and 1708, performed a small miracle. Before entering, remove your shoes and socks (check them at the counter on the left), get rid of cigarettes, and bring or find a piece of cloth to cover your head. As you walk up the stairs and enter the sanctum, you'll see people filling jugs of water from enclosed cisterns. Guru Hari Krishan used to distribute sanctified water to the sick, believing it had a miraculous healing effect on their mind, body, and soul, and people still treat the contents of these pools as holy water. Inside, devotees sit facing a small pavilion in the center that holds the *Granth Sahib* (Sikh scriptures). Hymns from the holy book are sung continuously from well before sunrise until approximately 9 PM, and you're welcome to sit and listen for a while; if you fancy something cultural in the evening, come at about 9 to see the ceremony by which the book is stored away for the night. As you walk around inside, be careful to proceed in a clockwise direction, and exit on the right side in back. Out the door to the right a priest distributes *prasad,* or communion: Take a lump of this sugar, flour, and oil concoction with both hands, pop it into your mouth with your right hand, then rub the remaining oil into your hands. ✉ *Baba Bangla Sahib Marg, across from Gole Post Office.* 🎫 *Free.* ⏲ *4 AM–9 PM.*

★ 20 **Bahai Temple.** The Bahai Temple celebrates the lotus flower, symbol of purity throughout India, and the number nine, which represents the highest digit and, in the Bahai faith, unity. The nine pools on the elevated platform signify the green leaves of the lotus and cool the stark, smooth, elegant interior. The sleek structure has two layers: nine white marble-covered petals that point to heaven, and nine petals that conceal the portals. From a short distance, it looks like a fantastic work of origami rising out of the earth. The interior conforms to that of all Bahai temples: There are no religious icons, just copies of the Holy Scriptures and sleek wooden pews. Completed in 1986, the temple was designed by Fariburz Sahba, an Iranian-born Canadian architect. ✉ *Bahapur, Kalkaji (9 km/5 mi southeast of Connaught Pl., near Nehru Pl.), South Delhi.* 🎫 *Free.* ⏲ *Apr.–Sept., 9–7; Oct.–Mar., 9:30–5:30. Closed Mon.*

13 **Crafts Museum.** Designed by the architect Charles Correa, this charming complex houses more than 20,000 artifacts and handicrafts from all over India. Located near the Old Fort, it's a great respite from Delhi's crowds and intensity, with terra-cotta sculptures from Tamil Nadu dotting the spacious grounds. The Folk and Tribal Art Gallery—a delightful mix of village and tribal India—has objects fashioned out of locally available materials, highlighting in various ways the mythology, ingenuity, and whimsy that characterize so much of India's folk art. A wooden temple car (built to carry deities in festive processions) stands in an open courtyard that leads to more buildings, including a lavishly decorated two-story Gujarati haveli. The Courtly Crafts section illustrates the luxurious lifestyle of India's onetime royalty. An upper floor celebrates the country's superb saris and textiles: brocades, embroideries, mirror work, and appliqués. In the village complex, with replicas of rural homes, artisans demonstrate their skills (weather permitting) and sell their creations. The museum has a shop and a snack bar. ✉ *Pragati Bhavan, Mathura Rd.,* ☎ *11/337–1353.* 🎫 *Rs. 5.* ⏲ *Tues.–Sun. 10–5:30.*

16 **Gandhi Smriti.** While Mahatma Gandhi lived a life of voluntary poverty, he did it in some attractive places. It was in this huge colonial bungalow, designed by a French architect for Indian industrialist G. D. R. Birla, that Gandhi was staying as a guest when he was assassinated. Gandhi's bedroom is just as he left it, with his "worldly remains" (only 11 items, including glasses and a walking stick) mounted on the wall. Pictures and text tell the story of Gandhi's life and the Independence movement; there is also a collection of dioramas depicting events in Gandhi's life. In the theater, 10 different documentaries are available for viewing upon request. Take off your shoes before entering the somber prayer ground in the back garden; an eternal flame marks the very spot where Gandhi expired. This, not the National Gandhi Museum at Raj Ghat, is the government's official museum dedicated to

the Mahatma. ✉ *5 Tees January Marg,* ☎ *11/301–2843.* 💵 *Free.* ⏲ *Daily 10–5.*

21 **Hauz Khas.** The road south to the village of Hauz Khas is lined on both sides by ancient stone monuments, and the entire village itself is dotted with domed structures, the tombs of minor Muslim royalty from the 14th to the 16th centuries. At the end of the road, all the way through the congested little village, is the tomb of Firoz Shah Tughluq, who ruled Delhi in the 14th century. Hauz Khas means "Royal Tank," referring to the now empty artificial lake visible from Firoz Shah's pillared tomb. The tank was actually built a century earlier by Allaudin Khiji as a water source for his nearby fort, then called Siri (the second city of Delhi; now the Asian Games Village, having housed athletes). Firoz Shah repaired the tank and built the now crumbling *madrasa* (Islamic college) on the edges of the tank. Wander around the ruins at leisure, and if you have energy left over, walk around the large tank with South Delhi's exercisers.

Back in the village itself, wander through the narrow *galis* (alleyways), where old and new exist in stark juxtaposition. In the 1980s Huaz Khas was designated an upscale tourist destination, but, fortunately, the process of redevelopment was never fully completed, so some of the village character persists. Check out the latest art gallery or stop into a jewelry shop; just watch your step or you may trip over a buffalo, chewing its cud as it lies on a bed of straw. After exploring, stop for a meal at one of the village's numerous restaurants, particularly Park Baluchi (a 5-minute walk to Deer Park) or Naivedyam (☞ Dining, *below*). ✉ *7 km (4 mi) south of Connaught Pl.*

★ 18 **Hazrat Nizamuddin Darga.** Here you may have a chance to enjoy one of Delhi's greatest treats—hearing devout Sufis sing qawwalis, hypnotically intense songs of religious ecstasy. To get here, follow the twisting narrow lanes in Nizamuddin, an old neighborhood about 3 km (2 mi) east of the Lodi Gardens—a smaller version of Chandni Chowk. You'll pass open-air stalls selling Islamic religious objects, butchers chopping buffalo meat (often with the knife held between dexterous toes), small restaurants cooking simple Indian meals and *paratha* (unleavened bread) that is given to the poor at day's end, and tiny shops selling cassettes, many by famous qawwali singers. When you see vendors selling flowers and garlands, you're getting close to the shrine (*darga*) of Hazrat Nizamuddin Aulia. Buy a few garlands (about Rs. 10 each) to present at the memorial for this Sufi saint, who died in 1325.

When you're asked to remove your shoes, you've arrived at the tomb's entrance. Within the small courtyard, considered extremely sacred, are three small mausoleums. The saint's tomb has a white, onion-shaped dome with thin black stripes, and the largest crowd of visitors. It's surrounded by a mosque and the graves of other important Muslims, including a daughter of the Mogul emperor Shah Jahan and another relative of the emperor Akbar, the 16th-century conqueror and reformer.

Hazrat Nizamuddin Aulia was born in Bukhara and later came to Delhi, where he became an important Sufi mystic with a dedicated following. His white mausoleum was built in 1562 after the destruction of two earlier tombs. Architecturally, the structure is modest: a little jewel that grows prettier the longer you study its inlay work and the carved parapet above the verandas. Evenings from around 5 to 7, especially Thursdays, the Sufi saint's male followers often (not always) sing their songs of ecstasy. You can sit in the courtyard and listen as the singers wail and gesture lovingly with their hands. ✉ *Old Nizamuddin Bazaar (5 km/3 mi southeast of Connaught Pl.)* 💵 *Free; make charitable do-*

nation and request that it be used to feed the poor; give small offering to musicians if you hear them perform. ⏲ *Daily 24 hours.*

★ 19 **Humayun's Tomb.** Erected in the middle of the 16th century by the wife of the Mogul emperor Humayun, this tomb launched a new architectural era that culminated in the Mogul masterpieces in Agra and Fatehpur Sikri. The Moguls brought to India their love of gardens and fountains, and left a legacy of harmonious structures, such as this mausoleum, that fuse symmetry with Oriental splendor.

Reminiscent of Persian architecture, this exquisite structure of red sandstone and white marble rests on a raised podium amid gardens intersected by water channels and enclosed by walls. The design represents India's first "tomb-in-a-garden" complex, and the marble dome covering the actual tomb is another first: a dome within a dome (the interior dome is set inside the soaring dome seen from the exterior), a style later used in the Taj Mahal.

Besides Humayun, seven other important Moguls are buried here, along with Humayun's wife, Haji Begum—who lies in the beautifully dilapidated octagonal shrine outside the gateway—and possibly his barber. As you enter or leave the gateway, stand a moment for the square, blue-domed structure to enjoy the view of the entire monument framed in the arch. The building's serenity belies the fact that many of the dead buried inside were murdered princes, victims of foul play. ✉ *Off Mathura Rd. (5 km/3 mi southeast of Connaught Pl.).* 🎫 *Sat.–Thurs. Rs. 5, free Fri.* ⏲ *Daily sunrise–sunset.*

17 **Lodi Gardens.** After Timur ransacked Delhi at the end of the 14th century, he ordered the massacre of the entire population—acceptable retribution, he thought, for the murder of some of his soldiers. As if in unconscious response to this horrific act, the subsequent Lodi and Sayyid dynasties built no city, only a few mosques and some mausoleums and tombs, the latter of which stand in what is now a lovely urban park. Winding walks cut through landscaped lawns with trees and small flowers, past schoolboys playing cricket and groups of friends relaxing in the greenery. Near the southern entrance on Lodi Road is the dignified mausoleum of Mohammed Shah, third ruler of the Sayyid dynasty, and some members of his family. This octagon, with a central chamber surrounded by verandas carved with arches, is a good example of the architecture of this period. The smaller, equally lovely, octagonal tomb of Sikandar Lodi, surrounded by a garden in the park's northwestern corner, has an unusual double dome. ✉ *Lodi Rd., 5 km/3 mi south of Connaught Pl..* 🎫 *Free.* ⏲ *Daily sunrise–sunset.*

10 **Lutyens's Imperial City.** Raj Path—the broadest avenue in Delhi—leads to Delhi's eighth capital: Sir Edwin Lutyens's Imperial City, built between 1914 and 1931 in a symbolically imperialistic design. Starting from India Gate at the lowest and eastern end of Raj Path, nearby land was allocated to numerous princely states, which built small palaces, such as the **Bikaner House** (now the Rajasthan tourism office) and **Jaipur House** (now the National Gallery of Modern Art). It might be said that this placement mirrored the British sentiments toward the princes, who lost much of their former power and status during the British Raj. Moving up the slowly inclining hill at the western end of the avenue, you also move up the British ladder of power, a concept inherent in the original design. First, you come to the enormous **North and South Secretariats,** facing each other on Raj Path and reflecting the importance of the bureaucracy, a fixture of Indian society since the time of British rule. Identical in design, the two buildings have 1,000 rooms and miles of corridors.

Directly behind the North Secretariat is **Sansad Bhavan,** a circular building in red-and-gray sandstone with an open colonnade that extends around the circumference. Architecturally, the Indian design is meant to mirror the spinning wheel that was the symbol of Mahatma Gandhi, but the building's placement (off of the main avenue) may suggest the attitude of the British toward the legislative assembly that was made up of Indians: not the ruling force.

At the top of the hill is the former Viceroy's House, now called **Rashtrapati Bhavan,** where the President of India (distinct from the prime minister) now resides. Though it was built in the 20th century, the building's daunting proportions seem to reflect an earlier, more lavish time. Its scale was meant to express British supremacy. The Bhavan contains 340 rooms and its grounds cover 330 acres, including a Mogul-style garden that opens to the public for several weeks in February. The shape of the central brass dome, the palace's main architectural feature, copies that of a Buddhist *stupa* (shrine).

The execution of Lutyens's design has two ironic twists. The entire palace was supposed to fill the vista as you approach the top of the hill, but because the gradient is actually too steep, only the dome dominates the horizon. And, of course, a few years after the Imperial City was completed, the British packed up and went home, and all of this became the grand capital of newly independent India. Permission to enter Rashtrapati and Sansad Bhavan is almost impossible to obtain; unless you have contacts in high places, satisfy yourself with a glimpse from outside. ✉ *2 km/1 mi south of Connaught Pl.*

12 **National Gallery of Modern Art.** Facing India Gate, this neoclassical building was built by the British in the early 20th century as a palace for the maharaja of Jaipur. With its small dome and large, open rooms, the structure makes a beautiful space for an art museum, and it's well maintained. The museum was established in 1954 to preserve Indian art forms (mainly painting) that have emerged since about 1850. The collection is broad, and well displayed by local standards, but still somewhat uneven and oddly arranged. The highlights—Bengali Renaissance works by such artists as Rabindranath Tagore and Jamini Roy—are all but hidden away in corner rooms upstairs, and the works chosen to represent contemporary masters such as M. F. Husain and Ganesh Pyne are disappointing. Documentaries shown daily at 11 AM and 3 PM discuss Indian art, but works in the museum are not contextualized with written commentary. ✉ *Jaipur House, India Gate,* ☎ *11/338–2835.* 🎫 *Rs. 5.* ⏲ *Tues.–Sun. 10 AM–5 PM.*

11 **National Museum.** The facade of this grand building imitates Lutyens's Rashtrapati Bhavan: A sandstone dome is supported by classical columns of brown sandstone on a red sandstone base. Upon entering, you're greeted by a 13th-century idol (from the Konark Sun Temple; ☞ Chapter 13) of Surya, the sun god, standing beneath the dome. The statue is emblematic of the National Museum's strength—ancient, mostly Hindu, sculptures. One whole room is dedicated to artifacts from the Indus Valley Civilization, circa 2,700 BC, while others display works from the Gandharan, Chandela, and Chola periods. In addition to sculpture, exhibits feature jewelry, painting, musical instruments, coins, carpets, and weapons. Alas, the museum is not terribly well maintained, and there's no brochure to aid your wandering. ✉ *Corner of Janpath and Rajpath,* ☎ *11/301–5938.* 🎫 *Rs. 5.* ⏲ *Tues.–Sun. 10–5.*

15 **Nehru Memorial Museum.** This massive colonial mansion was originally built for the commander of the British Indian Army. While the Viceregal residence (framed at the other end of South Avenue) became

the home of India's president, India's first prime minister, Jawaharlal Nehru, took up residence here. Those interested in the Independence movement should not miss this landmark, nor the nearby Gandhi Smriti (☞ *above*). The yellow two-story building is surrounded by beautiful flower gardens and punctuated by grand trees. Inside, several rooms are still decorated as Nehru left them, and extensive displays chronicle Nehru's life and the Independence movement. Move through the rooms in order: One by one, photographs, newspaper clippings, and personal letters tell the heart-stopping story of the birth of the world's largest democracy. On your way out, stop to see the 14th-century hunting lodge next to the Nehru Planetarium. (The latter, good for kids, has shows in English at 11:30 AM and 3 PM.) ✉ *Teen Murti Bhavan, Teen Murti Marg,* ☎ *11/301–3765.* 🎟 *Free.* ⏲ *9–5:30. Closed. Mon.*

14 **Purana Qila.** (Old Fort). India's sixth capital was the scene of a fierce power struggle between the Afghan Sher Shah and Humayun, son of the first Mogul emperor, Babar. Humayun, who believed deeply in astrology, probably considered himself star-crossed. When he started to build his own capital, Dinpanah, on these grounds in the 1530s, Sher Shah forced the emperor to flee for his life. Sher Shah destroyed what existed of Dinpanah to create his own capital, Shergarh. Fifteen years later, Humayun took revenge and seized control, but he died the following year, leaving Sher Shah's city for others to destroy.

Unfortunately, once you enter the massive **Bara Darwaza** (Western Gate), only two buildings are intact: the **Qila-i-Kunha Masjid,** Sher Shah's private mosque, an excellent example of Indo-Afghan architecture in red sandstone with decorative marble touches, and the two-story octagonal tower of red sandstone and white marble, the **Sher Mandal,** which ultimately became Humayun's library and his death trap: Hearing the call to prayer, Humayun started down the steep steps, slipped, and fell to his death. ✉ *Off Mathura Rd., near Delhi Zoo.* 🎟 *Free.* ⏲ *Daily sunrise–sunset.*

22 **Qutab Minar.** This 234-ft tower, called the seventh wonder of Hindustan, is the tallest stone tower in India, with 376 steps. Begun by the Muslim campaigner Qutab-ud-din-Aibak in 1193 to commemorate his capture of Delhi, it was completed by his son-in-law and successor, Iltutmish, who added the top four stories. This combined effort led to a handsome sandstone example of Indo-Islamic architecture with terracotta frills and outbursts of balconies to mark each story. Unfortunately, repairs by a 14th-century ruler destroyed the harmonious lines, adding not only height and marble to the two upper stories, but a silly dose of incongruity. The lower sandstone sections are fluted, with vertical lines; the renovation adopted a round motif with horizontal lines. The rulers also changed the degree of the taper. The decorative bands of intricately carved inscription are Arabic quotations from the Koran.

At the foot of the Qutab Minar lies the **Quwwat-ul-Islam Masjid,** the first Muslim mosque in India, erected in the 12th century after Muslims defeated the Hindu Chauhan dynasty and created the first capital not far from here. As if to prove their supremacy over the Hindus, the Muslims built their mosque on the site of a Hindu temple and used materials, especially columns, from 27 other demolished Hindu and Jain shrines, with the result that Hindu and Jain sculptures stand in various parts of the mosque. Because the mosque was probably built by Hindu craftsmen, the presence of the large stone screen across the front of the prayer hall may have been the Muslims' own attempt to block out the strong Hindu influence.

The mosque is also famous for a strange, 5th-century iron pillar, which originally stood before a temple of Vishnu and may have been brought here in the 11th century. A solid shaft of iron 24 ft high, the pillar is inscribed with six lines of Sanskrit. No one knows why it has remained rust-free for so many years. According to legend, if you stand with your back to the pillar and can reach around and touch your fingers, any wish you make will come true. (Alas, it's currently fenced off.) ✉ *Aurobindo Marg, near Mehrauli (14 km/9 mi south of Connaught Pl.).* 🎫 *Rs. 5; free Fri.* ⏲ *Daily sunrise–sunset.*

8 **Raj Ghat and National Gandhi Museum.** After Mohandas K. Gandhi was shot and killed by a Hindu fanatic on January 30, 1948 (the anniversary of which is now a national holiday), his body was cremated on the banks of the Yamuna River in Delhi. This site is now a national shrine to the Mahatma, as he is known (the honorific means "Great Soul"). Indian tourists and pilgrims from all walks of life stream across the peaceful lawn to pay their respects to "Gandhiji." At the center of a low, modern courtyard is a slightly raised black-marble slab covered with flowers. At its head is an eternal flame and an inscription of Gandhi's final words, "Hai Ram!" ("Oh God!"). The sandstone walls enclosing the shrine are inscribed with various passages written by Gandhi, translated into India's 13 national languages as well other languages, such as Spanish and Zulu. Raj Ghat was also the cremation site for two other assassinated heads of state, Indira Gandhi and her son, Rajiv. Back across the busy street from which you entered is the National Gandhi Museum, run by a private foundation, which houses a collection of photographs and some of Gandhi's personal effects. ✉ *Mahatma Gandhi Marg.* 🎫 *Free.* ⏲ *Raj Ghat, daily sunrise–sunset; museum, Tues.–Sun. 9:30–5:30.*

DINING

Delhi's restaurants are generally open daily 12:30 to 3 for lunch and 7:30 to 11 for dinner. Dry days are strictly observed on the first and seventh day of each month and all national holidays. Expect a 20% tax on your food and beverage bill. Imported liquor is extremely expensive; inquire before you imbibe.

North Indian

$$$$ ★ ✕ **Dum Pukht.** Like the *nawabi* (princely) culture from which it's drawn, the food at Dum Pukht is subtle and refined. The understated European decor, offset by embroidered ceiling fans mounted on the walls, creates an elegant, peaceful environment for cuisine from Lucknow and Hyderabad. The *habibia* and *kakori* kebabs are delicately spiced, with a touch of saffron. For vegetarians, the *baghare baigan* (baby eggplants slit and browned) are served in a peanut-sesame sauce that fills the mouth and bites the tongue. One section of the menu features fusion dishes that emerged when East India Company officers adapted to the nawabi way of life. Marinated mutton chops, served with a dark, rich pomegranate sauce, have a splendid sweet-savory balance with an occasional crunch from pomegranate seeds; river trout is cooked with a pomegranate-seed stuffing, then wrapped in silver foil and topped with a spinach leaf. The rich *rangeenaq* (Hyderabadi date pudding) goes well with coffee. All this is presented with almost Zen simplicity on silver service by precise waiters, whose silken *salwar-kameez* somehow do not clash with the old Hindi film songs drifting from the grand piano. ✉ *Welcomgroup Maurya Sheraton Hotel, Diplomatic Enclave,* ☎ *11/611–2233. AE, DC, MC, V.*

$$$ ✕ **Bukhara.** This small restaurant with stone walls, mounted Bukhara carpets, and hanging copper vessels is so crowded that it's hard to hear the taped Uzbeki music. Gleaming wide-plank tables fill the place, and more tables are set outside near the pool. By popular demand, the menu hasn't changed in years. The Northwest Frontier cuisine consists mainly of meaty morsels that are marinated, then cooked before your very eyes on a spit in a tandoori oven. The *Sikandari raan* (leg of lamb marinated in rum and cooked in the tandoor), which serves four, is heavenly; the delicately spiced meat is tender and moist without being oily. The *murgh malai kabab* (boneless chicken pieces marinated in cheese, cream, and lime) tastes of cardamom, and the hearty dal is so famous that it's now sold in cans. Although carnivores will be happier here, vegetarians can opt for a tandoori salad (slow-cooked vegetables and pineapple with Indian cheese). ✉ *Welcomgroup Maurya Sheraton Hotel, Diplomatic Enclave,* ☏ *11/611–2233. Reservations not accepted after 8:30. AE, DC, MC, V.*

$$$ ✕ **Haveli.** Every aspect of this restaurant's decor contributes to the look of an old haveli. Earthy colors speak of Rajasthan, antiqued walls showcase tiny replicas of exquisite *jharoka* (perforated-stone) balconies, miniature paintings depict Rajput scenes, and the elegant old samovars once held Rajputs' liquor. Clusters of yellow lights hang from gold-plated glass domes. The total effect is enchanting, and the North Indian food is superb, with a bonus: Some of Chef Rajeev Janveja's creations are cooked with minimal oil or no oil at all. Start with street food gone epicurean: have some marvelous *chaats* (tangy, moist delicacies made of lentils and potatoes). Move on to *murgh tikka Irani* (marinated chicken cooked in the tandoor), the marvelous *rogini gosht* (lamb curry), or *machli ke tikka* (fish marinated in coconut and mint and cooked in the tandoor). The excellent Indian desserts include *gulab jamun* and *rasmalai,* doughy sweets smothered in syrup and cream respectively. Folk dancers, singers, and musicians entertain. ✉ *Taj Mahal Hotel, 1 Mansingh Rd.,* ☏ *11/302–6162. AE, DC, MC, V.*

$$$ ✕ **Kandahar.** Named for a city in Afghanistan, this winning Oberoi eatery has cream-colored walls and pillars, a show kitchen, and stunning 19th-century Afghan etchings and handsome ethnic clothing mounted on the walls. The chef's newest menu is pan-Indian, with an emphasis on low-fat preparation and a line of wonderful *kadhai* (Indian wok) options. In dishes like *karara paneer aur khilley phool,* fresh ingredients such as broccoli florets and farmer's cheese are quickly stir-fried with Indian ingredients like chili batter, pepper, and fresh mint to create a crispy, spicy curry. Other standards like *dal makhani khandahari* are stripped of their excess fat, leaving only flavor and aroma. Explore the changing menu for modern adaptations of traditional dishes from all over India. Ghazals are performed every night except Tuesday by noted TV personality Ansar Sabri. ✉ *The Oberoi, Dr. Zakir Hussain Rd.,* ☏ *11/436–3030. AE, DC, MC, V.*

$$ ✕ **Chor Bizarre.** Expect a 1927 Fiat roadster for a salad bar, a spiral staircase that leads nowhere, an eclectic mix of tables (one created from a four-poster bed and another from an antique sewing-machine table), and a similar mix of chairs—all collected from *chor* (thieves') bazaars around India. You can also expect excellent North Indian cuisine, especially Kashmiri dishes. Try *ghazab ka tikka* (tandoori chicken coated with cheddar cheese), lightly cooked *haaq* (Kashmiri spinach), *dal* Chor B'zar (a thick, dark lentil preparation flavored with tomatoes and cream), or *dum aloo* Kashmiri (spicy potatoes), and follow it all with *kahwah,* fragrant Kashmiri tea. ✉ *Hotel Broadway, 4/15 A Asif Ali Rd.,* ☏ *11/327–3821. AE, DC, MC, V.*

Dining
Baan Thai, **17**
Basil and Thyme, **30**
Bukhara, **18**
Chor Bizarre, **3**
Coconut Grove, **9**
Curry on the Roof, **27**
Dum Pukht, **18**
Fa Yian, **4**
Farsaan, **26**
Haveli, **11**
Kandahar, **17**
Karim, **1**
Kovil, **5**
La Piazza, **23**
La Rochelle and Wine Bar, **17**
Las Meninas, **6**
Naivedyam, **24**
Orient Express, **21**
Park Baluchi, **25**
Rampur Kitchen, **13**
Sagar, **29**
Spice Route, **8**
Taipan, **17**
Tamura, **20**
Tea House of the August Moon, **21**
TK's, **23**

Lodging
Ambassador Hotel, **14**
Ashok Hotel, **19**
Claridges, **12**
Hans Plaza, **10**
Hyatt Regency, **23**
Imperial, **8**
Jukaso Inn, **16**
Maharani Guest House, **15**
The Oberoi, **17**
Oberoi Maidens, **2**
Park, **6**
Parkroyal, **28**
Radisson, **22**
Taj Mahal, **11**
Taj Palace, **21**
Welcomgroup Maurya Sheraton Hotel and Towers, **18**
YMCA Tourist Hostel, **7**

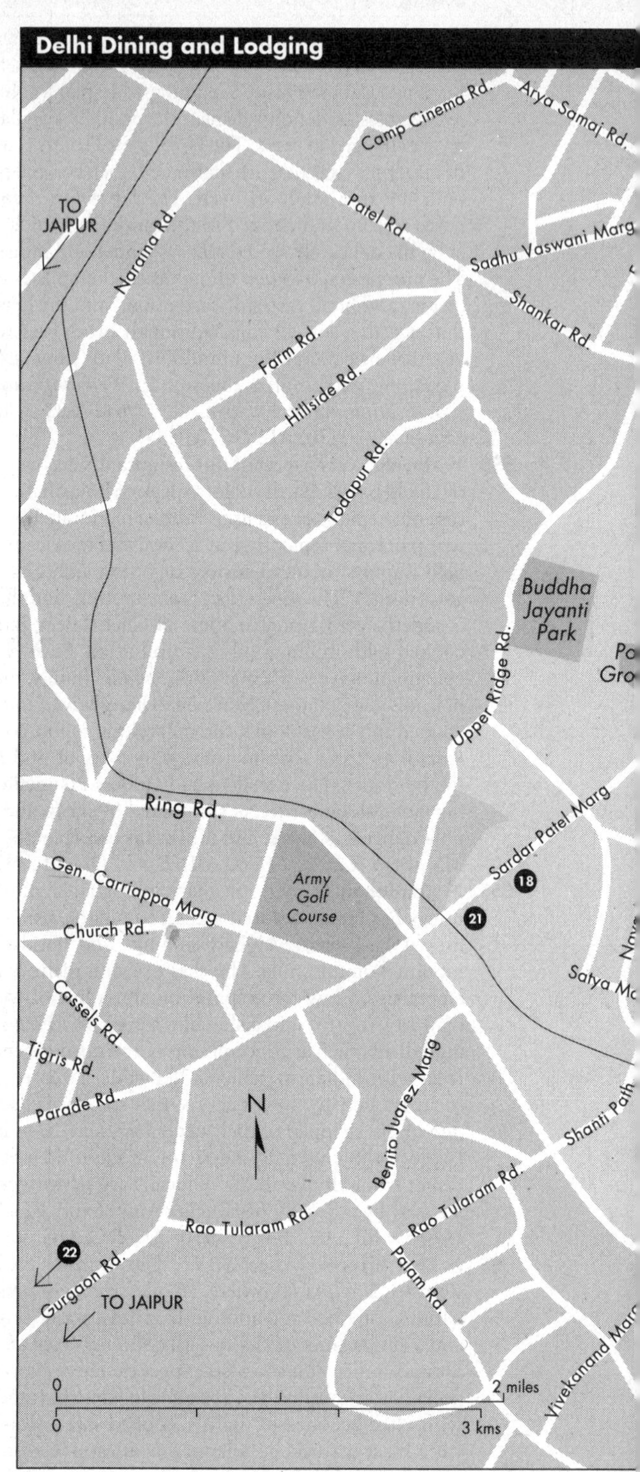

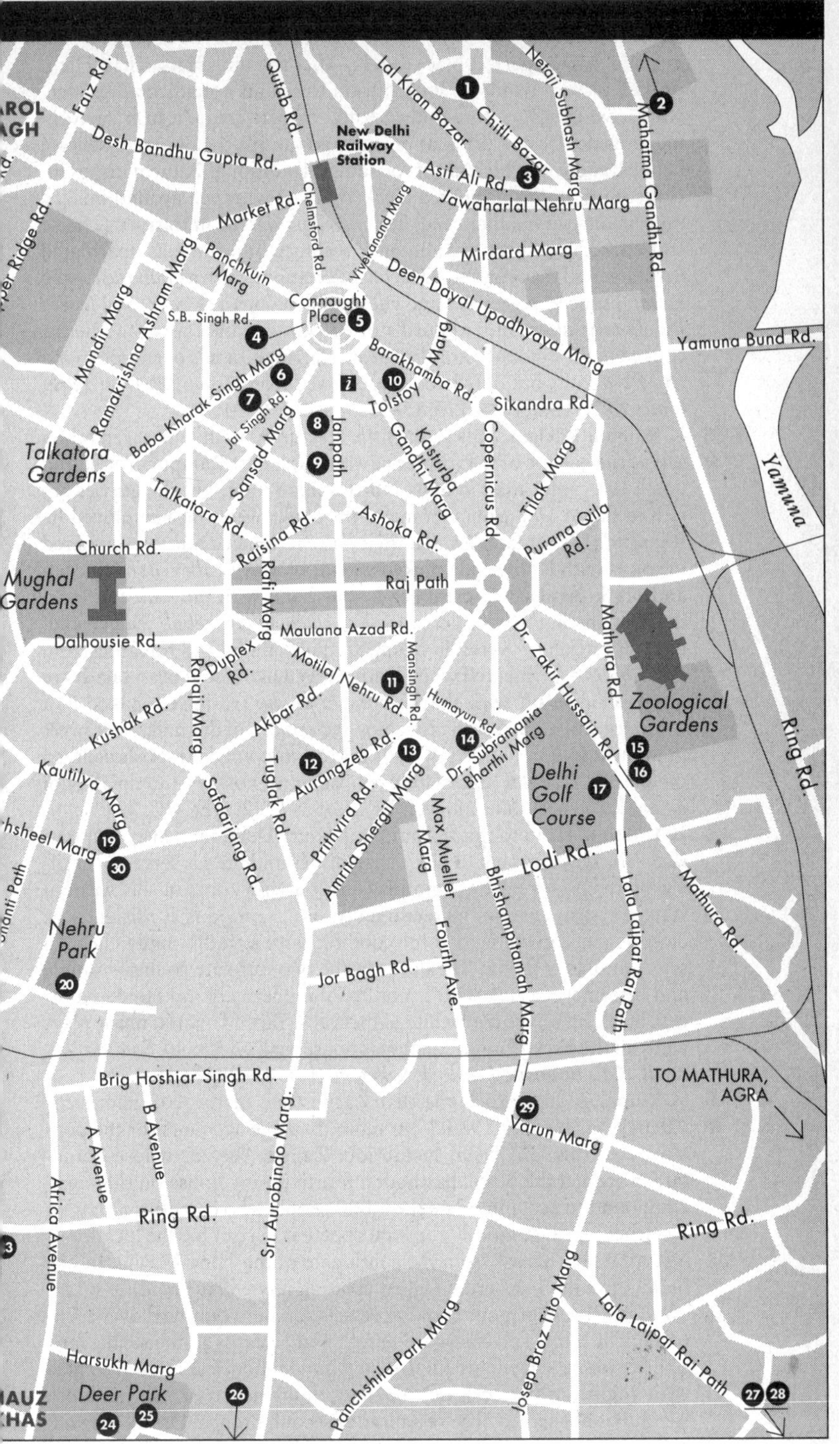
New Delhi Railway Station
Lal Kuan Bazar
Chitli Bazar
Netaji Subhash Marg
Mahatma Gandhi Rd.
Asif Ali Rd.
Jawaharlal Nehru Marg
Mirdard Marg
Deen Dayal Upadhyaya Marg
Yamuna Bund Rd.
Yamuna
Desh Bandhu Gupta Rd.
Qutab Rd.
Market Rd.
Chelmsford Rd.
Vivekanand Marg
Panchkuin Marg
Connaught Place
S.B. Singh Rd.
Mandir Marg
Ramakrishna Ashram Marg
Baba Kharak Singh Marg
Jai Singh Rd.
Sansad Marg
Janpath
Barakhamba Rd.
Tolstoy Marg
Kasturba Gandhi Marg
Copernicus Rd.
Sikandra Rd.
Tilak Marg
Purana Qila Rd.
Talkatora Gardens
Talkatora Rd.
Raisina Rd.
Ashoka Rd.
Church Rd.
Mughal Gardens
Raj Path
Rafi Marg
Dalhousie Rd.
Maulana Azad Rd.
Duplex Rd.
Motilal Nehru Rd.
Mansingh Rd.
Humayun Rd.
Dr. Zakir Hussain Rd.
Mathura Rd.
Zoological Gardens
Ring Rd.
Rajaji Marg
Kushak Rd.
Akbar Rd.
Aurangzeb Rd.
Dr. Subramania Bharthi Marg
Delhi Golf Course
Kautilya Marg
Safdarjang Rd.
Tuglak Rd.
Prithvira Rd.
Amrita Shergil Marg
Max Mueller Marg
Lodi Rd.
Lala Lajpat Rai Path
Bhishampitamah Marg
Fourth Ave.
Nehru Park
Jor Bagh Rd.
Brig Hoshiar Singh Rd.
TO MATHURA, AGRA
Varun Marg
A Avenue
B Avenue
Sri Aurobindo Marg
Africa Avenue
Ring Rd.
Ring Rd.
Josep Broz Tito Marg
Lala Lajpat Rai Path
Panchshila Park Marg
Harsukh Marg
Deer Park

$$ ★ ✕ **Park Baluchi.** Set in the wooded environs of Deer Park, this sumptuous restaurant probably serves the most distinctive barbecue dishes in Delhi. It's the perfect place to relax after roaming Hauz Khas: High-peaked picture windows look out on trees and a manicured garden, while cast-iron furniture and Oriental carpets create a lush environment inside. Have a drink at the bar and sample the uniquely delicate kebabs, some of which are stupendous. Traditional Baluchi dishes include *murg potli* (marinated chicken breast wrapped around minced mutton and served flambéed) and *mewa panier tukra* (farmer's cheese stuffed with mushrooms, almonds, walnuts, and sultanas, marinated in cream, and then roasted). The house creations, such as *Banarasi seekh kabab* (minced vegetables and cheese rolled onto a skewer) and *lazeez karela mussalam* (bitter gourd stuffed with cottage cheese and herbs, cooked in the tandoor), are also great. The restaurant is open from noon to 11 PM daily, but only kebabs are served from 3 to 6. ✉ *Deer Park, Hauz Khas Village,* ☎ *11/685–9369. AE, DC, MC, V.*

$–$$ ★ ✕ **Rampur Kitchen.** This funky little restaurant with only seven tables serves the cuisine of the former nawabi capital of Rampur. You'll find much less cream than in most North Indian food, but the gravies are rich in flavor and aroma. Some of the cooks were once employed by Rampur's richest families. Eat their *haleem* (minced mutton simmered in spices with lentils and cracked wheat) or *murg kalk mirch* (chicken and black pepper in a cream sauce) by hand with *mughali roti* (particularly thick, fluffy flat breads). The *murg gillafi kebab* (chicken kebabs beautifully covered in chopped mint, onions and tomatoes) and *dal Rampuri* (fermented white lentils served like a cold bean salad) are unique. Finish off with the *Rampur ki sevain* (vermicelli baked in a red sauce and topped with pistachios and crumbs of dry milk), less sweet than most Indian desserts. This is a Muslim-owned establishment, so the meat is all *halal* (the Islamic equivalent of kosher) and no alcohol is served. ✉ *8A Khan Market,* ☎ *11/463–1222. AE, MC, V.*

$ ✕ **Farsaan.** Head to this restaurant in South Delhi for a tasty Gujarati *thali* (fixed assortment of vegetarian dishes and breads served on a silver platter). Owned by a mother and son with roots in this western state, Farsaan changes its menu daily, but the food is consistently as close as you can come to home cooking, with a traditionally Gujarati sweet-and-sour flavor. The decor in the two intimate rooms is simple and extremely casual, with a mixture of modern art and Hindu paintings breaking up the cool white of the walls. Taped Gujarati music plays softly in the background. Alcohol is not served. ✉ *Kh. 30, Saidula Jab, M. B. Rd., opposite D-Block Saket,* ☎ *11/683–8827. AE.*

$ ★ ✕ **Karim.** A sign proclaims that Karim (one of the 100 names for Allah) was "born in 1913," but more than age accounts for the popularity of this Old Delhi institution. Zainul Abedin, whose grandfather opened the place, has built a fourth dining house on this small compound to accommodate the 1,000 people who come every day for his delicious "fast food." The atmosphere is perfect for the location—just off a lane across from the south gate of the Jama Masjid. In one building, a man sits cross-legged creating *naan* (flat bread) in a tandoor; nearby, enormous cooking vessels simmer your meal over a low flame. The tables and chairs are simple, and placards announce the fare. The fastest-moving items are *badam pasanda* (boneless mutton cooked with yogurt and spices), mutton stew, and chicken or fish tandoori. Alcohol is not served. The restaurant's second branch, **Dastar Khwan-E-Karim** (✉ 168/2 Jha House Basti, Hazrat Nizamuddin West, ☎ 11/469–8300), also known simply as Karim, works well if you don't want to go all the way into Old Delhi (or prefer a more upmarket setting), but the food just isn't the same. ✉ *Matiya Mahal, opposite Hotel Bombay Orient,* ☎ *11/326–9800. No credit cards.*

South Indian

$$ ✕ **Coconut Grove.** This cozy restaurant, with cane chairs, bamboo trim, subdued lighting, and taped South Indian classical music, serves the cuisines of Kerala and other southern coastal regions. Try the special *konju thenga* curry (prawns cooked in mildly spicy coconut sauce), *appams* (rice pancakes, here served with a rich coconut gravy and chicken or prawns), and pepper chicken Chettinad (spicy chicken cooked in a thick pepper gravy). Alcohol is not served. ✉ *Ashok Yatri Niwas, 19 Ashok Rd.,* ☎ *11/336–8553. AE, DC, MC, V.*

$$ ✕ **Curry on the Roof.** This is the only restaurant in Delhi serving Chettinad-style South Indian food, and while the ambience is nothing special, the food is fantastic. Every meal begins with a chick-pea starter served with grated coconut and lemon. As an entrée, the chicken *Amaravathi* (strips of marinated chicken fried with onions and cashews) is hard to beat, though it might burn your taste buds (as might anything marked with a bomb symbol on the menu). Seafood is a specialty; the prawns masala, served in a rich gravy, are wonderful. To add something green to your plate, order the beans *Porial,* chopped French beans cooked with lentils, curry leaf, and red chilis. All these foods are generally eaten with *idiappam* (steamed-rice pancakes); an order of creamy yogurt is another way to cool your palate. There is a full bar. The restaurant shares dining space with a Thai kitchen. ✉ *M-35 Greater Kailash I,* ☎ *11/641–8896. AE, MC, V.*

$ ✕ **Kovil.** Conveniently located on the inner circle of Connaught Place, this South Indian restaurant is popular with the business crowd. While service can be slouchy and the wash basin needs a thorough cleaning, Kovil's food is quite tasty and often original. The fixed lunch ("Executive Thali"), served from 11 to 3, sometimes contains unusual preparations, such as curried beet roots and sweet biriani, and the thali's seven components are served in paisley-shaped stainless-steel dishes around the traditional banana leaf. On the walls are some white line drawings on black fabric by the renowned M. F. Husain, depicting rustic scenes. ✉ *E-2 Connaught Pl.,* ☎ *11/371–0585. AE, DC, MC, V.*

$ ✕ **Naivedyam.** This charming restaurant was meticulously designed by artisans from the Tamil temple city of Thanjavur, complete with a polished stone Nandi (Shiva's faithful bull) facing its stained-glass entrance. The small dining room displays Tanjore religious paintings, and Carnatic instrumental tapes play in the background. Wearing *veshtis* (traditional South Indian men's skirts), the waiters serve delicately cooked Udupi food in almost comically dim lighting. All meals begin with a *rasam* (peppery soup) that must be the best in Delhi. For a snack try the *masala vadai* (fried lentil cakes), which are served with three distinctive chutneys—coconut, mint, and tomato. More filling is the *maharaja sajjasar masala dosa,* a lentil-flour crêpe filled with spicy potatoes and dried fruit. For dessert, try the *holige* (a sugary paratha mixed with coconut) with *ghee* (clarified butter). No alcohol is served. ✉ *1 Hauz Khas Village,* ☎ *11/696–0426. AE, DC, MC, V.*

$ ★ ✕ **Sagar.** This three-story family restaurant is a favorite with New Delhi's upper middle class. Always bustling, it's usually full at mealtimes. Service is efficient, and the premises are kept impeccably clean (watch out for the sweeper boy crouched on the floor). The *upma* (semolina mash with bits of cashew and peas) is especially good, as are the vegetable *uthapams* (fermented rice-flour pancakes with bits of vegetables). For dessert have fresh filtered Indian coffee and *kulfi falooda* (traditional green-cashew ice cream served over angel-hair pasta). No credit cards or traveler's checks are accepted, but that shouldn't be a problem—one person's bill is usually less than Rs. 100. The restaurant opens at

8 AM, and thali is served from noon to 3 and 6 to 11. ✉ *18 Defence Colony Market,* ☎ *11/461–7832. No credit cards.*

East and Southeast Asian

$$$$ ✕ **Baan Thai.** The corridor into this traditional Thai *baan* (house) is an Asian art gallery, with carved wood statues, "elephant" chairs, porcelain, and antiques. More statues and exquisite embroidered hangings adorn the dining room, and Burmese teak latticework covers the windows, the partitions that create private alcoves, and parts of the ceiling. Sit at a regular table or on a traditional Thai *khantok* (floor cushion) on the raised platform. The Thai chefs import special ingredients to create their authentic cuisine. This is a fantastic place for lunch, as the food is light and picture windows have lovely views of the garden and the hotel pool. ✉ *The Oberoi, Dr. Zakir Hussain Rd.,* ☎ *11/436–3030. AE, DC, MC, V.*

$$$$ ★ ✕ **Taipan.** This is without a doubt the best Chinese restaurant in Delhi. The food is authentic, luscious, and artfully presented, and the view from the top of the Oberoi—over the Delhi Golf Course toward the high-rise buildings of Connaught Circus—is grand. Waiters are attentive and precise. The menu encompasses various Chinese cuisines, but the highlight is dim sum, of which 18 varieties are intricately prepared under the direction of a special dim-sum chef from Singapore. Of particular interest are the prawn-banana rolls in rice paper and the steamed bean-curd skin with vegetables. Although dim sum is available weekdays à la carte, the real bargain is on weekends, when the fixed-price lunch includes an intensely flavored wonton soup, unlimited dim sum, and a dessert of lychees with ice cream for Rs. 695. Reserve in advance for this feast. ✉ *The Oberoi, Dr. Zakir Hussain Marg,* ☎ *11/436–3030. AE, DC, MC, V.*

$$$ ★ ✕ **Spice Route.** It took seven years to design and build this place, and it's not hard to imagine why—the interior of a mock trading ship is decorated with elements of Thai, Balinese, and Keralite temples, complete with antique teak columns and meticulous wall paintings of stories from the *Ramayana* and *Mahabharata.* The menu gathers cuisines from the lands of the ancient spice route—Kerala, Sri Lanka, Thailand, Malaysia, and Indonesia—and the flavors rely heavily on lemon grass, curry leaves, and coriander. The best dishes seem to be those from Kerala, including a pineapple *rassam* (a thin, spicy-sweet soup) and a vegetable stew (tempered with mustard seeds, curry leaves, and coconut paste), both eaten with appams. The Thai *kaeng khew waan kai* (chicken in green curry with baby eggplants) and *som tum chae* (a salad of raw papaya and peanuts) are also delicious, but the *nasi goreng* (a greasy Malay-style fried rice) should be avoided. The menu changes seasonally, and special menus coincide with traditional festivals on the spice route. ✉ *Imperial Hotel, Janpath,* ☎ *11/334–1234. AE, DC, MC, V.*

$$$ ✕ **Tamura.** Hidden away in a corner of Nehru Park, this Japanese restaurant gets the nod from local Japanese expats as the most authentic in Delhi. Despite a dearth of windows, the ambience is bright and airy, with white granite walls and prints of Japanese flowers. The food is light, and artfully presented. Try the prawn-tempura noodle dish, the "Tamura-style" fillet steak (flown in from Bangkok), and the mixed sushi roll (chef Takayuki Tamura wisely opts not to serve any raw fish in Delhi). You eat at upright tables or in one of three *tatami* rooms (floor-level dining alcoves surrounded by paper screens). The service is excellent: attentive, but not too much so. Alcohol is not served. ✉ *Inside the NDMC Swimming Pool Complex (Nehru Park), Vinay Marg,* ☎ *11/611–0552. No credit cards.*

$$$ ✕ **Tea House of the August Moon.** There's plenty of whimsy here, with enormous carved dragons on the ceiling and a narrow bridge across a goldfish pond leading to an elevated central pagoda. Brass lanterns create subdued lighting, and a full moon is projected onto an upper wall at night. The menu is predominantly Chinese, but the kitchen is in the process of diversifying, adding popular Korean, Mongolian, and Singaporean dishes. In this spirit, musicians from Vietnam, Korea, and elsewhere play during both lunch and dinner. The *konjee* (shredded lamb tossed in a piquant sauce, then lightly sautéed with bean spouts and capsicum) is still delicious, as are the delicately stir-fried seasonal vegetables with garlic (a special dish not listed on the menu). Balancing yin with yang, the hot toffee banana with vanilla ice cream is a nice way to end your meal. ✉ *Taj Palace Hotel, 2 Sardar Patel Marg, Diplomatic Enclave,* ☎ *11/611–0202. AE, DC, MC, V.*

$$$ ★ ✕ **TK's.** The focus of this restaurant is the *teppanyaki* grill, used as both a cooking tool and a performance space. Chef Huria has collected cooking ideas and specific dishes from all over Asia, though Japanese food is still the focus. You dine facing an informative cook who guides you through the meal. The set meals are best, especially the lighter "Orchid" and the seafood-oriented "Shima," as they're designed to combine styles and dishes in unusual ways. Each set meal includes an appetizer, soup, and your choice of various entrées as well as dessert and coffee served in a separate dining area. Particularly interesting are the jumbo prawns in yellow curry sauce, shredded chicken with black-bean sauce, and seasonal green vegetables with green curry. The meal lasts up to two hours: Time moves quickly as you watch each course being flamboyantly prepared before your eyes. At lunchtime, the popular Mongolian barbecue features great seafood. ✉ *Hyatt Regency, Bhikaiji Cama Pl., Ring Rd.,* ☎ *11/679–1234. AE, DC, MC, V.*

$$ ✕ **Fa Yian.** Don't let the dark, dingy location—the middle circle of Connaught Place—scare you away from this fabulous restaurant. Potted trees spruce up the exterior, where you may have to wait for one of the eight tables. Taped flute music and water spilling into a small fountain are soothing, but the decor takes second place to wonderful Chinese dishes that are either steamed or stir-fried in a minimum of oil. Many ingredients are imported, and the condiments, sauces, dumplings, and noodles are prepared daily. Try the delicate steamed wonton, honey chicken, fish steamed with black beans and ginger, or shredded lamb with garlic sauce; and if you have room, don't pass up the homemade date-coffee ice cream. ✉ *A block, 25/2 Middle Circle (behind Marina Hotel), Connaught Pl.,* ☎ *11/332–4603. AE, MC, V.*

European

$$$$ ★ ✕ **La Rochelle and Wine Bar.** Olaf Niemeier, appropriately called Chef Picasso, is arguably Delhi's best chef. His tantalizing cuisine, which he calls "West meets East," is so beautiful that it's almost painful to disturb the artworks placed before you. The menus, one of which is vegetarian, change every two months, but both feature Niemeier's special combination of natural ingredients, lovely colors, and light preparations. Tickle your taste buds with such inventions as chili sorbet served on a wheat lattice over yellow capsicum soup. A favorite entrée is the delicately flavored rack of lamb crusted with herbs, served in a spiral over gratin potatoes, and drizzled with a roasted summer-squash gravy. The lunch buffet is a joy to eat next to the floor-to-ceiling picture window overlooking the Oberoi's rose garden. La Rochelle also boasts a wine bar and one of the best selections of wines (mostly French) in Delhi. A jazz trio plays nightly and during Sunday brunch. ✉ *The Oberoi,*

Dr. Zakir Hussain Rd., ☎ 11/436–3030. Reservations essential for Sunday brunch. AE, DC, MC, V.

$$$$ ✕ **Orient Express.** This enchanting, intimate railcar with handsome teak walls and brass fittings has 10 softly lit tables, most separated by partitions of wood and beveled glass. A pianist plays light pop tunes in the adjoining bar. Like the decor, the service is self-consciously grandiose; napkins are snapped onto laps, and the silver covers on main courses are unveiled with a "Violà!" The French cuisine, in the form of four-course, fixed-price meals, is satisfying, if not especially dazzling. The turbot *en croûte d'olive* is well cooked, its delicate flavors enhanced by an olive crust and onion sauce; the lamb chops are less successful. The lunch for two is very reasonably priced. Note that children under 17 are not allowed at dinner. Jackets, while not required, are suggested for men. ✉ *Taj Palace Hotel, 2 Sardar Patel Marg, Diplomatic Enclave, ☎ 11/611–0202. AE, DC, MC, V.*

$$$ ✕ **La Piazza.** With an open kitchen and wood-fired ovens, this space feels more like an informal villa than a plaza. Dark wooden beams with concealed lights illuminate the brick-like tiles on the ceiling, and pale-yellow walls and massive pillars are delicately fluted and streaked with gold. The antipasto, with fresh mozzarella and carpaccio, is delicious, and the assortment of pizzas includes Chef Pien Mario Cremella's popular Pizza al Piazza—with goat cheese, sun-dried tomatoes, roasted garlic, and basil. You might also try the delicate fresh ravioli with ricotta cheese, panfried breaded Australian lamb chops flavored with fresh herbs, or any of the fresh fish, especially the tasty Norwegian salmon. There's an excellent lunch buffet. ✉ *Hyatt Regency, Bhikaiji Cama Pl., Ring Rd., ☎ 11/679–1234. Reservations not accepted after 8 PM. AE, DC, MC, V.*

$$$ ★ ✕ **Las Meninas.** Playful and artsy, Delhi's only Spanish restaurant is pop-Baroque: think Alice in Wonderland meets Pedro Alamdóvar. The centerpiece is an interpretation of Velázquez's masterpiece in bold colors like lime and fuchsia. Dressed like matadors, the attentive waiters begin dinner service with an array of olives and delicious fresh bread. Tapas are served in clay bowls; try the *calamares a la romana* (deep-fried marinated squid rings) with creamy *aioli* (a mixture of garlic and mayonnaise) or *jamón de jabugo* (cured Iberian ham with almonds). You can make a meal out of tapas, or, after some soup (chef Pedro Hoyos experiments with concoctions like green almonds in a garlic-cream base), sample entrées like *mero al ajillo en cama de patatas a lo pobre* (grilled red-snapper fillet with sweet roasted garlic and red chilis served over sea-flavored potatoes). Finish with *perfecto de platano* (banana-and-honey parfait) and an espresso or Spanish liqueur. There's a well-priced selection of Spanish wines. ✉ *The Park, 15 Parliament St., ☎ 11/373–3737. AE, DC, MC, V. No lunch.*

$$ ★ ✕ **Basil and Thyme.** Head chef Bhicoo Manekshaw is 76 years old, but that doesn't stop her from changing her menu every 90 days and overseeing a daily special. The mostly vegetarian food leans towards cheese and eggs, and is delicate and artfully presented. There's no telling what your choices will be, but you can bank on creative Continental concoctions like tomato-orange soup, chicken-liver pâté, leek tarts, and mint soufflé. The plain white decor pushes your gaze through the picture windows toward the greenery of Santushti. Alcohol is not served, but this little lunch spot is very popular with Delhi's upper class and the embassy crowd. ✉ *Santushti Shopping Complex, New Wellingdon Camp, ☎ 11/467–3322. Reservations essential. AE, DC, MC, V. Closed Sun.; no dinner.*

LODGING

Unless we note otherwise, Delhi hotels have central air-conditioning, bathrooms with tubs, currency exchange, and room service. Many also have a house doctor. In addition, most luxury hotels have executive floors with special privileges or facilities designed for the business traveler.

$$$$ **The Oberoi.** Delhi's first luxury hotel (built 1965) is perfect for those who want elegance and real quiet—an attribute that sets it apart from its counterparts. Even when the hotel is packed, the lobby is peaceful; and it's lovely in its own right, with a small, marble lotus fountain strewn with rose petals near the entrance, an illuminated carved Tree of Life set in the back wall, and stunning Indian artifacts. Adorned with valuable aquatints and lithographs, the spacious guest rooms have Western decor and warm color schemes. All rooms have multiple-line phones and well-stocked minibars; deluxe rooms have more amenities, such as fax machines and DVD players with a large library. The best views take in the Delhi Golf Course, where you can usually spot a peacock, but rooms on the other side face Humayun's Tomb. ✉ *Dr. Zakir Hussain Rd., New Delhi 110003,* ☎ *11/436–3030,* FAX *11/436–0484. 290 rooms, 31 suites. 5 restaurants, bar, no-smoking floor, pool, beauty salon, health club, golf privileges at 27-hole course, baby-sitting, business services, travel services. AE, DC, MC, V.*

$$$$ **Taj Mahal.** This jazzy hotel crackles with life. If you want to be near Connaught Place and surrounded by Who's Who in Delhi—flamboyant weddings and all—by all means stay here. The lobby's wall and ceiling domes are decorated with bright Rajasthani-style ceramics, and marble *jalis* (latticework screens) discreetly cover pool-facing windows and surround a central platform with a bubbling fountain. Room decor is largely Western, with Indian touches; the best rooms are on the upper floors, overlooking the pool and garden. Five floors are dedicated to business travelers, who enjoy a cozy private lounge and complimentary breakfast. ✉ *1 Mansingh Rd., New Delhi 110011,* ☎ *11/302–6162,* FAX *11/301–7299. 275 rooms, 15 suites. 5 restaurants, bar, coffee shop, pool, beauty salon, health club, baby-sitting, business services, meeting rooms, travel services. AE, DC, MC, V.*

$$$–$$$$ **Welcomgroup Maurya Sheraton Hotel and Towers.** Entering the Maurya, you're greeted by a flower-petal *rangoli* (floor painting) depicting the *namaste*—an Indian greeting you may already have seen, given with fingertips pressed together. The handsome sitting areas incorporate the colors of the gigantic folk painting set into the massive overhead dome, and fountains just outside the picture windows bring the entire lobby to life. The Maurya has fabulous facilities, including well-known restaurants, multiple business centers, a lovely pool, and a huge health club that's probably the nicest in town. Rooms have both Western and Indian element, including two large wall mirrors with silver filigree frames. At press time, 100 new guest rooms were under construction at the Maurya. The Sheraton Towers (much more expensive) has a small private lobby, an exclusive dining room, and swanker bedrooms that make this wing popular with corporate clients and dignitaries. ✉ *Diplomatic Enclave, New Delhi 110021,* ☎ *11/611–2233,* FAX *11/611–3333. 444 rooms, 44 suites. 5 restaurants, bar, patisserie, pool, beauty salon, health club, 2 tennis courts, nightclub, baby-sitting, business services, travel services. AE, DC, MC, V.*

$$$ **Ashok.** This enormous hotel across the street from beautiful Nehru Park has lovely gardens, some good restaurants, and a cheerful coffee shop. Alas, service, housekeeping, and maintenance are lax at best, but if you need to stay within walking distance of the embassies in the Diplo-

matic Enclave or just want to experience Delhi's leafiest neighborhood, the Ashok might suit your needs. ✉ *50 B Chanakyapuri, New Delhi 110021,* ☎ *11/611–0101,* FAX *11/687–3216. 571 rooms, 112 suites. 5 restaurants, 2 bars, pool, beauty salon, health club, putting green, 1 tennis court, billiards, baby-sitting, business center, travel services. AE, DC, MC, V.*

$$$ ★ **Hyatt Regency.** One of the city's spiffiest hotels, the Hyatt is in South Delhi, a short drive from the Diplomatic Enclave. The five restaurants are a high point, serving a variety of delicious cuisines—Indian, Japanese, Italian, Mediterranean, and Continental—and the bakery has the best Western-style bread in town. The lobby is filled with white and green marble and brass-trimmed mirrors; a lovely pool, with a statue of a dancing goddess, connects to a waterfall that spills down to the lower lobby. Standard guest rooms are not spacious, and have small double beds. Deluxe rooms are quiet and overlook the outdoor pool and handsome rock garden, while the less-expensive Superior doubles look out on Ring Road. ✉ *Bhikaiji Cama Pl., Ring Rd., New Delhi 110066,* ☎ *11/679–1234,* FAX *11/679–1212. http://delhi.hyatt.com. 518 rooms, 29 suites. 5 restaurants, bar, pool, beauty salon, health club, 2 tennis courts, baby-sitting, business services, travel services. AE, DC, MC, V.*

$$$ **Park.** A five-minute walk from Connaught Place, the Park Hotel is a bit pricey for what it delivers (though tour groups reportedly get great rates). The quiet lobby, filled with granite and marble, has circular sitting areas beneath small domes. The good-sized rooms have a warm color scheme and large windows that let in more sound than they should. The quietest rooms overlook the pool or (from the upper floors) Jantar Mantar, an 18th-century astronomical observatory. Guests in the deluxe rooms on the top floor have a private lounge with a library and a dining area that serves complimentary Continental breakfast. Each suite has its own decor; some, like the Black and Gold Suite, may be a bit too far-out for some tastes. ✉ *15 Parliament St., New Delhi 110001,* ☎ *11/373–3737,* FAX *11/373–2025. 226 rooms, 36 suites. 2 restaurants, pool, beauty salon, health club, dance club, business services, travel services. AE, DC, MC, V.*

$$$ **Parkroyal.** This new nine-floor hotel in South Delhi makes good use of its small property, with underground parking and a terrace over the the main entrance. The lobby is sedate, recalling the British Raj with wood paneling and columns, a fireplace, and a tea lounge. The spacious guest rooms have masculine decor and separate dressing rooms. Ordinary doubles have urban views; if you want a view of the Bahai Temple, splurge for one of the more expensive Lutyens Club rooms, which include complimentary breakfast and happy hour. ✉ *Nehru Pl., New Delhi 110019,* ☎ *11/622–3344,* FAX *11/622–4288. 216 rooms, 15 suites. 3 restaurants, bar, pool, beauty salon, health club, baby-sitting, business services, travel services. AE, DC, MC, V.*

$$$ **Taj Palace.** Facilities are top-notch in this deluxe hotel. The beautiful business center, done completely in rosewood, is well equipped; the uncrowded health club is amply outfitted with cardiovascular equipment and weights; and the pool is set in a sprawling flower garden that overlooks an expansive lawn on the level below. Three floors have special amenities for business travelers, including two floors of club rooms with a private lounge and business center. Room decor is Western. Deluxe suites, which cost over U.S. $500, have terraced gardens that can accommodate huge gatherings. ✉ *2 Sardar Patel Marg, Diplomatic Enclave, New Delhi 110021,* ☎ *11/611–0202,* FAX *11/301–1252. 455 rooms, 34 suites. 4 restaurants, pool, beauty salon, barber shop, health club, nightclub, baby-sitting, business services, travel services. AE, DC, MC, V.*

$$–$$$ ★ **Claridges.** In 1950, a Dutch hotel manager convinced an Indian family to build a hotel with a British name and aesthetic. The family accepted this advice, and to this day Claridges has a loyal following—many of them fussy, long-term visitors who appreciate the old-fashioned charm. The hotel also has a superior location, not far from the sights and the embassies but still in a quiet, leafy neighborhood; it's perhaps the only hotel in Delhi from which you can take a relaxing stroll around the block. The airy lobby is unique: One side is Victorian, while the other depicts an Indian courtyard. The carpeted bedrooms have Victorian furnishings. While the standard rooms are average in size, the "Regal" rooms are quite large, worth the extra money. The most popular rooms, slightly more expensive still, are on the third floor and have balconies overlooking the pool. ✉ *12 Aurangzeb Rd., New Delhi 110011,* ☎ *11/301–0211,* FAX *11/301–0625. 162 rooms, 11 suites. 4 restaurants, bar, pool, beauty salon, barber shop, health club, business services, travel services. AE, DC, MC, V.*

$$–$$$ **Radisson.** While the brand-new Radisson is some distance from the center of town (22 km/13 mi; about a 25-minute, Rs.-250 taxi ride), it suits short-term visitors, especially when you consider that most sights and restaurants are in South Delhi. The rooms are large, each with a foyer, king-size bed, spacious sitting area, and desk. The free-form pool in back is also large and luscious, complete with a gazebo bar and pool chairs. Like many of Delhi's major hotels, the Radisson suffers from an unfortunate setting: it's inches from the Delhi-Jaipur Highway. The hotel has addressed this by installing double-paned windows, but these don't improve the view. Free in-house movies attempt to distract you from your inability to take a peaceful evening walk. ✉ *National Hwy. 8, New Delhi 110037,* ☎ *11/612–9191,* FAX *11/612–9090. 256 rooms, 27 suites. 3 restaurants, 2 bars, pool, beauty salon, health club, squash, business services, travel services. AE, DC, MC, V.*

$$ ★ **Ambassador.** This comfortable, spacious hotel is now part of the Taj Group. Within easy walking distance of Lodi Gardens and Khan Market, the Ambassador is pleasingly quiet, set back from the road behind a private garden. The entrance brings you into an enclosed terrace and an adjoining lobby with marble and banquettes. The huge guest rooms have wall-to-wall carpeting and teak furnishings that lack elegance but are fine for the price. The bathrooms have modern fixtures and new tiles. All rooms have balconies; aim for one overlooking the front garden. ✉ *Sujan Singh Park, Cornwallis Rd., New Delhi 110003,* ☎ *11/463–2600,* FAX *11/463–2252. 88 rooms, 12 suites. 4 restaurants, bar, baby-sitting, business services. AE, DC, MC, V.*

$$ **Hans Plaza.** Delhi is crying out for more mid-priced hotels like this one near Connaught Place. From the outside, it looks like an office building, but the lobby is whistle-clean and cozy, with pleasant sitting areas and Victorian-style furnishings. The quietest and most spacious rooms overlook Barakhamba Road. All rooms have Western furnishings, but the deluxe rooms have bathtubs and dhurries on gleaming granite floors while lower-priced rooms have (less attractive) wall-to-wall carpeting and showers. The 21st-floor Club Cafe is inexpensive and has fabulous views; come for a buffet lunch or alfresco breakfast. ✉ *15 Barakhamba Rd., Connaught Pl., New Delhi, 110001,* ☎ *11/331–6860,* FAX *11/331–4830. 70 rooms, 3 suites. Restaurant, business services, travel services. AE, DC, MC, V.*

$$$ ★ **Imperial.** Built in 1933, this Delhi landmark near Connaught Place is gorgeous after its recent facelift. The entire place speaks of elegance. The driveway, bordered by palm trees, leads to a portico entranceway, and the lobby and other public spaces lift the eye from inlaid marble floors to three-story atriums. Water tinkles from Italian fountains as you examine British Raj lithographs and Italian bronze sculptures. The

Superior Deluxe rooms and executive suites are the best buys, spacious and sumptuous. Standard rooms are less expensive, but they're drab in comparison. ✉ *Jan Path, New Delhi 110001,* ☎ *11/334–1234,* FAX *11/334–2255. 245 rooms, 18 suites. 4 restaurants, 2 bars, pool, beauty salon, business services, travel services. AE, DC, MC, V.*

$–$$ 🏨 **Oberoi Maidens.** Unbeknownst to most travelers, this hotel has low rates, large rooms, and a unique location. Opened in 1907, before New Delhi was even a gleam in the Viceroy's eye, it's the oldest hotel in the city. The classic Raj building, with columns, high-arched windows, and deep verandas, shines white, and grand old trees and green lawns add to the sense of history. Named after its original owner, the Maidens is in North Delhi (near Old Delhi), so it's best suited for those doing business on that side of town or planning to move on to the Himalayas. Thanks to the building's age, the rooms are huge (if a bit dark and viewless); the Superior rooms are really suites, and in the low season (summer), they're priced at less than U.S. $100. The Curzon Room, the hotel's elegant Continental/Indian restaurant, is worth checking out if you're on this side of town. ✉ *7 Sham Nath Marg, Delhi 110054,* ☎ *11/291–4841,* FAX *11/398–0771. 53 rooms, 1 suite. 2 restaurants, bar, pool, 2 tennis courts. AE, DC, MC, V.*

$ ★ 🏨 **Jukaso Inn.** This large guest house has a shiny, white marble lobby and clean—albeit dark and drab—guest rooms. The bathrooms, smelling faintly of mothballs, have simple fixtures and no bathtubs. Meals are conveniently served in the ad hoc courtyard. ✉ *50 Sunder Nagar, New Delhi 110003,* ☎ *11/469–0754,* FAX *11/469–4402. 49 rooms, 2 suites. Restaurant AE, DC, MC, V.*

$ 🏨 **Maharani Guest House.** A small guest house in the same quiet neighborhood as the Jukaso Inn, the Maharani retains an essence of mothballs. It has a pleasant front lawn and upper-floor terrace. The lackluster rooms are small, as are many of the beds; if you're heavy or tall, request a room with a full-size bed. There is no restaurant, but there is a small room-service menu. ✉ *3 Sunder Nagar, New Delhi 110003,* ☎ *11/469–3128,* FAX *11/462–4562. 24 rooms. AE, DC, MC, V.*

$ 🏨 **YMCA Tourist Hostel.** Just south of the Park Hotel, about a 10-minute walk from Connaught Place, the YMCA has some singles and twin-bed doubles with private bathrooms (showers only) and air-conditioning. The rooms are small, uncarpeted, and endowed with modest furnishings that probably date from the hostel's construction in the late 1960s. But the linens are clean, hot water runs from the taps, and you can laze around on your own private balcony. Upper-floor rooms facing the back are the quietest. Other rooms in the hostel have shared bathrooms (also with showers) and overhead fans instead of air-conditioning. ✉ *Jai Singh Rd., New Delhi 110001,* ☎ *11/336–1915,* FAX *11/374–6032. 123 rooms (14 with attached bath), 1 suite. Restaurant, pool, business services, travel services. AE, DC, MC, V.*

NIGHTLIFE AND THE ARTS

The Arts

Respected Indian dancers and musicians perform in the capital often, and Indian films and slightly dated Western films are shown in Delhi's many theaters. The problem is that it's hard to find out what's going on; most events are publicized only a few days in advance. The most reliable sources are the monthly magazine *First City,* the weekly *Delhi Diary,* or the daily newspapers, especially *The Asian Age.* Your hotel may also have the scoop.

Art Galleries

While many of Delhi's arts are subsidized by the government, the visual arts—especially painting—have a life of their own. Private galleries selling works by contemporary Indian painters have proliferated in the last decade. Some of the work blending traditional Indian with modern Western styles is excellent and affordable. Galleries come and go quickly, but they generally cluster in several South Delhi neighborhoods, including Sunder Nager, Defence Colony, New Friends Colony, and Greater Kailash. Check the *Delhi Diary* for current listings.

Hauz Khas has three small galleries grouped together at 11, 12, and 14 Hauz Khas Village. The largest, **Delhi Art Gallery** (☎ 11/696–7619) has works by old masters and contemporary artists. **Image India** (☎ 11/652–4159) and **The Village Gallery** (☎ 11/695–3860) feature contemporary artists only. All are open from 10:30 AM until 7 PM, and all take credit cards.

Connaught Place is not noted for its galleries, but **Art Today** (✉ A-1 Hamilton House, Connaught Pl., ☎ 11/332–0689) has been around for a long time and often has good shows; it's open Monday through Saturday from 11 to 7. Several government institutions in the Connaught Place area also display modern Indian art. Stop in at **Lalit Kala Akademi** (✉ Rabindra Bhavan, ☎ 11/338–7243) or **Art Heritage** (✉ Triveni Kal Sangam, 205 Tansen Marg, ☎ 11/371–9470).

Music and Dance

Classical Indian recitals and dance performances tend to be stilted affairs in Delhi; polite applause often substitutes for the passionate outbursts you hear in such soulful cities as Varanasi. Still, great musicians and dancers are always passing through, and tickets are readily available and relatively cheap. The **Indian Habitat Centre** (✉ Lodi Rd., ☎ 11/469–1920) is the hot new venue for dance and music. More established performance spaces include the **Indian International Centre** (✉ 40 Lodi Estate, ☎ 11/461–9431), the **Kamani Auditorium** (✉ Copernicus Marg, ☎ 11/338–8040), and the **Triveni Chamber Theatre** (✉ 205 Tansen Marg, ☎ 11/371–9470). Check the local listings.

Theater

India has an ancient dramatic tradition. *Nautanki* plays, with their mixture of drama, comedy, and song, are still held in the surrounding villages. Delhi itself has an active theater scene, and many shows are locally written, produced, and acted. Oddly, most run only for one weekend and don't travel afterward, so they can seem a bit unpolished even when they're fundamentally good. In addition to the following venues, check those under Music and Dance (☞ *above*) and consult local listings. **FICCI Auditorium** (✉ Tansen Marg, ☎ 11/335–7369). **Sri Fort Auditorium** (✉ Asiad Village, ☎ 11/649–3370). **Sri Ram Centre** (✉ Mandi House, Safdar Hashmi Marg, ☎ 11/371–4307).

Nightlife

Delhi is not much of a party town. A traditional social evening involves having a drink at home with friends, enjoying a late dinner, and turning in. Note that women in Delhi, whether alone or in groups, do not go out unaccompanied at night.

Discos

Clubs have been dying a slow death in Delhi over the last several years (it's hard to make money on such limited opening hours), but there are still a few hip places to literally dance the night away. Wherever you go, know the facts of nightlife in Delhi. First, things don't get hopping until almost midnight, but liquor laws forbid the sale of alcohol after that time. Many solve this problem by getting blasted before they come, not always a pretty sight. Second, stag males are not welcome at most discos.

The Mirage (✉ Surya Hotel, New Friends Colony, ☎ 11/683–5070) is a hike from the center of town, but it's currently Delhi's most popular nightclub. If you have access to a car for the whole evening, head out to **The Fireball** (✉ 32nd Mile Stone, National Hwy. 8, ☎ 91/325554 or 91/322528), 19 mi (32 km) outside Delhi. This place was built just a few feet across the Delhi-Haryana state border to take advantage of looser liquor laws. **CJ's** (✉ Le Meridien Hotel, Janpath, ☎ 11/371–0101) is not the hippest place in town, but it's reasonably convenient. **Ghungroo** (✉ Welcomgroup Maurya Sheraton Hotel, ☎ 11/611–2233) is also convenient but is largely restricted to hotel guests.

Hotel Bars and Lounges

India does not traditionally have a bar culture. When Indian men drink (women generally don't), they do it discreetly, at home with their friends or at private parties. All the major hotels have bars, but most are better suited for a comfortable nap than a night of camaraderie. Richly decorated, often aiming for either a British Raj or a plush Continental look, these bars are generally open from 11 to 11 and closed on the 1st and 7th days of each month and national holidays. If you tend toward serious drinking, bring a credit card—these are pricey places.

The **Polo Lounge** (✉ Hyatt Regency, Bhikaiji Cama Pl., Ring Rd.) may be the most hopping hotel bar in Delhi. Paneled in wood, it has a leather sofa, a library with newspapers and an odd selection of books, sports on a cable TV, and a curved bar. **The Jazz Bar** (✉ Welcomegroup Maurya Sheraton Hotel, Diplomatic Enclave) is a classy place to hear jazz tunes sung with a five-piece band nightly from 9 to midnight. If you want to puff on a Cubano, try the austere **Club Bar** (✉ The Oberoi, Dr. Zakir Hussain Rd.). A pianist plays every night but Tuesday for those occupying discreetly positioned clusters of sofas and chairs in an elegant room. In the **Viceroy** (✉ Claridges, 12 Aurangzeb Rd.), a brass cannon and old rifles combine with dark Victorian antiques to create a manly ambience, and a pianist plays quietly every night except Tuesday, adding to the restful mood. **The Patiala Peg** (✉ Hotel Imperial, Jan Path) is an up-and-coming place for the younger set.

Pubs

Delhi's major hotels are slowly replacing their dance bars with what they call pubs—bizarre amalgams of English pubs and American sports bars, with a bit of dancing thrown in. These places tend to get going early in the evening, with happy-hour specials and menus featuring some sort of bar food. By far the trendiest pub is **Djinns** (✉ Hyatt Regency, Bhikaiji Cama Pl., ☎ 11/679–1212). You enter what looks like the set for a *Cheers* episode, complete with hardwood floors and brass fittings. Waiters in French café aprons serve up tasty Middle Eastern food, and a Caribbean band entertains. At press time this place was ragingly popular, and it was not always easy to get in; hotel guests have priority. Hotel pubs in the center of Delhi include the **Pegasus Bar** (✉ Nirula's Hotel, L-Block, Connaught Circus, ☎ 11/332–2419) and **Someplace Else** (✉ The Park, 15 Parliament St., ☎ 11/373–3737), the latter of which looks more like a disco. Also in the Park Hotel, the restaurant **Las Meninas** (☞ Dining, *above*) opens at 6 PM for delicious tapas, reasonably priced Spanish wines, and beer, and on Friday and Saturday nights Bobby Cash, a local celebrity, plays flamenco guitar mixed with country-western tunes. For a straightforward sports bar, complete with punching bags and bicycles hanging from the ceiling, head out to the **Sports Bar** (✉ Radisson Hotel, National Hwy. 8, ☎ 11/612–9191), near the airport.

Outside the hotels, **Rodeo** (✉ 12A Connaught Pl., ☏ 11/371–3780), a Mexican restaurant in the heart of town, has a guitarist in its bar nightly and karaoke on Tuesday. Also in Connaught Place is **Blues** (✉ Outer Circle, Connaught Pl.), currently quite popular. **TGIF** (✉ 62 Basant Lok, ☏ 11/614–0761) has garish American decor and four or five TV sets visible from any position. If you must go, take advantage of the drink specials, not the food. If you want to bowl a few frames, have your drink at **Essex Farms** (✉ 4 Aurobindo Marg, ☏ 11/686–2145).

SPORTS AND OUTDOOR ACTIVITIES

Participant Sports

Golf

Play golf against a backdrop of ancient monuments at the 27-hole **Delhi Golf Club** (✉ Dr. Zakir Hussain Rd., ☏ 11/436–2768 or 11/436–2235). Contact the club for reservations and the cost to play. Delhi's newest golf destination, **Classics,** is an hour's drive away in Haryana State (☏ 11/614–7507). This 27-hole, Jack Nicholas–designed course is great, even by international standards. You pay the price though—about U.S. $70 for 18 holes. Closer in but more difficult to get on is the **Army Golf Club** (✉ Delhi Cantonment, ☏ 11/569–1972).

Swimming

City pools should be avoided, as there's no way to judge the water quality. The top hotels have excellent pools, some open to outsiders for a fee.

Tennis

If your hotel doesn't have a tennis court, reserve one at the **Delhi Lawn Tennis Association** (✉ Africa Ave., ☏ 11/619–3955).

Yoga

The **Sivananda Yoga Vedanta Nataraja Center** (✉ 52 Community Center, east of Kailash, ☏ 11/648–0869) holds classes daily.

Spectator Sports

Check the newspaper or your hotel for **cricket** and **soccer** matches. Rivalries are intense, so these games are popular events; see if your hotel can get you tickets. Delhi's polo games (October–March) are another crowd-pleaser—contact the **Polo Club** (✉ 61 Cavalry Cariappa Marg, Delhi Cantonment, ☏ 11/569–9777).

SHOPPING

Delhi is the marketplace for all of India, and bargaining is the rule everywhere except fixed-price shops. Most shops are open six days a week; the day a shop is closed is determined by its location. Ask around—every taxi driver knows which markets are closed on a given day.

India has one of the world's foremost Oriental-rug industries, and there are carpet vendors all over Delhi. Unfortunately, carpet sellers are a notoriously dishonest crowd. In addition to being obnoxiously pushy, they are likely to sell you inauthentic merchandise at colossally inflated prices and then deny it later. The best exception to this rule is Jasim Jan (☞ Janson's Carpets *in* South Delhi, *below*).

Old Delhi

Chandni Chowk and the bazaar inside **Lal Qila** are good areas to hunt for bargains. On the streets behind the **Jama Masjid,** many shops sell metalware curios and old utensils, and one street specializes in paper and stationery, some of it handmade and hand-printed. On **Dariba Kalan,** stalls are filled with silver and gold jewelry. Except for the Lal Qila bazaar, most businesses in Old Delhi shut down on Sunday.

The small **Gems 'n' Jewels** (⊠ No. 31, Lal Qila, ☎ 11/327–0524) has good miniature paintings and silver jewelry. **Multan Enamel Mart Jewellers** (⊠ No. 246-247, Dariba Kalan, ☎ 11/325–5877) has fine old and new silver jewelry sold by weight with an add-on charge for labor. **Ram Chandra Krishan Chandra's** (Gali Parante Wali, ☎ 11/327–7869) is one of Delhi's oldest fabric shops; it has three floors of fine silks and handloomed fabrics from all over India. **Shivam Zari Palace** (2178 Kinari Bazaar, ☎ 11/327–1464) offers inexpensive Hindu wedding paraphernalia—turbans, fabric covered boxes, *torans* (auspicious door hangings), and tiny brass gods that you can dress as you like. **Singh Copper & Brass Palace** (⊠ 1167 Chah Rahat Gali, near Jama Masjid, ☎ 11/326–6717) has an entire building filled with old and new Indian brass, copper, and wood handicrafts. **Tula Ram** (⊠ No. 36, Lal Qila, ☎ 11/326–9937) sells traditional Indian handicrafts, especially wooden objects, tribal work, and brass items.

Around Connaught Place

This area, closed on Sunday, is the former commercial district of the British Raj. Beneath the green park at the center of Connaught Place is **Palika Bazaar,** an air-conditioned underground emporium with the ambience of a Times Square subway station. Avoid it: It's a favorite haunt of pickpockets and many shopkeepers are dishonest. Delhi's fixed-price **government emporia** are near Connaught Place and offer good values for visitors with limited time. There are more than 20 such emporia in Delhi; each state operates a store featuring its own native crafts and other products. The **State Emporia** (⊠ Baba Kharak Singh Marg) are three blocks of state-run shops with a wonderful selection of regional items. The Kashmir store specializes in carpets. The government-run **Central Cottage Industries Emporium** (⊠ Jawahar Vyapar Bhavan, Jan Path, opposite Imperial Hotel, ☎ 11/332–6790), housed in a spacious multistory building, has products from the entire country.

Banaras House (⊠ N-13 Connaught Pl., opposite Scindia House, ☎ 11/331–4751) sells sublime silks from all over India. **Natesans** (⊠ GF-2, Suryakiran Bldg., opposite *Hindustan Times* Bldg., Kasturba Gandhi Marg, ☎ 11/331–2603), with branches throughout India, sells magnificent curios and artifacts.

Diplomatic Enclave

The **Santushti Shopping Complex,** open every day but Monday, is a collection of upscale arty boutiques scattered around a small garden across the street from the Hotel Samrat. Prices are high, but this is a lovely place to stroll and browse. For funky printed apparel with a traditional Indian flair, try **Anokhi** (☎ 11/688–3076). **Tulsi** (☎ 11/687–0339) sells supple garments of hand-woven silk, linen, and cotton. Other shops in the complex sell jewelry, leather, pottery, and home furnishings. For a break, stop into **Basil and Thyme** (☞ Dining, *above*) for lunch or a snack; it's open 10 to 6 every day but Sunday.

Near Lodi Gardens

Sunder Nagar Market, a neighborhood shopping district near the Oberoi hotel and Delhi Zoo, specializes in jewelry, curios, artifacts, and artwork. It's closed Sunday.

Bharany's (✉ 14 Sunder Nagar, ☎ 11/461–8528) specializes in traditional Indian jewelry, exquisite old shawls, and textiles from all over India. **Padma Gems** (✉ 9-A Sunder Nagar, ☎ 11/461–1513) has lovely contemporary and antique gold jewelry and a good variety of semi-precious and precious stones. Designs can be made to order in four to five days. **Kumar Gallery** (✉ 11 Sunder Nagar, ☎ 11/461–1113) specializes in original tribal statues, old dhurries, Tibetan carpets and furniture, miniatures, temple art, and contemporary paintings by India's finest artists. The **Mittal Tea House** (✉ 12 Sunder Nagar, ☎ 11/461–0667) sells Indian teas, herbs, and spices. **Natesan's** (✉ 13 Sunder Nagar, ☎ 11/464–9320)sells art and antiques. **The Studio** (✉ 4 Sunder Nagar, ☎ 11/461–9360) has good contemporary silver jewelry, tribal jewelry, and some gold items.

South Delhi

INA Market and Dilli Haat (✉ Aurobindo Marg) are two colorful stops. INA Market is the place to experience a Delhi "wet market." Fruits and vegetables are sold in front, while the open-air butcher shops with chicken, fish, and mutton are on a slushy lane in the back. Wander around to see merchants devoted to spices, nuts, or dried fruits. The market is closed on Monday. Once you're overwhelmed, cross the street and enter Dilli Haat (☎ 11/611–9055), a government-run food and crafts bazaar open daily. More than 60 stalls sell handmade products from all over India, and 25 serve regional food. Open-air music and dance occasionally accompany the proceedings in mid-afternoon or evening. Dilli Haat charges an admission fee of Rs. 5.

In **Hauz Khas Village** (✉ Near Deer Park, 7 km/4 mi south of Connaught Pl.), boutiques and shops set in converted old homes up and down narrow alleys sell handicrafts, curios, old carpets and kilims, and designer clothing (both Indian and Western). Most stores are open Monday through Saturday from 10:30 to 7.

Proprietor Jasim Jan of **Janson's Carpets** (✉ A/375 Sarita Vihar, ☎ 11/694–2953 or –6325, cell phone 9811/129095) delivers exactly what he describes—carpets old and new, silk and wool, Persian and tribal—and at fair (not cheap) prices. Jan hawks his wares at trade fairs all over Delhi, often to the rich and famous.

Qutab Colonnade (✉ H 5/6 Mehrauli Rd., ☎ 11/696–7537), a newly restored haveli, houses a collection of shops that sell artifacts and attractive Indian clothing. A short walk from Qutab Minar, the complex is closed on Sunday. **Tandon's** (✉ 4 Aurobindo Pl., opposite Green Park Church, Hauz Khas, ☎ 11/696–6552) offers high-quality *chicken* (hand embroidery) on fine linen and traditional clothing. It's closed Tuesday. **Wild Orchid** (✉ 12 Siri Fort Rd., ☎ 11/644–9347; ✉ M-37, Main Market, Greater Kalash I, ☎ 11/643–2668) sells designer Indian clothing in exquisite hand-loomed cotton and silk and a good selection of Western wear for women. The family that runs **Novel Exports** (✉ D-23, Jangpura Extension, ☎ 11/431–2248) is from Kashmir, and they have absolutely stunning Kashmiri carpets as well as shawls, jewelry, and papier mâché items.

Sarojini Nagar Market and **Lajpat Nagar Market** are two very lively markets where middle-class locals shop. These are good places just to stroll around and take in the chaos, as they have pedestrian-only zones—a rarity in India. Shopkeepers boisterously hawk their wares while coolies unload goods from auto- and cycle-rickshaws, shoppers scurry about, and diners pause over plates of greasy street food. The back streets of Sarojini are famous for selling rejected export apparel at bargain prices. Both markets are open from about 10:30 AM to 7 PM and closed Monday.

DELHI A TO Z

Arriving and Departing

By Plane

International flights use **Indira Gandhi International Airport,** about 23 km (14 mi) southwest of Connaught Place. Domestic flights use **Palam Airport** (also called the "national" or "domestic" airport), which is near the international airport. Palam has two terminals: the Airbus Terminal for Indian Airlines airbuses serving Bangalore, Bombay, Calcutta, Hyderabad, and Madras; and the Boeing Terminal for other Indian Airlines flights and private domestic carriers. Most taxi drivers have no idea which terminals apply to which flights, so when you purchase or reconfirm any domestic ticket, find out which terminal to use. At Boeing Terminal, use the extreme right-hand entrance.

Major international carriers that use Indira Gandhi International Airport include **Air Canada** (☎ 11/372–0014), **Air France** (☎ 11/373–8004), **Air India** (☎ 11/373–1225), **Alitalia** (☎ 11/372–1006), **British Airways** (☎ 11/332–7428), **Cathay Pacific** (☎ 11/332–3332), **Gulf Air** (☎ 11/332–4293), **Japan Airlines** (☎ 11/332–4922), **KLM** (☎ 11/335–7747), **Kuwait Airways** (☎ 11/335–4373), **Lufthansa** (☎ 11/332–3310), **Malaysian Airlines** (☎ 11/332–4308), **Qantas** (☎ 11/332–9027), **SAS** (☎ 11/335–2299), **Singapore Airlines** (☎ 11/332–6373), **Swissair** (☎ 11/332–5511), **Thai Airlines** (☎ 11/623–9133), and **United Airlines** (☎ 11/371–5550).

The Indian government's open-sky policy for private domestic airlines keeps changing, so routes and schedules for domestic flights are often unsettled. **Indian Airlines** (☎ 11/462–0566 or 11/331–0517) is the national carrier; the top private carriers are **Jet Airways** (☎ 11/651–7443 or 11/685–3700) and **Sahara Airlines** (☎ 11/332–0013).

BETWEEN THE AIRPORT AND THE CITY

The trip between Delhi's airports and Delhi itself should take about 30 minutes if you arrive before 9 AM or after 8 PM. At other times, traffic can increase the time to an hour. All hotels provide airport transfers for Rs. 500 to Rs. 1,000, depending on their locations, and if you're staying in a suite on an executive floor, the transfer is on the house.

By Taxi: Taking a cab is the most convenient way to get to your hotel. Because taxi drivers are famous for rigging their meters and overcharging, use the prepaid taxi service offered at both airports—you can arrange a cab at designated counters outside the baggage-claim area and inside the arrival terminal. Unfortunately, hucksters have set up similar services, so make sure the counter is operated by the Delhi Traffic Police. Your destination and amount of luggage determine the rate, which you pay in advance at the counter. Take the receipt, go to a second prepaid taxi booth outside the terminal, and you'll be assigned a taxi. When you leave the terminal, drivers and touts will converge on you and offer assistance. Avoid them (don't be afraid to be aggressive) and wheel your own baggage cart, if you have one, to the designated taxi, which is normally waiting in a line near the terminal exit. Taxis are black with yellow tops. Once you get into the taxi, don't give the driver the payment slip until you reach your destination. If the driver demands more rupees, complain to the hotel doorman. A taxi from the international airport to the city center should cost Rs. 250 to Rs. 300; from the domestic airport, Rs. 200 to Rs. 250.

Be aware, too, that touts at the airports, even at hotel-reservation counters, may try to trick you into booking a hotel room by claiming that your prior reservation is invalid. Ignore them. If you do need a room, go to the Government of India Tourist Office counter.

By Limousine: There are no Western-style limousines in India. If you want a Mercedes-Benz to bring you to and from the airport, make arrangements with your hotel or travel agency. This can cost as much as Rs. 3,000 each way.

By Train

The **Delhi Railway Station** (commonly called the Old Delhi Railway Station) is about 7 km (4½ mi) north of Connaught Place. The **New Delhi Railway Station** is about 1 km (½ mi) north of Connaught Place. Most trains leave from New Delhi, but check before you set off. For tickets and information, you can save time and energy by using a travel agent (☞ *below*); otherwise, contact the **International Tourist Bureau** (✉ New Delhi Railway Station, 1st floor, ☏ 11/373–4164), open Monday through Saturday 8 to 5. At this window (for foreigners with tourist visas only), you must purchase tickets in foreign currency, usually dollars or pounds sterling, unless you have a valid encashment slip. If you don't have an encashment slip, you can purchase a ticket in rupees at the general ticket counter, open daily 9:30 to 8 at the same location, but this can be a long and complicated process. Before you board any train, you must have a confirmed ticket and a reservation, including a reservation for your sleeping berth if you're traveling overnight (☞ Rail Travel *in* Smart Travel Tips). If hotel touts approach you at either rail station to offer you a room or claim that your room reservation is bogus, ignore them.

Getting Around

Only people with nerves of steel should drive in and around Delhi. Traffic rules exist, but few drivers observe them, and even fewer police officers enforce them. Every major thoroughfare is packed from 9 AM to 7 PM with bullock carts, auto-rickshaws, overcrowded buses and trucks, bicycles and motorcycles, cows, horses, goats, and dogs. Major highways (oversize two-lane roads) from Jaipur, Agra, and northern Uttar Pradesh are famous for accidents, with overturned trucks and demolished cars as common as roadside restaurants. Even new roads can develop craters overnight, and badly designed culverts can lead to flooding during the monsoon season.

Except in the Old Delhi's Chandni Chowk, 6 km (4 mi) north of Connaught Place, the best way to travel around Delhi is by taxi or hired car with driver. To visit Chandni Chowk, take an auto- or cycle-rickshaw to Lal Qila, then walk or take a cycle-rickshaw through the market's maze of narrow lanes.

By Auto-Rickshaw

While they're a novelty to ride in once or twice, auto-rickshaws are not a safe, speedy, pleasant, or cheap way to get around Delhi. Poorly maintained, and seldom equipped with rear-view mirrors, they also tend to be driven in a maniacal fashion. The meter rate is not worth documenting, as most rickshaw-wallahs refuse to use it, preferring to quote fares 10 times higher than they should be. Those who do use their meters rig them to run faster than the rickshaw. Take a taxi and arrive safely, without the hassle.

By Cycle-Rickshaw

These have all but disappeared from most Delhi streets. If you do use a cycle-rickshaw (perhaps for a tour of Old Delhi), ask a local merchant to help you negotiate the fare, and remember that these guys pedal hard for a living.

By Hired Car with Driver

Let an experienced driver chauffeur you around Delhi and to nearby destinations. Expect to pay about Rs. 400 for four hours or 40 km (25 mi) and about Rs. 600 for eight hours or 80 km (50 mi) for sightseeing in an Ambassador without air-conditioning, the least expensive vehicle. Larger cars or those with air-conditioning cost more. Ask in advance about the cost for extra mileage or hours. If you're staying in an upscale hotel, you can often pay less if you arrange for a car from an outside travel agent. Stick with a government-recognized tour operator (☞ Travel Agencies, *below*).

By Taxi

Like rickshaw-wallahs, many cabbies rig their meters or refuse to use them, but here the situation is nowhere near as bad. At press time, the tariff (fare) was three times the meter (the meters are old), plus Rs. 3.50, with a 25% surcharge between 10 PM and 5 AM. If the tariff is revised again, drivers should carry a fare chart; ask to see it before you pay. If you don't have exact change, don't expect anything back; taxi drivers will tell you "No change" while small bills hang out of their breast pockets. Taxis are available at every hotel, at taxi stands in shopping areas, and in every neighborhood.

Contacts and Resources

Currency Exchange

Most Western-style hotels have foreign-exchange facilities for their guests and will cash traveler's checks with twice the speed and half the hassle of banks. **American Express** (✉ Wenger House, A-Block, Connaught Pl., ☎ 11/332–4149 or 11/332–4119), open Monday through Saturday 9:30 to 5:30, will cash its own traveler's checks. **Thomas Cook** (✉ Hotel Imperial, Jan Path, ☎ 11/336–8060 and International Trade Tower, 717–718 Nehru Pl., 7th floor, ☎ 11/646–7484) will cash Thomas Cook traveler's checks. The location in the Imperial Hotel is open Monday through Saturday 9:30 to 8; the branch at Nehru Place is open Monday through Saturday 9:30 to 6. The **Central Bank of India** (✉ Ashok Hotel, Chanakyapuri, ☎ 11/611–0101 ext. 2584) is open 24 hours daily, except national holidays. You can also cash traveler's checks at the **Bank of America** (✉ 15 Hansaslaya, 4 Barakhamba Rd., ☎ 11/372–2332), open weekdays 10 to 2 and Saturday 10 to noon, but only Visa traveler's checks issues by Interpayment Services are cashed. **Citibank** (✉ Jeewan Bharati Bldg., ☎ 11/371–4211) is open from 9:30 to 7 weekdays and 9:30 to 2 on Saturday.

Embassies

☞ Smart Travel Tips.

Emergencies and Late-Night Pharmacies

In any emergency, contact your embassy or the **East-West Medical Center** (☞ Emergencies *in* Smart Travel Tips). For significant non-emergency situations there are better private hospitals, such as **Privat Hospital** (DLF Enclave II, Mehraul Rd., Gurgaon, ☎ 91/353793), which is some distance out of town. Whatever happens, *do not* go to a government hospital. For dental problems contact U.S.-trained **Dr. Siddartha Mehta** (✉ 41 Khan Market, ☎ 11/461–5914), who looks after many in Delhi's expatriate community. Most hotels also have house physicians and dentists on call.

Most hotels have chemists (pharmacies) that stay open daily until about 9 PM. The chemist in **Super Bazaar** on Connaught Place is open 24 hours.

English-Language Bookstores

Delhi has great book bargains, including lower-priced Indian editions of new titles published abroad. Although better hotels have small bookshops, the best selections are at **Book Worm** (✉ B-29 Connaught Pl.), **New Book Depot** (✉ B-18 Connaught Pl.), **Oxford Book and Stationery** (✉ Scindia House, Connaught Pl.), and **Piccadilly Book Stall** (✉ Shop 64, Shankar Market, off Connaught Pl.). These stores are open Monday through Saturday 10 to 7. Oxford takes a lunch break from 1:30 to 2:30. Vendors on **Parliament Street** near Connaught Place also have stacks of books with negotiable prices. **Khan Market** has four excellent bookstores that are open Monday through Saturday 10 to 7. **The Bookshop** (✉ 14A Khan Market) has an excellent selection of fiction and non-fiction and a well-informed staff.

Post Offices

One centrally located post office is near American Express on Connaught Place. The Eastern Court Post Office on Jan Path is also convenient. Hotels have mailing facilities, and some sell stamps; but if you really want your postcards to reach their destinations, go to a post office and have them postmarked in front of you to make sure the stamp doesn't mysteriously disappear from the card en route.

Travel Agencies

Travel agencies are apt to offer varying rates for cars and drivers, tours, excursions, and even hotel rooms. Shop around and ask what the price includes. Use only government-recognized tour operators or travel agents—ask to see their license. **American Express** (✉ Wenger House, A-Block, Connaught Pl., ☎ 11/332–4149 or 11/332–4119) is open Monday through Saturday 9:30 to 6:30. **Ashok Travel and Tours** (✉ New Delhi House, 3rd floor, 27 Barakhamba Rd., ☎ 11/331–3233), open Monday through Saturday 10 to 5:30, has desks open into the evening at all Ashok hotels. The **Great India Tour Company** (✉ G-44 Triveni Community Centre, Sheikh Sarai, Phase I, ☎ 11/628–6804) not only helps you with Delhi but has great contacts if you're heading to South India. **Outbound Travels** (✉ 115 Arjun Nagar, opposite B-6/88 Safdarjung Enclave, ☎ 11/616–9285, 11/610–3902 or 11/621–5370 after hours) has a basement location. **RBS Travels** (✉ Shop G, Connaught Palace Hotel, 37 Shaheed Bhagat Singh Marg, ☎ 11/373–3950, and ✉ 5/47 W.E.A., Saraswati Marg, Karol Bagh, ☎ 11/576–1441; ☎ 11/461–0596 after hours), which offers extremely competitive rates, is open daily 9 to 8:30. **Thomas Cook** (✉ Hotel Imperial, Jan Path, ☎ 11/336–8060) is open Monday through Saturday 9:30 to 8.

Visitor Information

The **Government of India Tourist Office** (✉ 88 Jan Path, ☎ 11/332–0005) is open weekdays 9 to 6 and Saturday 9 to 2. Its airport counters are open for major flight arrivals, and its train-station counters are open 24 hours. Upholding an old tradition, employees at the **Delhi Tourism and Transportation Development Corporation** are poorly informed; don't waste your time.

4 NORTH CENTRAL INDIA

Anchored by Agra, Khajuraho, and Varanasi, this section of the traveler's trail heads southeast of Delhi into the state of Uttar Pradesh, detouring into Madhya Pradesh and Bihar. The history of these lands is ancient and vast, their religions spanning Hinduism, Islam, Buddhism, and even, in Lucknow, Christianity. The spectacular architecture includes Agra's incomparable Taj Mahal and Khajuraho's erotic Hindu temples. Varanasi, the holiest city in Hinduism, draws a constant stream of pilgrims to bathe in the Ganges River.

By Andy McCord, Smita Patel, and Vikram Singh

CENTERED ON THE STATE OF UTTAR PRADESH, the Hindi heartland has long held the balance of power in North India, from the ancient Gupta kingdoms through the Moguls and the British Raj to the present day. Together, Uttar Pradesh, Madhya Pradesh, and Bihar send far more representatives to Parliament than any other linguistic region in India. Sometimes disparaged as the Cow Belt, North Central India has often been slow to advance economically, but it remains a vital part of India's heritage and contemporary culture.

Agra was a seat of Mogul power. Dominated by Muslim influences in culture, art, architecture, and cuisine, the city is a testament to the beauty and grandeur of Mogul aesthetics—most notably in the form of the Taj Mahal, but also in the forms of some exquisite smaller Muslim tombs and monuments. Today Agra is dusty and crowded, the spectacular Taj Mahal is being damaged by air pollution, and the nearby Mogul ghost town of Fatehpur Sikri is being choked by commercial encroachments. Still, the courts have stepped in with far-reaching orders that should go a long way toward cleaning up the urban environment, including the closure of several factories near the Taj itself.

Southeast of Agra, in the northern part of Madhya Pradesh, the sleepy village of Khajuraho predates the Moguls: It was founded at the end of the classical age of Hindu civilization. Khajuraho's stunning temples celebrate an eroticized Hinduism that flourished when Hindu kings adopted Tantric religion. Recent excavations have also begun to uncover a previously unknown complex of Buddhist temples here.

In many ways, Varanasi (or Banaras, as it's commonly called), in southwestern Uttar Pradesh, is the antithesis of Khajuraho. The holiest city in Hinduism and one of the oldest continuously inhabited cities in the world, Varanasi is crowded, filled with pilgrims, hospice patients, ascetics, priests, Hindu pundits, and worldly citizens of many religions. Unlike those in Khajuraho, Varanasi's temples are squeezed into the city itself, and the *ghats* (wide stone stairways leading down to the Ganges) are both key religious sites and secular promenades.

The popular Agra–Khajuraho–Varanasi route has plenty of worthwhile tentacles. The emperor Akbar's deserted city at Fatehpur Sikri is just outside Agra, and a short drive from here across the Rajasthan border is the Keoladeo National Park in Bharatpur. A separate day trip takes you from Agra to the Mogul-influenced Hindu provincial capital at Gwalior. The magical town of Orccha, a two-hour drive from Gwalior toward Khajuraho, is riddled with 16th- and 17th-century ruins built by the Hindu Bundela rulers, including underground chambers and passageways. Buddha preached his first sermon in Sarnath, just outside Varanasi; and the international Buddhist center of Bodhgaya is east of Varanasi in the state of Bihar. The city of Lucknow, capital of Uttar Pradesh, was once the seat of an elegant Muslim province on a northern route between Varanasi and Delhi.

Pleasures and Pastimes

The Arts

This region provides ample opportunity to experience Indian classical music and dance. Both Agra and Khajuraho stage annual festivals in attractive milieus; Khajuraho's Festival of Dance, normally held in March, stages some performances in front of the Western Group of temples. Varanasi also maintains a vibrant local tradition of music and dance, noted particularly for its *tabla* (drum) players.

The visual arts are strong here as well, beyond the splendid architecture. Khajuraho's archaeological museum displays sculptures that once graced the niches of the town's temples. The Bharat Kala Bhavan at Banaras Hindu University is one of the most attractively arranged museums in India and has superb collections of both miniature painting and locally discovered classical sculpture. The archaeological museum in Mathura, some 56 km (35 mi) northwest of Agra on the road from Delhi, has one of the best collections of classical sculpture (from the Hindu Golden Age, the Gupta dynasty) in the country.

Dining

Restaurants on this route serve kebabs, other grilled meats, *birianis* (rice casseroles), and the rich, almond- and saffron-scented concoctions featured in Mughlai cuisine, a culinary counterpart to the Moguls' architecture. Hotels in Agra, not surprisingly, serve particularly good Mughlai dishes. Small restaurants in villages along the way, not always in hotels, feature simpler, local vegetarian dishes that are often delicious and cheap. Most restaurants in this region are open from 7 to 10 for breakfast, noon to 3 for lunch, and 7:30 to 11 for dinner.

Varanasi, with its abundant food for the soul, is extremely light on restaurants; orthodox Hindus do not eat meat, and prefer to keep food preparation a family affair. The major hotels serve standard Indian and Continental dishes and have branched out competently into Chinese cuisine. The city has lately come up with some excellent cafés, however, and is known for its sweets, which are mostly based on distillations of milk and cream; one, called the *lavan lata,* tastes like a supercharged baklava. A few cafés in Varanasi and Khajuraho even serve such exoticisms as tacos and yak-cheese pizza. Khajuraho, with its laid-back atmosphere, is a good place to venture into a roadside tea stall, a cultural institution as important to India as Parliament. Concerns about hygiene may ward you off sampling street food, but when it's hot from the fire it's generally quite safe.

Festivals

Agra's cultural festival, Taj Mahotsav (February), and the Khajuraho Festival of Dance (March) are geared primarily toward travelers. The Lucknow Festival (November–December) highlights the refined Indo-Muslim background of this state capital. In Varanasi, the religious calendar takes precedence, creating a major festival practically every week. The Hindu calendar follows lunar months, so Hindu festival dates shift back every year, catching up to the solar calendar when a leap month is added every third year. Varanasi's great bathing days, when thousands stream down the ghats into the Ganges, include Makar Sankranti (January), the full moon of the Hindu month Kartik (October or November), and Ganga Dussehra (May or June). Durga Puja (September or October) ends with the city's large Bengali community marching to the river at sunset to immerse large mud-daubed images of the goddess Durga. The month leading up to Dussehra, also in September or October, features nightly reenactments of the epic of Rama in the Ram Nagar palace, across the river from Varanasi (some episodes also take place in the city itself). Buddhists from Tibet and all over Asia celebrate their festivals in Sarnath and Bodhgaya, and Muslim holidays are observed by Varanasi's large Muslim minority as well as the more predominantly Muslim cities of Agra and Lucknow.

Lodging

India's main hotel groups are represented in this region, providing increased amenities and efficiency at increasing prices. More and more good, air-conditioned hotels here cater to India's burgeoning upper middle class, but these are often quite generic. Outside the old British cantonment areas where most hotels are clustered, a few clean, well-run guest houses have sprung up; these are often more convenient to town centers and may be attractive to those who like to venture out on their own. Unless we note otherwise, all hotels listed are air-conditioned.

Shopping

Agra and Varanasi are craft centers. Marble work, jewelry, and leather are renowned in Agra, and the Varanasi area has long been known for its silk (particularly brocade) and rug weaving and for block-printing. However, the virtues of the soft sell are only now becoming known to the touts and emporium owners in these cities—there is a rigorous commission system, and prices are likely to be as high as (or even higher than) those for similar goods at a five-star hotel in New Delhi. Visits to artisans' workshops are always interesting; just prepare to feel overt pressure to buy at the end of a guided tour.

Exploring North Central India

Agra and Varanasi are at opposite ends of India's largest state, Uttar Pradesh. Both lie on the Gangetic plain, and the countryside around each is similar—a dry landscape planted with sugarcane, mustard, and wheat in winter and inhabited by poor peasants and wealthier landowners. The monsoon hits harder to the east, around Varanasi, so the terrain there is a little more lush. The Yamuna River, backdrop to the Taj Mahal, joins the Ganges at Allahabad, about a hundred miles west of Varanasi. Khajuraho, in contrast, has a more dramatic setting at the edge of the hills and ravines that separate the northern plains south of the Vindhya hills from the Deccan plateau. This area, called Bundelkhand, has been notorious since British times for harboring *dacoits* (highway robbers), including Phoolan Devi, the "Bandit Queen," who now holds a seat in India's Parliament; yet the area is pacific from day to day.

Great Itineraries

Agra, Khajuraho, and Varanasi are well connected by air. The adventuresome can arrange to drive, but traffic is heavy between Agra and Delhi in particular, and the chances of an accident are not negligible. Train service between Delhi and Agra or Varanasi is reliable and comfortable; between Agra and Khajuraho, a comfortable morning train runs as far as Jhansi, with Orccha just a few miles away and a pleasant overnight stop. The scenic drive on to Khajuraho takes about four hours. From Khajuraho to Varanasi the rail and road connection is more complicated; you may prefer the afternoon plane. Agra makes a convenient starting point for this region: From there you can hop to Khajuraho (a 35-minute flight) and then Varanasi (40 minutes by plane) and then back to Delhi. If you fly from point to point, aim for at least five days in this region; if you stick to land travel, allow at least a week.

Numbers in the text correspond to numbers in the margin and on the North Central India, Agra, Khajuraho, and Varanasi maps.

IF YOU HAVE 4 DAYS

If time is limited and you're returning to Delhi, you may wish to drop either Khajuraho or Varanasi from this itinerary. Plane schedules make it necessary to stay overnight in each place. From Delhi, you can take a morning flight or a train to **Agra** and proceed immediately to the Taj Mahal while the morning light lasts. Allow several hours to wander the grounds and inspect the fine marble work inside the tomb itself. After lunch you can visit Agra Fort *or* take a perhaps more rewarding road trip to **Fatehpur Sikri.** Also worth wedging in is **Itmad-ud-Daulah's Tomb,** a stunning but little visited gem of Mogul architecture.

The next morning, fly to **Khajuraho** and explore the Western Group of Temples; on your third day you can briefly visit some other temples or the museum before flying to **Varanasi** for a late-afternoon boat ride on the Ganges. Art lovers may want to spend an afternoon at the Bharat Kala Bhavan, on the campus of Banaras Hindu University; returning to town, you can stop at the Durga and Sankat Mochan temples. A convenient side trip from Varanasi is the Buddhist center of **Sarnath.** The next morning, take a sunrise boat ride to see the ritual bathing and Varanasi's lovely skyline; then visit the main temple area around Kashi Vishvanath, the Golden Temple.

IF YOU HAVE 6 DAYS

Spend two days and two nights in **Agra;** visit Agra Fort, **Fatehpur Sikri,** and **Itmad-ud-Daulah's tomb** or **Akbar's tomb.** If you've had enough urban bustle, the bucolic Keoladeo National Park at **Bharatpur,** just over the Rajasthan border, is a hop, skip, and a jump from Fatehpur Sikri and has some nice lodges (☞ Chapter 5). Two days in **Khajuraho** will allow leisurely exploration of the temples or a trip to the wildlife park at Panna. With two days in **Varanasi** you can take at least one boat ride on the Ganges, visit the main temples, tour the palace at Ram Nagar, admire the artwork in the Bharat Kala Bhavan, and detour to **Sarnath.**

IF YOU HAVE 8 DAYS

If you're coming from Delhi, consider hiring a car for the potentially nerve-wracking three-hour trip to Agra, as driving will allow you to stop at Mathura, with its excellent archaeological museum; the tiny temple town of Vrindavan, where the god Krishna grew up as a cowherd; and Sikandra, site of **Akbar's tomb.** Spend two days in **Agra.** Then, instead of the 40-minute plane ride to **Khajuraho,** where you should also spend two days, take a two-day road trip, which involves a total of about 10 hours' driving and includes stops at **Gwalior,** with a spectacular Hindu fort, and **Orchha,** another seat of Hindu rajas on a picturesque river. To minimize your time on the road, you might arrange through a travel agent for a car to meet your train at Mathura, and perhaps travel from Agra to Gwalior or Orccha by train. Finally, fly from Khajuraho to **Varanasi** and spend the better part of two days here. The morning of your eighth day, head west toward **Lucknow** *or* east to **Bodhgaya.** (The latter will lengthen your stay in the region to nine days—to fly out of Bodhgaya you'll need to stay the night and drive early the next morning to Patna.)

When to Tour North Central India

Nowhere in India is the common advice to come between November and March more apt. This region is hot, and the sights in Agra and Khajuraho involve hours in the sun. (It can be chilly in late December and January, however.) The weather from early February to mid-March is temperate and beautiful. For adventurous travelers, the mid-monsoon period (late July and early August) is an attractive alternative: Temperatures are usually in the 70s and 80s, downpours are intermittent and impressive, hotel rates are much lower, and Varanasi is probably in the midst of a festival. Orccha is at its best during the monsoons, when the river is in full flow and the surrounding scrubland is green.

AGRA AND ENVIRONS

The journey from Delhi to Agra follows the Grand Trunk Road, a royal route established by India's Mogul emperors in the 16th and 17th centuries, when their capital alternated between Delhi, Agra, and Lahore (now in Pakistan). If you get an early start, you can see Agra's sights

North Central India

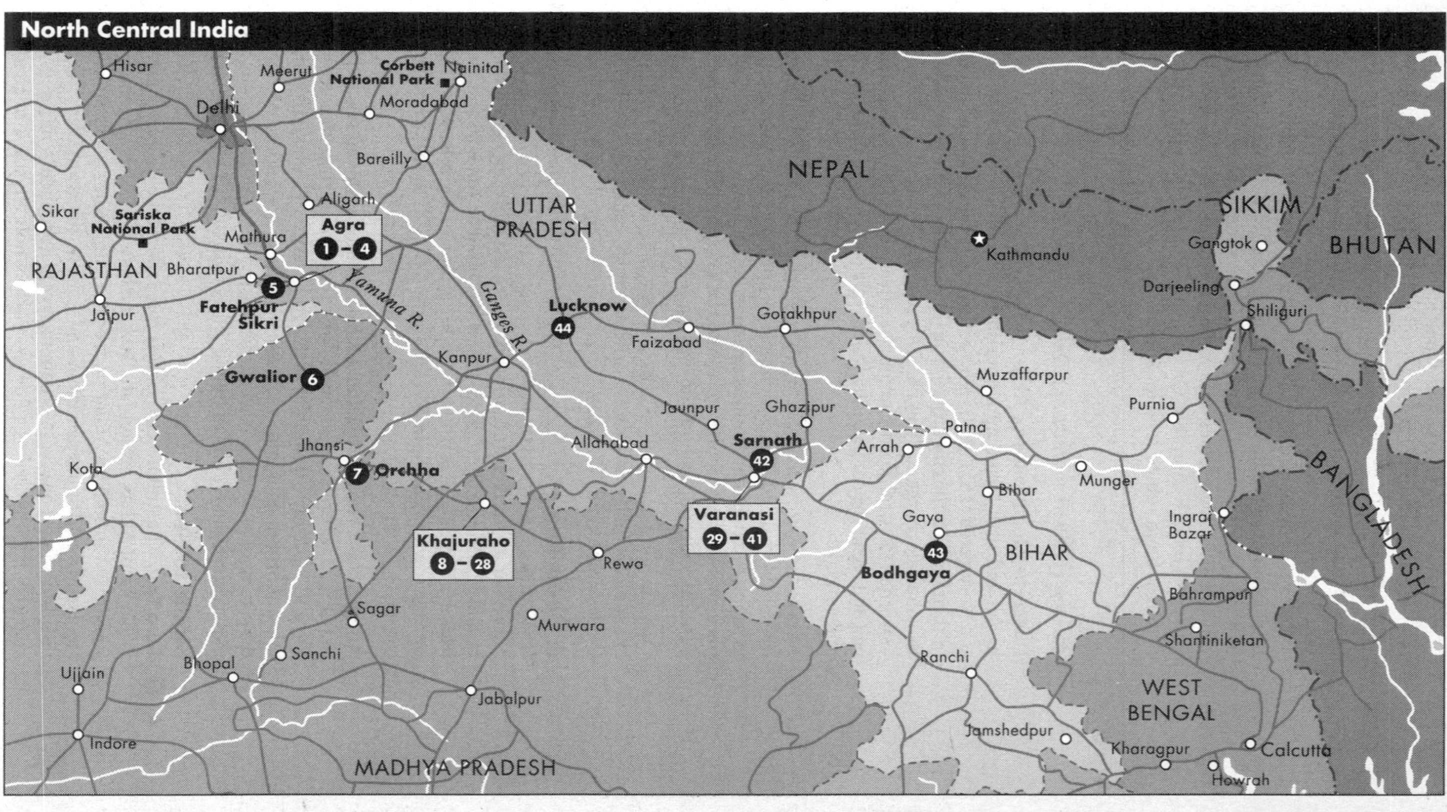

in one day: Turn off the Grand Trunk Road 10 km (6 mi) north of Agra to visit Akbar's Tomb, then move on to Itmad-ud-Daulah's Tomb, the Taj Mahal, and Agra Fort.

Several excursions from Agra make a trip here more interesting. Many find Akbar's deserted dream-city at Fatehpur Sikri as rewarding as the Taj Mahal. A short drive on from Fatehpur Sikri (toward Jaipur) brings you over the Rajasthan border to the Keoladeo National Park in Bharatpur, winter home of the Siberian crane. A separate trip takes you to the Mogul-influenced Hindu provincial capital at Gwalior. If you drive on to Khajuraho, Orccha makes an excellent place to spend the night amid ruined temples and palaces.

Agra

200 km (124 mi) southeast of Delhi

Under the Mogul emperor Akbar (1542–1605) and his successors, Jahangir and Shah Jahan, Agra flourished. After the reign of Shah Jahan's son Aurangzeb (1618–1707), however, and the gradual disintegration of their empire, the city passed from one invader to another before the British took charge early in the 19th century. The British, particularly Governor General Lord Curzon (in office 1898–1905), did much to halt and repair the damage inflicted on Agra's forts and palaces by raiders and vandals.

Agra today is crowded and dirty, and some of the Mogul buildings are irrevocably scarred. Other monuments, however, are strewn like pearls in ashes, evoking that glorious period in Indian history when Agra was the center of the Mogul empire, and the empire itself was the focus of political, cultural, and artistic evolution.

Opening hours and admission fees—especially those of the Taj Mahal—change constantly; inquire in advance with your hotel or the Uttar Pradesh State Tourist Office.

A Good Tour

If you arrive in Agra late in the day, set out very early the next day. Hire a car and driver, and stop first to see the morning light on the **Taj Mahal** ①. Drive from there to **Itmad-ud-Daulah's Tomb** ② and then to **Akbar's Tomb** ③. Return to Agra for a tour of **Agra Fort** ④ *or* drive outside town to **Fatehpur Sikri.** Return to the Taj to see the marble at sunset.

Alternately, if you leave Delhi at 5 AM by car, you should reach Sikandra at 7:30, where you can see Akbar's Tomb in less than an hour. From there it's roughly 20 minutes' drive to Itmad-ud Daulah's Tomb, another short but delightful visit; and from there it's a 30- to 45- minute drive to the Taj Mahal. You can then visit Agra Fort or Fatehpur Sikri in the afternoon and relax by the Taj at twilight.

Sights to See

★ ❹ **Agra Fort.** The architecture of this fort reflects the collective creative brilliance of Akbar, his son Jahangir, and his grandson Shah Jahan. The structure was built by Akbar on the site of an earlier fort, but, as with similar Mogul facilities in Delhi and Lahore, the word "fort" is a little misleading. The complex contains royal apartments, mosques, and assembly halls as well as a dungeon—the whole cityscape of an imperial capital. Its roughly triangular shape is surrounded by a massive wall 2½ km (1½ mi) long and 69 ft high; and with the Yamuna River running at its base, the fort was also protected by a moat and another wall, presenting a daunting barrier to anyone hoping to access the treasures within.

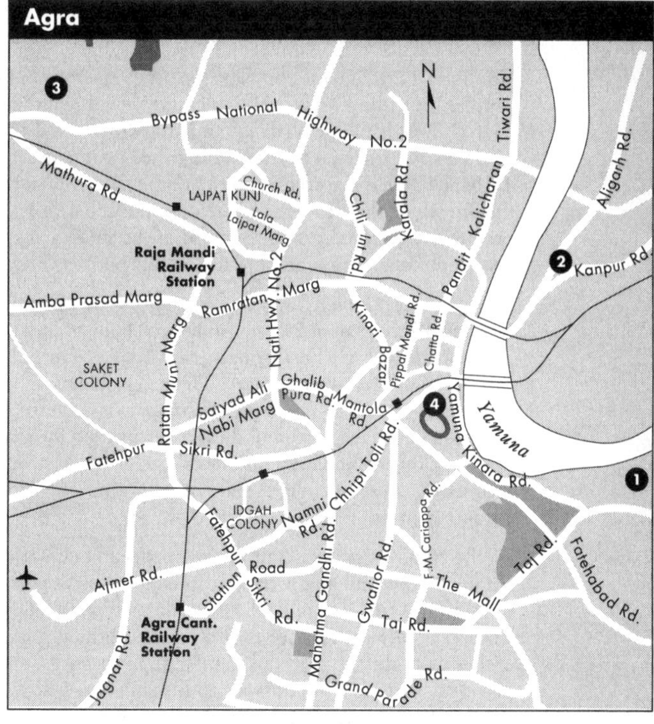

Today, entrance is easy through the Amar Singh Gate. North of this entrance is the fort's largest private residence, the **Jahangiri Mahal,** built as a harem for Akbar's son Jahangir. (Akbar's own palace, closer to the entrance, is in ruins.) Measuring 250 by 300 ft, the Jahangiri Mahal juxtaposes *jarokhas* (balconies) and other elements of Hindu architecture with pointed arches and other Central Asian influences imported by the Moguls—a mixture foreshadowing the stylistic synthesis that would follow at Fatehpur Sikri. The palace's central court is lined with two-story facades bearing remnants of the rich, gilded decoration that once covered much of the structure. Next to architecture and the arts, Jahangir's greatest loves were wine and his Persian-born wife Nur Jahan, who, failing to persuade him to pay some attention to his empire, did it for him, making short work of all rivals. This strong-willed woman was unable to consolidate her power after her husband died, however, and lived out her days in virtual seclusion in Lahore.

After Jahangir's death in 1628, Shah Jahan (whose mother was one of Jahangir's other wives) assumed the throne and started his own buildings inside the fort, often tearing down those built by his father and grandfather in the process. The **Anguri Bagh** (literally, Grape Arbor) shows the outlines of a geometric garden built around delicate water courses and chutes by Shah Jahan. The **Khas Mahal** (Private Palace) is an early masterpiece of Shah Jahan's craftsmen; it was built in 1637 overlooking the Yamuna and the Taj on one side and the Anguri Bagh on the other. The central pavilion, made of white marble, follows the classic Mogul pattern: three arches on each side, five in front, and two turrets rising out of the roof. Of the two flanking pavilions, one is of white marble and was supposedly decorated with gold leaf, while the other is made of red stone; these are said to have housed Shah Jahan's two daughters. The arched roofs of all three pavilions are stone translations of the bamboo architecture of Bengal. In one part of the Khas

Mahal, a staircase leads down to the palace's "air-conditioned" quarters, cool underground rooms that were probably used in the summer.

Continuing through the complex, the octagonal tower of the **Mussaman Burj** has fine inlay work and a splendid view down the river to the Taj Mahal. This is where Shah Jahan is sometimes said to have spent his last days, imprisoned but still able to see his greatest monument, the Taj Mahal. On the northeastern end of the Khas Mahal courtyard stands the **Sheesh Mahal** (Palace of Mirrors), built in 1637 as a bath for the private palace and dressing room for the harem. Each of the two chambers contained a bathing tank fed by marble channels.

The emperor received foreign ambassadors and other dignitaries in the **Diwan-i-Khas** (Hall of Private Audience), built by Shah Jahan in 1636–37. Outside, the marble throne terrace holds a pair of black and white thrones. The black throne, carved from a single block of marble, overlooks the Yamuna. The white throne was made of several marble blocks, and the inscription indicates it was used by Shah Jahan, while the black throne had been his father's seat of power. Both thrones face the **Machhi Bhavan,** an enclosure of fountains and shallow pools, and a number of imperial offices.

To the empire's citizens and to the European emissaries who came to see these powerful monarchs, the most impressive part of the fort was the **Diwan-i-Am** (Hall of Public Audience), set within a large quadrangle. This huge, low structure rests on a 4-ft platform, its nine cusped Mogul arches held aloft by rows of slender supporting pillars. Here the emperor sat and dispensed justice to his subjects; below the throne, his *wazir* (prime minister) sat on a small platform with a silver railing.

Northeast of the Diwan-i-Khas is the **Nagina Masjid,** a private mosque raised by Shah Jahan for the women of his harem. Made of white marble and walled in on three sides, it has typical cusped arches, a marble courtyard, and three graceful domes. Nearby is the lovely **Moti Masjid,** a perfectly proportioned pearl mosque built in white marble by Shah Jahan. At press time the Moti Masjid was closed for restoration. ✉ *Yamuna Kinara Rd., near Nehru Park.* 🎫 *Rs. 15; video cameras Rs. 25.* ⏲ *7–6.*

3 **Akbar's Tomb.** Akbar's resting place was begun by the emperor himself in 1602, and completed after his death by his son Jahangir. Topped with smooth white marble and flanked by graceful minarets, this mausoleum of rough red sandstone sits in a typical Mogul garden comprised of four quadrants separated by waterways. The garden is not well tended now, and much of the gold work that once adorned the tomb was destroyed in the 18th century by Jat raiders (who invaded Agra after the fall of the Mogul empire), though some of it was partially restored by the British. In a domed chamber three stories high, the crypt is inscribed with the 99 names of Allah, plus the phrases "Allah-o-Akbar" ("God is Great") at the head and "Jalla Jalalahu" ("Great is His Glory") at the foot. You can actually see the tomb's enormous gateway, topped with bright tilework, from the train from Delhi—look out the left window 10 or 15 minutes before the train is due to reach Agra. ✉ *Sikandra, 10 km (6 mi) north of Agra on Grand Trunk Rd. to Delhi.* 🎫 *Rs. 12, free Fri.; video cameras Rs. 25.* ⏲ *6–5:30.*

★ **2** **Itmad-ud-Daulah's Tomb.** The empress Nur Jahan (Jahangir's favorite wife) built this small but gorgeous tomb for her father, a Persian nobleman who became Jahangir's chief minister. One of Agra's loveliest monuments, it was supposedly built by workers from Iran (then Persia). The tomb incorporates a great deal of brown and yellow Persian marble, and shows the first use of Persian-style marble inlay in India—

both features that would later characterize the style of Shah Jahan. This building was a precursor to, and very likely an inspiration, for the Taj Mahal in its use of intricate marble inlay in particular. The roof is arched in the style of Bengali terra-cotta temples, and the minarets are octagonal, much broader than the slender cylinders of the Taj; yet in its fine proportions this mausoleum is almost the equal of that masterpiece. Inside—where the elegant decoration continues—the central chamber holds the tombs of Itmad-ud-Daulah and his wife, with other relations buried in adjacent rooms. Most travelers to Agra never see this place, yet its beauty and tranquility are extraordinary, and its well-maintained gardens make it a wonderful place to pause and reflect. You can see a bit of everyday Agra life on the river just below, and the Taj across the water to the south. ✉ *5 km (3 mi) north of Taj Mahal on left bank of Yamuna River.* 🎫 *Rs. 12, free Fri.; video cameras Rs. 25.* 🕓 6–6.

★ ❶ **Taj Mahal.** The architecture alone has inspired reams of rapture over the years, but what really makes this marble monument so endearing is its haunting tale of love and loss. Arjuman Banu, the niece of Jahangir's wife Nur Jahan, supposedly captured the heart of the young Shah Jahan the minute he saw her. In 1612, at the age of 21, she married him and became his favorite wife, his Mumtaz Mahal (the Exalted of the Palace) and Mumtazul-Zamani (the Distinguished of the Age). Numerous stories recall this woman's generosity and wisdom, both as a household manager and as an adviser to her husband, but even these qualities were diminished by the love that bound her to Shah Jahan. She bore him 14 children, and it was in childbirth that she died in 1630 while accompanying her husband on a military campaign. On her deathbed, it is said, she begged the king to build a monument so beautiful that the world would never forget their love. Shattered by the death of his favorite, legend claims, Shah Jahan locked himself in his private chambers for a month; and when he finally emerged, his hair was white. Six months after Mumtaz Mahal's death, a huge procession brought her body to Agra, where Shah Jahan began the process of honoring her request.

Shah Jahan's chief architect, Ustad Ahmad Lahori, oversaw the construction, which began in 1632. Shah Jahan put an army of 20,000 laborers to work, even building a new village (Taj Ganj, which still stands) to house them as they spent 17 years creating a vast tomb of white marble. On the banks of the Yamuna River—visible from Agra Fort—the Taj was completed on the exact anniversary of Mumtaz Mahal's death. The great emperor spent his last years locked in one of his own creations, gazing, according to the popular story, across the Yamuna at his wife's final resting place.

The Taj stands at the end of a large, four-quartered garden, or *charbagh,* symbolizing paradise, extending about a thousand feet in each direction from a small central pool. You enter the grounds through a huge sandstone gateway, with an arching Koranic inscription calibrated by its calligraphers to appear uniform in size. Ahead, facing the long reflecting pool, the Taj Mahal stands on two bases, one of sandstone and, above it, a marble platform measuring 313 ft square and worked into a chessboard design. A slender marble minaret stands at each corner of the platform, blending so well into the general composition that it's hard to believe each one is 137 ft tall. The minarets are actually built at a slight tilt away from the tomb so that, in case of an earthquake, they'd fall away from the building. Facing the Taj from beneath its platform are two majestic sandstone buildings, a mosque on the left and its mirror image (built purely for symmetry) on the right. Behind the tomb, the Yamuna winds through its broad, sandy bed.

The tomb's central archway is deeply recessed, as are the smaller pairs of companion archways along the sides, and the beveled corners of the 190-square-ft structure. The Taj's most extraordinary feature is its onion dome, crowned by a brass finial mounted in a scalloped ornament that inverts the Hindu motif of the lotus. The dome uses the Central Asian technique of placing a central inner dome, in this case 81 ft high, inside an outer shell to attain the extraordinary exterior height of 200 ft; between the two is an area nearly the size of the interior hall itself. Raising the dome above the minarets was the builders' great stroke of genius, and the dome is balanced by large *chattras* (umbrellas), another feature borrowed from Hindu design. It's easy to cling to the legendary narrative behind this building—as well as the equally undocumented story of Shah Jahan's plan to build a black-marble tomb for himself across the Yamuna—yet the Taj Mahal, along with only a handful of world treasures, speaks for itself. It is, somewhat paradoxically, both the culmination of and the best introduction to the elaborate aesthetic world that the Moguls created in India, sometimes at the expense of their political power.

Inside the mausoleum, the changing light creeps softly in through marble screens that have been chiseled like silver filigree. Look closely at the tiny flowers drawn of inlaid semiprecious stones—at the detailed stonework on each petal and leaf. The work is so fine that not even a magnifying glass reveals the tiny breaks between stones; yet a single one-inch flower on the queen's tomb contains 60 separate pieces. Shine a flashlight to see the delicate stones' translucence. Feel the perfectly smooth surfaces. Directly under the marble dome lie the tombs of Mumtaz Mahal and Shah Jahan, surrounded by a screen carved from a single block of marble, with latticework as intricate as lace. In the center of the enclosure, diminishing rectangles lead up to what looks like a coffin; in fact, both Mumtaz Mahal and Shah Jahan are buried in a crypt below these tombs in deference to the Islamic tradition that no one should walk upon their graves. After his death, Shah Jahan was buried next to his wife by his son Aurangzeb, upsetting the perfect symmetry, most likely a cost-cutting measure that forms an ironic postscript to the munificence of Shah Jahan. But it may be fitting that the emperor lies in perpetuity next to his favorite wife, and the romantically inclined give Aurangzeb credit for bringing the two together. Mumtaz Mahal's tomb bears a Persian inscription: "The illustrious sepulcher of Arjuman Banu Begum, called Mumtaz Mahal. God is everlasting, God is sufficient. He knoweth what is concealed and what is manifest. He is merciful and compassionate. Nearer unto him are those who say: Our Lord is God." The emperor's epitaph reads: "The illustrious sepulcher of His Exalted Majesty Shah Jahan, the Valiant King, whose dwelling is in the starry Heaven. He traveled from this transient world to the World of Eternity on the 28th night of the month of Rajab in the year of 1076 of the Hegira [February 1, 1666]."

It's worth making more than one trip to see the Taj in varying lights. In early morning, the pale rays of the sun give the marble a soft pink luster, while at sunset the west side of the monument turns lemon-yellow, then pumpkin-orange. Once the sun goes down, the marble is pure white on a white sky. At press time, a plan to open the Taj on moonlit winter nights was being pushed by tour operators and hotel owners but opposed by preservationists and some religious groups. Tourist traffic can be very heavy the week after Christmas, and you should try to avoid coming on Friday year-round, as admission is free and the crowds are awful. The complex is closed on Monday.

The Taj Mahal Museum stands near the mosque to the left of the Taj. Though small, it holds interesting Mogul memorabilia and provides some historical background to the Taj, as well as paintings of the famous couple. ✉ *Taj Rd., Taj Ganj.* *Taj Mahal: Rs. 105 between sunrise and 8 AM and 4 and 7 PM; Rs. 15 between 8 AM and 4 PM, both including museum entry (the higher fee includes entry to Agra's other monuments as well); free Fri.* ⌚ *Taj Mahal, Tues.–Sun. sunrise–7 PM; museum, weekends and Tues.–Thurs. 8–5.*

Dining and Lodging

$$$ ★ ✕ **Mahjong Room.** Enjoy excellent Chinese dishes in this intimate, dimly lit, wood-paneled restaurant with red and green linens and Chinese lanterns. Try the tangy hot-and-sour soup and the spicy chili chicken. The dining room, which has a non-smoking section, overlooks the hotel courtyard and gardens. ✉ *Welcomgroup Mogul Sheraton, 194 Fatehbad Rd., Taj Ganj,* ☎ *562/331701 (–28). AE, DC, MC, V.*

$$$ ★ ✕ **Mogul Room.** This dark, elegant top-floor restaurant is decorated in pinks and reds, with a ceiling of faux twinkling stars. At night you might catch a live performances of *ghazals* (Urdu-language love songs). The menu mixes Indian, Chinese, and Continental cuisines, but the Indian dishes are particularly delicious. For dessert, see if the *shahi tukra* ("toast of kings"), a rich, bread-based pudding, is on offer. ✉ *Clarks Shiraz, 54 Taj Rd.,* ☎ *562/361421 (–7). AE, DC, MC, V.*

$$$ ✕ **Nauratna.** Named for the "nine jewels" (ministers) of Akbar's court, this intimate restaurant has Mogul decor, with expanses of marble and lots of purple, the emperor's favorite color. The Mughlai cuisine is similar to what Akbar himself ate. Try a biriani, the quintessential Mughlai dish, or one of the excellent kebabs. Evening usually brings a live performance of ghazals. ✉ *Welcomgroup Mogul Sheraton, 194 Fatehbad Rd., Taj Ganj,* ☎ *562/331701 (–28). AE, DC, MC, V.*

$$ ★ ✕ **Kwality.** This restaurant is part of a chain that was the first to popularize dining out in Indian cities and resorts. Most evenings and weekends it's filled with lively middle-class families enjoying a rare treat. Though the menu has a Continental section, the Indian fare is best, particularly the rich butter chicken, delicious with hot naan. ✉ *2 Taj Rd., Sadar Bazaar,* ☎ *562/363524 or –848. No credit cards.*

$ ★ ✕ **Dasaprakash.** A far cry from the traditional cuisine of Agra, these light and spicy South Indian dishes can be a nice change from rich Mughlai fare. With its Formica tables and fake Tiffany lamps, Dasaprakash resembles an American pizza joint, but the food is excellent, and service is fast. Try the crisp *aplam* (fried wafers) and *rasam* (thin, spicy lentil soup), as well as fluffy *idlis* (steamed rice cakes) and crisp *dosas* (crisp rice crepes). There's also an unusual selection of fresh juices and a great dessert menu with ice creams and floats. ✉ *1 Meher Cinema Complex, (5 min from Taj Mahal, near Hotel Agra Ashok), Gwalior Rd., Agra Cantonment,* ☎ *562/260269 or 562/363368. DC, MC, V.*

$$$$ ★ **Welcomgroup Mogul Sheraton.** Winner of the Aga Khan Award for excellence in architecture, this brick-and-marble edifice is Agra's class act, though its size is a little overwhelming. The huge, landscaped gardens even hold a miniature lake. Most of the spacious rooms have low-key modern decor, their soft white walls accented by handsome, dark-wood trim, but you can actually request an Indian-style room with local fabrics and furniture. Some rooms have views of the Taj. Forgetting nothing, the hotel retains its own astrologer and snake charmer. ✉ *194 Fatehbad Rd., Taj Ganj, 282001,* ☎ *562/331701 (–28),* FAX *562/331730. 300 rooms, 12 suites. 5 restaurants, bar, no-smoking rooms, pool, miniature golf, 2 tennis courts, croquet, health club, boating, dance club, business services, travel services. AE, DC, MC, V.*

$$$ **Agra Ashok.** The architecture of this government-run Western-style hotel is Mogul-inspired, with lots of marble and red sandstone and an interior water fountain. Rooms are spacious and modern, and some have views of the Taj. ✉ *6B The Mall, 282001,* ☎ *562/361223 (–32),* FAX *562/361620. 53 rooms, 2 suites. 2 restaurants, bar, coffee shop, pool, babysitting, business services, travel services. AE, DC, MC, V.*

$$$ **Clarks Shiraz.** This Western-style high-rise, set on 8 acres with extensive gardens, evokes no era so much as the 1960s. The comfortable rooms have subdued contemporary decor. Odd-numbered rooms have distant views of the Taj; the newer rooms in the tower are more spacious and offer better views. Expect an evening barbecue on the beautifully lighted lawn. ✉ *54 Taj Rd., 282001,* ☎ *562/361421 (–7),* FAX *562/361428. 235 rooms, 2 suites. 4 restaurants, bar, pool, golf privileges, miniature golf, croquet, babysitting, business services, meeting room, travel services. AE, DC, MC, V.*

$$$ **Taj View.** This Western-style Taj-group hotel has a restful, brown-toned lobby, good service, and spacious modern rooms. The Taj Mahal views from the upper stories are the best in town, albeit still distant. ✉ *Taj Ganj, Fatehbad Rd., 282001,* ☎ *562/331841 (–59),* FAX *562/331860. 95 rooms, 5 suites. Restaurant, bar, coffee shop, pool, health club, badminton, babysitting, business services, meeting rooms, travel services. AE, DC, MC, V.*

$$ **Mansingh Palace.** This Western-style hotel has a spacious lobby with a fountain, and simply decorated modern rooms. ✉ *Fatehbad Rd., 282001,* ☎ *562/331771 (–5),* FAX *562/330202. 100 rooms, 3 suites. Restaurant, bar, coffee shop, pool, health club, meeting rooms, travel services. AE, DC, MC, V.*

$$ ★ **The Trident.** This Oberoi hotel is used to train Oberoi staff from all over India, and service is correspondingly excellent. Built around a lovely garden courtyard with stone pathways, fountains, a sandstone pavilion, and a pool, it's simple, clean, and elegant—one of Agra's best values, if a little farther from the Taj Mahal than the hotels in Taj Ganj. The rooms have subdued modern decor, individually controlled air-conditioning, and tile floors. ✉ *Taj Nagri Scheme, Fatehbad Rd., Agra 282001,* ☎ *562/331818* FAX *562/331827. 139 rooms, 1 suite. Restaurant, bar, pool, barbershop, beauty salon, badminton, volleyball, travel services. AE, DC, MC, V.*

$ **New Bakshi House.** If you'd like to stay in a middle-class Indian neighborhood, New Bakshi is perfect. The two-story house has a homey feel and is decorated with all kinds of mementos, including the owner's collection of old maps. Each room is cozy and clean. Air-conditioned rooms cost more, but they're still inexpensive. Guests are served home-cooked meals from an Indian or Continental menu. ✉ *5 Laxman Nagar, 282001,* ☎ *562/368159 or 562/261228,* FAX *562/363991. 10 rooms. Restaurant, golf privileges, travel services. No credit cards.*

Shopping

Many shops sell hand-knotted carpets and dhurries, precious and semiprecious stones, inlaid marble work, and brass statues. Beware of drivers and touts who want to take you to "bargains"; they receive huge commissions from shopkeepers, which you pay in the price of the merchandise. Beware, too, of soapstone masquerading as marble: This softer, cheaper stone is a convincing substitute, but you can test it by scraping the item with your fingernail. Marble won't scrape. Finally, for what it's worth, local lore has it that miniature replicas of the Taj Mahal bring bad luck. . . .

Cottage Industry (✉ 18 Munro Rd., ☎ 562/360417) features good dhurries and carpets. **Cottage Industries Exposition** (✉ 39 Fatehbad Rd., ☎ 562/360417) has a full selection of high-quality rugs, crafts, and gemstones at prices to match. **Ganeshi Lall and Son** (✉ Welcomgroup Mogul Sheraton, 194 Fatehbad Rd., ☎ 562/330181) is Agra's old-time reliable jeweler, established 1843; the store also sells objets d'art. **Kohinoor** (✉ 41 Mahatma Gandhi Rd., ☎ 562/364156) has also been selling jewelry for generations. **Ganesha** (✉ 18 Munro Rd., ☎ 562/353421) has brass, copper, and bronze curios. **Oswal Emporium** (✉ 30 Munro Rd., ☎ 562/363240 or -407) has excellent inlaid marble items; we did, however, hear of a stone item being shipped instead of the marble piece that was paid for. **Subash Emporium** (✉ 18/1 Gwalior Rd., ☎ 562/363867 or 562/264891) was the first store to revive Agra marble work in the 1960s. The **Handicrafts Gallery** (✉ 18A/54 Jasoria Enclave, Eatchabad Rd., ☎ 562/330188) sells jewelry, silk-embroidered "paintings," handicrafts, and musical instruments, and hosts free live Indian musical performances daily. Call for details.

Fatehpur Sikri

★ 5 *37 km (23 mi) southwest of Agra*

In the 16th century (the story goes), a mystic, Salim Chisti, blessed the Mogul emperor Akbar with a much-wanted male heir. To honor the saint, Akbar built a new capital in the saint's honor around 1571, adding "Fatehpur" to the name of the village where Salim Chisti had settled to form a name meaning "City of Victory." Standing on a rocky ridge overlooking the village, Fatehpur Sikri originally had a circumference of about 11 km (7 mi). Three sides were enclosed by massive walls; the fourth was protected by a lake. What remains now is a beautiful cluster of royal dwellings on the top of the ridge. When some Elizabethans came to Fatehpur Sikri in 1583 to meet Akbar, they were amazed to see a city that exceeded London in both population and grandeur; they lost count of the rubies, diamonds, and plush silks. The buildings, made mostly of red sandstone and remarkably well preserved, incorporate architectural styles from Akbar's various Indian holdings, a reflection of the synthesizing impulse that characterized the third and greatest of the Mogul emperors. Akbar ruled here for only 15 years before moving his capital—perhaps in pursuit of water, perhaps for political reasons—to Lahore (now in Pakistan) and eventually back to Agra. Fatehpur Sikri's elegant blend of cultures and styles stands now as an intriguing ghost town in a picturesque setting, reflecting a high point in India's cultural history.

The usual starting point for a walk through Fatehpur Sikri is the Buland Darwaza (Great Gate) at the city's southwestern end. Unfortunately, the adjoining parking lot is crowded with hawkers and guides, who can be unrelenting in their efforts to assist you. If you arrive by car, you can avoid this minor annoyance by asking to be dropped at the subsidiary entrance at the northeastern end of the city: Coming from Agra, bear right just after passing through Agra Gate. The entrance—the main one in Akbar's day—is beside the imperial mint. Your driver can meet you outside the Buland Darwaza. The walk outlined below wends through the city from the subsidiary entrance on the Agra side.

Approaching the complex, you'll walk through the **Naubat Khana,** which was manned by drummers and musicians during imperial processions. Just ahead on the right is the **Mint,** faced by the smaller **Treasury** across the road. Fantasy and whimsy prevail in the Treasury's decorative stone *makaras,* or sea monsters, who were said to keep thieves from the crown jewels believed to have been kept in secret niches carved into the walls.

A few steps lead into the **Diwan-i-Am** (Hall of Public Audience), a large courtyard 366 ft long and 181 ft wide, with cloisters on three sides. Ahead is the balcony, where the emperor sat on his throne to meet subjects or observe celebrations and other spectacles. Chiseled marble screens on either side allowed the women of the court to watch the proceedings in privacy. Here, as the empire's chief justice, Akbar handed down his decisions: Those condemned to die were reportedly impaled, hanged, or trampled under the feet of an elephant. In the courtyard behind the Diwan-i-Am, Akbar played pachisi (an early form of Parcheesi) using slave girls as life-size pieces.

The **Diwan-i-Khas** (Hall of Private Audience) is set back in the courtyard's far right corner. It looks like a two-story building with domed cupolas at each corner, but inside is one tall room where Akbar sat elevated on a platform connected by causeways to the balconies on four sides and supported by a stone column topped with an intricately carved lotus flower. The throne's position symbolized both the center of the world and the one god sought by several major religions (which might be represented among Akbar's visitors), and removed the emperor from would-be assassins. Here Akbar is said to have held discussions with his ministers, the "nine jewels," each of whom occupied a window seat on the surrounding balcony. Like all of Fatehpur Sikri, the column was assembled without mortar.

Next to the Diwan-i-Khas at the northeast end of the complex is a small platform topped with a *chattri* (umbrella) for Akbar's royal astrologer and constructed with brackets carved as elephant trunks. Close by is the **Ankh Michauli** (Hide and Seek), named for Akbar's reported habit of playing the game with his harem inside the broad rooms and narrow passageways of this building. **Akbar's private chambers** are on the south side of the courtyard, abutting the road; they're separated from the official buildings by a square fountain with a central platform where the famous court musician, Tansen, would sit and sing for the emperor. (The water softened the echo.) The small room near the fountain is thought to have been the **palace of Akbar's Turkish wife.** Covered with elaborate Persian carvings, many of them in angular zigzag patterns, this charming structure bears close inspection. The onetime sandalwood doors were supposedly plated with silver.

East of the Diwan-i-Khas, across a terrace designed as a life-size chessboard, rise the tiered colonnades of the five-story **Panch Mahal,** each floor smaller than the one below. The highest structure in Fatehpur Sikri, this pavilion combines primarily Hindu and Buddhist architecture. The upper stories have grand views of the city and the surrounding landscape. Behind the Panch Mahal, facing what was once a small garden, is the small **Nagina Mosque** used by the women of the court.

Farther along the terraces stands the Hawa Mahal (Palace of the Winds). Concealed by a red sandstone screen, this is a cool vantage point from which women could catch some breezes and peek out onto the trees or the court unseen. Past this, **Jodh Bai's Palace,** reputedly built for Akbar's Hindu wife, is the largest palace in the complex, comprising several apartments. The building incorporates elements of Gujarati design. The **House of Maryam** (on a diagonal between Jodh Bai's Palace and the Panch Mahal), supposedly the home of Akbar's Christian wife, is said to suggest the wooden architecture of the Punjab at that time. Look for the faded paintings of horses and elephants on the exterior walls. **Birbal's Palace,** said to have been housed the emperor's playfully irreverent Hindu prime minister, is northwest of Jodh Bai's Palace and the Hawa Mahal. Though its actual purpose is not certain, its ornamentation makes further use of Hindu motifs.

The city proper ends with Jodh Bai's Palace. As you emerge onto the road, the **Royal Stables** are on your left. Follow the left path down to the east gate of Akbar's **Jama Masjid** (Imperial Mosque—built around 1571 and designed to hold 10,000 worshipers, the mosque is still in active use. Note the deliberate use of Hindu elements in the design (especially the decorations on the pillars), another example of the desire for religious harmony so often reflected in Akbar's architecture.

In the courtyard of the Jama Masjid (opposite the Buland Darwaza) lies **Salim Chisti's tomb,** surrounded by walls of marble lace, each with a different design. Begun upon the saint's death in 1571 and finished nine years later, the tomb was originally faced with red sandstone but was refinished in marble by Jahangir, the heir Akbar received after the saint's blessing. Women of all faiths come here to cover the tomb with cloth and tie a string on the marble latticework in hopes of giving birth to a son. From here you can cross the courtyard, exit through the King's Gate (once reserved for Akbar alone).

Facing the mosque's southern gate is the exemplary **Buland Darwaza.** With its beveled walls and inset archways, the Great Gate rises 134 ft over a base of steps that raise it another 34 ft, dwarfing everything else in sight. Akbar built the gate after conquering Gujarat, in about 1576, and it set the style for later gateways, which the Moguls built habitually as symbols of their power. An inscription quotes Jesus from the Koran: "The world is but a bridge. Pass over it, but build no houses on it"—an ironic reference to the ephemeral nature of even an emperor's monuments. Directly ahead is the parking lot, where you can prearrange to have you driver meet you.

To reach Fatehpur Sikri from Agra, hire a car and driver or join a tour (☞ Guided Tours *in* North Central India A to Z, *below*). Plan to spend two or three hours touring the grounds. En route back to Agra, the small hotel in the **Gulistan Tourist Complex** (☎ 5619/2490) makes a convenient roadside lunch stop amid spacious gardens.

Gwalior

❻ *120 km (75 mi) south of Agra*

Now a bustling commercial city, Gwalior traces its history back to a legend: A chieftain named Suraj Sen was cured of leprosy by the hermit saint Gwalipa. On the hermit's advice, Suraj Sen founded his city here and named it for his benefactor. The city changed hands numerous times, and each dynasty left its mark. Gwalior was also the home of Tansen, whom many regard as the founder of North Indian classical music; and the annual Tansen Music Festival, in late November or early December, is one of the best in India.

Sitting on a high, rocky plateau, **Gwalior Fort** is a huge structure, its 2-mi-long, 35-ft-high wall dominating the skyline. The only pre-Mogul Hindu palace complex to survive in this region, the structure was admired by the first Mogul emperor, Babur. The fort was often captured, achieving its greatest glory under the Tomar rulers of the 14th century. The main palace, **Man Mandir,** was once resplendent in gold and mosaic tiles. If you can, take a flashlight to explore the underground dungeons where the Moguls kept their prisoners after finally capturing the fort in Akbar's time. Don't miss the beautifully carved 11th-century **Sas-Bahu** or the 9th-century **Teli ka Mandir** temples. The state museum in the **Gujari Mahal,** at the base of the fort, has an excellent collection of sculptures and archaeological treasures dating as far back as the 2nd century BC. Ask to see the statue of the goddess Shalbhanjika, an exquisite miniature kept in the curator's custody. ✉ *Gwalior*

Rd., ☎ *751/8641.* 🎫 *Fort Rs. 1, museum Rs. 2.* ⏲ *Fort daily sunrise–sunset, museum Tues.–Sun. 10–5.*

Belonging to the Scindias, Gwalior's rulers up through Indian Independence, the **Jai Vilas Palace** is an opulent structure with Tuscan and Corinthian architecture. The ceiling of the massive **Durbar Hall** is gilded and hung with enormous chandeliers. In the dining room below, you can see the crystal train that carried liqueurs along the maharaja's banquet table. ✉ *Jayandra Gang, Lashkar,* ☎ *751/23453.* 🎫 *Rs. 30.* ⏲ *Tues.–Sun. 10–5.*

Sarod Ghar is an elegantly designed museum with a collection of musical instruments from the family of India's best living sarod player, Amjad Ali Khan. ✉ *Jiwaji Ganj, Ustad Hafiz Ali Khan Marg, Lashkar* ☎ *751/425607.* ⏲ *Daily 10–1 and 2–5.* 🎫 *Rs. 10.*

Lodging

$$$ 🏨 **Welcomgroup Usha Kiran Palace.** This white palace, a Heritage Hotel, is trimmed with filigreed sandstone and has served as both a royal guest house and a royal residence. To see the view granted women of the royal family, stand in the passageway and look out through the stone screen over the beautifully landscaped lawns. The hotel exudes a gentle, Old World ambience, and while the Western-style rooms are not opulent, they're comfortable. Be sure to take a ride in the maharaja's buggy. ✉ *Jayendraganj, Lashkar, Gwalior 474009, Madhya Pradesh,* ☎ *751/323993 (–4) or 751/323213 (–4),* FAX *751/321103. 17 rooms, 10 suites. Restaurant, bar, indoor pool, badminton, croquet, horseback riding, billiards, meeting room. AE, DC, MC, V.*

$ 🏨 **MPSTDC Hotel Tansen.** Run by the Madhya Pradesh State Tourism Development Corporation, this two-story white hotel is surrounded by pleasant lawns. Two-thirds of the rooms are air-conditioned and have TVs; the rest have fans only. This place isn't luxurious, but it's clean and the staff is very friendly. 🏨 *6 Gandhi Rd., Gwalior 474009, Madhya Pradesh,* ☎ *751/340370 (–1) or 751/216064.* FAX *751/340371. 35 rooms, 1 suite. Restaurant, bar, meeting rooms. AE, MC, V.*

Orchha

❼ *119 km (74 mi) southeast of Gwalior, 16 km (9 mi) east of Jhansi, 170 km (102 mi) west of Khajuraho*

Set on the banks of the winding Betwa River, the sleepy town of Orchha was built up as a provincial capital in the 16th and 17th centuries by the Hindu Bundela rulers, who were allies of the Moguls. In 1787 the Bundela capital was shifted from this isolated (but easy to defend) location, and today the place is little more than a village crowded with beautiful palaces, temples, and *chattras,* funerary monuments that resemble Muslim tombs but of course contain no remains of the Hindu rulers, who were cremated on the banks of the river. Orccha's isolation proved useful in the 1920s to Chandrashekhar Azad, a nationalist leader who hid from the British here, and even today you may feel you've entered a sort of benignly protected corner of the world (though some townspeople are concerned that growing tourist interest may soon overwhelm them).

Orccha has no real beaten path, so it's a great place to poke around in peace. Take a flashlight so you can explore the underground rooms and passageways that riddle the land beneath the town. Most of the sites are accessible around the clock, but some are open only from 10 to 5; inquire at the Sheesh Mahal Hotel (☞ Lodging, *below*), which also rents an audio tour.

On the banks of the Betwa River next to Kanchana Ghat, a short walk upstream from the town proper, are 14 sandstone **cenotaphs** built in honor of the former rulers. The arches of these *chattras*—and their placement in a garden setting—suggest the architecture of the Moguls and other Muslim rulers, yet the structures are topped with spires, or *shikharas,* recalling North Indian Hindu temples.

Towering over the center of Orccha from opposite the fort, the **Chaturbhuj Temple** was built in the 16th century to house an image of the Hindu god Rama that would be brought to the capital by Kunwari, wife of Madhukar Shah (1554–92), the third and greatest of Orchha's kings. According to local lore, however, the temple was incomplete when Kunwari returned with the icon from Ayodhya, the mythic capital of Rama's kingdom. She installed it in her own palace, whence the image refused to move; that building is now the Ram Raja Temple. A temple that never was, Chaturbhuj remains desolate.

Facing the bridge to the palace complex, the **Ram Raja Temple** is the center of community life in Orchha. A large, low-rise palace building in the shadow of the Chaturbhuj Temple, it's fronted by a pleasant plaza filled with people and trees, and vendors selling snacks and religious items. The secular architecture and abandoned royal surroundings emphasize Rama's role as the ideal king in the Hindu pantheon. In late November, the temple is the site of an annual reenactment of the epic hero's marriage. ⏲ *8–12:30 and 7–9:30.*

Dinman Hardaul's Palace, below the fort, has some interesting underground rooms. The palace's **Phool Bagh** gardens have an ancient, intricate watering system.

★ The **Laxminarayan Temple,** less than 1 km (½ mi) west of town, is a 17th-century mix of temple and fort architecture. Its walls and ceilings are decorated with vibrant murals, and its upper terrace has lovely views of the surrounding countryside. The paintings, which are well preserved, illustrate both mythological and historical subjects, including the Queen of Jhansi's battles with the British during the Mutiny of 1857. ⏲ *8–12:30 and 7:30.*

Perched on a small seasonal island where the river splits as it passes ★ through town, the impressive **Sheesh Mahal** fort and palace is approached by a multiarched granite bridge. The first building you'll see is the 16th-century **Raj Mahal** (Royal Palace), which has beautiful murals and, from the upper stories, good views of the rest of the complex. Climbing further, the Sheesh Mahal Hotel is on your left; here you can pick up an excellent self-guided audio tour of the complex. Straight ahead is the largest palace in the complex, the three-story, 17th-century **Jahangir Mahal.** Built for an expected, but never realized, visit from the Mogul emperor Jahangir (who had married, among others, the sister of an Orchha king), it elegantly blends Hindu and Mogul themes. The main (east) entrance is flanked by two stone elephants. North of these buildings is the **Rai Praveen Mahal,** a two-story brick palace named for the consort of the Bundela king Indramani. This one has accessible underground rooms, and an interesting system of watering its adjacent gardens from two wells. Scattered over the flood plain north of the royal residences are a series of temples and ritual structures including a compound containing three temples and several royal *chattras.* The images have been removed from the temples themselves, but the entrance to the sanctum of the largest one, **Panchmukhi Mahadeva** ("Shiva with Five Faces"), holds an appealing carving of the elephant-headed god Ganesh.

Lodging

$$ **Orchha Resort.** This new, air-conditioned hotel on the river bank just opposite the cenotaphs has a helpful and pleasant staff and comfortable modern rooms. Its design echoes the local sandstone, yet it encroaches somewhat on its natural setting, near the river and some important monuments. The buffet restaurant serves a reasonable version of the standard Mughlai-meets-Continental hotel menu. ✉ *Kanchanaghat, Orchha, Tikamgarh district, 472246* ☎ *7680/52677 (–8) or 517/330759,* FAX *515/449817; or reserve through Oswal Motels and Resorts, 30 Munro Rd., Agra 282001,* ☎ *562/363240,* FAX *562/363407. 32 rooms. Restaurant, bar, pool, laundry service. AE, MC, V.*

$$ ★ **Sheesh Mahal.** Part of the fort-palace complex, this government-run hotel was built in 1763 and renovated in a comfortable, if not luxurious, style. It's a great way to experience Orchha's past. The rooms are simply furnished, but they're clean; ask for the Royal Suite on the top floor, or the slightly less palatial Deluxe room. Both have wonderful views and are huge and regally decorated with wooden furniture that recalls the British Raj. A lack of phones and TVs keeps things quiet. There's no air-conditioning, but you won't need it before March or April, and each room has a fan. ✉ *Orchha, Tikamgarh district, 472246,* ☎ *7680/52624; or reserve through MPSTDC, Gangotri Bldg., 4th floor, T. T. Nagar, Bhopal 462003,* ☎ *755/554340 (–3),* FAX *725/772384; local phone* ☎ *224. 8 rooms. Restaurant, bar. MC, V.*

$ **Betwa Cottages.** These charming modern cottages stand on the banks of the Betwa River. Each house has a little lawn outside, and the immaculate rooms have huge windows and are pleasantly furnished with comfortable beds and rugs. The bathrooms even have exhaust fans. Some rooms are air-conditioned; the rest have fans. The chef prepares excellent kebabs and Chinese food. ✉ *Orchha, Tikamgarh district, 472246,* ☎ *7680/52618; or reserve through MPSTDC, Gangotri Bldg., 4th floor, T. T. Nagar, Bhopal 462003,* ☎ *755/554340 (–3),* FAX *755/772384. 10 cottages. Restaurant. MC, V.*

Shopping

Just outside Orchha, where the road from town meets the main road between Jhansi and Khajuraho, **Taragram** (✉ 1077 Civil Lines, Jhansi, ☎ 910/5281) is an innovative development program focusing on the revival of traditional paper-making methods. Here you can buy handmade notebooks and other items.

KHAJURAHO

The Vidhya hills in Madhya Pradesh's Chatarpur district form the backdrop to the small village of Khajuraho. Located 395 km (244 mi) southeast of Agra, this place is so rural that it's hard to imagine Khajuraho as the religious capital of the Chandela dynasty (10th–12th centuries), one of the most powerful Rajput dynasties of Central India. The only significant river is some distance away, and the village seems far removed from any substantial economic activity. Yet this is where the Chandelas built 85 temples, 22 of which remain to give us a glimpse of a time when Hindu art and devotion reached their apex.

During the Chandelas' rule, India was the Asian El Dorado. The temples' royal patrons were rich, the land was fertile, and everyone lived the 10th-century good life, trooping off to fairs, feasts, hunts, dramas, music, and dances. This abundance was the perfect climate for creativity, and temple-building was emerging as the major form of expression. There were no strict boundaries between the sacred and profane, no dictates on acceptable deities: Shiva, Vishnu, Brahma, and the Jains' saints were all lavishly honored, and new excavations have begun to uncover a complex of Buddhist temples as well. Despite the interest in heaven, the real focus was earth, and particularly the facts of human life. Here, immortalized in stone, virile men and voluptuous women cavort and copulate in the most intimate and erotic of postures. Khajuraho represents the best of Hindu temple sculpture: sinuous, twisting forms—human and divine—throbbing with life, tension, and conflict.

The Chandela dynasty reigned for five centuries, succumbing eventually to invaders with a different moral outlook. In 1100, Mahmud the Turk began a holy war against the "idolaters" of India, and by 1200 the sultans of Delhi ruled over the once-glorious Chandela domain. Khajuraho's temples lapsed into obscurity until their rediscovery by a British explorer in 1838.

The temples have more to offer than erotic sculpture. Their soaring shikharas are meant to resemble the peaks of the Himalayas, abode of Lord Shiva: Starting with the smallest shikhara, over the entrance, each spire rises higher than the one before it, as in a range of mountains that seems to draw near the heavens. Designed to inspire the viewer toward the highest human potential, these were also the builders' attempts to reach upward, out of the material world, to *moksha*—the final release from the cycle of rebirth. One scholar has suggested that Khajuraho's temples were in effect chariots of the kings, carrying them off to a heavenly world resembling an idealized view of courtly life. Their combination of lofty structure and delicate sculpture gives them a unique sense of completeness and exuberance.

Of the 22 extant temples, all but two were made from sandstone mined from the banks of the River Ken, 30 km (19 mi) away. The stone blocks were carved separately, then assembled as interlocking pieces to form a temple. Though each structure is different, every temple observes precise architectural principles of shape, form, and orientation and contains certain essential elements: a high raised platform, an *ardh mandapam* (entrance porch), a mandapam (portico), an *antrala* (vestibule), and a *garbha griha* (inner sanctum). Some of the larger temples also have a walkway around the inner sanctum, a *mahamandapam* (hall), and subsidiary shrines on each corner of the platform, making a complete *panchayatana* (five-shrine complex).

A number of sculptural motifs run through the temples. The directional gods, for instance, have designated positions on each temple. Elephant-headed Ganesh faces north; Yama, the god of death, and his mount, the male buffalo, face south. The two goddesses guarding the entrance to the sanctum are the rivers Ganges and Yamuna. Other sculptures include the *apsaras* (heavenly maidens), found mainly inside the temples, and the Atlas-like *kichakas*, who support the temple ceilings on their shoulders. Many sculptures simply reflect everyday activities, such as a dance class. The sultry *nayikas* (human women) show various emotions, and the *mithunas* are amorous couples. The scorpion appears as an intriguing theme, running up and down the thighs of many female sculptures as a kind of erotic thermometer. It appears, too, on the breastbone of the terrible, emaciated goddess Chamundi on the corners of several temple platforms, suggesting a complex and imaginative view of sexuality on the part of the sculptors and their patrons.

No one knows for sure why erotic sculptures are so important here, though many explanations have been offered. The female form is often used as an auspicious marker on Hindu gateways and doors, in the form of temple sculptures as well as domestic wall paintings. In the late classical and early medieval period, this symbol expanded into full-blown erotic art in many places, including the roughly contemporary sun temple at Modhera, in Gujarat, and the slightly later sun temple at Konark, in Orissa. Khajuraho legend has it that the founder of the Chandela dynasty, Chandravarman, was born of an illicit union between his mother and the moon god, which resulted in her ostracism. When he grew up to become a mighty king, his mother begged him to show the world the beauty and divinity of lovemaking. A common folk explanation is that the erotic sculptures protect the temples from lightning; and art historians have recently noticed that many of the erotic panels are placed at junctures where some protection or strengthening agent might be structurally necessary. Others say the sculptures reflect the influence of a tantric cult that believed in reversals of ordinary morality as a religious practice. Still others argue that sex has been used as a metaphor: The carnal and bestial sex generally shown near the bases of the temples represent uncontrolled human appetites, while the couples deeply engrossed in each another, oblivious to all else, represent a divine bliss, the closest humans can approach to God. Some also contend that the erotic is confined to the outer, worldly walls of the temples while their interior decoration is uplifting and focused on God, but this view is contradicted by the sculptures at several temples. The mystery lives on, but it's clear that the sculptors drew on a sophisticated and sensual worldly heritage, including the *Kama Sutra,* the classical Hindu love manual, some of whose specific instructions are illustrated here.

The best way to see Khajuraho is to hire a guide (especially for the Western Group of temples) and to visit the Western Group in the first rays of the morning sun, follow them with the Eastern Group, see the museum in the afternoon, and make it to the Chaturbhuj Temple in the Southern Group in time for sunset.

Khajuraho holds an annual **dance festival** set in part against the backdrop of the temples. If you'll be in India anytime around the beginning of March, don't miss this superb event. Contact Khajuraho's regional tourist office for details (☎ 7686/44051).

Eastern Group of Temples

Interspersed around the edges of Khajuraho village, the Eastern Group of temples includes four Hindu and four Jain temples, whose proximity attests to the religious tolerance of the times in general and the Chan-
8 dela rulers in particular. Northernmost is the late-11th-century **Vamana Temple,** dedicated to Vishnu's dwarf incarnation (though the image in the sanctum looks more like a tall, sly child). The sanctum walls show unusual theological openness, featuring most of the major gods and goddesses; Vishnu appears in many of his form, including the Buddha, his ninth incarnation. Outside, two tiers of sculpture are concerned mainly with the nymphs of paradise, who strike charming poses under
9 their private awnings. The small, well-proportioned **Javari Temple,** just south of the Vamana Temple and roughly contemporary in origin, has a simplified three-shrine design. The two main exterior bands bear hosts of heavenly maidens.

10 The granite and sandstone **Brahma Temple,** one of the earliest temples here (c. 900), is probably misnamed. Brahma, a titular member of the triad of Hinduism's great gods, along with Shiva and Vishnu, rarely gets a temple to himself, and this one has a *linga,* the abstract, phallus-shape icon of Shiva. It differs in design from most of the other temples, particularly in the combination of materials and the shape of its shikhara.

Temples
Adinath, **12**
Brahma, **10**
Chaturbhuj, **16**
Chausath Yogini, **17**
Chitragupta, **25**
Devi Jagdamba, **23**
Duladeo, **15**
Ghantai, **11**
Javari, **9**
Kandariya Mahadev, **22**
Lakshmana, **21**
Lalguan Mahadeva, **18**
Mahadeva, **24**
Matangesvara, **19**
Nandi, **27**
Parsvanath, **13**
Parvati, **28**
Shantinath, **14**
Vamana, **8**
Varaha, **20**
Vishvanath, **26**

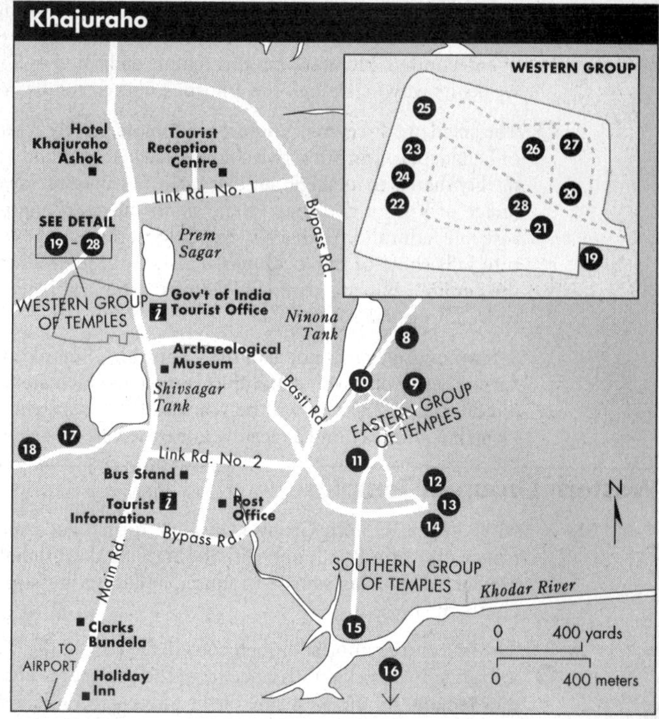

South of these three temples, toward the Jain complex, is a little gem
11 called the **Ghantai Temple.** All that's left of this temple are its pillars, festooned with carvings of pearls and bells. Adorning the entrance are an eight-armed Jain goddess riding the mythical bird Garuda and a relief illustrating the 16 dreams of the mother of Mahavira, the greatest religious figure in Jainism and a counterpart to the Buddha.

12 The late-11th-century **Adinath Temple,** a minor shrine, is set in a small walled compound southeast of Ghantai. Its porch and the statue of Tirthankara (literally, "Ford-Maker," a figure who leads others to liberation) Adinatha are modern additions. Built at the beginning of the Chandelas' decline, this temple is relatively small, but the shikhara and base are richly carved.

13 The **Parsvanath Temple** to the south, built in the mid-10th century, is the largest and finest in the Eastern Group's Jain complex and holds some of the best sculpture in Khajuraho, including images of Vishnu. In contrast to the intricate calculations behind the layout of the Western Group, the plan for this temple is a simple rectangle, with a separate spire in the rear. Statues of flying angels and sloe-eyed beauties occupied with children, cosmetics, and flowers adorn the outer walls. The stone conveys even the texture of the women's thin garments. The
14 third temple in this cluster, the **Shantinath,** bears an inscription dating it to the early 11th century. It has been remodeled extensively and is still in active use, but it does contain some old Jain sculpture.

Southern Group of Temples

15 Though built in the customary five-shrine style, the **Duladeo Temple** (about 900 yards south of the Eastern Group's Ghantai) looks flatter and more massive than most Khajuraho shrines. Probably the last temple built in Khajuraho, dated to the 12th century, the Duladeo Tem-

ple lacks the usual ambulatory passage and crowning lotus-shape finials. It has some vibrant sculptures, but many are clichéd and overdecorated. Here, too, in this temple dedicated to Shiva, eroticism works its way in, though the amorous figures are discreetly placed.

16 The small, 12th-century **Chaturbhuj Temple,** nearly 3 km (2 mi) south of Duladeo, has an attractive colonnaded entrance and a feeling or verticality thanks to its single spire. It enshrines an impressive four-handed image of Vishnu that may be the single most striking piece of sculpture in Khajuraho. With a few exceptions, the temple's exterior sculpture falls short of the local mark (a sign of the declining fortunes of the empire), but this temple is definitely the best place in Khajuraho to watch the sun set.

A few hundred yards north of the Chaturbhuj Temple are excavations for the newly discovered **Buddhist complex,** which archaeologists first announced in 1999. It will be years before reconstructions are complete, but you may find a recently unearthed piece of sculpture on view.

Western Group of Temples

Most of the Western Group is inside a formal enclosure with an entrance off Main Road, opposite the State Bank of India. The grounds are open daily from sunrise to sunset, and the admission fee, Rs. 1, includes the museum.

The first three temples, though considered part of the Western Group,
17 are actually at a slight distance from the enclosure. The **Chausath Yogini Temple,** on the west side of the Shivsagar Tank, a small artificial lake, is the oldest temple at Khajuraho, possibly built as early as AD 820. It is dedicated to Kali, and its name refers to the 64 (*chausath*) female ascetics (*yoginis*) who serve this fierce goddess in the Hindu pantheon. Unlike its counterparts of pale, warm-hued sandstone, this temple is made of granite and is the only one (so far excavated) in Khajuraho that's oriented northeast-southwest instead of north-south. It was originally surrounded by 64 roofed cells for the figures of Kali's attendants; only 35 cells remain. Scholarly supposition holds that this and a handful of other open-air temples, usually circular, in remote parts of India were focal points for an esoteric cult.

18 The Shiva temple **Lalguan Mahadeva** is a few hundred yards northeast of the Chausath Yogini. The structure is in ruins, and the original portico is missing, but this temple is historically significant because it was built of both granite and sandstone, marking the transition from Chausath Yogini to the later temples. Just outside the boundary of the
19 Western Group is the **Matangesvara Temple,** the only one still in use here; worship takes place in the morning and afternoon. The lack of ornamentation, square construction, and simpler floor plan date this temple to the early 10th century. The building has oriel windows, a projecting portico, and a ceiling of overlapping concentric circles. An enormous linga, nearly 8½ ft tall, is enshrined in the sanctum.

Across the street from Matangesvara, Khajuraho's **Archaeological Museum** has some exquisite carvings and sculptures recovered by archaeologists. The three galleries attempt to put the various sculptures into context according to the deities they represent. ⌚ *Sat.–Thurs. 10–5.*

20 As you enter the Western Group complex, you'll see the **Varaha Temple** (circa 900–925) to your left. This shrine is dedicated to Vishnu's Varaha avatar, or Boar Incarnation, which Vishnu assumed in order to rescue the earth after a demon had hidden it in the slush at the bottom of the sea. In the inner sanctum, all of creation is depicted on the

massive and beautifully polished sides of a stone boar, who in turn stands on the serpent Shesha. The ceiling is carved with a lotus relief.

21 Behind the Varaha Temple stands the **Lakshmana Temple,** also dedicated to Vishnu, and the only complete temple remaining. Along with Kandariya Mahadeva and Vishvanath (☞ *below*), this edifice represents the peak of achievement in North Indian temple architecture. All three temples were built in the early to mid-10th century, face east, and follow an elaborate plan resembling a double cross, with three tiers of exterior sculpture above the friezes on their high platforms. The ceiling of the mandapam is charmingly carved with shell and floral motifs. The lintel over the entrance to the main shrine shows Lakshmi, goddess of wealth and consort of Vishnu, with Brahma, Lord of Creation (on her left) and Shiva, Lord of Destruction (on her right). A frieze above the lintel depicts the planets. The relief on the doorway shows the gods and demons churning the ocean to obtain a pitcher of miraculous nectar from the bottom. The wall of the sanctum is carved with scenes from the legend of Krishna (one of Vishnu's incarnations). An icon in the sanctum with two pairs of arms and three heads represents Vishnu as Vaikuntha, or the supreme god, and is surrounded by images of his ten incarnations. Around the exterior base are some of Khajuraho's most famous sculptures, with gods and goddesses on the protruding corners, erotic couples or groups in the recesses, and apsaras and *sura-sundaris* (apsaras performing everyday activities) in-between. Along the sides of the tall platform beneath the temple, friezes depict social life, including battle scenes, festivals, and amorous sport.

22 The **Kandariya Mahadev,** west of the Lakshmana Temple, is the largest and most evolved temple in Khajuraho in terms of the blending of architecture and sculpture, and one of the finest in India. Probably built around 1020, it follows the five-shrine design; and its central shikhara, which towers 102 ft above the platform, is actually made up of 84 subsidiary towers building up in increments. The feeling of ascent is repeated inside, where each succeeding mandapam is a step above the previous one, and the garbha griha is higher still; dedicated to Shiva, this inner sanctum houses a marble linga with a 4-ft circumference. Even the figures on this temple are taller and slimmer than those elsewhere. The rich interior carving includes two beautiful *toranas* (arched doorways); outside, three bands of sculpture around the sanctum and transept bring to life a whole galaxy of Hindu gods and goddesses, mithunas, celestial handmaidens, and lions. A total of 872 statues—226 inside and 646 outside—have been counted.

23 The **Devi Jagdamba Temple** was originally dedicated to Vishnu, as indicated by a prominent sculpture over the sanctum's doorway. It's now dedicated to Parvati, Shiva's consort, but because her image is black—a color associated with Kali, goddess of wrath and an avatar of Parvati—it is also known as the Kali Temple. From the inside, its three-shrine design makes the temple appear to be shaped like a cross. The third band of sculpture has a series of erotic mithunas. The ceilings are similar to those in the Kandariya Mahadev, and the three-headed, eight-armed statue of Shiva is one of the best cult images in Khajuraho.

24 The small, mostly ruined **Mahadeva Temple** shares its platform with the Kandariya and the Devi Jagdamba. Now dedicated to Shiva, it may originally have been a subsidiary to the Kandariya Mahadev temple, probably dedicated to Shiva's consort. In the portico stands a remarkable statue of a man caressing a mythical horned lion.

25 The **Chitragupta Temple** lies slightly north of the Devi Jagdamba and resembles it in construction. In honor of the presiding deity, Surya—

the sun god—the temple faces east, and its cell contains a 5-ft image of Surya complete with the chariot and seven horses that carry him across the sky. Surya also appears above the doorway. In the central niche south of the sanctum is an image of Vishnu with 11 heads; his own face is in the center, and the other heads represent his 10 (9 past and 1 future) incarnations. A profusion of sculptural scenes of animal combat, royal processions, masons at work, and joyous dances depict the lavish country life of the Chandelas.

26 The **Vishvanath Temple** is on a terrace to the east of the Chitragupta and Devi Jagdamba temples. Two staircases lead up to it, the northern flanked by a pair of lions and the southern by a pair of elephants. The Vishvanath probably preceded the Kandariya, but here two of the original corner shrines remain. On the outer wall of the corridor surrounding the cells is an impressive image of Brahma, the three-headed Lord of Creation, and his consort, Saraswati. On every wall the form of woman dominates, portrayed in all her daily 10th-century occupations: writing a letter, holding her baby, studying her reflection in a mirror, applying makeup, or playing music. The nymphs of paradise are voluptuous and provocative, and the erotic scenes, robust. An inscription states that the temple was built by Chandela King Dhanga
27 in 1002. Facing the main temple, a simpler shrine, the **Nandi Temple,** houses a monolithic statue of Shiva's mount, the massive and richly harnessed sacred bull Nandi.

28 The small and heavily rebuilt **Parvati Temple,** near Vishvanath, was originally dedicated to Vishnu. The present icon is that of the goddess Ganga standing on her mount, the crocodile.

Dining and Lodging

$$$ ✕ **Apsara.** This pleasant restaurant has lattice screens of teak and bird paintings on silk. The chef prepares good Indian and Continental dishes; try the tandoori kebabs or the vegetable *korma* (creamy tomato-and-onion curry). ✉ *Jass Oberoi hotel,* ☎ *7686/42344. AE, DC, MC, V.*

$$$ ✕ **Bhoj Bundela.** Decorated in shades of gold, this small restaurant has tile floors, cane furniture, and elegant plants everywhere. The menu mixes Indian and Continental fare, and the chef is creative. Try the vegetable-coriander soup and the chicken *hara masala* (with green spices). ✉ *Clarks Bundela,* ☎ *7686/42386. AE, DC, MC, V.*

$ ✕ **Mediterraneo.** Eat on the rooftop or in a small dining room at this Italian restaurant near the Western Group. It has not a single frill, but the kitchen is spotless and the chef is from Italy. Go for pizza or one of the many pasta dishes. Payment is in rupees only. ✉ *Jain Temple Rd., opposite Surya Hotel,* ☎ *7686/42340. No credit cards.*

$ ✕ **Raja Cafe.** This little open-air restaurant is a popular meeting place for local guides, so you can easily hire one here (or at the tourist office next door). Set under towering peepul trees, it's a great place for a cup of tea or a snack. The food is pretty basic, but the Continental dishes are popular, such as the chicken pancake béchamel (chicken in white sauce served in a crepe). Payment is in rupees only. ✉ *Opposite Western Group entrance on main square,* ☎ *no phone. No credit cards.*

$$$ 🏨 **Clarks Bundela.** This two-story, white colonial-style hotel is nicely illuminated and has abundant marble, which gives it a generally cool feel. The rooms are Western and very comfortable, with French doors and balconies. ✉ *Khajuraho 471606, Madhya Pradesh,* ☎ *7686/42386 (–7),* FAX *7686/42385. 68 rooms, 2 suites. Restaurant, bar, pool, meeting room, travel services. AE, DC, MC, V.*

$$$ 🏨 **Holiday Inn Khajuraho.** From the outside, the Holiday Inn looks more like an American condo complex than a hotel, but its interior, with plenty of marble, chandeliers, and curving staircases, is surprisingly elegant. The Western-style rooms are decorated in soft cream shades and have large bay windows, some with temple views. Suites are decorated with cultural themes. ✉ *Airport Rd.,* ☏ *7686/50784,* FAX *7686/50749; reserve through* ✉ *Suite 7-B, Girdhar Apartments, 28 Feroz Shah Rd., New Delhi 110001,* ☏ *11/375–5501,* FAX *11/373–9260. 56 rooms, 8 suites. 2 restaurants, bar, coffee shop, pool, beauty salon, tennis court, health club, jogging, babysitting, meeting room, travel services. AE, DC, MC, V.*

$$$ 🏨 **Chandela.** Run by the Taj group, this elegant hotel centers on a lovely pool and is surrounded by gardens. The Western-style rooms are perfectly comfortable, and each has a balcony or patio. ✉ *Khajuraho 471606, Madhya Pradesh,* ☏ *7686/42355 (–65),* FAX *7686/42366. 94 rooms, 4 suites. 2 restaurants, bar, coffee shop, pool, beauty salon, miniature golf, tennis court, health club, badminton, croquet, babysitting, business services, meeting rooms, travel services. AE, DC, MC, V.*

$$$ ★ 🏨 **Jass Oberoi.** The main motifs at this Oberoi are white marble and plants in brass pots. Just over half a mile from the Western Group of temples, this two-story lodging has modern rooms with balconies overlooking either the pool or the hills around town. ✉ *Khajuraho 471606, Madhya Pradesh,* ☏ *7686/42344 or 7686/42376 (–77),* FAX *7686/42345. 91 rooms, 3 suites. Restaurant, bar, pool, tennis court, health club, travel services, meeting room. AE, DC, MC, V.*

$$ ★ 🏨 **Ken River Lodge.** Set near Panna National Park, 27 km (17 mi) from Khajuraho, this lodge offers village-style mud huts and spacious tents, all with running hot water and private baths and showers. The restaurant is a platform built on tree limbs on the banks of the Ken River. ✉ *Madla Village, Panna district; reserve through Ken River Lodge, c/o Pro-Host, A/C-456 Vasant Kunj, New Delhi 110070,* ☏ *11/613–4440,* FAX *11/689–3027. 4 cottages, 4 tents. Restaurant, beach, boating, fishing. No credit cards.*

$ ★ 🏨 **Jhankar.** This one-story government-owned hotel rents spacious, clean rooms with modern decor. Some rooms are air-conditioned; others have fans. ✉ *Airport Rd., Khajuraho 471606 Madhya Pradesh,* ☏ *7686/44063 or 7686/44194; or reserve through MPSTDC, Gangotri Bldg., 4th floor, T. T. Nagar, Bhopal 462003, Madhya Pradesh,* ☏ *755/774340 (–43),* FAX *755/774289 or 755/772384. 19 rooms. Restaurant, bar. MC, V.*

Shopping

Numerous curio shops around the Western Group of temples sell sundry souvenirs, including humorous knockoffs of erotic sculptures and examples of tribal metalwork. **Shilpgram** (☏ 7686/42280), just off the airport road, is a government project that hosts craftspeople from all over India for extended residences during the peak travel season; for Rs. 100 you can watch the artisans at work as you shop, and enjoy dance and drama performances in the evening. The campus is open daily from 11 to 9.

Side Trips

If you have time, take an extra day to explore and picnic in the beautiful country around Khajuraho. Backed by the distant mountains, **Khajuraho Village** (west of the main square, near the Jain temples) is a typical Indian village, its small streets crammed with animals and bicycles. For ★ a slightly longer excursion, drive or bike to the **Gharial Sanctuary** on the Ken River, 28 km (17 mi) away; the park was set up to protect the ★ slender-snouted crocodile and has some lovely waterfalls. At **Panna National Park** you can see the elusive tiger and a host of other wildlife.

Only 31 km (19 mi) from Khajuraho, it's still relatively undisturbed by visitors.

VARANASI AND LUCKNOW

Spread out along the Ganges River, the interior lanes and river ghats of ancient Varanasi throb with religious and commercial energy like no other place in India. Sarnath, just north of Varanasi, is the historic center of the Buddhist world, and Bodhgaya, east of Varanasi in the state of Bihar, is a present-day international center of Buddhist worship. European-flavored Lucknow, the capital of Uttar Pradesh, is an easy diversion between Varanasi and Delhi.

Varanasi

406 km (252 mi) east of Khajuraho, 765 km (474 mi) southeast of Delhi, 677 km (420 mi) northwest of Calcutta

Varanasi has been the religious capital of Hinduism through all recorded time. No one knows the date of the city's founding, but when Siddhartha Gautama, the historic Buddha, came here around 550 BC to deliver his first teaching, he found an ancient and developed settlement. Contemporary with Babylon, Nineveh, and Thebes, Varanasi has been called the oldest continuously inhabited city on earth.

Every devout Hindu wants to visit Varanasi to purify body and soul in the Ganges, to shed all sin, and, if possible, to die here in old age and achieve moksha, release from the cycle of rebirth. Descending from the Himalayas on its long course to the Bay of Bengal, the Ganges is believed by Hindus to hold the power of salvation in each drop. Pilgrims seek that salvation along the length of the river, but their holiest site is Varanasi. Every year, the city welcomes millions of pilgrims for whom these waters—fouled by the pollution of humans both living and dead—remain pristine enough to cleanse the soul.

Commonly called Banaras, and, by devout Hindus, Kashi ("Resplendent with Light"), Varanasi has about 1 million inhabitants. Its heart is a maze of streets and alleys, hiding a disorderly array of at least 2,000 temples and shrines. Domes, minarets, pinnacles, towers, and derelict 18th-century palaces dominate the river's sacred left bank. The streets are noisy and rife with color, and the air hangs heavy, as if in collaboration with the clang of temple gongs and bells. Some houses have simply decorated entrances; other buildings are ornate with Indian-style gingerbread on balconies and verandas. You're likely to encounter funeral processions, cows munching on garlands destined for the gods, and, especially near the Golden Temple and the centrally located Dashashvamedh Ghat, assertive hawkers and phony guides.

Its variety of shrines notwithstanding, Varanasi is essentially a temple city dedicated to Shiva, Lord of Destruction. Shiva is typically said to live in the Himalayas, but myths say he was unable to leave Kashi after manifesting himself here. Exiling the earthly maharaja to Ram Nagar, across the river, Shiva took up permanent residence here. (As a popular song has it, in Varanasi "every pebble is a Shiva linga.") The city itself is said to rest on a prong of Shiva's trident, above the cycles of creation, decay, and destruction that prevail in the rest of the world.

The maze of lanes may seem daunting, but you're never far from the river, where you can hire a boat for a quiet ride. Banarasis, as the locals call themselves, typically hire boats at sundown for twilight excursions, sometimes with tiny candlelit lamps made of leaves and flowers which they leave on the water as offerings. The Ganges turns sharply at Varanasi to flow south to north past the city, giving the riverbank a perfect alignment with the rising sun. In sacred geography the city is demarcated by the Ganges to the east and two small rivers—the Varana to the north, which winds by the cantonment area and joins the Ganges near Raj Ghat (site of some important archaeological excavations), and the Asi, a small stream in the south that was recently diverted as a sanitation measure.

Traditionally, Varanasi is seen as a field divided into three sections named after important temples to Shiva. Omkareshvara is the namesake temple in the northern section, which is probably the oldest area but is now impoverished and seldom visited by pilgrims. The central section is named after Kashi Vishvanath, the famous "Golden Temple." Vishvanath itself means "Lord of the Universe," one of Shiva's names, and there are actually many Vishvanath temples. The southern area, the Kedar Khand, is named for Kedareshvara, a temple easily picked out from the river thanks to the vertical red and white stripes painted on its walls, a custom of the South Indian worshipers who are among temple's devotees. The ghats stretch along the river from Raj Ghat in the north to Asi Ghat in the south; beyond Asi is the university, across the river from Ram Nagar Fort and Palace. The city itself spreads out behind the ghats, with the hotels in the cantonment area about 20 minutes from the river by auto-rickshaw.

A Good Walk

To get a sense of the pilgrim's experience, walk from Dashashvamedh Road down the relatively broad, shop-lined lane to Vishvanath Temple. The lane turns sharply right at a large image of the elephant-headed god Ganesh, then passes the entrance to the temple of Vishvanath's consort, Annapurna, on the right, and **Kashi Vishvanath Temple** ㉙ itself. Just past the temple complex the Vishvanath lane intersects with Kachauri Gali, a lane (*gali*) named for the small, deep fried puris, or *kachauris,* cooked here for pilgrims.

Turning left, the entrance to the **Gyanvapi Mosque** ㉚ compound (closed to non-Muslims) is on the left. The short, stepped lane passes under a room in a house than spans both sides of the lane; the compound around the mosque is now cordoned off with steel bars, in response to an intermittent movement to restore the mosque as a Hindu temple. On the left are the Gyanvapi well and a cluster of tree-shaded Hindu shrines. Here many Hindus begin their pilgrimage to Kashi, declaring their purpose with the help of a Brahmin *panda* (temple priest) in a rite known as *sankalp,* or declaration of intention. Here a young tout will probably offer to escort you to a rooftop from which you can see into the Vishvanath Temple compound. The view is fascinating; just know that this process will also involve offers of tea and and the display of various wares. Farther up Kachauri Gali, a lane on the right is marked by a sign pointing toward Lalita Ghat; take this lane to a junction beside a small temple dedicated to Neelkanth Mahadev. On the right, a lane marked Bishwanath Singh Lane leads to the main cremation ground, just upstream from **Manikarnika Ghat** ㉛. You can often find your way just by following the processions of funeral biers that pass with startling regularity toward Manikarnika, their bearers moving swiftly and chanting, "Ram nam satya hai" ("God's name is truth").

Manikarnika itself has a small, deep pool, or *kund,* at the top of its flight of stone steps. The pool is said to have been dug by Vishnu at the dawn of creation, and thus to be the first *tirtha*—literally, "ford," and figuratively a place of sacred bathing. Shiva is said to have lost an earring (*manikarnika*) as he trembled in awe before this place, one of the holiest sites in Varanasi. Walk north (upstream) past the broad, grad-

Alamgir Mosque, **32**
Bharat Kala Bhavan Museum, **40**
Chausath Yogini Temple, **35**
Dashashvamedh Ghat, **33**
Dhobi Ghat, **36**
Durga Temple, **38**
Gyanvapi Mosque, **30**
Kashi Vishvanath Temple, **29**
Kedareshvara Temple, **37**
Manikarnika Ghat, **31**
Ram Nagar Fort and Palace, **41**
Sankat Mochan Temple, **39**
Shitala Temple, **34**

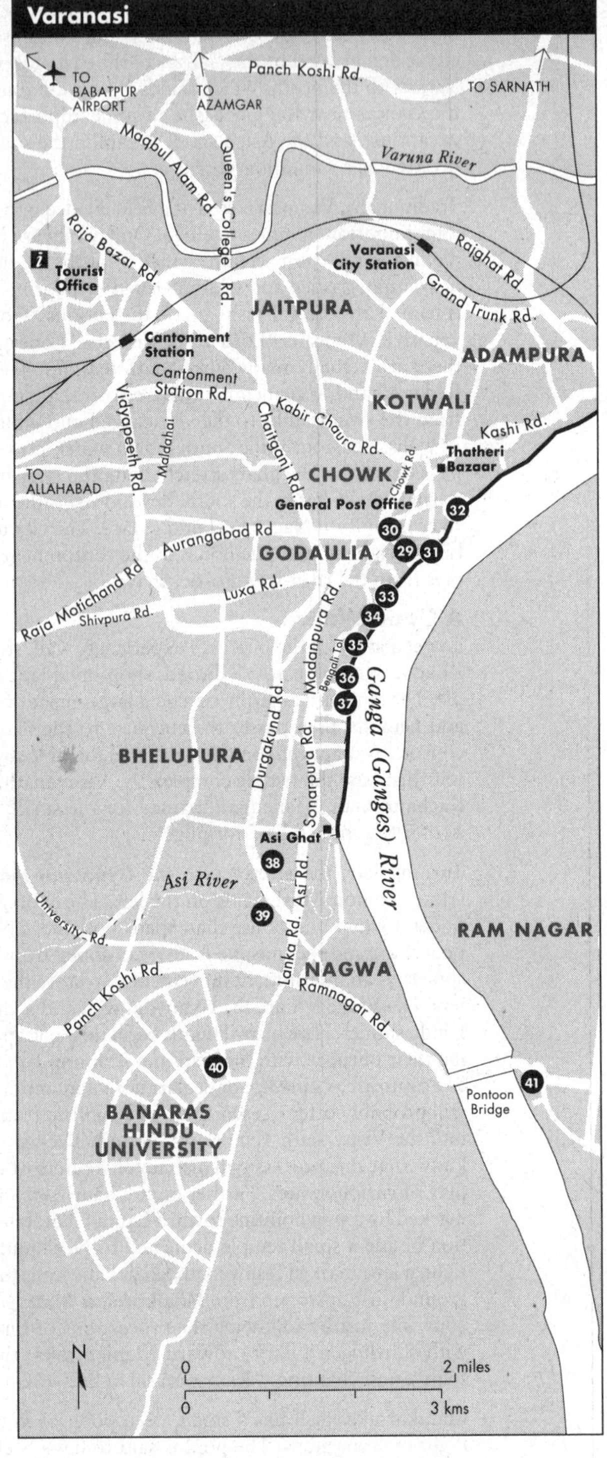

Finally, a travel companion that doesn't snore on the plane or eat all your peanuts.

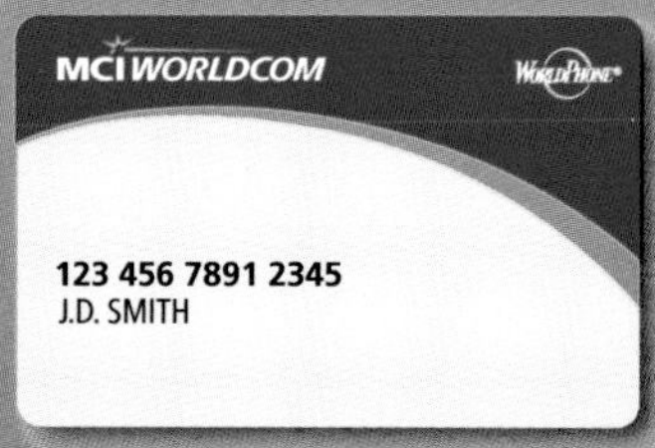

When traveling, your MCI WorldCom Card is the best way to keep in touch. Our operators speak your language, so they'll be able to connect you back home—no matter where your travels take you. Plus, your MCI WorldCom Card is easy to use, and even earns you frequent flyer miles every time you use it. When you add in our great rates, you get something even more valuable: peace-of-mind. So go ahead. Travel the world. MCI WorldCom just brought it a whole lot closer.

You can even sign up today at www.mci.com/worldphone or ask your operator to make a collect call to 1-410-314-2938.

EASY TO CALL WORLDWIDE

1. **Just dial the WorldPhone access number of the country you're calling from.**
2. **Dial or give the operator your MCI WorldCom Card number.**
3. **Dial or give the number you're calling.**

Australia ◆ To call using OPTUS To call using TELSTRA	 **1-800-551-111** **1-800-881-100**
Bahamas/Bermuda	**1-800-888-8000**
British Virgin Islands	**1-800-888-8000**
Costa Rica ◆	**0-800-012-2222**
Denmark	**8001-0022**
Norway ◆	**800-19912**
India For collect access	**000-127** **000-126**
United States/Canada	**1-800-888-8000**

For your complete WorldPhone calling guide, dial the WorldPhone access number for the country you're in and ask the operator for Customer Service. In the U.S. call 1-800-431-5402.

◆ Public phones may require deposit of coin or phone card for dial tone.

EARN FREQUENT FLYER MILES

Continental Airlines OnePass

Delta Air Lines SkyMiles

MILEAGE PLUS. United Airlines

MCI WorldCom, its logo and the names of the products referred to herein are proprietary marks of MCI WorldCom, Inc. All airline names and logos are proprietary marks of the respective airlines. All airline program rules and conditions apply.

The first thing you need overseas is the one thing you forget to pack.

FOREIGN CURRENCY DELIVERED OVERNIGHT

Chase Currency To Go® delivers foreign currency to your home by the next business day*

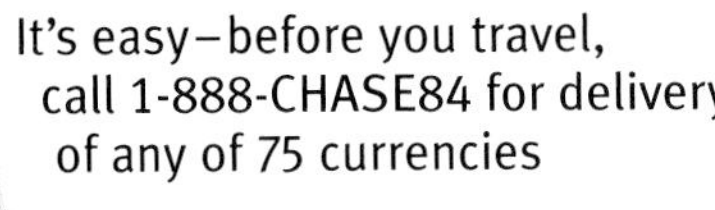

It's easy–before you travel, call 1-888-CHASE84 for delivery of any of 75 currencies

Delivery is free with orders of $500 or more

Competitive rates–without exchange fees

You don't have to be a Chase customer–you can pay by Visa® or MasterCard®

CHASE

THE RIGHT RELATIONSHIP IS EVERYTHING.®

1•888•CHASE84
www.chase.com

*Orders must be placed before 5 PM ET. $10 delivery fee for orders under $500.
©1999 The Chase Manhattan Corporation. All rights reserved. The Chase Manhattan Bank. Member FDIC.

ual steps of Scindia Ghat to the steps of Panchganga Ghat, the mythic confluence of five invisible rivers. The **Alamgir Mosque** ㉜ towers above Panchganga, and from its relatively short minaret you get a sweeping view of Varanasi and the Ganges. You can walk along the ghats back to **Dashashvamedh Ghat** ㉝, where a rickshaw-wallah can peddle you onward or you can take a boat.

Down the right fork of Dashashvamedh Road is Prayag Ghat. Here, at the top of the ghats on the right, is the white **Shitala Temple** ㉞. Continue south along the ghats fronting the somewhat quieter Kedar Khand section of town, which in ancient times was heavily forested and dotted with hermitages. After about 10 minutes you'll see steep steps leading up toward a house at the top of Chausath Yogini Ghat—a few yards up the lane on the right is the **Chausath Yogini Temple** ㉟, favored by the many Hindu widows who live in the surrounding Bengali quarter. Further south, you'll reach the **Dhobi Ghat** ㊱, where washermen beat clothes against stone slabs on the water's edge. A little farther south is the **Kedareshvara Temple** ㊲, recognizable from the river by its South Indian–style red and white stripes. Anywhere along this section, you can climb up the ghats and enter the city, where you'll soon reach a broader gali that runs parallel to the river through Bengali Tola, home to a large community from Bengal as well as from South India. You can pick up transport a little farther south, where a broad road reaches the river by the small burning ground at Harish Chandra Ghat, preferred cremation site of the *panditas,* or learned Brahmins. The large cement structure on stilts above the river is an electric crematorium built in the 1980s (the electric process is much cheaper than traditional cremation by flame on a wooden pyre). The restaurant Sindhi (☞ Dining and Lodging, *below*) is near here if you'd like to break for lunch.

Another half hour's walk brings you to Asi Ghat. Tulsi Ghat, just north of Asi, is where Tulsi Das, a medieval saint, is said to have composed his hugely popular Hindi version of the *Ramayana* epic (translated and revised from the Sanskrit). The ghat is now home to the offices of the Swachha Ganga Campaign, a movement led by a local priest to clean up the Ganges, first by building a series of sewage lagoons downstream. From the top of Tulsi Ghat, the lane to the right leads to **Lolark Kund,** a deep step well surrounded by several small but important shrines. This is an extraordinary place to visit just after sunrise, when people from the neighborhood offer devotions. Asi Ghat itself is an important bathing point and the only ghat in Varanasi where bathers access the river from a plain mud bank rather than stone steps. From here, walk or hire a cycle-rickshaw to take you to the **Durga Temple** ㊳, or Monkey Temple, a few hundred yards west of the river. From here you can walk or drive to **Sankat Mochan Temple** ㊴, whose *mahant,* or head priest, leads the Swachha Ganga Campaign. A 20-minute cycle-rickshaw ride or shorter cab ride takes you to the **Bharat Kala Bhavan Museum** ㊵ at Banaras Hindu University. Have your driver wait for you, and if you have time (and if, in the case of a cycle-rickshaw, your driver has the energy), proceed from the university across the Ganges to **Ram Nagar Fort and Palace** ㊶.

TIMING

The first part of this tour, starting and ending at Dashashvamedh Road, takes about two hours. The walk from Dashashvamedh to Kedareshvara takes 45 minutes if you stop to see the temples, plus 30 more minutes from Kedar Ghat to Asi Ghat. The last part of the tour, from Asi Ghat to Bharat Kala Bhavan, takes two more hours. A trip to Ram Nagar by car adds about two hours more. Varanasi is a labyrinth, however, so by all means allow some time to get lost. A boat ride will also stretch your sightseeing time.

Sights to See

32 **Alamgir Mosque.** Overlooking the Ganges from a dramatic high point, the Alamgir Mosque is a creation of the Mogul emperor Aurangzeb. Destroying the 17th-century temple Beni Madhav ka Darera, which had been dedicated to Vishnu, Aurangzeb built this mosque with an odd fusion of Hindu (lower portions and wall) and Muslim (upper portion) designs. Panchganga Ghat, down below, is an important bathing point, particularly on Makar Sankranti (January 14), when the sun crosses the Tropic of Capricorn as the earth shifts on its axis following the winter solstice. ✉ *From Dashashvamedh or Manikarnika ghats, head north along the river; the mosque towers above Panchganga Ghat.*

40 **Bharat Kala Bhavan Museum.** No one interested in Indian art should miss this museum on the campus of Banaras Hindu University, just south of Varanasi's traditional boundary. The permanent collection includes textiles, excellent Hindu and Buddhist sculptures, and miniature paintings from the courts of the Moguls and the Hindu princes of the Punjab Hills. One sculpture with particular power is from Varanasi's immediate area—a 4th-century Gupta-dynasty frieze showing Krishna (an incarnation of Vishnu) holding up Mt. Govardhan to protect his pastoral comrades from the rain. Have your car or rickshaw wait, as transport can be hard to find on the university's sprawling campus. ✉ *Banaras Hindu University, Lanka,.* ⏲ *Mon.–Sat. 10:30–4.* 🎟 *Free.*

35 **Chausath Yogini Temple.** The interesting temples between Prayag and Asi ghats include this one, which is at the top of a particularly steep set of steps by the ghat of the same name. Originally devoted to a tantric cult that is also associated with an important ruined temple at Khajuraho, it's now devoted to Kali (the goddess most popular with Bengalis), who is known here simply as "Ma"—Mother. The worshipers here now are mainly widows from Varanasi's Bengali quarter; in the early morning you'll see these women coming for the *darshan* (vision) of Kali after bathing in the Ganges. ✉ *Just above Chausath Yogini Ghat.*

★ 33 **Dashashvamedh Ghat.** About 70 stepped ghats line a 4-mi stretch of the Ganges, effortlessly wedding the great Hindu metropolis to the river. Numerous lingas remind pilgrims that they're under Shiva's care here. If you decide to hire a boat, an essential Varanasi experience, go to Dashashvamedh Ghat, the unofficial "main" ghat for most purposes. The best time to see the ghats is at sunrise, when a solemn group of people and even animals—lit by the sun's darkly golden first rays—hover on the water's edge, bent on immersion in the holy stream. As you float on the river, you'll see young bodybuilders exercising: these are members of some of the city's many wrestling clubs. Older men sit cross-legged in meditation or prayer, and pandas seated under huge umbrellas offer prayers for their pilgrim clients. Some devotees drink from the polluted water. A carcass may even float by. ✉ *Head east to the water from Godaulia Crossing, the central traffic circle in the Chowk district.*

36 **Dhobi Ghat.** At the Dhobi Ghat, south of Dashashvamedh, washermen and -women do early-morning laundry by beating it against stones in the river while their donkeys bray disconsolately on the bank. This may be the sight that moved Mark Twain to declare that "a Hindu is someone who spends his life trying to break stones with wet clothes."

38 **Durga Temple.** Dedicated to the goddess Durga, Shiva's consort, this 18th-century shrine stands besides a large, square pool of water due

west of Asi Ghat. The shikhara is formed on top of five lower spires, a convergence symbolizing the belief that all five elements of the world (earth, air, wind, water, and ether) merge with the supreme. This shrine is also called the Monkey Temple—the pests are everywhere, and they'll steal anything. ✉ *Durgakund Rd.*

NEED A BREAK? The **Vaatika Café** on the riverbank at Asi Ghat serves excellent pizza made with yak-milk cheese from Nepal, as well as pasta dishes, bona fide espresso, and other unlikely delicacies.

30 **Gyanvapi Mosque.** Mogul emperor Aurangzeb pulled down the original Vishveswara Temple to erect this mosque, and the building's foundation and rear still show parts of the original temple. The tallest of the mosque's minarets, which dominated the skyline of the holy city, collapsed during a flood in 1948. The surrounding area—just next to Kashi Vishvanath, the Golden Temple—has been the focus of Hindu revivalist attempts to reconsecrate the site of the former temple, and is currently staffed with police and fenced with barbed wire. It's normally very sedate, however, and is an important starting point for Hindu pilgrims.

29 **Kashi Vishvanath Temple.** Dedicated to Shiva, this temple in the old city is the most sacred shrine in Varanasi. Known as the Golden Temple for the gold plate on its spire—a gift from the Sikh maharaja Ranjit Singh in 1835—the temple is set back from the Ganges between the Dashashvamedh and Manikarnika ghats. Vishvanath is technically off-limits to non-Hindus, so your best bet is to glimpse it from the top floor of the house opposite (pay the owner a small fee). You'll see men and women making offerings to the linga in the inner shrine. The present temple was built by Rani Ahalyabai of Indore in 1776, near the site of the original shrine, which had been destroyed by Aurangzeb. ✉ *Vishvanath Gali.*

NEED A BREAK? From the lane that leads from Kashi Vishvanath Temple to Dashashvamedh Road, turn right toward Godaulia Crossing. To the left, in the second-to-last cul de sac before the crossing (opposite a sign for the Union Bank of India), a short lane lined with cloth merchants leads to the friendly, slightly divey **Ayyar's Café** (✉ Raman Katra, Dashashvamedh Rd.). Here milky, sweet South Indian filter coffee and South Indian desserts are served on worn marble tables at a slight remove from the city's tumult.

37 **Kedareshvara Temple.** You'll recognize this temple, the most important Shiva temple in this part of town, by its candy-stripe red and white walls. Take off your shoes at the small rear door at the top of the ghats to enter. The linga here is an unsculpted stone and is said to have emerged spontaneously when a pure-hearted but feeble devotee of Shiva prayed for a chance to visit the famous Kedareshvara Shiva temple in the Himalayas. Shiva is the god of destruction and fierce in aspect but, paradoxically, he is famously kind to his devotees, or *bhaktas*; in this myth, Shiva was touched by his bhakta's piety, so instead of bringing him to the mountain, Shiva brought his own image to the bhakta. The linga emerged out of a plate of rice and lentils, called *kicchari,* which believers see in the rough surface of the linga's natural stone. ✉ *Bengali Tola.*

31 **Manikarnika Ghat.** Thin blue smoke twists up to the sky from fires at Varanasi's chief cremation center (Harish Chandra Ghat, upstream, is the smaller one), which is actually adjacent to the ghat itself. Bodies wrapped in silk or linen—traditionally white for men and red or orange for women—are carried through the streets on bamboo stretchers to

the smoking pyres. After a brief immersion in the Ganges and a short wait, they body is placed on the pyre for the ritual that precedes the cremation. Funeral parties dressed in white, the color of mourning, hover with their deceased. Photographing funeral ghats is strictly forbidden, but you are allowed to watch.

★ 41 **Ram Nagar Fort and Palace.** Across the Ganges from town is the residential palace of the former maharaja of Varanasi, who still lives here and performs important ceremonial and charitable functions. The **Durbar Hall** (Public Audience Chamber) and **Royal Museum** have collections of palanquins, furniture, arms, and costumes. The palace was built to resist the floods of the monsoon, which play havoc with the city side of the river. ✉ *End of Pontoon Bridge.* 🎫 *Rs. 5.* ⏲ *Daily 9–noon and 2–5.*

39 **Sankat Mochan Temple.** Sankat Mochan, meaning "Deliverer from Troubles," is one of the native Banarasis' most beloved temples. While the city has now encroached all around it, the building still stands in a good-sized, tree-shaded enclosure, like temples elsewhere in India. (Most temples in Varanasi are squeezed between other buildings.) While most of the city's major shrines are dedicated to Shiva or various aspects of the mother goddess, Sankat Mochan belongs to Hanuman, the monkey god revered for his dedicated service to Rama, an incarnation of Vishnu whose story is told in the *Ramayana* epic. The best time to see Sankat Mochan is in the early evening, when dozens of locals stop by for a brief visit at the end of the work day. ✉ *Durgakund Rd.*

34 **Shitala Temple.** This unassuming but very popular white temple is dedicated to Shitala, the smallpox goddess. Despite the eradication of smallpox, Shitala is still an important folk goddess in North India. Here, as in many Shitala temples, a new shrine has been added in honor of Santoshi Mata, the "Mother of Contentment"—a goddess who gained popularity in the 1970s when a Hindi movie was made about her. ✉ *Shitala Ghat.*

Dining and Lodging

$ ✕ **Anandaram Jaipuriya Bhavan.** Most Hindu pilgrims in Varanasi dine in a sort of cafeteria called a *bhojanalaya,* where they get reliable, affordable meals cooked in the style of the region they come from. Housed in the third story of a building that is also a guest house for affluent Rajasthani pilgrims, this one is considered the best in the city. Large meals of vegetables, dal, rice, chapatis, and yogurt are served on *thali* platters to patrons seated in rows on planks on the floor. The food is delicious, and mineral water is available. Lunch is served 11–2, dinner 8–10. ✉ *About 100 yards north of Godaulia Crossing, on west side of road to Chowk,* ☎ *542/352674. No credit cards.*

$ ★ ✕ **Bread of Life Bakery.** Specializing in "European breads and American cookies," this pristine café makes a great place for breakfast after a morning boat ride—it's about 10 minutes' walk from Asi Ghat. Lunch and dinner are also served. ✉ *B 3/322 Shivala (on east side of main road to Godaulia Crossing),* ☎ *542/313912. No credit cards.*

$ ✕ **Sindhi.** This unprepossessing restaurant is your best bet for a meal in central Varanasi. Packed at both lunch- and dinnertime, it serves delicious thalis (combination meals) as well as omelets and side dishes of fresh local vegetables. Try the creamy *malai kofta* (minced vegetables in a spicy cream sauce) or, for a lighter dish, *aloo methi* (potatoes and fenugreek greens). ✉ *Opposite Lalita Cinema, near Bhelupura Police Station. No credit cards.*

$$$ 🏨 **Clarks Varanasi.** This modern hotel has attractive rooms with light and cheery decor; the best overlook the pool or the lawn. Clarks maintains a traditional *haveli* (traditional Rajput mansion) on the Ganges

at Raja Ghat, for cultural programs in the evening and demonstrations of Hindu ritual in the morning; trips are arranged for groups, but individual travelers can sign on if space is available. ✉ *The Mall, Varanasi 221002, Uttar Pradesh,* ☎ *542/348501 (–12),* FAX *542/348186. 140 rooms. Restaurant, bar, pool, travel services. AE, DC, MC, V.*

$$$ ★ **Taj Ganges.** Abutting the grounds of an old palace of Varanasi's maharaja, this Western-style high-rise has a large, pleasant lobby and spacious modern rooms. It's the quietest hotel in town, particularly if you get an upper-story room facing the palace grounds. The restaurant's patio tables and the nicely landscaped pool area make lovely places to grab some tranquility before plunging back into the city. ✉ *Nadesar Palace, Raja Bazaar Rd., Varanasi 221002, Uttar Pradesh,* ☎ *542/345100 (–17),* FAX *542/348067. 120 rooms, 10 suites. 2 restaurants, bar, coffee shop, pool, beauty salon, tennis court, meeting rooms, business services, travel services. AE, DC, MC, V.*

$ **Diamond.** This is not a top-of-the-line hotel, but it's centrally located, the staff is friendly, and the restaurant is fairly good. ✉ *Bhelupura, Varanasi, Uttar Pradesh,* ☎ *542/310696 (–9),* FAX *542/310703. 40 rooms. 2 restaurants, bar, travel services. MC, V.*

$ **Ganges View.** This excellent guest house has small, immaculate rooms and a veranda with little tables overlooking the river and Asi Ghat. The owner is a repository of information on local culture, particularly Indian classical music. Delicious vegetarian meals are prepared with advance notice. This place is very popular; book months in advance to stay during peak season. ✉ *Asi Ghat, Varanasi 221006, Uttar Pradesh.* ☎ *542/313218. 8 rooms. Restaurant. No credit cards.*

$ **Hotel de Paris.** Set on pretty grounds, this rambling old bungalow with a handsome cream-and-pink exterior is an elegant—if slightly shabby—relic of the British cantonment. Service is friendly and efficient. The rooms are spacious and simple, but lit with fluorescent lights; some are air-conditioned. ✉ *15 The Mall, Varanasi 221002, Uttar Pradesh,* ☎ *542/346601 (–8),* FAX *542/348520. 50 rooms. 2 restaurants, bar, travel services. AE, DC, MC, V.*

$ **Ideal Top.** The salmon-pink and white exterior of this modern hotel hides a spacious, white-marble lobby. The rooms are large and actually nicer than many of their pricier counterparts. ✉ *The Mall, Varanasi 221002, Uttar Pradesh,* ☎ *542/348091 (–2) or 542/348250 (–1),* FAX *542/348685. 40 rooms, 4 suites. Restaurant, bar, travel services, airport shuttle. AE, MC, V.*

$ **Pradeep.** This well-maintained small hotel is near Lahurabir, on the north side of the city. The multicuisine restaurant, Poonam, is popular with locals, and a rooftop barbecue offers informal alfresco dining. Rooms have air-conditioners and are comfortably furnished; ask for one away from the road. ✉ *C 27/153, Chetganj, Varanasi 221002, Uttar Pradesh,* ☎ *542/344963 or –594,* FAX *542/344898. 45 rooms. Restaurant, bar, travel services. MC, V.*

Shopping

Varanasi is one of India's chief weaving centers and is famous for its silk-brocade saris, many adorned with real gold and silver. Most hotels sell samples of this work in their shops, but the main bazaars for Banarasi saris are in the **Vishvanath Gali**—the lane leading from Dashashvamedh Road to the Kashi Vishvanath Temple, where the customers are mainly pilgrims and tourists. Among the brass vendors in **Thatheri Bazaar** (Brass Market), some shops sell silks and woollens to a local crowd. **Dharam Kumar Jain & Sons** (✉ K 37/12 Sona Kuan, ☎ 542/333354), operating out of their home near Thatheri Bazaar, have an extraordinary private collection of old brocade saris, Pashmina shawls, and other textiles, and can help you find the best examples of contemporary weaving. **Mehta International** (✉ S 20/51 Varuna Bridge, ☎ 542/344489), near the major hotels, is a large showroom with a wide selection of saris and scarves.

Nightlife and the Arts

Nagari Natak Mandal (✉ Kabir Chowra) presents regular concerts of some of Varanasi's—indeed, India's—best musicians. There are also numerous seasonal music festivals; ask your hotel to check the local Hindi newspaper, *Aj*.

Sarnath

42 *11 km (7 mi) north of Varanasi*

In 528 BC Siddhartha Gautama preached his first sermon in what is now Sarnath's Deer Park. Here he revealed his Eightfold Path leading to the end of sorrow and the attainment of enlightenment.

Three hundred years later, in the 3rd century BC, the Mauryan emperor Ashoka arrived. A zealous convert to Buddhism, he built in Sarnath several *stupas* (large, mound-shape reliquary shrines) and a pillar with a lion capital that was adopted by 20th-century India as the national emblem. The wheel motif under the lions' feet represents the *dharma chakra*, the wheel (*chakra*) of Buddhist teaching (*dharma*), which began in Sarnath. The chakra is replicated at the center of the national flag. Sarnath reached its zenith by the 4th century AD, under the Gupta dynasty, and was occupied into the 9th century, when Buddhist influence in India began to wane. By the 12th century, Sarnath had more or less fallen to Muslim invaders and begun a long decay. In 1836, Sir Alexander Cunningham started extensive excavations here, uncovering first a stone slab with an inscription of the Buddhist creed, then numerous other relics. It was only then that the Western world realized the Buddha had been an actual person, not just a mythical figure.

In the 16th century, the Mogul emperor Akbar built a brick tower on top of the 5th-century **Chaukhandi Stupa** to commemorate his father's visit some years earlier. It's on the west side of Ashoka Marg, just south of the archaeological museum.

★ The excellent **Sarnath Archaeological Museum** houses a copy of Ashoka's lion pillar and some other beautiful sculpture. Still more of Sarnath's masterpieces are in the National Museum, Delhi, and the Indian Museum, Calcutta. ✉ *Ashoka Marg at Dharmapal Marg,* ☎ *542/385002.* *50 paise.* ⏲ *Sat.–Thurs. 10–5.*

The **Ashoka Pillar,** on Ashoka Marg north of the museum, is one of many inscribed monuments that Ashoka erected throughout his empire. This one stands in front of the main stupa where the emperor used to sit in meditation.

Dappled with geometric ornamentation, the **Dhamekh Stupa** (northeast of the museum) is, at 102 ft tall, the largest surviving monument in Sarnath. Built around AD 500, Dhamekh is thought to mark the place where the Buddha set the Wheel of Law in motion, though excavations have unearthed the remains of an even earlier stupa of Mauryan bricks of the Gupta period (200 BC).

Due east of the Dhamekh Stupa, and joining the old foundations of seven monasteries, is a the **Mulagandha Kuti Vihari Temple,** built in 1931. The walls bear frescoes by a Japanese artist, Kosetsu Nosu, depicting scenes from the Buddha's life. On the anniversary of the temple's foundation—the first full moon in November—monks and lay devotees from all parts of Asia assemble here.

Before you leave Sarnath, walk north from the Dhamekh Stupa into **Deer Park** and buy some carrots (Rs. 1) to feed the deer. Legend has it that Buddha was once incarnated as King of the Deer here.

Bodhgaya

43 *266 km (165 mi) east of Varanasi*

A short drive from Varanasi (followed by a train connection from Gaya or an air connection from Patna), Bodhgaya seems an oasis in central Bihar, one of the poorest states in India. In perhaps 530–520 BC (though the consensus on these dates is currently shifting), Gautama Buddha meditated under a peepul tree here until he achieved enlightenment. What's believed to be a descendant of a cutting of that tree still stands, and in recent decades Buddhists from around the world have built monasteries nearby. In the winter months Bodhgaya teems with the faithful and the curious, particularly when the Dalai Lama is delivering lectures, usually in December. Around town you'll encounter lay Buddhists from Maharasthra (center of a 20th-century Buddhist revival); Tibetan monks in maroon robes, some approaching the temple by prostrating themselves repeatedly; Sri Lankan and Thai *bhikkus* in yellow robes; and a growing number of Westerners. The contradictions between local poverty and the prosperity of these international monasteries have not been completely resolved; but most of Bodhgaya's Buddhist institutions do run a school, a dispensary, or another charitable project, and the global spirit in Bodhgaya today in some ways reenacts that of Buddhism during its early Indian history. Since many of India's other old Buddhist centers are primarily archaeological monuments, Bodhgaya gives you some idea of how Buddhism thrives as a contemporary faith.

The **Mahabodhi Temple** is the physical as well as the symbolic center of town. Though it has been remodeled several times over the centuries, Mahabodhi may date from as early as the 2nd century AD and was certainly built before the 7th century, when the Chinese pilgrim Hsuan Tsang visited. It's one of the earliest examples of the North Indian *nagara* style, which emphasizes the shikhara; rising some 160 ft, the spire can be seen far and wide from the surrounding flat country. The temple's four flat sides are tiered with niches for Buddha images offered by pilgrims, though only a few of these are still here. At the top of the spire is a stone *stupa,* a representation of the reliquary mounds that the first Buddhists built all over the subcontinent, topped by a series of of stone *chattris,* or parasols, symbols of both the Buddha's princely lineage and the shelter provided by the faith he founded.

You enter the temple down a long flight of steps through its eastern gate, which faces an attractive pedestrian plaza. The temple itself is enclosed on three sides by a four-tier carved stone railing, which opens under a high torana (archway) on the eastern side. Much of the original railing has been carted away to museums and replaced by less elaborate reproductions, but you can see examples of the carving here and there, and more in Bodhgaya's archaeological museum. Pilgrims typically circumambulate the temple before entering the tall central chamber, which now houses a large gilt image of the Buddha in meditation. (According to Hsuan Tsang, in his day the image was made of a sandalwood paste.) The sanctum is strung with colored lights, and the surrounding space is enlivened by the obvious emotion of pilgrims. The **Bodhi tree,** standing outside the temple directly behind the inner sanctum, gives a more visceral feeling of sanctity. The railing around the tree forms a small courtyard, and pilgrims enter through a gate to place flowers on the stone slab representing the **vajrasan** ("diamond seat") where the Buddha meditated and to tie bits of colored cloth to the tree. Contemporary Buddhists often sit in emulation of the founder's practice along the railing under the tree. Dotted around the large temple compound, shaded by several trees, are small stone stupas sponsored by pilgrims over the centuries. The pathway of carved stone next to the north wall is said to mark the track of the Buddha's walking meditation, and he is thought to have bathed in the pretty lotus pond on the southeast side. *Free, camera Rs. 5. 6–12 and 2–6:30 in winter; midday break longer in summer.*

The area around the temple compound is a mixture of shops for pilgrims, simple restaurants, and international monasteries, each built in the style of its home country. You can cover Bodhgaya on foot or in a cycle-rickshaw. The main **Tibetan Monastery,** representing the Dalai Lama's *gelugpa* tradition (or Yellow Hat Tradition) is on the north side of town; the man himself teaches under a large tent in an adjacent field. The **Mahabodhi Society,** a Sri Lankan organization that played a key role in reviving the practice of pilgrimage to Buddhist centers in India, has its complex on the main road just across from the temple's northern wall. The attractive **Thai Monastery** is at the southern end of town. Bodhgaya's **Archaeological Museum** is also on the south side of town, off the short road leading up to the Hotel Bodhgaya Ashok; it holds some of the temple's original carved-stone railing and some good classical sculpture. **Rajgir** was capital of the ancient kingdom of Magadha and site of the first Buddhist Council in Buddha's time. If you can stay in Bodhgaya overnight, the ruins of the great Buddhist university at **Nalanda,** northeast of Bodhgaya, make a long but fascinating day trip.

Dining and Lodging

$ ✕ **Cafe Om.** In winter, this seasonal restaurant serves soups and other Tibetan dishes to pilgrims and tourists alike. Try the *momos,* classic Tibetan dumplings. ✉ *Opposite Tibetan Monastery,* ☎ *no phone. No credit cards.*

$$$ **Bodhgaya Ashok.** The Indian government's Ashok chain is generally in decline, with frequent proposals to privatize, but this one retains some of the project's earlier strengths. Guest rooms are large and comfortably furnished, with individual air-conditioners, and the restaurant is quite good. Service is friendly and efficient. ✉ *Bodhgaya, Gaya district 824231, Bihar,* ☎ *631/400789 (–92),* FAX *631/400788. 30 rooms, 2 suites. Restaurant, bar, laundry service, travel services. AE, DC, MC, V.*

$$ **Sujata.** One of several new private hotels that have sprung up to accommodate the increase in travel to Bodhgaya, the Sujata has smallish, plain but comfortable rooms, some with air-conditioners. Its restaurant is the best in town for the typical hotelier's selection of North Indian, Chinese, and Continental dishes. ✉ *Bodhgaya, Gaya district 824231, Bihar,* ☎ *631/400761 or –481,* FAX *631/400515. 25 rooms, 2 suites. Restaurant, bar, laundry service, travel services. MC, V.*

$ **Bihar State Tourist Bungalow.** This new building on the western outskirts of Bodhgaya offers clean, simple rooms, two of which are air-conditioned, and an attached restaurant. ✉ *Bodhgaya, Gaya district 824231, Bihar,* ☎ FAX *631/400445. 13 rooms. Restaurant, laundry service, travel services. No credit cards*

Lucknow

44 *300 km (186 mi) northwest of Varanasi, 516 km (320 mi) southeast of Delhi*

Lucknow is—in its lingering self-image, anyway—a city of almost ridiculously ornate manners, inherited from the last significant Muslim court to hold sway in North India. Though settled here on the banks of the Gomti River in the earliest period of Indian history, it came to its present prominence in 1775 (after Mogul power had declined in Delhi) as capital of the independent kingdom of Avadh. It is now capital of the state of Uttar Pradesh. Much of Lucknow's old lazy charm is being superseded, yet people still think of the city as one where passengers miss their train connections by getting caught up in elaborate exchanges of "*Phele aap*" ("You first") on the platform. Even the cycle-rickshaw wallahs are said to speak only the most high-falutin' Urdu.

Lucknow's famous Nawabs of Avadh were members of the Shia sect of Islam, and the city is still an important center for that minority. Shia *imambaras*—gathering places used during Muharram, the month of mourning for Hussain, fifth Caliph of Islam—are Lucknow's most important monuments. Wajid Ali Shah, the last nawab and a legendarily impractical aesthete, was deposed by the British in 1856. Resentment over that act, combined with the decades of indirect control that preceded it, contributed to Lucknow's strong support for the rebels during the Mutiny of 1857, with members of Avadh's disbanded army manning the barricades against the British. British residents and troops, and an equal number of Indian troops and servants, were besieged for almost five months, an event that now figures in the national myths of both India and England.

The city's plan was drastically altered after the Mutiny and is now crisscrossed with broad avenues. Driving along the Gomti at the eastern end of the city, you'll see the Bara Imambara, passing the **Rumi Darwaza,** or Turkish Gate, as you approach the complex. The **Bara Imambara** is Lucknow's largest, preceded by a wide plaza and set at an oblique angle to its accompanying mosque. Guides will pester you to avail yourself their services, and you may need them when you climb up to the top floor: Here a labyrinth of identical doorways, passages, and stairways, with hidden routes and many dead ends, makes up the *bhul bhulaiya* (roughly, "place of forgetting") leading back down to the ground level. You can go through the warren solo, but it takes time and patience. The imambara's raison d'être is the **tomb of Nawab Asaf-ud-Daulah,** who built his own resting place in 1784. The excellent views from the top floor take in a deep step well on the opposite side of the plaza from the mosque. The imambara is open daily from 6 to 5, and admission is Rs. 10.West of here is the elegant **Hussainabad Imambara,** built in 1837 with a gilt dome. The city's **clock tower** is, along with the train station, Lucknow's most remarkable Victorian Gothic structure.

Heading back toward the city center, you'll come to the **Residency** compound, where the British garrison was besieged on June 30, 1857. A relief force entered (as you will) through the **Baillie Guard Gate** on September 25, only to end up besieged themselves. On the right is the **Treasury,** and behind that a large **Banquet Hall** that served as a hospital. (About 2,000 people died in the siege, more from disease than from gunfire.) Up a slight rise is a large open green, with an active shrine to a Muslim *pir* (holy man) under a tree to the left and an obelisk on the right commemorating Henry Lawrence, the Chief Commissioner who gathered his people here only to fall to gunfire on July 4. The Residency itself is largely in ruins, but you can see how its stone walls mimic European plaster, and the first floor displays a model of the compound under siege as well as cannonballs and other artifacts. Below ground are the *tikhana* (cellar) chambers, where many of the women and children escaped intermittent fire from the rooftops of surrounding buildings. Down the slope on the far side of the Residency is a **cemetery** for the many who did not last until the siege was finally broken on November 17. Pre- and post-Independence markers and signs indicate graphically the differences in how events here have been viewed. (Until August 15, 1947, a Union Jack flew over the compound.) Other buildings are scattered throughout, and you'll want at least an hour and a half to absorb the Residency's melancholy significance. ⏲ *Daily 9–5:30.* 🎫 *Rs. 10.*

At the eastern edge of the city, on the banks of the Gomti, is **La Martinière College,** the most outlandish building in town. Now a high school, it was built as a palace by Major-General Claude Martin, an 18th-century French adventurer who profited handsomely from his military service to the nawabs and happily spread his epicurean tastes. The building's lower stories were designed to flood in the summer—an innovative, if malarial, cooling system. With its oddly angled wings, towering cupola, and assorted Baroque gargoyles, the college suggests a fevered dream of Versailles. You can get a good sense of it from the outside, but can also arrange a tour in advance through the school administration (contact Uttar Pradesh Tourism, ☎ 522/228349).

Dining and Lodging

$ ★ ✕ **Prakash Kulfi.** "Beware of imitations," warns a signboard, and there are plenty all around this famous dessert joint. On a rooftop overlooking the Akbari Gate, *kulfi*—an ice cream with hints of almond and cardamom—is served with *faludi,* noodles floating in a sweet cream sauce. ✉ *12–13 Fruit La., Aminabad.* ☎ *522/226–6737. No credit cards.*

$ ★ ✕ **Tunday Kababi.** Here's the downtown branch of a local institution named after the one-armed kebab artist who founded it. You won't find much in the way of vegetables here, but the grilled meats are delicious, accompanied by naan and a range of other breads. The open-air cooking area fronts the street, facing a busy bazaar. ✉ *Near Ghari Wali Masjid, Nazirabad.* ☎ *522/216535. No credit cards.*

$$$ 🏨 **Clarks Avadh.** Lucknow's original high-class hotel is bearing up well against new competition, helped by its central location. It features a rooftop restaurant and a higher-priced "privilege floor" with a separate lounge. The rooms are spacious, if somewhat dimly lighted. ✉ *8 Mahatma Gandhi Marg, Lucknow 226001, Uttar Pradesh,* ☎ *522/216500 (–9) or 522/220131 (–3),* FAX *522/216507. 98 rooms, 3 suites. Restaurant, coffee shop, beauty salon, laundry service, business services, travel services. AE, D, MC, V.*

$$$ ★ 🏨 **Taj Mahal.** Newly constructed in the British colonial style, this luxury hotel is a bargain compared to its counterparts in more popular destinations. The Oudhayana restaurant serves near-perfect samples of Lakhnavi cooking. Rooms are spacious and, like the public areas, appointed with pleasing period detail. The remote location makes transport difficult to arrange on your own; reserve a car through the travel desk. ✉ *Vipin Khand, Gomti Nagar, Lucknow 226010, Uttar Pradesh,* ☎ *522/393939,* FAX *522/392282. 106 rooms, 4 suites. 2 restaurants, bar, pool, beauty salon, golf privileges, health club, laundry service, business services, meeting rooms, travel services. AE, DC, MC, V.*

$ 🏨 **Carlton.** If the remains of the Raj appeal, this may be the place for you, though the furnishings seem nearly as moth-eaten as the stuffed tiger in the lobby. The rooms are palatial, however, and some are air-conditioned. The central location is key. ✉ *Rana Pratap Marg, Hazratganj, Lucknow 226001, Uttar Pradesh,* ☎ *522/224021 (–4),* FAX *522/229793. 10 rooms, 18 suites. Restaurant, bar, laundry service, travel services. AE, DC, MC, V*

$ 🏨 **Arif Castles.** This new hotel near the Carlton caters to local business travelers and tourists alike. Guest rooms are comfortable, and service is pleasant and efficient. ✉ *4 Rana Pratap Marg, Hazratganj, Lucknow*

226001, Uttar Pradesh, ☏ *522/211313 (–7),* FAX *522/211360. 46 rooms, 6 suites. Restaurant, laundry service, travel services. MC, V.*

Shopping

Lucknow is famous for a style of straight-stitch embroidery on fine cotton cloth known as *chikan.* This is fashioned into *kurtas* (long tunics for both men and women) as well on larger pieces that can serve as bedspreads or tablecloths. You'll see examples in hotel shops, but the bazaar at **Aminabad** is the place to go for bargains and variety. Start at Chikan Paradise, near Akbari Gate. Lucknow's other characteristic product is *attar,* the essential oils used in perfumes. **Ram Advani's Bookshop** (✉ Mayfair Cinema Building, Mahatma Gandhi Rd., Hazratganj) stocks a good selection for general reading as well as works of Lakhnavi history by scholars from around the world.

Nightlife and the Arts

The courtly cultivation of singing, dance, and poetry that characterized Lucknow in earlier eras has waned, but efforts are on to revive it. The Uttar Pradesh tourist office (☞ Visitor Information, *below*) stages occasional evenings of **ghazal singing,** once the specialty of the city's famous courtesans; and in February there's a music and dance festival. **Bhat Khande Maha Vidhyalaya,** in Kaiserbagh (☏ 522/222926), also hosts performances.

NORTH CENTRAL INDIA A TO Z

Arriving and Departing

By Car

AGRA

Agra is 200 km (124 mi) south of Delhi on roads built by the Mogul emperors to connect their two capitals. The roads are good, but heavily used—don't expect to travel much above 50 kph (30 mph). The best route is probably the Mathura Road (NH 2).

KHAJURAHO

Madhya Pradesh is one of the most scenic Indian states to drive through. You can tailor a delightful trip covering Agra, Gwalior, Orchha, and Khajuraho over four or five days; hire a car in Delhi or Agra from a tour operators or travel agency (☞ *below*).

VARANASI

If you come by car, you'll take National Highway (NH) 2 or NH 56 from the northwest, NH 29 from Gorakhpur in the north, NH 2 from Calcutta, or NH 30 and NH 2 from Patna.

A taxi from Varanasi will drop you in **Sarnath** for Rs. 50 and wait about three hours for Rs. 200. Auto-rickshaws will make the round trip for about Rs. 120. The Grand Trunk Road (NH 2) east of Varanasi passes south of **Bodhgaya.** The local connecting roads, for which you turn off just east of Auranagabad, are in poor condition and sometimes beset by robbers.

LUCKNOW

Lucknow is connected to Delhi by NH 2, the Grand Trunk Road, which runs through Agra and the industrial city of Kanpur before NH 25 turns north to Lucknow. This is one of the most heavily used truck routes in India, and is for the most part devoid of lanes. An alternate route is NH 24 through Bareilly and central Uttar Pradesh. NH 56 links Lucknow with the Grand Trunk Road at Varanasi, and allows a stop in little-visited Jaunpur, capital of an early Muslim sultanate.

By Plane

AGRA

Agra's Kheria Airport is roughly 7 km (4½ mi) from the Taj Mahal. **Indian Airlines** (☎ 562/360982, airport 562/268453) flies daily between Agra and Delhi, Khajuraho, and Varanasi. Contact your travel agent for other domestic carriers that may have flights into Agra.

You can get a fixed-rate taxi (Rs. 100) or auto-rickshaw (Rs. 75) from the airport to the city center. Ask your hotel if it participates in the local airport shuttle.

KHAJURAHO

Indian Airlines (☎ 7686/44035, airport 7686/44036) and **Jet Airways** (☎ 7686/44409 [–11], 7686/44406; airport 7686/44408) fly daily in peak season between Delhi, Agra, Khajuraho, and Varanasi. The airport is 5 km (3 mi) from Khajuraho; the taxi ride to town costs about Rs. 50.

VARANASI

Regular flights connect Varanasi with such major cities as Delhi, Bhubaneshwar, and Kathmandu. Note that some flights to Delhi on **Indian Airlines** (☎ 542/433746 or 542/433832) fly first to Bhubaneshwar, a four-hour detour. **Jet Airways** (☎ 542/511555 or 542/511444; airport 542/622577) and **Sahara Airlines** (☎ 542/342355 or 542/343094; airport 542/622334) also connect Varanasi to Lucknow and other destinations.

The airport is about 45 minutes by car from most hotels. A taxi costs about Rs. 300 to the cantonment area, Rs. 350 into the city proper. Of the airport's two prepaid-taxi counters, **Airport Rent A Car Service**, inside the terminal, is more reliable. The shuttle bus is only convenient if your hotel is in the cantonment; otherwise, you'll simply be dropped on the far side of the cantonment train station.

BODHGAYA

The nearest airport is in the city of Patna; from here it's a four-hour, 125-km (75-mi), Rs.-1,000 taxi ride to Bodhgaya. Between them, **Indian Airlines** (☎ 612/227310, airport 612/223199), **Jet Airways** (☎ 11/566–5404) and **Sahara Airlines** (☎ 612/661109 or 612/661289, airport 612/220954 [–8] offer regular flights from Varanasi and Delhi.

LUCKNOW

Lucknow is well connected by air to Delhi, Varanasi, and Calcutta. **Indian Airlines** (☎ 522/224030, airport 522/256132), **Jet Airways** (☎ 522/239612 [–4], airport 522/434009 [–10]) and **Sahara Airlines** (☎ 522/377675 or 522/323126; airport 522/436188) all have regular service. The airport is about 30 minutes by car from most hotels; a taxi costs about Rs. 200.

By Train

AGRA

Air-conditioned coaches run daily on the Delhi–Agra–Gwalior–Jhansi–Bhopal route (☎ 562/131 for inquiries, 562/364244 for reservations, 562/362252 for a supervisor) of the ***Shatabdi Express.*** The slightly slower *Taj Express* is a comparable option. In winter, trains may actually be a more reliable way to get to Agra from Delhi than planes, because Delhi's airport is often plagued by fog delays.

A one-hour train trip links Agra and **Gwalior** (120 km/75 mi). **Orchha** is 16 km (9 mi) from Jhansi, a major rail junction.

KHAJURAHO

The **MPSTDC** (☞ Visitor Information, *below*) runs a daily air-conditioned deluxe train from Jhansi to Khajuraho.

VARANASI

India's premier train, the *Rajdhani Express,* has overnight service to and from Delhi twice a week. The *Kashi Vishvanath Express* also serves **Lucknow.** The best transport between Varanasi and **Bodhgaya** is the mid-morning *Poorva Express* train to Gaya (16 km/10 mi from Bodhgaya). Gaya is also served by the *Rajdhani Express* between Delhi and Calcutta five days a week. On days when the Rajdhani and Poorva expresses bypass Varanasi, they stop in Mughal Sarai, about an hour away by car.

Getting Around

By Auto-Rickshaw

In **Agra,** you can hire an auto-rickshaw for a half day (Rs. 75) or full day (Rs. 150).

Auto-rickshaws are a fast way to scoot through **Varanasi**'s crowded streets. Ask your hotel or the tourist office for the going rate and agree on a fare in advance. These and other motor vehicles are not allowed into Godaulia Crossing, the traffic circle near the central bathing ghat, Dashashvamedh; they'll drop you off a short walk from the river if that's where you're headed.

By Bicycle

Renting a bike in Khajuraho should cost about Rs. 10 per day and is one of the most popular ways to get around this tranquil town. You can rent bikes across from the bus stand, behind the museum, or from some hotels.

By Cycle-Rickshaw

Cycle-rickshaws should cost no more than Rs. 20 per hour in **Agra.** They're a particularly pleasant way to get around **Khajuraho,** especially to the outlying temples, and the rate starts at around Rs. 30 per hour. (Get the latest rate estimates from the Government of India Tourist Office, ☎ 7686/44047). Distances are long in **Varanasi,** so a cycle-rickshaw is better for a leisurely roll through the old city (it frees you from fighting the crowds) than for cross-town transport. A trip from the cantonment to the ghats should cost about Rs. 30. If you hire a cycle-rickshaw for the day, agree on the price in advance and expect to pay at least Rs. 100 for the service.

By Boat

Boat rides on the Ganges in **Varanasi** should cost Rs. 40–60 an hour. At Dashashvamedh Ghat, however, touts will demand a lot more. If you just show up at sunrise, you'll have limited time to shop around; for a reasonable rate, chat with some boatmen the previous evening and arrange to meet one by the river the next morning. A boat from the main ghats to Ram Nagar should cost about Rs. 150 round trip.

By Car

Hire a car and driver only through your hotel, your tour operator, or a recommended local travel agent.

AGRA

Prices are generally Rs. 4–Rs. 8 per km. A non-air-conditioned car for two hours or 20 km (12 mi) should cost about Rs. 80, the minimum charge. A non-air-conditioned car for eight hours or 100 km (62 mi) should cost about Rs. 400. For overnight excursions, add a halt charge of Rs. 100.

Budget Rent-a-Car (✉ Fatehbad Rd., ☎ 562/331771) has a second office in the Mansingh Palace hotel. In peak season, reserve a car and driver in advance. You can also hire a taxi at the train station under a fixed-rate system. If you would prefer not to be taken to the driver's choice of stores, restaurants, or hotels (where he gets a commission), say so firmly up front.

KHAJURAHO

A car may be convenient if you want to wander outside Khajuraho or can't walk the 3 km (2 mi) to the most distant temples. A non-air-conditioned car should cost about Rs. 175 for two hours or 30 km (19 mi). You can hire a taxi for about Rs. 4 per km.

VARANASI

A three- to four-hour car excursion should cost Rs. 200–Rs. 300.

Contacts and Resources

Currency Exchange

AGRA

Besides your hotel, which is easiest and most convenient, you can change money at the **State Bank of India** (✉ Mahatma Gandhi Rd., Rakabganj, ☎ 562/26322). The **Canara Bank** (✉ Sanjay Pl., Sadar Bazaar) also changes money.

KHAJURAHO

The **State Bank of India** (☎ 7686/44173) is opposite the entrance to the Western Group of temples.

VARANASI

The **State Bank of India** has a branch in the Hotel de Paris.

LUCKNOW

The **State Bank of India** (✉ Main branch: 15 Ashok Marg, ☎ 522/213074) is in Hazratganj.

Guided Tours

AGRA

The **Uttar Pradesh State Road Transport Corporation** (✉ 96 Gwalior Rd., ☎ 562/72206; Platform No. 1, near inquiry window, Agra Cantonment Railway Station) offers a daily guided bus tour of Fatehpur Sikri, Agra Fort, and Taj Mahal for Rs. 100 per person. For a personal guide, ask your hotel or contact the **Approved Guide Association** (✉ B-18/163 Fatehbad Rd., ☎ 562/268255, FAX 562/311120), west of the Taj View Hotel. Full-day charges for a group of four run up to Rs. 300.

KHAJURAHO

Hire a licensed guide through the **Government of India Tourist Office** (☞ Visitor Information, *below*).

Travel Agencies

KHAJURAHO

Touraids (☎ 7686/44060). **Travel Bureau** (☎ 44686/2037). **Khajuraho Tours** (☎ 7686/44033).

BODHGAYA

Middle Way Travels (✉ 7/11 Main Rd., ☎ 631/400648).

Visitor Information

AGRA

The **Uttar Pradesh State Tourist Office** (✉ 64 Taj Rd., ☎ 562/360517) is open Monday–Saturday 10–5 (closed second Saturday of each month). The **Uttar Pradesh State Tourism Development Corporation** (✉

Tourist Bungalow, near Raja Mandi Station, ☎ 562/350120) arranges tours and cars; it's open Monday–Saturday 10–5. The **Government of India Tourist Office** (✉ 191, The Mall, ☎ 562/363959 or 562/363377) is open weekdays 9–5:30 and Saturday 9–1.

For information on Gwalior and Orchha, contact the **Madhya Pradesh State Tourism Corporation** (✉ Gangotri Bldg., 4th floor, T. T. Nagar, Bhopal, ☎ 755/554340, FAX 755/552384; ✉ Kanishka Shopping Plaza, 2nd floor, 19 Ashoka Rd., New Delhi, ☎ 11/332–1187, FAX 11/332–7264).

KHAJURAHO

The **Madhya Pradesh State Tourism Development Corporation** (MP-STDC, ✉ Gangotri Bldg., 4th floor, T. T. Nagar, Bhopal, ☎ 755/774289; in New Delhi, 11/336–6528) is one of India's better tourist offices. The **Khajuraho regional MPSTDC office** (✉ Tourist Bungalow Complex, ☎ 7686/44051) is open Monday–Saturday 10 to 5. The **Government of India Tourist Office** (✉ opposite Western Group of temples, ☎ 7686/44047) is a good place to get maps and hire guides. It's open weekdays 9–5:30, Saturday 8–12:30.

LUCKNOW

Uttar Pradesh Tourism (✉ Chitrahar Building, 3 Nawal Kishore Rd., ☎ 522/228349 or 522/225165) has general information.

VARANASI

The **Government of India Tourist Office** (✉ 15B, The Mall, ☎ 545/343744) in the cantonment is open Monday–Saturday 10–5; there's also an information desk at the airport. The best information at the **Uttar Pradesh (UP) Government Tourist Office** (✉ Parade Kothi, opposite train station, ☎ 545/341162) is in Hindi, but the staff can still help you. The UP tourist office also has a desk at the train station.

5 RAJASTHAN

Steeped in tales of chivalry, romance, and revelry, Rajasthan has a timeless spirit and haunting magic that draw travelers by the thousand. From its legendary cities of Jaipur, Jodhpur, Udaipur, and Jaisalmer, built by the mighty Rajputs, to its indigenous tribal and artisan communities, Rajasthan is veritably packed with awe-inspiring forts, sparkling palaces, soothing lakes and gardens, exquisite temples and shrines, and world-renowned craft and folk arts.

Updated by Vidhi Jain, Manish Jain, and Michael W. Bollom

ONCE CALLED RAJPUTANA—"Abode of Kings"—this vast land consisted of more than 22 princely states before they were consolidated into modern Rajasthan in 1956. Each state was ruled by a Rajput, an upper-caste Hindu warrior-prince, and the Rajputs were divided into three main clans: the Suryavanshis, descended from the sun, the Chandravanshis, descended from the moon, and the *agnikuls,* who had been purified by ritual fire. When they were not fighting amongst themselves for power, wealth, and women, the Rajputs built the hundreds of forts, palaces, gardens, and temples that make this region so enchanting to this day.

For centuries, many Hindu Rajputs valiantly resisted invasion, including attempts by the Muslim Moguls. Their legendary codes of battle emphasized honor and pride, and they went to war prepared to die. When defeat on the battlefield was imminent, the strong Rajput women would perform the rite of *jauhar,* throwing themselves onto a flaming pyre en masse rather than live with the indignity of capture. With the prominent exception of the princes of Mewar, major Rajput states such as Jaipur, Bikaner, Bundi, and Kota, eventually stopped fighting and built strong ties with the Moguls. The Mogul emperor Akbar was particularly skilled at forging alliances with the Rajputs; he offered them high posts in his darbar, or court, and sealed the deal with matrimonial ties. (He himself married two Rajput princesses.) Those kingdoms who sided with Akbar quickly rose in importance and prosperity.

Maharaja Man Singh of Jaipur was the first to marry his sister to Akbar. As the emperor's brother-in-law and trusted commander-in-chief, Man Singh led Mogul armies to many a victory. Both rulers benefited immensely, as a traditional saying indicates: *"Jeet Akbar ki, loot Man Singh ki"* ("The victory belongs to Akbar, the loot to Man Singh").

In addition to securing wealth, these marriages opened the gates of the royal Rajput households to the Moguls' distinctive culture. Ironically, the same people who initially sacrificed their lives to resist the Moguls quickly adapted themselves to Mogul domination and started borrowing heavily from Mogul aesthetics. Skilled craftsmen from the Mogul courts were enticed to Rajasthan to start craft schools, fomenting what would become a golden age of Indian art and architecture. The Moguls' influence in Rajasthan is still visible in everything from food to palace architecture, from intricate miniature paintings to new musical styles, and from clothing to the tradition of *purdah* (women covering their head and face with a veil).

The beginning of the 18th century marked the decline of the Mogul period, and with it came the decline of the Rajputs. The incoming British took advantage of the prevailing chaos. Not only did they introduce significant administrative, legal, and educational changes in Rajasthan, they also exposed the Rajputs to new levels of decadence. The British introduced polo and other equestrian sports, the latest rifles and guns, *shikar* (hunting) camps, Belgian glass, English crockery, French chiffons, Victorian furniture, European architecture, and eventually fancy limousines. The influence extended to Rajput children: sons were sent to English universities, and daughters to the best finishing schools in Switzerland.

Ironically, in their struggle to free India from British rule, many Rajput princes ended up defending the Raj. Unwilling to give up their world of luxury and power, they did their best to suppress rebellion in other parts of the country by sending their soldiers to help the British forces.

When India won independence, the Rajput princes and kings were forced to merge their kingdoms into one state as part of the new nation, but they still kept the titles to their palaces, forts, lands, jewels, and other sumptuous possessions. Since then, the government has taken over much of this land and many of the palaces and forts. Stripped of their feudal powers, many of the maharajas have become hotel owners, while others have turned their properties over to leading hotel chains. A few have become paupers or recluses.

Rajasthan's heritage goes well beyond the illustrious maharajas, however. The Marwari trading community is known far and wide for its dynamic entrepreneurial spirit and its ornate *havelis* (mansions with interior courtyards). Semi-nomadic indigenous tribes such as the Bhils, Meenas, Garasias, and Sahrias create a rich canvas of folk life and folklore, their art, dance, music, and drama contributing much to Rajasthan's vibrant, festive culture. The exquisite craft work of the state's rural artisan communities is celebrated around the world. The presence of saints and spiritual leaders from a variety of religious communities has, over the years, made Rajasthan a trove of shrines, temple art, and religious architecture. These and other communities give rise to tremendous revelry in fairs and festivals throughout the year.

Cultures within Rajasthan vary in everything from the colors of their sandstone buildings to the languages they speak. Though five principal Rajasthani dialects are spoken here (Marwari, Mewari, Dhundari, Mewati, and Hadauti), a local saying has it that you hear a new language every 4 km. And despite the overwhelming spread of both English and Hindi, villagers continue to maintain the rich literary traditions, both oral and written, of their local tongues. Also regionally significant—and perhaps more noticeable to the traveler—are the brilliant colors of the women's *lehangas* (long skirts with separate veils), designed to stand out against the potentially maddening starkness of the desert. Women complete this garb with various forms of elaborate jewelry. Rajasthani men are famous for their turbans, which vary in style from region to region and caste to caste; the *saafa* style (high turbans with a tail) is preferred by Rajputs, for instance, while *pagris* (compact turbans, often orange) are worn by businessmen. Even facial hair is unique in these parts: Rajputs, in particular, sport long, Salvador Dali–like moustaches full of twists and turns.

The region's natural variety is just as compelling. The Aravalli Hills divide Rajasthan into two natural parts, northwest and southeast. The northwest is characterized by arid sand dunes: The sizzling Thar Desert is referred to in the ancient Hindu epic *Mahabharata* as the Maru-Kantar, "Region of Death." The southeast belies Rajasthan's image as a desert state with its craggy hills, lush forests, and shimmering lakes. A rich array of birds, animal life, and insect species makes its home in each environment.

With all this color and tradition, Rajasthan is perennially one of India's most popular tourist destinations. Recent nuclear tests in Pokharan and continuing tensions with Pakistan have made some people wary of coming here, but there is really nothing to fear. The cities and people remain lively and unaffected.

Pleasures and Pastimes

Dining

Rajasthan's culinary spread will stretch your palate. Both North and South Indian food are available, and many hotels also serve Chinese and/or Continental cuisine, but you shouldn't leave the region without trying some local delicacies, such as *dal baati churma* (lentils with wheat-flour dumplings), *gatte ki subzi* (graham-flour dumplings), and *ker sangri* (dried fruits; also known as *pachkuta*). Breads include *bajra ki roti* (maize bread), *makki ki roti* (corn bread), and *missi ki roti* (graham- and wheat-flour bread). *Mirchi baras* (fried, breaded peppers) and *kachoris* (fried stuffed pastries) make hearty appetizers. Dessert is a highlight here—in some parts of Rajasthan, sweets actually open the meal. Favorites include *ghevar* (layer cake), *laddus* (sugar balls), *malpuas* (syrupy pancakes), and *diljani* (mini sugar balls). The classic Rajasthani *thali* (sampler plate; often a giant metal platter with a series of smaller dishes on it) is a good way to try a bit of everything.

Lodging

The most opulent hotels in India—perhaps in the world—are in Rajasthan. You can literally live like a king in one of several converted palaces: Stay in a pillared room surrounded by glittering mirrored walls, tiger skins, and stained-glass windows, dine in a vaulted, chandeliered ballroom, and still enjoy the best of the modern conveniences. The best-known of these lush lodgings are Udaipur's Lake Palace, Jodhpur's Umaid Bhawan Palace, and Jaipur's Taj Rambagh Palace. Unique to Rajasthan, too, are the Heritage Hotels, a group of castles, forts, and havelis that have been converted to charming accommodations; these give you a real taste of each site's history, traditions, and ancestral heritage. Samode Haveli (Jaipur), Castle Mandawa (Shekhavati), Rohetgarh (near Jodhpur), and Fateh Prakash Palace (Udaipur) are among the finest. All hotels are air-conditioned unless we note otherwise.

Shopping

JEWELRY

Rajasthani women bedeck themselves with spectacular jewelry: bangles, tinkling anklets, armbands, finger rings, and nose-, toe-, and earrings. Men are also fond of wearing gold hoops in their ears and amulets around their arms. In Jaipur, look for gold settings of *kundan* (a glasslike white stone) and *mina* (enameled) work. Udaipur, Nathdwara, and Jaisalmer all feature antique and contemporary silver jewelry. Decorated *lac* (lacquer) bangles are worn for good luck. Rajasthan also specializes in cutting precious and semiprecious stones, including emerald, garnet, agate, amethyst, topaz, and lapis lazuli. Jaipur is one of the emerald capitals of the world.

LEATHER

Men and women work together to produce Rajasthan's fantastic leather work: While men do the tanning, cutting, and stitching, women add embroidery and ornamentation. Look for leather shoes, sandals, fans, pouches, saddles, and even musical instruments.

PAINTINGS

Rajasthan has long been famous for its miniatures. Painted on paper, silk, marble, and bone, these astonishingly intricate works depict animals at play; religious stories; mythological themes; and princes and princesses in love, in court, or on parade. Originally created by the *chittrekar* (artist) community, miniatures now usually blend both Rajput and Mogul styles. Building on the Rajputs' bright colors and courtly themes, the Moguls added more detail to the faces and the landscapes. You'll find a concentration of the best miniatures in Udaipur. Rajasthan is also famous for paintings in the *phad* and *pichwai* styles. The phad is a red, green, and yellow scroll depicting the life of a local hero; the dark and richly hued pichwais, hung in temples, are cloth paintings depicting Lord Krishna in different moods. Equally popular are reproductions of *mandana* art, designs traditionally drawn by women on the walls and floors of rural homes using a chalk solution on a crimson cow-dung background. These unique works serve as ritual decorations for festivals and ceremonial occasions.

PUPPETS

Puppet art has a proud history here. Most villages have a resident puppeteer, and many hotels and restaurants stage daily puppet shows. The wood-and-string creatures are sold throughout the state.

TEXTILES

Rajasthan is famous for its dyed and hand-blocked printed fabric, often further embellished by embroidery. Some hand-blocked patterns are familiar in the West, but the range of colors here is stunning: scarlet, shocking pink, purple, orange, green, and saffron appear on almost all fabrics. Of particular note are the *bandhani* (tie-dye), embroidered-mirror, and appliqué (patchwork) styles.

Exploring Rajasthan

This large state could easily fill a month-long trip of its own. The state's southwestern corner centers on Udaipur, a hilly town of palaces and artificial lakes. Central Rajasthan is anchored by Jodhpur, home to a glorious fort and the eye-catching blue houses of the Brahmin caste. Jaipur, the state capital, is in the east (toward Delhi). Western Rajasthan, largely given over to the Thar Desert, can best be explored via camel or jeep from the golden city of Jaisalmer. In the northeast, between Jaipur and Delhi, the Shekhavati region is home to lovely painted havelis, built by merchants of yesteryear to celebrate their prosperity. The southern and eastern regions also have a number of first-rate wildlife parks.

Numbers in the text correspond to numbers in the margin and on the Rajasthan and Jaipur maps.

Great Itineraries

Distances here are long, and transportation is relatively slow. The best way to see Rajasthan is to fly to Jaipur, Jodhpur, and/or Udaipur and make excursions from each.

IF YOU HAVE 3 DAYS

Fly into **Udaipur** and spend the day wandering the narrow, hilly lanes of the old city and visiting the vast City Palace. That evening, take a boat ride on Lake Pichola or a cab up to the Monsoon Palace at sunset. If you can, stay at the Lake Palace Hotel, smack in the middle of the lake—it's a sight in itself. The next day, fly to **Jaipur** and explore the pink-hued Old City. Take a taxi out of town to the Amer Fort and Palace, then spend the night in one of Jaipur's havelis or palace hotels. On your third day, hire a car and driver to explore **Shekhavati,** stopping in villages such as Jhunjhunu and Mandawa to see the lovely havelis, some with magnificent frescoes. Treat yourself to a meal at one of the Heritage Hotels. From here you can easily drive to Delhi.

IF YOU HAVE 6 DAYS

As on the three-day itinerary, fly into **Udaipur** and spend a day and a night here. Try to pop outside the city to the crafts village of Shilpgram. The next day, drive northwest to the Jain temple at **Ranakpur,** and spend a few hours exploring the temple and the surrounding countryside. Continue on to **Jodhpur** and spend the night in one of the city's splendid hotels. Head up to the fort the next morning, then spend the day exploring Jodhpur itself. Take the overnight train to **Jaisalmer** and spend day four and the following night here. The morning of day five, embark on a half-day camel trek. Return to Jaisalmer in time for dinner and the overnight train back to **Jodhpur.** On your last day, fly to **Jaipur** to see the Amer Fort and Palace and the pink of the Old City.

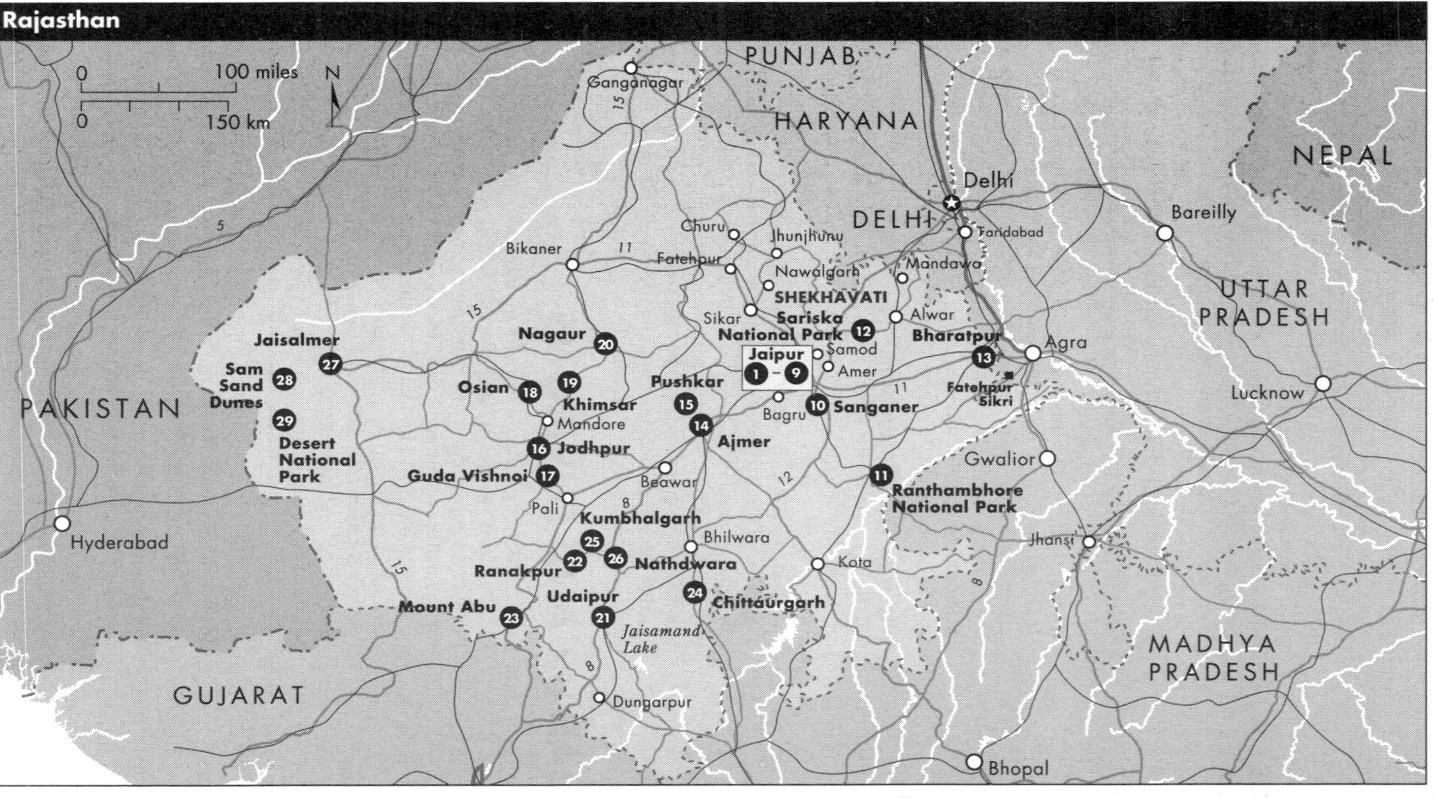
Rajasthan
0
100 miles
0
150 km
N
PUNJAB
HARYANA
NEPAL
DELHI
Delhi
Faridabad
Bareilly
UTTAR PRADESH
Ganganagar
Bikaner
Churu
Jhunjhunu
Fatehpur
Nawalgarh
Mandawa
SHEKHAVATI
Sikar
Sariska National Park 12
Alwar
Bharatpur 13
Agra
Lucknow
Jaisalmer 27
Sam Sand Dunes 28
29 Desert National Park
PAKISTAN
Nagaur 20
Osian 18
19 Khimsar
Mandore
16 Jodhpur
Guda Vishnoi 17
Pali
Jaipur 1–9
Samod
Amer
Bagru
10 Sanganer
Pushkar 15
14 Ajmer
Beawar
Fatehpur Sikri
Gwalior
11 Ranthambhore National Park
Hyderabad
Kumbhalgarh 25
Bhilwara
26 Nathdwara
Ranakpur 22
Udaipur 21
Mount Abu 23
24 Chittaurgarh
Kota
Jhansi
Jaisamand Lake
Dungarpur
GUJARAT
MADHYA PRADESH
Bhopal
5
8
11
12
15

IF YOU HAVE 10 DAYS

Spend your first day exploring **Jaipur.** After a night in one of Jaipur's sybaritic hotels, hire a car and leave early for a trip to one of Rajasthan's wildlife parks. **Bharatpur,** on the eastern edge of the state, is one of the finest bird sanctuaries in India; if you prefer tigers, head to **Sariska** or **Ranthambhore** national park. Spend the afternoon in the great outdoors and the night at a park lodge, then venture out early the following morning to watch the animals as they wake. Leave the park on day three for **Shekhavati** (an easy hop from Bharatpur and Sariska, a longer drive from Ranthambhore). Spend your third night at one of the Heritage Hotels in this region, and drive back to Jaipur on day four.

From Jaipur, fly to **Jaisalmer** and consider devoting days five and six to a camel safari, which will have you sleeping in the desert those two nights. Fly or take the overnight train to **Jodhpur** for day seven. Fly the next morning to **Udaipur,** and splurge on one of the city's magical hotels for your last two nights here. If you like temple architecture, detour to the Jain temples at **Ranakpur** and **Mount Abu** or the Hindu temples at **Nathdwara.** Leave Rajasthan on day 10. This is a crowded schedule, but it exposes you to most of Rajasthan's highlights.

When to Tour Rajasthan

Rajasthan is best visited from October to March. Unfortunately, everyone knows this, so the sights can be crowded. If you want to get away from the hordes and can bear the heat of a desert summer, April is a good time to come. By May and June, it's so hot that even the merchants spend the afternoons sleeping in their shops. The monsoon season (July–September) is fine unless you want to see the wildlife parks, which tend to flood. If you want to see a festival: The Pushkar camel fair is in November, the Shekhavati art festival is in December, the Jaisalmer desert festival is in January, Udaipur's Gangaur festival is in April, and Mount Abu's summer festival is in June.

JAIPUR AND ENVIRONS

Loads of day trips beckon from the countryside near Rajasthan's capital. The craft villages of Sanganer and Bagru, just outside Jaipur, are populated almost entirely by artisans, and you're free to stop in and watch them make fine paper and block-print textiles by hand. The town of Ajmer, a blend of Hindu and Muslim elements, is the final resting place of an important Muslim saint. The Hindu pilgrimage town of Pushkar is known for its annual camel fair. To escape civilization altogether, go animal-spotting at the Ranthambhore, Sariska, or Keoladeo national parks.

Jaipur

261 km (163 mi) southwest of Delhi, 343 km (215 mi) east of Jodhpur, 405 km (251 mi) northeast of Udaipur

A Rajasthani proverb asks, *"Je na dekhyo Jaipario, To kal men akar kya kario?"* ("What have I accomplished in my life, if I have not seen Jaipur?")

Surrounded on three sides by the rugged Aravalli Hills, and under the benevolent watch of weathered fortresses, Jaipur is well protected. It's a fine starting point for a trip through Rajasthan, not only for its pleasing location but also for its significance as one of the few planned cities in the world.

The city takes its name from Maharaja Sawai Jai Singh II, an avid scientist, architect, and astronomer, and is said to epitomize the dreams of the ruler and the creative ideas of his talented designer and builder, Vidhydar. Jaipur was founded in 1727, when Sawai Jai Singh moved down from Amer (commonly misrendered as Amber), the ancient rockbound stronghold of his ancestors. Rectangular in shape, the city is divided into nine blocks based the principles of the ancient architectural treatise *Shilp Shastra*. Every aspect of Jaipur—streets, sidewalks, building height, and number and division of blocks—was based on geometric harmony, sound environmental and climatic considerations, and the intended use of each zone. Originally colored yellow (a color you can still see on the backs of the buildings), it was washed in pink when Prince Albert, consort of Queen Victoria, visited India in 1883; thus is Rajasthan's blushing capital known as the Pink City.

At the moment, Jaipur is a bustling metropolis-in-the-making, with a population of almost 2 million. It has grown tremendously in the last two decades, and some speculate that in 20 years it will be as large (and as painful) as Delhi. Part of the city is still enclosed in fortified walls 20 ft high and guarded by eight gates. Head down any of the 108-ft-wide main roads and you'll see the unusual ways in which traditional Rajasthan meets modern India here. Wandering camels get into the same traffic jams as veiled or jeans-clad young women on motor scooters.

Timelessly appealing bazaars full of colorful textiles and trinkets—lac bangles, steel utensils, copper ornaments—and *mendhi* (henna) artisans form an integral part of the city center and its outlying villages. Another cultural highlight of Jaipur is its mouthwatering cuisine, particularly desserts: Ghevar, *pheeni* (strawlike sweet), *jalebis* (fried, pretzel-shape sweet), *churmas* (tasty wheat-flour dumplings), and *baati* (baked bread) are unbeatable, and set the tone for a serious rendezvous with the land and its people. The sensory whirl and jumble of rainbow-color *ghagharas* (skirts), turbans, camel carts, cycle-rickshaws, towers of quilts, and sturdy *jutis* (pointed shoes) makes Jaipur a city like no other in the world.

A Good Tour

Start outside the walled Old City at the **Albert Hall Museum** ①, then walk north on Chaura Rasta into the Old City. Turn right on Tripolia Bazaar to reach the **Jantar Mantar** ② observatory. A left onto Sireh Deorhi Bazaar takes you to the **Hawa Mahal** ③ and **City Palace** ④. After a break for lunch, take a taxi north of town to the **Amer Fort and Palace** ⑤. Spend the afternoon here and at **Nahar Garh Fort** ⑥, and watch the sun set at the nearby **Kanak Vrindavan Gardens** ⑦.

The next day, visit **Sisodia Rani ka Bagh** ⑧ and, if you'd like to meet some local artists, **Jawahar Kala Kendra** ⑨.

TIMING

Start early, as the Amer Fort closes at 4:30. If you're running late, save it for the next day.

Sights to See

❶ **Albert Hall Museum.** Worth a visit just for its architecture, this sandstone-and-marble building was built in the late 19th century in the Indo-Saracenic style. The collection includes folk arts, miniature paintings, traditional costumes, unexpected exhibits of yoga postures, and visual explanations of Indian culture and traditions. ✉ *Ram Niwas Gardens.* 🎫 *Weekends and Tues.–Thurs. Rs. 3, free Mon.* ⏲ *Sat.–Thurs. 10:30–4:30.*

★ ❺ **Amer Fort and Palace.** Surrounded by ramparts, this comely fortress sits on a hill behind Maota Lake. Built by Raja Man Singh, Mirza Raja

Albert Hall Museum, **1**
Amer Fort & Palace, **5**
City Palace, **4**
Hawa Mahal, **3**
Jantar Mantar, **2**
Jawahar Kala Kendra, **9**
Kanak Vrindavan Gardens, **7**
Nahar Garh Fort, **6**
Sisodia Rani ka Bagh, **8**

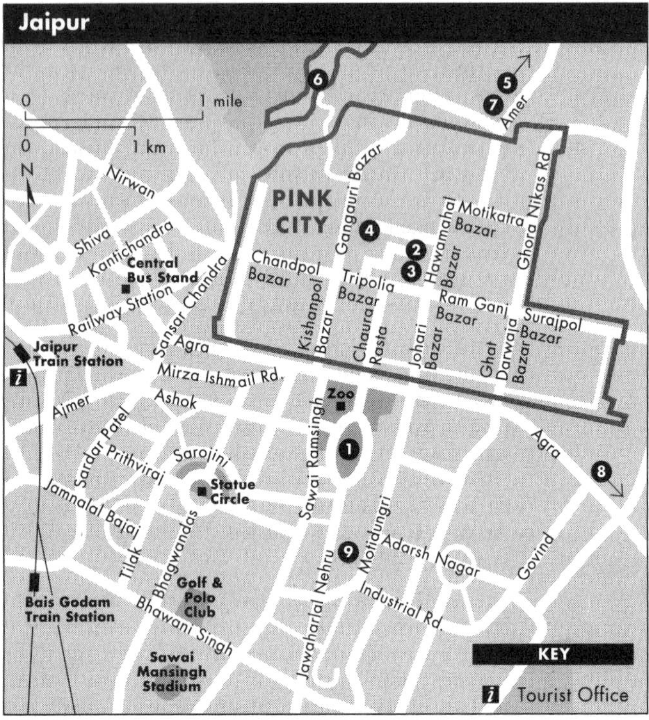

Jai Singh, and Sewai Jai Singh over a period of 125 years, it was for centuries the capital of the Kachhawah Rajputs. When the capital shifted to Jaipur in the early 18th century, the site was abandoned, but, while the fort is in ruins, the interior palaces, gardens, and temples retain much of their pristine beauty. Both the art and the architecture combine Rajput and Mogul influences in felicitous ways. To reach the palace, you can walk or ride up the gentle incline on an elephant.

The palace complex is approached through a steep path to the **Singh Pole** gate and **Jaleb Chowk,** the preliminary courtyard. Two flights of stairs lead up from the chowk; for now, skip the one leading to the Shila Mata temple and take the one leading to the palace itself. In the next courtyard, the pillared **Diwan-i-Am** (Hall of Public Audience) contains alabaster panels with fine inlay work of the most tender hues, the kind of craftsmanship for which Jaipur is famous. Typical of the Mogul period, the rooms are small and intimate, whereas the palace's successive airy courtyards and narrow passages are characteristically Rajput.

From the latticed corridor atop the elaborately carved and painted **Ganesh Pol,** or elephant gate, the queen would await the king's return from battle and sprinkle scented water and flowers down upon him. Each room shows some vestige of its former glory, especially the **Sheesh Mahal** (Palace of Mirrors). Step inside, close the doors, strike a match if you can, and watch the ceiling twinkle. Narrow flights of stairs lead up to the lavish royal apartments, and beyond the corridors and galleries here you'll find the small, elegant **Char Bagh** garden. Drink in the views of the valley, the palace courtyards, the formal gardens abutting the octagonal pool that edges the lake, and the vast **Jaigarh Fort,** the ancient fortress on the crest of the hill above you. Also on the upper floor is **Jas Mandir,** all intricately carved marble *jalis* (screens) and delicate mirror and stucco work.

On your way out, peek into the 400-year-old **Shiladevi Temple** to the goddess Kali, with its silver doors and marble carvings. Raja Man Singh installed the image of the Mother Goddess after bringing it here from lower Bengal (now Bangladesh). Exit the palace by the gate near the temple, and just a few minutes down the road is the 450-year-old **Jagat Shiromani** temple. Dedicated to Krishna, this exquisitely carved marble and sandstone temple was built by Raja Man Singh I in memory of his son. ✉ *Delhi Rd., 11 km (7 mi) north of Jaipur.* 🎟 *Rs. 4; cameras Rs. 50.* ⏲ *Daily 9–4:30.*

★ ❹ **City Palace.** This complex of pavilions, courtyards, chambers, and palace was begun by Jai Singh II, with further additions from later maharajas. Once you're in the outer courtyard, the marble-and-sandstone building directly in front of you is the **Mubarak Mahal** (Guest Pavilion), built by Maharaja Madho Singh in the late 19th century. Now a museum, it's an ideal place to admire at close range some of the royals' finest brocades, silks, and hand-blocked garments and robes, many made in nearby Sanganer and some dating from as far back as the 17th century. The collection also includes musical instruments. The **armory** in the northwest corner of the courtyard has one of India's best collections of arms and weapons, including an 11-pound sword belonging to Akbar's Rajput general. Some of the paints on the beautiful, 250-year-old ceiling are said to be made of crushed semiprecious stones.

In the inner courtyard, through the gateway guarded by two stone elephants, is the art gallery housed in the cavernous **Diwan-i-Am** (Hall of Public Audience). Built in the late 18th century, the building has rows of gray marble columns, the second-largest chandelier in India, and a magnificent, vintage-1930s painted ceiling. The art includes scores of miniatures from the Mogul and various Rajput schools, rare manuscripts, and 17th-century carpets from the Amer Palace. From the inner courtyard, enter the Zenana courtyard on the left to see the seven-story **Chandra Mahal** (Moon Palace). Built by Jai Singh II, this attractive cream-hue building is still the official residence of the present maharaja, "Bubbles"—Lieutenant Colonel Sawai Bhawani Singh—who lives on the upper floors. The ground floor has sumptuous chandeliers, murals, and a painting of an old maharaja. ✉ *City center.* 🎟 *Rs. 70; cameras extra.* ⏲ *Daily 9:30–4:45.*

❸ **Hawa Mahal.** Jaipur's photogenic Palace of Winds was built by Maharaja Sawai Pratap Singh in 1799 so that the women of the court could discreetly take some air and watch the activity on the street below. Every story has semi-octagonal overhanging windows, each with a perforated screen, and it's fun to walk through the little chambers behind each one, as this curious five-story structure—which draws its name from the westerly winds that send cool breezes through the windows—is just one room deep. Its delicate honeycomb design, fashioned of pink sandstone, seems to glow in the evening light. While you're here, check out some of the nearby shops (a row of which you can scan from above) for great deals on antiques and handicrafts. ✉ *Sireh Deorhi Bazaar.* 🎟 *Rs. 2; cameras Rs. 30.* ⏲ *Sat.–Thurs. 10–5.*

❷ **Jantar Mantar.** The Newton of the East, Jai Singh II was well aware of European developments in the field of astronomy, and wanted to create the world's finest observatories. He eventually supervised the design and construction of five remarkable facilities in northern India, of which this is the largest and best preserved. Built in 1726 of masonry, marble, and brass, it's equipped with large solar instruments called *yantras,* which have an avant-garde look and are uncannily precise in measuring celestial data. If you don't have a guide with you, try to recruit one to explain how these devices work, as they're fascinating and, for nonscientists, somewhat complicated. ✉ *Tripoliya Bazaar (near entrance to City Palace).* 🎫 *Rs. 4; cameras Rs. 50.* ⏲ *Daily 9–4:30.*

9 **Jawahar Kala Kendra.** Jaipur's center for art and crafts was founded by the state government with a specific vision: to create a space for understanding and experiencing culture and folk traditions amid the chaos and traffic of urban life. It's also becoming a venue for theatrical and musical performances. If you're an arts connoisseur, drop in to meet and talk with some of the local artisans, artists, and theater people who exhibit and perform here, or just to collect information on local cultural events. ✉ *Jawaharlal Nehru Marg (opposite Jhalana Institutional Area).* ⏲ *Daily 10–6; concerts some evenings.*

7 **Kanak Vrindavan Gardens.** This picturesque set of gardens and temples is just below the majestic Amer and Nahar Garh forts. From here you can take a good look at the Jai Mahal palace in Man Sagar Lake. The gardens also make a great picnic spot, especially if you like to people-watch: honeymooners and other fetching couples like to stroll here, and if you're lucky you might even catch a glimpse of Bollywood's brightest filming a Hindi movie. ✉ *Amer Rd.*

6 **Nahar Garh Fort.** Perched on a scenic hill, the Nahar Garh Fort offers a breathtaking view of all Jaipur. Initially built by Sawai Jai Singh in 1734, it was enlarged to its present-day glory in 1885 by Sawai Madho Singh, who commandeered it as a lookout point. Cannons loom behind the walls. The Rajasthan tourist board runs a snack bar here, and indeed it's a great place for a picnic. ✉ *10 km (6 mi) north of Jaipur off Amer Rd.*

★ 8 **Sisodia Rani ka Bagh.** On the road to Bharatpur stands one of many palaces built for the *ranis,* or royal Sisodia Rajput queens, of Sawai Jai Singh II. Built in 1779, the palace still looks lovely against the backdrop of the hills. Its terraced garden is punctuated with fountains, and the palace itself is furnished with painted murals illustrating hunting scenes and the romantic legend of Krishna and Radha. From the terrace, you'll glimpse dancing peacocks and plenty of monkeys. Come during the day, as the site is often reserved for weddings and parties at night. ✉ *8 km (5 mi) east of Jaipur on road to Bharatpur.*

Dining and Lodging

$$$$ ★ ✕ **Panghat.** Starting at 8, this dinner theater in a grove provides an exquisite performance of traditional Rajasthani dance and music while you sip cocktails in a small open-air amphitheater. After the performance (depending on the season) you can sit on cushions or chairs and watch a puppet show, or watch women prepare different traditional breads over a wood fire. Thalis are served with freshly baked breads. ✉ *Taj Rambagh Palace,* ☎ *141/381919. Reservations essential. AE, DC, MC, V. No lunch.*

$$$ ✕ **Suvarna Mahal.** Once the maharaja's royal banquet hall, this room is so grand—with a soaring, painted ceiling, handsome drapes, and tapestry-covered walls—that it's hard to concentrate on the menu, which offers Indian, Chinese, and Continental dishes. Regional specialties include *murgh tikka zaffrani* (chicken marinated in yogurt and saffron and cooked in a tandoor) and *dahi ka mass* (lamb cooked in a yogurt-based curry). Go for the enormous thali, which mixes things up deliciously. ✉ *Taj Rambagh Palace,* ☎ *141/381919. Reservations essential for dinner. AE, DC, MC, V.*

$$ ★ ✕ **Apno Gaon.** If you won't have time to visit a small village, here's your chance to get a feel for Rajasthani folk culture. Like the state's many simulated villages, Apno Gaon offers camel rides, playground swings, live traditional music, and puppet shows. Here, though, the

food is so good that even locals come to feast. Along with farm-fresh, organically grown vegetables, try the *bhajra* (maize) delicacies and milk products, like *kheech* (maize or wheat porridge) and *rabardi* (hot, soupy buttermilk cooked with maize). Be prepared to sit on the ground and eat with your hands. Apno Gaon is open all day, but it's better at night, when the folk spirits seem to rise and shine. ✉ *Sikar Rd. (past Vishwa Karma Industrial Area),* ☎ *141/331582. No credit cards.*

$$ ✕ **Niros.** This Jaipur institution is probably the most popular restaurant with the city's upper middle class. (Look for young couples on their first dates.) Amid mirrors and marble floors, it serves good Indian and Chinese food, and Continental dishes that actually taste Continental. Most of the curries and *subzis* (vegetables) are served in cute little bronze *kadhais* (pots). Specialties include *reshmi* kebab (skewered boned chicken), paneer tikka (Indian cheese with skewered tomatoes, onions, and capsicum), and mutton tikka masala (tandoori lamb simmered in a spicy tomato-and-butter sauce). Niros also has the best cold coffee in town, topped with a scoop of ice cream. ✉ *Mirza Ismail (M. I.) Rd.,* ☎ *141/374459. Reservations essential for dinner. AE, DC, MC, V.*

$$ ✕ **Shivir.** This cozy rooftop restaurant has plush carpeting, a fine city view, and good Indian fare. Live *ghazals* (Urdu-language love songs) set the mood during lunch and dinner. Shivir is known for its tandoori dishes, baked breads, and curries; try *aloo bhojpuri* (potato stuffed with paneer) and chicken *lajawaab* (boneless chicken served in a nicely spiced gravy). Top things off with a creamy dessert of *ras malai* (paneer in thickened milk flavored with cardamom). ✉ *M. I. Rd., Govt. Hostel Junction,* ☎ *141/378771. AE, DC, MC, V.*

$ ✕ **Chanakya.** Subdued lighting, table linen, and taped Indian classical music create an appealing ambience for terrific Indian, Continental, or Chinese vegetarian meals. The Chanakya special is a tasty mixture of dried fruits, cottage cheese, vegetables, and spices, topped with edible pure silver. *Gatta,* a spicy dish of graham flour rolled in herbs and spices and cooked in tasty tomato sauce, is a Rajasthani standard. ✉ *M. I. Rd.,* ☎ *141/376161. AE, DC, MC, V.*

$ ★ ✕ **Chokhi Dhani.** An evening excursion to this village complex allows you to sit on the floor in a lantern-lit hut and eat (with your hands) Rajasthani vegetarian dishes on the original disposable tableware—plates and bowls made of leaves. Come hungry! Wandering around the compound, you'll take in traditional dances, singing, puppet shows, and juggling by villagers. Entertainment is included in the cost of the meal, and tipping is discouraged. The temples in the complex are real, and if you're there at sunset, you'll see the traditional village *aarti* (prayer ceremony). Camel and boat rides cost Rs. 5, and only rupees are accepted throughout. ✉ *Tonk Rd. (19 km, or 12 mi, south of Jaipur via Vatika),* ☎ *141/374137. No credit cards.*

$ ✕ **Handi Restaurant.** This no-frills restaurant with bamboo walls and a thatch roof has some of the best nonvegetarian Mughlai food in town. One bite of the *kathi* kebab (garlicky mutton wrapped in thinly rolled bread with onions and tomatoes) and you'll forget all about the plastic chairs. Other specialties include a tangy butter chicken (chicken marinated in yogurt and baked in a tandoor, then cooked in a tomato curry) and the specialty, *handi* meat (a spicy mutton dish cooked in a handi, or clay pot). Only rupees are accepted. ✉ *M. I. Rd., opposite General Post Office,* ☎ *141/364839. No credit cards.*

$ ✕ **Laxmi Misthan Bhandar.** Known affectionately as LMB, this institution is known for fresh and sumptuous sweets, including *ghevar, mave ki kachori* (a milk-based pastry), and other savory snacks and meals. The rest of the food is average, though the *shahi* thali has an impressive 15 items. ✉ *Johari Bazar,* ☎ *141/565844. No credit cards.*

$ ✕ **Natraj Hotel.** The guest rooms aren't recommended, but Natraj is a terrific place for coffee and dessert. The house specialty is *bundi ki laddu* (sweet graham balls), and the *rasgullas* (doughy cheese balls in a syrupy sauce) and *rasmalai* (doughy cheese balls smothered in cream) melt in your mouth. ✉ *M. I. Rd.,* ☏ *141/371863 or 141/375804. AE, MC, V.*

$ ★ ✕ **Sharma Dhaba.** A treat for the adventurous, this popular place simulates an Indian *dhaba* (truck stop). The hot, fresh Punjabi food is extraordinary: mouthwatering and finger-licking good. It's amazing to watch the tandoori chefs in action here, pounding dough and stir-frying vegetables with grace. Sharma Dhaba may well serve the best naan bread in all of Rajasthan, and the *aloo jira* (potato with cumin seeds), *palak paneer* (spinach with Indian cheese), and garlic chutney are other choice sides. Ask them to spice to your taste. ✉ *Sikar Rd.,* ☏ *141/331582. No credit cards.*

$ ✕ **Swad.** This safe little joint offers a variety of cuisines but specializes in South Indian food. Try the classic *masala dosas* (paper-thin crepes stuffed with potatoes) and *chaats* (rice wafers topped with a sauce of yogurt and tamarind). ✉ *Ganpati Plaza,* ☏ *141/360750. AE, MC, V.*

$$$$ ★ **Rajvilas.** Any hotel with a helipad has to be swank. This Oberoi property has 30 acres of orchards, gardens, and fountains and a haveli that houses an ayurvedic spa. The rooms—some of which are tents, with billowy ceilings—are arranged around courtyards. The separate villas have private pools. Horseback rides and elephant safaris are optional excursions. Rajvilas is a 20-minute drive outside Jaipur; the Oberoi Group also runs the Trident ($$$) in the city itself. ✉ *Near Goner Rd., 303012,* ☏ *141/640101,* FAX *141/640202; reserve through Oberoi Group, New York,* ☏ *212/223–8800 or 800/562–3764,* FAX *212/223–8500, 54 rooms, 14 tents, 3 villas. Restaurant, bar, pool, health club, spa, 2 tennis courts, horseback riding, helipad, business services, meeting room, travel services, airport shuttle. AE, DC, MC, V.*

$$$$ ★ **Taj Rambagh Palace.** Once home to the maharaja of Jaipur, this airy, cream-color palace is relaxing and wistfully romantic, right down to the peacocks strutting across the manicured lawns and the dangling strands of beads that serve as doors in the open-air hallways. The arcaded back patios are lovely places to take tea. Standard rooms are spacious and largely contemporary; Superior and Luxury rooms have traditional decor, including colorful, Shekhavati-style painting. Most higher-end rooms have original (if not opulent) furnishings. The suites are above and beyond: The Maharani Suite is an Eastern fantasy, complete with an intimate, ruby-red cushioned alcove; the enormous Prince's Suite has its own fountain. The grandest suites are on ground level, their floor-to-ceiling windows nuzzling the surrounding trees. The beauty salon gives a wonderful scalp massage; ask for Rajendra. The hotel is on the edge of Jaipur. ✉ *Bhawani Singh Rd., 302005,* ☏ *141/381919,* FAX *141/381098. 106 rooms, 4 suites. 2 restaurants, bar, indoor pool, barbershop, beauty salon, golf privileges, 3 tennis courts, badminton, health club, Ping-Pong, squash, baby-sitting, business services, meeting rooms, travel services. AE, DC, MC, V.*

$$$$ **Welcomgroup Rajputana Palace Sheraton.** This sprawling brick structure, designed as a haveli, has four courtyards and numerous fountains, but it's more chic than it is reminiscent of Rajputana. The Western-style rooms are plush and comfortable. The pool, set in the main courtyard along with an outdoor bar, is lovely. This is the place to be if you value comfort over nostalgia. ✉ *Palace Rd., 302006,* ☏ *141/360017,* FAX *141/367848;* ☏ *in the U.S., 800/325–3535. 200 rooms, 16 suites. 3 restaurants, 2 bars, pool, barbershop, beauty salon, health club, dance club, billiards, recreation room, business services, travel services. AE, DC, MC, V.*

$$$ ★ **Jai Mahal Palace Hotel.** This 250-year-old palace is not as grand as the maharaja's other ancestral homes, and is farther from the city center, but the elegant white structure is extremely romantic. The lavish, Mogul-style garden has a row of fountains and an enormous chessboard with virtually life-size pieces. The interior has been restored with Rajasthani handicrafts and heirlooms: The suites are sumptuous, with priceless antiques and artwork, and the other rooms are Western-style comfortable. Rooms look out over the lawns or the pool. Puppet shows and folk dances provide on-site entertainment. ✉ *Jacob Rd., Civil Lines, 302006,* ☎ *141/371616,* FAX *141/371640. 102 rooms, 6 suites. Restaurant, coffee shop, bar, pool, barbershop, beauty salon, meeting rooms, travel services. AE, DC, MC, V.*

$$$ **Samode Palace.** Nestled in a narrow valley between red and green hills 45 km (28 mi) from Jaipur, this 18th-century palace, built in the shadow of a small fort, towers over its little village. The palace has splendidly painted and enameled public rooms, including a grand 250-year-old audience hall now used for gala dinners. Guest rooms, which have their own pillars and arches, are furnished with traditional Rajasthani-style chairs and beds with mosquito-net canopies. They're not regal, and they lack phones, but they're clean and comfortable. The staff can arrange horse, camel, and jeep safaris. ✉ *Samode, Jaipur district; reserve through Samode Haveli, Gangapole, 302002,* ☎ *141/630943,* FAX *141/632370. 35 rooms. Restaurant, bar, horseback riding, travel services. AE, MC, V.*

$$ **Alsisar Haveli.** This cheerful yellow haveli is close to the Pink City, but its large lawn removes you from urban noise. Once the city residence of Shekhavati Rajputs, the 105-year-old bungalow offers elegant rooms with antique carved furniture, bedspreads with traditional Rajasthani prints, rug-covered tile floors, and brass-frame mirrors in the bathrooms. The public areas are hung with crystal chandeliers, hunting trophies, and various weapons. Jeep and camel safaris can take you to a nearby village and fort. ✉ *Sansar Chandra Rd., 302001,* ☎ FAX *141/368290. 22 rooms. Restaurant. AE, MC, V.*

$$ **Raj Mahal Palace.** Built in 1729 by Sawai Jai Singh II, this small palace has a world-weary air, hardly surprising considering its turbulent history: It was first used as a refuge by a queen who feared her son might be in danger from rivals to the throne. It was then the residence of a British political officer in 1821 and of the Jaipur royal family in 1958. Now a Heritage Hotel run by the Taj Group, the Palace offers spacious, if modest, rooms with high ceilings and few windows. The restaurant serves Indian and Continental food. ✉ *Sardar Patel Marg, C-Scheme, 302001,* ☎ *141/381676 or 381757,* FAX *141/381887. 21 rooms, 5 suites. Restaurant, bar, pool, badminton, croquet. AE, MC, V.*

$$ ★ **Samode Haveli.** Tucked away in a corner of the Pink City, this lemon-yellow haveli is hidden from the noise and hustle. Now a Heritage Hotel, it was built for a prime minister of the royal court in the mid-19th century. Arranged around two courtyards, the haveli still has an air of stately grace and some original colorful frescoes. The rooms are spacious and simply furnished. If you want opulence, stay in one of the two Sheesh Mahals, the luxurious quarters of the local Rajput himself (still moderate in price), which have antique furniture and walls and pillars elaborately inlaid with mirror work. The best views take in the elegant palace gardens. Camel and elephant rides are easily organized. The restaurant serves Indian buffets. The haveli also runs the **Samode Bagh** luxury-tent encampment in Fathepur village, Shekhavati. ✉ *Gangapole 302002,* ☎ FAX *141/632407 or 141/630943. 25 rooms, 2 suites. Restaurant, travel services. AE, MC, V.*

$ 🏨 **Bissau Palace.** A sweeping drive leads to the veranda of this two-story 1919 bungalow, now a Heritage Hotel, on the outskirts of the Old City. The lounge, library, and intimate dining room are filled with mementos, paintings, and artifacts, and the small Royal Museum displays weapons from the 17th century. Guest rooms in the old wing have original furniture, cotton dhurries on the floors, and murals; those in the new wing are furnished with four-poster beds and divans and decorated with pieces from the armory. Though they're not fancy (no phones or TVs), the rooms have Rajasthani touches and are neat and clean. The family also has a beautiful retreat (visited by British royalty) 16 km (10 mi) outside town, where you can relax by the pool, sleep in a quaint two-room bungalow, and take a camel ride through surrounding villages. ✉ *Outside Chand Pol (near Sarod Cinema), 302016,* ☎ *141/304371 or 304391,* FAX *141/304628. 40 rooms, 13 suites. Restaurant, pool, tennis court, baby-sitting, travel services. AE, MC, V.*

$ 🏨 **Chokhi Dhani.** Separated by a wall from the restaurant of the same name, this little hotel south of Jaipur lets you stay in a village setting without giving up modern conveniences. Opt for a room in one of the mud huts, with wooden doors and carved furniture, or live like a landowner in the large painted haveli, with its marble floors. The bathrooms in the haveli are modern. The complex mirrors a village right down to the swimming pool, designed to look like a village water tank. The vegetarian restaurant does, however, have Western-style tables and chairs. ✉ *Tonk Rd. (19 km, or 12 mi, south of Jaipur via Vatika), 302015,* ☎ *141/550118 or 141/382034,* FAX *141/381888. 40 rooms, 8 suites. Restaurant, bar, pool, meeting room. AE, DC, MC, V.*

Nightlife and the Arts

Your best bet for a night out is one of the hotel bars, which are usually open from about 11 AM to 3 PM and 7 PM to 11:30 PM. Hotel discos kick in from about 7 to 11:30 as well.

Many hotels stage cultural programs for their guests, such as the dance performances with dinner in Panghat, at the Rambagh Palace. In addition, **Apno Gaon** (☞ Dining and Lodging, *above*) and the **Chokhi Dhani** (☞ Dining and Lodging, *above*) village complex offer excellent performances of Rajasthani folk dance coupled with traditional regional meals. **Ravindra Rang Manch** (✉ Ram Niwas Garden, ☎ 141/49061) hosts occasional programs.

To experience a contemporary Indian institution, head to the movies. **Rajmandir Movie Theatre** (✉ 16 Bhagwandas Rd., near Panch Batti, ☎ 141/379372) has a beautifully ornate interior and is known as the best movie hall in Asia. The theater disperses different blends of incense at occasional points in the film. Widely visited by Indian and foreign tourists, Rajmandir is still constantly flooded with locals, who sing, cheer, and whistle throughout each film.

Sports and Outdoor Activities

Polo is a passion in Jaipur. In season (late March and late October), matches are held at the **Rajasthan Polo Club.** Call the Taj Rambagh Palace (☎ 141/381919) or the Jaipur Polo Club (☎ 141/69235) for information. The Rajasthan Mounted Sports Association (☎ 141/366276) gives polo lessons.

Golf lovers can phone the **Taj Rambagh Palace** (☎ 141/381919) to reserve access to a driving range.

Shopping

Rajasthan's craftspeople have been famous for centuries for their jewel settings; stonework; block-printed silk and muslin; tie-dye; blue pottery; and enamel, lacquer, and filigree work. You'll find all this and more in Jaipur, but watch out: your drivers and/or guides are likely to insist that they know the best shops and bargains in the city ("I'll take you to my uncle's jewelry store," etc.). Unfortunately, their interest in your shopping excursion stems from the fact that they get a commission on whatever you purchase, which increases the price of your "bargain" as well as limiting your say in where you go. If you have a specific shop in mind, be firm. Also, don't rely on the words "government approved"—easily painted over a shop door, they're essentially meaningless. The shops below are reliable, with good service and excellent merchandise, and you're bound to find others in your explorations. Note that many shops are closed on Sunday.

ARTS AND CRAFTS

If you have limited time and lots of gifts to buy or don't relish bargaining, head to an emporium. The enormous, government-run **Rajasthali** (✉ Government Hostel, M. I. Rd., ☎ 141/367176 or 141/372974) is always flooded with interesting crafts of every stripe. **Tharyamal Balchand** (✉ M. I. Rd., ☎ 141/370376 or 141/361019) sells a variety of authentic, good-quality crafts ranging from jewelry and brass work to textiles, blue pottery, and wood work. You'll get a good feel for the diversity of crafts and textiles from the different parts of Rajasthan. **Manglam Arts** (✉ Amer Rd., ☎ 141/37170) is filled with exquisite old and new fine art, including Hindu pichwais, Jain temple art, tantric and folk art, terra-cotta sculptures, silver furniture, hand-woven dhurries, wood carvings, and wonderful old fabrics. If you miss the store here, check it out in Udaipur.

If you'd rather delve into specialty shops, wander through the **Kazana Walon ka Rasta** lane in the Old City (accessible from Chand Pol) and watch stone-cutters create artworks in marble. For brass or other metal work, visit **P. M. Allah Buksh and Son** (✉ M. I. Rd., ☎ 141/40441)—established in 1880, it still sells the finest hand-engraved, enameled, or embossed brassware, including oversize old trays and historic armor. The tiny, unpretentious shop **Bhorilal Hanuman Sahar** (✉ Shop 131, Tripoliya Bazaar, ☎ no phone) has burlap bags full of old brass, copper, and bronze pieces that are sold by weight at bargain prices. The **Popular Art Palace** (✉ B/6 Prithviraj Rd., C-Scheme, ☎ 141/360368) is great for both brass and wooden furniture and miniature crafts and also carries antiques.

For demonstrations of hand-block printing and other craftsmanship, visit **Rajasthan Cottage Industries** (✉ Shilpgram Complex, Golimar Garden, Amer Rd., ☎ 141/601091) or **Rajasthan Small Scale Cottage Industries** (✉ Jagat Shiromani Temple Rd., Amer, ☎ 141/530519). Both sell good selections of textiles, gems, and handicrafts, and purchases are guaranteed.

A special treat for lovers of miniature paintings is a trip to the home of award-winning artist **Tilak Gitai** (✉ E-5 Gokhle Marg, C-Scheme, ☎ 141/372101), who creates exquisite miniatures in the classic Mogul, Rajput, Pahari ("hilly"), and other styles. Using antique paper, Gitai applies colors made from semiprecious stones, then real gold and silver leaf, in designs so fine he'll give you a magnifying glass to admire them. This is not a quick visit—it's a lovely way to spend a few hours with a friendly Rajasthani family and learn more about Indian art.

JEWELRY

Gem Palace has Jaipur's best gems and jewelry, a small collection of museum-quality curios, and a royal clientele; prices range from U.S.$2 to $2 million (✉ M. I. Rd., ☎ 141/37175). **Amprapalli Jewels** has some great silver and ornamental trinkets as well as semiprecious stone artifacts (⊠ Panchbatti, M. I. Rd., ☏ 141/377940 or 141/362768). For precious jewels, including gold ornaments, find the **Bhurmal-Rajmal Surana Showroom** (⊠ J. L. N. Marg, ☏ 141/570429 or 141/570430) known worldwide for its kundan and mina work. If you want something less expensive and are willing to bargain, you'll find your niche on **Chameli Valon ka Rasta** (⊠ off M. I. Rd.). Walk among the shops on this lane for silver and semiprecious jeweled ornaments, trinkets, and small toys.

POTTERY

Jaipur Blue Pottery Art Center (⊠ Amer Rd. (near Jain Mandir, ☏ 141/48952) sells a broad selection of Rajasthan's fetching blue pottery. Pots are thrown on the premises. The blue pottery at **Neerja Internationals** is particularly funky—the designer and owner, Lela Bordie, has exhibited all over the world, and she runs this shop for a discriminating crowd (⊠ S-19 Bhagwan Singh Rd., C-Scheme Extension, ☏ 141/380395 or 141/383511).

TEXTILES

Channi Carpets and Textiles (⊠ Mount Rd. opposite Ramgarh Rd., ☏ 141/40414) has an excellent selection of handwoven merino-wool carpets, cotton dhurries, and hand-blocked cottons and silks. The staff can also tailor clothes on short notice. **Anokhi** (⊠ 2 Tilak Marg, opposite Udhyog Bhawan, C-Scheme, ☏ 141/381247) is a leading shop for designer and ethnic wear, mostly in cotton. The selection includes beautiful bedspreads, quilts, cloth bags, saris, and other clothing, both Indian and casual Western. You can also visit the on-site workshop.

Catering to the aesthetically discriminating, **Soma** (⊠ 5 Jacob Rd., Civil Lines, ☏ 141/222778) is a second-floor paradise of incredibly vibrant colors. Here you'll find everything from clothing to pickles and chutneys to decorative fabrics, including fabulous, hand-painted white cloth lamp shades. It's an unusually refreshing shopping experience. Run and managed by women, the cute **Cottons** boutique (⊠ 4 Achrol Estate, Jacob Rd.) sells simple, attractive clothes for both men and women, little bags, quilts, and other decorative household items. For fine hand-blocked fabrics, visit the towns of Sanganer and Bagru (☞ *below*).

Sanganer

❿ *16 km (10 mi) south of Jaipur up Tonk Rd., near the airport*

Watch artisans in action throughout this well-known craft town, where nearly every family is involved in the production of block- and screen-printed textiles, blue pottery, or handmade paper. Whatever handmade paper you've seen back home may well have come from **Salim's Paper** (⊠ Gramodyog Rd., ☏ 141/550552 or –772), in whose factory you can see each step of the fascinating process. Some of these thick, beautiful papers are made with crushed flower petals, and it's fun to see them thrown into the mixture of cotton and resin. Another highlight of Sanganer is the **Shri Digamber Jain Temple,** roughly 1,000 years old and covered with amazingly ornate carvings from its piled spires on down. The temple is right in town, and the inner shrine has no roof, yet somehow the space achieves total tranquility. On your way into or out of town, check out the line of blue potters on Tonk Road.

The small Rajput township of **Bagru,** 35 km (22 mi) southwest of Sanganer on Ajmer Road, is also famous for its hand-printed cloth industry. Bagru's simple, popular designs feature earthen colors of green, brown, black, and blue.

Ranthambhore National Park

11 *161 km (100 mi) south of Jaipur*

The locale is spectacular: The rugged Aravalli and Vindhya hills, highland boulder plateaus, and lakes and rivers provide homes for hundreds of species of birds, mammals, and reptiles. Ranthambhore is noted for its tiger and leopard population, although you still have only a so-so chance of seeing a large cat on any given expedition. What you will see are numerous peacocks, deer (including large sauras), wild pigs, and often sloth bears as well.

Now incorporating several nearby sanctuaries in its borders, the park encompasses 1,334 square km (512 square mi). Run by the Indian government, it has somewhat inflexible rules. You can only enter the park in an official government jeep, and the jeeps keep strict hours: 6:30 AM–9:30 AM and 3:30 PM–6:30 PM. In the off-hours, you can explore the surrounding region; **Ranthambhore Fort,** atop one of the nearby hills, is more than a thousand years old, and one of Rajasthan's more spectacular military bastions.

Within the park itself are two government-run hotels, **Jhoomar Baori** and **Jogi Mahal.** Both are decent and, more important, offer the chance to spend a night with the animals. *For information call Sawai Madhopur Tourist Information Center, ☎ 7462/20808. Rs. 575 per jeep. ⏲ Oct.–June.*

Lodging

The neighboring town of Sawai Madhopur has numerous hotels, but most are extremely basic.

$$$ **Sawai Madhopur Lodge.** The one luxurious accommodation near the park is this Taj-run property. Like most of Rajasthan's former hunting lodges, it provides comfortable, atmospheric rooms, smooths out all safari details with the forestry office, and has a good—and expensive—restaurant. Ask about packages that include meals in the room price. ✉ *Ranthambhore Rd., Sawai Madhopur 322001, ☎ 7462/20541, FAX 7462/20718. 20 rooms, 2 suites. Restaurant, bar, tennis court, croquet, billiards, travel services. AE, DC, MC, V.*

Sariska National Park

12 *110 km (68 mi) northeast of Jaipur, 110 km (68 mi) southwest of Delhi, 40 km (25 mi) southwest of Alwar*

Sariska was once the exclusive game preserve of the rulers of the princely state of Alwar. Today, this sanctuary in the hills of the Arvalli Range makes a great weekend escape from Delhi. Traditionally a tiger reserve, Sariska is now better endowed with other carnivorous animals, including the leopard, jackal, caracal, and jungle cat (though the cats' nocturnal habits make sightings rare). The terrain—mostly scrub and lush stands of forest and grasslands—also provides an excellent habitat for herbivores. Peacocks abound here, as do monkeys, blue bulls, spotted deer, and wild boars. You do have a good chance of seeing langurs and other monkeys, porcupines, hyenas, and numerous species of deer (including the *chowsingha,* a four-horned deer unique to India) and a great variety of birds.

Forest officials have created water holes for the animals, which aid in catching glimpses. The best times to view animals at Sariska are early morning and evening from November through June (though it starts getting hot by March). Jeeps are available through the hotels. Wear neutral colors to avoid frightening the animals away, and take a jacket in winter.

Keeping the animals company in Sariska are a number of historic monuments. Within the park is the **Pandupol,** a huge hole in the rock supposedly made by Bhim, one of the five Pandava brothers who are celebrated in the *Mahabharata* epic. Outside the sanctuary, but still close by, is the **Neelkanth Mahadev,** an ancient ruin comprising bits and pieces from about 300 Hindu and Jain temples. Among these are some beautiful sculptures and an entire Shiva temple as well as the ruins of the Kankwari Fort perched high on a hill (a good picnic spot).

Lodging

$$ **Sariska Palace Hotel.** This former palace and royal hunting lodge was built in 1892 by the maharaja of Alwar for the visit of Queen Victoria's son, the Duke of Connaught. Now a Heritage Hotel, it blends French-regal architecture with Eastern details. The interior is not opulent, but it has some Louis XIV and Art Deco furniture, along with wicker chairs and Victoriana. The high-ceiling rooms and suites are gigantic and clean, with phones but no TVs; some are air-conditioned. The lovely flower-speckled grounds are encircled by a large wall to keep out the animals, but they often find their way in, so you may see wildlife while relaxing on the terrace. Horse, camel, and jeep safaris are easily arranged. The dining room serves Continental and Indian cuisine. ✉ *Alwar district, 301022,* ☎ *144/41322 or 144/41360; reserve through* ✉ *1/1-B, Mohammedpur, Bikhaji Cama Pl., New Delhi 110066,* ☎ *11/617–2346 or 11/618–8862,* FAX *11/618–8861. 40 rooms, 5 suites. Restaurant, bar, pool, tennis court, horseback riding, travel services. AE, DC, MC, V.*

Bharatpur

⓭ *150 km (93 mi) east of Jaipur, 55 km (34 mi) west of Agra, 18 km (11 mi) west of Fatehpur Sikri*

Founded by the Jat ruler Suraj Mal in 1733 and named for the brother of Lord Ram, the city of Bharatpur is famous for the **Keoladeo National Park** (also known as the Ghana Bird Sanctuary), once the duck-hunting forest of the local maharajas. People now come here to watch birds. This famous waterbird haven is an ornithologist's dream—29 square km (12 square mi) of forests and wetlands inviting 400 species, over 130 of these resident year-round, such as the Saras crane, gray heron, snake bird, and spoonbill. In winter birds arrive from the Himalayas, Siberia, and even Europe.

The best way to see the park is on foot, but there are plenty of other options. The park's main artery is a blacktop road that runs from the entrance gate to the center. Surrounded by marshlands but screened by bushes, this road is the most convenient viewpoint for bird-watching, and is also plied by cycle-rickshaws (Rs. 30 per hour), a horse and buggy, and the park's electric bus. The rickshaw drivers are trained by the forest department and are fairly good at finding and pointing out birds. You can also rent a bicycle (about Rs. 20) and head into some less-traveled areas; just note that most roads are unpaved. There's even a limited boating area. The excellent guides at the gate (Rs. 35 per hour per person or Rs. 75 for a group) are familiar with the birds' haunts and can help you spot and identify them.

The park is also home to mammals and reptiles, including ungainly blue bulls; spotted deer; a few otters; and Indian rock pythons, which bask outside their burrows during the day in winter.

Try to bring a bird guidebook: former royal-family member Salim Ali's *The Birds of India* is a good choice. The best time to see the birds is early in the morning or late in the evening, November–February; by the end of February, many birds start heading home. Stick around at sunset, when the water takes on a mirrorlike stillness and the air is filled with the calls of day birds settling down and night birds stirring. ✉ *For information, contact the Tourist Reception Center, Hotel Saras, Agra Rd., Bharatpur 321001,* ☎ *5644/22542. Park:* ⏲ *Daily 6 AM–6:30 PM.* 🎫 *Rs. 100; cameras Rs. 10; video cameras Rs. 250.*

Northwest Bharatpur holds the **Lohagarh Fort,** also known figuratively as the Iron Fort. Built of mud, the structure might seem fragile, but it was tested by a British siege in 1805: Armed with 65 pieces of field artillery, 1,800 European soldiers and 6,000 Indian sepoys did manage to win the battle, but they failed to break the invincible fort.

The town of **Deeg,** 34 km (21 mi) north of Bharatpur, is known for its graceful palaces and gardens, complete with swings and ancient fountains. (The latter are now pressed into service as musical fountains, in which capacity their waters dance to the rhythm of taped classical music.) Also built in the 1730s, Deeg was the first capital of the Jat state.

Dining and Lodging

$$ ✕🏨 **Ashok Bharatpur Forest Lodge.** This ivy-covered bungalow inside the sanctuary offers clean, comfortable rooms, some with decorative interior swings. All rooms have balconies, and you may see spotted deer nibbling the grass outside your window. The Indian and Continental food in the restaurant, served buffet-style, is excellent. ✉ *Bharatpur 321001,* ☎ *5644/22722 or 5644/22760,* FAX *5644/22864. 17 rooms. Restaurant, bar. AE, DC, MC, V.*

$ ★ 🏨 **Laxmi Vilas Palace Hotel.** Still home to the former maharaja's uncle and his family, this cozy Heritage Hotel is a two-story haveli built in 1899 for the maharaja's younger brother. Blending Mogul and Rajput styles, the building sits on a 40-acre estate covered with mustard flowers. Each room is different, but many contain old brass beds and antique furniture. Pricier rooms have original tiles and painted walls and fireplaces; the others are smaller and have newer furniture, but they're still pleasant. The dining room serves a variety of cuisines. The family is happy to organize jeep safaris or excursions to surrounding areas, such as Deeg, Agra, and Fatehpur Sikri. ✉ *Kakaji Ki Kothi, Bharatpur 321001,* ☎ *5644/25259 or 5644/23523,* FAX *5644/25259. 7 rooms, 11 suites. Restaurant, travel services. AE, MC, V.*

Ajmer

⓮ *131 km (81 mi) southwest of Jaipur*

Situated in a green oasis roughly three hours' drive from Jaipur, Ajmer has an interesting past. Founded by Raja Ajay Pal Chauhan in the 7th century, the town was a center of Chauhan power until 1193, when Prithvi Raj Chauhan lost the kingdom to Mohammed Ghori. From then on, many dynasties contributed to making Ajmer what it is today—a fascinating blend of Hindu and Islamic culture. In the heart of the city is **Darga Sharif,** the tomb of Khwaja Moin-ud din Chisti. This site is comparable to Mecca in significance for South Asian Muslims, and is frequented by Muslims and non-Muslims alike, especially during Urs (six days in the Islamic month of Rajab). If you visit, be sure to cover your head, and feel free to give *namaz* (prayers) and lay a *chaddhar* (sheet) on the saint's tomb.

Pushkar

15 *11 km (7 mi) northwest of Ajmer*

The beautiful Hindu pilgrimage town of Pushkar lies right on the edge of the desert. It's commonly held among Hindus that one must bathe in the Pushkar Lake if one's *other* pilgrimages are to be successful. The Vedic text *Padma Purana* says that Brahma, creator of the universe, was once contemplating a suitable place on earth to perform a *yajna* (sacrificial ritual). He dropped a lotus from his hand and it struck the earth in three places, all in close proximity; this 9-square-km (5½-square-mi) area became known as Pushkar. Today, Pushkar is also known for its annual November **camel festival,** to which decorated camels and horses are brought from all over Rajasthan to be traded, sold, and entered in races. For added adventure, take an overnight elephant safari from Jaipur to Pushkar; contact the Rajasthan Tourism Development Corporation (RTDC) or a local travel agency for more information (☞ Rajasthan A to Z, *below*).

Lodging

$$$ 🏨 **Pushkar Palace.** Considered one of the best Heritage Hotels in Rajasthan, this one combines fabulous views of sand dunes, the Aravalli Hills, and 400 temples. Built by the maharaja of Jaisalmar in the 15th century, it was later presented to the maharaja of Kishangarh. If you like the swimming pool, thank Kate Winslet: The *Titanic* star came to Pushkar for a few days and the pool was constructed in her honor. Horse, camel, and jeep safaris are available. ✉ ☎ *145/72001 or 145/72401,* FAX *145/72226. 34 rooms, 2 suites. Restaurant, bar, pool, horseback riding, travel services. AE, MC, V.*

SHEKHAVATI

This large chunk of northeastern Rajasthan is renowned for its painted havelis and old forts. The name Shekhavati literally means "Garden of Shekha": Rao Shekhaji, born 1433, was a Rajput king of this region. He was so named by his father because his parents were only able to bear a son after being granted a boon from a *fakir* (Muslim holy man) named Sheikh Burhan. In another unwitting contribution to history, the sheikh had come to India with the Mongol invader Tamerlane in 1398 dressed in a blue robe—hence the color of Shekhavati's flag. The region has had a colorful history ever since, experiencing the rise and fall of many a Rajput prince, alliances with the Moguls after Akbar, and finally suzerainty under the British Raj. The region is made up of smaller principalities, including Sikar, Lachhmangarh, Churi Ajitgarh, Mukundgarh, Jhunjhunu, Mandawa, Fatehpur, and Churu.

A regional center of trade between the 18th and 20th centuries, Shekhavati is now known as Rajasthan's open-air art gallery, as its ornate havelis bear fantastically realistic frescoes. Influenced by the Persian, Jaipur, and Mogul schools of painting, Shekhavati's frescoes illustrate a variety of subjects—from mythological stories and local legends, to hunting safaris and scenes of everyday life, to experiences with the British and the impact of technology (cars, planes, telephones, and more). The introduction of photography in 1840 gave Shekhavati's painters yet more to work with. The painters themselves were called *chiteras* and belonged to the caste of *kumhars* (potters). Initially, they colored their masterpieces with vegetable pigments, such as indigo, lime, saffron, and yellow clay; after mixing these with lime water and treating the wall with three layers of a very fine clay, the chiteras painstakingly drew their designs on a last layer of filtered lime dust. Time was short, as the design had to be completed before the plaster dried, but the highly refined technique assured that the images would not fade as long as the building was standing.

The haveli homes of these masterpieces are equally spectacular. With indoor and outdoor courtyards, exquisitely latticed windows, intricate mirror work, vaulted ceilings, immense balconies, and ornate gateways and facades, they're the perfect settings for Shekhavati's frescoes. The havelis of Shekhavati date from the British Raj, during which traditional overland trading routes to Central Asia, Europe, and China were slowly superseded by rail and sea routes. In the 19th century, Marwari traders (Hindus from the *vaisha,* or trading, caste) who had profited from the overland trading system migrated to Calcutta, Bombay, and Madras to seek new fortunes. These came to be some of India's wealthiest families; but even in their distant prosperity, the Marwaris maintained connections with their ancestral homes, sending remittance from their new enterprises. Often this money was used to build havelis, adorned with elaborate frescoes depicting family life and wealth. Many of the havelis, as well as some old Rajput forts, are now open to the public, and some have been converted to Heritage Hotels. Stay in one if you can, and take a day or two to explore the dusty towns around them.

Unfortunately, the golden age of fresco painting came to an end in the 1930s with the mass exodus of the Marwaris. Since then, many of these beautiful mansions and their paintings have fallen into disrepair, succumbed to water damage, been whitewashed, or been obscured by new construction. A few, however, have been restored by their owners. In **Sikar,** formerly the wealthiest trading center, look for the Biyani, Murarka, and Somani havelis. **Lachhmangarh** features the grand Char Chowk Haveli, particularly evocative of the prosperous Marwari lifestyle. A planned city like Jaipur, Lachhmangarh is also home to a popular ayurvedic center, **SPG Kaya Kalp and Research Center** (✉ Tara Kung, Salasar Rd., ☎ 1573/64230), which teaches yoga, meditation, and various therapies. In the village of **Churi Ajitgarh,** unusually erotic frescoes are painted behind doors and on bedroom ceilings in the Shiv Narain Nemani, Kothi Shiv Datt, and Rai Jagan Lal Tibrewal havelis. The frescoed temples of **Jhunjhunu** make for interesting comparisons: Visit Laxmi Nath, Mertani Baori, Ajeet Sagar, and Qamrudin Shah Ki Dargah Fatehpur. **Mukandgarh** has an excellent craft market, known especially for textiles, brass ware, and iron scissors, in addition to the Kanoria, Ganeriwala, and Bheekraj Nangalia havelis. Warrior-statesman Thakur Nawal Singh founded **Nawalgarh** in 1737, and the town boasts some of the best frescoes in Shekhavati in its Aath, Anandilal Poddar, Jodhraj Patodia, and Chokhani havelis, as well as in Roop Niwas Palace (☞ Dining and Lodging, *below*).

Dining and Lodging

$$ ★ ✕🏨 **Castle Mandawa.** Towering high above the town of Mandawa, this rugged, miragelike fort has been converted by its owners (descendants of the local *thakur,* or feudal lord) to a luxury Heritage Hotel. Sword-bearing guards welcome you at the immensely tall, spiked gate; inside, the walls bear 16th-century portraits of the Mandawa family. The spacious, airy rooms are charmingly furnished with period furniture. In the evening, you can sip tea on the main terrace and behold the town and the Rajasthan desert spreading out below; the canopied balconies and turreted battlements also have panoramic views. Dinner is an enchanting candlelit affair in the rear open-air courtyard. The highlight of the evening is the spectacular Fire Dance (a Mandawa specialty), where eight men in traditional attire follow an elderly retainer who dances with torches in his hands. Camel, horse, and jeep safaris offer still more adventures. ✉ *Mandawa, Jhunjhunu district, 333704, ☎ 1592/23124 or 1592/23480; reserve through 306 Anukampa Tower, Church Rd., Jaipur 302001, ☎ 141/371194, FAX 141/372084. 56 rooms, 14 suites. Restaurant, bar, horseback riding. AE, MC, V.*

$$–$$$$ ★ **Neemrana Fort Palace.** Sitting on a plateau in the Aravalli Hills, this 15th-century fort was the home of a Hindu prince killed in battle with invading Muslims in 1192. Now a Heritage Hotel, Neemrana is a true gem, one of the finest retreats in India. The rooms, which vary in size and price, are furnished with antiques and decorated with Rajput mementos and indigenous crafts. The architecture is characterized by wooden jalis (latticework screens), cusped arches, gleaming pillars, squinches, and niches of various sizes. Swatches of the original royal-blue paint remain. Forget about phones and TVs—just relax and watch preening peacocks and swooping parrots from the various terraces, balconies, and courtyards. The restaurant serves fixed Rajasthani and French menus; breakfast and lunch or dinner are included in the room rate. Most bathrooms do not have tubs. The village nearby has an ancient step well—an enormous underground well with wraparound staircases and sitting areas on each level, where people once took refuge during the heat. ✉ *Off National Hwy. 8, Alwar district, 301705, ☎ 1494/6007 or 1494/6008; reserve through A-58, Nizamuddin East, New Delhi 110013, ☎ 11/461–6145, FAX 11/462–1112. 42 rooms, 8 suites. Restaurant, bar, travel services. AE, DC, MC, V.*

$$ **Hill Fort, Kesroli.** This stone fort overlooking farmland and distant hills has been turned into a Heritage Hotel by the same duo responsible for Neemrana (☞ *above*). While Kesroli does not have the same grandeur or scale, it's still an elegant base for exploration. The origins of the seven-turreted fort go back over six centuries. Built by Yaduvanshi Rajputs, the building was later conquered by the Moguls and then the Jats before reverting to the Rajputs in 1775. The hotel is decorated with a tasteful mix of Indian antiques and traditional crafts, and the price includes breakfast. The evening meal is a sumptuous event, with table-side braziers for warmth in winter. ✉ *Kesroli village, Alwar district, 301030, ☎ 0144/81312; reserve through A-58, Nizamuddin East, New Delhi 110013, ☎ 11/461–6145, FAX 11/462–1112. 21 rooms. Restaurant. AE, DC, MC, V.*

$$ **Mukandgarh Fort.** Founded in the mid-18th century by Raja Mukand Singh, this picturesque fort in the artisans' town of Mukandgarh is now a Heritage Hotel. A bar overlooks the courtyard, where an outdoor barbecue serves kebabs and curry in the evenings. Guest rooms have painted walls and ceilings, tie-dye curtains, and fat-legged beds under patchwork bedspreads. ✉ *Mukandgarh, Jhunjhunu district, 333705, ☎ 1594/52396 or 1594/52397, FAX 1594/52395. 42 rooms, 4 suites. 2 restaurants, bar, travel services. AE, DC, MC, V.*

$ **Dera Dundlod Kila.** In the heart of the Shekhavati region, Dundlod was built in 1750 by Kesari Singhji. Now a Heritage Hotel, the fort is still owned by the descendants of the former thakur. Surrounded by a moat, it has an interesting mix of Mogul and Rajput architecture; inside, the stunning Diwan-i-Khas (Hall of Private Audience), has original wall frescoes in shades of yellow and orange, European-style portraits, Louis XIV furniture, and a well-stocked library. The clean, simple bedrooms have painted walls. The family has 20 horses and is mainly involved in promoting horse safaris (as well as camel and jeep trips), using the hotel as a base. Dine under the light of rustic oil lamps in the rooftop restaurant. ✉ *P.O. Dundlod, Jhunjhunu district, 333702, ☎ 15945/2519 or 15945/2180, FAX 15945/2519; reserve through Dundlod House, Civil Lines, Jaipur 302019, ☎ FAX 141/211276 or –118. 30 rooms, 12 suites. Restaurant, bar, pool, horseback riding. AE.*

$ ★ **Desert Resort.** The interiors of these clay-covered "village huts" on a large sand dune sparkle with the glass inlaid in their walls, and glow with the warmth of Rajasthani fabrics and handicrafts. Even the main lounge is made of mud, and the dining room gleams from the bits of glass and cowrie shells in *its* walls. Sit by the pool or in the garden and enjoy beautiful views of the surrounding area. ✉ *Mandawa, Jhunjhunu district, 333702,* ☎ *1592/23151; reserve through 306 Anukampa Tower, Church Rd., Jaipur 302001,* ☎ *141/371194,* FAX *141/372084. 40 rooms, 1 suite, 12 cottages. Restaurant, bar, pool. AE, MC, V.*

$ **Roop Niwas Palace.** This Heritage Hotel on the outskirts of town combines Rajput and European architecture in its beautiful gardens and private cottages. It's far from grand, but the owners, descendants of the former thakur, aim to please. The rooms have Victorian furniture and are modest but clean; the dining room is quaint; and the grounds are lovely. Jeep and camel safaris and bird-watching trips can be arranged. ✉ *Nawalgarh, Jhunjhunu district, Shekhavati 333042,* ☎ *1594/22008,* FAX *1594/23388. 30 rooms, 1 suite. Restaurant, bar, pool, horseback riding. AE.*

JODHPUR AND ENVIRONS

Jodhpur is rich in fort and palace treasures and well endowed with side trips, such as Guda Vishnoi, home of the gentle Vishnoi community and a haven for wildlife, and the Thar Desert temple town of Osian. Two other forts beckon: the 16th-century Khimsar Fort, now a Heritage Hotel and a destination in its own right, and Nagaur, in whose fort you can camp during the town's winter cattle fair.

Jodhpur

16 *343 km (215 mi) west of Jaipur, 266 km (165 mi) northwest of Udaipur*

Guarded by one of the most imposing fortresses of Rajputana, Jodhpur sits at the base of a golden sandstone ridge. Capital of the Marwar kingdom for five centuries, the city is named for its 15th-century founder, Rao Jodha, chief of the Rathore clan of Marwar (which traces its lineage back to Lord Rama, hero of the Hindu *Ramayana* epic). The city is on the fringe of the Thar Desert, so a wall 9 km (6 mi) in circumference keeps out the desert sands. Not to be outdone by the Pink City, Jodhpur is famous for its blue houses, painted with blue dye mixed into white cement. From Meherangarh Fort the city looks like a sea in the desert.

Getting around Jodhpur is relatively easy, and rewards you with walks through a massive fort, palaces, and gardens as well as markets full of fruit, textile, and handicraft stalls. Take special note of Jodhpuri *pathar,* the peach-color stone that makes these houses and buildings stand apart from others in Rajasthan. If you have extra time, take a desert safari on camelback.

Jodhpur is also well-known for its food and hospitality, especially its *mithai* (sweets) and the *manuhar* ritual that accompanies its food. When you're offered a *mave ki kachori* (milk-based pastry) or *basin ki baarfi* (graham-flour cookie), along with *mirchi bada* (fried breaded pepper) and *kofta* (fried breaded potato), don't resist: The offer will be repeated until you take some.

A Good Tour

This plan covers Jodhpur in two days, covering the essentials first. Start your first day early at the **Meherangarth Fort,** where you're bound to spend a few hours. Take one of the waiting rickshaws down the mountain and north to the **Jaswant Thada** memorial. After a break for lunch, hire a car and driver for the short drive north of Jodhpur to the **Mandore Gardens.** From there, it's a hop, skip, and a jump to **Balsamand Lake and Garden.** If you have a little extra time, visit **Mahandir.** End your day at the **Umaid Bhawan Palace Museum**—walk through the museum before it closes at 5, then stay for dinner and fabulous sunset views.

If you have two days here, drive out of town once more to see the nature-loving town of **Guda Vishnoi,** where deer and birds feed at water holes early in the morning. Return to Jodhpur for lunch and a bit of shopping. In the early evening, make a pilgrimage to the temple town of **Osian.**

Sights to See

★ **Balsamand Lake and Garden.** This public park (cum wildlife sanctuary) has a picturesque view of its 12th-century artificial lake and the royal family's beautiful 19th-century summer palace, now a hotel. The lake is surrounded by a thick jungle of fruit trees called *badis.* It's the perfect place for a tranquil stroll—just beware the mischievous monkeys, who are always on the watch for good pranks (and good *pakoras,* vegetable fritters). Don't try to pluck the fruit from the trees, as the monkeys will catch you red-handed. ✉ *5 km (3 mi) northeast of Jodhpur.*

Jaswant Thada. The royal marble crematorium was built in 1899 for Maharaja Jaswant Singh II. Capping the enormous white structure are marble canopies under which individual members of the royal family are buried. You may see people bowing before the image of the king, who is considered to have joined the ranks of the deities. ✉ *Near Mehrangarh Fort.* 🎫 *Free.* ⏲ *Daily 8–6.*

Mahamandir. Built in 1812 just outside Jodhpur, this old, walled monastery complex still has a few hundred houses. The monastery belongs to the Nath community, warrior-priests who worked closely with the royal family to arrange support in times of war. Mahamandir is best known for the 84 beautifully carved pillars that surround it. ✉ *9 km (6 mi) from Jaipur.*

Mandore Gardens. Within the old Marwar capital at Mandore, these gardens house the exquisitely sculpted red-sandstone *davals* (cenotaphs) of former rulers. The Hall of Heroes depicts 16 colorfully painted heroes and deities carved from a single piece of stone. The small **museum** on the grounds has sculptures from the 5th to the 9th centuries as well as ivory and lacquer work. There's even a **cactus nursery.** Unfortunately, due to the large number of picnics and dal baati churma feasts held here, the gardens have grown dirty and are not terribly well-maintained. ✉ *Mandore (8 km/5 mi north of Jodhpur).* 🎫 *Free.* ⏲ *Gardens daily sunrise–sunset, museum Sat.–Thurs. 10–4.*

★ **Mehrangarh Fort.** Perched on the top of a hill, this enormous fort was built by Rao Jodha in 1459, when he shifted his capital from Mandore to Jodhpur. Looking straight down a perpendicular cliff, the fort has been thus far impregnable and is a mighty imposing landmark, especially at night, when it's bathed in yellow light. You approach the fort up a steep walkway (the 40-minute hike is much more enjoyable than the rickshaw alternative), passing under no fewer than eight huge gates. The first, the Victory Gate, was built by Maharaja Ajit Singh to commemorate his military success against the Moguls at the beginning of the 18th century; the other seven commemorate victories over other Rajput states. The last gate, as in many Rajput forts, displays the haunting handprints of women who immolated themselves after their husbands were defeated in battle.

Inside the rugged fort, delicate latticed windows and pierced sandstone screens are the surprising motifs. The palaces—**Moti Mahal** (Pearl Palace), **Phool Mahal** (Flower Palace), **Sheesh Mahal** (Glass Palace), and the other apartments—are exquisitely decorated, their ceilings, walls, and even floors, covered with murals, mirrorwork, and gilt. The palace museum has exquisite rooms filled with lavish royal palenquins, thrones, paintings, and even a giant tent. The ramparts provide an excellent city view. ✉ *Fort Rd.* 🎫 *Rs. 50, camera Rs. 50.* ⏲ *Daily 8:30–1 and 2:30–5.*

★ **Umaid Bhawan Palace Museum.** Built between 1929 and 1942 as a public-works project during a long famine, by 3,000 workers at the behest of Maharaja Umaid Singh this palace is now part museum, part royal residence, and part Heritage Hotel. Its Art Deco design makes it unique in the state. Amazingly, no cement was used in construction; the palace is made of interlocking blocks of sandstone, a fact to bear in mind when you stand under the imposing 183-ft-high central dome. The collection includes royal finery, local arts and crafts, miniature paintings, and a large number of clocks. You may catch a glimpse of the maharaja of Jodhpur, who still lives in one large wing of the palace; but in any case you won't miss seeing the magnificent peacocks who dance around the palace's marble *chattris* (canopies) and lush back lawns.

One of Jodhpur's most exquisite places to watch the sun set is **Pillars,** the restaurant on the palace's elegant, colonnaded veranda. As you contemplate the immaculately manicured gardens, peacocks strut up the steps and strains of sitar music fill the air. ✉ *Umaid Bhawan Palace.* ☎ *291/510101.* 🎫 *Rs. 40.* ⏲ *Daily 9–5.*

Dining and Lodging

Watch the hearty consumption of local delicacies at the local eating area **Rawat Mishtan Bhandar,** next to the train station. Your system might find the street food problematic, but the sight of crowds tucking into hot and spicy kachoris, koftas, and mave ki kachori can be phenomenal.

All the hotels listed below can arrange camel and jeep safaris, and usually other excursions as well, upon request.

$$$ ✕ **Kabab Korner.** This open-air restaurant at Umaid Bhawan Palace has breathtaking views of Jodhpur by night. The tandoori food is excellent, as are the kebabs, skewered vegetables and meats cooked over an open flame. ✉ *Welcomgroup Umaid Bhawan Palace,* ☎ *291/510101. AE, DC, MC, V.*

$$$ ✕ **Marwar Hall.** Huge chandeliers hang from the high vaulted ceilings of this gorgeous palace dining room. The chef prepares very good Continental and Indian food, including tasty Mughlai and regional Marwari dishes. Meals are served buffet-style. ✉ *Welcomgroup Umaid Bhawan Palace,* ☎ *291/33316. AE, DC, MC, V.*

$$ ✕ **Khamaghani.** The walls of this classy restaurant are decorated with Rajasthani saris bunched up into circles. Half the tables, along with their red velvet–covered chairs, are in a sunken enclave in the center of the room. Classical Indian music plays in the background. The menu mixes local, Indian, Chinese, and Continental fare; the chicken tikka is particularly good, as are the Chinese dishes. ✉ *Ratanada Polo Palace Hotel, Residency Rd.,* ☎ *291/31910. AE, DC, MC, V.*

$ ✕ **Midtown Vegetarian Restaurant.** This unpretentious but spotlessly clean joint has Rajasthani decor and specializes in Rajasthani and South Indian cuisine. Midtown specials include a *dosa* (Indian-style crepe) filled with potato and cashews and *kabuli* (rice layered with vegetables, bread, and dried fruits and nuts). A salad bar rounds out the vegetarian menu. ✉ *Hotel Shanti Bhawan, Station Rd.,* ☎ *291/621689,* FAX *291/639211. No credit cards.*

$ ✕ **On the Rocks.** Here you can tuck into a buffet of traditional Rajasthani food in the cozy flagstone courtyard of the Ajit Bhawan Hotel. Chinese and other Indian options are on offer as well. ✉ *Ajit Bhawan Hotel,* ☎ *291/612410. MC, V.*

$ ✕ **Sukh Sagar.** Specializing in South Indian food, Sukh Sagar also serves North Indian and Chinese dishes. Try the *rava idli* (steamed semolina and rice cakes) and *vada sambar* (fried rice-and-lentil doughnuts served with spicy stew), taking care to specify how spicy you like your food. Down some South Indian filter coffee for an extra kick. ✉ *Ratanada Bazaar,* ☎ *291/511450 or 291/621450. No credit cards.*

$$$$ ★ **Welcomgroup Umaid Bhawan Palace.** Built in the 1930s of pink sandstone, in the Art Deco style peculiar to colonial India, this magnificent fort palace is one of the grandest of Rajasthan's many such hotels. Still home to the maharaja of Jodhpur, it has served as a backdrop for many an Indian and foreign film. The public rooms are lavish, and filled with objets d'art; many of the rooms, though not opulent, have period decor. The newer rooms tend to be small and ordinary. Weary travelers can take a refreshing dip in the cool blue of the beautiful underground pool. ✉ *Jodhpur 342006,* ☎ *291/510101,* FAX *291/510100. 98 rooms, 4 suites. 3 restaurants, bar, indoor pool, sauna, golf privileges, 2 tennis courts, health club, horseback riding, squash, billiards, travel services. AE, DC, MC, V.*

$$$ **Ratanada Polo Palace.** This hotel is dedicated to the Rajasthani polo player Raorajahanut Singh and owned by his son. One section was actually once a stable for polo players' steeds. The marble entrance hall is lined with numerous paintings and photos of Singh playing polo or shaking the hands of international aristocracy; horses' heads and profiles form a related motif throughout the building. Guest rooms are fairly simple—marble on the ground floor, carpeted upstairs—and bathrooms are on the small side. The furnishings are dark wood, and the suites have frilly Victorian lamps and flowery sofas. This place is popular with both business travelers and wedding parties; you'll find it easy to gate-crash, and join the fun of a traditional Indian wedding. ✉ *Residency Rd., 342001,* ☎ *291/31910 (–14),* FAX *291/33118. 80 rooms, 9 suites. Restaurant, bar, pool, tennis court, business services, meeting room, travel services. AE, DC, MC, V.*

$$$ ★ **Rohetgarh.** This 17th-century desert fortress 40 km (25 mi) south of Jodhpur is both Heritage Hotel and the home of its Rajput family, whose members are your hosts. It's a great place to experience the lifestyle of Rajput nobility. The public rooms are decked out in original paintings and weapons; guest rooms, some of which have air-conditioning, are decorated in various ways with traditional carved furniture and colorful hand-blocked prints. Some even have swings, but none has a phone or TV. Horseback safaris are a specialty, as there are plenty of bird species and other animals nearby. ✉ *Rohetgarh Village, Pali district,* ☎ *2932/682321; reserve through Rohet House, P. W. D. Rd., 342001,* ☎ *291/31161,* FAX *291/649368. 23 rooms, 2 suites. Restaurant, pool, horseback riding, travel services. MC, V.*

$$$ **Sardarsamand Lake Resort.** The hunting lodge of Jodhpur's former maharaja, Umaid Singh, is now a resort. Built in 1933, the verandas of this pink sandstone-and-granite building have fabulous views of an artificial lake that attracts migrating birds from October to March. Just beyond the lake are the expansive sands of the Thar Desert. Rooms retain their original fittings, helped by Art Deco–style furnishings. ✉ *Sardarsamand; reserve through Balsamand Lake Palace (**☞ below**). 18 rooms. Restaurant, pool, tennis, horseback riding. MC, V.*

$$ ★ **Ajit Bhawan.** For an abundance of charm with little regal display, stay in this small but enchanting palace and village complex, designed and owned by the maharaja's uncle. The palace rooms are now suites; each bungalow, which can sleep up to four, is decorated with its own Rajasthani motif and named after a month of the Hindu calendar. With painted tables and doors and traditional Rajasthani fabrics, the rooms are colorful and quaint. Outside, paths wind through greenery and over little bridges. Some rooms are air-conditioned, but, as in some other Heritage Hotels, there are no phones or TVs. ✉ *Near Circuit House, 342006,* ☎ *291/510410 or 511410,* FAX *291/510674. 40 rooms, 13 suites. Restaurant, bar, pool, horseback riding. AE, MC, V.*

$$ ★ **Balsamand Lake Palace.** A fine specimen of Rajput architecture in red sandstone, this Heritage Hotel is surrounded by lush, expansive green gardens on the outskirts of Jodhpur. Set on the banks of Balsamand Lake, an artificial lake built in the 12th century, the palace has long made a dreamy setting for royal R & R. The park around the lake contains a small bird sanctuary; just beware of overenthusiastic monkeys. Meals are prepared for guests only. ✉ *Mandore Rd., 342006,* ☎ *291/571991,* FAX *291/571240. 26 rooms. Restaurant, bar, pool, tennis court, horseback riding. MC, V.*

$$ **Jhalamand Garh.** Run and managed by the extremely hospitable Jhalamand family, this small Heritage Hotel 10 km (6 mi) outside town is an ideal setting for a peaceful holiday. You'll feel like a member of the family—in addition to making sure you're comfortable, the Jhalamands will help you plan your stay. The terrace has stunning views of Jodhpur. ✉ *Village and Post Jhalamand, 342005,* ☎ *291/40481,* FAX *291/41125. 18 rooms, 6 suites. Restaurant, bar, horseback riding. AE, DC, MC, V.*

$$ **Karni Bhavan** This (late-)colonial bungalow was built of red sandstone in 1947 and is now a Heritage Hotel. Famous for its personalized service, the hotel has great views of Mehrangarh Fort and Umaid Bhawan Palace. The rooftop restaurant serves Indian, Continental, and exquisite Rajasthani food. Complete with a beautiful pool and safari excursions around Jodhpur, Karni Bhavan makes a comfortable home away from home. ✉ *Palace Rd., 342006,* ☎ *291/432220, 639380,* FAX *291/433495. 27 rooms, 5 suites. Restaurant, bar, pool. AE, DC, MC, V.*

$ **Fort Chanwa.** Out in the dusty village of Luni, 58 km (36 mi) south of Jodhpur, is this somber red fort, now a charming Heritage Hotel. A century old, it has spacious courtyards and delightful rooms, complete with small arched windows called *jharokhas,* Rajasthani-style furniture and fabrics, and old photographs. Many of the small rooms have stairways leading to an alcove or to the bathroom. The water wheel—now a fountain in the bar—was originally used to channel water around the fort. The restaurant has a fixed Indian menu. ✉ *Luni,* ☎ *291/84216; reserve through Dilip Bhawan, House 1, P. W. D. Rd., 342001,* ☎ *291/32460. 20 rooms, 5 suites. Restaurant, bar, pool, horseback riding. V.*

Nightlife and the Arts

Your best bet for Jodhpur nightlife is one of the hotel bars, which are usually open from 11 AM to 2:30 PM and 6 PM to 11 PM. The **Trophy Bar** (✉ Umaid Bhawan Palace, ☎ 291/33316), with its richly paneled walls and carpeted floors, has a regal yet intimate atmosphere.

Mehrangarh Fort stages festivals and exhibits throughout the year; inquire at the **Tourist Information Center** (☎ 291/44010) or your hotel to see if anything's on.

Sports and Outdoor Activities

Many hotels offer safaris to outlying villages. If yours doesn't, try one of the horse or camel trips offered by **Rohet Safaris** (☎ 291/31161).

Shopping

Jodhpur's vibrant bazaars are among the city's key sights, particularly **Sardar Bazaar** and the nearby **Girdikot Bazaar.** Wandering among the tiny shops dotting narrow lanes in the heart of town, you'll get a real feel for the life and color of Marwar. Everything from jewelry to underclothes, steel utensils to leather shoes, and trinkets to wedding clothes is sold here. Polish off your bargaining skills.

Outside the bazaars, **Lalji Handicrafts Emporium** (✉ opposite Umaid Bhawan Palace, ☎ 291/511378) also has woodwork and antiques but adds leather work and brass furniture to the mix. The collection includes unique artistic boxes and *jharokhas* (carved doorways or windows) made of dark wood with brass decoration. This place is a haven for antiques-lovers; it even smells antique. **Bhandari Handicrafts** (✉ Old Police Line, Raika Bagh, ☎ 291/510621) also features wood items and antiques. For textiles, including cotton dress fabric, and other handicrafts, check out the four-story emporium **National Handloom** (✉ Nayee Sadak, ☎ 291/638144). For high-end gifts, **Shenai** (✉ Ratanada Polo Palace Hotel, ☎ 492/431910 or –1) sells fine arts and crafts from all over Rajasthan, such as marble inlaid with gold and colored paints; silk scarves; and a wide range of silver jewelry.

Guda Vishnoi

⑰ *25 km (16 mi) south of Jodhpur*

Guda Vishnoi is one of several immaculately kept villages of the Vishnoi community, a Hindu caste that takes its name from the 29 saints its members worship. Staunch believers in the sanctity of plant and animal life, the Vishnois are very protective of their environment and look harshly on anyone who appears to hurt their animals, especially deer and antelope, whom they consider extensions of their families. Khejri trees and wild deer thrive here, and your hotel can help you arrange some amazing safaris, especially to see endangered and migratory birds such as the Godavan and Saras cranes. Guda Vishnoi also makes an excellent picnic spot (just save the venison sandwich for another day). On your way out, ask directions to the nearby village of **Salawas,** where shops such as Roopraj Udhyog and Jagthamba Durry Udhyog sell beautiful hand-crafted dhurries.

Osian

⑱ *58 km (36 mi) north of Jodhpur*

The **Jain temples** in this Thar Desert city were constructed in two periods, the 8th–9th and 11th–12th centuries. Here you can feel the rugged sand dunes beneath your feet while standing in awe of a desert sunset. Depending on the weather and the moods of the beasts, you can also take a leisurely camel ride.

Khimsar

⑲ *90 km (56 mi) northeast of Jodhpur*

The 16th-century **fort** at Khimsar, a three-hour drive from Jodhpur, was once the province of one of Rao Jodha's sons, and his descendants still live in the palace. Surrounded by a small village, green fields, and sand dunes, it's now a Heritage Hotel, and a delightful place to relax. The building is gorgeously floodlit at night.

Lodging

$$ ★ **Welcomgroup Khimsar Fort.** The best rooms in this graceful pile are in the original palace, hidden around enclosed courtyards and color-

fully decorated with traditional fabrics. These older rooms are large, and some have furniture dating back to the 1920s. You can take a horse, camel, or jeep safari to see black buck and take tea on the nearby sand dunes. Dinner, Rajasthani or Continental, is served by candlelight in the crumbling ruins of one of the original fort towers. Relax and enjoy the fine service, as well as the peace and quiet—none of the rooms has a phone or TV. ✉ *P.O. Khimsar, Nagaur district, 341025,* ☎ *1585/62345 or -6,* FAX *1585/62228; or reserve through Welcomgroup Khimsar Fort, 27 Shivaji Nagar, Civil Lines, Jaipur, 302006,* ☎ *141/382314 or 141/384931,* FAX *141/381150. 15 rooms, 35 suites. Restaurant, bar, pool, horseback riding. AE, MC, V.*

Nagaur

20 *30 km (19 mi) northeast of Khimsar, 150 km (94 mi) northeast of Jodhpur*

Try to visit Nagaur during its colorful **cattle fair,** in late January or early February, as only then can you can camp out royally at the historic Nagaur Fort. The fort's crumbling walls show remnants of beautiful frescoes, and the complex has an amazing engineering system that supplied enough water for the fountains and royal baths and provide simple air-conditioning in this otherwise arid land. The local area is famous for its clay toys.

Lodging

$$$ ★ **Nagaur Fort.** Built between the 4th and 16th centuries, this enormous fort serves as backdrop to a royal camp of spacious tents with hand-blocked designs inside, electric lanterns, and attached bathrooms with flush toilets (hot water comes by the bucket). To signal for service, you hang a little red flag outside your door. Meals are served in a marble pavilion in what was once a Mogul garden; in the evening, you can sip cocktails and sit back on cushions laid out before a bonfire to watch a performance of traditional folk dances. Note that the camp is open only during the cattle fair or by special arrangement; reserve at least 60 days in advance. ✉ *Nagaur,* ☎ *1582/42092; reserve through Umaid Bhawan Palace, Jodhpur 342006,* ☎ *291/33316,* FAX *291/635373. 35 tents. Restaurant. No credit cards. Closed Mar.–Dec.*

UDAIPUR AND ENVIRONS

Cradled in the green Aravalli Hills, the Mewar Region captivates with marble palaces, elaborate gardens, serene temples, lush forests, and sparkling lakes. The best ways to take in this part of Rajasthan are quiet walks, long treks, and leisurely bike rides. Its rich cultural tradition, marked by a blend of chivalry, tribal and village folk revelry, and spirituality, makes Mewar especially intriguing.

Claiming descent from the divine Lord Rama, the Sisodia rulers of Mewar are considered the most senior and respected members of all Rajput clans. The Mewar rulers were among the most determined foes of the Moguls, continuing to resist them long after other Rajput rulers had given up. The name Maharana Pratap still conjures the pride of people all over Mewar, as this man resisted Emperor Akbar's reign through several guerilla wars. Pratap's struggle against Akbar is celebrated in murals and ballads all over Rajasthan, and it has been said that "As a great warrior of liberty, his name is, to millions of men even today, a cloud of hope by day and a pillar of fire by night." As famous as Pratap was his trusted horse, Chetak, who rescued him from certain death on more than one occasion.

Mewar is famous for the vibrant festivals that take place in both its cities and its villages. A motto here is "*Saat vaar, aur nau tyauhaar*": "Seven days, nine festivals." The biggest festival of the year is the annual Gangaur, held in April in honor of the goddess Parvati and observed primarily by girls of marriageable age. In the villages, the ancient tradition of *raati jagga*—all-night singing of mostly devotional songs by such saint-poets as Kabir and Mira—survives here as a form of thanksgiving to a particular deity, particularly after weddings, childbirth, and sometimes even mourning. Mewar has two major indigenous tribal groups, the Bhils (also called *van putras,* or sons of the forest) and the Garasiyas. The tribes' festivals are renowned for their lively songs, music, art exhibits, and dances; particularly memorable is the Ghoomer dance, in which hundreds of women dance in a giant circle. If you're here during a festival, try to see the *terahtal* dance, in which women sit and dance with *manjiras* (little brass discs) tied to their wrists, elbows, waists, arms, and hands. For added effect, the women may hold a sword between their teeth or balance pots or even lighted lamps on their heads. Mewar also has several famous temples and religious sites attended yearly by thousands of pilgrims.

To get a real feel for the culture, style, and spirit of the Mewar region, plan at least two or three days here, if not a whole week. From the dreamy city of Udaipur, you can explore the incredible Jain temples of Ranakpur; watch the sun set over Nakki Lake at Mount Abu; absorb the passionate history of Chittaurgarh; take in sweeping views from the fort at Kumbalgarh, perhaps followed by a wildlife safari; and learn more about pichwai paintings at Nathdwara's Krishna temple. Hope for a good monsoon the summer before your trip: without rains to fill its lakes and quench its thirsty gardens, Udaipur isn't the same.

Udaipur

21 *335 km (207 mi) southeast of Jodhpur*

The jewel of Mewar is Udaipur, the City of Lakes. In his *Annals and Antiquities of Rajasthan,* Colonel James Tod described the valley of Udaipur as "the most diversified and most romantic spot on the subcontinent of India." Some have dubbed it the Venice of the East. The city of Udaipur was founded in 1567, when, having grown weary of repeated attacks on the old Mewar capital of Chittaur, Maharana Udai Singh asked a holy sage to suggest a safe place for his new capital. The man assured Udai Singh that his new base would never be conquered if he established it on the banks of Lake Pichola, and thus was born Singh's namesake, Udaipur.

Modern Udaipur comprises the old city and the newer parts. Five main gates lead into the old city: Hathi Pol (Elephant Gate) to the north; Kishan Gate to the south; Delhi Gate to the northeast, Chand Pol (Moon Gate) to the west; and Suraj Pol (Sun Gate) to the east. Anchored by the City Palace and, in the lake itself, the Lake Palace, the old city itself is built on tiny hillocks and raised areas, so its lanes are full of twists and turns, leaving plenty of shady little niches to be discovered. Many lanes converge on the Jagdish Temple area, near the northeastern corner of Lake Pichola. The major landmarks in the new section are Chetak Circle, Sukhadia Circle, and Sahelion Ki Bari gardens.

The Mewar region is famous for its silver jewelry, wooden folk toys, miniature paintings, tribal arts, *molela* (terra-cotta work), applique, and embroidery. The landscape around Udaipur is dotted with crafts villages, whose unique creations are also sold in the city itself. Udaipur is also one of Rajasthan's great centers of contemporary art. Mewar gastronomy features diljani and *imarti* (pretzel-shape pastries dipped in sugary syrup) sweets, dal baati churma, *chaach* (buttermilk), various *makhi* (corn) products, and the guava. Most smaller shops and restaurants here accept rupees only.

Udaipur is also known for its spirit of voluntarism, boasting one of the largest numbers of non-government organizations (NGOs) in India. Of late these groups have been grappling with crucial social and environmental issues such as drought, deforestation, dowry, and the displacement of tribes. Despite being one of Rajasthan's largest cities, Udaipur retains a small-town atmosphere, and its weather and people are balmy year-round.

A Good Tour

Start with a wander around the **Sahelion Ki Bari** gardens. Heading south, walk or hire a car to the folk museum **Bharatiya Lok Kala Mandal.** Continue to the **City Palace** and Jagdish Temple area, where you can have some lunch and just wander around; from here you can embark on a boat ride to see the two palaces on **Lake Pichola.** Finish your day with dinner at the legendary Lake Palace Hotel (make reservations).

You can cover this ground in one very full day, but you should really spend at least two days in this glorious city, especially if you want to fit in a trip to the arts-and-crafts village of Shilpgram (☞ *below*), drink in an aerial view from **Sajjan Garh** or **Neemach Mata,** and see some of Udaipur's art galleries.

Sights to See

Bharatiya Lok Kala Mandal. This folk-art museum displays a collection of puppets, dolls, masks, folk dresses, ornaments, musical instruments, and paintings. The nightly puppet shows are cute, but the museum is not well maintained. ✉ *Near Chetak Circle.* 🎫 *Rs. 7 (evening program Rs. 20).* ⏲ *Daily 9–6; evening program, 6–7. Closed roughly Apr.–Aug.*

★ **City Palace.** The imposing maharana's palace—the largest in Rajasthan—its white exterior weathered to ivory, stands on a ridge overlooking the lake. Begun by Udai Singh and extended by subsequent maharanas, the sprawling structure retains its harmonious design, enhanced by tall octagonal towers surmounted by cupolas and connected by a maze of narrow passageways. The fifth-floor courtyard centers on a thriving tree. Inside, the rooms contain beautiful paintings, colorful enamel, inlay glasswork, and antique furniture. Each room has its own tale to tell; this is one place to have a full-fledged site publication (buy one in the bookshop) or a guide (hire one at the gate). The City Palace is actually one of a complex of palaces, two of which have been converted to hotels and one of which houses the current maharana, Arvind Singh of Mewar. ✉ *City Palace Complex.* 🎫 *Rs. 20.* ⏲ *Daily 9:30–4:30.*

★ **Lake Pichola.** You can't leave Udaipur without seeing its **Lake Palace** (Jag Niwas), floating surreally on the waters of Lake Pichola. A vast, white-marble fantasy, it's been featured in many Indian and foreign films, including the James Bond film *Octopussy.* Unfortunately, the palace's apartments, courts, fountains, and gardens are off-limits unless you're a guest at the Lake Palace Hotel or have reservations at the restaurant, but it's fun just to daydream about staying here. The equally inspiring, three-story **Jag Mandir** occupies another island at the southern end of the lake. Built and embellished over a 50-year period beginning in the 17th century, it's made of yellow sandstone, lined with marble, and crowned by an imposing dome. The interior is decorated with arabesques of colored stones. Prince Khurrum (later known as Shah Jahan), son of the Mogul emperor Jahangir, was given refuge in Jag Mandir after leading an unsuccessful revolt against his father. One legend has it that Shah Jahan's inspiration for the Taj Mahal came from this marble masterpiece. *Boats to both islands leave from the jetty at the base of City Palace.* *Fare: Rs. 125 round trip to islands; Rs. 60 for ½-hr cruise.* *Daily 2–6.*

MLV Tribal Research Institute. Stop in here if you have a serious interest in Mewar's tribal communities. The institute has a compact museum of tribal culture and a good library on tribal life and issues. ✉ *Ashok Nagar, University Rd.,* ☎ *294/410958.*

Neemach Mata. This hilltop temple, dedicated to the goddess of the mountain, has a good view of Udaipur. Because no taxis or cars are allowed, you must make the climb up on your own, so have comfortable shoes ready. We recommend the less paved, more scenic path, but formal steps have been etched out for the more cautious. ✉ *North of Fateh Sagar Lake.*

Sahelion Ki Bari (Garden of the Maidens). Udaipur is famous for its gardens; don't miss this one. Founded by Maharana Sangam Singh for the 48 young ladies-in-waiting who were sent to the royal house as dowry, the garden features exotic flowers, theme fountains, and a playful ambience. In the 18th century, men were forbidden entrance when the queens and their ladies-in-waiting came to relax (though the king and his buddies still found their way in). Interestingly, the fountains, with their carved pavilions and monolithic marble elephants, don't have pumps—their design utilized principles of gravity to run solely on water pressure from the lakes. Because of this, the garden is actually quite depressing when the lakes are comparatively dry. If the fountains are not on, ask one of the local attendants to open the floodgates. The pavilion opposite the entrance houses a small **children's science center.** For a moment of touristy fun, you can dress up in gaudy (and sometimes smelly) traditional Rajasthani garb and have your picture snapped by a local photographer. ✉ *Saheli Marg.* *Rs. 5.* *Daily 8–7.*

Sajjan Garh. High in the Aravalli Hills just outside Udaipur, this fort-palace glows a golden orange in the Udaipur night sky. Once the maharana's Monsoon Palace, it's now a radio station for the Indian Army. The panoramic view is spectacular from the fort's lofty tower, and locals claim you can see Chittaur on a clear day (almost 110 km/70 mi away). The winding road to the top, surrounded by green forests, is best covered by car; you can take an auto-rickshaw, but it's a long and bumpy ride.

OFF THE BEATEN PATH

SHILPGRAM – This rural arts-and-crafts village 3 km (2 mi) west of Udaipur includes a complex with 26 re-creations of furnished village huts (authentic right down to their toilets) from Rajasthan, Gujarat, Maharashtra, Goa, and Madhya Pradesh. It comes alive in December with the **Shilpgram Utsav**, when artists and craftspeople from around India arrive to sell and display their works; but puppet shows, dances, folk music, and handicrafts sales go on year-round as well. You can see it all slowly on a camel ride. ✉ *Rani Rd.* *Rs. 20.* *Daily 8–5.*

Dining and Lodging

$$$$ ★ ✕ **Gallery.** Overlooking Lake Pichola from a gallery adjoining magnificent Durbar Hall in Fateh Prakash Palace, this restaurant offers one of the most lavish dining experiences in Udaipur. The menu changes regularly, but the Continental food is consistently delicious, and is accompanied by a selection of imported and local wines and beers. You can also stop by in the afternoon for an English cream tea with all the trimmings, and for U.S. $5 you can take a guided tour of the crystal gallery above the restaurant. The palace's 200-year-old collection of Birmingham crystal includes everything from wine decanters to tables, chairs, and beds. ✉ *Fateh Prakash Palace, City Palace Complex,* ☎ *294/528016. Reservations essential. AE, DC, MC, V.*

$$$ ✕ **Aravalli.** This restaurant has local, Indian, and Continental fare covered. The *gatte ki subzi* (graham-flour dumplings), *lal maas* (lamb with a thick, spicy Rajasthani gravy), and *ker sangri* (dried fruits) are local traditional delicacies, and the *dal makhani* (lentils in a rich, buttery tomato sauce) is excellent. The pastas, particularly the cheese ravioli, are very good, and the dark-chocolate mousse is a treat. Avoid the dinner buffet; like so many others, it's overpriced and not overly fresh. Be sure to specify how spicy you like your food. You can also dine outside, on the Aravelli Terrace, which features regional thalis and evening cultural shows. ✉ *Trident Hotel, Haridasji Ki Magri, Mulla Tulai,* ☎ *294/432200,* FAX *294/432211. AE, DC, MC, V.*

$$$ ✕ **Neelkamal.** Looking back on the City Palace from Lake Pichola, the top Lake Palace restaurant serves both Indian and Continental cuisines, including Rajasthani specialties. Try the *sula chat* (cold, thin strips of mutton in a spicy chutney) or the vegetable biriani. The buffet is expensive and much less tasty. The room is small, so non-guests must reserve in advance. ✉ *Lake Palace,* ☎ *294/527961. Reservations essential for non-guests. AE, DC, MC, V.*

$$ ✕ **Sunset Terrace.** Overlooking Lake Pichola from the mainland, this café is great for an afternoon snack (it's open daily 11–6) and an equally delicious view. Have a cold coffee, munch on pakoras and samosas, and bask in the sun. ✉ *Fateh Prakash Palace, City Palace Complex,* ☎ *294/528016. No dinner. AE, DC, MC, V.*

$ ✕ **Jagat Niwas Palace.** A converted haveli, Jagat Niwas has retained the mansion's lovely design and atmosphere, and its open-air restaurant has spectacular views of the Lake Palace. Between them, the premises and surroundings more than make up for the mediocre food and service. If you can't afford to dine at the Gallery, this is the place to go for a truly romantic evening. ✉ *Lal Ghat, Jagdish Mandir,* ☎ *294/529728. MC, V.*

$ **Berry's.** An old favorite with tourists, Berry's makes the best pizza in Udaipur. The Chinese food is also decent. The menu includes something called Mexican food, but you may not be desperate enough to attempt this. The decor is a bit dingy. ✉ *Chetak Circle,* ☎ *294/419927. No credit cards.*

$ **Santosh Dal Bhati.** For the adventurous: Santosh Dal Bhati is Udaipur's best bargain for traditional Rajasthani food. The place is a dive, but the dal baati churma is fantastic, and deservedly popular with locals. Roll up your sleeves, wash your hands, and dig in. ✉ *Suraj Pole,* ☎ *no phone. No credit cards.*

$ ✕ **Shilpi.** A 15-minute cab ride from the city center, this casual garden restaurant serves good Indian and Chinese food. Dine on the huge lawn or under the thatch roof of the dining room. Try the missi ki roti and the butter chicken, baked in spices and then cooked in rich tomato curry. Equipped with an outdoor swimming pool and bar as well as kitchen, Shilpi is a good place to relax in the sun. ✉ *Rani Rd., near Shilpgram Village,* ☎ *294/522475. AE, MC, V.*

$$$$ **Fateh Prakash Palace.** Standing next to the City Palace, this small but grand palace was built by Maharana Fateh Singh at the turn of the 20th century and has suitably excellent views of Lake Pichola. The suites are elegantly furnished with period furniture (some of it once used by the royal family), heavy drapes, and brass fixtures, but have neither TVs nor air-conditioning. Oddly enough, the standard rooms—which are also luxurious—*do* have TVs and air-conditioning, as well

as black stone and marble floors. ✉ *City Palace Complex; reserve through City Palace, 313001,* ☎ *294/528016,* FAX *294/528006 or 294/528012. 9 rooms, 6 suites. Restaurant, bar, pool, health club, Ping-Pong, squash, boating, billiards. AE, DC, MC, V.*

$$$$ ★ 🏨 **Lake Palace.** Now run by the Taj Group, this 250-year-old white-marble palace floats like a vision in the middle of Lake Pichola, looking back at Udaipur from its watery perch. You arrive, of course, by boat. The standard rooms are contemporary; if you want a room to match the nonpareil setting, opt for a suite. The fantastical Khush Mahal Suite takes its sunlight through stained-glass windows; the peach-tone Sarva Ritu Suite has a small interior porch with three arched windows and a window seat. Most rooms have lake views, though some look onto the lily pond or the courtyard. You might be able to take a meal on the hotel's wooden barge, *Gangaur.* ✉ *Lake Pichola 313001,* ☎ *294/527961 (–73),* FAX *294/527974. 76 rooms, 8 suites. Restaurant, bar, coffee shop, pool, exercise room, boating, baby-sitting, laundry service, meeting room, travel services. AE, DC, MC, V.*

$$$$ ★ 🏨 **Shivniwas Palace.** Laid out like a white crescent moon around a large pool, this palace next to the City Palace was once a royal guest house. Standard rooms, set apart from the main building, have contemporary decor. The regal suites are gorgeous, with molded ceilings, elaborate canopy beds, and original paintings and furniture; some have private terraces, and all have excellent views of Lake Pichola. The Baneera Bar has a pleasant Victorian ambience, and the restaurant's *pudina paratha* (mint-flavored bread) is delicious. ✉ *City Palace Complex; reserve through City Palace, 313001,* ☎ *294/528016,* FAX *294/528006. 13 rooms, 18 suites. Restaurant, bar, pool, tennis court, health club, boating, billiards, meeting rooms, travel services. AE, DC, MC, V.*

$$$$ ★ 🏨 **Trident.** Removed from the bustle of downtown Udaipur, the Trident is down a long and solitary road, set among acres of beautiful gardens. While the hotel's architecture is striking, the interior is somewhat lacking in aesthetic sensibility; rooms are well equipped but modern and nondescript. The pool is heated and pleasant both day and night; if you don't actually want to get wet, the hotel also offers boat rides around Lake Pichola. The smiling and attentive staff aim to please. ✉ *Haridasji Ki Magri, Mulla Tulai,* ☎ *294/432200,* FAX *294/432211. 143 rooms. Restaurant, bar, pool, beauty salon, exercise room, boating, meeting room, travel services. AE, DC, MC, V.*

$$$ 🏨 **Laxmi Vilas Palace.** A nostalgia for times past clings to this former royal guest house, built in 1933. Set on a hillside above the banks of Fateh Sagar Lake, the hotel affords a lovely view of the lake and the Sajjan Garh from its verandas and gardens. Rooms in the new wing are modern; the old wing, though not lavish, has far more atmosphere. The restaurant has good Indian food, though it's a little too dimly lit for some. ✉ *Sagar Rd., 313001,* ☎ *294/529711,* FAX *294/25536. 54 rooms, 10 suites. Restaurant, bar, pool, travel services. AE, DC, MC, V.*

$$ 🏨 **Hilltop Hotel Palace.** Perched on a hill overlooking Fateh Sagar Lake, this building has splendid views of the city as well. With its spacious marble lobby, glass elevator, elegant garden, and many rooftop terraces, the hotel may not take you back in time, but it's an excellent value. The Western-style rooms are simple but clean, and each has a balcony. ✉ *5 Ambavgarh, Fateh Sagar 313001,* ☎ *294/521997 (–9),* FAX *294/525106. 62 rooms. 2 restaurants, bar, pool, meeting room. AE, DC, MC, V.*

$$ 🏨 **Jaisamand Island Resort.** This large, white hotel leans against a brown and green slope on an island in Jaisamand Lake, one of the largest artificial lakes in the world. The spacious lobby and the bar have granite floors and Rajasthani furniture. The rooms are Western-style and comfortable. Catch the hotel boat on the lake's boardwalk. ✉ *51 km (32 mi) southeast of Udaipur, P.O. Jaisamand Lake,* ☎ *2906/2222,*

FAX 294/523898. 20 rooms. Restaurant, bar, boating, fishing, meeting rooms, airport shuttle. AE, DC, MC, V.*

$$ **Paras Mahal.** Half a kilometer (¼ mi) from Udaipur's train station, this hotel is clean and modern, lacking in atmosphere but convenient to transport and a Hindi-movie theatre. The main attraction is a glass elevator that shoots up through the central atrium. Rooms have low-lying beds, with lavish, colorful bedspreads, and the walls are hung with Rajasthani paintings. All rooms have TVs, phones, sofas, and desks. ✉ *Near Paras Cinema, Hiran Magri, Sector 11, 313001,* ☎ *294/483381 (–94),* FAX *294/584103. 60 rooms. Restaurant, bar, pool, shops, laundry service, business services, travel services. MC, V.*

$$ ★ **Shikarbadi.** Just outside the city, this former hunting lodge of the local royal family is a Heritage Hotel and a lovely, rustic retreat, complete with a private lake. The rooms are attractive, with tile ceilings and stone walls, and deer and monkeys come nearly to the door. The open-air restaurant serves traditional Mewari fare. Try one of the horseback-riding excursions. ✉ *Goverdhan Vilas,* ☎ *294/583201,* FAX *294/584841; reserve through City Palace, 313001,* ☎ *294/528016,* FAX *294/528006. 21 rooms, 4 suites. Restaurants, bar, pool, horseback riding, travel services. AE, DC, MC, V.*

$ **Caravanserai.** Run by a friendly family, this 150-year-old former haveli is a Heritage Hotel, and the most charming of Lake Pichola's many budget lodgings. The spotlessly clean guest rooms have marble floors and bright-blue patterned bedspreads and drapes; deluxe rooms have coffee tables and large paintings. None of the bathrooms has a tub. You get an unbeatable panorama of the lake from the rooftop restaurant. ✉ *14 Lalghat,* ☎ *294/411103,* FAX *294/521252. 24 rooms. Restaurant, bar. AE, MC, V.*

Shopping

Udaipur's main shopping area surrounds the **Jagdish Temple.** It's fun to walk around here—you'll happen on interesting nooks and crannies—but beware that would-be guides are out in full force. Here, along with wooden toys, silver, and Udaipuri and Gujarati embroidery, you'll find several shops that sell miniature paintings in the Mogul and Rajput styles. Most of these paintings are machine-made prints, a fact ultimately reflected in the wide disparity in prices in this genre; if you want to buy some original art, push the proprietor to show you what's in the back room. Do try your hand at bargaining. While you're in the area, check out the **University of Arts** (✉ 166 Jagdish Marg, City Palace Rd., ☎ 294/422591), featuring a collection of over 500 handmade wooden puppets. Ask the proprietor, Rajesh Gurjarjour, for a private demonstration. From Jagdish Temple, stroll down to **Ganta Ghar** (Clock Tower), ground zero for silver jewelry. Browse freely, but take care not to purchase items that are merely coated with silver-tone paint. **Gehrilal Goverdhan Singh Choudhary** (✉ 72 Jagdish Marg, Clock Tower, ☎ 294/410806) has a good selection of fixed-price, antique jewelry as well as contemporary designs with stonework. Choudhary has been in the business for over 22 years and has exhibited several times abroad. Right next door is a sweet stall, Lala Mishtan Bhandar, where you can satisfy your sweet tooth and refuel with the best gulab jamuns and imarti in town.

If your time is limited, you'll find everything under the sun under a few key roofs. Government-run **Rajasthali** (✉ Chetak Circle, ☎ 294/528768) sells high-quality arts and handicrafts from all over Rajasthan. The **Manglam Arts** (✉ Sukhadia Circle, ☎ 294/560259) emporium deals in Rajasthani handicrafts such as rugs, block-printed textiles, knickknacks, and furniture. Both places are great for those who get bargain-shy in bazaars.

Serious art collectors should know that Udaipur is home to many galleries exhibiting original work by internationally renowned and soon-to-be-renowned artists. Feel free to stop in and meet the artists. **Pristine Gallery** (✉ 6 Kalapi House, Bhatiyani Chohatta, Palace Rd., ☎ 294/415291) specializes in both contemporary and folk art, with many small pieces by Shail Choyal, a guru of contemporary Indian painting. Other highlights are the stylized work of Shahid Parvez, a very fine up-and-coming local artist; and the mandana designs. Just up the road is the **Traditional Art Gallery** (✉ 13 Bhatiyani Chohetta, Jagdish Mandir, ☎ 294/529095), where talented young artist Anil Sharma specializes in watercolor tribal portraits and village scenes. **Ganesh Art Emporium** (✉ 152 Jagdish Chowk, ☎ 294/422864) is a trendy little shop focusing on another gifted young artist, Madhu Kant Mundra, whose oeuvre includes over 125 highly funky representations of Lord Ganesh. Don't miss the artistic refrigerator magnets, sculptures, or antique photographs. At **Sharma Art Gallery** (✉ 15-A New Colony, Kalaji - Goraji, ☎ 294/421107), Kamal Sharma paints mainly birds and animals on paper, marble, silk, and canvas. Apart from being the chief resident artist at Udaipur Medical College, **S. N. Bhandraj** has been creating sculpture out of sea foam for over 20 years; he demonstrates this unique craft in his home studio (✉ Studio 70, Moti Magri Colony, ☎ 294/561396). Last but not least, the **B. G. Sharma Art Gallery** (✉ 3 Saheli Marg, ☎ 294/560063) holds 45 years of work by B. G. Sharma himself, one of the most eminent painters in India. Unlike most miniature artists, who copy traditional pictures, Sharma has made huge contributions to advancing the Mogul, Kishangarh, and Kangra painting styles.

Sadhana (✉ Seva Mandir Rd., Fatehpura, ☎ 294/560951), open weekdays 11–6, is run by Seva Mandir—one of the oldest non-government organizations in India, working for the advancement of the village poor. Among Seva Mandir's activities is a rural women's income-generation program that encourages women to produce traditional appliqué work on cushion covers and bedspreads. The lovely results are sold in the organization's office building, and the full proceeds are returned to the women (rather than pocketed by middlemen, as they would be if the work was sold in stores).

Ranakpur

★ 22 *96 km (60 mi) northwest of Udaipur*

Nestled in a glen northwest of Udaipur is one of the five holy places for the Jain community. Legend has it that this 15th-century **Jain temple,** dedicated to Lord Rishabadeva, was built after it appeared in a dream to a minister of the Mewar king. The three-story temple is surrounded by a three-story wall, which contains 27 halls supported by 1,444 profusely carved pillars—no two carvings alike. Below the temple are underground chambers where the Jains' idols were hidden to protect them from the Moguls. As you enter, look for the pillar on the left where the minister and the architect provided themselves with front-row seats for worship. Another pillar is intentionally warped, to separate human works from divine ones. Outside are two smaller Jain temples and a shrine adorned with erotic sculptures and dedicated to the sun god. *Free; camera charge. Non-Jains, daily 11–sunset.*

Dining and Lodging

$ **Maharani Bagh Orchard Retreat.** This 19th-century pied-à-terre for the maharani of Jodhpur is perfect for relaxing. Scattered among huge mango trees, the little brick cottages have traditional decor, with painted wooden beds and tile floors. The kitchen serves Indian and Rajasthani specialties under small thatched shelters to the sound of water rushing through a canal in the middle of the property. The rooms do not have phones or air-conditioning. ✉ *Sadri, Ranakpur,* ☎ *2934/85105; reserve through Welcomgroup Umaid Bhawan Palace, Jodhpur 342006,* ☎ *291/510101,* FAX *291/510101. 19 rooms. Restaurant, pool. MC, V.*

Mount Abu

23 *185 km (115 mi) west of Udaipur*

High in the Aravallis, Mount Abu was long the site of one of Hinduism's most sacred rites, the *yagya*. Legend has it that the clan of the mighty *agnikula* Rajputs rose from this mystical fire. Today Mount Abu is Rajasthan's only hill station, and a great stopping point if you like long walks. **Nakki Lake,** resting between green hills, is believed to have been carved out by the gods' fingernails. The far side of the lake is quieter and cleaner. At **Sunset Point** you can imbibe a romantic Mount Abu sunset. It often gets crowded here, however; finding a private spot takes some doing.

Mount Abu's newest landmark is the **Brahma Kumaris Spiritual University.** Thousands of followers of this sect come from all over the world, don white robes or saris, and study spiritual knowledge or Raja Yoga meditation. The Brahma Kumaris have also designed the **Peace Park,** which has some beautiful gardens. Beyond the park on Guru Shikhar road is **Guru Shikhar,** the highest point between South India's Nilgiri Hills and the far-northern Himalayas. The point has excellent views of the countryside. The stunningly carved, unforgettably beautiful **Dilwara Temples,** dedicated to Jain saints, were built entirely of marble between the 11th and 13th centuries.

Dining and Lodging

$$ ✕🏨 **Cama Rajputana Club Resort.** Cradled in the hills, this 100-year-old club combines modern amenities with country style. Its peaceful atmosphere gives the weary walker a chance to rest and recharge. ✉ *Mount Abu,* ☎ *2974/38205,* FAX *2974/38206; or reserve through* ✉ *Cama Hotel Ltd., Khanpur Rd., Ahmedabad 380001, Gujarat,* ☎ *79/550–5281,* FAX *79/550–5285. 40 rooms, 2 suites. Restaurant, pool, tennis court, squash. AE, MC, V.*

$$ 🏨 **Palace Hotel (Bikaner House).** Formerly the summer residence of the maharaja of Bikaner, this place was the hub of Mount Abu's aristocratic social life for decades. Now a Heritage Hotel, it still feels something like a hunting lodge and is a good place to retreat and relax for a few days. Service is excellent. The gardens are nice, but the tennis court is a bit dilapidated. ✉ *Delwara Rd.,* ☎ *2974/38673,* FAX *2974/38674; or reserve through* ✉ *Rajvir Sinh Jadeja, Landmark, Flat No. 121, Carmichael Rd., Bombay 400026,* ☎ *22/492–6579. 24 rooms, 11 suites. Restaurant, tennis court. AE, DC, MC, V.*

Chittaurgarh

24 *112 km (69 mi) northeast of Udaipur*

If any one of Rajasthan's myriad forts had to be singled out for its glorious history and chivalric lore, it would be Chittaurgarh. Prior to Udai Singh's move, from the 8th to the 16th centuries, this was the capital of the Mewar princely state. The **fort** sprawls over 700 acres on a hill over 2,000 ft high. It was surrounded and sacked three times: After the first two conquests, the Rajputs recovered it, but the third attack clinched it for the Moguls for several decades.

Chittaur's maharanis were better known than their male counterparts. The beauty of Rani Padmini so enamored the Sultan of Delhi, Allauddin

Khilji, that he set out to attack the fort and win her in battle. Seven thousand warriors lost their lives in this struggle, yet the Sultan did not get Padmini: The maharani, along with her entire entourage, committed jauhar rather than submit to him. Frustrated, Khilji entered the city in a rage, looting and destroying much of what he saw—one of Chittaurgarh's enduring tragedies. This was also the home of saint-poetess Mira, a devotee of Lord Krishna who gave up her royal life to sing *bhajans* (hymns) in his praise.

The massive fort encompasses the **palaces** of Maharana Kumbha and Maharani Padmini, victory towers such as **Vijay Stambh** and **Kirti Stambh,** and a huge variety of temples including **Kunbha Shyam** and **Kalika Mata.** The **Fateh Prakash Mahal** displays some fine sculptures.

Kumbhalgarh

25 *84 km (52 mi) north of Udaipur*

Isolated and serene, this formidable **fort** was a refuge for Mewari rulers in times of strife. Built by Maharana Kumbha in the 15th century, the fort covers 12 square km (7 square mi). At one time, its ramparts nearly encircled an entire township, self-contained to withstand a long siege. The fort fell only once, to the army of Akbar—whose forces had contaminated the water supply. The fort was also the birthplace of Maharana Pratap. The **Badal Mahal** (Cloud Palace), at the top, has an awesome view of the surrounding countryside. Surrounding the fort, the modern-day **Kumbalgarh Sanctuary** is home to wolves, leopards, jackals, nilgai deer, sambar deer, and various species of birds, and makes for delightful treks. Have a leisurely lunch at the open-air restaurant of the Aodhi Hotel.

Nathdwara

26 *48 km (30 mi) north of Udaipur*

The town of Nathdwara is totally devoted to the **Shrinathji Temple,** visited by thousands of pilgrims each year. Built in the 18th century, this simple temple is one of the most celebrated shrines to Lord Krishna, and features a unique image of the deity sculpted from a single piece of black marble. Nathdwara is known for its pichwais, large cloth paintings depicting legends from Krishna's life, and its devotional music.

A few minutes outside Nathdwara is **Rajsamand Lake,** which attracts a large number of migratory birds. Maharana Raj Singh ordered the construction of the lake in 1662 as a famine-relief work project, so a workforce of 60,000 people wrestled it into being over the course of 10 years. The architecture of its main dam, **Nauchowki** (Nine Pavilions), combines Rajput and Mogul traits; interestingly, the Rajaprashasthi (Royal Eulogy) is engraved on 25 of the dam's niched slabs. Locals come here early in the morning to learn to swim.

Also near Nathdwara is the village of **Molela,** where artisans craft and paint fine terra-cotta images of gods, goddesses, and animals, as well as more functional pots and utensils.

Dining and Lodging

$$ **Deogarh Mahal.** Built in the 17th century, this Heritage Hotel is run by its resident once-royal family. Set in the rugged countryside of the Aravalli Hills, it offers jeep and camel safaris and excellent views of the region's migratory birds. Don't miss the family's exquisite collection of miniature paintings. ✉ *Deogarh, Madarja, Rajsamand,* ☎ *2904/52777,* FAX *2904/52555. 17 rooms, 5 suites. Restaurant, travel services. AE, DC, MC, V.*

JAISALMER AND ENVIRONS

The desert is the draw to far-western Rajasthan. Resplendent with golden sandstone, Jaisalmer is also an anchor for camel safaris to the Thar Desert. Short trips to the photogenic Sam Sand Dunes and animal-happy Desert National Park round out the regional experience.

Jaisalmer

★ 27 *663 km (412 mi) northwest of Udaipur, 285 km (160 mi) northwest of Jodhpur, 570 (353 mi) west of Jaipur*

Soaring out of the Thar Desert like a giant sandcastle, Jaisalmer is a totally improbable city. Its sandstone buildings look like something out of an armchair traveler's daydream, and the way the light plays against these golden buildings is magical. Approach this ancient city slowly and savor the gold-tone fortress, its carved spires and palaces jutting above its imposing wall. Founded in 1156 by Rawal Jaisal, a descendent of the Yadav clan and a Bhatti Rajput, Jaisalmer lies near the extreme western edge of Rajasthan, about 100 mi east of the Pakistan border. It began life as an important caravan center: From the 12th through the 18th centuries, rulers amassed their wealth from taxes levied on those passing through here from Africa, Persia, Arabia, and other parts of Central Asia. This was also a smuggler's paradise, with opium the longtime best-seller. The rise of Bombay as a major trading port in the 19th century eclipsed Jaisalmer's role as a staging post.

Today Jaisalmer attracts travelers who want to taste the magic, mystery, and charisma of the desert. A welcome change from crowded, polluted cities, this architectural masterpiece never fails to amaze, its havelis drawing you toward their lacelike facades. Unfortunately, following the nuclear tests in nearby Pokharan in May 1998, and given the ongoing border tension with Pakistan, travelers have lately been wary of going as far west as Jaisalmer. These concerns are understandable, but they'll dissipate as soon as you meet the people of Jaisalmer, whose strength, courage, and indomitable spirit will not be diminished by the respective political agendas of the Indian and Pakistani governments. To skip Jaisalmer is to skip the real jewel of Rajasthan.

With clean lanes, no traffic, and small, friendly crowds, the walled city is easily covered on foot. Camel safaris beckon from the desert. These are great fun, but choose one carefully; if you skimp and choose a cheap outfitter, you might get sick. Bring your own cutlery, and a light scarf to protect your face in case of a sandstorm.

Spend at least two nights in Jaisalmer. Nothing is more spectacularly romantic than a Thar Desert sunset; and the city's cultural festivities, at the heart and soul of its people, begin at night. For the traveler these can reach once-in-a-lifetime levels of passion: Around blazing bonfires, dancers and musicians gather in a fragrant and colorful folk mosaic. It's intoxicating. To get a full dose of this *mahole* (atmosphere), try to visit Jaisalmer during the Desert Festival, held in late January and early February: Then, in addition to desert rhythms, you'll see camel races, turban-tying contests, and special craft bazaars with traders from around the region.

A Good Tour

Jaisalmer is like Venice in that it's next to impossible to follow a straight path: The warren of streets and lanes flow into each other. Trust your instincts and/or don't be afraid to ask the locals for directions. The overriding landmark is the **fort**, which is every bit as mazelike as the rest of the city; allow several hours to explore the attractions within. From here, walk north and west to the **havelis.** Finally, hop a camel and head southeast toward **Gadsisar Lake** and the nearby Folklore Museum.

If you spend a second day in town, visit the lovely **Bada Bagh,** and drive northwest from there to the **Ludarva Temples.**

Sights to See

Bada Bagh. This garden lies on the banks of an artificial lake. More like a giant orchard than a garden, much of the city's vegetables and fruits are grown here, 6 kms (4 mi) northwest of the city. This lush greenery in the middle of the dry desert will remind you of a beautiful oasis. You'll also see royal cenotaphs, with canopies under which members of the royal family are buried. Notice the beautifully carved ceilings and equestrian statues of the former rulers.

★ **Fort.** What's absolutely extraordinary about this fort is that 5,000 people live here, just as they did centuries ago. Standing guard some 250 ft above the town, the fort is protected by a 30-ft-high wall and contains 99 bastions. Several great *pols* (gateways) approach and pierce the towered battlements of this 12th-century citadel. Built of sandstone and extremely brittle, the fort is rumored to be an architectural time bomb, destined to collapse in the face of a particularly aggressive sandstorm. Yet so lovely is this structure in the meantime that the poet Rabindranath Tagore composed *Sonar Kila* (*The Golden Fort*) after seeing it, and inspired another creative Bengali in turn: Satyajit Ray made his famous film *Sonar Kila* after reading Tagore's work.

Inside the web of tiny lanes are Jain and Hindu temples, palaces, and charming havelis. The seven-story **Juna Mahal** (Old Palace), built around 1500, towers over the other buildings and stands under a vast metal umbrella mounted on a stone shaft. At the **Satiyon ka Pagthiya** (Steps of the Satis), just before the palace entrance, the royal ladies performed the rite of *sati,* immolating themselves when their husbands were slain.

Within the fort are eight **Jain temples** built from the 12th to 16th centuries: These house thousands of carved deities and dancing figures in mythological settings. No photography is allowed here, and you'll have to leave your leather items at the gate. The **Gyan Bhandar** (Jain Library) inside the Jain temple complex contains more than 1,000 old manuscripts—some from the 12th century, written on palm leaf, with painted wooden covers—and a collection of Jain, pre-Mogul, and Rajput paintings.

The historic **Tazia Tower** is a delicate pagoda rising five tiers from the **Badal Mahal** (Cloud Palace), each tier graced with an intricately carved balcony. Muslim craftsmen built the tower in the shape of a *tazia*—replica of a bier carried in procession during Mohurram, a Muslim period of mourning. ✉ *Juna Mahal:* 🎫 *Rs. 5.* ⏲ *Daily 8–5. Jain temples:* 🎫 *free.* ⏲ *Daily 7–noon. Library:* 🎫 *Free.* ⏲ *Daily 10 AM–11 AM.*

Gadsisar Lake. Just south of Jaisalmer is a rainwater lake (otherwise known as Gadsisar Sagar, or Tank) built in the 12th century. Surrounded by numerous golden-hued shrines, it's also frequented by a diverse, spectacular avian community. Plan for a camel ride, a picnic, and perhaps a short paddle-boat excursion. Near the shrines is a charming little **Folklore Museum,** built in the style of a traditional home. Filled with memorabilia, it's the perfect place to ground yourself in local history and culture. ✉ *Museum: Behind main bus stand.* 🎫 *Rs. 2.* ⏲ *Daily 9–noon and 3–6.*

Havelis. Outside the fort, in a narrow lane with more delicate, lacy architecture that shimmers in soft yellow, stand a string of five connected havelis built by the Patwa brothers in the 1800s. The Patwas were highly influential Jain merchants back when Jaisalmer was an independent principality. They and their counterparts forbade the repetition of any motifs or designs between their mansions, so each one is distinctive.

Two of the five havelis are now owned by the government and open to the public, and you can explore the interiors of the others by offering a small fee (not more than Rs. 50) to the residents. Three havelis are noteworthy in this part of the walled city: **Patwon Ki Haveli** is arguably the most elaborate and magnificent of all Jaisalmer's havelis. In addition to exquisitely carved pillars and expansive corridors, one of the apartments in this five-story mansion is painted with beautiful murals. The 19th-century **Nathamalji Ki Haveli** was carved by two brothers, each working independently on his own half; the design is remarkably harmonious, though you can spot small differences. The interior of the late-18th-century **Salim Singh Ki Haveli** is in sad disrepair, but the mansion's exterior is still lovely, with an overhanging gallery on its top floor. Note the havelis' ventilation systems: The projecting windows and stone screens keep them cool even in the searing summer months.

Ludarva Temples. Rawal Jaisal lived here before shifting to his new capital, and you can still see the ruins of his former city. The Jain temple complex here is known for its *nag devta* (snake god), a live snake that appears on auspicious days and nights. The snake is worshiped—said to have been protecting this temple for thousands of years. The temples are famous for their graceful architecture and detailed carving. ✉ *16 km (10 mi) northwest of Jaisalmer.*

Dining and Lodging

There are very few decent restaurants in Jaisalmer. The good hotels are your best bet for a savory meal.

$ ✕ **8 July Restaurant.** Run by an eccentric Indo-Australian, this restaurant serves simple snacks, pizzas, vegetable dishes, and wonderful coffee milkshakes throughout the day. Literally next door to the fort, it has a breathtaking view of Jaisalmer. ☎ *No phone. No credit cards.*

$$$ 🏨 **Himmatgarh Palace.** Just opposite the royal cenotaphs, this hotel is about 1 km (½ mi) from the city, but it offers one of the best views in town, especially at sunset, and performances of folk dance and music. The standard rooms are modern and comfortable, but the small, circular *burj* (tower) rooms are the most charming, with marble beds and lights concealed in the nooks of their stone walls. ✉ *1 Ramgarh Rd., 345001,* ☎ *2992/52002 (–4),* FAX *2992/52005. 40 rooms. Restaurant, bar, pool, travel services. AE, MC, V.*

$$ 🏨 **Gorbandh Palace.** Built of golden sandstone, this fairly new hotel is spacious and elegant. Rooms are arranged in haveli-style blocks around a series of small interior courtyards with skylights and fountains. Interiors are Western-style, with some Rajasthani touches and large, lovely windows. Some rooms are air-conditioned. ✉ *1 Tourist Complex, Sam Rd., 345001,* ☎ *2992/53111,* FAX *2992/52749. 64 rooms, 3 suites. Restaurant, bar, pool, travel services. AE, DC, MC, V.*

$$ 🏨 **Heritage Inn.** A short distance from the town center, this hotel has a functional, subdued interior. Accommodations are in bungalows dotted around the garden. Beds are set into depressions in the floor, walls are of rustic stone, and the bathrooms lack tubs. Ask for a suite: They're much plusher and not much more expensive. There's a tandoori barbecue in the garden, and evenings bring Rajasthani folk dance. ✉ *PB-43 Sam Rd., 345001,* ☎ *2992/52769 or 50901,* FAX *2992/51638. 45 rooms, 6 suites. Restaurant, bar, coffee shop, meeting room, travel services. AE, DC, MC, V.*

$$ **Narayan Niwas Palace.** This carved stone palace was once a caravansary, and its interior courtyard still feels like an oasis. Now a Heritage Hotel, it has unassuming modern rooms, a lovely pool, sprawling lawns, a well-stocked bar, and a warm, smiling staff (who can help arrange camel and jeep safaris). Rooms are furnished with carved wooden furniture from the craft village of Barmer, and sandstone beds—stone frames filled with sand and covered with a sheet to give you the feel of sleeping in the desert. Some rooms are air-conditioned. ✉ *Near Malka Prol, 345001,* ☎ *2992/52408, or 51901 (–4),* FAX *2992/52101; or reserve through* ✉ *D18, 2nd floor, Pamposh Enclave, Greater Kailash 1, New Delhi 110048,* ☎ *11/648–6807,* FAX *11/648–6806. 38 rooms, 5 suites. Restaurant, bar, pool. AE, DC, MC, V.*

$ **Dhola Maru.** This government-run hotel is much cleaner and tidier than its counterparts elsewhere in the state. Outside, there are good facilities for camping and for nighttime bonfires, at which performing groups pull you in to dance and have fun with them. ✉ *Near Malka Prol, 342006,* ☎ *2992/52408 or 2992/52801,* FAX *2992/52101. 38 rooms, 5 suites. Restaurant, bar, health club. AE, DC, MC, V.*

Camel Safaris

Royal Safaris (✉ Gandhi Chowk, ☎ 2992/52538) is the recommended agent, tailoring trips to nearby villages or overnight sojourns in the desert. You can also contact the Rajasthan Tourism Development Corporation in the Hotel Moomal (☞ Visitor Information, *below*), or the Indian Tourism Development Corporation at the Dhola Maru hotel (☞ *above*), for reservations. Note that safari prices vary dramatically depending on the itinerary and the level of tourist crush.

Shopping

Jaislamer is famous for its mirror work, embroidery, and woolen shawls. Local artisans also make attractive, good-quality wooden boxes, silver jewelry, and curios. The main shopping areas are **Sadar Bazaar, Sonaron Ka Bas, Manak Chowk,** and **Pansari Bazaar,** all within the walled city, near the fort and temple areas. Sonaron Ka Bas, in particular, has exquisite silver jewelry. Avoid touts, take time to browse carefully, and bargain.

Visit the government emporium **Rajasthali** (✉ Gandhi Chowk) to get a feel for appropriate prices. **Khadi Graamudyog,** in the walled city, for an array of *khadi* (hand-spun cotton) shawls, Nehru jackets, scarves, and rugs. **Damoder Handicraft Emporium** (✉ Fort, near Rang Prol) has an excellent selection of local handicrafts, especially old textiles.

Sam Sand Dunes

28 *42 km (26 mi) west of Jaisalmer*

No trip to Jaisalmer is complete without a visit to Sam, a photographer's feast. The ripples of these wind-caressed dunes create fantastic mirages. Take a camel safari here, if you can, and stay for the sunset and an evening with artists and melodious folk singers who reinforce the beauty and romance of the setting.

Desert National Park

29 *45 km (28 mi) Southwest of Jaisalmer*

Wildlife-lovers will delight in this place. The desert birds include everything from birds of prey, such as vultures and desert hawks, to sandgrouses, doves, shrikes, bee eaters, and warblers. The rarest, most remarkable bird is the great Indian bustard, a large, majestic crane said to be found only in the Thar Desert.

RAJASTHAN A TO Z

Arriving and Departing

By Hired Car with Driver

The roads in Rajasthan are not in good shape, and the truck and bus drivers can be pretty reckless, particularly at night. In any case, the going is slow—when calculating driving time, plan to cover 40–50 km (25–31 mi) per hour at most. Driving is an excellent way, however, to see the Indian countryside and glimpse village life. A stop in a traditional village that's off the trodden path could turn into the highlight of your trip. Hire a car with driver from a government-licensed operator (☞ Travel Agencies, *below*). The cost should be about Rs. 10–Rs. 12 per km.

Jaipur is a 5½-hour drive from Delhi on National Highway (NH) 8. This is a congested industrial road with a high accident rate, so prepare for a trying experience.

The **Shekhavati** region is usually a three- to four-hour drive from Delhi (the distance varies depending on your destination within the region). Driving is much quicker and smoother than train travel in this case. Hire a car and driver through a Delhi travel agency (☞ Delhi A to Z *in* Chapter 3). Plan to pay about Rs. 10 per km, with a halt charge of Rs. 200–Rs. 250 per night.

Roads are rough in and out of **Jodhpur,** and the going is slow. Don't expect to average more than 40 km (25 mi) per hour.

Udaipur is on NH 8, which links Bombay and Delhi. Again, road speed is bound to top out at 40 km (25 mi) per hour.

If you have time, you can design a delightful road trip to **Jaisalmer** by traveling from Delhi through Khimsar and Shekhavati, spending each night in a Heritage Hotel. You can also fly into Jodhpur and continue to Jaisalmer by road.

By Plane

There are domestic airports in Jaipur, Jodhpur, Udaipur, and Jaisalmer. Each is a short drive from the city. **Indian Airlines** flies between these four (less often to Jaisalmer) and connects Rajasthan with Delhi, Bombay, and Aurangabad (☎ 141 in Delhi, 11/329–5121 from elsewhere). Ask your travel agent about service on private domestic airlines. Flights to Rajasthan fill up, so reserve in advance.

JAIPUR

Indian Airlines flies daily between Jaipur and Delhi, Bombay, Jodhpur, and Udaipur (✉ Nehru Pl., Tonk Rd., ☎ 141/514500 or –407). Jaipur's Sanganer Airport is about 13 km (8 mi) south of town; a taxi to the city costs about Rs. 150. **Air India** now has an office in Jaipur as well (☎ 141/68569).

JODHPUR

Jodhpur is connected to Jaipur, Udaipur, Delhi, Bombay, Aurangabad, and occasionally Jaisalmer by **Indian Airlines** (☎ 291/636757 or 291/636758). The airport (☎ 291/30617) is 5 km (3 mi) from the city center. A taxi to town costs about Rs. 150.

UDAIPUR

Indian Airlines (✉ outside Delhi Gate, ☎ 294/527711) flies daily between Udaipur and Jaipur, Jodhpur, Delhi, Aurangabad, and Bombay. Dabok Airport is 25 km (16 mi) from the city center; the cab ride costs about Rs. 200.

JAISALMER

In peak season, **Indian Airlines** and private carriers fly from Jodhpur to Jaisalmer three times a week. The airport is about 10 km (6 mi) from the city, and a taxi to town runs about Rs. 100.

By Train

Rajasthan is still in the process of converting all its lines to broad gauge, a change that is improving train service but altering most of the train routes and schedules. If you want to travel overnight, it's safer and more comfortable to take a train than a bus or car. Trains offer various classes of service (according to seating or sleeper, air-conditioning, and whether or not you reserve ahead) to meet any budget. Call the nearest tourist office (☞ Visitor Information, *below*) or Indian Railways for updated information.

JAIPUR

The *Shatabdi Express,* an air-conditioned chair-car train, travels daily (except Sunday) from New Delhi to Jaipur, a roughly five-hour trip. The *Pink City Express* to Jaipur from New Delhi takes about six hours. For inquiries, call 131; for reservations, 135.

SHEKHAVATI

The *Shekhavati Express* runs daily from Delhi to Jaipur, stopping at Jhunjhunu, Mukungarh, and Sikar. The daily *Bikaner Express* from Delhi also passes through Shekhavati en route to Bikaner.

JODHPUR

The overnight *Superfast Express* leaves New Delhi at 8 PM and reaches Jodhpur at 5:30 AM (inquiries ☏ 291/131 or 291/132). Another *Superfast Express* connects Jodhpur with Jaipur in four hours; contact the **Tourist Information Center** (☏ 291/44010) for more information.

UDAIPUR

Daily trains connect Udaipur with Jaipur, Ajmer, Chittaurgarh, Jodhpur, Ahmedabad, and Delhi. For more information, call ☏ 294/131 or the **Tourist Reception Center** (☏ 294/41535).

JAISALMER

Trains run out to Jaisalmer from Jodhpur and Udaipur, but they're significantly slower than the road routes.

Getting Around

Your mode of transport within Rajasthan depends on your budget and the length of your trip. It's a big state, with long stretches of territory between the most popular destinations. If you have very limited time here, it's best to stay in one city and explore the surrounding area rather than try to rush through the entire state.

By Auto-Rickshaw

Auto-rickshaws in Jaipur are metered, though the meters are often ignored. Insist on adhering to the meter, *or* set the price in advance. The rate should be no more than Rs. 4.50 per km, with a minimum total of Rs. 10. Auto-rickshaws in Jodphur and Udaipur are unmetered, so you *must* agree on a price before departing. You can also hire an auto-rickshaw by the hour, for about Rs. 30 per hour. Note that all of these rates go up by about 50% after 11 PM.

By Bicycle

You can hire bikes from some hotels, and from shops around Jagdish Temple in Udaipur. Rates are typically Rs. 15–20 per hour. Biking in Jaipur can be dangerous, but elsewhere it's a nice way to tool around.

By Cycle-Rickshaw

This option is quickly dying out in Rajasthan, but if you find one in, say, Jaipur, it should cost about Rs. 30 per hour. Agree on a rate in advance.

By Hired Car with Driver

It's not cheap, but having a car and driver to yourself is highly efficient if you're short on time, and aids greatly in exploring forts and small towns just outside the major cities. Hire a car through your hotel or a recognized travel agent (☞ *below*); the latter option may be cheaper.

By Taxi

Taxis are unmetered in Jaipur, Jodhpur, and Udaipur, so be sure to ask your hotel for the going rate and negotiate with the driver before you set off. In Jodhphur and Jaipur, you can hire a cab through the RTDC's **Tourist Information Center** (☞ Visitor Information, *below*). Depending on the distance to be covered, a taxi for half a day will cost about Rs. 600, for a full day about Rs. 1200.

Contacts and Resources

Currency Exchange

Most Western-style hotels will change money for their guests. You can also change money at the **State Bank of India** (✉ Tilak Marg, C-Scheme, Jaipur, ☎ 141/380421; High Court Rd., Jodhpur, ☎ 291/45090 or 291/44169; Hospital Rd., Udaipur, ☎ 294/528857).

Homestays

The **RTDC** (☎ Jaipur, 141/370180; Delhi, 11/389525 or 11/383837) has developed a program that allows travelers to stay in private homes. These lack the facilities of hotels, of course, but they're an authentic and much cheaper option. The RTDC has a directory that describes each accommodation.

Tour Operators

Alternative Travels (✉ Nawalgarh 333042, Shekhavati, ☎ 1594/22129, FAX 1592/32280) organizes terrific stays in artisan villages; trips focusing on music and dance; treks; and bike, jeep, horse, and camel safaris. **Historic Resort Hotels** (✉ Shikarbadi, Udaipur 313001, ☎ 294/83200) leads horse safaris around the Udaipur area, with night halts in tented camps or in hotels. The **Rajasthan Mounted Sports Association** (✉ c/o Dundlod House, Hawa Sarak, Civil Lines, Jaipur 302006, ☎ 141/366276, FAX 141/366276) gives riding and polo lessons in Jaipur; runs elephant, horse, and camel day trips in Shekhavati; and leads horse and jeep safaris that may include stays at palaces and forts. **Rajasthan Safaris and Treks** (✉ Birendra Singh Tanwar, Bassai House, Purani Ginani, Bikaner, 334001, ☎ 151/28557, FAX 151/24321) offers less luxurious but more authentic camel, camel-cart, or jeep safaris out of Bikaner. While food (traditional desert fare) and water are provided, you're on your own when it comes to toilet facilities. **Roop Nivas Safaris** (✉ c/o Roop Nivas Palace, Nawalgarh, Jhunjhunu district, Shekhavati 333702, ☎ 15941/22008; in Jaipur, 141/46949 or 141/351511) leads a Shekhavati Brigade Horse Safari around the colorful painted towns of this region, and longer safaris from Nawalgarh to Pushkar or Bikaner. You sleep in tents with bathroom facilities or at palace and fort hotels. **Royal Safari** (✉ Royal Safari, Box 23, Nachna Haveli, Gandhi Chowk, Jaisalmer 345001, ☎ 2992/52538 or 2992/53202) administers treks, camel safaris, and nights in the desert around Bikaner, Jodhpur, and Jaisalmer, as well as visits to traditional villages, craftspeople's homes, little-known fairs, and ashrams. The **RTDC** (☞ *below*) also leads tours.

Travel Agencies

These agents can help with travel arrangements generally, including a hired car with driver.

JAIPUR

Karwan Tours (✉ Bissau Palace Hotel, outside Chand Pol, ☎ 141/304854). **TGS Tours and Travels** (✉ Tholia Circle, Mirza Ismail Rd., ☎ 141/367735) represents American Express.

JODHPUR

Rajasthan Tours (✉ Airport Rd., ☎ 291/36942 or 291/628265).

UDAIPUR

Meera Tour and Travels (✉ 14 Badu Ji, ☎ 294/415249). **Rajasthan Tours** (✉ Garden Hotel, ☎ 294/525777). **TGS Tours and Travels** (✉ Chetak Circle, ☎ 294/29661) represents American Express.

Visitor Information

Many hotels can provide regional information and travel services. The Tourist Information Centers of the **Rajasthan Tourism Development Corporation** provide information, travel assistance, and guides in **Jaipur** (✉ Paryatan Bhawan, Government Hostel Campus, ☎ 141/376362; main railway station, ☎ 141/69714), **Jodhpur** (✉ Hotel Ghoomar, High Court Rd., ☎ 291/44010), **Udaipur** (✉ Shastri Circle, ☎ 294/411535), and **Jaisalmer** (✉ Hotel Moomal, Station Rd., ☎ 2992/52392).

The **Government of India Tourist Office** has a **Jaipur** branch (✉ Hotel Khasa Kothi, ☎ 141/372200). *Jaipur Vision* and the *Jaipur City Guide,* available in most hotels, are periodicals with visitor information and up-to-date phone numbers. A **Tourist Information Bureau** serves **Shekhavati** (✉ Hotel Shiv Shekhawati, Jhunjhunu, ☎ 15945/32909).

6 GUJARAT

High art, ancient civilizations, wildlife, and folk crafts all prosper in this northwestern coastal state. Le Corbusier built more buildings in Ahmedabad than he did in all of the United States; lions roam about the ildlife Sanctuary; Dhola Vira has the remains of a 4,000-year-old city; and crafts villages around Bhuj are known for their hand-woven textiles.

By Andy McCord and Julie Tomasz

GUJARAT IS ONE OF THE RICHEST states in India, both economically and culturally. The arts flourish in its cities, and artisanship thrives in its villages. At the Gir Wildlife Sanctuary, the last prides of Asiatic lions are growing in number, and at Dhola Vira, the spectacular remains of a 4,000-year-old Indus Valley city have only recently been excavated. The Hindu Solanki dynasty produced a flowering of architecture late in the classical period, and some of the earliest Muslim kingdoms in India were founded here a few centuries later. The cross-fertilization of Hindu and Muslim cultures is as pronounced, and successful, in Gujarat as anywhere in the country. Previous neglect of tourism delivers a bonus to travelers now in that the hard-sell approach is rare among guides, touts, and taxi drivers. Gujaratis are relatively unfazed by visitors from over the oceans: They themselves are India's greatest travelers, composing about a quarter of Indian immigrants around the world. Their most famous son, Mahatma Gandhi, began his adult life as an immigrant lawyer in South Africa. After a few days here, you will feel you've discovered a hidden gem.

Ahmedabad, the state's capital, is a remarkable repository of architectural styles: from the early Indo-Saracenic forms of the 15th-century Muslim sultans to the modern forms of Le Corbusier, the contemporary Indian architect Charles Correa, and the American Louis Kahn. The city is congested and hectic, but its wealth of museums, performing-arts centers, and galleries makes it a rewarding stopping point. In Ahmedabad and elsewhere, curious and ornately decorated step-wells, or *baolis,* plunge fathoms down into the earth to the water table.

Elsewhere in the state, Vadodara (a Sanskrit name commonly anglicized as Baroda), the former headquarters of an important princely state, is a pretty college town with vibrant cultural life. The Kutch region, on the state's northwestern edge bordering Pakistan, has superb artisans, the remains of an ancient city at Dhola Vira, and miles of pristine, undeveloped beaches on the Arabian Sea.

Southwest of Ahmedabad, the region of Saurashtra has remarkable wildlife preserves, and the palaces of the dozens of princes who ruled here before Independence. Scattered about the state are pilgrimage centers of the Jains, members of an ancient religion that practices strict nonviolence; more Jains live in Gujarat than anywhere else in India.

Pleasures and Pastimes

Beaches

The beach in Diu, a former Portuguese enclave just off the coast of Gujarat, is pretty, though it's no match for India's best. At Mandvi, in Kutch, the beach is truly beautiful, pristine, and unpopulated, with clear water and a calm surf.

Dining

The rich sauces and meats of North India are foreign here, though many hotels have restaurants featuring classic Mughlai cuisine. Gujaratis prefer a delicious variety of vegetable dishes stir-fried in light vegetable oils, served with unleavened breads—fritters made from bean flours and rice—and washed down with *lassi,* a cold drink made with yogurt. You can try all of the above by ordering a *thali,* the traditional sampler platter. Note that Gujarat is a dry state: Alcohol is available only in a few hotel shops, and then only for consumption in your room. Ask your hotel how to obtain a permit from the Excise Department to purchase from these stores. Note also that restaurants tend to close for two or three hours in the late afternoon.

Festivals

Makar Sankranti—the point when the sun reaches the Tropic of Capricorn after the winter solstice—is celebrated on January 14 with a tremendous kite festival in Ahmedabad. A dance festival is organized immediately afterwards at the sun temple at Modhera, about 100 km (62 mi) north of Ahmedabad. The Gujarat tourist board sponsors the Kutch Utsav in February or early March, a cultural festival with crafts fairs, folk dances, and air-conditioned buses to Dhola Vira.

Navaratri, the goddess festival in late September or early October, is celebrated throughout the state with performances of Ras Garba, Gujarat's folk dance, nowadays often embellished with disco moves and amplified music. Tarnetar, northeast of Rajkot in the center of the Kathiawar Peninsula, is the site of a large folk fair in October or November. Diwali—the November or December festival of lights marking the return of the epic hero Rama from exile with his wife, Sita—is celebrated distinctively here by the Jains, as is the birthday of their ancient founder, Mahavira, in April. When the monsoon rains are good—every fourth or fifth year—the Hindu month of Shravan, in July or August, brings Kutch to life as nomads return to their villages and the rare season of plenty is celebrated.

Lodging

Ahmedabad and some other cities have some good business hotels, and in the countryside some formerly state-run tourist facilities have been refurbished under private ownership. Several of the modest palaces of former princes are being converted to Heritage Hotels in charming rural locations. Still, accommodations in Gujarat are largely works in progress, particularly in Kutch.

Shopping

Gujarat remains a premier design center, and its traditional crafts are nurtured by modern institutions like Ahmedabad's National Institute of Design. In Kutch, you can admire and buy these crafts in the villages where they're made; in Ahmedabad, emporia and street markets deliver a wide selection. It is now very difficult to buy pieces made with the mind-boggling detail you see in museums and private collections, but contemporary crafts are still vibrant with color and with charming vernacular design.

Visual Arts and Architecture

If you visit only one museum in India, make it Ahmedabad's Calico Museum of Textiles. The displays here will convince you that weaving and embroidery are fine arts. The art school in Vadodara is the best in India, so Ahmedabad and Vadodara both have good collections of Indian sculpture and painting from various periods as well as galleries of contemporary Indian art. Architecture enthusiasts have the rare opportunity to see three buildings by Le Corbusier in Ahmedabad (he built only one in the United States); and the city's Indian Institute of Management Studies was designed beautifully by Louis Kahn. Ahmedabad's pre-Mogul Muslim buildings have a lightness and exuberance equal to that of the better-known architecture that followed.

Wildlife

Even if you don't see lions in the Gir Wildlife Sanctuary, you won't leave disappointed. Gujarat's hilly landscape is beautiful in its own right and teeming with deer and other animals, giving a sense of the natural landscape celebrated in Indian art and literature. At Velavadar Wildlife Sanctuary, you're likely to see great herds of blackbuck, the most graceful Indian antelope, on a large, grassy plain, and in Kutch and at the Nalsarovar Bird Sanctuary in Saurashtra, you'll see an unparalleled variety of bird life in the winter months.

Exploring Gujarat

Great Itineraries

Numbers in the margin correspond to points of interest on the Gujarat map.

IF YOU HAVE 2 DAYS

Spend one day sampling the sights and culture of **Ahmedabad.** The next day, venture out to the ruined capital of the Solanki dynasty at **Patan** and the ornately carved sun temple at nearby **Modhera,** a structure that predates the more famous sun temple at Konark, Orissa, and rivals it in beauty if not in scale. *Alternately,* take a fast train to **Vadodara** and visit the palace and excellent museums of the maharaja as well as the charming ghost town of Champaner nearby.

IF YOU HAVE 4 DAYS

Visit **Ahmedabad,** then venture south onto the Kathiawar Peninsula. Leave Ahmedabad early so as to arrive at **Gir Wildlife Sanctuary** in time for a late-afternoon game drive. The next morning, take another game drive just after dawn and end the day on the beach at **Diu.** Alternately, if you leave **Ahmedabad** in the late afternoon, spend the night at the delightful Palace Utelia, near **Lothal,** and arrange for transport the next morning to **Velavadar Wildlife Sanctuary** in the morning and **Palitana** in the afternoon. Spend the night at **Bhavnagar** before flying out to Bombay.

You can also spend half a week in Kutch, accessible by a short flight from Bombay to **Bhuj** or an overnight train ride from Ahmedabad. Wander the charming walled city of Bhuj, then spend a long day traveling to **Dhola Vira.** The chance to wander around ruins more than 4,000 years old outlining a once-prosperous city larger than Bhuj, and to see the tremendous salt pans of the Rann of Kutch, is worth every bit of the effort it takes to get here. Spend a day visiting **crafts villages** north of Bhuj, and another relaxing on the beach in **Mandvi.**

IF YOU HAVE 7 DAYS

Fly into **Bhuj** and wander around Kutch for three days as outlined above. Then hire a car to drive you to **Gir Wildlife Sanctuary** and the Saurashtra coastline. From **Diu** you can drive up to **Palitana, Velavadar Wildlife Sanctuary,** and **Ahmedabad.**

When to Tour Gujarat

As in much of India, the months between October and March are the best times to come here. In Kutch, the strong sea breeze can make January very cold, but it also extends the period of comfortable dry weather into early April. A very light monsoon comes to Kutch in rare years, causing the desert to bloom.

AHMEDABAD AND ENVIRONS

Gujarat's richness and variety are apparent in the immediate region of its capital. The ruins at Patan and Modhera bear striking testament to the classical Hindu period, and Ahmedabad itself shows how a winning sense of style persisted through eras of Muslim rule and the modern period. At the Little Rann of Kutch, the state's natural beauty is on display, as well as rural Gujarati crafts and traditions.

Ahmedabad

❶ *545 km (338 mi) north of Bombay*

Founded in AD 1411 by the Muslim Sultan Ahmed Shah, Ahmedabad flourished under the Gujarat dynasty and subsequently became the seat of the Mogul governors of Gujarat—Jahangir, Shah Jahan, and Aurangzeb—all of whom later became emperors. At one time it was said that Ahmedabad hung on three threads: gold, silk, and cotton. The city's present prominence is due largely to one family of textile magnates, the Sarabhais, who were patrons of the arts (they invited Le Corbusier to build here) and supporters of Mahatma Gandhi. Members of the family are still active in the city's cultural life. Although textiles are still a principal industry in Ahmedabad, today the city is also a booming national and international center for the mineral, power, agribusiness, petro-chemical, scientific-development, computer-software, and pharmaceuticals industries.

Ahmedabad is divided into old and new by the Sabarmati River, a now mostly dry riverbed; most of the new development is on the west side of the river. The pace and scope of the development are amazing: Brand-new towering office complexes, designed by well-known Indian architects, are going up everywhere, particularly along C. G. Road, the up-and-coming business and shopping strip where real-estate prices already challenge those of Bombay.

In some ways, Ahmedabad doesn't quite look the part of a major international business hub. Ashram and C. G. roads, the city's main streets, lined with exclusive shopping complexes and office buildings, are perpetually under construction, with deep, dusty shoulders instead of sidewalks and a constant crowd of camels, cows, and monkeys. Amid this turmoil is a self-confident city full of cultural attractions and intellectual life, accessible and welcoming.

A Good Tour

To see the main sights of Ahmedabad in a single day, arrange for a car to pick you up early in the morning, before the traffic kicks in at 9 AM. Head first to the **Jama Masjid,** then to **Ahmed Shah's Tomb** and the **Sidi Saiyad Mosque,** all in the central, walled part of town. Then proceed north to the **Hatheesing Jain Temple.** A few kilometers farther north is the **Calico Museum of Textiles**—take the tour, which starts at 10:30. If you prefer, skip the second (religious) part of the Calico tour and go directly on to **Sabarmati Ashram,** just across the river to the west.

TIMING

This tour should take about six hours in its entirety. You'll probably spend the biggest chunks of time in the Hatheesing Jain Temple, the Calico Museum, and the Sabarmati Ashram.

Sights to See

Ahmed Shah's Tomb. The grave of Ahmedabad's founder is venerated with incense, flowers, and colorful cloths called *chadars,* in the manner of a Muslim saint. ☒ *Gandhi Rd.* *Free.*

★ **Calico Museum of Textiles.** Considered one of the best textile museums in the world, this vast collection is a rich way to experience the lavish colors and textures of Ahmedabad's age-old primary industry. Housed in a composite *haveli* (traditional Gujarati carved mansion), the museum buildings are connected by paths through lush gardens of shady trees and exotic flowers. The museum is filled with beautiful examples of myriad varieties of embroidery, dyeing, weaving, and other textile traditions from all over India: heavy royal costumes with gold brocade (including one worn by Shah Jahan), battle scenes embroidered on silk, silver gilt, 12-ft-long Banarasi silk cummerbunds, 17th-century painted prayer cloths, and so on. For reasons of security and preservation, you must go on a guided tour. The tour of the first section, the larger historical exhibit, begins promptly at 10:30 and ends at 11:30, when part two, comprising religious textiles, begins (it, too, lasts one hour). The same two-part sequence begins again at 2:45. If you miss the first tour, you can't enter until the next one begins. ☒ *Retreat Bungalow, near Shahibag overpass,* ☎ *79/786–8172.* *Free.* ⏲ *Mon.—Tues. and Thurs.–Sun. 10:30–12:30 and 2:45–5.*

Hatheesing Jain Temple. This elaborately carved white-marble temple and is the finest of Ahmedabad's beautiful Jain temples. Dedicated to Dharmanath, the 15th Jain apostle, it took 25 years to complete in the mid-19th century. Every surface of every pillar and arch is intricately carved with dancing figures and curling ornaments; just pick a spot and allow yourself to get lost in the details. The main structure is surrounded by 52 miniature temples. The magnificent stone lattice screens of the second-floor windows appear to be woven of stone threads. A few restrictions: Photography of gods or goddesses is prohibited, and menstruating women are theoretically banned from entry. ☒ *By Delhi Gate, Balvantrai Mehta Rd.* *Free.* ⏲ *Daily 5:30–1 and 3:30–7:30.*

Jama Masjid. The city's largest mosque is best seen before business hours congest the surrounding streets. The mosque was built in 1424 by Ahmed Shah. The prayer hall, with its niche facing Mecca, is covered by five domes held up with 260 pillars, carved in a style reminiscent of Hindu and Jain temple architecture. ☒ *Gandhi Rd.* *Free.*

Sabarmati Ashram. Born in Gujarat, Mahatma Gandhi established his simple retreat, the Satyagraha (literally, "seizing truth") here when he returned from South Africa in 1915. Eventually the nerve center of the Indian independence movement, this ashram occupies a tranquil spot on the bank of the nearly dry Sabarmati River just outside the rush of the city center. It was from here, in 1930, that Gandhi and 79 followers began the 241-mile march to the seacoast at Dandi to protest the British salt tax, an event which galvanized the movement that would bring India independence after World War II. The main, open-air building houses exhibits, including a moving photo display documenting the major points of Gandhi's life and work; and the grounds give a deep, if less tangible, impression of Gandhi's legacy. Under shade trees on the green lawns, students and others come in pairs or small groups to talk quietly or reflect on the history of this place and on modern India. When you sign the register in the humble cottage where Gandhi lived, your name will share the pages with those of Nelson Mandela and other foreign dignitaries and peace workers who come to pay homage to the father of India. ✉ *Ashram Rd. and Sabarmati River, 7 km (3 mi) north of city center.* 🎟 *Free; sound-and-light show Rs. 5.* ⏲ *Daily 8:30–6:30; sound-and-light show in English Wed., Sat., and Fri. 8:30 PM; tickets on sale at box office after 2.*

Sidi Saiyad Mosque. Named for a slave in Ahmed Shah's court, this intimate mosque stands at a busy intersection in the heart of Ahmedabad, but the chiseled stone friezes on its western wall, depicting the tree of life, will transport you out of the hubbub. Built in the late 1500s, the mosque is a masterpiece: Its stonework has the delicacy of filigree (though the full effect is reduced, as the central screen is now in Delhi's National Museum). Women are not allowed under the dome, but you can see the friezes from a small garden outside it. ✉ *Relief Rd.* 🎟 *Free.*

Dining and Lodging

Gujarati food is excellent, and Ahmedabad is one of the few places in Gujarat with modern restaurants serving non-Indian food as well.

To accommodate a rapidly growing number of business travelers, new hotels are popping up left and right in Ahmedabad. Room prices are generally lower than those in other Indian cities. Hotels with alcohol permits are indicated below.

$$$ ✕ **The Waterfall.** Named for the simulated waterfalls cascading behind a glass window in the dining room, the Holiday Inn's restaurant is intimate and elegant, with candlelit tables. The menu has an impressive variety of excellent Indian and Continental cuisine as well as Chinese items. Specialties include Kerala kebab (a moist, spicy chicken leg stuffed with dried fruits, nuts, and paneer and baked in a tandoor oven) and *kadai* chicken (boneless chicken chunks in tangy brown sauce named for, and served in, the traditional Indian woklike pot in which it's cooked). ✉ *Holiday Inn Ahmedabad, Chand Suraj Estate, Khanpur,* ☎ *79/550–5505. Reservations essential. AE, DC, MC, V.*

$$ ★ ✕ **Mirch Masala.** Done up in imitation of a roadside truck stop, with painted murals of rural scenes, this basement restaurant on Ahmedabad s main shopping strip draws a congenial affluent crowd of young people and families. The house specialties include a variety of Jain-inspired selections—vegetarian dishes made without resort to onions or garlic. You can also sample traditional street snacks, prepared in a cleaner environment than the street. Expect to wait for a table. ✉ *Chandan Complex, C. G. Rd., near Swastik Char Rasta, Navrangpura,* ☎ *79/640–3340. AE, MC, V.*

$$ ✕ **Rajwadu.** Like the better-known Vishalla, this outdoor restaurant in a residential suburb serves Gujarati meals in a faux-rural ambience. Relatively new in town, it already has a loyal local following. The menus are only in Gujarati, so you're best off asking for help. ✉ *Jivaraj*

Tolanaka, near Ambaji Temple, Malar Talav, ☎ 79/664–3845. No credit cards. No lunch.

$$ ✕ **"10."** As its numerical name implies, this classy restaurant strives for perfection. Special touches, like heated plates, complimentary bottled water, and linen napkins embroidered with the names of the restaurant's many regulars, reflect the management's mission of personalized service and attention to detail. The chef prepares top-notch Punjabi, Continental, and Chinese fare. Try the *paneer khada masala* (cheese chunks in a spicy clove and nutmeg gravy) with some floppy garlic *naan* (bread), and save room for the excellent desserts. ✉ *Urja House, Swastik Char Rasta, ☎ 79/642–5703. AE, MC, V.*

$$ ★ ✕ **Vishalla.** No matter how tight your schedule is, try to make time for this famous outdoor restaurant, a re-created Gujarati village outside Ahmedabad. You're welcomed with a flower garland, and a *bindi* (colored dot) is placed on your forehead. Once you've placed your order at the entrance, try a sugarcane aperitif from the village-style juice bar, a thatch-roof hut where a young boy cranks a giant cog-and-wheel contraption that mashes and squeezes the sweet juice out of the sugarcane stalks. Stroll on worn dirt paths lit by candles and lanterns and discover a Rajasthani puppet show performed under a palm tree, or wander into a clearing where musicians sing Gujarati folk songs. When your order is ready—they run around calling your name until they find you—you sit (amid locals) on straw mats at low, rough wood tables while turbaned young waiters serve an exceptional, authentic thali on banana leaves. Come hungry, be prepared to eat with your hand, and bring insect repellent. ✉ *Vasana Tol Naka, ☎ 79/643–0357. Reservations essential. No credit cards.*

$ ✕ **Gopi Dining Hall.** This popular sit-down lunchroom in the center of town is a good place to restore yourself after a morning's sightseeing. Serving hundreds of hungry office workers at once, it specializes in large Gujarati thalis. The setting is hectic, with service to match, but you'll have a tasty and filling vegetarian meal. ✉ *Opposite Town Hall, Ashram Rd., Ellisbridge, ☎ 79/657–6388. V*

$ ✕ **South-Indian Restaurant.** Tucked into the hotel pocket on the east side of the Sabarmati River, this tiny, simple restaurant fills up at lunchtime with neighborhood businesspeople and hotel staff enjoying large portions of tasty, cheap southern vegetarian fare. Choose from nearly 30 different *dosas* (stuffed Indian crepes), or try the fixed thali menu. Service is prompt and efficient. ✉ *Opposite Ministry Chambers, near Cama Hotel, Khanpur, ☎ 79/550–1343. No credit cards.*

$ ★ ✕ **Toran Dining Hall.** This Ahmedabad institution is a great place to get the full experience of a Gujarati thali meal. Barefoot waiters dressed in plain gray uniforms swarm around the dining room tossing handfuls of *chapati* and *puri* bread and spooning refills of the various vegetarian concoctions, chutneys, and condiments into your stainless-steel thali bowls and onto the tray. Each waiter carries just one garnish or type of food and will hover over you throughout the meal, replenishing your tray before you can eat the last bite. Come hungry. The large, simple room is strongly air-conditioned and dark, with pale-gray walls, dim lighting, and dark mirrors set into pillars. ✉ *Opposite Sales India, Ashram Rd., ☎ 79/754–2197. No credit cards. No dinner Mon.*

$$$$ 🏨 **Fortune Hotel Landmark.** This new business hotel is challenging its more-established competitors. Guest rooms are comfortably furnished and spacious, and service is excellent. The location—near the central business district—is more convenient than that of Ahmedbad's other upscale hotels, which are out in Khanpur. ✉ *Ashram Rd., Osmanpura, Ahmedabad 380013, ☎ 79/755–2929, FAX 79/755–2912. 96 rooms, 2 suites. 2 restaurants, coffee shop, pool, dry cleaning, laundry service, business services, meeting rooms, travel services. AE, DC, MC, V.*

$$$$ **Holiday Inn Ahmedabad.** A pair of glass-capsule elevators glides up and down the soaring atrium lobby of Ahmedabad's classiest hotel. Gleaming with glass and polished marble, the lobby is a hushed bustle of local and international businesspeople. Rooms are contemporary and elegant, with occasional clashes among the fabric colors and furniture styles. Set on the east bank of the Sabarmati River, the hotel is slightly removed from the city center, a short trip across the Nehru Bridge. Rooms facing west have river views with a tragic twist on the modern Indian paradox: Just below the towering white hotel, a dense stretch of a box-like slum housing lines the shore. ✉ *Chand Suraj Estate, Khanpur, Ahmedabad 380001,* ☎ *79/550–5505,* FAX *79/550–5501. 61 rooms, 2 suites. 2 restaurants, coffee shop, patisserie, pool, health club, babysitting, dry cleaning, laundry service, business services, meeting rooms, travel services, free parking. AE, DC, MC, V.*

$$$ ★ **Cama.** Once the only upscale hotel in town, the 40-year-old Cama now faces stiff competition, but it still has the loveliest grounds in the city. The green lawns, palm trees, chirping birds, and small swimming pool in the back garden grant respite after a hectic day. The interior has an old, slightly worn Indian elegance, with wide, cold hallways and a faded white-marble lobby decorated with Gujarati handicrafts and antiques. Rooms are large and modern, with pale floral bedspreads and curtains and painted wood furniture. Request a room facing the river—the Cama's views of the Sabarmati are the best in town. The hotel has a liquor store. ✉ *Khanpur Rd., Khanpur, Ahmedabad 380001,* ☎ *272/550–5281 (–89),* FAX *272/550–5285. 46 rooms, 5 suites. Restaurant, coffee shop, pool, dry cleaning, laundry service, business services, meeting rooms, travel services. AE, DC, MC, V.*

$$ **Inder Residency.** The central location of this promising, young upmarket, between Ashram and C. G. roads, is a prime selling point. The lobby has low ceilings, white pillars, and a kitschy, rainbow-colored water sculpture on the back wall. With clean white walls, modern blond wood furniture, aqua carpeting, and coordinating geometric-pattern fabrics, the guest rooms feel cool and bright, and all face the pool on the front terrace. Rates are at the low end of this price category. ✉ *Opposite Gujarat College, Ellisbridge, Ahmedabad 380006,* ☎ *79/656–5222 (–31),* FAX *79/656–0407. 74 rooms, 5 suites. Restaurant, coffee shop, patisserie, pool, dry cleaning, laundry service, business services, meeting rooms. AE, DC, MC, V.*

$$ **Shalin.** Designed for business travelers, all the rooms in the Shalin are suites, each with a tiny sitting and working area and a small bedroom separated by a sliding glass door. Modern, functional furnishings are uniform throughout. The rooms, alas, tend to show signs of wear and tear quickly, but the sleek lobby is immaculate, sparkling with marble and teakwood and flooded with light from a large bank of windows. Rooms facing the pool and street have the best views; but for less street noise, request a room at the back or on an upper floor. The location, near the new stock-exchange building and busy M. G. Road, is convenient for business travelers, and there's a liquor store on the premises. ✉ *Gujarat College Cross Rds., Ellisbridge, Ahmedabad 380006,* ☎ *79/642–6967 (–76),* FAX *79/656–5334 or –0022. 70 suites. 2 restaurants, pool, dry cleaning, laundry service, business services, meeting rooms, travel services. AE, DC, MC, V.*

$ **King Palace.** This addition to the main strip of hotels in Khanpur is a clean and attractive option for travelers on a budget. The rooms are carpeted, and furnished with basic upholstered chairs. ✉ *Khanpur, Ahmedabad 380001,* ☎ *79/550–0276 (–82),* FAX *79/550–0275. 37 rooms, 2 suites. Restaurant, laundry service, meeting room, travel services. AE, DC, MC, V.*

$ ★ **Rock Regency.** A giant, red neon sign blazes above this white, four-story hotel, just off C. G. Road. The lobby is stylish and contemporary, with polished granite floors and twisting white pillars; in the rooms, pea-green floral upholstered chairs and headboards with white wooden frames create a garden look. ✉ *Law Garden Rd., Navrangpura, Ahmedabad 380006,* ☎ *79/656–2101 (–5),* FAX *79/642–3694. 37 rooms, 2 suites. Restaurant, coffee shop, dry cleaning, laundry service, meeting rooms, travel services. AE, DC, MC, V.*

Nightlife and the Arts

You won't find discos in this dry city, but you may well discover a new master of the sitar or the next great Indian painter. The **Darpana Academy of the Performing Arts** (☎ 79/755–1389, FAX 79/755–0955) in Usmanpura, a neighborhood just north of the Khanpur hotel district, has regular performances ranging from classical dance to folk puppet shows. The complex also has an arts bookstore.

Other performances are held in the **Tagore Auditorium** (✉ Sanskar Kendra municipal complex, Bhagtacharya Rd.), designed by Le Corbusier. The Sanskar Kendra also houses an intriguing kite museum.

The **Amdavad-ni-Gufa** (✉ Gujarat University) is an eccentric collaboration between the painter M. F. Husain and the prominent local architect Balkrishna Doshi, who collaborated with Le Corbusier. It displays contemporary arts and crafts in a cave-like space.

The **National Institute of Design** (✉ Paldi, ☎ 79/663–9692, FAX 79/663–8465) holds regular exhibitions. For classical art, the **N. C. Mehta Gallery** and the **L. D. Institute of Indology Museum** (✉ L. D. Institute of Indology, opposite Gujarat University, Navrangpura) have excellent collections of medieval sculpture and miniature painting, respectively. Open Tuesdays to Sundays from 11 to 6.

The **Archer Art Gallery** (✉ Archer House, Gurukul Rd., Paldi, ☎ 79/741–3594) is a leading gallery for modern and contemporary art.

Shopping

Ahmedabad is a great place to buy authentic Gujarati handicrafts, famous throughout India. Textiles are outstanding, from finely woven silk *patola* fabrics and *bhandej* (tie-dyed) materials to elaborately embroidered vests, purses, wall hangings, slippers, and bedspreads from the Kutch desert and Saurashtra. Look also for *moti-kaam* (beadwork) textiles and figures, and for copper, brass, and bronze metalwork. Mobiles and chains of small stuffed parrots, horses, and other figures of various sizes make inexpensive decorative accents or cheerful baby toys. Most shops are open Monday through Saturday, 10 to 6 or 7. Some stores accept credit cards.

Banascraft (✉ 8 Chandan Complex, near Mirch Masala Restaurant, C. G. Rd., Swastik Char Rasta, Navrangpura, ☎ 79/640–5784) is a boutique featuring embroidery and other high-quality craftwork by members of the Self-Employed Women's Association (SEWA), a highly successful women's cooperative. The organization works with slum dwellers in Ahmedabad and with rural craftswomen in Kutch.

Gurjari (✉ opposite La-Gajjar Chamber, Ashram Rd., ☎ 79/658–9505), also known as the Gujarat State Handicrafts Emporium, is a fixed-price government shop with low prices, no taxes, and guaranteed quality. It sells an impressive variety of brightly embroidered dresses, hand-woven wall hangings, beaded tribal jewelry, brass figures, traditional silver and brass *pataris* (jewelry boxes), and other examples of Gujarati craftwork.

Kapasi Handicrafts Emporium (✉ 105 B. K. House, C. G. Rd., near Stadium Circle, ☎ 79/754–1092) has a good selection of handicrafts, particularly brass and other metalwork.

The **Law Garden Market** (✉ Netaji Rd.) gets going only at around 7 or 8 each night, when the road is transformed into a vibrant, chaotic scene. Vendors from the Kutch and elsewhere drape their stalls with exquisitely embroidered wall hangings, shirts, vests, bedspreads, and more, studded with tiny mirrors. Bargain like mad.

Manek Chowk (✉ off Ramanlal Jani and Desai Rds.) is a colorful bazaar in the old city where crowded, narrow streets are packed with stalls and shops selling excellent fabrics and ready-made clothes.

Patan and Modhera

❷–❸ *Patan is 30 km (20 mi) northeast of Modhera. Modhera is 100 km (62 mi) northwest of Ahmedabad.*

Northwest of Ahmedabad, these two groups of ruins can be combined in a day trip or worked into a longer road trip to or from Rajastan. **Patan** was capital of the Hindu Solanki dynasty from the 8th to 12th centuries. The ornately carved **Rani-ka-Vav,** built in 1050, is the most stunning baoli in Gujarat. A great flight of steps leads down into the well, halting at a covered colonade just above the waterline; the walls are covered in finely executed sculptures of Vishnu, Ganesh, and other Hindu gods. The nearby **Sahasra Linga Tank** once housed a thousand *lingas* (abstract stone icons of the great god Shiva, sometimes characterized as phallic symbols). Little remains of the shrines today, but the outlines of the extensive water tanks are impressive in themselves, eerily reminiscent of the waterworks from three thousand years earlier that archeologists have recently uncovered at Dhola Vira in Kutch. On the way into town from the Sahasra Linga Tank, you can see the last makers of **patola saris,** who use a weaving technique called *ikat*—threads used for both warp and weft are tie-dyed before they're woven into saris. It can take up to seven months for two weavers to produce a single six-yard-long sari, and the results are stunning; the slightly blurred but intricate pattern recalls an impressionist painting. The process is fascinating to watch—ask for directions to the Salvi family. (Their shop, Patolawala, is at ⊞ Salviwado, Patolawala St., ☎ 2766/32274). In the center of the sleepy contemporary town of Patan there is an attractive Jain temple complex, and next to the temple a "Jnan Mandir," or temple of knowledge, with an important collection of illuminated manuscripts. Mornings from 8 to 10 and afternoons from 2 to 4, young monks come to study the manuscripts. The caretaker has a photo album of the collection, and upon request he'll bring out a few of the original works, which are masterpieces of miniature painting. Make a small donation in return for his help.

The 11th-century sun-temple complex at **Modhera** is the Solanki dynasty's most striking architectural achievement. The main temple sits on a moderately high plinth, which is now missing its spire, or *shikara.* Fronting this is the ornately carved *ranga mandapa,* or hall for dance and other entertainments, and a large stone bathing tank, which itself contains some 108 small shrines. The temple, mandapa, and tank were lined up so that on the fall and spring equinoxes, the sun rose to shine directly on the temple's main image of Surya, the sun god. All three structures are embellished with high-quality sculpture reminiscent of the better-known temples at Khajuraho, which date from the same period. A guide can point out scenes of the Hindu epics *Mahabharata* and *Ramayana,* as well as various images of the sun god on the temple walls and numerous well-carved erotic scenes. On the east side of the bathing tank, a shrine houses a fine relief of Vishnu reclining on the serpent Anant Nag, preparing for the sleep that follows the cosmic dissolution and precedes the rejuvenation of the universe.

NEED A BREAK? **Hotel New Janapath** (☎ 2762/52441), on the highway near Radhanpur Char Rasta, Mahesana, 80 km (48 mi) north of Ahmedabad, has an excellent air-conditioned vegetarian restaurant where you can break your journey between Ahmedabad and Patan or Modhera.

Lodging

$$ **Balaram Palace Resorts.** If you plan to enter or leave Gujarat via Rajasthan, this Heritage Hotel at the edge of the Aravalli Hills makes an ideal base. Patan and Modhera are 73 and 112 km (50 and 67 mi) away, respectively, and Mount Abu, in Rajasthan, is even closer. Once a princely mansion, it's well restored and professionally run. Palanpur, a stop on the main rail line between Ahmedabad and Delhi, is 15 km (10 mi) away. ✉ *Chitrasani Village, off Abu-Palanpur Hwy No. 14,* ☎ *2742/84278 (–80),* FAX *2742/84336. 17 rooms. Restaurant, pool, health club, laundry service, travel services. AE, D, MC, V.*

Little Rann of Kutch

❹ *93 km (60 mi) northwest of Ahmedabad, 400 km (240 mi) east of Bhuj*

The salt-pan and swamp territory separating the main area of Gujarat from Kutch is home to a sanctuary populated by the last herds of Asian wild ass, a species of small wild horses that recall the zebras of Africa in their exuberance and herding behavior. In prehistoric times, this area was an estuary flowing into the Arabian sea, and the desert countryside is still interspersed with small mounds that were once islands. The Little Rann of Kutch connects with the Great Rann (which separates Kutch from the Pakistani province of Sind) to form a huge wild area that is also home to blackbuck, wolves, and a wide array of birdlife. Villages on the firm soil abutting the Rann maintain old craft traditions. It's a great place to escape the urban chaos of Ahmedabad, or to break up the long road journey between Ahmedabad and Bhuj.

Lodging

$$ **Desert Coursers Zainabad Camp.** Just outside the sanctuary, this camp is rustic but impeccable. The twelve small huts have clean linen, clean bathrooms, and running water. Meals are served buffet-style in an open-air dining room. The camp has its own game-viewing vehicle and can arrange camel safaris and trips to meet local craftswomen; just note that it's closed in late spring and summer. ✉ *Zainabad Camp, via Dasada, Surendranagar district 382751,* ☎ *2757/41333 (–5). No credit cards. Closed mid-April to September.*

KUTCH

Isolated by history and geography, with blue skies and a blue seacoast, Kutch has preserved its easygoing manners even as it has entered the modern economy by mining the mineral resources of the huge salt flat known as the Rann of Kutch. Birds and wildlife live here in abundance. The climate is dry, with a cool sea breeze reaching far inland. The Rann—a shimmering gulf of salt and marshland where water ran in prehistoric times—the Arabian Sea, and the Gulf of Kutch make the region a virtual island; until 1947 it was a princely state outside the British customs union. The dry, flat landscape is punctuated by worn dark hills.

Kutchis speak their own language, which is related to the Sindhi tongue of neighboring Pakistan, and have retained a distinct regional identity, though more Kutchis have now migrated elsewhere in India and the world than remain in this drought-prone region. The Hindus, Jains, and Muslims who live here have a remarkable record of intercommunity tolerance, even from the time of Partition in 1947, when much of northern India was plagued with communal violence. Groups of nomadic and sedentary tribes in Kutch still make many traditional crafts.

The relatively sparse population of about one million has helped maintain diverse wildlife in this region—great flocks of flamingos appear on the salt pans and coast in winter along with wild asses, monitor lizards, and a great variety of bird life, including the Indian bustard. Recent enthusiasm for Kutch as a travel destination has spawned small lodges for budget travelers and some better-equipped re-creations of Kutchi villages outside the city of Bhuj; but amenities here are less extensive than in other parts of India. The tourist impulse has also eased some restrictions in this sensitive border area, but you'll still need to get a permit from the District Collector (☞ Gujarat A to Z, *below*) specifying to which places you can travel north of Bhuj. Because Kutch is delightful in itself, relatively unpolluted, and—with the recent excavations at the 4,000-year-old city of Dhola Vira—possessed of a spectacular historical monument, few who reach Kutch use anything other than superlatives to describe their experiences.

Bhuj

❺ *300 km (180 mi) northwest of Ahmedabad*

You can easily explore the walled old city of Bhuj on foot. Visit the covered **vegetable market** in Shroff Bazaar, at the center of town, early in the morning, when the light bounces off the produce and the people of Bhuj come out to stock up for the day.

West of the vegetable market is the pastel-painted **Old Satyanarayan Temple** complex, which serves as the center for a communitarian religious movement focused on Krishna, a popular deity in Gujarat since the 19th century. Men and women congregate here to worship, hear lectures, and speak with the *sadhus* (holy men) who live in the complex. The assembly hall adjoining the temple is open only to men. ✉ *Old city.*

Just north of the Old Satyanarayan Temple is the eclectic main palace of Kutch's ruler, the maharao. A clock tower that wouldn't look out of place in Oxford dominates the **maharao's complex,** and a more traditional 17th-century structure, the **Aina Mahal,** or Hall of Mirrors, houses a collection of royal furnishings and art. One room includes indoor fountains and a platform where the maharao reclined to watch dancing girls or other performers. ✉ *Center of old city.* 🎟 *Rs. 3.* ⏲ *Sun.–Fri. 9–noon and 3–6.*

Outside the walled city, near the mostly dry Hamirsar Tank, is the **Kutch Museum,** the oldest museum in Gujarat. The collection includes some Indus Valley artifacts and Hindu and Jain sculpture from the late classical period. One 11th-century frieze depicts a boat at sea, a reminder of Kutch's age-old maritime history. ✉ *Museum Rd.,* ☎ *2832/20541.* 🎟 *Free; photos Rs. 2 per exposure.* ⏲ *Thurs.–Tues. 9–noon and 3–5. Closed 2nd and 4th Sat. of every month.*

A local family's excellent collection of Kutchi folk arts is now housed at **Bharati Sanskruti Darshan.** Call for an appointment. ✉ *College Rd.,* ☎ *2832/21518.* 🎟 *Free; photos Rs. 2 per exposure.* ⏲ *Mon.–Sat. 9–noon and 3–5.*

Dining and Lodging

$ ★ ✕ 🏨 **Hotel Prince.** This well-equipped hotel fronts a busy street on the outskirts of Bhuj. Rooms are large and comfortable, and those with air-conditioning are in the quieter rear section. The owner is a helpful, disinterested source of information and advice on travel in Kutch, and the two restaurants are excellent. The popular **Jesal** restaurant upstairs serves North Indian Mughlai cuisine, considered exotic by locals who have their fill of light Gujarati cooking at home. Don't miss **Toral,** the Gujarati restaurant downstairs. ✉ *Station Rd., Kutch 37000,* ☎ *2832/20370 (–2),* FAX *2832/50373. 2 restaurants, room service, business services. No credit cards.*

$ 🏨 **Ghara Safari Lodge.** This small resort in the countryside outside Bhuj makes an attractive base for excursions to the crafts villages. For small groups, the lodge can arrange camel and Jeep trips, including overnight tented expeditions. Rooms are a somewhat fancier version of the round huts found in Kutchi villages; some are air-conditioned. At press time a pool was in the works. ✉ *Bhuj, Kutch 37000; reserve through Ghara Hospitalities Pvt. Ltd., 109 Anil Kunj Rd., Ahmedabad 38006,* ☎ *79/657–9672,* FAX *79/657–6680, or through Ghara Tours & Travels, Elve Chambers, Green St., Fort, Bombay 400023,* ☎ *22/266–1186 or 266–5160,* FAX *22/266–2923. 16 huts. No credit cards.*

Shopping

To see samples of exquisite Kutchi embroidery and other textiles, contact **A. A. Wazir** (✉ Plot No. 107/B-1, Lotus Colony, Prankumar Mehta Marg, ☎ 2832/24187, FAX 2832/55500), a collector with some astounding materials from this region and elsewhere in India. Wazir has some priceless pieces, but he also sells some cheaper items that are still of very high quality, and can also help arrange trips to the crafts villages north of Bhuj. Shops in the walled city's **Shroff Bazaar** sell local handicrafts of varying quality.

Crafts Villages

Outside Bhuj, several villages maintain traditions of embroidery, weaving, block-printing, tie-dyeing, and other textile arts. You can visit a selection of these in a day for a glimpse of village life and culture; just note that you need a permit (☞ Gujarat A to Z, *below*). At **Sumrasar,** about 20 km (12 mi) north of Bhuj, a cooperative called **Kala Raksha** (☎ 2832/77238 or 77507) has helped revive embroidery among immigrants who came here from the Pakistani province of Sind after the brief 1971 Indo-Pakistan war. You'll see women busily embroidering cloth sent from crafts cooperatives elsewhere in India; they earn about Rs. 50 a day for their efforts, about the same as they would at road work or other manual labor. Other villages are less organized, but when people see you arrive, they'll usher you into their houses to show you their wares and how they make them.

Ludia, Hudko, Dhordo, and Khavda, all north of Sumrasar, are all worth seeing for their craftwork. In **Nirona,** about 30 km (19 mi) west of Sumrasar, a man believed to be the last practitioner of a technique known as Rogan art has a small workshop. This unusual craft, involving dyes boiled into a thick oil paste and applied to fabric, resembles the way henna is applied to hands and feet for Indian marriage ceremonies.

Lodging

$ 🏨 **Malir Garden Resort.** Located near Nakhatrana, about 40 km (25 mi) from Bhuj, Malir Garden is a collection of eight cottages modeled on Kutchi village architecture. The resort organizes camel safaris and tours of surrounding villages as well as performances of folk music in the evenings. ✉ *Vithon, Nakhatrana, Kutch 370615,* ☎ *2835/22288* *or 83344; or reserve through Florican Tours, Old Electricity House, Lal Darwaza, Ahmedabad 380001, ☎ 79/550–6590, FAX 79/642–6545. 8 cottages. No credit cards.*

En Route On a back road between Bhuj and Mandvi, the village of **Tunda Vandh** is the base camp for a group of Rabari nomads, a Muslim group that traditionally herds camels for its livelihood. The central packed-earth avenue is lined with well-made circular mud huts covered in thatch. Inside, the huts' walls are lined with fantastic cabinets, also made out of mud and ornamented with small mirrors, that look like something by the Catalan architect Antoni Gaudí. Many local women still practice their community's particular style of embroidery. Except during the monsoon, when the herders return, the village is peopled mainly by women; respect their customs of modesty, and wait for someone to invite you in before you approach individual huts.

Mandvi

6 *60 km (36 mi) southwest of Bhuj, 310 km (186 mi) west of Dhola Vira*

Outside the town of Mandvi, the maharao's seacoast retreat, **Lakshmi Vilas Palace,** is a dusty reminder of past glory in the middle of a desiccated coconut plantation. The beach here is lovely and uninhabited; you can use it for the day by paying a fee at the museum entrance or staying in the attractive but basic palace guest house.

Up the coast from Mandvi, the towns of **Lakhpat** and **Narayan Sarovar** are important Hindu pilgrimage centers. Until an earthquake cut off the westernmost branch of the Indus River delta in the 19th century, Lakhpat, in fact, was the richest city in Kutch. Because of the towns' proximity to the border, permits to come here are rarely issued to individual travelers, but you can join one of the group tours organized by the Gujarat tourist office during the Kutch Utsav each February.

Lodging

$ **Lakshmi Vilas Palace Guest House.** The four simply furnished rooms attached to the maharao's palace, 8 km (5 mi) south of Mandvi, have a spectacular setting. A pristine private beach lies down a short dirt road, with only the tomb of a Muslim saint overlooking it. You can see for miles up and down the beach; look for the temple in the middle distance. Don't expect full service here: Meals are cooked by the caretaker's wife, and the town of Mandvi has little in the way of restaurants. The nine extra rooms used for overflow are much less appealing than those in the guest house. ✉ *Lakshmi Vilas Palace, Mandvi, Kutch, ☎ 2834/20043; or reserve through North West Safaris, ☎ 79/661–0609, FAX 79/656–0962. 13 rooms. Restaurant. No credit cards.*

Dhola Vira

7 *250 km (155 mi) northeast of Bhuj*

Some 4,000 years ago there was a tremendous flowering of urban life in the northwest quadrant of the Indian subcontinent. This highly developed society, which traded with Sumeria, was christened the Indus Valley Civilization when archaeologists found cities near the Indus River in what is now Pakistan. Little is known of how this culture—whose script still has not been deciphered—rose and fell, but the current excavations at Dhola Vira may help to change that, as Dhola Vira was inhabited throughout the civilization's history. Artifacts were discovered here in the 1960s, but it wasn't until the Archaeological Survey of India began digging in earnest twenty years later that Dhola Vira's full significance became clear.

The city lies on an island in the middle of the Rann of Kutch, part of the reason for its excellent state of preservation. You approach over a long causeway, drive across the island, and park at the archaeologists' camp. From there, Dhola Vira looks like a large mound with a few rough stones sticking up. The archaeologists welcome visitors, and indeed, in recent years they have concentrated on excavating those portions of the site that are likely to be most easily comprehended by nonspecialists. World Bank funds are expected to help develop Dhola Vira as a full-fledged tourist attraction.

A watchman will lead you around the mound, pointing out the outlines of several enormous reservoirs and the channels that link them, and taking you up through one of the city's four impressive gates. At the summit of this three-tiered city, which is as large as the walled city in Bhuj, is an enormous well (about 12 ft across), with a stone chute to channel water into a series of bricked-in channels. The channels appear to have filled a set of two large pools or baths. Steps lead down to the north gate, where a huge, perfectly flat surface the size of a football field appears to have been some sort of stadium: Tiers of brick benches are built into the wall of the upper city.

Beyond this are what the archaeologists call the middle and lower towns, precisely laid-out lanes lined with small enclosures of one or two rooms, in which most of the inhabitants lived. The chief find of the excavation so far—unique in Indus Valley archaeology—is a signboard with a series of nine characters measuring about 10 inches high. Other discoveries include seals, beadwork, pottery, and large, smooth columns that stood at the gates of the city. You can see the most recent finds and photos from past excavations at the archaeologists' office outside the ruins. The digging season normally runs from November to early April, and it's easier to obtain a permit for Dhola Vira when the archaeologists are there.

The round-trip drive to Dhola Vira from Bhuj takes about eight hours. If you carry food and bedding, arrange to camp at a temple compound or village guest house along the way, but to do this you need advance permission from the District Collector (☞ Gujarat A to Z, *below*). Two charming temple compounds, **Ravechi** and **Akali Mata,** each dedicated to a Kutchi folk goddess, make good places to stop for a packed lunch or breakfast. An excursion to this pair actually shortens the journey by about 100 km (62 mi), because you reach them via back routes that are more direct than the main road; just make sure you bring a local guide with a good knowledge of the country roads.

KATHIAWAR PENINSULA

Gujarat's Kathiawar Peninsula, fanning out west of Ahmedabad and bounded by the Gulf of Kutch to the north and the Gulf of Khambat to the south, once comprised dozens of small princely states, lending the region the name Saurashtra, or the "Hundred Kingdoms." Mahatma Gandhi's father was an official in Porbandar, on the coast, and the grandfather of former Pakistani prime minister Benazir Bhutto was a minister in Junagadh, near the center of the region. The landscape is dry and flat, but dotted with worn, ancient hills, many of which hold temples on their summits.

Krishna, the incarnation of Vishnu whose story is told in the epic *Mahabharata,* is believed to have lived his last years in the legendary kingdom of Dwarka, at the peninsula's northwest tip. Somnath, site of one of the most famous Shiva temples in India, is also on the Saurashtra coast, and just off it is Diu, an island enclave settled by the Portuguese in the 16th century. Though cities like Rajkot and Surat are booming industrial centers, Saurashtra is entirely rustic. Men and women both wear traditional costumes: an all-white ensemble of turban, jodhpurs, and a pleated shirt for men, backless embroidered blouses, called *cholis,* for women. The land supports limited agriculture, a fact that has inadvertently led to the preservation of two excellent wildlife preserves. Good hotels, including Heritage Hotels, are gradually being established here. The easiest way to get around is by hired car; trains are slow, and air connections are few except to Bombay.

Gir National Park and Wildlife Sanctuary

8 *60 km (37 mi) southeast of Junagadh via Visavadar, 400 km (240 mi) southwest of Ahmedabad*

The Gir National Park and Wildlife Sanctuary (informally known as Sasan Gir for its entrance town) is a remarkable success story. Established in 1965 to protect a dwindling population of lions, it is now preparing to export prides to other areas. The sanctuary and the national park it surrounds encompass about 1,400 square km (540 square mi) of hill country covered in teak forest southeast of the town of Junagadh, an important religious center since at least the time of Ashoka in the 3rd century BC. About 300 lions live here, along with leopards, spotted deer, *sambhal* (another deer), king cobras, langur monkeys, and hundreds of peacocks and other birds. A project to stock the reservoir with *makara,* the Indian crocodile, is also underway.

The male lions are smaller, have sparser manes than their African relations, and are quite used to the presence of humans. A cattle-herding people known as the Maldhari lives inside the sanctuary. In dry weather the lions are more easily encountered, as they tend to take the Jeep roads to water points in the park. The park is most beautiful, however, from October to March, when the forest is green and teeming with life. The Kamaleshwar Reservoir is a fine place for a picnic under the watchful eyes of crocodiles in the water and eagles in the air.

To tour the park, you need to hire a Jeep from your hotel or the orientation center and a tracker from the orientation center. ✉ *Gir Wildlife Sanctuary and National Park, Sasan Gir district, Junagadh 362135,* ☎ *2877/85540.* 🎫 *Rs. 15 for 3 days, plus small additional charges for vehicles and cameras. Tracker: Rs. 10 for three hours, Rs. 4 for each additional hour; tipping encouraged.* ⏲ *Oct. 15 (or Nov. 15, depending on rainfall)–June 15, sunrise–sunset.*

Lodging

$$ ★ 🏨 **Gir Lodge.** Run by the Taj Group, this modern cement structure at the edge of the sanctuary has comfortable rooms. The staff is knowledgeable about the park and can take you on dawn or dusk game-viewing rides—these are expensive, but the hotel's open Jeeps are quieter than the others available here, i.e., less likely to disturb the animals. The staff can also book cars for excursions *from* Sasan Gir. Simple Indian buffet meals are included in the room rate. At press time, air-conditioning was being installed in most rooms and a swimming pool was under construction. ✉ *Sasan Gir district, Junagadh 362135.* ☎ *2877/85521 or 85501 (–4),* FAX *2877/85528. 27 rooms, 2 suites Dining room, laundry service, travel services. AE, DC, MC, V.*

$ 🏨 **Maneland Jungle Lodge.** This small lodge is a slight distance from the road, giving an impression of remoteness. The stone rooms are simple and well appointed. Jeeps are available for trips to the park. ✉ *Sasan Gir district, Junagadh 36215,* ☎ *2877/85555; or reserve through North West Safaris* ☎ *79/661–0609,* FAX *79/656–0962. 10 rooms. Dining room. No credit cards.*

$ **Sinh Sadan Guest House.** This forest-department guest house has large rooms, some with air-conditioning, surrounding a British-style flower garden next to the park orientation center. Breakfast and thali lunch and dinner are served for an additional charge. Reserve in advance, as the guest house can fill up with officials. ✉ *Deputy Central Forest Service Superintendent, Wildlife Division, Sasan Gir district, Junagadh 362135,* ☎ *2877/85540. 20 rooms plus a dormitory. Restaurant, laundry service. No credit cards.*

Somnath

9 *45 km (25 mi) southwest of Sasan Gir*

The Gujarati coastline has attracted traders and invaders for centuries. The **Shiva temple** at Somnath, which is believed to hold a naturally occurring Shiva linga, was a landmark to mariners from time immemorial until it was destroyed in the 11th century by Mahmud of Ghazni, an iconoclastic invader from Afghanistan. Since then the temple has been rebuilt several times, most recently in 1950 under the patronage of Sadar Patel, a Gujarati minister in Jawaharlal Nehru's post-Independence government.

The modern structure is not architecturally spectacular, but its setting right on the beach is. Devotees stream in—through metal detectors, due to ongoing Muslim anger at the reconstruction—and pay homage to one of the most sacred Shiva shrines in the country. At dawn, noon, and sunset, great kettle drums are beaten and conch shells blown while a large oil lamp is circled around the icon before being brought out to worshippers. This mesmerizing ceremony, known as *arati,* is meant to summon the god's presence in the temple. A small museum holds remnants of the temple's earlier incarnations. ⏲ *Thurs.–Tues., 9–12 and 3–6.* 🎫 *50 paise. Closed 2nd and 4th Sat. of each month.*

Diu

10 *90 km (48 mi) southeast of Somnath*

Diu, a narrow island measuring 11 by 3 km (7 by 2 mi), is an early Portuguese enclave that was taken over by the Indian government in 1961 and is now administered as a federal Union Territory, separate from Gujarat. The Portuguese first sought the island—then held by the Ottoman empire—in 1520, but they did not gain possession until a representative of the Mogul emperor Humayun granted it to them in 1535. An isolated enclave, it's popular with budget travelers as well as Gujaratis taking advantage of its free-flowing liquor laws.

Once you cross the short causeway that separates Diu from the mainland, you'll feel as though you've entered a sleepy Mediterranean market town. The streets are lined with two- and three-story buildings bearing the names of similar towns in Portuguese Africa. An enormous **fort** dominates the seaward end of the island, and when you walk along its ramparts you'll understand just how tenuous these seafaring colonists felt their hold on India was. Toppled gravestones alongside the fort's **chapel** date from as early as 1608. The fort is open daily 7–6.

The churches of **St. Paul, St. Thomas,** and **St. Francis of Assisi,** all with large, whitewashed Baroque facades, hold faded paintings from the Portugese era. St. Thomas's, at the north end of the market square, is now a **museum** with some interesting artifacts and a small café. There are several small **beaches** on Diu, but the nicest one in the vicinity is at Ahmedpur Mandvi, on the Gujarati mainland just before you reach the causeway. Note that, because Gujarat's prohibition of alcohol does not apply here, there are many small beer halls in Diu, but the island's restaurant fare is mostly disappointing.

Lodging

$$ ★ **Magico do Mar Beach Holiday Resort.** The town of Diu has a variety of fairly new hotels and, for budget travelers, older Portuguese-style lodgings. None are as attractive, however, as this complex of rooms and cottages just across the border in Gujarat, within striking distance of the town of Diu. The resort looks out over a wide, clean beach, and meals, which are included in the room rate, are served under a thatched canopy right on the beach. Some rooms are air-conditioned. ✉ *Diu Checkpost, Ahmedpur Mandvi, Una district, Junagadh 362510,* ☎ *28758/52216, 28758/52567, or 28758/52568,* FAX *28758/52569. 32 rooms, 15 cottages. Restaurant, laundry service, airport shuttle. No credit cards.*

Palitana

11 *150 km (90 mi) northeast of Diu, 277 km (166 mi) southwest of Ahmedabad*

Hilltop pilgrimage sites are a common feature in Saurashtra, but none is quite so expansive as **Shatrunjaya,** a city of some 900 temples built by followers of the Jain religion near modern-day Palitana. A prosperous but small merchant community, the Jains have maintained and refurbished the temples over the centuries; so while many of the temples here date back to the 1600s, the attraction is not that of an ancient ruin but that of a living faith. High above the surrounding flood plain, the place has an eerie calm about it. The temples are only open to the public during the day; at night, the gates are closed, and the temples' only inhabitants are their figures: white marble sculptures that each represent a Jina, one of the extremely few human souls in myth and history who, the Jains believe, have been able to liberate themselves from the cycle of rebirth. This hill marks the spot where, according to myth, such a Jina was liberated; he is worshiped in Shatrunjaya's largest temple as Adinath, the original master. You reach the temples by climbing the mountain—a mile-long stretch of 4,000 steps rising some 2,000 ft to the summit. Accompanying you will be lay pilgrims and white-garbed monks and *sadhvis* (female sadhus). The central tenet of Jain philosophy is nonviolence, or *ahimsa,* and the Jains' practice thereof is believed to have influenced Mahatma Gandhi. Some of the ascetics here wear gauze filters over their mouths so as not to harm micro-organisms with their breathing; and before they prostrate themselves at the shrines, they take care to sweep the ground of any tiny creatures beneath them. There is a small fee for both still and video cameras within the temple complex, and photography is not allowed inside the individual temples.

Lodging

$$$ **Nilambag Palace.** The former palace of Bhavnagar's local raja is now a Heritage Hotel and the most upscale lodging in the area. It makes the most comfortable base for excursions to Palitana (50 km/31 mi southwest of here) and Velavadar. ✉ *Bhavnagar 364002,* ☎ *278/429323, 278/424241, or 278/432295,* FAX *278/428072. 25 rooms, 2 suites. Restaurant, pool, laundry services, travel services. AE, D, MC, V.*

$ **Sumeru.** Run by the Tourism Corporation of Gujarat, this hotel is the best place to stay in Palitana itself. Still, the rooms are no more than basic (though some are air-conditioned), and the dining room keeps an erratic schedule. ✉ *Station Rd., Palitana,* ☎ *2848/2327; or reserve through the Tourism Corporation of Gujarat, Ltd., H. K. House, Ashram Rd.,* ☎ *79/449683 or 79/449172,* FAX *79/656–8183. 13 rooms plus a dormitory. Restaurant. No credit cards.*

Velavadar Wildlife Sanctuary

12 *65 km (40 mi) north of Bhavnagar, 85 km (53 mi) north of Palitana, 140 km (84 mi) south of Ahmedabad*

Once a hunting reserve, this small grassland sanctuary is home to large herds of the Indian blackbuck. Often depicted in miniature paintings, this elegant and fast-running antelope has been hunted almost to extinction elsewhere, but here its only predator is the Indian wolf, also an endangered species. The park is only 36 kilometers (22 mi) square, but it's home to about a thousand blackbuck, with more coming in from surrounding areas when foraging is plentiful. Chances of seeing both are best in October–November and February–March, the blackbuck's mating and foaling seasons, respectively. ✉ *10 km (6 mi) off main Bhavnagar-Ahmedabad highway; turnoff is between the towns of Vallabhipur and Barvala.* *Rs. 15 for foreigners, camera Rs. 15, car Rs. 5.*

Lodging

$ **Kaliyan Bhavan Forest Lodge.** This forest-department lodge is right outside the sanctuary. It has five small rooms and serves a fixed Gujarati menu. ✉ *Reserve through Gujarat Forest Department, Multistory Building, Annex F/10, Bhavnagar,* ☎ *278/426425. No credit cards.*

Lothal

13 *105 km (63 mi) north of Bhavnagar, 70 km (42 mi) southwest of Ahmedabad*

Gujarat's most accessible Indus Valley Civilization site is the prehistoric port center at Lothal. Now some 10 km (6 mi) inland from the Gulf of Khambat, the excavated area reveals a large dry dock as well as kilns and other work areas for a once-renowned manufacturing center. Archaeologists have also discovered signs of communication with sites on the Persian Gulf. The remains don't have the monumental grandeur of Dhola Vira, but the adjacent **Archeological Museum** displays a good selection of seals, tools, and artifacts from the site. *Free.* ⏲ *Sat.–Thurs. 9–5.*

Lodging

$$ ★ **Palace Utelia.** This family-run Heritage Hotel is on the edge of a small, picturesque village very close to Lothal and within day-tripping distance of the Velavadar Wildlife Sanctuary and Nalsarovar Bird Sanctuary. At press time, the hotel's large open rooms and verandas were being meticulously restored by local craftsmen using only traditional materials. Besides the excursions possible from here, the village itself is a major attraction, and the family's cordial relations with the villagers make it possible to receive an intimate welcome. The rooms, some with small balconies and some air-conditioned, are furnished with attractive old bedsteads, tables, and wardrobes. Meals, which include both local and Rajasthani specialties, are served buffet-style. ✉ *Village Utelia, Via Lothal Burkhi,, Ahmedabad district, 382230,* ☎ *2714/62222; or reserve through Utelia House, 9 Gandhi Bagh, Ahmedabad, 380006,* ☎ *79/656–9937,* FAX *79/644–5770. 20 rooms. Restaurant. No credit cards.*

Vadodara

14 *112 km (68 mi) south of Ahmedabad, 419 km (260 mi) north of Bombay*

Vadodara—commonly called Baroda—was until recently a laid-back garden city and college town on the banks of the Vishwamitri River. It's now a booming urban center with a population of just over a million people. The city dates back to the days of legend, and before Independence it was the capital of one of the largest and (with Mysore) best-administered princely states of the British period. Its ruler, called a Gaekwad, helped his people prosper and accumulated for himself a great many artistic treasures from all over India and the world. The city retains a pleasant and civic atmosphere, though much of its greenery has been overwhelmed by urban sprawl.

The **College of Fine Arts** at Maharaja Sayajirao University is known as the best in India, and its graduates include India's best-known contemporary painter, M. F. Husain. Many graduates stay in town, exhibiting their work at the **Nazar Arts Gallery** (☎ 265/322945). The university's **Archaeology Faculty** has a small display area with an excellent rendition of life and crafts in the ancient Indus Valley Civilization. The large park known as Sayaji Bagh, on University Road, contains the **Vadodara Museum and Art Gallery,** open daily 9:30–4:45, which has an excellent collection of Hindu and Jain sculpture as well as miniature paintings.

The former royal collection is housed in the **Maharaja Fateh Singh Museum** on the run-down grounds of the maharaja's palace. It includes a fine collection of works by the important 19th-century painter Raja Ravi Verma, as well as pictures attributed to Titian, Poussin, and Raphael. ✉ *Nehru Rd.,* ☎ *265/56372.* ⏲ *Tues.–Sun. 9–noon and 3–6.* 🎟 *Rs. 2.*

Better-maintained examples of the maharaja's architectural taste are the **Naya Mandir,** or Law Courts, and the **Kothi Building,** or Secretariat, both in the center of town. Both structures display the mixture of Mogul and Gothic elements common to the public works of British India. The **Kirti Mandir,** a memorial to the Gaekwad family, is decorated with murals painted by Nandalal Bose, a leader in the Bengal school of painting that launched contemporary art in India early in the 20th century. The **Makarpura Palace,** designed in an Indo-Italianate style, now houses a training school for the Indian Air Force; take an auto-rickshaw through the campus to get a glimpse of the grounds.

If you stay in Vadodara, you can make side trips to some truly out-of-the-way medieval sights. **Champaner,** 47 km (28 mi) northwest of Vadodara in the Girnar Hills, was an old Rajput and later Muslim capital; it's now an intriguing ghost town full of wonderful architecture. Preservation groups are working to spruce it up, but the place is not yet on many travelers' itineraries. Most of the buildings date from the 15th century and blend Muslim and Jain influences; a few Hindu temples date from as early as the 11th century. On the way back to Vadodara you can stop at **Pawagadh Fort,** just a few km outside Champaner, for an impressive view. The fort is mostly in ruins, but the Hindu and Jain temples here remain active pilgrimage centers. Overshooting Vadodara brings you to **Dabhoi Fort** (30 km, or 18 mi, southeast of town), built by the Raja of Patan in the 13th century. The fort's four ornate gates are early masterpieces of the Solank Rajput style. Nearby, the town's **Kali temple** also has beautiful carvings. Dabhoi is also home to the world's largest collection of steam locomotives. To make travel arrangements or change money in Vadodara, ask your hotel or contact **Narmada Travels** (✉ 19–21 Panorama, 2nd floor, R. C. Dutt Rd., ☎ 265/333941).

Lodging

$$$ 🏨 **Welcomgroup Vadodara.** This luxury hotel with relatively inexpensive rates is an excellent place to relax after the rigors of traveling. The restaurant Ruchika serves good North Indian Mughlai food; the Cascade features Western and Chinese dishes. There's also a 24-hour coffee shop. ✉ *R. C. Dutt Rd., Vadodara 390005,* ☎ *265/330033,* FAX *265/330050. 102 rooms. 2 restaurants, coffee shop, pool. AE, DC, MC, V.*

$ 🏨 **Aditi.** Well run and centrally air-conditioned, the Aditi is within walking distance of the university and a short auto-rickshaw ride from the train station and most of Vadodara's sights. The restaurant serves a range of North Indian and Gujarati dishes. ✉ *Opposite Sadar Patel Statue, Sayajigunj, Vadodara 390005,* ☎ *265/361188,* FAX *265/362257 (–59). 64 rooms. Restaurant. AE, DC, MC, V.*

GUJARAT A TO Z

Arriving and Departing

By Plane

Indian Airlines (☎ 79/550–3061, –2, or –3 in Ahmedabad, ☎ 2832/21433 in Kutch, ☎ 278/426503 on Kathiawar Peninsula) flies to Ahmedabad from Bombay, Delhi, Bangalore, and Madras. You can also fly to Vadodara from Bombay or Delhi. Four flights a week connect Bombay with Bhuj and Bhavnagar, and regular flights leave Bombay for Diu and Keshod (the nearest airport to Sasan Gir) as well. **Jet Airways** (✉ Madhuvan Complex, ground floor, Ellisbridge, Ahmedabad 380006, ☎ 79/656–1290 or 79/754–3304 [–10]) connects Ahmedabad with Delhi and Bombay, and Vadodara and Bhuj with Bombay. Contact your travel agent or the Government of India Tourist Office for the latest on other domestic carriers.

Ahmedabad Airport is 15 km (9 mi) from the city center. You'll find plenty of taxis, and a booth selling fixed-rate tickets for cab rides into town. The trip should cost roughly Rs. 150 to Rs. 200.

By Train

Ahmedabad and Vadodara are connected to Bombay, Delhi, and Rajasthan by good, fast trains, including the *Rajdhani Express.* The *Shatabdi Express,* an air-conditioned chair-car service, travels between Ahmedabad and Vadodara in 1½ hours every day except Friday. Bombay Central Station is 5½ hours beyond Vadodara on the Shatabdi. Because Gujarat was ruled separately from British India, by various local princes, its rail network has yet to be fully integrated into the Indian grid; many lines are on slow, meter-gauge tracks. If you want to travel from Ahmedabad to Bhuj, the *Bombay-Gandhidham Express, Delhi-Gandhidham Express,* and *Gandhidham-Vadodara Express* can bring you from Ahmedabad to Gandhidham in about six hours, and you can arrange to have your Bhuj hotel pick you up at Gandhidham for the two-hour drive into Bhuj. Tickets on the tourist quota are more easily obtained in Ahmedabad than in other Gujarati towns, as there is a separate line for tourists at the Ahmedabad Junction reservation counter.

Getting Around

By Auto-Rickshaw

It's not the most luxurious way to go, but in congested traffic, a savvy auto-rickshaw driver can reach your destination faster than a taxi or car. At press time, fares in Ahmedabad were about Rs. 1 per km, with a starting charge of about Rs. 4; but rates change as fuel prices increase, and fares are theoretically calculated by matching the meter amount to the adjusted rate on the driver's tariff card. If the driver refuses to show you the tariff card, either get another rickshaw or agree on a fare. Ask your hotel or a passerby what an appropriate fare would be.

Bicycle and auto-rickshaws can easily take you around Bhuj, and drivers here are not likely to overcharge.

By Car

With a car and driver at your disposal, you can move around without having to spar over fares. Rates for cars without air-conditioning start between Rs. 4 and Rs. 8 per km, usually with a minimum of 250 km per day and with additional charges for overnight stays and the driver's return trip. Arrange for a car and driver through a travel agency or tourist office. (Your hotel can arrange a car and driver for you, but hotels tend to charge more.)

By Foot

Traffic in Ahmedabad is chaotic. Lanes exist, but largely in theory. Getting around on foot in busy areas is tricky because there are no sidewalks to speak of, just dirt. Practice defensive pedestrianism: Traffic will hurtle toward you from every conceivable direction.

By Taxi

You can catch a taxi at the Ahmedabad or call one through your hotel. They're not plentiful, however, so if you prefer to get around by car it's easiest to hire a car and driver for the day.

By Train

A comfortable but expensive way to see Ahmedabad, Sasan Gir, Diu, and Palitana is on the *Royal Orient* luxury train recently launched by the Tourism Corporation of Gujarat. The train makes a seven-night round trip from Delhi, stopping for sights in both Rajasthan and Gujarat. Rates in season are $200 per person per night for a double-occupancy berth, $175 for triple occupancy.

Vadodara is two hours from Ahmedabad on the fast *Shatabdi Express* train. A slow train leaves Bhuj in the evening for Ahmedabad (16 hours), but more, faster trains connect with Gandhidham, about 50 km (30 mi) east of Bhuj.

Two express trains run daily between Bhavnagar and Ahmedabad, and there is slower service on the meter-gauge line between Palitana and Ahmedabad. The nearest train station to Diu is at Veraval, near Somnath, on the Gujarati mainland 90 km (50 mi) to the northwest. Overnight trains connect Ahmedabad with Veraval and Junagadh, and taxis outside the Junagadh station can take you the 60 km (37 mi) to Sasan Gir for about Rs. 500 if you haven't arranged to be picked up by your hotel.

Contacts and Resources

Currency Exchange

Nearly all hotels exchange foreign currency for their guests. You might get slightly better rates at state banks, but the hassle of waiting in line may defeat the purpose. Try a branch of the State Bank of India or the **Bank of Baroda** (✉ Ashram Rd., Ahmedabad, ☎ 79/656–1835), which is open weekdays 10 to 2 and Saturdays until noon. **Green Channel Travel Services** (✉ 576 Sun Complex, Navrangpura, Ahmedabad, ☎ 79/656–8457) can also change money.

Permits

To see Dhola Vira or the crafts villages north of Bhuj, you must have a permit listing the places you plan to visit and the points of any overnight stays. To get this permit, start with the **District Superintendent of Police** in Bhuj, off College Road; the office is open Monday to Saturday, 10:30 to 6. Bring photocopies of your passport's information page and your visa. The police will issue an application form, which you then take to the nearby **District Collector's Office,** open weekdays 10:30 to 1 and 2 to 6. Contact the tourism corporation (✉ Nigam Bhavan, Sector 16, Gandhinagar 382016, ☎ 2712/22645 or 22523, FAX 2712/22189) for an update.

Travel Agencies

If you need help with travel arrangements or hiring a car and driver, contact one of these agencies in Ahmedabad. **Alka Travel Service** (✉ Ashish Complex, C. G. Rd., near Swastik Cross Rd., ☎ 79/642–1197). **Green Channel Travel Services** (✉ 576 Sun Complex, Navrangpura, ☎ 79/656–8457). **Travel Corporation of India** (✉ Ashram Rd., behind Handloom House, ☎ 79/658–7601, –2, or –3).

Visitor Information

Tourism Corporation of Gujarat, Ltd. (✉ H. K. House, Ashram Rd., Ahmedabad, ☎ 79/658–9683 or 79/6589172 or 79/6587217, FAX 79/658–2183), the state government tourist office, provides information, organizes sightseeing tours, and arranges car-and-driver hire.

The tourist office in **Kutch** (✉ Aina Mahal, Bhuj, ☎ 2832/20004) gives excellent advice on Kutchi sights and history and can arrange for a guide and/or driver. It's open Sunday to Friday 9 to noon and 3 to 6. **Raysinhji Rathod** (✉ 7/A Shakti Nagar/B, Bhuj, Kutch 37001, ☎ 2832/22187) is a self-taught guide whose experience of Kutch's landscape, culture, and monuments stems from years of exploration here.

In Diu, the **Union Territory's Office of Tourism, Information, and Publicity** (✉ Marine House, Bunder Rd., ☎ 28758/52653) is near the market square.

7 BOMBAY AND THE AJANTA AND ELLORA CAVES

Bombay is urbane, stylish, and as hip as India gets. Curving dramatically around the Arabian Sea, this giant metropolis crackles with local color, international commerce, and the glamour of its enormous film industry. But behind its East-West exterior, Bombay remains exuberantly Indian, its streets packed with traffic of every kind. Northwest of the city, the spectacular 2,000-year-old cave temples of Ajanta and Ellora span three religions: Buddhism, Hinduism, and Jainism.

By Julie Tomasz and Vaihayasi Pande Daniel

RAZZLE-DAZZLE INDIAN-STYLE—that's Bombay, the country's seaside financial capital and trendsetting East-West nexus. India's greatest port, the capital of Maharashtra sits on the Arabian Sea, covering an island separated from the rest of India by a winding creek. A world unto itself, Bombay hits you with an intensity all its own. It's distinctly tropical, with pockets of palm trees and warm, salty breezes; and its culture is contemporary, vibrant, and often aggressive, reflecting the affluence—and lack thereof—of a crowded 10 million people. Behind all this, weathered Victorian mansions, some still privately owned, and grand public buildings, many beautifully lit at night, stand as lingering reminders of the British Raj.

Following the 1995 election in Maharashtra of the extreme right-wing regionalist party Shiv Sena, Bombay's name was officially changed to Mumbai, after Mumba Devi, the patron Hindu goddess of the island's original residents, the Koli fishermen. Because of the political overtones of this name change, however, many residents continue to call their city Bombay. It's all rather confusing, but in many ways this is but another chapter in the city's labyrinthine history.

Bombay initially consisted of seven marshy islands—probably Colaba, Old Woman's Island, Bombay, Mazgaon, Worli, Mahim, Parel—belonging to the Muslim kings of the Gujarat sultanate. The Muslims passed the parcel to the Portuguese (who occupied much of western India in the 16th and 17th centuries), who in turn passed it in 1661 to England's King Charles II as part of a dowry in his marriage to the Portuguese Princess Catherine de Braganza. The British established a fort and trading post that grew quickly in size and strength.

Soon enough, land reclamation joined the seven small islands into one, grafting a prototype for today's multifarious metropolis. The pride of the British in Bombay, and in their power over western India, is memorialized in the city's most celebrated landmark, near a statue of the young 17th-century Marathi leader Shivaji: the Gateway of India, built to welcome King George V to India in 1911.

The Bombay you see today is a city of mind-boggling contrasts: sometimes exciting, sometimes deeply disturbing. As your plane descends toward the runway, usually late at night, your first view of Bombay takes in vast stretches of slums, stacked and piled onto each other like cardboard boxes—only a fleeting glimpse of the staggering poverty that coexists with the dazzling wealth flashed in trendy boutiques and deluxe hotels. In the neighborhoods of Churchgate or Nariman Point, Bombay's slick hotel and business centers, a fleet of dark-suited executives may breeze by on their way to a meeting while a naked little girl with matted hair scavenges in the gutter beneath them. Bombay is a city, a journalist once pointed out, where the servant walking the pedigreed, handsomely groomed dog has no formal education but his charge has been to an expensive training school.

For the fortunate traveler, Bombay is both disturbingly eye-opening and incredibly exciting. Here in the heady sun and breeze of the Arabian Sea you can feast in fabulous restaurants, bargain in street bazaars, browse in exclusive boutiques, take a horse-drawn ride past stately old Victorian buildings, get lost in the stone carvings of the 7th-century Elephanta Caves, watch the sun rise over the Gateway of India, and stroll at sunset along Marine Drive's endless waterfront promenade.

Pleasures and Pastimes

Dining

Bombay is known for its chic restaurants and Western-style pubs. You can expect great meals and a wide choice of cuisines—Continental, Chinese, Italian, Thai, and Mexican—in addition to numerous regional Indian styles. You may also encounter some Jain fare, cooked without onions, garlic, and other ingredients banned for religious reasons. Many restaurants are pricey by Indian standards, but some tasty bargains will leave you and your wallet equally satisfied.

Many hotels have good restaurants and all-night coffee shops that serve full meals. Although popular with foreigners, buffet meals can be risky if the food has been sitting out too long; if you're a buffet diner, just make sure the food you select is steaming-hot and well cooked.

Lodging

Both Bombay and Aurangabad (base of operations for the Ajanta and Ellora caves) have hotels ranging from the skid-row to the palatial. Here, unlike elsewhere in India, even mid-range hotels can cost a pretty rupee. The Taj and Oberoi chains run several massive lodgings, most of them deluxe, catering to leisure travelers, business travelers, and movie stars with money to burn. If you reserve with a hotel directly, rather than through a travel agent, ask for a discount.

Bombay's cheaper hotels are often decent, offering good value for the money. During the monsoon season, from mid-June through late September, these hotels are overrun by large groups of vacationers from various Arab nations, during which time noise levels can be very high and solo women travelers should probably stay elsewhere.

Unless otherwise indicated, hotels have room service, doctors on call, and currency exchange, and rooms have cable TVs and private bathrooms. Many luxury hotels also have exclusive floors with special privileges or facilities for the business traveler.

EXPLORING BOMBAY

There's plenty to see in Bombay, but not generally in the form of stationary monuments like those in London, Paris, or even Delhi. The art of experiencing Bombay lies in eating, shopping, and wandering through strikingly different neighborhoods and markets, immersing yourself in the city's pulsing life and soaking up the intangible essences that blend and clash to make Bombay utterly unique. This city is essentially a 30-mile-long open-air bazaar.

Churchgate and Nariman Point are the business and hotel centers, with major bank and airline headquarters clustered in skyscrapers on Nariman Point. The district referred to as Fort—which includes Bombay's hub, Flora Fountain, in a square now called Hutatma Chowk—is the city's commercial heart, its narrow, bustling streets lined with small shops and office buildings, as well as a number of colleges and other educational facilities. Farther north, Kemps Corner is a trendy area with expensive boutiques, exclusive restaurants, and high-priced homes. Another upscale residential neighborhood, Malabar Hill, is older—leafy, breezy, and lovely, with fine, old stone mansions housing wealthy industrialists and government ministers.

Shopping and people-watching are most colorfully combined in Bombay's chaotic bazaar areas, such as Chor Bazaar, Zaveri (Jewelry) Bazaar, and Mahatma Jyotiba Phule (Crawford) Market. More recently, Bombay's suburbs have seen explosive business and residential development, as more and more people move out of Bombay center to escape its soaring real-estate prices and simple lack of space. Many of the city's newest and trendiest shops and restaurants are out here. A number of travelers opt to stay in Juhu Beach, a popular coastal suburb between Bombay and the airports (about 20 km [12 mi] north of the city center). Alas, Juhu's beaches are polluted and unsafe for swimming, and the general look of the place is scruffy and honky-tonk, but staying out here is a nice way to observe everyday Indian life outside the shadow of Bombay's skyline. Sunday nights bring families down to the beach for an old-fashioned carnival, complete with small, hand-powered Ferris wheels and lantern-lit snack stalls hawking sugar cane.

Great Itineraries

India's most cosmopolitan city gives way to a rugged interior that hides the spectacular Ajanta and Ellora caves, 370 km (229 mi) northeast of Bombay. Maharashtra's landscape fuses stark, semi-arid mountains and rock formations with lush, green countryside and virgin beaches. To see this state well, you should really spend the better part of a week here.

Numbers in the text correspond to numbers in the margin and on the Bombay, Ajanta Caves, Ellora Caves, and Maharashtra Beaches maps.

IF YOU HAVE 2 DAYS

On your first day, wander around Bombay's **Fort** district, home to the city's museums and such trappings of the British Raj as the stone Gateway of India. Spend the next morning at the **Elephanta Caves,** an hour's ferry ride away: Although not as spectacular as those at Ajanta and Ellora, these 7th-century cave temples are much more accessible for those with little time in Bombay. That afternoon, take a taxi to **Malabar Hill** and spend some time exploring Kamala Nehru Park, the Jain Temple, Banganga, Babulnath Temple, and Gandhi's former home, Mani Bhavan.

IF YOU HAVE 4 DAYS

Follow the 2-day itinerary. On your third day, visit the **Haji Ali Shrine,** a mosque set on a rocky jetty in the Arabian Sea; then drive outside the city center to the South Indian enclave of **Matunga,** where (every day but Monday) an array of temples, bazaars, and casual restaurants will more than eat up the lunch hour. Devote this afternoon to a walk around **Colaba.** On your fourth day, go shopping—hit the bazaars, craft emporiums, shops, and boutiques in earnest—and/or take an adventurous tour of Bombay's old **synagogues.**

IF YOU HAVE 7 DAYS

Follow the four-day itinerary, then hire a car or join a bus tour down the coast to the **Maharashtra beaches.** These are remote and beautiful, with only rudimentary development; spend two nights at one of the area's comfortable resorts before returning to Bombay.

When to Tour Bombay

Maharashtra is best explored between November and February, when the weather is warm but not unbearable and the monsoons are absent. Ajanta and Ellora explode with life during and after the monsoon season, if the rains have been good; at Ajanta, a river springs into being at the bottom of the gorge into which the caves are cut. If the rains *haven't* been good, it can be quite hot.

Fort District and Environs

The most manageable, and probably the most colorful, walks in Bombay center on the Fort district. If this is your first experience of India, as well as Bombay, remember that sightseeing here is nothing like sightseeing in, say, Europe—the streets are crowded, some lack sidewalks, traffic takes many forms, crosswalks are a rarity, and people may stare or call out to you with sales pitches as you pass. Stopping to take a picture can make you feel terribly conspicuous. You'll get used to it soon enough, and learn to revel in the whole *masala* whirlwind.

A Good Walk

Start your walk by exploring the **Mahatma Jyotiba Phule Market** ①, commonly known as Crawford Market, and the surrounding lanes. Abdul Rehman Street will take you north into **Zaveri Bazaar** ②. At all bazaars, be sure to keep your eyes and hands on your wallet. From Crawford or Zaveri you can either head south to the main Fort district or, if you're up for more narrow-lane navigation, detour to Chor Bazaar, a bustling old antiques market.

To find **Chor Bazaar** ③, walk or cab it (15 minutes by taxi) north from Crawford Market on Mohamed Ali Road, which joins Rahimtulla Road to bring you into South Bombay's main Muslim quarter. After passing the Beg Muhammed School, Mandavi Telephone Exchange, and Mandavi post office on the left, you'll hit Sardar Vallabhbhai Patel Road: Turn left and you can enter Chor Bazaar on Mutton Street. When you're almost bazaared out, retrace the route back down to Crawford Market, either on foot or by taxi.

To move south toward the center of the Fort district, follow A. Rehman Street until it becomes Dr. D. Naoroji Road: You are now in the heart of downtown, an area of broader streets and crowded sidewalks. On your right is the imposing, V-shaped, early-Gothic-style Municipal Corporation Building, vintage 1893, with Indian motifs and a large dome; on your left is Bombay's chief train station, the huge **Chhatrapati Shivaji Terminus,** also called by its old name, Victoria Terminus. Push your way through the crowds of people and cars to cross the chaotic roundabout; rejoin Dr. D. Naoroji Road on the other side, and continue heading south. After about fifteen minutes you'll arrive at the **Flora Fountain** ④, the true center of Bombay.

Take a right here onto Veer Nariman Road, pass the Central Telegraph office and its open-air book bazaars, and in a few minutes you'll hit K. B. Patil Marg. Turn left, keep heading south, and on your left you'll see the High Court, built in the early Gothic style in 1878. Farther south on the same street you'll see Bombay University's 260-ft Rajabhai Clocktower, also Victorian Gothic. Turn left onto Mahatma Gandhi Road (also known as M. G. Rd.) and you'll soon reach a cluster of three major museums. The **Jehangir Art Gallery** ⑤ will be on your left. Across the street from Jehangir, in the lane heading behind the music store Rhythm House, is the Keneseth Eliyahoo Synagogue (☞ Off the Beaten Path, *below*). From Mahatma Gandhi Road, hang a left down K. Dubash Marg to the **Prince of Wales Museum** ⑥. The **National Gallery of Modern Art** ⑦ is across the street. From here, take C. Shivaji Maharaj Marg to the **Gateway of India** ⑧, where you can relax among locals at the water's edge.

Right across the square from the Gateway of India is the historic Taj Mahal hotel (☞ Lodging, *below*). Even if you can't afford to stay here, it's a treat just to walk around the lobby and shopping areas (they don't mind) and perhaps have an Indian meal at the Tanjore restaurant or Sea Lounge coffee shop.

TIMING

This walk takes a full day: The going is relatively slow, the bazaars eat up time in a stealthy manner, and you'll probably want to spend close

Babulnath Temple, **13**
Banganga, **12**
Chor Bazaar, **3**
Flora Fountain, **4**
Gateway of India, **8**
Haji Ali Shrine, **9**
Jain Temple, **11**
Jehangir Art Gallery, **5**
Kamala Nehru Park, **10**
Mahatma Jyotiba Phule Market, **1**
Mani Bhavan, **14**
National Gallery of Modern Art, **7**
Prince of Wales Museum, **6**
Zaveri Bazaar, **2**

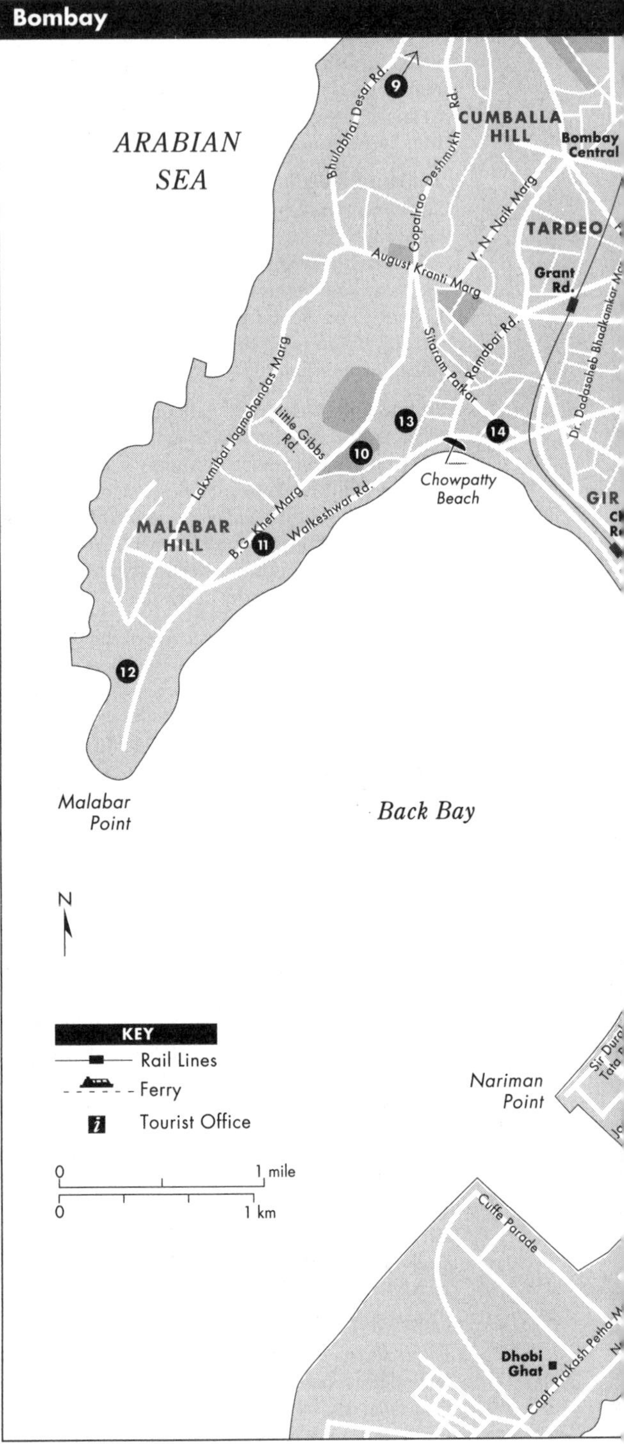

Byculla
Sant Savta Marg
Reay Rd.
Boatyard Rd.
Dr. Anandrao Nair Rd.
Mohd Shahid Marg
Maulana Azad Rd.
Dr. Mascarenhas Rd.
Dr. Motishah Rd.
BOMBAY CENTRAL
Sir Jamshedji Jijibhoy Rd.
Mirza Galib Marg
MAZAGAON
Jehangir Boman Behram Marg
Marg
Dockyard Rd.
R. S. Nimbkar Rd.
Dimtimkar Rd.
Dockyard Rd.
KAMATIPURA
Wadi Bunder Rd.
Ramchandra Bhatt Marg
Maulana Shaukatali Rd.
KHARA TALAO
Sandhurst Rd.
ETWADI
Jail Rd.
Jail Rd. (East)
Rahimtulla Rd.
Ibrahim Mohamed Ali Rd.
Malet Rd.
UMERKHADI
Cawasji Patel Tank Rd.
MANDVI
Keshavji Naik Rd.
BHULESHWAR
Manson Rd.
Babasaheb Jaykar
Bhuleshwar Rd.
Yusuf Meherali Rd.
KALBADEVI
Masjid
A. Rehman St.
N. Natha St.
Jagannath Shankarshet Rd.
Kalbadevi Rd.
S. Gandhi Marg
PYDHUNI
P. D'Mello Rd.
K. Sharma St.
Lokmanya Tilak Rd.
Cross Island
Marine Lines
Polton Rd.
Police
Dr. D. Naoroji Rd.
A. Poddar Marg
Netaji Subhash Rd.
Municipal Corporation Building
Chhatrapati Shivaji Terminus
TO ELEPHANTA CAVES
Mahatma Gandhi Rd.
General Post Office
Marine Drive
Sahid Bhagat Singh Marg
Churchgate Station
Shoorji Vallabhdas Marg
Veer Nariman Rd.
Dr. D. Naoroji Rd.
Jamshetji Tata Rd.
Maidan
Patil Marg
High Court
FORT
M. Gandhi Rd.
Rajabhai Clocktower
Custom Basin
Madam Cama Rd.
K. Dubash Marg
Maharshi Karve Rd.
Oval Maidan
Cooperage Maidan
Bhaurao
C. Shivaji Maharaj Marg
Free Press Journal Rd.
Maharshi Bhonsale Marg
Nathalal Parekh Marg
Taj Mahal Hotel
COLABA
Gen. Jagannathrao Bhonsale Marg
Shahid Bhagat Singh Marg (Colaba Causeway)
Mereweather Rd.
P. J. Ramchandani Marg
A. Bunder Rd.
Middle Ground
Sassoon Dock

to an hour at both the Prince of Wales Museum and the Jehangir Art Gallery. Note that Crawford Market is closed Sunday, the Prince of Wales Museum is closed Monday, and Chor Bazaar shuts down on Friday. Early morning tends to be less humid, so you may want to set off then.

Sights to See

Chhatrapati Shivaji Terminus. Built by the British in 1888 at an supposed cost of £300,000, this is one of Bombay's busiest train stations, overflowing at rush hour with enormous, surging, scurrying crowds. Formerly called Victoria Terminus, and bearing a hefty statue of Queen Victoria on its imposing dome, the haughty structure combines Indian and Victorian Gothic architecture for an Eastern version of London's St. Pancras station. ✉ *D. Naoroji Rd.*

3 **Chor Bazaar.** With a colorful name meaning "Thieves' Bazaar," this narrow thoroughfare is lined with stores crammed with both antiques and general bric-a-brac—clocks, old phonographs, brassware, glassware, and statues. Over the years the value of much of this stock has dwindled, but there's still a chance that you'll find some unusual, memorable piece. Haggle. In the same lane a number of shops are engaged in the profitable business of constructing new furniture that looks old; many will openly tell you as much. Some shops do stock genuine antique furniture from old Parsi homes. ✉ *Mutton St., off Sardar Vallabhbhai Patel Rd.* ⏲ *Sat.–Thurs. 11–7.*

4 **Flora Fountain.** Standing tall in the middle of a major five-way intersection, this fountain marks the heart of Fort. The ornately sculpted stone fountain was created as a memorial to one of Bombay's early governors, Sir Bartle Frere, who was responsible for urban planning in the 1860s. The square in which it stands is called Hutatma Chowk (Martyr's Square) in honor of those who died in the violence surrounding the establishment of Maharashtra in the 1960s (the Bombay Presidency was split into the states of Maharashtra and Gujarat). It's a hot spot for rallies, political and otherwise. ✉ *M. G. Rd. at Veer Nariman Rd.*

★ 8 **Gateway of India.** Bombay's signature landmark, this elegant 85-ft stone archway was hastily erected as a symbol of welcome to Queen Mary and King George V of England when they paid a visit to India in 1911. In the years following, artisans added decorative carvings and lovely *jharoka* work (window carvings), finishing in 1923. Less than 25 years later, the last British troops departed India through the same ceremonial arch. The monument serves as a launching point for boats going to Elephanta Island; this is also where the *Queen Elizabeth* 2 and other luxury liners dock on their cruises. The majestic Taj Mahal hotel, built before the Gateway of India, in 1903, now stands just behind it. ✉ *Peninsula at end of C. Shivaji Maharaj Marg.*

OFF THE BEATEN PATH

COLABA Bombay's budget-tourist district is often packed with vacationing Arabs in the rainy season and Western backpackers in the winter. Cheap boarding houses, handicraft stalls, and eating places stand cheek-by-jowl on the tip of Bombay's peninsula.

One of Colaba's most interesting sights is its fishing dock, built back in 1875. Extraordinarily smelly, mucky, and noisy, **Sassoon Dock** must be seen at dawn, when most of Bombay's seafood catch is unloaded. Piles of pink prawns are sorted, and grisly-looking fish are topped and tailed. The odor is severe, but you won't see this kind of chaos and five-sensory color anywhere else in the world. Out toward the ocean, Bombay duck, a fish peculiar to this coastline, dries on endless racks in the sun.

Walk north toward Navy Nagar (the naval cantonment area) on Shahid Bhagat Singh Marg for about 10 minutes. Just beyond Colaba Post Office is the old **Afghan Memorial Church of St. John the Baptist.** Rather out of place in the heart of Colaba, this somewhat imposing structure honors British soldiers lost in the Afghan wars of the late 19th century. The plaques inside say things like, "In the memory of Captain Conville Warneford of the Bombay Political Dept and the Gurkha Rifles who was born 13th October 1871 and was treacherously murdered by an Arab at Amrija in the Aden hinterland. . . ."

From the church, retrace your steps on Shahid Bhagat Singh as far as the fork outside Colaba Post Office; take Wodehouse Road to Panday Road, then turn left and you'll see Capt. Prakash Petha Marg. Turn left again, walk for five minutes (past the Taj President hotel), and just beyond the Colaba Woods park on your right is a **Dhobi Ghat,** behind a facade of huts. (If you get lost, just ask a local for help.) Another fascinating open-air sight, the *ghat* consists of a square half-kilometer of cement stalls where *dhobis,* or washermen, pound their garments to what seems like pulp to get them threadbare-clean. Rows of racks flutter with drying laundry, and in little huts nearby the incorrigibly dirty stuff is boiled with caustic soda. ✉ *Sassoon Dock: Shahid Bhagat Singh Marg, near Colaba Bus Station; Dhobi Ghat: Cuffe Parade, Colaba.*

5 **Jehangir Art Gallery.** Bombay's chief contemporary-art gallery hosts changing exhibits of well-known Indian artists. Some of the work is lovely, and all of it is interesting for its cultural perspective. There's plenty of art outside as well—the plaza in front of the building is full of artists offering their works for sale and their talents for commission assignments. ✉ *M. G. Rd., Fort,* ☎ *22/284–3989.* *Free.* ⏲ *Daily 11–7.*

NEED A BREAK?

Cafe Samovar (✉ M. G. Rd., Fort, ☎ 22/284–8000), next to a bit of courtyard greenery in the Jehangir Art Gallery, is a popular, arty place for a quick snack or a glass of lime juice.

★ 6 **Mahatma Jyotiba Phule Market.** Also known by its former name, Crawford Market, this building was designed in the 1860s by John Lockwood Kipling, father of Rudyard—who was born in this very neighborhood. Check out the stone relief depicting workers on the outside; the market's stone flooring supposedly came from Caithness. Come here early one morning for the most colorful walk through Bombay's fresh-produce emporium, and if it's late spring or early summer, treat yourself to a delicious Alphonso mango, a food fit for the gods. The meat section can be a bit hair-raising. Across the street from the market's main entrance, spread across a trio of lanes, is the popular bazaar area Lohar Chawl, where the selection ranges from plastic flowers to refrigerators. Farther up the middle lane, Sheikh Memon Street, is the chaotic **Mangaldas Market** (closed Sunday), a covered, wholesale cloth market with a tremendous variety of fabrics at hundreds of indoor stalls. ✉ *D. Naoroji Rd. at L. Tilak Rd.* ⏲ *Mon.–Sat. 11–8.*

NEED A BREAK?

Rajdhani (✉ Sheikh Memon St., ☎ 22/342–6919) serves up hot, hygienic Gujarati and Rajasthani *thalis* (combination platters; Rs. 160) from 11 to 3:30 in spartan but clean surroundings near Crawford Market. Eat sparingly so you don't live to regret the meal; the restaurant uses a lot of ghee, or clarified butter, in its preparations.

7 **National Gallery of Modern Art.** This museum is housed in a circular building resembling New York's Guggenheim Museum. Modern Indian art is displayed in an uncrowded, easy manner on four floors. It's

not as spectacular as the Prince of Wales Museum (across the street), but it's worth a visit for art lovers. ✉ *M. G. Rd.,* ☎ *22/285–2457 or 22/204–4285.* *Rs. 5.* ⏲ *Tues.–Sun. 11–6.*

❻ **Prince of Wales Museum.** Topped with Moorish domes, Bombay's finest Victorian building and principal museum was completed in 1911 and named for King George V, who laid the cornerstone in 1905. It's divided into three sections: art, archaeology, and natural history. The picture gallery contains scores of Mogul and Rajput miniature paintings, works by European and contemporary Indian artists, and copies of magnificent cave temple paintings from Ajanta. ✉ *M. G. Rd.,* ☎ *22/284–4519 or 22/284–4484.* *Rs. 5.* ⏲ *Tues.–Sun. 10:15–6.*

❷ **Zaveri Bazaar.** Zaveri and Dagina bazaars, a little beyond Fort in Kalbadevi, are Bombay's crowded, century-old jewelry markets, where the shops are filled with fabulous gold and silver in every conceivable design. At the end of Zaveri Bazaar is the **Mumbadevi Temple,** a noisy, busy structure that houses the mouthless but powerful patron goddess for which Mumbai is named. In front of the temple is the *khara kuan,* or salt-water well, actually an age-old water station funded by the jewelry bazaar. Free water is doled out to the thirsty from giant copper drums. One of the lanes leading off Zaveri Bazaar is called Khao Galli (literally "Eat Lane"), as its endless food stalls feed most of the bazaar workers daily. ✉ *Sheikh Memon St.* ⏲ *Mon.–Sat. 11–7:30.*

OFF THE BEATEN PATH

SYNAGOGUES Jews were a prominent stream in Bombay's population until most of them migrated to Israel in the 1950s. Left behind is an assortment of synagogues, some in what seem like strange locales. None is striking by itself, but a tour of four gives you a rare peek into one of India's oldest communities. Hire a car or hail a taxi for this two- to three-hour excursion.

The most attractive structure is the old Baghdadi synagogue at the southern edge of Fort: The ornate, sky-blue **Keneseth Eliyahoo Synagogue** (✉ Forbes St., Kala Ghoda, Fort), across from Jehangir Art Gallery, has some interesting stained-glass windows and balconies. You can visit daily between 10 and 6:30, and you're welcome for Sabbath prayers between 6:30 and 7:30 on Friday.

A few miles north (beyond Crawford Market via P. D'Mello Road, past Carnac Bunder and near the Masjid train station), in the heart of the wholesale district, is the hard-to-find **Shaare Rahamim** (Gate of Mercy; ✉ 254 Samuel St., Masjid). This sleepy, mildly dilapidated synagogue seems totally out of place in its surroundings, which bustle with trucks, handcarts, and workers unloading sacks, boxes, and crates into scruffy warehouses. Tiny and relatively plain, the building is set apart from its drab neighbors by its traditional blue and cream colors. The synagogue is still in use, and you're free to peek inside.

At Jacob Circle, a 20-minute taxi ride north of Shaare Rahamim (✉ Khare Rd., past Chinchpokli station, near Shirin Talkies) is **Tiphaereth Israel Synagogue,** home of the Bene Israel Jews—a still-thriving Maharashtrian Jewish community. Tiny and shiny, this synagogue is charming; unlike Shaare Rahamin, it seems well loved and maintained. Have a chat with the slightly woozy caretaker, if he's around to take you inside.

The same caretaker can guide you to the **Magen Hassidim Synagogue,** a few streets away (✉ Morland Rd./Maulana Azad Rd., near Fancy Market and Jula Maidan, Agripada). Another Bene Israel shrine, this one is in the strongly Muslim area of Madanpura. The congregation and caretakers at this prosperous, well-attended shrine can lend insight into the future of this community: Magen Hassidim is the face of India's modern Jews, the ones who generally don't plan to migrate to Israel.

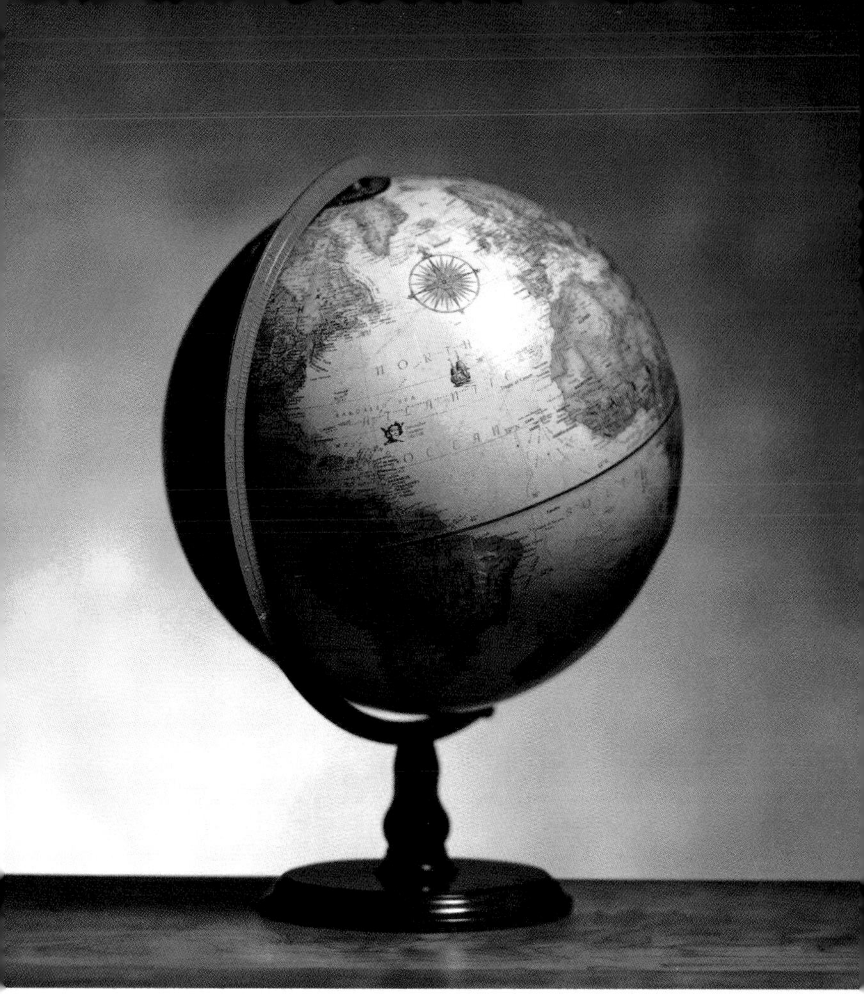

In case you want to see the world.

At American Express, we're here to make your journey a smooth one. So we have over 1,700 travel service locations in over 130 countries ready to help. What else would you expect from the world's largest travel agency?

do more 

Travel

Call 1 800 AXP-3429 or visit
www.americanexpress.com/travel

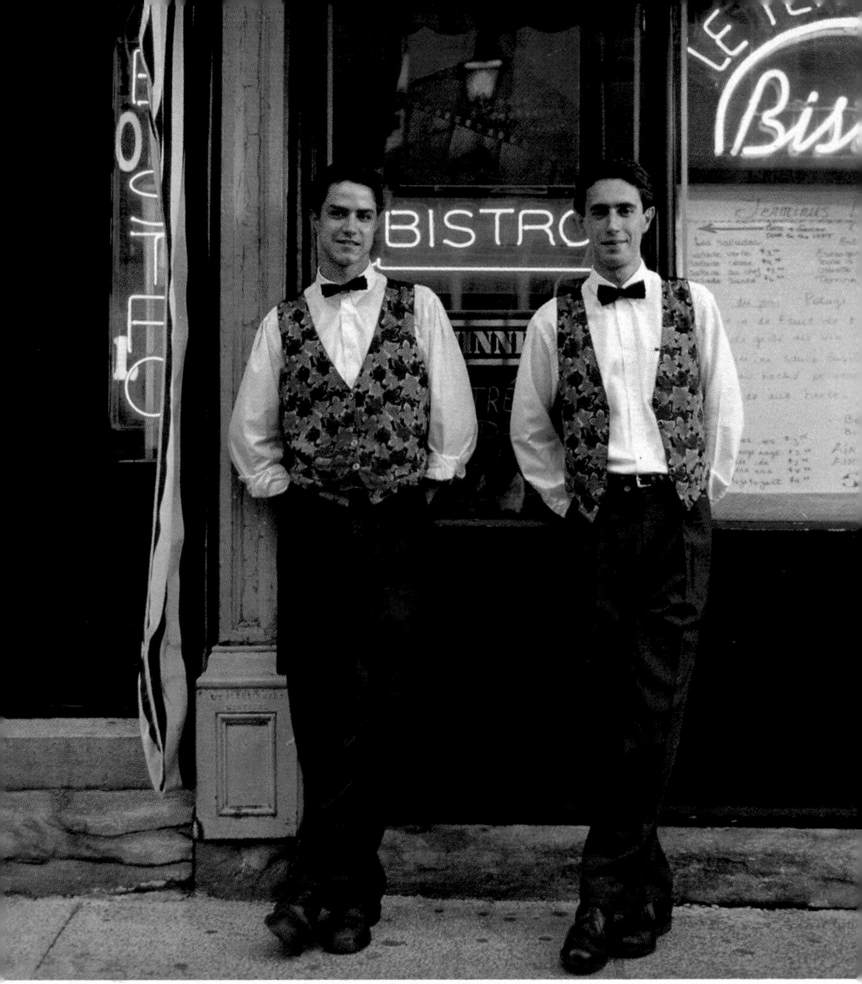

In case you want to be welcomed there.

We're here to see that you're always welcomed at establishments everywhere. That's why millions of people carry the American Express® Card – for peace of mind, confidence, and security, around the world or just around the corner.

do more 

Cards

**To apply, call 1 800 THE-CARD
or visit www.americanexpress.com**

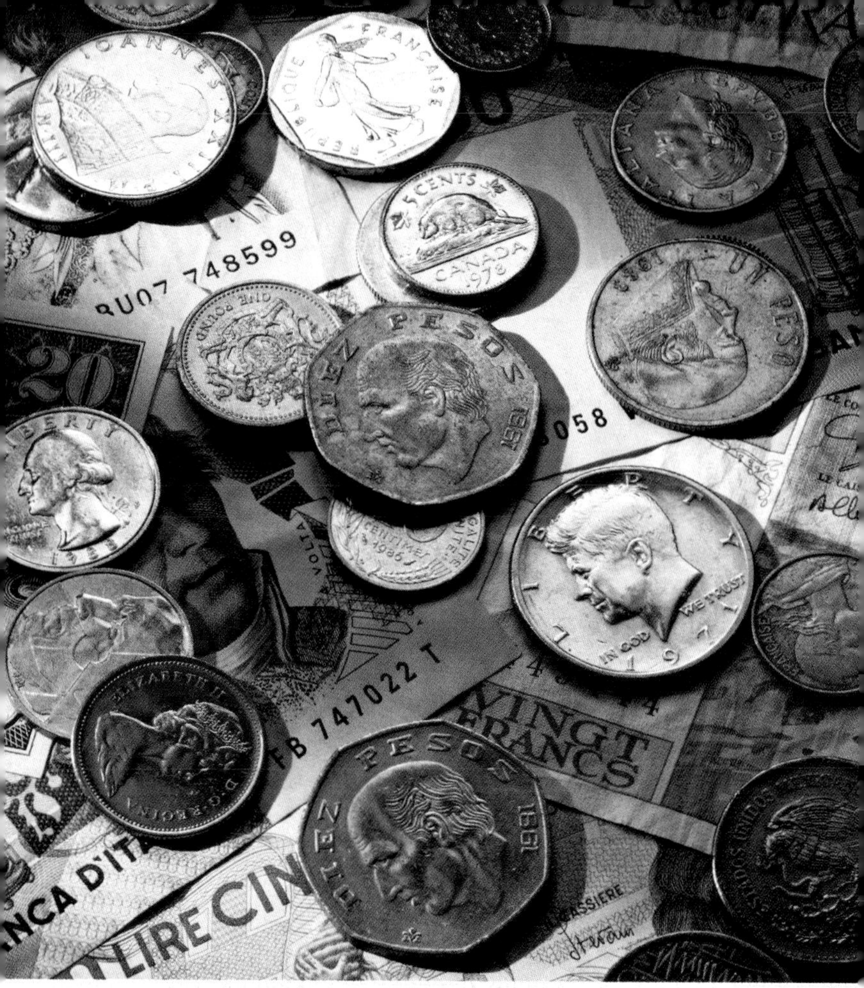

In case you're running low.

We're here to help with more than 190,000 Express Cash locations around the world. In order to enroll, just call American Express at 1 800 CASH-NOW before you start your vacation.

Express Cash

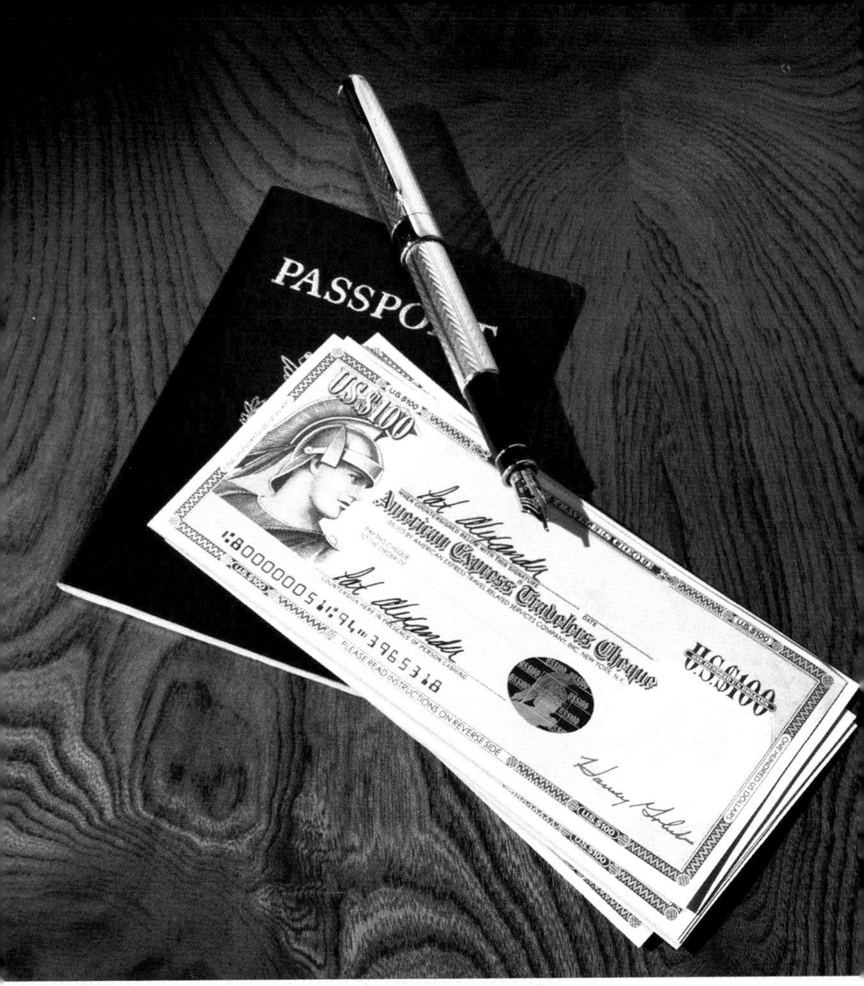

And in case you'd rather be safe than sorry.

We're here with American Express® Travelers Cheques. They're the safe way to carry money on your vacation, because if they're ever lost or stolen you can get a refund, practically anywhere or anytime. To find the nearest place to buy Travelers Cheques, call 1 800 495-1153. Another way we help you do more.

Travelers Cheques

©1999 American Express

Malabar Hill and Environs

Several of the attractions in this upscale residential area have stunning views of the city across Back Bay.

A Good Tour

After checking the tides, take a taxi to the **Haji Ali Shrine** ⑨, passing **Chowpatty Beach and Marine Drive** en route. At Haji Ali, have your taxi wait for you; then drive to **Kamala Nehru Park** ⑩, take some air, enjoy the views, and walk to the **Jain Temple** ⑪. From here you can either walk or take a taxi along Walkeshwar Road to the **Banganga** ⑫ area. Finally, have your taxi take you to **Babulnath Temple** ⑬ and Gandhi's former home, **Mani Bhavan** ⑭. If you're interested in South Indian culture and have some extra time, drive out to **Matunga.**

Sights to See

⑬ **Babulnath Temple** To get the flavor of a large traditional Indian temple, a visit to the Babulnath Temple is a must. Built at a height, this temple can be reached by climbing a few hundred steps and affords a panoramic view of south Bombay. The first Babulnath Temple was apparently built by Raja Bhimdev in the 13th century and named after the *babul* trees that forested this area. The architecture of this imposing shrine, one of Bombay's most important, is not remarkable, but it's interesting to watch the melée of worshipers coming, going, and milling about. Outside are rows of flower sellers hawking a temple-visitation kit—coconut plus flowers plus rock sugar—and a cluster of vendors concocting sweetmeats in *karhais* (large woks) in the open air. Temple authorities are sometimes sticky about allowing foreigners into its innermost areas, but it's worth a try. ✉ *Babulnath Rd..*

★ ⑫ **Banganga.** This undervisited temple complex in the Malabar Hill area is considered one of the city's holiest sites. It is also the oldest surviving structure in Bombay. The small, sometimes dilapidated temples are built around a holy pool of water and surrounded by the ever-encroaching houses of Bombay's newer residents. Cows and people mingle freely here, as do bathers who come to sample the healing powers of the water. ✉ *Walkeshwar Rd.* 🎫 *Free.*

★ **Chowpatty Beach and Marine Drive.** Chowpatty is not much of a beach in the resort sense, but this and the rest of Bombay's long, spectacular, perfectly curved Marine Drive capture at once the mammoth, cheeky, beautiful seaside beast that is Bombay. Chowpatty is a taste of the Bombay bazaar and *mela* (festival; hullabaloo) rolled into one. A hundred species of salesmen throng the sands in the evening, especially Sunday, selling everything from glow-in-the-dark yo-yos and animal-shaped balloons to rat poison. Men stand by with bathroom scales, offering complacent strollers a chance to check their heft. Hand-operated Ferris wheels and carousels are packed with children. Stalls distribute Bombay's own fast food—crunchy *bhelpuris* (puffed-rice snacks), *ragda pattices* (spicy potato cakes), and *paav bhaji* (fried vegetable mash eaten with bread). From the beach, walk east down Marine Drive toward Nariman Point and you'll bump into flotillas of evening exercisers, cooing couples wandering past the waves in a daze, and dogs and kids being walked by their respective nannies.

⑨ **Haji Ali Shrine.** Set far out on a thin, rocky jetty in the Arabian Sea, this striking white shrine was built in honor of the Muslim saint Haji Ali, who drowned here some 500 years ago on a pilgrimage to Mecca. When a coffin containing his mortal remains floated to rest on a rocky bed in the sea, devotees constructed the tomb and mosque to mark the spot. The shrine is reached by a long walkway just above the water, lined with destitute families and beggars ravaged by leprosy, some writhing, chanting, and (calling on the Muslim tradition of giving alms) perhaps beseeching you as you make your way down—a deeply discomfiting experience, but one that is unfortunately quintessentially Bombay. Inside, the shrine is full of colored-mirror mosaics and crowded with worshippers praying over the casket, which is covered with wilted flower garlands. Men and women must enter through separate doorways. ✉ *Off Lala Lajpatrai Marg, near Mahalaxmi Race Course, Breach Candy. Approachable only at low tide.*

⓫ **Jain Temple.** This may be the most impressive temple in Bombay. Belonging to the prosperous, strictly vegetarian Jain community—the largely Gujarati followers of Lord Mahavira—its colorful but attractive and peaceful interiors have a certain understated elegance. Check out the intricate work on the walls and ceilings. Worship at this shrine takes a somewhat different form than the *hungama,* or chaos, at Hindu temples; it's muted, less robust, more introspective and humble in aspect. Around 8 AM, freshly bathed Jains in swaths of unstitched off-white cloth, walk here barefoot from their nearby homes to pay homage to the splendid idol of Adinath, an important prophet. If you arrive just before noon, you'll see Jain housewives completing their morning prayers while a fragrant community lunch is prepared next door. ✉ *B. G. Kher Marg, Teen Batti, near Walkeshwar.*

❿ **Kamala Nehru Park.** On the eastern side of the top of lovely Malabar Hill, this small, unpretentious park is primarily a children's playground (kids look especially cute popping out of the "Old Woman Who Lived in a Shoe" boot), but it offers gorgeous panoramic views of the city below. From the special viewpoint clearing, you can see all of Marine Drive and the Bombay skyline, from Chowpatty Beach to Colaba Point. Try to come up after dark to see why Marine Drive, sparkling with lights, is known as the Queen's Necklace. Just across the road, another park, the **Hanging Gardens,** has pleasant views as well. A few minutes north of here are the **Towers of Silence,** where Bombay's Parsi community—followers of the Zoroastrian faith—dispose of their dead. Pallbearers carry the corpse to the top of one of the towering cylindrical bastions, where it is left to be devoured by vultures and crows (a roughly 2-hr process) and decomposed by the elements. None of this is visible to would-be onlookers, even relatives, and high walls prevent any furtive peeping. ✉ *B. G. Kher Marg.* ⏲ *Daily 6 AM–9 PM.*

★ ⓮ **Mani Bhavan.** This charming, three-story Gujarati house, painted brown and yellow and ensconced in a quiet, tree-shaded Parsi neighborhood on Malabar Hill, was the home of Mahatma Gandhi from 1917 to 1934. Now overseen and maintained by the Gandhi Institute, it houses a library and a small museum on Gandhi's life and work. Gandhi's simple belongings are displayed in his room, including his original copies of the Bible, the Koran, and the *Bhagavad Gita*; other displays include colorful dioramas and some important and moving letters from the fight for Indian independence. ✉ *19 Laburnam Rd.,* ☎ *22/380–5864.* 🎟 *Rs. 3.* ⏲ *Daily 9:30–6.*

Matunga. About 30 minutes west of Bombay's business district, this suburb is home to a sizable chunk of the city's South Indian population. A little bit of Madras up north, it even has a few South Indian temples complete with distinctive *gopurams* (towers), like the **Asthika Samaj Temple** on Bhandarkar Road. Bazaars and shops sell banana leaves, Kanchipuram saris, and typical South Indian vegetables, flowers, and pickles (bottled relishes); nearby eating houses serve clean, simple South Indian thali lunches on banana leaves or hot crispy *dosas* (lentil pancakes). **Shree Sunders** (☎ 22/416–9216) is known for its large variety of dosas. The legendary banana-leaf-lunch provider **A Ra-**

manayak Udipi Shri Krishna Boarding (☏ 22/414–2422; no dinner) is near the train station. Matunga's shops and restaurants are closed on Monday. ✉ *Telang Rd., near Matunga Central Railway Station.*

Side Trip: Elephanta Caves

★ *9 nautical mi from Gateway of India*

Exactly who carved these 7th-century cave temples on Elephanta Island is not known. We do know that the island was originally called Gharapuri; the Portuguese renamed it Elephanta after they found a large stone elephant near their landing place. (The figure collapsed in 1814 and was subsequently moved to the far-off Victoria Gardens and reassembled.) Shortly before these temples were created, Bombay had experienced the golden age of the late Guptas, under whom the talents of artists had free range. Sanskrit had been finely polished, and under the court's liberal patronage, Kalidasa and other writers had helped incite a revival of Hindu beliefs. It was Shivaism, or the worship of Shiva, that inspired the building of these temples.

The outside of the main cave consists of a columned veranda 30 ft wide and 6 ft deep, which you approach on steps flanked by sculptured elephants. The entire temple, carved out of the basalt hillside, is 130 ft square. The principle sculptures are on the southern wall at the back. The central recess in the hall contains the most outstanding sculpture, the unusual Mahesamurti, the Great Lord Shiva—an 18-ft triple image. Its three faces represent three aspects of Shiva: the creator (on the right), the preserver (in the center), and the destroyer (on the left).

Other sculptures near the doorways and on side panels show Shiva's usefulness. Shiva brought the Ganges River down to Earth, the story says, letting it trickle through his matted hair. He is also depicted as Yogisvara, lord of Yogis, seated on a lotus, and as Nataraja, the many-armed cosmic dancer. The beauty of this stonework lies in the grace, balance, and sense of peace conveyed in spite of the subject's multiple actions.

In winter the Maharashtra Tourism Development Corporation (MTDC) organizes a top-notch dance festival in this memorable setting. The island itself is quiet and picturesque, with light-green foliage and monkeys scampering about. The MTDC (☞ Visitor Information *in* Bombay A to Z, *below*) leads an excellent daily tour and runs a tiny restaurant on the island for refreshments and beer. ✉ *Motor launches (1 hr each way) depart daily every half hour, 9–2:30 from Gateway of India and 1–5 from Elephanta Island, unless sea is very choppy.* 🎫 *Round-trip fare Rs. 70; caves 50 paise.*

DINING

$$$$ ✕ **Biscotti.** Bombay's hippest shopping center, Crossroads, is the home of this fine new Italian restaurant. Decorated in bright creams and cool blues, it has a refined, somewhat snobby air. Conjured by a Swiss-Italian chef, the meals are highly authentic, fortunately more so than the decorative pièce de resistance, a center-stage gondola (apparently an import from Kerala). Try the wood-oven pizzas, chicken tenderloin Maria Luisa, or *gamberoni ai finocchi con sals alla sambuca* (tiger prawns sautéed in a tomato sauce). Tiramisu heads the dessert list. ✉ *28 Pandit M. M. Malviya Rd., opposite Haji Ali,* ☏ *22/495–5075 or –55, 22/285–6316, or 22/202–3592. Reservations essential. AE, DC, MC, V.*

Dining
Ankur, **18**
Biscotti, **10**
Café Churchill, **29**
Café Indigo, **26**
Café Mondegar, **24**
Casa Mexicana, **16**
Chetana, **22**
Khyber, **19**
Konkan Café, **35**
Leopold Café, **27**
Ling's Pavilion, **23**
Mahesh Lunch Home, **17**
Oriental Blossom, **14**
Palkhi, **28**
Sanuk Thai, **37**
Sheetal Samudra, **6**
Sidewok, **38**
Society, **12**
Thai Pavilion, **35**
Trishna, **20**
Wayside Inn, **21**
Zodiac Grill, **25**

Lodging
Ambassador, **12**
Ascot, **32**
Cowie's, **28**
Fariyas, **33**
Garden, **31**
Godwin, **30**
Holiday Inn, **1**
Juhu Centaur, **4**
The Leela, **8**
Marine Plaza, **14**
Mercure Guestline, **3**
The Oberoi, **15**
Oberoi Towers, **16**
The Orchid, **9**
Ramada Palm Grove, **5**
The Regent, **7**
Ritz, **36**
Sea Green, **13**
Shelley's, **34**
Sun 'n' Sand, **2**
Taj Mahal, **25**
Taj President, **35**
West End, **11**

Greater Bombay Dining and Lodging

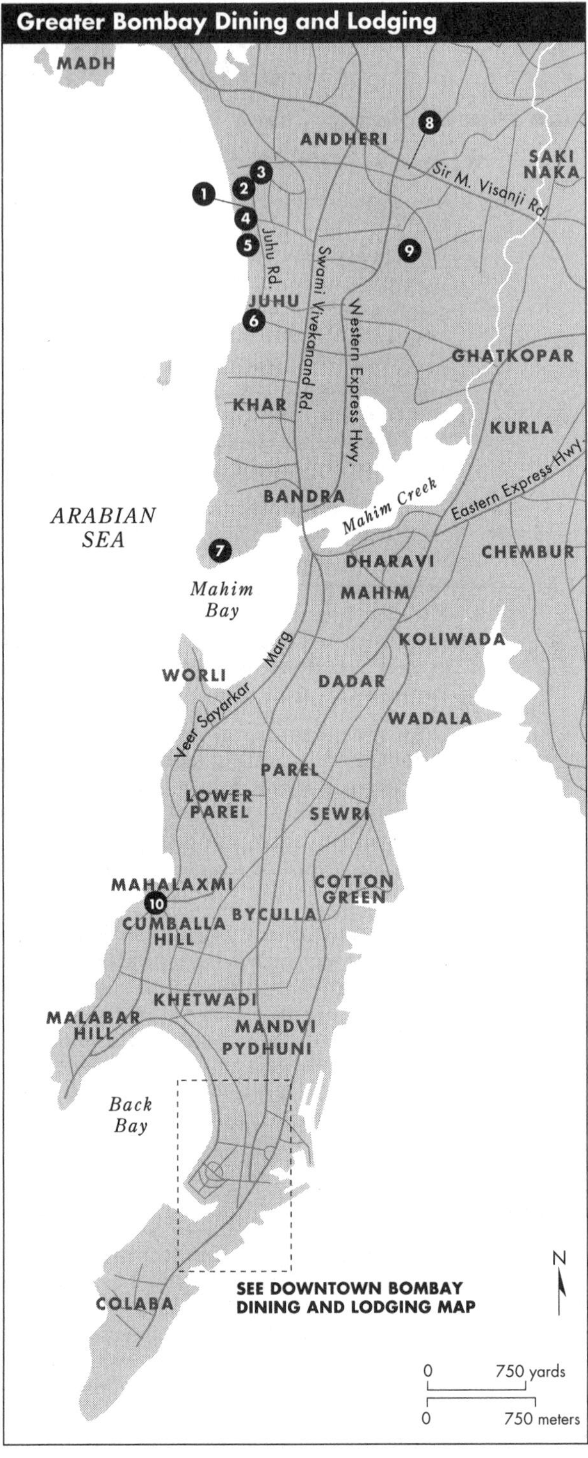

Downtown Bombay Dining and Lodging

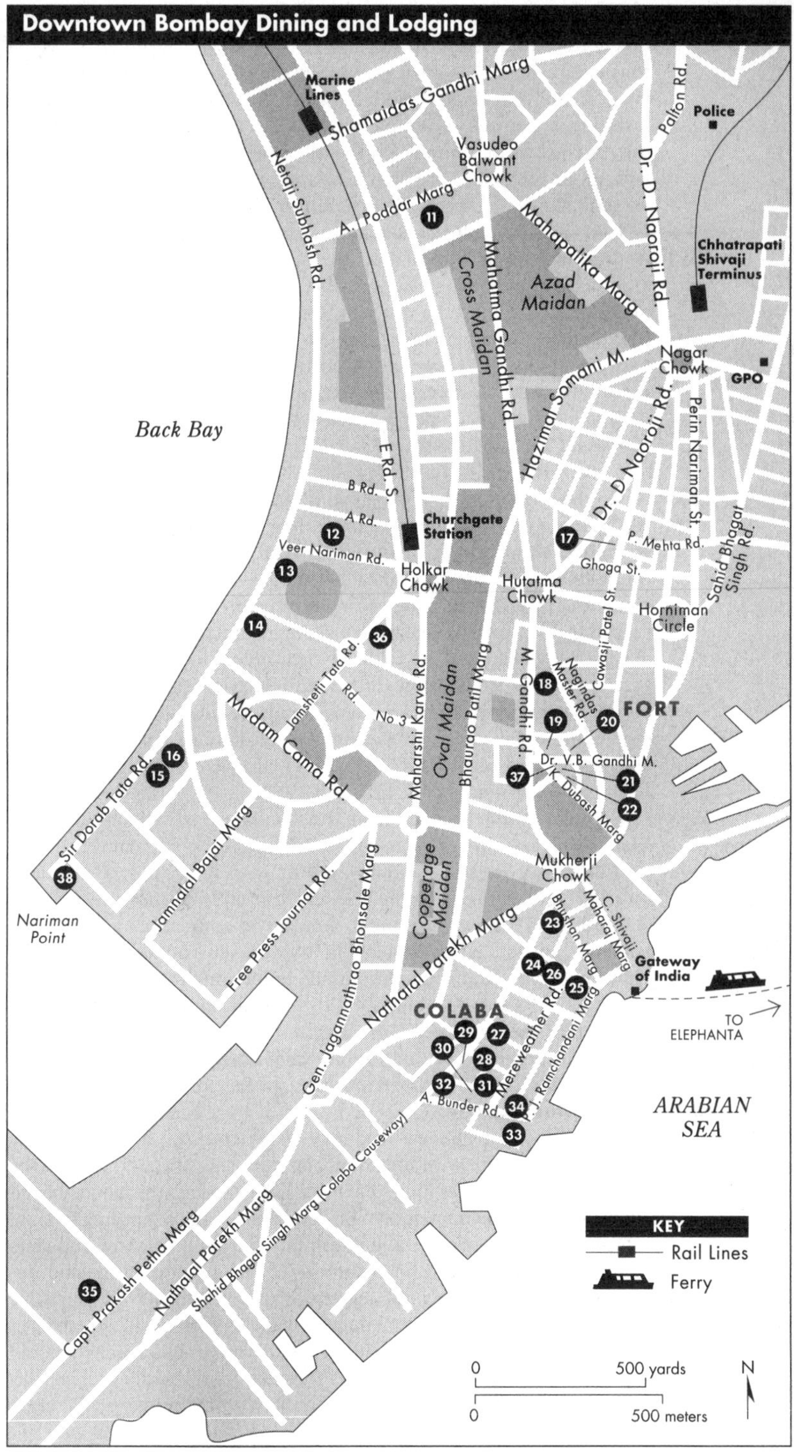

$$$$ ✕ **Café Indigo.** The narrow lane out front fills with a queue of cars at lunch- and dinnertime. Reservations are a must at Bombay's newest tony eatery, housed in an attractive old mansion on a side street in Colaba. A nouvelle Indo-Anglian cuisine is served to Bombay's most fashionable denizens in simple, woodsy but elegant surroundings. Try the *rawas* (Indian salmon) fry, the fillet mignon, or the big *raviolo*; in fact, all of the pastas are commendable. Save room for the tempting desserts. ✉ *Mandalik Rd. (near Cotton World), Colaba,* ☎ *22/285–6316 or 22/202–3592. Reservations essential. AE, DC, MC, V.*

$$$$ ✕ **Casa Mexicana.** Situated on the mezzanine floor of the gleaming Oberoi Towers hotel, this cheerful restaurant features a special view of Marine Drive and the Arabian Sea as well as the hotel's pool. The Mexican food—albeit more Tex-Mex than authentic Mexican—is first-rate, the best in Bombay. A buffet lunch is served from 12:30 to 2:30. Fill up on blackened chicken, grilled lobster with salsa, fajitas, or chimichangas, each perhaps chased by tequila. ✉ *Oberoi Towers, Nariman Point,* ☎ *22/202–4343 or 22/202–5757. Reservations essential. AE, DC, MC, V.*

$$$$ ★ ✕ **Khyber.** Named for the Himalayan mountain pass between Afghanistan and northwestern India, Khyber is one of Bombay's most attractive and popular restaurants, with three floors of delightful rooms done up in Northwest Frontier decor—white marble floors, terracotta urns, carved stone pillars, low wooden rafters, and handsome fresco murals by local artists. The waiters, dressed in Pathan tribal garb, serve delicious kebabs, rotis, and other North Indian food. Try the pomfret green *masala* (fried pomfret stuffed with tangy green chutney and scallions), Khyber *raan* for two (leg of lamb marinated overnight, then roasted in a clay oven), or *paneer shaslik* (cottage cheese marinated with spices and roasted). ✉ *145 M. G. Rd., Fort,* ☎ *22/267–3228. Reservations essential. AE, DC, MC, V.*

$$$$ ✕🏨 **Konkan Café.** Seafood from the Konkan coast (which runs from Maharashtra south through Goa to Mangalore, Karnataka) is extraordinarily popular in Bombay, yet for years it was only available in no-frills "lunch homes" in the business district. In opening the Konkan Café, the Taj President is trying to do what no one else has attempted—serve fish-curry rice-plate lunches in luxurious surroundings. Although crummy taverns and souped-up lunch homes might still be said to do it better, the food here is tasty, and the coastal-home ambience charming. Opt for the steamed pomfret, coastal *maida* (white-flour) paratha, or mixed vegetable curry. ✉ *Taj President hotel, 90 Cuffe Parade, Colaba,* ☎ *22/215–0808. Reservations essential. AE, DC, MC, V.*

$$$$ ★ ✕ **Ling's Pavilion.** Baba Ling and his family have been providing Bombay with excellent Chinese food for two generations, formerly in tiny Nanking, a favorite with film stars and yuppies alike, and now in the much bigger and fancier Ling's Pavilion. Enter through the moon-shaped door and you find yourself on a bridge overlooking a gurgling stream, complete with fish. Some tables look down from a balcony, and stars twinkle from the ceiling. A testimony to Ling's popularity and authenticity is the number of Chinese tourists and consular corps visible on any given evening, tucking into their meals with gusto. The barbecue platter, which arrives with a flourish on its own mini-charcoal, should not be missed, nor should the baby lobsters or steamed fish. The Chinese bread is soft and succulent—terrific with the ginger-garlic crab. ✉ *19/21 Mahakavi Bhushan Marg (behind Regal Cinema),* ☎ *22/285–0023 or 22/282–4533. Reservations essential. AE, DC, MC, V.*

$$$$ ✕ **Oriental Blossom.** Honey-glazed spare ribs, deep-fried corn curd, coconut pancakes, dim sum . . . the Chinese food at the Marine Plaza hotel's showcase restaurant is lightly spiced, a mixture of Cantonese and Szechuan. The decor is simple and elegant, the service unobtrusive. If you want seclusion, book a table in one of the almost-private dining alcoves. ✉ *Hotel Marine Plaza, 29 Marine Dr.,* ☎ *22/285–1212. Reservations essential. AE, DC, MC, V.*

$$$$ ✕ **Palkhi.** Much-ballyhooed when the restaurant opened some years ago, Palkhi's decor was designed by leading socialite Parmeshwar Godrej. In fact, it looks like something out of a Meat Loaf music video. Giant electric candles drip faux plastic wax, and little caverns in the wall hide tableaux by the well-known Indian artist Subhash Awchat. It's startling, rather Halloween-like, yet the effect is not unappealing. The menu includes some relatively unusual tandoori and North Indian dishes, thoughtfully seasoned. The mixed Palkhi platter of kebabs is a good bet, as are the ring kebab, vegetable kebabs, *murg kali mirchi* (chicken with black pepper), seafood in "Delite" sauce (spicy), and the *paneer* Amritsari (cottage cheese cooked in a white gravy). Save room for the special dessert, "Hot Romance"—gulab jamuns flambéed with Cointreau. ✉ *Walton Rd., near Electric House, Colaba,* ☎ *22/284–0053. Reservations essential. AE, DC, MC, V.*

$$$$ ✕ **Society.** If you're in the mood for Continental cuisine—or just want a good steak—pay a visit to this elegant Victorian restaurant, decked out in mirrors and handsome, rich maroon velvet. The best steak, "à la Fernandes"—named after a former maître d'—is richly seasoned with cinnamon, spices, and cream and cooked and flambéed at your table. The crêpes suzette are delectable. Excellent Indian dishes are also served. ✉ *Ambassador hotel, Veer Nariman Rd., Churchgate,* ☎ *22/204–1131. Reservations essential. AE, DC, MC, V.*

$$$$ ★ ✕ **Thai Pavilion.** A Thai woman kneels on banana leaves, carving flower blossoms out of carrots and watermelons. This small dining room is tastefully decorated with inlaid teak surfaces, candles, and orchids, and the Thai chef's cuisine is exceptional. Portions are unusually generous. Start with a clay crock of *tom yum koong,* a spicy prawn soup aromatic with lemongrass and fiery with chilis (not for the faint of palate). A fabulous entrée is *kai haw bai toey,* sweet marinated chicken chunks wrapped in pandanus, or screw-pine, leaves (don't eat them), then steamed and deep-fried. Knowledgeable, attentive waiters provide fantastic service. ✉ *Taj President hotel, 90 Cuffe Parade, Colaba,* ☎ *22/215–0808, ext. 5621. Reservations essential. AE, DC, MC, V.*

$$$$ ✕ **Zodiac Grill.** This Continental restaurant in the legendary Taj Mahal hotel is Western in style, with subdued lighting, handsome chandeliers, captains in black jackets, and waiters in black or white (including white gloves). Specialties include Camembert *dariole* (soufflé) and a creamy Kahlua mousse for dessert. The entrées center on meat and seafood, such as New Zealand steak, Cajun lobster, and grilled lobster served with flavored butter. ✉ *Taj Mahal hotel, Apollo Bunder,* ☎ *22/202–3366. Reservations essential. Jacket and tie. AE, DC, MC, V.*

$$$ ★ ✕ **Ankur.** If you're a seafood fanatic, make immediate tracks for Ankur—named for the spicy seafood of the Konkan coast, garnished with coconut and *kokum* (a tangy tamarind) and now ragingly hot in Bombay. Once a down-market fish house, Ankur does the popular Manglorean and Konkan dishes rather well. The decor has wood and glass accents. Dine on semolina-fried jumbo prawns; fried *kane* (ladyfish); tandoori crab; or *teesri* (clams) in pepper sauce served with *sana* (fluffy rice cakes tempered with toddy) or *neer dosa* (lacy rice pancakes) and you're sure to attain nirvana. Vegetarians can choose from a number of Mughlai dishes and *sana* with chutney. You may want to call before you arrive to ascertain the catch of the day. ✉ *Meadows House, Tamarind La. (behind Kendeel bar), Fort,* ☎ *22/265–4194 or 22/263–0393,. Reservations essential on weekends. AE, DC, MC, V.*

$$$ ★ ✕ **Mahesh Lunch Home.** One of the first Bombay restaurants to popularize the seafoods of the Konkan coast, the formerly humble Mahesh, a two-level eatery tucked away on a narrow street, has gone upmarket with marble, brass, plastic floral arrangements, and smartly clad waiters. (The diners have gone upmarket too; no more leaving fish bones on the side of the table.) This kitchen still, however, serves what may be Bombay's freshest and best seafood, personally selected at the nearby Fort fish market every morning for the last 20 years by the owner, Mr. Karkera. Local office workers, bankers, five-star hoteliers, suburban families, and cricket and film stars in the know come here for giant portions of exquisite crab, and *rawas* (Indian salmon), and pomfret dishes, all succulently tender and light, essentially oil-free, and seasoned with tangy tandoori or Mangalorean spices. The seafood dishes prepared with butter, garlic, and pepper are also popular. ✉ *8-B Cawasji Patel St., Fort,* ☎ *22/287–0938. AE, DC, MC, V.*

$$$ ✕ **Sanuk Thai.** Thailand is thousands of miles away, but walk into Sanuk Thai and you're pretty much there, only better: In this magical Thai kingdom, stars twinkle, orchids sparkle, and Buddhist artifacts and pagoda-style decor create a special charm. The Thai curries are excellent, as are the pepper-and-garlic prawns and the crispy bean sprouts. Start with corn curd, if you're extra-hungry, and wind up with banana fritters. ✉ *30 K. Dubash Marg, Kala Ghoda, Fort,* ☎ *22/204–4233 or –4239. Reservations essential. AE, DC, MC, V.*

$$$ ✕ **Sidewok.** The Taj Group runs this happening new restaurant at the National Centre for the Performing Arts, serving up pan-Asian food and cheerful music. Between handing out courses, waiters hit the danc floor to their own special numbers. Aim for the lemon-grass pomfret, tandoori salmon, house chicken, Asian wok (grilled vegetables), and orange-marmalade crème brûlée. ✉ *Nariman Point,* ☎ *22/281–8132. Reservations essential. AE, DC, MC, V.*

$$$ ✕ **Trishna.** This small restaurant near busy M. G. Road was once just another neighborhood lunch place, but it's very much been discovered. Today, yuppies and film stars crowd into the rows of benches and tables alongside Trishna's old-time regulars, all devouring fresh seafood or Indian and Chinese cuisine, both vegetarian and nonvegetarian. Favorites include squid or oyster chili and salt-and-pepper butter crab. Ask to see the crab before it's cooked: the creature's giant, snapping claws will dispel any doubts about freshness. Call in advance to inquire about the daily catch and make a reservation. ✉ *7 Rope Walk La. (next to Commerce House), Fort,* ☎ *22/267–2176, 22/265–9644, or 22/261–4991. Reservations essential. AE, DC, MC, V.*

$$ ✕ **Café Churchill.** The size of a handkerchief, this six-table eatery serves up fresh, delicious pasta, pizza, and other simple Continental dishes cooked just right. The desserts are also first-class. It's a simple place: The only decor is a television, perpetually tuned to MTV. At lunchtime, the line outdoors outnumbers the café's entire seating capacity. Open from early in the morning until late at night, and kindly providing any kind of takeout, Churchill is unusually convenient. ✉ *103-B Colaba Causeway (opposite Cusrow Baug),* ☎ *22/284–4689. No credit cards.*

$$ ★ ✕ **Chetana.** Rajasthani decor—hand-blocked fabrics on the ceiling and traditional *toranas* (ornamental carvings above temple entrances) on the walls—provides a cozy ambience for tasty vegetarian Rajasthani and Gujarati thalis. Sample Rajasthani *dal bati* (lentils), *kadhi* (curd curry), and mint *raita* (yogurt-and-mint salad). Service is excellent, and the owners' adjacent philosophy bookshop–cum–craft store is well worth a visit after your meal. Note that the restaurant is closed between 3 and 7. ✉ *34 K. Dubash Marg, Kala Ghoda,* ☎ *22/284–4968 or 22/282–4983. AE, DC, MC, V.*

$$ ★ **Sheetal Samudra.** Gourmands regularly make the one-hour trip from central Bombay to dine at one of the city's best suburban restaurants, on the main road between Bombay and Juhu Beach. The decor is unexceptional, but the cuisine—Punjabi and Chinese, with an accent on fresh seafood—is creative and delicious. Try the prawns in buttery, mild crab sauce or the batter-fried prawns in green or red sauce; alternately, opt for boneless fish steak, also in green or red sauce. Live crabs are sold by weight and cooked any way you choose. The waiters, dressed in black vests and red bowties, are skilled and attentive. ✉ *Unity Compound, Juhu Tara Rd., Juhu Beach,* ☎ *22/612–6218 or 22/618–2872. Reservations essential. AE, DC, MC, V.*

$ **Café Mondegar.** Next door to the vast Regal Cinema, this Western joint is one of Bombay's hippest hangouts. The jukebox, at full volume, has a wide selection of jazz and pop anthems, and the walls are adorned with cartoons and glib quotes from the likes of George Bernard Shaw. The café is open all day, and is usually jam-packed. The onion rings and french fries are as greasy as you could wish for, and the coffee float is delicious. ✉ *Colaba Causeway,* ☎ *22/202–0591 or 22/283–0585. MC, V.*

$ ★ **Leopold Café.** Founded in 1871, this is one of the city's oldest restaurants and a popular tourist haunt. With a highly international, eclectic, sometimes outlandish clientele, it's a great place to people-watch. The tables are well spaced, and the paintings and posters recall a French café; at the back is a fruit bar lined with mangos, papayas, and pineapples. The selection of tandoori and Chinese food is broad, and the milkshakes are delicious. Portions are very large. ✉ *Colaba Causeway,* ☎ *22/287–3362 or 22/202–0131. AE, MC, V.*

$ **Wayside Inn.** The sleepy ambience hasn't changed in 50 years at this mildly seedy institution: Plants at open windows, red-and-white checked tablecloths, whirring overhead fans, and the owner's collection of crockery and mugs on walls and in sideboards create a casual, inviting look. On Tuesday, Wednesday, and Thursday, enjoy Parsi cuisine, such as *dhansak* (brown rice served with chicken cooked with lentils) or chicken pillau. The rest of the week, it's Continental fare or the popular pomfret and chips. ✉ *38 K. Dubash Marg, Kala Ghoda,* ☎ *22/284–4324. No credit cards.*

LODGING

All hotels listed are air-conditioned.

$$$$ **The Leela.** Close to both airports, 25 km (16 mi) outside the city, this stylish, extremely posh hotel is the stopover hub for high-powered businesspeople and airline employees; its airport location is not convenient if you'll be sightseeing or doing business for a few days in Bombay proper. Although the consistently high occupancy rate detracts somewhat from the personalized service, all else is superior five-star deluxe. Rooms are spacious, immaculate, and sumptuous, with plush carpeting, armchairs in white and ivory, exquisitely comfortable beds. Outside, 11 acres of beautifully maintained gardens include lotus pools and a small waterfall. ✉ *Sahar, 400059,* ☎ *22/836–3636,* FAX *22/836–0606. 425 rooms, 32 suites. 4 restaurants, 2 bars, pool, steam room, 2 tennis courts, health club, business services, meeting rooms, travel services, airport shuttle. AE, DC, MC, V.*

$$$$ ★ **Marine Plaza.** The polished, smoky-glass exterior of this Marine Drive hotel promises elegance, and the Marine Plaza—which calls itself a "fashionable small hotel"—delivers with a sleek, modern, black-marble interior and a clean, uncluttered feel. Glass elevators whiz you up to rooms that are small but very comfortable and offer sea views and dressing

rooms. Breakfast is included in the room rate. At press time the glass-bottomed pool was under renovation. ✉ *29 Marine Dr., 400020,* ☎ *22/285–1212,* FAX *22/282–8585. 28 rooms, 40 suites. Restaurant, bar, coffee shop, in-room data ports, in-room safes, refrigerators, health club, dry cleaning, laundry service, business services, meeting rooms, travel services. AE, DC, MC, V.*

$$$$ ★ **The Oberoi.** This elegant high-rise in the heart of the business district caters to business travelers. From service to decor, everything is sleek and efficient, yet the fabulous, high-ceilinged lobby and various public spaces are punctuated with traditional pieces for warmth. Each floor is staffed with a butler for personal assistance, and each room has small, separate dressing and luggage areas to allow for clutter-free in-room meetings. A superior business center and complimentary personalized stationery are extra touches. If at all possible, arrange for a room with a view of the Arabian Sea. The Oberoi's Indian restaurant, Kandahar, serves memorable, healthy meals prepared with little or no oil, and the Brasserie coffee shop serves 80 dishes from around the world. ✉ *Nariman Point, 400021,* ☎ *22/202–5757,* FAX *22/204–1505. 350 rooms, 22 suites. 3 restaurants, bar, pool, barbershop, beauty salon, sauna, Turkish bath, health club, dry cleaning, laundry service, business services, meeting rooms, travel services. AE, DC, MC, V.*

$$$$ **Oberoi Towers.** Adjoining the Oberoi, this enormous, 35-story high-rise is geared toward the business traveler but hosts a mixed international crowd of both executives and tourists. True to the Oberoi chain's characteristic efficiency, it runs like a well-tuned instrument. Public spaces are many and varied, some overlooking the vast, gleaming, glass-walled lobby from smart mezzanines. Guest rooms are modern and classy, with patterned bedspreads and drapes, brass-framed prints of Indian monuments, and smooth, contemporary wood furniture. Sea-facing rooms on high floors have stunning views of the Arabian Sea and Marine Drive, which turns into the "Queen's Necklace" at night. The forthcoming Frangipani restaurant will have an international menu, as does the laid-back coffee shop, The Palms. A Hard Rock Café is slated to open downstairs by 2001. ✉ *Nariman Point, 400021,* ☎ *22/202–4343,* FAX *22/204–3282. 546 rooms, 54 suites. 3 restaurants, 2 bars, pool, sauna, health club, laundry service, business services, meeting rooms, travel services. AE, DC, MC, V.*

$$$$ ★ **The Regent.** In a city where space is extremely tight and real-estate prices are some of the highest in the world, the opening of a brand-new five-star hotel is an event. The Regent opened in 1999 after almost 15 years of no such construction, and it does seem worth the wait. Opulent and swish, its portals open onto what seems like an acre of marble, oversize sparkling chandeliers, fountains, purring elevators, automatic revolving doors, and tinkling china. Facing the ocean from the suburb of Bandra, the Regent has some remarkably luxurious modern rooms, complete with bedside controls for the lights, curtains, and air-conditioning. Bathrooms have both shower and tub. ✉ *Lands End, Bandstand, Bandra West, 400050,* ☎ *22/655–1234,* FAX *22/651–2471. 610 rooms, 40 suites. 3 restaurants, bar, coffee shop, patisserie, in-room data ports, in-room safes, minibars, pool, barbershop, beauty salon, health club, dance club, baby-sitting, dry cleaning, laundry service, business services, meeting rooms, travel services. AE, DC, MC, V.*

$$$$ ★ **Taj Mahal.** The first hotel in what is now a pan-India luxury chain, this Victorian extravaganza was built in 1903. Looking past the Gateway of India to the Arabian Sea, its brownstone exterior is stunning, with rows of jutting white balconies and some Gothic windows. The high, central Italianate dome is echoed in the onion domes on the corner turrets. A 19-story modern wing called the Intercontinental, which throws in some Moorish elements, towers just inland from its older

sister. Every corner of the older building is exquisitely decorated, often with antiques (for which the hotel's decorator scours India) and always with warm, tasteful colors. Rooms and suites here, some of which surround small, quiet interior verandas, retain their Victorian character with high ceilings, pastel colors, antiques such as lanterns or beveled mirrors, and sometimes cane furniture. Rooms facing the harbor from the lower floors can be noisy, so ask for a higher room with the same view. Rooms in the Intercontinental, slightly less expensive, are spacious, with contemporary decor. ✉ *Apollo Bunder, Colaba, 400039,* ☎ *22/202–3366,* FAX *22/287–2711. 80 rooms, 2 suites. 3 restaurants, 4 bars, coffee shop, patisserie, pool, barbershop, beauty salon, health club, dance club, baby-sitting, dry cleaning, laundry service, business services, meeting rooms, travel services. AE, DC, MC, V.*

$$$$ **Taj President.** In a residential neighborhood near the World Trade Center shopping emporium, this luxury hotel and its buffet breakfast are very popular with business travelers, not least because of its e-mail provisions—every room has a data port. The driveway is lined with trees, and the rooms have high ceilings and modern furnishings. While the Taj President is not as extravagant as some others in its price range, the service here stands out. Ask for one of the slightly more expensive "superior rooms" that dominate the upper floors. ✉ *90 Cuffe Parade, Colaba, 400005,* ☎ *22/215–0808,* FAX *22/215–1201. 310 rooms, 21 suites. 3 restaurants, café, bar, pool, beauty salon, health club, laundry service, business services, travel services. AE, DC, MC, V.*

$$$ **Ambassador.** Once an apartment house, this nine-story 1940s hotel in the heart of Bombay is less sleek in service and appearance than its South Bombay counterparts but offers a bit more old-fashioned personality. Rooms are furnished in a functional modern style, each with the Ambassador chain's signature brass knocker on its door. The hotel is topped with India's first revolving restaurant, offering gorgeous views over the city and the Arabian Sea. ✉ *Veer Nariman Rd., Churchgate, 400020,* ☎ *22/204–1131,* FAX *22/204–0004. 123 rooms, 3 suites. 3 restaurants, bar, coffee shop, dry cleaning, laundry service, travel services. AE, DC, MC, V.*

$$$ **Holiday Inn.** Built in the 1970s, this Western-style high-rise on Juhu Beach has a spacious lobby, executive floors for business travelers, and rooms that are uniformly decorated with standard contemporary furniture and pastel wall-to-wall carpeting and fabrics. The best standard rooms have limited views of the beach; only deluxe rooms face the sea directly. ✉ *Balraj Sahani Marg, Juhu Beach, 400049,* ☎ *22/620–4444 or 22/670–4444,* FAX *22/620–4452. 191 rooms, 13 suites. 2 restaurants, bar, coffee shop, pool, health club, dry cleaning, laundry service, business services, meeting rooms, travel services. AE, DC, MC, V.*

$$$ **Juhu Centaur.** Fairly far outside the center of town, the Centaur is one of the more expensive hotels on Juhu Beach. Built in the 1980s, this sprawling, five-story cement building has a truly immense lobby and a quiet public sitting area on each floor, near the elevator. Rooms are contemporary, with plush carpeting, and each has two sofas or armchairs; all have balconies. Ask for a room overlooking the beach, and watch the Juhu locals take their seaside constitutionals early in the morning. ✉ *Juhu Tara Rd., Juhu Beach, 400049,* ☎ *22/611–3040,* FAX *22/611–6343. 365 rooms, 20 suites. 3 restaurants, bar, pool, health club, laundry service, business services, travel services. AE, DC, MC, V.*

$$$ ★ **The Orchid.** This small eco-hotel is right next to Bombay's domestic airport and a few minutes' drive from the international airport. The rooms are brightly lit, decently sized, and very comfortable. Boasting proudly of "eco-friendly waste management and recycling policies," the hotel built its "green" rooms with a minimal amount of wood, plastic, and paper. A bedside button allows you to turn up your air-conditioning thermostat by two degrees to save energy. ✉ *Nehru Rd., Vile Parle East, 400050,* ☎ *22/616–4040,* FAX *22/616–4141. 201 rooms, 55 suites. Restaurant, bar, pool, health club, dry cleaning, laundry service, business services, baby-sitting, meeting rooms, travel services, airport shuttle. AE, DC, MC, V.*

$$$ **Ramada Palm Grove.** The long lobby of this Juhu Beach high-rise is lined with marble and etched glass. Rooms are fairly large, with subdued contemporary decor in shades of mauve and green, and each has a small sitting area. Only deluxe suites and executive salons face the water; the rest of the rooms have limited views. The modest pool is a pleasant, if slightly cramped, place to unwind. ✉ *Juhu Tara Rd., Juhu Beach, 400049,* ☎ *22/611–2323,* FAX *22/611–3682. 114 rooms, 3 suites. Restaurant, bar, pool, beauty salon, health club, windsurfing, business services, meeting rooms, travel services. AE, DC, MC, V.*

$$$ **Sun 'n' Sand.** There's a tangibly friendly atmosphere at this 1963 Juhu Beach hotel. A small circular driveway curves up to the intimate lobby, which leads out to a lovely garden terrace and pool overlooking the sand. In spite of its upscale facilities, there is something mildly seedy about the place—a sort of B-grade Hindi-movie air—which can perhaps be attributed to its age. The rooms have basic, modern decor; about 60 face the sea. Breakfast is included. ✉ *39 Juhu Beach, 400049,* ☎ *22/620–1811 or 22/620–4821,* FAX *22/620–2170. 120 rooms, 9 suites. 2 restaurants, bar, pool, beauty salon, health club, business services, meeting rooms, travel services, airport shuttle. AE, DC, MC, V.*

$$ **Fariyas.** The cool, shiny marble lobby is full of glass chandeliers and brass and carved-wood details. With contemporary furnishings and wall-to-wall carpets, the rooms are inviting, and the facilities and location—half a block from the eastern shore in trendy Colaba, near the Gateway of India—combine to make the Fariyas among the best buys in its price range. Only two suites have tubs; the rest of the rooms have showers. ✉ *25 Devshankar V Vyas Marg (at Shahid Bhagt Singh Marg), off Arthur Bunder Rd., Colaba, 400005,* ☎ *22/204–2911 or 22/285–5431,* FAX *22/283–4992. 86 rooms, 6 suites. Restaurant, bar, pool, health club, meeting rooms, travel services. AE, DC, MC, V.*

$$ ★ **Mercure Guestline.** Small, compact, and right across the road from the ocean in Juhu, this business hotel has attractive, plush rooms with all the standard amenities, such as fridges and minibars. The accent is on practicality and comfort rather than charm. The Ivy Club serves healthy breakfasts, salad lunches, and a cake buffet to executives and their clients in a quiet lounge atmosphere. Slightly less expensive than Bombay's top hotels, the Guestline is nonetheless very competent. ✉ *462 A. B. Nair Rd., Juhu Beach, 400049,* ☎ *22/670–5555,* FAX *22/620–2821. 91 rooms, 2 suites. Restaurant, bar, coffee shop, pool, health club, dry cleaning, laundry service, business services, meeting rooms. AE, DC, MC, V.*

$$ **Ritz.** Quaint and charming, this vintage 1930s hotel has a small lobby and simple, pleasant rooms. White with green trim on the outside, the building is centrally located but peaceful, on a tree-lined side street just off Marine Drive. Fifteen of the rooms have balconies, but not all of these have scenic views. The bathrooms, in tile and white stone, are clean and supplied with small baskets of toiletries. Note that the water heater, or "geyser," must be switched on manually 30 minutes before you use the hot water. ✉ *5 Jamshedij Tata Rd., 400020,* ☎ *22/285–0500 or 22/283–7623,* FAX *22/285–0494. 72 rooms, 10 suites. 2 restaurants, coffee shop, dry cleaning, laundry service, meeting room, travel services. AE, DC, MC, V.*

$ **Ascot.** True, the facade is grim, but the spacious, deeply carpeted rooms in this no-frills hotel are atmospheric and very clean: Their old wooden furniture is upholstered with red velvet, and the bathrooms have vintage, freestanding bathtubs. All rooms have working, if antiquated, refrigerators. The Ascot has no restaurant, but there are many fine options nearby. This is one of the better deals in its price range, even if most rooms lack any kind of soul-stirring view. ✉ *38 Garden Rd., Colaba, 400039,* ☏ *22/284–0020 or 22/287–2105,* FAX *22/204–6449 or 22/284–6006. 28 rooms. Refrigerators. AE, DC, MC, V.*

$ **Cowie's.** Minutes from the Gateway of India promenade, Cowie's has a few rooms in an old, roughly turn-of-the-20th-century building. The rooms are very simple, but they're clean and equipped with refrigerators. Three or four rooms have balconies, and these are the most charming overall. Splurge on dinner at popular Palkhi, next door, run by the same management: A Mughlai meal here costs about what your room does (☞ Dining). ✉ *15 Walton Rd. (off Colaba Causeway, near Electric House), Colaba, 400039,* ☏ *22/284–0232 or 22/284-5727,* FAX *22/283–4203. 20 rooms. Restaurant, laundry service. AE, MC, V.*

$ **Garden.** On a small side street in Colaba, minutes from major sights and shops, Garden offers good value for the money. Rooms are clean, comfortable, and equipped with refrigerators, TVs, and some even have bathtubs. Book a deluxe room; the standard rooms are not as recommendable. The only drawback is the lack of a pleasant view. The restaurant serves both Indian and Chinese food. ✉ *42 Garden Rd., off Colaba Causeway (near Electric House), Colaba, 400039,* ☏ *22/283–1330, 22/283–4823, or 22/284–1476,* FAX *22/204–4290. 31 rooms, 3 suites. Restaurant, laundry service. AE, MC, V.*

$ **Godwin.** A sister concern of the Garden, the nine-story Godwin is another good, low-frills bargain next door. Accommodations vary widely. Opt only for one of the 10 recently renovated deluxe rooms, with clean marble floors and in-room amenities; the non-deluxe rooms are rather shabby. Most rooms have window air-conditioning units, but several are centrally air-conditioned. Request a room with a view (albeit distant) of the Taj Mahal hotel and Gateway of India—many rooms have no view or an outright depressing view. The restaurant serves Indian and Chinese food. ✉ *41 Garden Rd. (off Colaba Causeway, near Electric House), Colaba, 400039,* ☏ *22/287–2050 or 22/282–1226,* FAX *22/287–1592. 44 rooms, 3 suites. Restaurant, bar, refrigerators, laundry service. AE, MC, V.*

$ **Sea Green.** The green trimmings on this five-story building have been weathered by the Arabian Sea (and pollution) over its more than 50 years of hosting guests on Marine Drive. Beyond the location and friendly service, the Sea Green's only virtue is that it's a remarkable bargain if you don't mind the lack of facilities and worn, government-office look. Narrow halls open onto surprisingly large rooms with window air-conditioners and clean but institutional (think 1960s-asylum) furnishings, such as metal wardrobes and turquoise vinyl couches. All rooms but one have small balconies, a few looking across to the sea. The bathrooms have only open showers, no stalls or tubs. Room service brings beverages and simple breakfasts. ✉ *145 Marine Dr., 400020,* ☏ *22/282–2294,* FAX *22/283–6158. 30 rooms, 4 suites. AE, DC, MC, V.*

$ ★ **Shelley's.** This attractive, old-fashioned hotel has a marvelous ambience and sits right on the waterfront in the shadow of the Gateway of India. Despite the lack of facilities, it's a memorable place to stay, and the rooms are clean. The seafacing rooms (called apartments) are set aside for extended stays only. ✉ *30 P. J. Ramchandani Marg, Apollo Bunder,* ☏ *22/284–0229,* FAX *22/288–1436. 34 rooms. Breakfast room, refrigerators. AE.*

$ **West End.** Over half a century old, the West End has a simple charm. The spacious rooms have private balconies, bathtubs, and outdated furniture (that is, modern items that are not modern anymore). The restaurant, the lobby, and even the bellboys still have a 1940s look.

Indian, Chinese, and Continental food are served on site, and the popular Gujarati-thali restaurant Panchvati Gaurav is two minutes away. The building is centrally located near the humming Bombay Hospital, where doctors and relatives swarm in and out until late at night. ✉ *45 New Marine Lines, 400020,* ☎ *22/203–9121 or 22/205–7484,* FAX *22/205–7506. 55 rooms, 25 suites. Restaurant, bar, meeting rooms. AE, DC, MC, V.*

NIGHTLIFE AND THE ARTS

The Arts

The best source of arts information is the fortnightly culture calendar "Programme of Dance, Music and Drama," free at the Government of India Tourist Office. The daily *Times of India* newspaper usually lists that day's films, concerts, and other events on the last two or three pages; on Friday, the afternoon paper *Midday* publishes "The List" to highlight the coming week's events. Program information and details usually appear on the MTDC's city-guide programs, shown regularly on hotels' in-house TV stations. The **National Center for the Performing Arts** (NCPA; ✉ Nariman Point, ☎ 22/283–3737, 22/283–3838, or 22/283–4678) posts its performance schedule on the bulletin board at the main entrance and at the entrances to its Tata and Experimental theaters. Note that many NCPA performances are open to members only; a year's membership is Rs. 900. Other performance tickets in Bombay are usually very inexpensive (from entirely free to Rs. 240) and can be purchased from box offices or from the ticket counter at **Rhythm House Private Ltd.** (✉ 40 K. Dubash Marg, Rampart Row, ☎ 22/285–3963), near the Jehangir Art Gallery, one of Bombay's main music stores and another source of information on what's happening.

Dance

The restaurant **Tanjore** (✉ Taj Mahal hotel, ☎ 22/202–3366) doubles as a dance venue, where local performers present a classical Indian dance demonstration with explanation every evening from 7:45 to 8, 8:30 to 8:45, and 9:15 to 9:30. Confirm exact times with the Taj Mahal concierge. The **NCPA** complex (☞ *above*) also houses the **Godrej Dance Academy Theater,** a main venue for classical Indian dance performances as well as workshops and master classes, and the **Drama Opera Arts Complex,** a 1,000-seat auditorium planned as Bombay's ballet and opera theater.

Film

Bombay, a.k.a. "Bollywood," is the center of the Indian film industry—the largest film producer in the world. Most of the epic Indian musicals shown in movie theaters are in Hindi. The **Regal Cinema** (✉ Shaheed Bhagat Singh Rd., opposite Prince of Wales Museum, Colaba ☎ 22/202–9271 or 22/202–1017) usually shows current English-language movies. The **Sterling Cinema** (✉ Tata Palace, Murzban Road, off D. Naoroji Rd., near Victoria Terminus, ☎ 22/207–5187 or 22/207–5189) also shows current English-language films. Interesting art films, some in English, are sometimes shown at the **Nehru Center Auditorium** (☞ *below*) in the Worli area. Also check listings for the **NCPA** (☞ *above*).

Music and Theater

The **National Center for the Performing Arts** complex (☞ *above*) includes the **Tata Theater,** a grand 1,000-seat auditorium that regularly hosts plays, often in English, and classical concerts by major Indian and international musicians. The **Little Theater** is the NCPA's smallest, hosting small-scale plays and Western chamber music. The **Experimental Theater,** with 300 seats, is usually used for avant-garde drama and occasionally for concerts and small-scale dance performances. The **Nehru Center Auditorium** (✉ Dr. Annie Besant Rd., Worli, ☎ 22/496–4676) is Bombay's second major venue, where theater, music, and dance performances are regularly held. The **Prithvi Theatre** (Janaki Kutir, Church Rd., Juhu, ☎ 22/614–9546), run by the famous Kapoor acting family, stages a variety of plays each week, some in English, with reasonably priced tickets.

Nightlife

Between couples strolling on the breezy promenade around the Gateway of India and fashion-forward twenty-somethings dancing at Three Flights Up, Bombay has what may be the most vibrant nightlife in India. Because of astronomical real-estate prices and bullying by racketeers, however, only a few private groups have opened their own bars or clubs. Quite a few of the nightspots in Bombay proper are in established hotels and restaurants; many of the rest are in wealthy suburbs like Juhu and Bandra, where the after-dark scene thrives on suburbia's young nouveau riche as well as city folk willing to travel for a good night out.

Note that many clubs and bars have "couples" policies, whereby a lone man is not permitted to enter without a woman—a circuitous attempt to prevent brawls, pick-up scenes, and prostitution. To avoid an unpleasant encounter at the door, check with your hotel staff if you are a man traveling alone or in a group of men. Dress nicely (jackets for men) and you'll probably get in; an advance call from your hotel concierge might also make your entry smoother. Most nightspots, even pubs that would otherwise be conducive to cozy talks over beers, tend to have extremely loud music and are very smoky. If you'd like to converse beyond a few shouts over blaring rock music, opt for the more reserved bars and lounges in hotels.

Revelry peaks from Thursday to Sunday nights, with primarily an older crowd—i.e., late 20s to mid-30s—on Sunday. Pubs open at around 7 or 8 (except a few that open in the afternoon) and close by midnight; only few remain open longer, depending on current police rules in the area. Some places collect a nominal cover charge at the door. As in any metropolis, the reign of a nightspot can be ephemeral; ask a young hotel employee to brief you on the scene.

Bars and Lounges

The **Bay View Bar** (✉ The Oberoi, Nariman Point, ☎ 22/202–5757), facing the Arabian Sea, is elegant and more reserved than many of its peers. Rather expensive, it has live music and a dance floor. **Club Abyss** (✉ Turner Rd., opposite Moti Mahal and near the Popley jewelry showroom, Bandra, ☎ 22/ 640–8577 or 22/640–1931) is a tiny, swank suburban pub. The **Copa Cabana** (✉ 39D Chowpatty Beach, ☎ 22/368–0274) is a small, Spanish-style tapas bar with an open loft upstairs and a trendy crowd. The popular **Fashion Bistro** (✉ Next to Sterling Cinema, off D. Naoroji Rd., near Victoria Terminus, ☎ 22/204–7270) pub gets packed to suffocation late at night. The Continental and Lebanese snacks are tasty, and the music is often from the late sixties. The Bistro organizes a variety of weekly activities, from kiddie lunches, workouts, and makeovers during the day to Latino nights (Tuesday) and ladies' nights (Thursday) after dark. **Geoffrey's** (✉ Hotel Marine Plaza, 29 Marine Dr., ☎ 22/285–1212) draws a relatively staid yuppie crowd with golden oldies and a clubby setting. **The Ghetto** (✉ 30 Bhulabhai Desai Rd., ☎ 22/492–4725) is a psychedelic/rave bar with a fairly grungy clientele, a strange combination of sixties and techno music, and convincingly graffitied walls. It can be fun late in the evening. **HQ** (✉ Above Cafe Royal, near Regal Cinema, ☎ 22/288–3982 or 22/288–3983) plays modern favorites from techno to rap. It has a phantasmal look, with lots of chrome and glass. **The Tavern** (✉ Fariyas Hotel, Colaba, ☎ 22/204–2911), a friendly, small, dark room with wooden rafters, is open noon to midnight with very loud pop and rock music. **Three Flights Up** (✉ Apollo Bunder, next to Central Cottage Industries Emporium, ☎ 22/285–2298) is an ongoing hot spot. It has an enormous dance floor, serves overpriced Western cocktails, and encourages its guests, who pay a hefty cover charge for the privilege, to dance the night away.

Clubs and Discos

Cyclone (✉ The Leela, Sahar, ☎ 22/836–3636), which admits only hotel guests, members, and invitees, nearly outdoes every disco in town with its flashing electronic gadgetry, sophisticated sound system, and posh decor. Ask your concierge for help getting in. **Fire and Ice** (✉ Phoenix Mills Compound, 462 Senapati Bapat Marg, Lower Parel) is Bombay's newest and biggest club, with room for 100 dancers. **J-49** (✉ Juhu Residency, Juhu Tara Rd., ☎ 22/618–4546) is the hottest disco in the 'burbs. One wonders why, as it's small and has little in the way of decor, but it packs in rockers of all ages, even on weekdays. **Not Just Jazz By The Bay** (✉ 143 Marine Dr., ☎ 22/285–1876 or 22/282–0957) is one of Bombay's few jazz venues, with live music several nights a week. Beautifully located, it serves a buffet lunch and stays open until 12:30 AM. **Beyond 1900s** (✉ Taj Mahal hotel, Apollo Bunder, ☎ 22/202–3366), intended primarily for Taj Mahal guests, is an upmarket club with a high-tech, Gotham City theme—full of metal girders and waiters dressed like the Joker's henchmen. It's open 8:30 PM–2 AM. At **Razzberry Rhinoceros** (✉ Juhu Hotel, Juhu Tara Rd., Juhu Beach, ☎ 22/618–4012) the feel is young and casual, the look rustic, and the music loud rock, pop, or jazz.

SPORTS AND OUTDOOR ACTIVITIES

Billiards and Bowling

Bowling and pool have captured the imagination of Bombay-wallahs in a big way. Hundreds of pool parlors have sprung up in the last few years, and the city's few bowling alleys are doing a brisk business. These three are open daily from noon to midnight. **The Bowling Company** (✉ Phoenix Mills Compound, 462 Senapati Bapat Marg, Lower Parel, ☎ 22/491–5677 or 22/491–4000) is the fanciest alley in town, with 20 lanes. Fees are Rs. 50–Rs. 125 per game depending on the day of the week. The Bowling Company also has six pool tables, for which it charges Rs. 50 per frame. The attached café serves drinks as well as a variety of coffees and exotic desserts to live jazz. **Buddy's** (✉ Jyoti Studio, next to Kennedy Bridge, near Nana Chowk, ☎ 22/387–5495) has four lanes, for which it charges Rs. 150 per game, and eight pool tables, for which it charges Rs. 50 per frame. There's a Rs. 50 cover charge on weekends and holidays. **Superdrome** (✉ Film Centre Building, Tardeo, ☎ 22/491–2313) has four lanes and charges Rs. 75–Rs. 250 per game depending on the day of the week. For use of one of the eight pool tables, you'll pay Rs. 100 per frame. Superdrome also has a video arcade and a snack bar serving pan-Asian food. The cover charge of Rs. 100 goes toward your first game of any kind.

Cricket

Wankhede Stadium (✉ D. Rd., Churchgate) hosts Bombay's major domestic and international cricket matches. In season—October through March—there are usually several matches a week. You can buy tickets, which range in price from Rs. 150 to Rs. 3,400, through the **Bom-**

bay Cricket Association (✉ D. Rd., Churchgate, ☎ 22/281–9910 or 22/281–2714).

Golf

The **Willingdon Sports Club** (✉ K. Khadye Marg, ☎ 22/494–5754) has an 18-hole golf course. Nonmembers can usually play as "guests" of the secretary on weekdays; just call ahead to make arrangements.

Horse-and-Buggy Rides

For a quick tour of Bombay's illuminated sights by night, hop in one of the horse-drawn buggies parked at Nariman Point, next to the Oberoi Towers; at the northern end of Marine Drive; or at the Gateway of India. Neither the carriages nor the horses are in particularly good shape, let alone elegant; but if you don't require luxury, this can be an enjoyable jaunt. A spin from the Gateway of India to Churchgate and back, taking in key sights on the way, takes about an hour and should cost less than Rs. 150 (agree on the price ahead of time).

Horse Racing

Bombay's **Mahalaxmi Race Course** (✉ Mahalaxmi, near Nehru Planetarium, ☎ 22/307–1401) is one of the finest courses in the East. A visit here in season is a social experience: For a few months each year this green patch in central Bombay becomes Ascot in the 1950s, with faux British accents and outfits to kill. The season usually runs from November through April, with races on Thursdays and Sundays.

Sailing

Members of any yachting association affiliated with the **Royal Bombay Yacht Club** (✉ Apollo Bunder, Bombay 400039, ☎ 22/202–1880) can charter a boat for local sailing, October to June. The club also offers visiting memberships for a reasonable Rs. 450; just contact the secretary.

SHOPPING

From crowded street bazaars to exclusive air-conditioned boutiques, Bombay can keep the shopper riveted for days. Colaba Causeway, Flora Fountain, Kemps Corner, and Breach Candy are all trendy shopping areas, with the latter two very chic and very pricey. The air-conditioned World Trade Centre on Cuffe Parade, at the southern tip of Bombay, looks discouraging from the outside but houses a useful cluster of government-run emporiums with fixed-price crafts from all over India. Crossroads is Bombay's newest mall, and a swanky one at that: unusually spacious and attractive, and open daily. India's most fashionable clothing labels have stores here, and the rest of the 130 shops sell everything from napkins to videos. The arcades in top hotels—those at the Oberoi, Oberoi Towers, and Taj Mahal are particularly good—offer a little bit of everything for a lot more money than anywhere else, but the merchandise is beautiful and the atmosphere unhurried and climate-controlled. For lower prices and a more vibrant atmosphere, throw yourself into the middle of one of Bombay's famous bazaars.

Once you've exhausted Bombay proper, you can venture out to the suburbs, where prices can be lower. Linking Road in Bandra is a trendy place to shop, and Juhu's main strip, Juhu Tara Road, is lined with trendy new boutiques, shops, art galleries, and restaurants. Note that each neighborhood has a different closing day for shops. In Colaba, up to Worli, shops are closed Sunday; in Worli, up to Bandra, they're closed Monday; and in Bandra, up to the suburbs, they're closed Thursday. Throughout Bombay, many shops are closed on Sunday.

Bazaars and Markets

Chor Bazaar (✉ Mutton St., near Kutbi Masjid) is a bustling flea market where you can find exactly what you don't need but have to have—old phonographs, broken nautical instruments, dusty chandeliers, furniture, and brass objects ranging from junky knickknacks to valuable antiques and curios. Keep an eye on your purse or wallet and come relaxed—it can be chaotic. **Fashion Street** (✉ M. G. Rd., opposite Bombay Gymkhana) is a cotton bargain trove set in a row of open-air stalls, with mounds of colorful, cheap, mainly Western clothing for all ages. Come around 11 AM, when the crowds are thinner and the sun has not yet peaked—and bargain. **Zaveri Bazaar** (✉ Near V. Vallabh Chowk) is the place to go for diamond, gold, and silver *zevar* (jewelry). The tumultuous streets are lined with tiny, decades-old family jewelry businesses. Duck into one and sip a customary cup of tea or coffee while a salesperson shows you the merchandise. Most shops are authentic, but beware of false silver and gold; it's difficult to spot.

Specialty Stores

Art and Antiques

The **Jehangir Art Gallery** (✉ Kala Ghoda, Fort, ☎ 22/284–3989), has at least three art shows on every week either on the main floor or at the Gallery Chemould ☎ 22/283–3640 or even on the pavement racks outside in fair weather. Prices vary vastly. **Natesans Antiquarts Ltd.** (✉ Basement of Jehangir Art Gallery, Fort, ☎ 22/285–2700; Taj Mahal hotel, ☎ 22/202–4165), which has branches in many Indian cities, sells magnificent but expensive curios, subcontinental antiquities, wood carvings, sculptures, and paintings, even registered national monuments (not exportable!). **Phillips Antiques** (✉ Madam Cama Rd., opposite Regal Cinema, ☎ 22/202–0564) has the best old prints, engravings, and maps in Bombay. Phillips also sells many possessions left behind by the British—Staffordshire and East India Company china, old jewelry, crystal, lacquerware, and sterling silver.

Books

Most large hotels have small bookshops, but Bombay's best selection is at **Crossword** (✉ Mahalaxmi Chambers, Bhulabhai Desai Rd., Breach Candy, near Mahalakshmi temple, ☎ 22/492–0253), probably the largest bookstore in Bombay and a comfortable place to browse. **Danai** (✉ Khar Danda Rd., Khar, ☎ 22/648–7123) is the largest suburban bookstore and also sells CDs and cassettes. **Fountainhead** (✉ C-401, Crossroads, 28 Pandit M. M. Malviya Rd., opposite Haji Ali, ☎ 22/495–5149 or 22/495–5159) is Bombay's newest bookstore and one of its largest. **Nalanda** (✉ Taj Mahal hotel, ☎ 22/202–2514), open until midnight, has plenty of books on India, including travel guides and fiction, and the latest foreign papers. The **Strand Book Stall** (✉ Dhannur Sir P. M. Rd., Fort, ☎ 22/266–1994 or 22/266–1719) offers good discounts. The sidewalk book market on **Veer Nariman Road,** opposite Flora Fountain (near the Central Telegraph office) and toward Victoria Terminus, is a great source for secondhand books. You can score some rare finds here—bargain.

Carpets

The **Central Cottage Industries Emporium** (✉ Apollo Bunder, Colaba, ☎ 22/202–2491) stocks an excellent selection of traditional Kashmiri carpets at reliable prices. **Coir Board** (✉ 5 Stadium House, Veer Nariman Rd., Churchgate, ☎ 22/282–1575) has cheap jute and coir matting. There are several Kashmiri-run carpet shops in **The Oberoi** and on **Colaba Causeway** (between Regal Cinema and Cusrow Baug, and on lanes leading off the causeway). You may find a genuine, well-priced carpet in any of these shops, but you're on your own vis-a-vis unscrupulous shopkeepers. A carpet's mix of silk, wool, and cotton has a lot to do with its price; visit several shops, including the government emporiums, to get a sense of the market before cutting a deal in an independent shop. A small, fixed-price outlet for the well-known brand **Shyam Ahuja** (✉ Crossroads, 3rd floor, 28 Pandit M. M. Malviya Rd., opposite Haji Ali, ☎ 22/460–3074, 22/460–3075, or 22/460–3077) has cotton dhurries and wool carpets.

Children's Clothing and Toys

The **Central Cottage Industries Emporium** (✉ Apollo Bunder, Colaba, ☎ 22/202–7537 or 22/202–6564) has a small but imaginative assortment of Indian costumes for kids and traditional Indian toys. Mirror-work elephants, Indian dolls, wood and cane doll furniture, tiny brass tea sets, stuffed leather animals, and puppets can all be found on the second floor, as can *kurtas* (collarless or band-collar shirts) and long skirt ensembles in cotton and silk. **Colaba Causeway** is lined with pavement stalls selling various children's trinkets—leather animals, small drums, beads, peacock-feather fans. A number of shops here also sell Indian clothing for kids. Several shops in the **Oberoi Towers** sell Indian children's clothes, cool cotton dresses, and wooden dolls.

Clothing

The large, attractive, and friendly **Bombay Store** (✉ Sir Pherozeshah Mehta Rd., Fort, ☎ 22/288–5048 or 22/287–3443) has a good-size selection of men's shirts, kurtas, ties, women's *salwar kameez* (a 2-piece outfit of long, loose-fitting tunic over loose pants tapered at the ankle), blouses, skirts, shawls, saris, silk by the meter, and cotton clothes for children. **Charagh Din** (✉ 64 and 81 Wodehouse Rd., Colaba, ☎ 22/218–1375) is one of the best-known Indian names for top-quality, pure silk shirts for men in a tremendous variety of styles and patterns. **Christina** (✉ The Oberoi, ☎ 22/282–5069) is a tiny, classy boutique with a whole range of exquisite silk blouses and shirts, scarves, ties, *dupattas* (long, thin scarves for draping), and silk-edged purses and wallets. **Cotton World** (✉ Ram Nimi, Mandlik Rd., Colaba,, ☎ 22/285–0060 or 22/283–3294; ✉ Vipul Apartments, near Podar High School, Tagore Rd., Santa Cruz, ☎ 22/605–1602) is small but has some excellent Western cotton items at reasonable prices. **Ensemble** (✉ Great Western Building, 130/132 Shahid Bhagat Singh Marg, ☎ 22/287–0277 or –2882), a pricey boutique not far from the Taj Mahal hotel, has exclusive salwar kameez for women, kurtas for men, Western fashions, saris, and lovely costume jewelry, all by high-profile Indian designers. Ask to see the rare Banarasi silk saris, in rich colors woven with real gold and silver thread. The Bombay branch of the famous Madras store **Nalli** (✉ Trimurti Apartments, Bhulabhai Desai Rd., Breach Candy, ☎ 22/496–5577 or 22/496–5599), one of the largest sari stores in India, has a fair selection of classic silk saris. Have a look at the authentic *zari* Kanchipuram saris (their borders embroidered with gold), the Bangalore saris, and the uncut silk, sold by the meter. **Ravissant** (✉ Kemps Corner, ☎ 22/368–4934) was India's first haute-couture salon; it sells its own women's and men's clothing in exquisite patterns and fabrics, from rich silks to feather-light moiré. The branch in the Taj Mahal hotel (☎ 22/281–5227) also sells unique silver housewares and furnishings. A few shops in the **Taj Mahal** sell quality silks; try Burlington or the Indian Textiles Company. **Vama** (✉ 72 Peddar Rd., ☎ 22/387–1450) looks like another Benetton or Lacoste outlet, but it also has racks and glass counters full of gorgeous, high-fashion Indian women's and men's wear. Ask to see the nearly sacred Paithani saris—hand-woven of brilliantly colored silk and real gold and silver thread, they have gorgeous border designs.

Handicrafts

Aurocraft (✉ Swami Vivekanand Rd., Bandra) features crafts made at the Auroville commune in Pondicherry (☞ Chapter 11), including crocheted shoes, earrings, pottery, and toys. **The Bombay Store** (✉ Sir Pherozeshah Mehta Rd., Fort, ☏ 22/288–5048 or 22/287–3443) has a classy collection of popular Indian handicrafts such as metal work, sandalwood, china, marble, carpets, linens, and lamps. Prices are a tad higher here than at the government emporiums, but the store is enticingly laid out and service is competent. The **Central Cottage Industries Emporium** (✉ Apollo Bunder, Colaba, ☏ 22/202–7537 or 22/202–6564) is packed with textiles, carvings, and myriad other traditional Indian handicrafts from all over the country. It's a wonderful place to buy souvenirs, despite less-than-brilliant service. **Contemporary Arts and Crafts** (✉ 19 Nepean Sea Rd., opposite Baskin-Robbins, ☏ 22/363–1979; ✉ Juhu Vile Parle Shopping Centre, Gul Mohar Rd., Juhu, ☏ 22/620–4668) has a small but nicely representative selection of Indian handicrafts at reasonable prices. **Gangotri** (✉ World Trade Centre, Cuffe Parade, Colaba, ☏ 22/218–8187) sells lovely stone and wood carvings from the state of Uttar Pradesh. If you won't be traveling farther south, peruse regal Mysore silks at **Mysore Sales International** (☏ 22/218–4952). Browse Maharashtra's own crafts and an outstanding collection of statues, sculptures, and idols at **Trimourti** (☏ 22/218–9191 ext. 278). The **World Trade Centre** (✉ Cuffe Parade, Colaba, ☏ 22/218–9191) gathers government-run handicrafts emporiums and boutiques from most of India's states under one air-conditioned roof. Fixed prices offer respite from bazaar-style haggling.

Incense and Perfumes

Ajmal (✉ 4/13 Kamal Mansion, Arthur Bunder Rd., Fort, ☏ 22/285–6976) has a wonderful selection of rare Indian and French perfumes stored in huge decanters. It also stocks Agra wood, a rare incense base, 100 grams of which costs as much as a night at the Taj Mahal.

Jewelry

In business since 1865, the venerable **Tribhovandas Bhimji Zaveri** (✉ 241–43 Zaveri Bazaar, ☏ 22/342–5001) is said to be the largest jewelry showroom in India, with five floors of gorgeous 18-, 22-, and 24-karat gold, diamond, and silver jewelry. Do tour this palace of jewelry, if only to gaze at the mind-boggling range of designs. It's *much* more cost-effective, however, to buy from a smaller outfit such as Narandas and Sons, Zaveri Naran Das, or Ram Kewalram Popley, all on Sheikh Memon Street. Insist on knowing how many karats you're buying and whether or not the store will stand by the piece's purity. For silver jewelry, try **The Bombay Store** (☞ Handicrafts, *above*) or the arcade at **The Oberoi;** otherwise, head for the heart of **Colaba Bazaar,** a little south of the Taj Mahal hotel, where a series of tiny jewelry shops sells rings, earrings, necklaces, and more. Haggling is a must here.

Leather and Shoes

The posh shopping arcade at **The Oberoi** includes a variety of leather and shoe shops whose stylish goods are still priced lower than they would be in the West. Brave bargain-hunters have a cheaper and more adventurous alternative: **Daboo Street** (off Mohammed Ali Rd., a five-minute walk from Chor Bazaar, near Shalimar Hotel).

Music and Musical Instruments

If you want to take home some Indian recordings, especially classical music, head for the **Rhythm House** (✉ Kala Ghoda, Fort, ☏ 22/285–3963). Along with pop, jazz, and everything else, it has an excellent selection of *pacca gana* (classical vocal music) and Indian instrumental music. For Indian musical instruments try **Bhargava Musical Enterprise** (✉ 156 Khetwadi, Vallabhai Patel Rd.), a tiny, hard-to-find shop selling tablas, harmoniums, sitars, and tanpuras. **Swami Music City** (✉ Sayani Rd., opposite Ravindra Natya Mandir, near Siddhi Vinayak Temple, Prabhadevi, ☎ 22/430–6024) stocks all the traditional Indian instruments.

Tailoring

It can be disappointing to walk into a Bombay fabric shop, see bales and bales of splendid cloth, and realize you have no use for such raw materials. But a number of Bombay tailors can turn that fabric into custom-made clothing—Indian or Western—in a matter of hours. **Kala Pushp** (✉ Oberoi Towers shopping arcade, 2nd floor, ☎ 22/287–0654) has a tailoring department for both ladies and gents, ready to make suits, trousers, shirts, and even complicated women's ensembles in a very short time. Armed with the latest catalogs from Europe, these tailors will faithfully copy a design from a picture if you so desire. Bring fabric from elsewhere or choose from the store's own assortment of silk, linen, cotton and rayon cloth. **Narisons Khubsons** (✉ 49 Colaba Causeway, opposite police station, ☎ 22/202–0614) carries fine cotton and silk and can make excellent shirts, trousers, or women's outfits in one day if need be. They also sell ready-made women's clothing. There are two shops named Khubsons, back to back; make sure you have the right one. **Raymond** (✉ Bhulabhai Desai Rd., Breach Candy, opposite Breach Candy Hospital and Research Centre, ☎ 22/368–2644) is an outlet for Raymond Mills, which makes some of India's finest men's suits. Drawing on a tremendous range of material, the store can tailor a first-rate suit for about Rs. 3,000 in three days to a week. Call ahead to ask about delivery time; during the wedding season (winter) they can get very busy.

AJANTA AND ELLORA CAVES

Dating back more than 2,000 years, the cave temples of Ajanta and Ellora rank among the wonders of the ancient world. Here, over a period of 700 years—between the 2nd century BC and the 5th century AD—great armies of monks and artisans carved cathedrals, monasteries, and whole cities of frescoed, sculptured halls into the solid rock. Working with simple chisels and hammers and an ingenious system of reflecting mirrors to provide light, they cut away hundreds of thousands of tons of rock to create the cave temples. Driven by a religious fervor and sustained by a sacred patience beyond our contemporary grasp, these craftsmen inspired perpetual awe with the precision of their planning, their knowledge of rock formations, and the delicacy and profusion of their artwork. Together, the cave temples span three great religions—Buddhism, Hinduism, and Jainism. For optimum absorption of the vast and phenomenal caves, allow one full day for each site, remembering that both are closed on Monday. To get to Ajanta and Ellora, take a train, bus, or plane to Aurangabad, the nearest major city. From Aurangabad you can hop on a tour bus or hire a car and driver for about Rs. 1,300 to the Ajanta caves (a two- to three-hour trip), Rs. 550 to the Ellora caves (30 minutes).

Aurangabad

388 km (241 mi) east of Bombay, 30 km (18 mi) southeast of Ellora, 100 km (62 mi) southwest of Ajanta

With several excellent hotels and a growing number of good restaurants, Aurangabad serves as a base of exploration for the cave temples at both Ajanta and Ellora. The city has an interesting old bazaar, and is known for its *himru* (cotton and silk brocade) shawls and saris and its rich Paithani saris. If you're interested, pop into the Aurangabad Standard Silk Showroom or Aurangabad Silk, both near the train station; Ajanta Handicrafts in Harsul, on the highway to Ajanta; or Himroo Saris, on the highway to Ellora.

More than a mere gateway, Aurangabad has a number of ancient sites of its own, such as the imposing **Daulatabad Fort** (⊠ 13 km, or 8 mi, west of Old Town), built in 1187 by the Hindu king and surrounded by seven giant walls over 5 km (3 mi) long. The 17th-century **Bibi-ka-Maqbara** is also known as the mini–Taj Mahal; located 550 yards north of the old town, you can usually see it from the plane if you fly into Aurangabad. A pale but noble imitation of the original Taj Mahal, the tomb is dedicated to the wife of the last of the six great Mogul emperors, Aurangzeb (founder of Aurangabad and son of the Taj Mahal's creator, Shah Jahan). It was supposed to be a shining, white-marble edifice, but due to a paucity of funds only the bottom two feet of the monument were built with marble; the rest is probably stone faced with plaster. Somewhat awkwardly proportioned, the structure can be said to illustrate the decline of Mogul architecture.

Dining and Lodging

Most hotels in Aurangabad will discount their rates upon request; push for 15 percent off. Unless otherwise noted, all hotels listed are fully air-conditioned.

$$$$ ★ ✕ **Madhuban.** A central fountain of white marble; tables of dark wood; and fabrics of burgundy, ivory, and gold set a regal Mogul tone at this top restaurant. One wall of windows opens onto lovely tropical trees and flowers; another displays the busy kitchen, where you can watch chefs in tall, stiff white hats skewering meats for the tandoor oven. The menu also includes Chinese and Continental dishes, and there's a popular buffet lunch. ⊠ *Welcomgroup Rama International hotel, R-3 Chikalthana,* ☎ *240/485441. AE, DC, MC, V.*

$$$ ✕ **Angeethi.** One of Aurangabad's most popular restaurants, Angeethi is packed on weekends with locals enjoying their evening off. Named for a traditional Indian cooking vessel, this dark, cozy restaurant serves reasonably priced Punjabi, Continental, and Chinese fare, with a special knack for tandoori items. Other specialties include Afghani kebab masala (boneless chicken pieces in sweet, white cashew-nut gravy) and the two-person *sikendari raan* (a large leg of goat marinated in rum and spices and seared in a tandoor oven). There are plenty of tasty vegetarian choices. Service is friendly but not terribly efficient. The restaurant serves only Indian food between 3 and 7. ⊠ *6 Mehar Chambers, Vidya Nagar, Jalna Rd.,* ☎ *240/441988. MC, V.*

$$ ✕ **Master Cook.** Another hot favorite with Aurangabadis, Master Cook offers a mixed Chinese and Punjabi/Mughlai menu. Service is efficient and the food, above average; ask your waiter for recommendations. The kitchen is obliging enough to cook a dish to your specifications. The garden out back has a pleasant ambience. ⊠ *1 Surana Nagar, Jalna Rd.,* ☎ *240/340280. MC, V.*

$ ✕ **Bhoj.** Both branches of this thali restaurant serve a quick, tasty but light vegetarian Gujarati or Rajasthani platter for lunch and dinner. The choice of preparations is wide, and the price is right. Decor is purely functional, however, and the din deafening; this is not a place for leisurely dining. Alcohol is not served. The restaurant is closed between 3 and 7. ⊠ *Kamdar Bhavan, CBS Rd., no phone; Hotel Sai, Jalna Rd.,* ☎ *240/329915. No credit cards.*

$ ✕ **Woodlands.** Carnivores can move on: This primarily South Indian eatery is strictly vegetarian, offering tasty dosas and tangy *paneer makhanwala* (curd steaks spiced with chili), as well as thali options and a few Punjabi dishes. Alcohol is not served, and the restaurant is closed daily between 3:30 and 7. ✉ *Akashay Deep Plaza, near CIDCO Bus Stand, Jalna Rd.,* ☎ *no phone.*

$$$ **Taj Residency.** Inside and out, this gleaming Mogul palace is done in bright-white marble and stone with gold accents. The windows and doors arch to regal Mogul points, and the grand dome over the lobby is hand-painted in traditional Jaipuri patterns of bright yellow and white. Rooms have smooth teak furniture with matching headboards and mirror frames. All rooms open onto the garden and have balconies or patios, most with a teak swing. Stone paths wind through five acres of beautifully landscaped lawns, flower beds, and blossoming hedges. The most expensive hotel in Aurangabad, the Taj is not the best value in town. ✉ *8-N-12 CIDCO, Aurangabad 431003,* ☎ *240/381–1106 (–08),* FAX *240/381053. 38 rooms, 2 suites. Restaurant, pool, exercise room, dry cleaning, laundry service, business services, meeting room, travel services. AE, DC, MC, V.*

$$$ ★ **Welcomgroup Rama International.** A long driveway takes you away from the main road and through spacious grounds to this attractive hotel, with red bands of elephants chiseled on its bleached-white facade. The efficient and friendly staff provide personalized service of the highest order and create the kind of warm, intimate atmosphere you'd normally associate with a smaller hotel. Standard rooms are spacious and comfortably elegant, with views onto the verdant garden of palms and bright flower beds. Corner suites are like vast living rooms. Rooms in the old wing are substandard but are slated for renovation. ✉ *R-3 Chikalthana, 431210,* ☎ *240/484768 or 240/485854,* FAX *240/484768. 87 rooms, 3 suites. Restaurant, bar, coffee shop, pool, barber shop, beauty salon, massage, sauna, steam room, miniature golf, 2 tennis courts, croquet, exercise room, Ping-Pong, dry cleaning, laundry service, business services, meeting room, travel services. AE, DC, MC, V.*

$$ **Ambassador Ajanta.** Next door to its rival, the Rama, this five-story marble hotel sits amid sweeping lawns, well-kept flower beds, and towering trees alive with singing birds. Filled with brass goddesses, marble elephants, wood carvings, and myriad other Indian antiques, it's a haven of dark, Indian elegance. The rooms have garden-view windows and authentic decorative details but are slightly dreary. Don't miss a dip in the pool, where you can imbibe midswim at the sunken bar at the shallow end. The restaurant offers live ghazal music on weekends. ✉ *Jalna Rd., CIDCO, 431003,* ☎ *240/485211 or 240/485214,* FAX *240/484367. 78 rooms with bath, 18 suites. Restaurant, bar, pool, tennis court, badminton, dry cleaning, laundry service, business services, meeting rooms, travel services. AE, DC, MC, V.*

$$ **Hotel President Park.** All curves and semicircles, this attractive contemporary building was designed to embrace its central garden and give every room a view of the pretty pool. Ground-floor rooms open directly onto the garden. Rooms have balconies or patios and are cheerful inside, with teak-trimmed furniture, dark-toned fabrics, and brass fixtures, though bathrooms are on the small side. Overall the feel is very pleasant. The restaurant serves vegetarian food only. ✉ *R 7/2 Chikalthana, Airport Rd., 431210,* ☎ *240/486201,* FAX *240/484823. 56 rooms, 4 suites. Restaurant, bar, coffee shop, pool, sauna, steam room, tennis court, exercise room, dry cleaning, laundry service, meeting room, business services, meeting room, travel services. AE, DC, MC, V.*

$$ **The Meadows.** A little far (5 km/3 mi) from the city center, the Meadows offers the services of a tropical resort. Accommodations are in simple (carpet-free) but ultramodern cottages, each with a private lawn. The hotel prides itself on its architectural awards and environmental record—it uses a biotechnological system of plant roots to purify its air and waste water. The grounds are planted with a splendid variety of trees and flowers and house a number of rare birds. At night the silence of the countryside descends. This is a good place to stay if you want some creature comforts without urban bustle; and it's ideal for kids, with rabbits, parrots, ducks, and ample space to run around. Rusticity costs: Prices are a bit higher than at comparable hotels in the city itself. A courtesy coach runs into Aurangabad twice daily. ✉ *Village Mitmita, Padegaon, Bombay-Nasik Hwy., 431002,* ☎ *240/677412 or 240/677415,* FAX *240/677416. 44 rooms. Restaurant bar, pool, health club, beauty salon, business services, laundry, travel services, meeting room. AE, DC, MC, V.*

$ **Hotel Windsor Castle.** You enter the tiny lobby of this small, pale-pink brick budget hotel through teak-framed glass doors carved with elephants—at which point you see electric-purple, red, and black modular couches and chairs on red marble floors. The place does not resemble its namesake. Rooms are reasonably clean and functional but quite small and unusually polyhedral, with simple, modern furniture and clashing curtains and upholstery. Only 12 rooms have air-conditioning. ✉ *Jalgaon Rd., opposite CIDCO Office, 431003,* ☎ *240/484818 or 240/486011,* FAX *240/488250. 56 rooms, 2 suites. Restaurant, bar, coffee shop, meeting rooms. AE, DC, MC, V.*

$ **MTDC Holiday Resort.** If you don't mind a bleary-eyed staff and listless ambience, this centrally located hotel offers excellent value for the money. The strictly no-frills rooms are recommended for their cleanliness. Only six rooms have air-conditioning; don't try the others. ✉ *Station Rd., 431001,* ☎ *240/331513,* FAX *240/331198. 6 air-conditioned rooms. Restaurant. No credit cards.*

Ajanta Caves

It is thought that a band of wandering Buddhist monks first came here in the 2nd century BC searching for a place to meditate during the monsoons. Ajanta was ideal—peaceful and remote, with a spectacular setting: a sharp, wide horseshoe-shape gorge that fell steeply to a wild mountain stream flowing through the jungle below. The monks began carving crude caves into the rock face of the gorge, and a new temple form was born.

Over seven centuries, the cave temples of Ajanta evolved into works of incredible art. Structural engineers continue to be awestruck by the sheer brilliance of the ancient builders, who seem to have created this marvel of artistic and architectural splendor undaunted by the limitations of their implements, materials, and skills. In all, 29 caves were carved, 15 of which were left unfinished; some of them were *viharas* (monasteries)—complete with stone pillows carved onto the monks' stone beds—others were *chaityas* (Buddhist cathedrals). All of the caves were profusely decorated with intricate sculptures and murals depicting the many incarnations of Buddha.

As Buddhism declined, the monk-artists abandoned their work, and the temples were swallowed up by the jungle. A thousand years later, in 1819, Englishman John Smith was tiger-hunting on a bluff nearby in the dry season and noticed the soaring arch of what is now dubbed Cave 10 peeking out from the thinned greenery; it was he who subsequently unveiled the caves to the modern world.

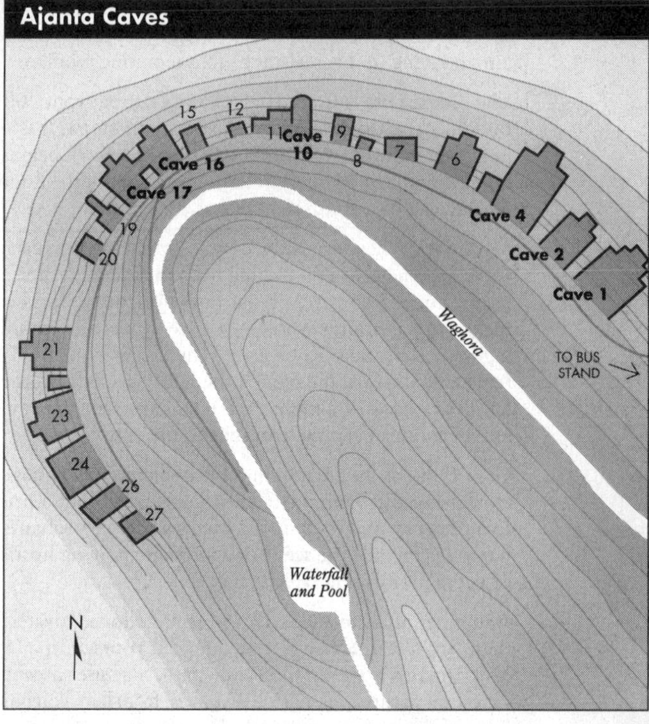

At both Ajanta and Ellora, monumental facades and statues were chipped out of solid, particularly hard rock, but at Ajanta, an added dimension has survived the centuries—India's most remarkable cave paintings. Monks spread a carefully prepared plaster of clay, cow dung, chopped rice husks, and lime onto the rough rock walls and devotedly painted pictures on it with only natural local pigments: red ocher, burnt brick, copper oxide, lampblack, and dust from crushed green rocks. The caves are now like chapters of a splendid epic in visual form, recalling the life of the Buddha and illustrating tales from Buddhist *jatakas* (fables). As the artists lovingly told the story of the Buddha, they portrayed the life and civilization they knew; the effect is that of a magic carpet flying you back into a drama of ancient nobles, wise men, and commoners. When the electric spotlights flicker onto the paintings, the figures seem to come alive.

Opinions vary on which of the Ajanta caves is most exquisite. Caves 1, 2, 16, 17, and 19 are generally considered to have the best paintings, Caves 1, 4, 17, 19, and 26 the best sculptures. (The caves are numbered from west to east, not in chronological order.) The guides hanging around the entrance to the caves are useless at best: Don't waste your money. The attendants at each cave, however, can be helpful.

Most popular at Ajanta are the paintings in **Cave 1,** depicting the Bodhisattva Avalokitesvara and Bodhisattva Padmapani. Padmapani, or the "one with the lotus in his hand," is considered the alter ego of the Lord Buddha, who assumed the duties of the Buddha when he disappeared. Padmapani is depicted with his sinuous-hipped wife, one of Ajanta's most widely reproduced figures.

Cave 2 is remarkable for its ceiling decorations and its murals relating the birth of the Buddha. For its sheer exuberance and joie de vivre, the painting of women on a swing is considered the finest.

Sculpture is the main interest in **Cave 4.** The largest vihara in Ajanta, this one depicts a man and a woman fleeing from a mad elephant and a man giving up his resistance to a tempting woman.

The oldest cave is **Cave 10,** a chaitya dating from 200 BC, filled with Buddhas and dominated by an enormous stupa. It is only in AD 100, however, that the exquisite brush-and-line work begins. In breathtaking detail, the Shadanta Jataka, a legend about the Buddha, is depicted on the wall in a continuous panel.

The mystical heights attained by the monk-artists reach their zenith in **Cave 16,** where you're released from the bonds of time and space. Here a continuous narrative spreads both horizontally and vertically, evolving into a panoramic whole—at once logical and stunning. One painting here is riveting: Known as "The Dying Princess," it is believed to represent Sundari, the wife of the Buddha's half-brother, Nanda, who left her to become a monk. Cave 16 has an excellent view of the river and may have been the entrance to the entire series of caves.

Cave 17 holds the greatest number of pictures undamaged by time. Luscious heavenly damsels fly effortlessly overhead, a prince makes love to a princess, and the Buddha tames a raging elephant. Other favorite paintings include the scene of a woman applying lipstick and one of a princess performing *sringar* (her toilet).

A number of unfinished caves were abandoned mysteriously, but even these are worth a visit if you can haul yourself up a steep 100 steps. You can also walk up the bridle path, a gentler ascent in the form of a crescent pathway alongside the caves; from here you have a magnificent view of the ravines of the Waghura River.

A trip to the Ajanta caves needs to be well planned. You can see the caves at a fairly leisurely pace in two hours, but the drive to and from the caves takes anywhere from two to three hours. Come prepared with water, snacks (from a shop in Aurangabad; there are no snack stands here), comfortable walking shoes, a flashlight, and patience. Aurangabad can be hot year-round, and peering into a succession of 29 caves can be tiring. The paintings are only dimly lit (to protect the artwork) and a number of them are badly damaged, so deciphering the work takes some effort. The caves are connected by a fair number of steps, both up and down; it's advisable to start at the far end and work your way back, to avoid a hot trek back at the end. Flash photography and video cameras are both prohibited inside the caves; the admission fee includes having the lights turned on as you enter one. ✉ *100 km (62 mi) northeast of Aurangabad.* 🎫 *Rs. 5 per party, video cameras Rs. 25.* ⏲ *Tues.–Sun. 9–5:30 (arrive by 4).*

Ellora Caves

In the 7th century, for some inexplicable reason, the focus of activity shifted from Ajanta to a site 123 km (76 mi) to the southwest—a place known today as Ellora. Unlike the cave temples at Ajanta, those of Ellora are not solely Buddhist. Instead, they trace the course of religious development in India—through the decline of Buddhism in the latter half of the 8th century, the Hindu renaissance that followed the return of the Gupta dynasty, and the Jain resurgence between the 9th and 11th centuries. Of the 34 caves, the 12 to the south are Buddhist, the 17 in the center are Hindu, and the five to the north are Jain.

At Ellora the focus is on sculpture, which covers the walls in exquisitely ornate masses. The carvings in the Buddhist caves are a serene reflection of the Buddhist philosophy, but in the Hindu caves they take on

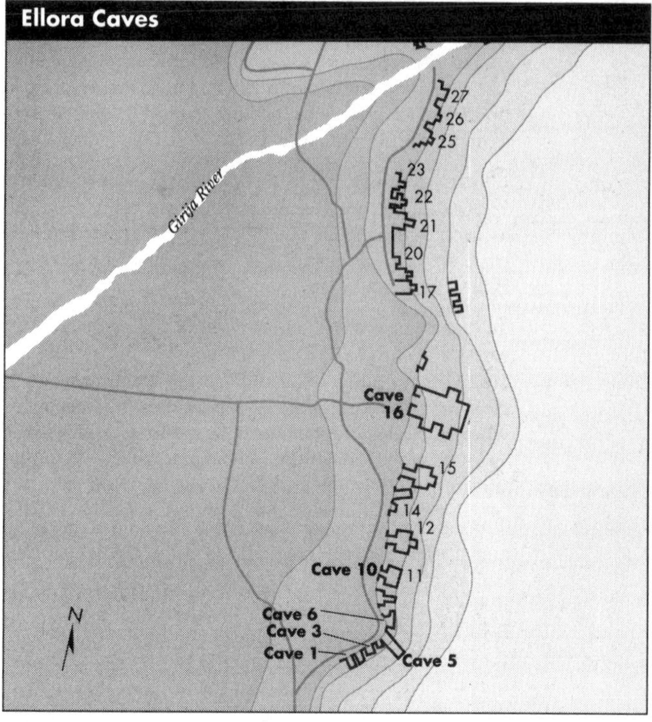

a certain exuberance, a throbbing vitality. Gods and demons do fearful battle, Lord Shiva angrily flails his eight arms, elephants rampage, eagles swoop, and lovers intertwine.

Unlike Ajanta, where the temples were chopped out of a steep cliff, the caves at Ellora were dug into the slope of a hill along a north-south line, presumably so that they faced west and could thus receive the light of the setting sun.

Cave 1 (two stories) and **Cave 3** (three stories) are remarkable for having more than one floor. The two caves form a monastery behind an open courtyard. The facade looms nearly 50 ft high, but it's simple, belying the lavish interior beyond. Gouged into this block of rock are a ground-floor hall, a shrine above that, and another hall on the top story with a gallery of Buddhas seated under trees and parasols.

The largest of the Buddhist caves is **Cave 5,** 117 ft by 56 ft. This was probably as a classroom for young monks. The roof appears to be supported by 24 pillars; working their way down, sculptors first "built" the roof before they "erected" the pillars.

Cave 6 contains a statue of Saraswati, the Hindu goddess of learning—also identified as Mahamayuri, the Buddhist goddess of learning—in the company of Buddhist figures. **Cave 10** is the "Carpenter's Cave," where Hinduism and Buddhism meet again. Here the stonecutters reproduced the timbered roofs of their day over a richly decorated facade that imitates masonry work. Inside this chaitya—the only actual Buddhist chapel at Ellora—the main work of art is a huge image of Buddha.

The immediate successors to the Buddhist caves are the Hindu caves, and a step inside these is enough to pull you up short. It's another world—another universe—in which the calm contemplation of the seated Buddhas gives way to the dynamic cosmology of Hinduism. Thought to have been created around the 7th and 8th centuries, these kinetic sculptures depict goddesses at battle; Shiva waving his eight arms; life-size elephants groaning under their burdens; lovers striking poses; and boars, eagles, peacocks, and monkeys prancing around what has suddenly turned into a zoo.

Ellora is dominated by the mammoth Kailasa temple complex, or **Cave 16.** Dedicated to Shiva, the complex is a replica of his legendary abode at Mount Kailasa in the Tibetan Himalayas. The largest monolithic structure in the world, the Kailasa reveals the genius, daring, and raw skill of its artisans.

To create the Kailasa complex, an army of stonecutters started at the top of the cliff, where they removed 3 million cubic ft of rock to create a vast pit with a freestanding rock left in the center. Out of this single slab, 276 ft long and 154 ft wide, the workers created Shiva's abode, which includes the main temple, a series of smaller shrines, and galleries built into a wall that encloses the entire complex. Nearly every surface is exquisitely sculpted with epic themes.

Around the courtyard, numerous friezes illustrate the legends of Shiva and stories from the great Hindu epics, the *Mahabharata* and the *Ramayana.* One interesting panel on the eastern wall relates the origin of Shiva's symbol, the linga, or phallus. Another frieze, on the outer wall of the main sanctuary on the southern side of the courtyard, shows the demon Ravana shaking Mount Kailasa, a story from the *Ramayana.*The Jain caves are at the far end. If you have a car, consider driving there once you've seen the Hindu group of caves. The Jain caves are attractive in their own right and should not be missed on account of geography. **Cave 32,** for one, is as complex as a rabbit burrow; it's marvelous to climb through the numerous well-carved chambers and study the towering figures of Gomateshvara and Mahavir.

Ellora is said to be the busiest tourist site in the state of Maharashtra. The Ajanta caves are a bit off the beaten track, but Ellora, a mere half an hour from Aurangabad, bristles with crowds—honeymooners, picnic-wallahs, and students—and is none too peaceful. Try to avoid coming here during school holidays. *Rs. 5; Video cameras Rs. 25. Tues.–Sun. 9–5:30.*

NEED A BREAK?

Ellora Restaurant (✉ Parking lot, Ellora Caves) is a convenient place to stop for a cold drink and a hot samosa (fried meat or vegetable pastry). The outdoor patio is pleasant, with fruit trees (home to many monkeys) and floods of pink bougainvillea flowers spilling down the arbor.

Nightlife and the Arts

The annual **Ellora Dance Festival,** held in December, draws top classical Indian dancers and musicians from around the country to perform outdoors against the magical backdrop of the Ellora Caves.

Ajanta and Ellora Caves A to Z

Arriving and Departing

BY BUS

Several competing companies run luxury overnight buses to Aurangabad from Bombay, a 12-hour journey. You can arrange such a ride through your hotel or travel agent in Bombay. This is not the most comfortable option.

BY PLANE

Aurangabad and Bombay are only about 45 minutes apart by air; a one-way ticket costs about Rs. 2,000. **Indian Airlines** (☏ 240/485421 or 240/483392; Aurangabad airport, ☏ 240/482111 or 240/485780) flies regularly. Ask your travel agent about the current status and schedules of other domestic airlines.

BY TRAIN

Slow trains run to Aurangabad from Bombay, Hyderabad, Delhi, and other major cities. Ask a travel agent for details.

Contacts and Resources

CURRENCY EXCHANGE

Hotels generally change money for their guests. The **State Bank of India** (✉ Kranti Chowk, ☏ 240/331386 or 240/331872) is open weekdays 10–2:30 and Saturday 10–12:30. **Trade Wings** (✉ Near Bawa Petrol Pump, Jalna Rd., Aurangabad, ☏ 240/357480 or 240/332952) is open Monday–Saturday from 9:30 to 6:30 or 7.

GUIDED TOURS

The **Government of India Tourist Office** (☞ Visitor Information, *below*) in Aurangabad oversees about 56 expert, polite, multilingual tour guides. You can hire one through the tourist office itself; the MTDC office, also in Aurangabad (☞ Visitor Information, *below*); and most travel agents. For parties of one to four, the fees are Rs. 230 per half day (four hours) and Rs. 345 for a full day (up to eight hours). An extra Rs. 225 is charged for trips of more than 100 km (60 mi); a guided day trip to the Ajanta caves, for example, would run around Rs. 570. It's best to book ahead. The self-employed guides at the caves themselves will waste your time and money.

Once you have a guide, your best bet for transportation is to hire a car and driver. Rates are unusually high in Aurangabad, but moving around by auto-rickshaw is a slow business. A full-day trip in an air-conditioned Ambassador with a driver may cost around Rs. 2,250 to Ajanta and Rs. 850 to Ellora. A full-day trip in a non-air-conditioned Ambassador with driver may cost around Rs. 1,250 to Ajanta and Rs. 550 to Ellora. You can arrange car hire through your hotel travel desk, one of the travel agencies listed below, or the Government of India Tourist Office.

TRAVEL AGENCIES

Classic Travel Related Services (✉ MTDC Holiday Resort, Station Rd., Aurangabad, ☏ 240/335598 or 240/337788). **Aurangabad Tours and Travels** (a.k.a. Aurangabad Transport Syndicate, ✉ Welcomgroup Rama Hotel, Airport Rd., Aurangabad, ☏ 240/482423).

VISITOR INFORMATION

The **Government of India Tourist Office** (✉ Krishna Vilas, Station Rd., Aurangabad, ☏ 240/331913 or –513), across from the train station, provides a warm and informative welcome to Aurangabad. It's open weekdays 9 to 6, Saturdays and holidays 9 to 1:30. Ask for the helpful Mr. Yadav or Mr. Rao. The **MTDC** (✉ MTDC Holiday Resort, Station Rd., Aurangabad, ☏ 240/331513) is extremely helpful and stays open 24 hours. (Its airport counter opens when flights arrive.) In addition to these offices, most hotels have travel desks and informed concierges who can help you plot your moves.

MAHARASHTRA'S BEACHES

The Maharashtra coastline north of Goa may yet become the most beautiful resort area in India. Some of this region's many 17th-century forts are actually built on tiny offshore islands that are dwarfed by the ramparts. The coastline creates wide panoramas without any encroachment of the modern world, and you pass traditional villages that are usually the home of Kolis, one of the original fishing tribes. Koli women walk with a fine stride, their saris worn in the Marathi fashion, skin-tight between their legs; the men master the waves and bring back the fish, which is then cooked in the zesty Konkan style.

In the early 1990s, the state of Maharashtra enacted a plan to control the growth of resorts, protect valuable marshlands, and restore at least one coastal fort. There are no upscale accommodations here, but you can still spend a few nights under rustling palm fronds in idyllic coves and harbors at simple yet enjoyable tented beach resorts set up by the MTDC (☞ Visitor Information *in* Contacts and Resources, *below*).

Because these areas are still only minimally developed, the beaches at or near the tented resorts are your best bets for comfortable sun and sand. (The resorts and beaches are grouped together below.) Each resort has walk-in two- and four-bed tents with windows, front and back entrances, and plenty of interior space. All provide comfortable cots, clean linens, electricity, fans, filtered drinking water, and separate bathrooms and shower facilities in clean, if unappealing, concrete buildings. The restaurants are often open-air affairs under thatched roofs, and usually offer Indian (sometimes Konkan) and limited Continental menus that may include the catch of the day. All of these resorts, except Ganapatipule and Bordi, which offer cottages in addition to tents, close for the monsoon between June 15 and November 1. Each tent costs about Rs. 300 per day, double occupancy, and occupation is restricted to couples and families. MTDC also has a rent-a-tent scheme that allows you to choose your own private beach hideaway.

To get here, hire a car and driver from Bombay (☞ Visitor Information *in* Bombay A to Z, *below*).

15 **MTDC Bordi Beach Tented Resort.** The town of Bordi, north of Bombay, is a favorite holiday spot for urban escapees. Dormitories, cottages, and tents are on an isolated beach backed by casuarina trees. ✉ *Thane district, 130 km (81 mi) north of Bombay* ☎ *2424/51632,* FAX *2424/51632. 8 5-bed tents with shared bath, 4 rooms, 1 dormitory.*

16 **MTDC Harihareshwar Beach Tented Resort.** Set on an inlet backed by hills, this delightful complex stands near two beaches, of which the more secluded one is preferable. Authentic Konkan fare is served in a rustic restaurant, often followed by a crackling campfire. ✉ *Raigad district, 230 km (143 mi) south of Bombay* ☎ *2147/26036,* FAX *2147/26036. 20 2-bed and 10 4-bed tents.*

17 **MTDC Murud Janjira Beach Tented Resort.** This complex serves good local Konkan cuisine alongside a palm-fringed beach. ✉ *Ratnagiri district, 247 km (153 mi) south of Bombay. 5 4-bed tents with shared bath.*

18 **MTDC Ganapatipule Beach Tented Resort.** Nestled in a coconut grove, the cottages and tents in this complex have views onto the white-sand beach and plenty of privacy. Because Ganapatipule is an important Hindu pilgrimage site, liquor is not available, but the restaurant serves good food. There is now also an MTDC hotel here, the Konkani House, in which some rooms are air-conditioned; reserve through the number below or the MTDC in Bombay. ✉ *Ratnagiri district, 375 km (233 mi) south of Bombay* ☎ *2357/35248 or 2357/35061,* FAX *2357/35328. 60 beds in 2-bed and 4-bed tents with shared bath, 1 tent with private bath, and cottages.*

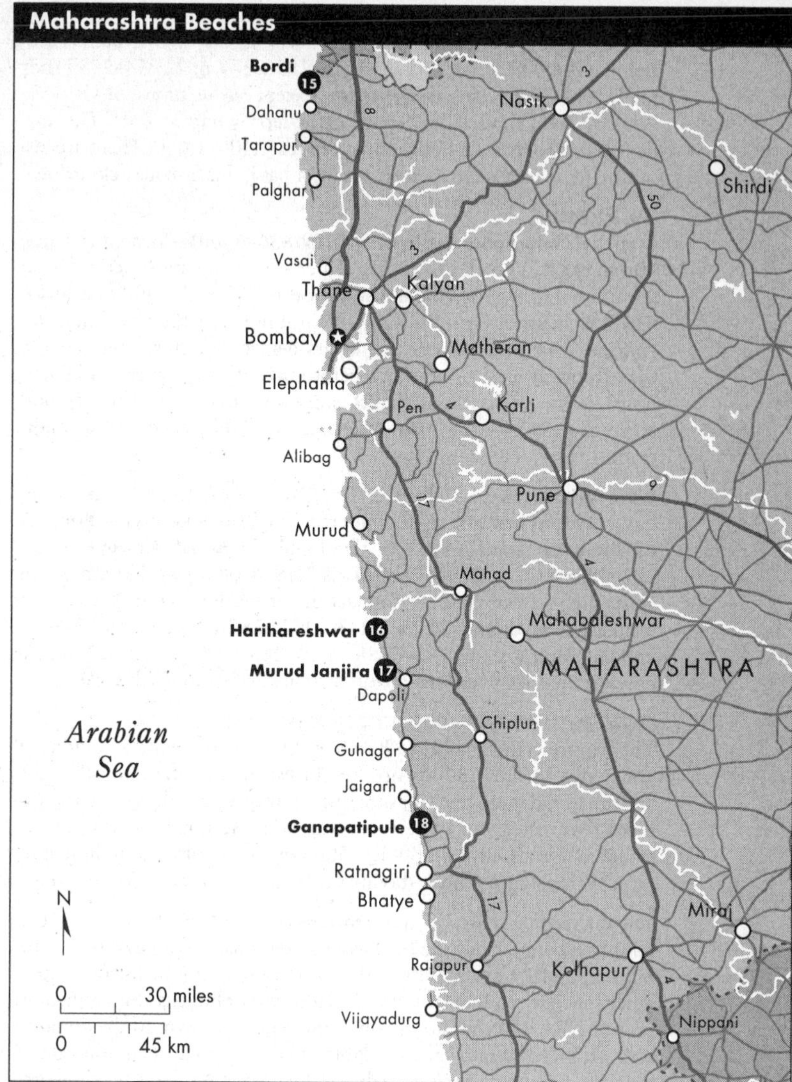

BOMBAY A TO Z

Arriving and Departing

By Car

Fairly good roads connect Bombay to most major cities and tourist areas. Hiring a car and driver gives you a chance to watch the often beautiful surroundings whiz by, but it can also be loud, hair-raising, and less than time-efficient. If you have the time and the nerves for a road trip, you'll experience what many people miss when they fly. Some distances from Bombay: Pune, 172 km (101 mi); Panaji (Goa), 597 km (373 mi); Ahmedabad, 545 km (341 mi); Hyderabad, 711 km (444 mi). Bombay is 1,033 km (650 mi) northwest of Bangalore, 432 km (268 mi) northwest of Madras, and 1,408 km (873 mi) southwest of Delhi.

By Catamaran

Frank Shipping Ltd. (✉ Shed 2, New Ferry Wharf, Mallet Bunder Rd., Bombay 400009, ☎ 22/285–2272, 22/285–2274, or 22/374–3737) normally runs a daily catamaran service (except during monsoon) between Bombay and Panaji, Goa, departing the ferry wharf at 7 AM. The journey takes about seven hours and costs Rs. 1,400–1,600. There are also overnight boats. *Call to inquire,* as rumor has it this firm may close down.

By Plane

Bombay's **international airport** (☎ 22/836–6700)—located in Sahar, 30 km (18 mi) north of the city center—is India's most active for international flights. The **domestic airport** (☎ 22/615–6400 or 22/615–6367) is at Santa Cruz, 26 km (15½ mi) north of the city center. *Reconfirm your flight* at least 72 hours before departure and arrive at the airport at least 60 minutes before takeoff for domestic flights, 2 hours before international flights (some airlines require 3 hours). Both airports have 24-hour business centers available to holders of major credit cards.

Delta Airlines (☎ 22/288–5659) has flights to and from Bombay every day via Frankfurt hub. Other international carriers serving Bombay: **Air-India** (☎ 22/202–4142 or 22/836–6767). **British Airways** (☎ 22/282–0888 or 22/832–9061). **KLM** (☎ 22/838–0838) works with Northwest; flights from the U.S. connect in Amsterdam. Domestic carriers include **Indian Airlines** (☎ 22/202–3031, 22/287–6161, or 22/615–6850) and **Jet Airways** (22/285–5788 or 22/283–7570 or 22/615–6666); check with your travel agent for current carriers and schedules.

BETWEEN THE AIRPORTS AND CENTER CITY

The trip from the airport to Bombay should take about 45 minutes if you arrive before 7:30 AM or after 11 PM (many international flights arrive around midnight). At other times, traffic near the city center can increase transfer time to more than an hour. All hotels provide airport transfers for about Rs. 200–Rs. 300, and some offer complimentary airport transfers to those staying in a suite or on an exclusive floor.

The international airport has a **prepaid taxi service.** Head to the prepaid-taxi counter outside the baggage-and-customs area to hire a regular cab, either air-conditioned or non-air-conditioned. Your rate is determined by your destination and amount of luggage, and is payable up front; Rs. 450 should get you to the center of town. At the domestic airport, metered taxis are available outside; a policemen notes down the taxi's license plates before dispatching you on your way. A metered (not prepaid) taxi from the domestic airport to the city center should cost about Rs. 150; from the international airport, about Rs. 200.

By Train

Bombay has two train stations. **Chhatrapati Shivaji Terminus** (✉ D. Naoroji Rd., Fort, ☎ 134), formerly Victoria Terminus, is the hub of India's Central Railway line. **Bombay Central Station** (✉ Phalke Rd., ☎ 131) is the hub of India's Western Railway line. Be sure to go to the right train station—check before you set out. To avoid the pandemonium at the stations, have a travel agent book your ticket; this costs a bit more but saves time and stress. If you do it yourself, head for the tourist counter established specially for foreign travelers. For more information and recommended trains, *see* Train Travel *in* Smart Travel Tips A to Z.

Getting Around

Having a car and driver for a day is usually the most convenient way to sightsee. In certain areas, however—in the bazaars, for instance—you really have to walk for the full experience.

By Auto-Rickshaw

Auto-rickshaws are permitted only in Bombay's suburbs, where you can flag them down on the street. The rate is about Rs. 7 for the first kilometer, Rs..70 per additional kilometer. As with regular taxis (☞ *below*), insist on paying by the meter and ask to see the tariff card.

By Hired Car with Driver

Having a car at your disposal zips you around town without the repeated hassle of hailing taxis and haggling over fares. To arrange a hired car, inquire at your hotel's travel desk or contact one of the travel agencies listed below. (You'll probably pay more if you book through your hotel.) You'll get lower rates from the India Tourism Development Corporation (☞ Travel Agencies, *below*): Rs. 850 for a full day (8 hours, or 80 km) in a non-air-conditioned Premier NE; Rs. 1,225 for a car with air-conditioning. Rates go up for Toyotas, Mercedes, and other "luxury" cars.

By Hydrofoil

Swift, air-conditioned hydrofoils connect Bombay with points in the suburbs, but service is discontinued during the monsoon and at press time had been suspended indefinitely. Contact the MTDC for current schedules.

By Taxi

Yellow-top black taxis or silver and blue air-conditioned taxis can be flagged down anywhere in the city. Insist that the driver turn on the meter, a rusty mechanical contraption on the hood of the car, before setting off. Because the development of taxi meters cannot keep up with the rising costs of fuel, it takes some arithmetic to compute the latest (higher) fares, based on the meter reading. Drivers are required to show you their revised tariff cards for easy reference, but they sometimes conveniently misplace them, or whip out a chart for air-conditioned cabs, or show you fares chargeable after midnight; examine the card carefully, and look for a policeman if you have doubts. At press time the legal fare was 10 times the total amount shown on the meter, based on roughly Rs. 11 for the first kilometer and Rs. 1 for each additional kilometer. Air-conditioned taxi fares are 25 percent higher. Ask your hotel what the going rates are.

Contacts and Resources

Currency Exchange

Most luxury hotels will change money for their guests. **American Express Travel Services** (✉ Regal Cinema bldg., Chhatrapati Shivaji Maharaj Rd., Colaba ☎ 22/204–8291) is open Monday–Saturday 9:30–6:30. **Thomas Cook India, Ltd.** (✉ Thomas Cook Bldg., D. Naoroji Rd., Fort ☎ 22/204–8556) is open Monday–Saturday 9:30–7. The **State Bank of India** (✉ Madame Cama Rd., Fort, ☎ 22/202–2426) is open weekdays 10:30–4:30, as are most other banks.

Consulates

The **U.S. Consulate** (✉ Lincoln House, 78 Bhulabhai Desai Rd., Warden, ☎ 22/363–3611) is open weekdays 7–11 AM; the staff is on duty until 5 PM in case of emergency. The **Canadian Consulate** (✉ 41–42 Makers Chambers VI, 4th floor, Nariman Point, ☎ 22/287–6027, 22/287–6028, 22/287–6029, or, in an emergency, 011/687–6500) is open Monday–Thursday 9–1 and 1:30–5:30, Friday 1:30–3:30. The **British Consulate** (✉ Makers Chambers IV, 1st floor, 222 J. Bajaj Marg, Nariman Point, ☎ 22/283–2330, 22/283–0517, or, in an emergency, 22/283–4040) is open weekdays 8–1, and for visas 2–4.

Emergencies

Police: ☎ 100. **Fire:** ☎ 101. **Ambulance:** ☎ 102.

Most hotels have house physicians and dentists on call. Your consulate can also give you the name of a reputable doctor or dentist. Otherwise, try the emergency room at **Breach Candy Hospital and Research Center** (✉ Bhulabhai Desai Rd., Breach Candy,, ☎ 22/363–3651) or **Jaslok Hospital** (✉ Dr. G. Deshmukh Marg, near Haji Ali, ☎ 22/493–3333).

Guided Tours

The **Government of India Tourist Office** (☞ *below*) trains and oversees knowledgeable, multilingual tour guides available directly from the office (22/203–7654) or through the MTDC (☞ *below*) or just about any travel agency. Rates are approximately Rs. 230 per half day for groups of one to four, Rs. 345 for a full eight-hour day with no lunch break (Rs. 460 with lunch break). Additional fees apply for trips beyond 100 km (62 mi) and for those involving overnight stays.

Late-Night Pharmacies

Most hotels have pharmacies that are open daily until about 9 PM. **Royal Chemists** (✉ Acharya Dhonde Marg, opposite Wadia Hospital, Vishwas Niwas Bldg. 8, Shop 3, Parel, ☎ 22/411–5028) is open 24 hours.

Travel Agencies

These agencies are the best for general travel assistance and car hire: **American Express** (☞ Currency Exchange, *above*). **Ashoka Travels** (✉ Kothari Mansion, 9 Parekh St., opposite Girgaon Court, ☎ 22/385–7622 or 22/387–8639). The transport department of the **India Tourism Development Corporation** (ITDC; ✉ 11th floor, Nirmal Bldg., Nariman Point, ☎ 22/288–0992 or 22/202–6679) is also helpful with travel arrangements. For a complete list of travel agencies, pick up a copy of the ITDC's "Mumbai" brochure.

Visitor Information

You cannot count on hotels to stock general tourist information, such as maps and brochures. The **Government of India Tourist Office** (✉ 123 Maharishi Karve Rd., Churchgate, ☎ 22/203–3144 or 22/203–2932), near the Churchgate train station, has useful material; it's open weekdays 8:30 to 6, Saturday and holidays 8:30 to 2. The **MTDC** Tours Division (✉ Madame Cama Rd., opposite L.I.C. Bldg., ☎ 22/202–6713 or 22/202–7762) is open daily from 8:30 to 7. Both bureaus have counters at the airports; the MTDC also has counters at Chhatrapati Shivaji Terminus and the Gateway of India.

8 GOA

The former Portuguese colony of Goa is India's most famous beach destination. Silvery strips of sand are never more than a short walk from charming villages here, and the towns—among the cleanest in India—are a pleasing blend of Portuguese and Indian culture and architecture, including a number of historic churches.

By Julie Tomasz

Updated by Jayanth Kodkani

IT'S HARD TO TELL where the coast ends and the towns begin in Goa. With more than 36 gorgeous beaches down the west side of its 2,295 square mi, this tiny state (population 1.2 million)—a Portuguese colony until 1961—is India's most famous resort destination. With the exception of the monsoon season (June to September), the temperature stays warm and the air stays dry. Wide, palm-bordered rivers move lazily down to the Arabian Sea, and in small towns the houses gleam with a light wash of color set off by brightly painted front porches.

Goa was already a flourishing trade center before the arrival of the Portuguese in the sixteenth century—a marketplace for spices, silk, Persian corals, porcelain, and pearls. Yet ever since Alfonso de Albuquerque defeated Adil Shahi and established what turned out to be a 450-year dominance, the Latin influence has defined Goan culture. The quintessential Goan is fun-loving and extroverted—Goans love a good drink and a hearty meal—yet always has time for an afternoon nap. Even today, most shopkeepers lower their shutters for a long siesta. Beer is cheap, and *feni*—cashew or coconut-palm hooch—is a favorite local drink at the state's 6,000 watering holes.

But the sweep of development and modernity is gradually undermining Goa's vestigial Portuguese culture in favor of Indian culture at large. Fewer houses and lodges begin their names with "Casa" or "Loja"; barbers are no no longer known as *barbarias,* nor tailors as *alfaitarias.* A few signs remain: HOSPICIO on the hospital in Margao, CINE NACIONAL on the movie theater in Panaji, and some shop signs with a Portuguese twist on common Hindu names, like POY for Pai, QUEXOVA for Keshava, and NAIQUE for Naik.

Although most travelers come to Goa for its beaches, both Margao, in the south, and the state capital of Panaji, farther north, are worth visiting for their sights alone. Panaji has whitewashed churches, palm-lined plazas, and clean streets and is a short taxi ride from the exquisitely beautiful Portuguese church town of Old Goa, the final resting place of St. Francis Xavier. Margao's Sunday food market is a chaotic spectacle, highlighted by garrulous fisherwomen selling their fish out of baskets.

Pleasures and Pastimes

Architecture

Goa is best known for its grandiose churches, exquisitely sculpted temples, and mosques, all three to four centuries old. The most illustriuos structures are Old Goa's *sé* (cathedral) and Basilica of Bom Jesus, where the remains of St. Francis Xavier lie in a silver casket entombed in a Florentine-style marble mausoleum.

Carnival

If you're here in February just before Lent, you'll see the Goans' zest for life in its finest form. Carnival time remains the official season for nonstop revelry, directed by King Momo ("King of Misrule"), a Goan appointed by his peers as the life of the party. Festivities include fanciful pageants (with some 50 floats depicting elements of Goa's folk culture, or more contemporary messages like preservation of the environment), hordes of musicians strumming the guitar or playing the banjo, and dancers breaking into the *mando* (a folk fusion of the Portuguese *fado* and the waltz)—all in streets spangled with confetti. This is prime time to have a beer or a feni and savor Goa's legendary warmth.

Dining

The Goans' legendary passion for seafood is borne out in the lines of the state's Poet Laureate, B. B. Borkar: "O, God of Death! Don't make it my turn today, because there's fish curry for dinner!" Portuguese dishes are generally adapted to Goan tastes with a healthy pinch of red chili, tempered with coconut milk. Typical local dishes include zesty-sweet prawn-curry rice, *chouris pao* (sausage bread), chicken *cafreal* (amply seasoned with ginger, garlic, green chilis, and lime), and ultra-hot vindaloo dishes. Goa's seafood is superb, especially fresh crabs, pomfret, squid, lobster, and prawns. Try pomfret in a red or green sauce, or tiger prawns *baffad* (in the spicy Goan style). For dessert, *bebinka* is a wonderfully rich layered pastry dense with butter, egg yolk, and coconut. And no Goan experience is truly complete without at least a taste of feni, the potent local brew made of either palm sap or cashew fruit.

Lodging

Most of Goa's ritziest hotels are in the Bardez district, north of Panaji, but you might want to try one of the little lodging houses that have sprung up along the coast in recent years. If you want to explore Old Goa, Panaji has several grand hotels, most notably the Hotel Fidalgo, complete with a shopping arcade that sells everything from postcards to pearls. From December to February, traveling hordes often fill the hotels, so be sure to reserve in advance. During the monsoon season, prices fall by up to half. Unless mentioned otherwise, hotels have central air-conditioning, room service, doctors on call, and currency-exchange facilities, and rooms have cable TV and bathrooms with tubs.

EXPLORING GOA

Closest to the capital of Panaji (also called Panjim) are Miramar and Dona Paula beaches, both city beaches written up in tourist brochures. Avoid them. At Miramar, the swimming is marred by a strong undertow, broken glass and garbage litter the sand, and some of the buildings are architectural eyesores. Dona Paula is a glorified cement dock crowded with vendors.

For the most seclusion, head north toward Arambol Beach, cloistered in cliffs (and popular with European hippies), or, farther south, to Palolem Beach or another less-developed beach below Colva. For pure beauty coupled with the comforts of a beach resort, opt for either Colva or Baga beach. If you want to windsurf or waterski, go to Sinquerim or Bogmalo beach, both an easy drive from Panaji. Surfers find that Goa's waves and wind generally only rise high enough during monsoon season.

Integral to the Goan beach experience are the vendors. You'll be approached constantly by men and women offering "Pineapples?" "Cheese?" "Cold drink?" "Drums?" Their persistence can drive you into the water. Nomadic Lambani women dressed in vibrant colors and silver jewelry set up blankets cluttered with handicrafts, jewelry, embroideries, and quilts.

For a slice of native Goan life, visit a weekly market. On Wednesday between September and May, vendors sell mostly Indian and Tibetan crafts and artifacts on Anjuna Beach, where a strong smell of fish fills the air. Friday is the big market day in Mapusa, the main town in the Bardez district; people from adjoining villages and even transplanted hippies convene to sell everything from vegetables to blue jeans to handicrafts. It's an ideal place to buy souvenirs.

Great Itineraries

Goa is a small state, so everywhere is within a few hours of everywhere else and taxis are affordable, even between Panaji and Margao. It's a leisurely, pleasure-oriented place, best seen in a state of relaxation.

IF YOU HAVE 3 DAYS

If you have only a few days in Goa, you might well spend them all swimming in the warm waters of the Arabian Sea and eating delicious fresh fish. Base yourself in the Bardez district and spend your first day on **Baga Beach.** Drive the next day to **Old Goa** for a few hours of sightseeing *or* take a longer, tourist-office bus tour of either south or north Goa. Stretch out on **Calangute Beach** on day three.

IF YOU HAVE 5 DAYS

Start your trip in the north. Spend a day and night at **Baga Beach** or the isolated, ruggedly beautiful **Arambol Beach** even farther north. The next day, explore **Panaji** and **Old Goa,** and in the evening take a boat ride from Panaji. On your third day, hit **Colva Beach** or **Sinquerim Beach** and linger to watch the sun set. The next day, if you're up for more traveling, take a taxi down the coast to **Palolem Beach,** another isolated and beautiful stretch of sand. Spend your valuable time on all of these beaches both swimming and exploring: walks away from the designated swimming areas are both enchanting and—a rare blessing in India—sometimes solitary. Taxi back to Panaji or **Margao** to leave Goa.

When to Tour Goa

It's best to come to Goa in winter or early spring. During the rainy season, which stretches from the end of May to September, most beach-shack restaurants are closed due to heavy winds and violent surf. April and May are the best months for lolling around on the beach. If you come in early February, you'll experience the added excitement of Carnival.

Beaches

The state of Goa is divided into 11 *talukas* (districts). Beach reviews below end with the name of the district. All beaches have lifeguards theoretically on duty every day from 6 AM to 6 PM, but their chairs are often empty.

Numbers in the text correspond to numbers in the margin and on the Goa Beaches map.

★ 1 **Arambol Beach.** Also known as Harmal, Goa's northernmost beach is ruggedly lovely. You enter through a lively but slow-paced hippie colony where young foreigners live in small huts. The best beach is a 20-minute walk to the right, beyond the ragged food and drink shacks. Here, the scenery is spectacular: a freshwater pond nestles at the base of the hillside just 50 yards from the crashing surf below, and the ocean foams around dark rocks rising just offshore. The sea is rougher here than at other beaches, still good for swimming but a bit more fun for surf-seekers. It can be crowded in season, but if you walk beyond the pond you'll find quieter tide-dependent inlets and rock ledges. *Pernem district.*

3 **Baga Beach.** This small beach north of (and technically part of) Calangute Beach is a lively place known for its hopping "shack life." The many popular food and drink joints are headlined by St. Anthony's for seafood and Tito's Bar for nighttime revelry. The beach drops steeply to the shoreline, where fishing canoes make use of the easy boat-

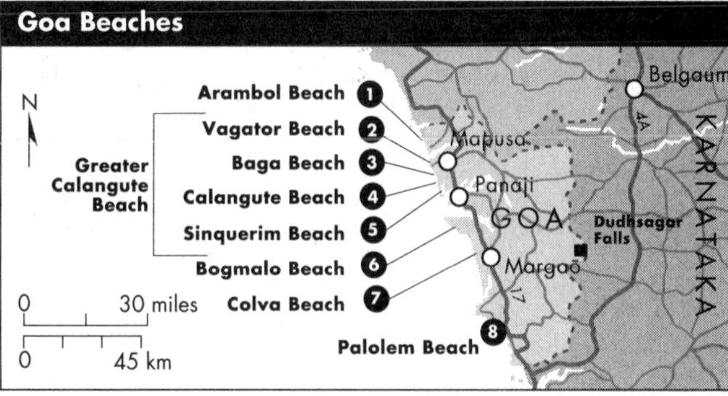

launching conditions to provide rides, often to the Wednesday market at Anjuna Beach just around the bend (the ride to Anjuna takes 15 minutes by sea, but significantly longer by road). Farther down the beach to the left of the entrance are more open, less crowded areas where you can spread out your towel and sunbathe. *Bardez district.*

6 **Bogmalo Beach.** Picturesque and rarely overcrowded, this tiny crescent of fine sand is perfect for swimming and sunning. It's overlooked by a low, verdant hill topped by a few modern buildings on one side and the Bogmalo Beach Resort on the other. Two tiny islands look back at you from about 10 km (6 mi) out to sea. For the most privacy, walk down to the far right—fewer fishing boats, shacks, and people. Another of Bogmalo's assets is its boating and water sports facilities. **Watersports Goa,** operating out of a shack on the beach, offers instruction in various sports and excursions to nearby islands. Trips to the islands are also run by the experienced young staff at the **Sandy Treat** snack shack (the first one jutting out on the right); reserve in advance. For a lunch break, try the **Seagull:** This simple, thatched-roof shack right on the beach serves some of the best prawn-curry rice in Goa. *Bardez district.*

4 **Calangute Beach.** Stretching some 16 km (10 mi) from Sinquerim Beach north through Vagator Beach, Calangute actually comprises several smaller beaches including Baga and Anjuna. The main part of Calangute Beach, about two thirds of the way down (just south of Baga Beach) is an open stretch of sand accessible by cement steps. Palm trees provide patchy shade. A sign warns that swimming is dangerous, as there's a fairly strong undertow. Calangute itself is bustling: the entrance area is crammed with stalls and shops. The government-run **Calangute Tourist Resort** (☎ 832/276024) has general information and changes currency and traveler's checks. *Bardez district.*

7 **Colva Beach.** About 6 km (4 mi) west of Margao, this is the most crowded beach in south Goa. Its large parking and entrance areas are crowded with shacks selling snacks and souvenirs and young men offering their mopeds for rent. The first 1,000 ft of the beach feel hectic—they're stuffed with vendors, cows, and fishing boats—but the sand, backed by palm groves, stretches in both directions, offering plenty of quieter spots to settle down. The water is good for swimming, with only nominal waves. The row of restaurant and bar shacks is the focus of nightlife for the whole region. Colva Beach officially stretches nearly the entire length of the Salcete district, but it's broken up into smaller sections. The government-run **Tourist Cottages** (☎ 832/222287) doubles as an information center. *Salcete district.*

8 **Palolem Beach.** For seclusion and idyllic scenery, Goa's southernmost sandy stretch—nicknamed "Paradise Beach"—is a dream. Palolem receives only those nature lovers and privacy-seekers willing to make the rugged, two-hour drive from the nearest resort (Leela Beach). It's a long, curving stretch of white sand backed by palm groves and low, green mountains, and, depending on the tides, you can wander past secluded coves and nooks sheltered by rocks. Far to the right, the beach ends in a rugged, rocky point teeming with crabs. The water is shallow and warm, with very little surf. Shacks sell refreshments near the main entrance; an occasional vendor dispenses pineapples and bananas from a weathered basket on his head; and local men entice people into wooden canoes to go and look for dolphins. *Canacona district.*

5 **Sinquerim Beach.** Along with Bogmalo Beach, Sinquerim is one of the few beaches where you can rent windsurfers, water skis, and other aqua toys without having to be a guest at a hotel. Stretching in front of the three Taj resorts, this small sandy beach gets fairly crowded with tourists and vendors. The water is warm and clean, and its slightly higher waves are good for bodysurfing. *Bardez district.*

2 **Vagator Beach.** At the north end of Calangute Beach (entrance beyond Mahalaxmi Bar and Restaurant), this tiny, semicircular getaway is backed by high palms. To the right and behind, Fort Chapora's dark-red walls rise above a low hill; to the left, a rock jetty is topped by a striking white cross. The picturesque setting makes Vagator a popular lunch spot on organized sightseeing tours. The surf is gentle, good for swimming. Some shacks sell food just beyond the dirty, rocky rise on the right. *Bardez district.*

Sights to See

Goa's inland sights are somewhat scattered, but taxis and hired cars connect them easily. Panaji and Margao are about a 40-minute drive apart.

Margao, a busy commercial center, is a jumping-off point for south Goa's beaches and one of the state's most exciting natural sights: Combine the beach with a taxi ride to Collem one afternoon to see the **Dudhsagar Waterfalls.** En route north to Panaji is Loutolim, where the **Big Foot Museum** presents an open-air re-creation of a 19th-century village.

Panaji and Goa command a few hours each. In Panaji, walk around and visit the **Church of Our Lady of Immaculate Conception,** built into a hillside next to the Municipal Garden. Another 20 minutes' drive brings you to Old Goa. Park at the **Basilica of Bom Jesus** (the huge building on your right as you drive into town), see St. Francis Xavier's tomb, cross the road to the imposing white Sé (St. Catherine's Cathedral), and perhaps explore some of Old Goa's smaller churches. If you have time, drive out to Rachol's **Museum of Christian Art** before driving back to Panaji. By now, the Goan heat might have tired you out: Drive along the river in Panaji, on 18th June Road, to the Hotel Mandavi and have lunch or a coffee at the hotel's relatively sumptuous Rio Rico Restaurant. If your driver knows the local back roads, make a trip north to **Anjuna.** Even when it isn't market day (Wednesday), this town is spectacular, with windswept palm trees and a splendid coastline of sand and rock. It's a wonderful place to watch the sun set.

Basilica of Bom Jesus. Dedicated to the worship of the infant Jesus, the basilica is also known throughout the Christian world as the tomb of St. Francis Xavier, patron saint of Goa. The saint's incorruptible body has "survived" almost 500 years now without ever having been embalmed, and now lies in a silver casket. Built under the guarantee of the Duke of Tuscany, the basilica itself took the Florentine sculptor Giovanni Batista Foggini 10 years to complete around the turn of the 17th century. ✉ *Old Goa. Free.* ⏲ *Mon.–Sat. 9–6:30, Sun. 10–6:30.*

Big Foot Museum. Also known as the Ancestral Goa Museum, this private facility re-creates in miniature a 19th-century Goan village. Guides explain the utility and significance of every object and article on display; highlights are the fishermen's shack, a mock feni distillery, and the spice garden. Within the museum's sprawling confines is an enormous, canopied dance floor, used for open-air private parties. ✉ *Near Saviour of the World Church, Loutolim,* ☎ *834/777034 or 834/735064.* 🎫 *Rs. 5.* ⏲ *Daily 9 AM–6 PM.*

Church of Our Lady of Immaculate Conception. This grand shrine was a mere chapel before 1541. Soon after it became a parish in 1600, it structure was rebuilt entirely, and it now almost presides over one of Panaji's beautiful squares. The building's most distinguishing stamp may be its beautiful zig-zag staircase. The church's annual December festival draws huge crowds. ✉ *Near Municipal Garden, Panaji,* 🎫 *Free.* ⏲ *Mon.–Sat. 9–6, Sun. 10–6.*

★ **Dudhsagar Waterfalls.** With a name that means "Sea of Milk" in Konkani, Dudhsagar is suitably spectacular and imposing, with water cascading almost 2,000 ft down a cliff to a rock-ribbed valley. The regular train here—which passes over the falls on a rocky viaduct—from Collem, in east Goa, has been temporarily suspended, but you can still access the foot of the falls via a rough, 10-km (6-mi) jeep ride (Rs. 300 per person round trip). The journey traverses rugged rolling plains, lagoons, and narrow mud paths hemmed in by bushes. Pack refreshments and bath towels, and plan to spend a morning here. It isn't difficult to find a private nook, but watch your step—the rocks are slippery. Monkeys, birds, bees, butterflies, and thick foliage complete the wild experience. The ideal time for a trek here is early summer or just after the monsoon; during monsoon season the approach road is often inaccessible. The Goa Tourism Development Corporation (GTDC) organises day trips from Panaji for Rs. 400; you can also take a taxi from Margao to the town of Collem, then hire a private jeep with driver to see the falls. *Sanguem district.*

Museum of Christian Art. Housed in a magnificent church (also a seminary) near the Zuari River, this large collection is the only one of its kind in Asia. When in Goa, the Portuguese recruited local talent—Hindus as well as Christians—to create their sacred images, so many of these paintings and sculptures are curious blends of European and traditional Indian styles. ✉ *Rachol, Salcette,* 🎫 *Rs. 5.* ⏲ *Mon.–Sat. 9:30 AM–5 PM.*

Sé (St. Catherine's Cathedral). The largest church in Old Goa, the sé was built between 1562 and 1652 by order of the King of Portugal. Fine carvings depict scenes from the life of Christ and the Blessed Virgin over the main altar, which commemorates St. Catherine of Alexandria. Several splendidly decorated chapels are dedicated to St. Joseph, St. George, St. Anthony, St. Bernard, and the Holy Cross. The cathedral has only one of its original two majestic towers; the other collapsed in 1776. The huge belfry contains the "Golden Bell," the largest bell in Goa. 🎫 *Free.*

NEED A BREAK? Goa's first cybercafé is in the heart of Panaji. The approach to **Cybercafe 2000** (✉ Shop No. 1, Sapana Center, ☎ 832/231892) snakes through narrow alleys, but once you get here you can relax. Surf the Web for Rs. 70 an hour or just treat yourself to a coffee, snack, or ice cream. If you need to send e-mail from south Goa, make use of the **Cyber Inn** (✉ 105, Kalika Chambers, behind Grace Church, Varde Valaulikar Rd., Margao, ☎ 834/731531).

DINING

Goa's best upscale restaurants are in the Bardez district, north of Panaji, but most travelers enjoy exploring the clusters of shack restaurants that line every major beach, serving up whatever the local fishermen happened to catch that day.

$$ ★ ✕ **Cajueiro.** This local favorite serves up tasty Goan cuisine. You dine outdoors, on a raised platform under a large straw-thatched roof supported by long betel-nut tree trunks. Candles and wood lanterns provide soft lighting at night. Specialties include pomfret fillets stuffed with prawns, and hearty mutton dishes. ✉ *Mapusa Hwy., Alto Betim, Bardez district,* ☎ *832/217375. MC, V.*

$$ ★ ✕ **O Coqueiro.** Here the extensive, well-worn menu features fresh prawn curries, hearty Goan sausages, and other local dishes. You dine outdoors, at rustic wood tables under a large thatched roof. If you have your own ideas, the chef is happy to cook up Goan dishes that don't appear on the menu. ✉ *Alto Porvorim, Bardez district,* ☎ *832/217271. AE, DC, MC, V.*

$ ✕ **St. Anthony's.** This simple restaurant–cum–beach shack serves an astonishing variety of fish dishes, and possibly the best sweet *lassi* in India. The tuna steaks and pomfret dishes are particularly good. ✉ *Baga, Bardez district. No credit cards.*

LODGING

$$$$ ★ **Aguada Hermitage.** If you crave seclusion and luxury—and can afford them—by all means stay at this Taj property. Set on a hill overlooking Sinquerim Beach and the Arabian Sea, the units in these Goan-style villas are like separate, elegant homes. Each has a large terrace with upholstered garden furniture, one or two bedrooms, and several other rooms. A regular car service shuttles you down the hill to the nearby Taj Fort Aguada Beach Resort (☞ *below*), with which it shares reception and all facilities. You may also use the facilities at the Taj Holiday Village next door. ✉ *Sinquerim, Bardez 403515, Goa,* ☎ *832/276201,* FAX *832/276044. 15 villas. Golf course (for other facilities, see Taj hotels, below). AE, DC, MC, V.*

$$$$ **Leela Beach.** You're greeted with a coconut drink and a map, and you'll need the latter to explore this 60-acre resort with a gorgeous secluded beach. The two-story, salmon-colored cement villas arranged along a winding artificial lagoon recall a South Florida condo colony; inside, the rooms have cool tile floors, dark-wood furniture, well-appointed bathrooms, and private balconies. Rooms in the villas ("Pavilion" rooms) are better and only slightly more expensive than the standard rooms in larger buildings. Children are welcome, and there's a play center for them. Power outages can be frequent depending on the season, and not all bathrooms have tubs. ✉ *Mobor Cavelossim, Salcete, Bardez 403731, Goa,* ☎ *834/746363,* FAX *834/746352. 219 rooms, 21 suites. 5 restaurants, bar, pool, 9-hole golf course, 3 tennis courts, barbershop, beauty salon, outdoor hot tub, sauna, steam room,*

exercise room, horseback riding, Ping-Pong, squash, beach, snorkeling, windsurfing, boating, jet skiing, parasailing, waterskiing, fishing, bicycles, dance club, dry cleaning, laundry service, business services, meeting rooms, travel services, airport shuttle. AE, DC, MC, V.

$$$ **Cidade de Goa.** Built into a hillside near Panaji and modeled after a Portuguese hill town, this stylish resort works well if you prefer an urbane beach scene to a rustic retreat. The building has open, multilevel corridors, and the public areas feature flat matte surfaces painted with contrasting oranges, tile floors in geometric patterns, and murals depicting the travels of Vasco da Gama. The rooms offer two distinct decors: "Damao" rooms have a Gujarati ambience with terra-cotta, mirror work, and a sleeping platform; "casa" rooms are faintly Iberian, with white walls, blue tiles, and wicker furniture. Request a terrace and a sea view. ✉ *Vainguinim Beach, Dona Paula, Tiswadi 403004, Goa,* ☎ *832/221133,* FAX *832/223303. 205 rooms, 5 suites. 5 restaurants, 2 bars, pool, beauty salon, massage, sauna, 2 tennis courts, exercise room, volleyball, beach, windsurfing, boating, jet skiing, parasailing, waterskiing, baby-sitting, dry cleaning, laundry service, meeting rooms, travel services, airport shuttle. AE, DC, MC, V.*

$$$ **Taj Fort Aguada Beach Resort.** Set within the ramparts of a 17th-century fort, this hotel's dark exterior blends well with its dramatic surroundings. The view from the chic, open-air lobby—of the fort, sea, and beach—is gorgeous. All rooms face the sea and are furnished with contemporary Goan-style dark wood and cane furniture; you can also stay in intimate, tile-roofed, two-unit cottages. All facilities at the resort's sister Taj properties next door are open for collective Taj use. ✉ *Sinquerim, Bardez 403515, Goa,* ☎ *832/276071,* FAX *832/276044. 106 rooms, 24 suites. 3 restaurants, bar, pool, barbershop, beauty salon, tennis court, health club, beach, windsurfing, boating, parasailing, waterskiing, baby-sitting, travel services, airport shuttle. AE, DC, MC, V.*

$$$ ★ ✕ **Taj Holiday Village.** Designed as a sort of ritzy Goan village, this delightful tropical resort is made up of tile-roofed villas scattered around gardens and lawns that face Sinquerim Beach. All rooms have private terraces and are elegantly rustic. The staff is friendly, helpful, and effective. For a great dining experience, head to the Banyan Tree restaurant, renowned for its Chinese and Thai cuisine—specialties include *gaeng kiaw waan goong* (king prawns cooked in green curry) and *phad Thai* (noodles tossed with bean sprouts and garnished with peanuts). Facilities at the adjoining Taj properties are shared by all three resorts. ✉ *Sinquerim, Bardez 403519, Goa,* ☎ *832/276201 or 832/276210,* FAX *832/276045. 142 rooms, 7 suites. 4 restaurants, bar, pool, beauty salon, 5-hole golf course, tennis courts, health club, Ping-Pong, squash, volleyball, beach, windsurfing, boating, jet skiing, parasailing, waterskiing, dance club, baby-sitting, dry cleaning, laundry service, business services, meeting room, travel services, airport shuttle. AE, DC, MC, V.*

$$ **Hotel Baia Do Sol.** This modern hotel on Baga Beach offers the best accommodation in Baga; the only drawback is the 200-yard arrival walk along an earthen track. The rooms are average in size but cool and breezy, and some have good views of the sea and countryside. The staff is courteous, and in the shoulder season (Oct.–Nov. and Mar.), rates are discounted by 20%. ✉ *Baga, Bardez, Goa,* ☎ *832/276084 or 834/721141,* FAX *834/731415. 22 rooms. Restaurant, pool, beach, travel services. AE, DC, MC, V.*

$$ **Hotel Fidalgo.** Panaji is not on the coast, but it's a convenient stopping point, and this majestic, neo-Victorian red and white hotel is its best-known lodging. The rooms are spacious, with wooden bedsteads and velvet drapes; bathrooms are merely adequate. A shopping arcade dominates the ground floor, and the vegetarian restaurant (A Machila) and coffee shop (Piri Piri) are popular with locals. ✉ *18th June Rd.,*

Panaji, Goa, ☎ 832/226291 or 832/2262919, FAX 832/225061. 123 rooms. Restaurant, coffee shop, pool, travel services. DC, MC, V.

$$ **Hotel Nova Goa.** This modern hotel in the center of Panaji is best if you prefer amenities and comfort to stylish decor. The rooms are large and fairly crowded with furniture; bathrooms are also spacious. Some of the deluxe suites have bars and refrigerators. Ask for a room overlooking the Mandovi River. ✉ *Dr. Atmaram Borkar Rd., Panaji, Goa, ☎ 832/226231 or 832/226237, FAX 832/224958. 85 rooms, 6 suites. Restaurant, bar, pool, travel services, business services. AE, DC, MC, V.*

$$ **Silver Sands Hotel.** A simple, minimalist building set slightly back from the road, this is the best hotel in Colva. It's low on atmosphere, but the rooms are good-sized and clean, and some have air-conditioning. In the evenings, an outdoor barbecue is served poolside and there's often live music, sometimes Western pop. ✉ *Colva, Bardez, Goa, ☎ 834/721645 or 721651, FAX 834/737749. 67 rooms. 2 restaurants, bar, pool, health club, beauty salon, travel services, airport shuttle. AE, DC, MC, V.*

$$ **Stirling Holiday Resort.** This secluded, Goan-style complex of white tile-roofed cottages is set in a palm grove just 43 yards from the high-tide line on pretty Vagator Beach. The rooms have pale gold stone floors, geometric-print upholstery, and painted wood furniture. At the lower end of its price category, this is a good deal. ✉ *Vagator, Bardez, Goa, ☎ 832/273276 or 832/273273. 38 rooms. 2 restaurants, 2 bars, pool, beach, travel services. AE, DC, MC, V.*

NIGHTLIFE AND THE ARTS

Head straight to the beaches for Goan nightlife. On Sunday night, all of southern Goa seems to descend on Colva for a night of drinking, eating, dancing, and playing *hausi,* a local version of bingo. Dancing and partying also happen at Baga, Anjuna, and any of the more remote beaches. The arts scene in Panaji and Margao is generally limited to Konkani-language theater and music.

SPORTS AND OUTDOOR ACTIVITIES

There's plenty to do in the Arabian Sea—in addition to swimming, you can waterski, jet ski, windsurf, and so on. Rent sports equipment from any of the major resorts or from **Watersports Goa,** which operates out of a shack on Bogmalo Beach. The **Aqua Sports Association** (☎ 832/224706), based in Panaji, can refer you to other local outfitters. Contact the **Yachting Association** (☎ 832/223261) in Panaji for the scoop on local sailing. **Odyssey Tours**(☎ 832/232586) rents out a luxury yacht.

River cruises, complete with live music and folk dance, leave Panaji's Nehru Bridge hourly to ply the Mandovi River. The short, hourly cruise costs Rs. 50–Rs. 60; the three-hour cruise (Rs. 150) goes up to the village of Aldona and a natural spring. You can even hire the piloted *Santa Monica* launch (☎ 832/230496) for Rs. 4,000–Rs. 6,000 an hour.

In Calangute, you can hop aboard a **dolphin- or crocodile-spotting tour,** which winds past thick mangroves along the Zuari and Mandovi rivers, or even take a ride on a **banana boat.** For information, stop into **Casa Goana Restaurant** (☎ 832/276362) or **Cats Cruise Boats** (☎ 832/276060).

SHOPPING

Most of the arts and crafts sold in Goa come from elsewhere in India, and the state has few flashy shopping areas. Between September and May, head to Anjuna's Wednesday flea market to browse through Rajasthani bags and clothing or Kashmiri blankets. Margao has a food market on Sunday, and Mapusa has a big, multifarious market on Friday. In March, Panaji hosts the spring festival of Shigmo, which fills the streets with stalls selling blankets, furniture, and sweets.

The **Silk House** (✉ Dr. Atmaran Rd., ☎ 832/231136) sells saris and colorful salwar-kameez; credit cards are accepted. **The Khadi Shop** (✉ Dr. Atmaran Rd., across from the Silk House), purveyor of hand-woven cotton clothing, was established as part of the Gandhian tradition of economic self-sufficiency. The shopping arcade at the **Hotel Fidalgo** (☞ Lodging, *above*) is worth a short visit for jewelry, hand-woven textiles, and general knick-knacks. In south Goa, check out the **Handicrafts and Silk Emporium** (✉ Shopping Arcade, Silver Sands Hotel, ☎ 834/721646) in Colva.

GOA A TO Z

Arriving and Departing

By Boat

A catamaran ride from Bombay to Panaji takes about seven hours and comes complete with beer and live bands. Contact **Frank Shipping Ltd** (In Bombay, ✉ Shed 2, New Ferry Wharf, Mallet Bunder Rd.,, ☎ 22/373–1855, –8788, or –5564; in Goa, Fisheries Bldg., opposite Hotel Mandovi, Panaji, ☎ 832/228712 or 832/228713). The first-class fare is Rs. 1,600 per person.

By Bus

The easiest way to reach Goa from Bombay over land is by bus, a 17-hour trip. The most reliable and comfortable bus company is **Quickways Travel** (✉ 1st Dhobitalao La., near Lalit Bar, Bombay, ☎ 22/209–1645; ✉ 8 Gasalia Bldg., Margao, Goa, ☎ 832/721808). The trip costs Rs. 479.

By Plane

Goa's airport is in Dabolim, 29 km (18 mi) south of Panjim. It's usually best to take a taxi from here to your destination; buses are not frequent. **Indian Airlines** (✉ Dempo House, Deyanand Bandodkar Marg, Panaji, ☎ 832/223826) connects Goa to all major cities in India, including Bombay, Delhi, Madras, Ahmedabad, Calcutta, Cochin, and Hyderabad. **Jet Airways** (✉ 102, Rizvi Chambers, Caetano Albuquerque Rd., Panaji, ☎ 832/221472 or 832/230956) flies between Goa and Bombay, Cochin, and Delhi. Check with your travel agent for the current schedules of other domestic airlines. **Air India** (✉ Hotel Fidalgo, Panaji ☎ 832/224081, 832/513251, or 832/512781) makes international connections from Goa.

FROM THE AIRPORT

Goa's airport is in **Dabolim** (☎ 832/512644), 29 km from Panaji. You can arrange pre-paid taxi service at a counter inside the airport, or go straight outside and hire a private cab. Either way, the fare to Panaji should not exceed Rs. 250.

By Train

For train schedules and fares, contact the rail station in **Margao** (☎ 834/722255) or the Tourist Information Centre in **Panaji** (☎ 832/225620).

To arrive in Goa via the **Konkan Scenic Railway** from Karnataka, board in Mangalore at 7 AM and plan to reach Margao at 1:30 PM if all goes well. If you find the landscape arresting, get off at Karwar, just an hour and a half before Margao; spend the afternoon in that picturesque town, then take a bus or taxi to Goa. If you're coming from Bombay, get schedule and fare information at the Tourist Information Centre in the Central Railway Station (☎ 22/308–6288). Hop off at Margao.

Getting Around

By Bus

Local buses are cheap and frequent. They are also terrifyingly overcrowded; be prepared to fight your way on and off them.

By Taxi

Try to negotiate a price before you set off. A six-hour day should cost about Rs. 500, but drivers will probably insist on your paying more. Many people rent motorbikes for the short trips between beaches.

Contacts and Resources

Currency Exchange

Most major hotels will change money for their guests. **State Bank of India** (✉ Near Municipal Garden, Margao, ☎ 832/721882 or 832/721889; 18th June Rd., Panaji, ☎ 832/224662 or 832/224566). **Thomas Cook** (✉ 8 Alcon Chambers, D. B. Marg, Panaji, ☎ 832/204–8556; 18th June Rd. at market, Panaji, ☎ 832/221312; Roadside between Calangute and Baga, ☎ no phone). In Anjuna, go to **Oxford Money Exchange/Bureau de Change** (✉ 111/6, Mazal Vaddo, opposite chapel, ☎ 832/273251 or 832/273269). In Colva, hotels run by the Goa Tourism Development Corporation (GTDC) have exchange desks.

Communications

There are many telephone kiosks in market areas. The best one in Margao is the **Cyberlink Advertising and Communications Centre** (✉ 9 Lower Ground Floor, Rangavi, opposite Municipal Bldg., ☎ 834/734414).

Singbal's Book House, opposite the Mary Immaculate Conception Church in Panaji, sells English-language newspapers and books; it's open Monday to Saturday, 9 to 4.

Late-Night Pharmacies

Neha Chemists and Druggists (✉ Mala, near market, Panaji, ☎ 832/222677) and **Holy Spirit Medical Stores** (✉ Old Market, Margao, ☎ 832/732553 or 737433) are open 24 hours.

Tour Operators and Travel Agencies

There are literally dozens of private tour operators in Goa, most offering 10-hour tours of the state. Contact the following for details: **Coastal Tours and Travels** (✉ 31st January Rd., Panaji, ☎ 832/43072). **Trans Goa Tours and Travels** (✉ G-11, Shankar Parvati, 18th June Rd., Panaji, ☎ 832/220975). **Tourist Home** (✉ Patto Bridge, Panaji, ☎ 832/224483). **Trade Wings** (✉ 6 Mascarenhas Bldg., Mahatma Gandhi Rd., Panaji, ☎ 832/222430 or 832/222435). **Goa Sea Travels Agency** (✉ opposite Tourist Hotel, Panaji, ☎ 832/225925).

For a private guide, contact a tourist office (☞ Visitor Information, *below*). The transport wing of the **Goa Tourism Development Corporation** (☞ Visitor Information, *below*) runs day-long bus tours of both north and south Goa—departing from Panaji, Margao, and Colva Beach—as well as river cruises from the Santa Monica pier in Panaji.

Visitor Information

Margao's **Tourist Information Centre** (✉ Tourist Hostel, near Municipal Garden, ☎ 834/722513) is a good source of information, including details on the Konkan Railway, and has maps of the state. In Panaji, the **Directorate of Tourism** (✉ Government of Goa, Tourist Home, Patto Bridge, Panaji, ☎ 832/228819) fields general inquiries. For assistance with reservations, including bus tours, contact the **Goa Tourism Development Corporation (GTDC)** (✉ Trionara Apartments, Dr. Alvares Costa Rd., Panaji, ☎ 832/226515, 832/226728, or 832/224132).

9 KARNATAKA

Outside Bangalore, Karnataka's high-tech tropical capital, village life transports you to an earlier time. Mysore is a city of palaces—the former maharaja's palace is an architectural tour de force. Near Mysore, the villages of Belur and Halebid have meticulously wrought 12th-century temples. The medieval city of Hampi is a hodgepodge of gorgeous ruins.

By Julie Tomasz

Updated by Jayanth Kodkani

KARNATAKA IS A MICROCOSM of the most colorful and fascinating aspects of India, presented at a comfort level that can be Oriental-sumptuous and Occidental-efficient. Roughly the size of New England, Karnataka has probably hosted human civilization as long as any place on earth. Scattered throughout the state, in such places as Belur, Halebid, and Hampi, are some of the greatest religious monuments in India. The climate is as varied as the culture, ranging from humid to dry and cool, the result of a geography that combines sea coast with tropical uplands and arid zones.

Karnataka's 46 million people—called Kannadigas after their language, Kannada—are sinewy and robust in build, docile in disposition. In villages, women wait patiently with their jugs at the well, which doubles as the social center. Men, often scantily dressed in *lungis* (colorful skirtlike wraps) or *dhotis* (white skirtlike wraps) work in the fields, walking slowly behind oxen dragging plows that have not changed much in 3,000 years. The climate makes it possible to live perpetually outdoors—village huts are often of rudimentary construction, and people frequently set up their beds outside.

The simplicity of Karnataka's countryside is balanced by the grand palaces and formal gardens of Mysore, the youthful cosmopolitanism of Bangalore, and the relics, both Hindu and Muslim, of centuries of royal living. Even the outdoors can impress if you spend a few days on safari in Nagarhole National Park.

Although Bangalore and Mysore are well connected by express trains and comfortable buses, there are advantages to traveling by car: The countryside along the way is lovely, verdant with palms and rice paddies and brightened by colorfully dressed women washing clothes in the roadside streams. Timid passengers and back-seat drivers, of course, may be put off by the Indian driver's way of roaring around curves marked with skull-and-crossbones signs that read "Accident Zone"—past giant buses, plodding oxcarts, and men pushing bicycles laden with bunches of coconuts.

Pleasures and Pastimes

Architecture

Karnataka is most famous for its astonishing Hindu temples and its Indo-Saracenic palaces: the Hoysala-dynasty temples of Belur and Halebid in the south, the enormous ruined town of Hampi in the center of the state, and the Maharaja's Palace in Mysore.

Dining

Karnataka is famed for its *thali,* a South Indian staple made up of rice surrounded by several bowls of vegetables and sauces, all mopped up with large helpings of *roti* (unleavened bread). The thali is cheap, filling, and usually fairly easy on a foreigner's stomach. Also, unlike most parts of India, Karnataka brews a fine cup of coffee.

Bangalore has an up-and-coming restaurant scene, but options for dining out in the rest of Karnataka are few, with good food but limited menus. You'll almost always find tasty, predominantly vegetarian southern favorites like *dosas* (Indian-style stuffed crepes) and *idlis* (steamed rice cakes), both served with coconut chutney and other condiments. A popular rice dish is *bisi belebath,* spicy lentil curry and mixed vegetables topped with wafers.

Konkan Railway

For a scenic panorama of India's Western coast from Bombay clear down to Cochin, there's no topping the new Konkan Railway, which stretches 470 miles across the states of Maharashtra, Goa, Karnataka, and Kerala. In its very first year, the train became the lifeline of this region, and a spectacular one at that, with more than 170 major bridges, 1,800 minor bridges, and 92 tunnels cutting through the imposing Western Ghats (a chain of highlands covered with tropical evergreen forests). To make the most of the Konkan Railway in Karnataka, take a ride on the Mangalore-Margao passenger train, which runs to and fro every day at a fare of just under Rs. 100. It isn't terribly plush, but the sights and sounds outside will absorb you. The train chugs across bridges—the longest on this route is the 2-km (1-mi) stretch over the river Sharavathi—and past rice paddies, sleepy villages, fishermen's backyards, hills, and marshy stretches where children play and cattle wander. Keeping you company inside is a mixed crowd: traders, nuns, students, laborers, fishermen, hawkers of snacks and beverages, and fellow travelers staring happily into the distance.

Lodging

Both Bangalore, the affluent state capital, and Mysore have sumptuous hotels set in verdant tropical gardens: Since 1954, when the princely state of Mysore was incorporated into India, the maharaja's numerous summer palaces have been converted to luxury accommodations for travelers, including elegant restaurants in former grand ballrooms. Both cities also have some excellent hotels with very moderate rates. Options outside Bangalore and Mysore are few and far between.

Unless we indicate otherwise, hotels have central air-conditioning and bathrooms with tubs. In addition, many luxury hotels have exclusive floors with special privileges or facilities for the business traveler.

Performing Arts

Karnataka has a rich and ancient tradition of folk drama and dance, as well as a colorful contemporary scene featuring classical music and dance from throughout India. In Bangalore and Mysore, performances are frequent, sometimes daily, during the high tourist season (December through March) and major festivals; the rest of the year, there's usually something cultural brewing each weekend. Restaurants popular with foreigners sometimes have live music and even dance performances during dinner. Most events are free; if advance tickets are required, you can generally buy them at the venue for Rs. 10–Rs. 20.

Safaris

In southern Karnataka, thick forests—preserved from destruction by their status as national parks—are home to large elephant herds, tigers, wild bison and pigs, peacocks, and crocodiles. Ecotourism is taking off here, and some of the resorts (jointly sponsored by the government and private capital) are quite delightful. Here, at least, the Indian infrastructure seems to run as smoothly as anywhere else on earth. If you're interested, inquire with **Jungle Lodges and Resorts** (⊠ Shrungar Shopping Centre, 2nd floor, M. G.Rd., Bangalore, ☎ 80/559–7025 or 558–6163) about Nagarhole National Park, Ranganthittu Bird Sanctuary, Bhadra Wildlife Sanctuary, Bandipur, and Kabini.

Shopping

Karnakata's artisans flourish, creating exquisite hand-loomed silk fabrics, intricately inlaid rosewood furniture, and smooth sandalwood carvings. Sandalwood incense sticks, oils, and soaps make great, easy-to-carry gifts. Mysore is especially known for its incense and sandalwood, both of which are sold at the numerous spice-and-smell stalls lining the Devaraja Market. Bangalore also has curio shops. If you're not in a fixed-price government shop, bargain hard and remember that "old" often means 24 hours old.

Exploring Karnataka

Karnataka is a large state packed with fascinating places and historic sights. The main transport hub is Bangalore, so it's easiest to start your trip here. Both Bangalore, which considers itself the Silicon Valley of India, and Mysore (2½ hours away by train) are worth exploring in themselves. Bangalore is a boom town, with a population now in excess of five million; huge municipal gardens and a teeming old commercial district are interspersed with cybercafés. Mysore, in contrast, is an elegant old royal town, center of the princely state that existed from the mid-19th to the mid-20th centuries. It's small in scale, tropical in appearance, and has India's finest zoo.

From Mysore, you can make two-day trips to Nagarhole National Park, on the Kerala border, home to elephants and tigers; or to the 11th- and 12th-century temples at Belur and Halebid, which between them hold more than 30,000 intricately carved sculptures; or to Sravanabelagola, with its awesome monolithic statue of the Jain saint Gomateshwara. For a refreshing outdoor stint, try the fishing camp on the banks of the Cauvery river. If you have time and stamina to spare, venture out from Bangalore to the spectacular abandoned city of Hampi.

Great Itineraries

Numbers in the text correspond to numbers in the margin and on the Bangalore and Mysore maps.

Distances are long here, and road and rail transport are very slow. Don't try to see too much in a limited time.

IF YOU HAVE 2 DAYS

If you only have a few days in Karnataka, skip Bangalore and head straight to **Mysore.** Spend the day exploring the Mysore Palace in the center of town and wandering the teeming Devaraja Market. In the afternoon, visit the sprawling zoo, where animals roam in open areas separated from onlookers by moats. Treat yourself to dinner at the Lalitha Mahal Palace Hotel, former home of the local maharaja.

For day two, hire a driver and leave Mysore early in the morning for a day trip to **Belur** and **Halebid,** 2½ hours away. Their temples are breathtaking, and if you're lucky, you might happen upon a Hindu wedding ceremony in the wedding temple at Belur.

IF YOU HAVE 5 DAYS

Spend your first day in **Bangalore.** You can wander on your own or join a bus tour sponsored by the tourist office; just make sure you don't miss the Lal Bagh gardens or the fancy shopping arcades on Brigade and Mahatma Gandhi roads. After dinner, take the commuter train 2½-3 hours to **Mysore** for your first night and second day. For day three, either book a safari in **Nagarhole National Park,** with an overnight stay at the Kabini River Lodge, or take a car up to **Belur** and **Halebid** for the day, spending the night there (at nearby Hassan) or returning to Mysore in the evening.

Take a car back to Bangalore and then the overnight train to Hospet, arriving the morning of day four. Take a taxi or auto-rickshaw at Hospet and go straight to the astonishing ruins of **Hampi,** 13 km (8 mi) outside town. Hire a guide at Hampi Bazaar and spend your last two days exploring the ruins. From Hospet you can make train connections to Guntakal, and from there to most major cities in India.

IF YOU HAVE 10 DAYS

If you have time to spare, first follow the five-day itinerary above, but make sure you see **Nagarhole National Park.** Return to Bangalore and take the train to Hospet. Spend two days at **Hampi** and return by the same train to Bangalore or take a bus to Hassan. On day eight, explore **Belur** and **Halebid** and return to your hotel in Hassan. Take an early-morning bus to **Mangalore,** about 4½ hours away. Spend the day roaming the beaches at Panambur, Malpe, or Ullal (by the Summer Sands Beach Resort) and the temple town of **Udupi.** The next morning, experience sustained coastal scenery with a trip on the scenic **Konkan Railway.** You can hop off at Karwar for lunch in the afternoon and take an evening train back to Mangalore, or take the train right out of Karnataka to Goa or Bombay.

When to Tour Karnataka

Like most of India, Karnataka is nicest between October and February, when the weather is sunny and dry but not unbearably hot. March through May is very hot, particularly in Hampi, and June through September is very wet, especially along the coast. If you can bear the heat, however, Karnataka's main attractions are much emptier in the hot months, and many hotels offer major discounts; just try to visit ruins in the early morning or late afternoon to avoid the hot sun. Many towns hold long religious festivals just prior to the monsoon.

BANGALORE

1,040 km (645 mi) southeast of Bombay, 140 km (87 mi) northeast of Mysore, 290 km (180 mi) west of Madras

Bangalore exudes a modernity that's unmatched by any other Indian city. Relatively new—at the end of the 16th century there was nothing here but a mud fort and a small bull temple, both built by the founding chieftain Kempe Gowda—it's also India's most anglicized metropolis. The name-changing bug hasn't touched most of Bangalore; Brigade Road, St. Marks Road, Fraser Town, Cubbon Road, and Queen's Circle have all retained their names from the British days. Yet the city's Janus-faced profile takes another form: There's a clear divide between the Cantonment and the City areas, separated by Cubbon Park. The Cantonment is cosmopolitan, its yuppies leading a Western lifestyle, while the City is more conventional, guarding middle-class values and an old section once ruled by the princely state of Mysore. While M. G. Road and the adjacent Brigade Road constitute the center of the garrison, where old and quaint buildings lie near latter-day shopping malls, K. G. Road, also known as the Majestic area, near the train station forms the focus of the city belt, abounding in offices, shops, cinemas, hawkers, and travelers.

Bangalore's salubrious climate (which has earned it the sobriquet "Pensioners' Paradise") and green environs have attracted so many scientists, industrialists, academics, and defense personnel since the 1980s that Bangalore is now the fastest-growing city in India and the national center of telecommunications and information technology. This explosive boom has drawn multinational corporations (Oracle, Motorola, Sun Microsystems) and the combination of money and international influence has made the city increasingly snazzy, with such Western commercial elements as trendy boutiques and nearly 200 pubs, where beer is drunk with gusto (although local authorities have recently enforced an 11 PM closing time). Students, software engineers, and even families huddle in pubs, pizza parlors, and cyber kiosks and window-shop in splendid malls. Yet effective urban planning—rare in India—has given the city a serene, orderly feel.

It's hard to spend more than a day seeing Bangalore's historic sights. You'll have plenty of time left over to soak up the city's fresh, contemporary feel by browsing its shops, trying some of its excellent restaurants, and knocking back a beer or two in a pub.

A Good Walk

Bangalore's heart is the area near Mahatma Gandhi, Brigade, and Residency roads. The bustling streets around the train station and Race Course Road are also well worth getting lost in for a couple of hours. For a good tour, start with a taxi to the **Bull Temple** ①. A 20-minute walk east on B. P. Wadia Road brings you to the tropical **Lal Bagh Botanical Gardens** ②. Head north through the gardens and come out on the Lal Bagh Fort Road side; turn left onto this road and continue to a large intersection. On your left is Krishnarajendra Road; on your right, Avenue Road. Turn onto Avenue Road, and shortly, on your left, where Avenue Road is intersected by Albert Victor Road, you'll come to **Tipu's Palace** ③.

Outside the palace, the urban scenery is rather dull, so you might decide to cheat and take an auto-rickshaw. If you do, stop at Mysore Bank Circle and walk down K. G. Road for 10 minutes to get a feel for this crowded area. Alternately, follow the narrow, busy Avenue Road for about 2 km (1 mi) to reach Mysore Bank Circle and K. G. Road. From some point on K. G. Road, take an auto-rickshaw to **Vidhana Soudha** ④, on Dr. Ambedkar Veedi Road, the spectacular building that houses the state legislature. To your right is the red-brick High Court of Karnataka. Continue up Dr. Ambedkar Veedi Road until you come to Cubbon Road (here, again, the scenery is insignificant, so you may want to cut to an auto-rickshaw). From Minsk Square you can walk left along Cubbon Road or straight toward Queen's Circle, with the cricket stadium on your left and Cubbon Park on your right. From either one, return to Queen's Circle, where M. G. Road starts.

By now you may need refreshment. Head across M. G. Road to Brigade Road and you'll see the Cyber Café on your left. After putting up your feet for a bit, head back to M. G. Road: To your left and right are several ritzy shopping arcades and state-run crafts and silk emporiums. Wandering in and out of these can eat up a happy afternoon.

TIMING

You'll need the best part of a day for this walk, though taking auto-rickshaws on the plainer stretches can save a few hours. The Lal Bagh Gardens deserve at least an hour, Tipu's Palace half an hour, and the Vidhana Soudha another half an hour. Shoppers will have a grand old time, but even diehards will probably want to call it a day after three hours. It's best to set off fairly early in the morning, as the gardens are most pleasant then (and in the early evening).

Sights to See

❶ **Bull Temple.** This small temple houses the enormous 1786 monolith of Nandi, the sacred Hindu bull, vehicle of Shiva. The temple's front yard bustles with activity: Peddlers sell coconuts, bananas, and jasmine blossoms for offerings. Don't be alarmed if a woman sitting on the pavement suddenly yanks out a live cobra from a straw basket in front of her, taunting it to fan out its collar: For a few rupees, you can snap a photo of the angry creature from as close (or as far) as you wish. Inside, Nandi lies in his traditional position, leaning slightly to one side with his legs tucked beneath him. The bull's hefty black bulk is beautifully carved and ornamented with bells, and glistens with coconut oil that priests apply regularly to keep the stone moist. ✉ *Bull Temple Rd.* 🎫 *Free.* ⏲ *Daily 6 AM–8 PM.*

Bull Temple, **1**
Lal Bagh Botanical Gardens, **2**
Tipu's Palace, **3**
Vidhana Soudha, **4**

2 **Lal Bagh Botanical Gardens.** This 240-acre park is one of the remaining reasons for Bangalore's increasingly obscure nickname, "The Garden City." Closed to auto traffic, the park is laced with pedestrian paths past more than 100 types of trees and thousands of varieties of plants and flowers from all over the world. Most of the flora are in their fullest bloom between October and December. Some trees, like the venerable 200-year-old elephant tree near the western gate entrance, date from the time of Tipu Sultan, who continued to develop the park in the late 18th century after the death of his father, Hyder Ali, who designed the grounds in 1760. Marking the heart of Lal Bagh is the **Rose Garden,** a square, fenced-in plot blooming with some 150 different kinds of roses. Just beyond, near the north gate entrance, is the **Glass House,** a cross-shaped pavilion built in 1881 with London's Crystal Palace in mind. Twice a year, around Independence Day (August 15) and Republic Day (January 15), week-long flower shows are held here. ✉ *Lal Bagh Fort Rd.,* ☎ *80/602231.* 🎫 *Free; Rs. 3 during flower shows.* ⏲ *Daily sunrise–sunset.*

3 **Tipu's Palace.** Tipu Sultan built this palace for himself in 1789. Made of wood, it's a replica of his summer palace on Srirangapatnam (a river island near Mysore), sans the elaborate fresco painting inside. The building now houses a modest photo exhibit about Tipu and his times. ✉ *Albert Victor Rd.* 🎫 *Rs. 2.* ⏲ *Daily 8–5:30.*

4 **Vidhana Soudha.** Bangalore's most beautiful building is a relatively recent addition to the city, built between 1954 and 1958 to house the state legislature and secretariat. The sprawling granite structure was designed in the Indo-Dravidian style, studded with pillars and carved ledges and topped with a central dome that's crowned, in turn, with a golden four-headed lion, emblem of the great 3rd-century BC Buddhist king Ashoka. The interior is not open to visitors. Facing the Vidhana Soudha head-on across the street is another of Bangalore's attractive public buildings, the pillared, red-brick High Court of Karnataka, built in 1885 as the seat of the then-British government. ✉ *Dr. Ambedkar Veedhi Rd.*

NEED A BREAK? For Rs. 20 you can take a delicious cup of cappuccino at the **Cyber Café** (✉ Windsor House, Brigade Rd., ☎ 80/555–0949). Sandwiches and other snacks are available. The atmosphere is friendly and hip, the air-conditioning is a welcome relief, and another Rs. 60 buys you an hour of surfing the Web or e-mailing friends back home. If you don't need the caffeine, there are scores of e-mail kiosks throughout Bangalore (especially on M. G. Rd.), some with rates as low as Rs. 40 an hour.

Dining and Lodging

Bangalore has an up-and-coming restaurant scene, growing more and more cosmopolitan by the month. Chinese restaurants abound, as do Italian, American, and other ethnic eateries. The scene is changing, but for now many of the best restaurants are still those in the major hotels. For the latest hot spots, consult your concierge, the city pages of the *Times of India,* the *Deccan Herald,* or the brochure "Agrus Bangalore," available in bookstores.

The city is also experiencing a lodging boom, with dozens of business-oriented hotels going up in the prime commercial areas. Competition is stiff, keeping the majority of hotels in the moderate price range.

$$$$ ✕ **Dum Pukht.** This posh restaurant is one of very few in India serving Nawab of Avadh cuisine, born in Mogul times and traditionally slow-cooked in sealed clay ovens over a low fire. (In Urdu, *dum* means "breathe in," and *pukht* means "cooking.") Specialties include *subz purdah* (vegetable and pineapple casserole baked in puff pastry), *kakori* (finely minced mutton spiced with cloves and cinnamon and grilled on a skewer), and the 100-layer *lachchedor paratha* bread. Arched ceilings and white pillars frame the elegant dining room, and the unusual menu made of ivory silk is literally presented to you on a silver platter. ✉ *Welcomgroup Windsor Manor, 25 Sankey Rd.,* ☎ *80/226–9898. AE, DC, MC, V.*

$$$ ✕ **Karavalli.** At this top restaurant you dine on a shady terrace walled in by hedges, or in an adjoining cottage. Waiters wear dhotis, and South Indian classical music sets the tone. The menu features coastal cuisines from Goa, Kerala, and Mangalore; two regional specialties are *kori gassi* (chicken pieces simmered in coconut gravy) served with *neer dosa* (a Karnataka-style crepe), and *kane bezule* (fish marinated in ground Mangalorean spices, then deep-fried). Save room for *bebinka,* the sinfully rich Goan dessert of egg yolk, butter, and coconut. ✉ *Taj Gateway Hotel, 66 Residency Rd.,* ☎ *80/558–4545. AE, DC, MC, V.*

$$$ ★ ✕ **Paradise Island.** India's very first Thai restaurant is set in a cross-shaped gazebo, surrounded by water and lush plants. The menu has evolved to incorporate Chinese, Japanese, Singaporean, and other Asian cuisines, but the emphasis remains on Thai food. Specialties include *som tam* (spicy-sweet raw-papaya salad tossed with peanut sauce) and *hormok* (curried prawns or fish steamed and wrapped in banana leaves). Try to save room for the coconut ice cream, or coconut pancakes topped with orange sauce. ✉ *Taj West End hotel, Race Course Rd.,* ☎ *80/225–5055. AE, DC, MC, V.*

$$$ ★ ✕ **Tandoor.** The extensive menu offers cuisine from all over the subcontinent, with a focus on tandoori items that you can watch being skewered and cooked by white-capped chefs behind a large window into the kitchen. Particularly good are the chicken *seekh kabab* (think

shish kebab) and the fish *tikka.* Gold-trimmed ivory walls and pillars, dimmed glass-bead chandeliers, and tables with red roses in silver vases create a look of traditional Indian splendor. ✉ *28 M. G. Rd.,* ☎ *80/558–4620. AE, DC, MC, V.*

$$ ✕ **Ebony.** This popular rooftop restaurant sits unsuperstitiously on the 13th floor of a hotel. The tables on the two outdoor terraces have lovely views of Bangalore and are in high demand in the evening, when the South Indian sun cools down and the city lights come on. The excellent chef specializes in Parsi cuisine, unusual in Bangalore, and also cooks good North and South Indian and Continental fare. On Saturdays you can sample unusual, spicy Balti food from the Indian-Afghan border. Warning: The food is very spicy. ✉ *Ivory Tower Hotel, 13th floor, 84 M. G. Rd.,* ☎ *80/558–9333 or 80/560–001. Reservations essential for dinner. AE, DC, MC, V.*

$$ ✕ **Nagarjuna Savoy.** Indian food from the state of Andhra Pradesh is the focus of this smart modern restaurant, the upscale sister of the original Nagarjuna eatery next door. Zesty-sweet chicken, mutton, and vegetable *biriani* (rice casseroles) are served on plates, not plantain leaves—not entirely authentic, but fair enough if you're not used to eating with your hands. The dining room is decorated with brass and copper masks and framed prints of Indian folk art. ✉ *45/3 Residency Rd.,* ☎ *80/558–7775. AE, DC, MC, V.*

$$ ★ ✕ **Only Place.** Since its humble 1965 beginnings as a place where American Peace Corps volunteers could get a wholesome taste of home and shoot the breeze with the kind and colorful owner, Haroon, the Only Place has become a Bangalore institution. Haroon still serves up what might well be the best American-style food in India. Best of all are his steaks—Haroon supplies beef to the American embassy and consulates, as well as other Western missions throughout India. The restaurant is conveniently located at the mouth of an ultramodern shopping mall. ✉ *Mota Royal Arcade, 158 Brigade Rd.,* ☎ *80/558–8678. AE, DC, MC, V.*

$$ ✕ **Sunny's.** Small and elegant, Sunny's is best known for its French and Italian specialties—pizzas, pastas, and seasonal salads—along with deli items like hot dogs and sausages. Call ahead to reserve: Lunchtime gets crowded. ✉ *215 St. Marks Rd.,* ☎ *80/558–7417. AE, MC, V.*

$ ✕ **Chung Wah.** Modern Oriental decor—wooden latticework, Chinese fans and paintings on the wall, and lanterns—defines this cozy, popular restaurant, which offers most of China's several cuisines. Two favorite dishes are *huli* chicken (sliced chicken simmered with soy sauce and onions) and deboned pomfret with a choice of sauces from mild to spicy. Expect crowds in the afternoon. ✉ *45/1 Residency Rd.,* ☎ *80/558–2662. AE, MC, V.*

$ ✕ **Koshy's.** For a coffee, beer, sandwich, or full-blown biriani, this may be the quietest hideaway near busy M. G. Road. The wood furniture is rather old-fashioned and the decor, plain, but the friendly waiters here won't blink an eye if you want to hang around for an hour just sipping coffee and scribbling. Try the tender coconut soup. A separate dining section is called the Jewel Box. ✉ *35/2 Kasturba Rd., off Lavelle Rd.,* ☎ *80/221–3793 or 80/221–5030. No credit cards.*

$ ★ ✕ **Mavalli Tiffin Rooms.** Come to this bustling Bangalore institution, established in 1924, for Indian vegetarian food. The front rooms, which have ceiling fans, are crowded with marble tables; the small back room is air-conditioned. You won't find better dosas in Bangalore, and you can't beat the prices. Desserts are also tasty, and the coffee is superb. You'll probably wait quite a while for a table, but once the dhoti-clad bearer takes your order, food materializes quickly. ✉ *Lalbagh Rd.,* ☎ *80/222–0022. No credit cards.*

$ ✕ **Rice Bowl.** This crowded restaurant serves enormous helpings of Chinese food. The soup and vegetable dishes are particularly good. The decor is not enticing, but for Rs. 80 for an ample meal, who's looking around? ✉ *215 Brigade Rd.,* ☎ *80/558–7417. No credit cards.*

$$$–$$$$ 🏨 **Welcomgroup Windsor Manor Sheraton and Towers.** Bangalore's prettiest hotel has a striking white exterior with arched windows and wrought-iron ornaments. In the lobby, a marble fountain sits beneath a domed skylight and massive teak pillars. The smaller, atrium lobby area in the Towers gleams with polished marble and brass, a suitable introduction to this opulent five-story wing geared toward business travelers. The handsome Manor rooms in the original wing have modern furnishings with endearing Victorian touches. ✉ *25 Sankey Rd., 560052,* ☎ *80/226–9898,* FAX *80/226–4941. Manor: 88 rooms, 12 suites. Towers: 139 rooms, 1 suite. 2 restaurants, bar, coffee shop, pool, health club, dry cleaning, laundry service, business services, travel services. AE, DC, MC, V.*

$$$ 🏨 **Ashok.** Built in 1971 in the park where Mahatma Gandhi once meditated, this hotel has a small memorial to Gandhi on the extensive grounds behind it. Guest rooms look fresh, with blue-gray and pale green decor and light-painted wood furnishings; the best rooms overlook the pool. The small marble lobby has low ceilings and comfortable wicker chairs. ✉ *Kumara Krupa, High Grounds, 560001,* ☎ *80/226–9462,* FAX *80/225–0033. 164 rooms, 17 suites. 2 restaurants, bar, coffee shop, pool, tennis court, beauty salon, exercise room, dry cleaning, laundry service, meeting rooms, travel services. AE, DC, MC, V.*

$$$ 🏨 **Le Meridien.** The enormous atrium lobby of this modern high-rise sparkles with white marble and shiny brass carriage lamps. The hallways and rooms, in contrast, are surprisingly dark. The modern room decor includes burnt-orange carpeting, upholstered chairs and ottomans, and floral drapes and bedspreads. Windows are double-glazed. ✉ *28 Sankey Rd., 560052,* ☎ *80/226–2233,* FAX *80/226–7676. 196 rooms, 30 suites. Restaurant, bar, coffee shop, pool, beauty salon, sauna, steam bath, tennis court, exercise room, baby-sitting, laundry service, business services, meeting rooms, travel services. AE, DC, MC, V.*

$$$ ★ 🏨 **Oberoi.** Slick, elegant, and well run, this young hotel has a stunning lobby with a green marble floor, a central fountain, and a bank of windows overlooking the landscaped garden—which, in turn, is dominated by a gorgeous blossoming rain tree and a small waterfall cascading into a fish-filled lotus pond. The spacious rooms have polished green-marble entryways, private balconies, and handsome brass-and-teak furnishings. Each floor has a private butler. ✉ *37/39 M. G. Rd., 560001,* ☎ *80/558–5858,* FAX *80/558–5960. 130 rooms, 9 suites. 2 restaurants, bar, outdoor pool, barber shop, hair salon, health club, laundry service and dry cleaning, business services, meeting rooms, travel services, airport shuttle. AE, DC, MC, V.*

$$$ 🏨 **Taj Residency.** The large, white-marble lobby in this high-rise bustles with activity. Guest rooms are furnished with contemporary teak furniture and blue-and-green upholstery. Ask for a room on an upper floor with a lake view. ✉ *41/3 M. G. Rd., 560001,* ☎ *80/558–4444,* FAX *80/558–4748. 163 rooms, 5 suites. 2 restaurants, bar, coffee shop, patisserie, pool, exercise room, baby-sitting, business services, meeting rooms, travel services. AE, DC, MC, V.*

$$$ ★ 🏨 **Taj West End.** More than 100 years old, this hotel has a decidedly Victorian look outside and in the public rooms. Most of the guest rooms are elegantly contemporary, with brass lamps and teak or solid cane furniture. The slightly more expensive "old world" rooms have a turn-of-the-century look, with mahogany writing desks and brass four-poster beds. The best rooms in the main building are on the second floor; they open onto a veranda overlooking the pool. Suites have pri-

vate verandas and sunlit alcoves. The setting is tropical, with 20 acres of lush gardens. ✉ *23 Race Course Rd., 560001,* ☎ *80/225–9281 or 80/225–5055,* FAX *80/220–0010. 131 rooms, 9 suites. 3 restaurants, 2 bars, patisserie, outdoor pool, sauna, 2 tennis courts, exercise room, baby-sitting, laundry service and dry cleaning, business services, travel services. AE, DC, MC, V.*

$$ **Central Park.** Tucked behind the Manipal Centre, a large commercial complex, this 10-story building is one of Bangalore's newer business hotels. Glass-backed elevators afford a view of the city en route to your room. Standard rooms are small, with standard modern furnishings and a few tartan-plaid details, but at almost the same price, the "park chamber" rooms on the executive floors are slightly larger, better-appointed, and include breakfast. ✉ *47 Dickenson Rd., 560042,* ☎ *80/558–4242,* FAX *80/558–8594. 126 rooms, 4 suites. Restaurant, bar, coffee shop, patisserie, book store, business services, meeting rooms, travel services. AE, DC, MC, V.*

$$ **New Victoria.** Set back off the road and surrounded by palm trees and other tropical vegetation, this hotel is one of the best bargains in Bangalore. The airy rooms, with white walls sans embellishment, are average in size, and the atmosphere is friendly. ✉ *47–48 Residency Rd., 560025,* ☎ *80/558–4076,* FAX *80/558–4945. Restaurant, bar, travel services. AE, DC, MC, V.*

$$ **St. Mark's Hotel.** A short walk from the British Library and about 1 mi from the center of town, this huge new hotel welcomes you with a marble-floored lobby. Rooms are carpeted in plush red, and come with coffee tables and flowery armchairs. The suites have separate living rooms and large wooden bars. ✉ *4/1 St. Mark's Rd., 560001,* ☎ *80/227–9090,* FAX *80/227–5700. 78 rooms, 18 suites. 2 restaurants, bar, café, business services, laundry service, travel services. AE, DC, MC, V.*

$$ **Taj Gateway Hotel.** This Western-style Taj property offers cleaner and better-equipped rooms than its peers among the new, low- to mid-range business hotels, but it's on a very noisy street. The walls are adorned with framed abstract prints throughout; guest rooms have modern wood and wicker furniture and pale blue carpeting. Only the suites have bathtubs. ✉ *66 Residency Rd., 560025,* ☎ *80/558–4545,* FAX *80/558–4030. 94 rooms, 4 suites. 3 restaurants, bar, pool, exercise room, laundry service, business services, travel services. AE, DC, MC, V.*

$ **Quality Inn Kensington Terrace.** This property was the first in India to install an interactive television system with information ranging from sightseeing recommendations to the status of your hotel bill. Rooms are on the small side, and are unobtrusively decorated with dark green and brown fabrics. Breakfast is included in the room rates. ✉ *Kensington Rd., off M. G. Rd., 560042,* ☎ *80/559–4666,* FAX *80/559–4029. 98 rooms, 10 suites. Restaurant, bar, coffee shop, pool, exercise room, laundry service, business services, meeting rooms, travel services. AE, DC, MC, V.*

Nightlife and the Arts

The Arts

Your best sources for information on cultural happenings are the newspapers: the *Deccan Herald*'s column "In the City Today," usually on page 3, and the *Times of India*'s "Events" column on page 2. Other sources are posters, the Karnataka Department of Tourism, the *Bangalore Weekly* magazine, and the staff at your hotel.

Bangalore has a number of venues for classical Indian music and dance and for plays, some in English. **Chowdiah Memorial Hall** (✉ Gayathri Devi Park Extension, Vyalikaval, ☎ 80/344–5810). **Sri Puttanachetty Town Hall** (✉ Sri Narasimharaja Circle, J. C. Rd., ☎ 80/222–1270).

Ravindra Kalakshetra (✉ Jayachamarachendra Rd., ☎ 80/222–1271). **Dr. H. Narasimaiah Kalakshetra** (✉ Jayanagar, 7th Block, ☎ 80/649684). The **Yavanika State Youth Center** (✉ Nrupathunga Rd., ☎ 80/221–4911) hosts free Indian classical music and dance performances and other cultural events most evenings.

On the outskirts of Bangalore, the **Nrityagram Dance Village** (☎ 80/558–5440) is a dance institution founded by the late Odissi dancer Protima Bedi. Here you can watch students (many Indian and some foreign) at work while sampling aspects of Karnataka folk culture. The premises, which include a guest house, are modeled on a Karnataka village and designed for holistic living, with granite, stone, mud, and thatch the chief architectural ingredients. Nrityagram is the only village of its kind in India, devoted to the promotion and preservation of ancient classical-dance styles and two martial-art forms. For a taste of Indian mythology and cultural traditions, this is worth a visit.

OFF THE BEATEN PATH

For an eyeful of Karnataka's folk traditions, hire a car or take a bus 53 km (33 mi) southwest toward Mysore to the **Janapada Loka Folk Arts Museum.** Puppets, masks, agricultural implements, and household articles are on display, and performances feature drummers, snake-charmers, and exponents of gypsy dances. Facilities include a simple restaurant and a dormitory. For information contact the Karnataka Janapada Trust (✉ Subramanyaswami Temple Rd., 5th Cross, 4th Block, Kumara Park West, ☎ 80/362768).

Nightlife

Bangalore is famous in India for its pubs. Over the last 15 years, nearly 200 have sprung up throughout the city, providing a variety of hangouts where people of all types and trades can meet over a beer or other drink and listen to music or watch television. Most pubs are styled according to themes, such as a cricket stadium (New Night Watchman) or a subway station (The Underground). In an effort to curb local students' alcohol consumption, the government requires pubs to close for a few hours in the afternoon and shut down altogether by 11 PM; live bands must also call it a day at 11. Further regulations aimed at preventing prostitution and go-go club scenes have forbidden late-night dancing in clubs. A few major hotels, however, have special permits. All this may change, but it's at the whim of the government; check with your hotel for the latest on the entertainment scene.

The atmosphere in all pubs is casual, upbeat, and decidedly friendly. The music, played by a DJ, tends to be very loud, despite the fact that there's usually no dancing. Weekends, particularly Saturday, are the most popular nights to go pubbing; expect large crowds, as you would anywhere else. At **Black Cadillac** (✉ 50 Residency Rd., Mohan Towers, ☎ 80/221–6148), a slightly corporate, upscale crowd relaxes inside on red-upholstered stools at tables with psychedelic, swirly-painted tops, or out in the backyard amid store awnings, yellow-striped curbs, and painted street scenes. **Guzzlers' Inn** (✉ 48 Rest House Rd., off Brigade Rd., ☎ 80/558–7336) is a small, crowded and boisterous place packed with young drinkers swaying to MTV. The **Jockey Club** (✉ Taj Residency, 41/3 M. G. Rd., ☎ 80/558–4444) is a small, posh bar and restaurant where white-gloved waiters serve silver steins of beer in a room with richly carved teak walls, Belgian mirrors, and subdued lantern light. **NASA** (✉ 1/4 Church St., ☎ 80/558–6512) has the look and feel of a space shuttle; you duck through an oval door into two oblong, oval-shaped rooms decorated in metallic silver and black. The **New Night Watchman** (✉ 46/1 Museum Rd., ☎ 80/558–8372), designed like a miniature cricket stadium, is popular with students. At the **Polo Club** (✉ Oberoi Hotel,

37–39 M. G. Rd., ☎ 80/558–5858) stained-glass windows and beautiful views of lush gardens and a cascading waterfall provide a peaceful setting. True to its name, **The Pub World** (✉ 65 Residency Rd., Laxmi Plaza, ☎ 80/558–5206) has polished wood, shiny brass fixtures, and a low ceiling with wooden rafters. **The Underground** (✉ 65 Blue Moon Complex, M. G. Rd., ☎ 80/558–9991) is divided into three sections, one designed after London's tube. Slightly cheesy but generally fun, it's a good place to end a night on the town.

On weekends only, the elegant **Midnight Express** (Welcomgroup Windsor Manor Sheraton and Towers, 25 Sankey Rd., ☎ 80/226-9898) dims its chandeliers, turns on its strobe lights, and goes disco. **Time and Again** (✉ Brigade Rd., ☎ 80/558–5845) is popular with the young set for dancing.

Sports and Outdoor Activities

Bowling

If bowling strikes your fancy, walk down the road to **G's Alley** (✉ Mota Arcade, Brigade Rd., ☎ 80/558–8211). You can use the 4-lane alley for Rs. 100 per game on weekdays, Rs. 125 on weekends and holidays. Tibetan and Chinese snacks are served.

Golf

The **Bangalore Golf Club** (✉ 2 Sankey Rd., ☎ 80/225–7121 or 80/226–6713), designed by the British in 1876, has a lovely 18-hole course open to the public. Call ahead to reserve your game. The restaurant serves some mouthwatering Chinese cuisine, among other options.

Health Clubs

Facilities at **Le Meridien** (☎ 80/226–2233 ext. 412) and the **Taj Residency** (☞ Lodging, *above*) are open to nonguests for around Rs. 200 a day.

Horse Racing

Thoroughbred racing is a major sport in Karnataka. The **Bangalore Turf Club** (✉ 1 Race Course Rd., ☎ 80/226–2391) goes into high gear from mid-May through the end of July and November through March, with races every Saturday and Sunday afternoon.

Shopping

M. G. Road is one of Bangalore's main shopping pockets, with government shops and some giant silk emporiums. **Brigade Road** is lined with flashy stores, foreign boutiques, and a number of multilevel shopping arcades. **Commercial Street** is a narrow, eclectic area packed with old and new shops selling everything from suitcase locks to Kashmiri hats to precious jewelry.

Antiques and Handicrafts

The state-run, fixed-price **Cauvery** (✉ 49 M. G. Rd., ☎ 80/558–0317) sells all of Karnataka's craft products: sandalwood handicrafts, terracotta pots, carved rosewood furniture, silk, leather work, jute products, lacquered toys, *bidri* ware (decorative metal ware in black and silver tones), embossed bronze, soaps, perfumes, incense, and sachets. The **Central Cottage Industries Emporium** (✉ 144 M. G. Rd., ☎ 80/558–4083 or 558–4084) is part of the nationwide government chain of fixed-price cottage-industry stores selling authentic crafts from all over India. It closes every day from 2 to 3. **Natesan's Antiqarts** (✉ 76 M. G. Rd., ☎ 80/558–8344) sells an unusual collection of high-quality stone, bronze, and wood antiquities; old paintings; and exquisite new artifacts, plus silver jewelry and precious stones.

Books

Bangalore has about 10 large English-language bookstores. All have good bargains, but the best are on or near M. G. Road. **Gangaram's Book Bureau** (✉ 72 M. G. Rd., ☎ 80/558–6783) is a four-story megastore selling books, CDs, cards, stationery, and toys. **Premier Bookshop** (✉ 46/1 Church St., ☎ 80/558–8570), closed Sunday, is a small store crammed with books and owned by a friendly bibliophile named Shanbhag, who will attend to you personally. The **Strand Book Stall** (✉ 113 Manipal Centre, Dickenson Rd., ☎ 80/558–0000), closed Sunday, has a wide selection of new and used books.

Silks

A number of giant silk emporiums on M. G. Road sell top-quality Karnataka silk products, from solid-color material by the meter to bright, ornately hand-blocked saris and scarves. **Deepam Silk International** (✉ M. G. Rd., ☎ 80/558–8760) has been in business for 25 years. **Karnataka Silk Industries Corporation Showroom** (✉ Leo Complex, Residency Rd. Cross, off M. G. Rd., ☎ 80/582118; also at Gupta Market, K. G. Rd., ☎ 80/262077), a fixed-price government shop, sells silks hot off the government silk looms in Mysore. **Lakshmi Silk Creations** (✉ 144 M. G. Rd., below Central Cottage Industries Emporium, ☎ 80/558–2129) has excellent silks. **Nalli Silks Arcade** (✉ 21/24 M. G. Rd., ☎ 80/558–3178) sells silks of all kinds and some cotton clothing. **Salonee**(✉ 8 Commercial St., ☎ 80/5589637) has designer silks, chiffons and cottons. **Vijayalakshmi Silks** (✉ Blue Moon Complex, M. G. Rd., ☎ 80/558–7395) is another reliable option.

MYSORE

140 km (87 mi) southwest of Bangalore, 1,177 km (730 mi) southeast of Bombay, 473 km (293 mi) north of Madras

No longer the capital of the princely state of Mysore, this palace-rich city survives as the principal residence of the former royal family. When you see what the maharajas accomplished in the way of arts and culture—not only developing palaces, temples, and schools but supporting the traditional Mysore school of painting—you'll understand why Prince Jayachamaraja Wodeyar (father of the current prince, Srikandatta Wodeyar) was appointed the first actual governor of Karnataka. Mysore had been known for its progressivism during his reign.

Mysore has been called the City of Palaces. You can explore its main attraction, the Mysore Palace, in a few hours, and if you can manage a stay in the Lalitha Mahal Palace Hotel, the simple combination of the two will make your trip to Mysore worthwhile. An evening visit to Brindavan Gardens is a nice way to experience the Indian fascination with kitschy but charming colored musical fountains.

Despite its opulent past, there is nothing flashy or fancy about Mysore, at least not in the modern, commercial sense. There are relatively few places to wine and dine, and the streets are lined with far more dozing cows than boutiques. The congenial climate and small-town surroundings, replete with leafy avenues, make a trip to Mysore enchanting. Here you can admire (and buy) some of India's richest silks, woven with real gold, and other elements of an age-old spirit of elegance that endures even as it deteriorates over the years.

Palace Area

A Good Walk

Mysore is a small city, and its center is easy to walk around. Start your walk at the conveniently central **Mysore Palace** ⑤. Exit on the Albert Victor Road side and turn left; then, at the traffic circle with the clock tower, turn right. On the left you'll see the entrance to the **Devaraja Market** (☞ Shopping, *below*). When you've had your fill of shopping, return to the clock tower and go back along the Albert Victor Road past the palace. At Hardinge Circle, turn right onto Lok Ranjan Mahal Road. A few more minutes will bring you to the **Zoological Garden** ⑥. After strolling through the gardens, take a taxi to the top of **Chamundi Hill** ⑦ for a beautiful panorama of Mysore. Walk down the hill's 1,000 steps and catch a taxi, bus, or auto-rickshaw back to the city.

TIMING

You'll need at least five hours for this walk, and probably most of the day if you make it to Chamundi Hill. The distances are not long, but you'll probably want more than an hour or two at the palace, an hour at the market, and two or three hours at the zoo. Note that the zoo is closed on Tuesdays.

Sights to See

❼ **Chamundi Hill.** Mysore looks its panoramic best from the top of this hill. The hill's 1,000 steps take you past a 16-ft stone **Nandi** (Shiva's holy bull), and the **Sri Chamundeswari Temple** on the summit is dedicated to the royal Wodeyar family's titular deity, the goddess Chamundi, an avatar of Parvati (Shiva's consort). The base of the temple dates from the 12th century; the ornately sculptured pyramidal tower was built in the 1800s. Because it's still an active religious site, the entire area surrounding the structure teems with beggars and peddlers. The temple's inner entrances are staffed by aggressive priests hassling tourists into buying flower offerings and *bindis* (forehead dots), applied by a fat thumb right between your eyes. Tuesdays and Fridays, auspicious days, are the most crowded. Near the temple is a giant **statue of Mahishasura,** the demon killed by the goddess Chamundi so that the region would be at peace; Mysore, originally called Mahishur, was named for him. The kitschy **Godly Museum** has gaudy paintings depicting eternal life and harmony. ✉ *Southeast Mysore, 2½ km (1½ mi) south of Lalitha Mahal Palace Hotel.* ⊙ *Temple daily 6:30–12:30 and 4–8:30, Godly Museum daily 9–6.* 🎫 *Free.*

★ ❺ **Mysore Palace.** By far the most impressive structure in Mysore is the maharaja's palace, a massive edifice that took 15 years to build (starting in 1897). One of the largest palaces in India, it's set on 73 acres and designed in the Indo-Saracenic style—a synthesis of Hindu and Islamic architecture. The main rooms and halls are a profusion of domes, arches, turrets, and colonnades, all lavishly carved, etched, or painted, with few surfaces spared. The halls and pavilions glitter with unabashed opulence: giant brass gates for grand elephant entrances; silver-plated doors encrusted with patterns and figures; richly carved teak ceilings; ivory gods and goddesses; a 616-pound solid-gold howdah. The cavernous **Kalyana Mantap** (Marriage Hall), where women sat behind screened balconies, exudes royal wealth, its turquoise-painted cast-iron pillars soaring up to a translucent dome of Scottish stained glass with brilliantly colored peacocks and flowers. A massive brass chandelier from the former Czechoslovakia hangs far below, above a floor of colorful English tiles. The impressive **Durbar Hall,** where public gatherings were held, is an elegant historical chamber, with floors of white Italian marble inlaid with semi-precious stones. The present-day maharaja (technically a prince—the last maharaja died in 1974) lives in

Brindavan Gardens, **10**
Chamundi Hill, **7**
Government Silk Weaving Factory, **9**
Mysore Palace, **5**
Sri Jayachamarajendra Art Gallery, **8**
Zoological Garden, **6**

a private wing at the rear of the palace. The small **Residential Museum** exhibits the prince's private collection of artwork and artifacts illustrating royal life of the past. On Sundays from 7 to 8 PM and on holidays, the palace is illuminated with thousands of tiny lights that turn it into a glittering statement of wealth. Negotiate the price for a guide; Rs. 50–Rs. 100 is optimal. For the ultimate palace experience, time your visit to coincide with the annual **Dussehra** festival in September or October, commemorating the victory of the goddess Durga (also known as Chamundi) over the demon Mahishasura. Mysore is known for its intensely colorful Dussehra celebrations: For 10 days palaces and temples are illuminated and cultural and sports events abound, culminating in a torchlight procession led by an elephant carrying an idol of the goddess herself in a howdah of pure gold. ✉ *Mizra Rd.,* ☎ *821/22672.* 🎫 *Palace, Rs. 10; museum, Rs. 10.* ⏲ *Palace daily 10–5; museum daily 10:30–6:30. Shoes and cameras prohibited in palace.*

❻ **Zoological Garden.** This well-maintained 250-acre zoo is more than 100 years old (founded 1892). Today it's populated by lions, white tigers, giraffes, African elephants, hyenas, kangaroos, rhinos, and a variety of other animals from all over the world. One section is devoted to reptiles and snakes. A small **museum** has effigies of rare animals and birds. ✉ *Indiranagar,* ☎ *821/520302.* 🎫 *Rs. 10.* ⏲ *Wed.–Mon. 8:30–5:30.*

Around Mysore: Art, Silk, and Gardens

A Good Tour

Hire a taxi for the whole day, or take auto-rickshaws from point to point. Start with a visit to the **Sri Jayachamarajendra Art Gallery** ⑧. After a tour of the **Government Silk Weaving Factory** ⑨, break for shopping and lunch. Finish with a trip to the **Brindavan Gardens** ⑩, 19 km

(12 mi) northwest of Mysore, in time for the evening fountain show before returning to Mysore for a late dinner.

TIMING

This leisurely day trip gives you some free time in the afternoon to have a relaxed lunch and shop for silks and handicrafts. Plan to spend at least an hour at each attraction and some time traveling between them; the gardens are about half an hour's drive away.

Sights to See

10 **Brindavan Gardens.** Extending from the side of one of India's largest dams, this vast, terraced garden is the pride of Mysore and a magnet for tourists. The park is rigidly laid out and carefully manicured, laced with long symmetrical paths and scores of fountains. Exposed metal pipes and concrete curbs betray its unnatural origins, but the profusion of fragrant flowers and the absence of cows and honking cars make it a comparatively peaceful place to stroll. Hordes of people flock to the far end of the gardens to see water spout into the air only slightly out of sync with recorded pop-classical Indian music and pulsing colored lights. To get here, hire a taxi for the roughly 30-minute ride or take Bus 303/304 from the city bus station. ✉ *Krishnaraja Sagar Rd., 19 km (12 mi) northwest of Mysore.* 🎫 *Rs. 5; cameras Rs. 10.* ⏲ *Gardens: Mon.–Sat. 9–7:45, Sun. and holidays 9–8:30; fountain show fall–spring, weekdays 7–7:55 PM, weekends 8–8:55 PM; winter, daily 6:30–7:25 PM.*

9 **Government Silk Weaving Factory.** The late maharaja created this factory in 1932, both to ensure the finest hand-loomed silks for himself and his royal family and to arrange for some profitable exportation. Now run by the Karnataka Silk Industries Corporation, the slightly dilapidated factory continues to produce the sumptuous Mysore silks coveted by women throughout India. From simple cocoons to crepe de Chine, chiffon, and other regal fabrics, the spinning, soaking, weaving, and dyeing are all done here. Accompanied by a factory official, you can stroll through the numerous giant workrooms busy with whirring spooling machines and clanking mechanical looms, and witness the transformation of hundreds of hair-thin, colorless threads into a sari fit for a queen. Ask to see the work stations where threads of real gold are woven into elaborate *zari* borders. Bring your wallet for a post-tour spree in the factory showroom, where the prices are as appealing as the selection. ✉ *Mananthody Rd.,* ☎ *821/21803.* 🎫 *Free.* ⏲ *Mon.–Sat. (except 2nd Sat. of month) 10:30–5. No cameras.*

8 **Sri Jayachamarajendra Art Gallery.** Housed in the tired, 150-year-old Jaganmohan Palace, this slightly run-down museum displays paintings from various schools and periods of Indian art as well as beautiful antique inlaid wood, antique sandalwood and ivory carvings, and a variety of other decorative pieces. Some exhibits are truly esoteric, such as a set of carved-ivory vegetables and the amazing "rice paintings"—portraits painted on single grains of rice. The service of a guide is free, but most expect a tip. ✉ *Jaganmohan Palace, Dewan's Rd., Devaraj Mohalla,* ☎ *821/23693.* 🎫 *Rs. 10.* ⏲ *Daily 8:30–6. No cameras.*

Dining and Lodging

Mysore has a relative dearth of sophisticated dining options. You can generally dine well in the hotels.

$$$ ✕ **Lalitha Mahal Palace Hotel.** Here you'll dine in the maharaja's cavernous former ballroom, a Baroque tour de force with stained-glass domes and sky-blue walls enhanced by ornate, white plaster moldings and pillars. Try the Mysore thali or the mutton *ulathiyathu* (mutton

cooked with coconut, red chili, and curry). There's a flutist at lunch and a sitarist or vina player at dinner. You can even shoot some pool on your way out. ✉ *T. Narsipur Rd.,* ☎ *821/571265. Reservations essential for dinner. AE, DC, MC, V.*

$$ ✕ **Gardenia.** The Quality Inn's restaurant has a contemporary Indian look, with upholstered rattan chairs and brass candle-lanterns on the tables at night. The menu features mostly North Indian fare, with some Chinese and Continental options. The tandoori items are delicious: Try *malai murgh tikka* (tender, boneless chicken chunks seasoned with Mughlai masala spices) with some *paneer kulcha* (bread stuffed with cottage cheese and masala spices). ✉ *Quality Inn Southern Star, 13–14 Vinoba Rd.,* ☎ *821/27217. AE, DC, MC, V.*

$$ ✕ **Ilapur.** Specializing in spicy foods from Andhra Pradesh, this fresh, clean restaurant serves good biriani dishes—chicken, mutton, or vegetable—as well as various curries, North Indian tandoori items, and an economical vegetable thali. Avoid the attempts at Chinese cuisine. The decor is contemporary, with plastic plants and colorful paintings of Krishna. ✉ *2721/1 Sri Harsha Rd.,* ☎ *821/32878. AE, MC, V.*

$ ✕ **Green Hotel.** The restaurant at this novel hotel (☞ *below*) is superb. You dine outdoors in comfortable wicker chairs around tables dotted throughout the gardens. The spicy vegetable starters are particularly tasty. This is also a quiet place to nurse a cool beer after dark. ✉ *2270 Vinoba Rd.,* ☎ *821/512536 or 821/512817. AE, DC, MC, V.*

$ ✕ **Jewel Rock.** Candlelight and red-checked linens create a cozy, romantic atmosphere at this multicuisine restaurant. Chinese dishes, including nonspicy chicken in wine sauce (not on the menu) and sliced lamb with chilis, are the most popular entrées. ✉ *Hotel Maurya Palace, 2-3-7 Sri Harsha Rd.,* ☎ *821/35912. AE, DC, MC, V.*

$$$ ★ **Lalitha Mahal Palace Hotel.** Just outside the city center, the gleaming-white 1920s palace of the former maharaja—built to host his most important guest, the British Viceroy—is now a sumptuous hotel. The public areas are lavishly trimmed with ornate plaster moldings, huge pillars, and gorgeous domes; broad marble staircases rise and curve majestically up through the three floors. The best rooms are in the older section and have appealing, if not necessarily grand, Victorian furnishings. The suites are palatial, favored by film stars, Arabian sheiks, and honeymooners. The rooms in the new wing have a contemporary decor. Staying here is a delightful and unique experience, but not without occasional reminders of the palace's age: The hot water and air-conditioning are not entirely reliable. ✉ *T. Narsipur Rd., 570011,* ☎ *821/571265 or 821/571276,* FAX *821/571770. 45 rooms, 10 suites. Restaurant, bar, pool, beauty salon, 2 tennis courts, health club, billiards, babysitting, meeting rooms, travel services, helipad. AE, DC, MC, V.*

$$ **Hotel Metropole.** This lovely, old British bungalow from the 1920s, a guest house of the former maharaja, is low on frills but faultlessly maintained. All rooms face the busy main road and can be noisy; the best rooms are on the upper floor of a sweeping veranda with rattan furniture and potted plants. Furnishings are basic but charming, evoking the 1940s; all beds come with romantic mosquito-net curtains. Not all rooms have air-conditioning. There's a barbecue every weekend, so you might enjoy taking a seat in the garden to dine, but guard against mosquitoes. ✉ *5 Jhansi Lakshmibai Rd., 570005,* ☎ *821/420681 or 821/420871,* FAX *821/420854. 16 rooms, 4 suites. Restaurant, bar, laundry service, travel services. AE, DC, MC, V.*

$$ ★ **Quality Inn Southern Star.** Opened in 1985, India's first Quality Inn property may also be its best. Some of the large guest rooms have floral drapes and bedspreads and coordinating pastel carpeting; other rooms are much darker and have dated '80s decor. The cozy back lawn is surrounded by high hedges, removing it in spirit from the busy city road

out front. Children love the cage of chattering parakeets and the tame white rabbits that hop lazily around the pool. ✉ *13–14 Vinoba Rd., 570005,* ☎ *821/438141 or 821/429686,* FAX *821/421689. 72 rooms, 1 suite. 2 restaurants, bar, pool, beauty salon, health club, laundry service, meeting rooms, travel services. AE, DC, MC, V.*

$ **Green Hotel.** This ex-palace-cum-ex-film studio is run by a British charity whose profits fund environmental projects. The drawing rooms are furnished in an Edwardian style and have chess boards and libraries. Guest rooms, while lacking air-conditioning, have delicate furnishings and high, wood-beamed ceilings. ✉ *2270 Vinoba Rd., 570012,* ☎ *821/512536,* FAX *821/516139. 12 rooms, 8 suites. Restaurant, bar, travel services. AE, DC, MC, V.*

$ **Kings Kourt Hotel.** This three-story lodging is clean and new but lacks charm and historic appeal. The midsize rooms have modern furnishings in dark red and black, and small bathrooms. Those facing the back are quieter. ✉ *Jhansi Lakshmibai Rd., 570001,* ☎ *821/421142,* FAX *821/563131. 58 rooms, 2 suites. Restaurant, bar, laundry service, meeting room, business services, travel services. AE, DC, MC, V.*

Nightlife and the Arts

Your best bet for a drink is a hotel bar or lounge. The **Lalitha Mahal Palace Hotel** has a good bar, with Victorian furnishings and a casual ambience; if you don't stay here, it's worth stopping in for a drink just to see the majestic building. **The Derby,** at the Quality Inn, has an equestrian motif, complete with saddle-topped barstools and staff dressed as jockeys.

To find out what's happening in Mysore, check with the Karnataka Department of Tourism and look for posters around town. **Kalamandir Auditorium** (✉ Vinoba Rd., ☎ 821/28185) hosts theater, dance, ballet, folklore, and classical Indian music. Admission is usually free or nominal. Other performances are sometimes held at the **Jaganmohan Palace** (☎ 821/23693) and the **Mysore Palace** (☎ 821/22672).

Outdoor Activities and Sports

Health Clubs

The mediocre health club at the **Quality Inn Southern Star** charges guests and nonguests alike Rs. 180 a day. The many Westerners studying yoga in Mysore tend to congregate here.

Horse Racing

The **Mysore Race Club** (✉ Race Course Rd., ☎ 821/521675) is a scene from August through October, with races about twice a week.

Shopping

Mysore is famous for its exquisite silks, fragrant jasmine, sandalwood products—oils, incense sticks, soaps, and carvings—and rosewood inlay work. The main shopping area is along **Sayaji Rao Road,** beginning at K. R. Circle in the center of town, with a plethora of silk emporiums, sweet stalls, and shops and hawkers of all kinds. Most shops are closed on Sunday.

Antiques and Handicrafts

Cauvery Art and Crafts Emporium (✉ Sayaji Rao Rd., ☎ 821/21258) is the fixed-price government showroom for sandalwood carvings, rosewood figurines, brassware, and other Karnataka handicrafts. **Mysore Crafts Emporium** (✉ 70-D Devaraja Urs Rd., ☎ 821/30294), the largest handicrafts showroom in Mysore, has a good selection of very reasonably priced local sandalwood and rosewood products, as well as crafts from other regions of India.

Markets

Devaraja Market (✉ Devaraja Urs Rd.; ⏲ open daily 6 AM–9 PM) is a bustling, old indoor fruit, vegetable, and flower market where you can immerse yourself in the vibrant colors and smells of Karnataka's bounteous produce.

Silks

Karnataka Silk Industries Corporation, the state body that runs the Government Silk Weaving Factory, has several fixed-price showrooms where you can buy or just admire the profusion of silks created at the factory (✉ **Government Silk Weaving Factory Complex,** Mananthody Rd., ☎ 821/21803; **city center,** ✉ Visveshwaraiah Bhavan, K. R. Circle, ☎ 821/22658; **Zoological Garden,** ✉ Zoo Complex, Indiranagar, ☎ 821/25502). The factory complex has a "seconds" showroom where a limited selection of silks with barely perceptible flaws are sold at up to 40% off. **Lakshmi Vilas** (✉ K. R. Circle, ☎ 821/420730) has a large selection of silks and other fabrics.

Side Trips

Cauvery River

Karnataka's rivers teem with fish and crocodiles, and fishing expeditions are becoming an important part of the state's tourist industry from December through March. The mammoth mahseer fish swim in the Cauvery River near Bhimeswari, about 100 km (60 mi) south of Bangalore and 75 km (46 mi) east of Mysore. Anglers fishing from *coracles* (round, basket-like boats) regularly hook mahseers weighing upwards of 50 pounds here, as well as smaller Carnatic carp, pink carp, and the good old catfish. The largest recorded catch was by an Englishman in 1992: 120 pounds. Catch can be weighed and photographed for proof but must be returned to the river.

LODGING

$$ **Cauvery Fishing Camp.** This peaceful camp is on the bank of the Cauvery River. You sleep overlooking the river in basic, twin-bedded tents with attached bathrooms; simple, healthy meals, included in the room price, are served in an open-air dining area around a campfire. Trained guides take you to the prime angling spots in Jeeps or coracle boats, but fishing equipment is not provided. Reserve far in advance. ✉ *Bhimeswari, Karnataka; reservations through Jungle Lodges & Resorts Ltd. (☞ Contacts and Resources in Karnataka A to Z, below). 6 tents. AE, DC, MC, V.*

Nagarhole National Park

The Karapur Forest of southwestern Karnataka has long provided India's now-defunct royalty—not to mention the world's zoos and circuses—with elephants. Many years ago, an infamous practice called *khedda* (wild-elephant roundup) was common, pitting swarms of skilled tribesmen against a herd of trumpeting elephants. Today, the kheddas have stopped, and instead of animals in terror you can watch wild elephants moving around the Nagarhole National Park (also known as Rajiv Gandhi Memorial Park), established in 1954.

From Kabini River Lodge (☞ *below*) you can join a fantastic game-viewing tour—from your Jeep you might spot dholes (wild dogs), a massively muscular Indian gaur (wild ox), barking deer, sambars (reddish-brown wild deer), sloth bears, crocodiles, and families of elephants (mothers, calves, "aunt" elephants, and tuskers), and, if you're lucky, an elusive leopard or tiger. You can also glide around in a coracle, a round, basket-shaped boat (lined with buffalo hide) that's so slow and quiet that you can draw very close to wild animals and the abundant birds (more than 225 different species) without disturbing them. The best viewing times are early morning and evening from October through March. The area surrounding Nagarhole is home to the Jenu Kurubas (traditionally beekeepers) and Betta Kurubas, two tribes currently fighting with the government over the rights to this land, which they consider their historical home. ✉ *Coorg region (between Kadagu and Mysore districts), 93 km (58 mi) southwest of Mysore,* ☎ *8236/334–1993.* *Rs. 150.*

LODGING

$$$ **Kabini River Lodge.** Once the hunting lodge of the viceroy and maharaja, this resort within Nagarhole National Park is a charming combination of comfort and rusticity. The cabins are surrounded by colorful trees, and monkeys roam through the grounds. The ambience is peaceful, with a languid daily routine: long Jeep safaris or coracle boating are broken up by morning and afternoon tea on the veranda and hearty open-air meals (included in the room rate; drinks are extra) with a variety of cuisines. At night, before dinner, guests can gather in the common room to watch a wildlife video. The rooms have overhead fans and stone floors; you can also stay in safari-style tents. ✉ *Karapur; reservations through Jungle Lodges & Resorts Ltd. (☞ Contacts and Resources in Karnataka A to Z, below),* ☎ *80/559–7021 or 80/559–7025,* FAX *80/558–6163. 14 rooms, 6 cottages. Restaurant, bar, travel services. AE, DC, MC, V.*

Sravanabelagola

If you have time en route between Mysore and Belur or Halebid, stop in the small town of Sravanabelagola to see the **colossal monolithic statue** of the Jain saint Gomateshwara, carved in AD 981 and alleged to be one of the largest monolithic statues in the world. Stark naked and towering 58 ft high, with 26-ft wide shoulders, 10-ft feet, and other similarly massive endowments, Gomateshwara is at once imposing and soothing. Once every 12 years, thousands of devotees congregate here for the Mahamastakabhishekha, a ceremony in which the 1,000-year-old statue is anointed with milk, ghee, curds, saffron, and gold coins. You have to climb 600 big steps to get there. Another site worth a visit is the Chandragupta Basti Jain temple, which has 600-year-old paintings. ✉ *84 km (52 mi) north of Mysore.*

MANGALORE

There's not much grand heritage in this coastal business center, but Mangalore is a mellow place to sample Karnataka's largely untouched beaches and jump on or off the deliciously scenic Konkan Railway. Once acclaimed as Karnataka's port city and pepper center, Mangalore has ceded the pepper honor to Cochin and now has the low-pressure feel of a breezy seaside town along with some bustling bazaars.

Upon arrival, take a taxi toward Malpe beach. En route, you'll pass the temple town of **Udupi,** once home of the ancient Sanskrit philosopher Madhwacharya. Udupi is known for both its Lord Krishna temple, trimmed with gold, and its vegetarian restaurants, so it's a nice place to break for a cup of coffee and a *masala dosa.* Upon the quiet yellow sands of **Malpe beach** you can hire a boat to the rocky **St. Mary's Island,** where Vasco da Gama is believed to have landed in the 15th century before he stopped at Calicut.

Back in Mangalore, snatch some time after dinner to watch some **Yakshagana,** an ancient folk form of dance-drama performed in colorful costumes and greasepaint. Usually a night-long program performed in open fields, the Yakshagana involves robust dancing and mime; an interpreter tells a story drawn customarily from mythology and sings to the accompaniment of drums and cymbals. Performances are now often held on stages.

Lodging

$$ **Taj Manjarun.** This is the best lodging in Mangalore, with a pleasant sea view and a lovely pool. The rooms, painted in light hues, are bright and cozy, and a bit breezy in the evening. The Galley restaurant offers both buffet and à la carte meals, and sometimes Indian and Western pop music. The Captain's Cabin pub is a nice, quiet corner for a quiet beer. ✉ *Old Port Rd., 575001,* ☎ *824/420420,* FAX *824/420585. 100 rooms. Restaurant, coffee shop, pub, pool, beach, travel services. AE, DC, MC, V.*

$ **Summer Sands Beach Resort.** This budget hotel is an option if you want to be near the sea upon arrival. Only 24 of the rooms have air-conditioning, so request one when booking. The villas, set in coconut groves, are cool and detached, and the Ullal beach is a treat. ✉ *Chota-Mangalore, Ullal,* ☎ *824/467690 or 467691,* FAX *824/467693. 75 rooms. Restaurant, in-room safes, some air-conditioning, billiards, playground, travel services. AE, DC, MC, V.*

BELUR AND HALEBID

Once flourishing cities of the 12th-century Hoysala dynasty, Belur and Halebid are now just fading rural villages. Both, however, hold some of the finest examples of stone carving in South India, called "the signs of a very confident Hindu culture" by writer V. S. Naipaul.

Hassan, an otherwise unexceptional town, is the gateway to the temples at Belur and Halebid—it's about 35 km (22 mi) away from each of the two, forming a triangle. Lodging options in Belur and Halebid are still few and far between, so you may want to base yourself in Hassan for a night or two.

To get the most out of the temples, hire a guide to show you around. You must remove your shoes before entering, so bring socks along on your visits; the stones can be painfully hot in the midday sun, particularly at Belur. If possible, bring a flashlight to see the temples' interior sculptures in full detail.

Belur

192 km (120 mi) northwest of Mysore; 240 km (150 mi) west of Bangalore

Set in a lush tropical landscape, the old city of Belur is dusty and rundown, with only one vestige of its splendid past. Still a functioning temple dedicated to a Vishnu incarnate, the **Temple of Lord Channakeshava** stands almost as pristine as it did the day it was completed in 1119—103 years after it was begun by the Hoysala king Vishnuvardhana. Legend claims that when Muslim conquerors came to Belur to destroy the temple, they were so awed by its magnificence that they left it alone.

Carved of soapstone, the temple is shaped like a star to allow maximum surface area for carving: a total of 32 corners. Squat and flat on top, it sits on a platform of the same shape; to its left is a small prototype (without the ornate stonework), built just before the temple as a study. Inside, some 10,000 impossibly intricate sculptures ornament every possible surface, a profusion of gods and goddesses in all their varied aspects and incarnations— scenes from the great Hindu epic, the *Ramayana,* as well as hunters, dancers, musicians, and beautiful women dressing and adorning themselves.

In the center of the temple, the domed ceiling is supported by four pillars surmounted by sculptures of voluptuous women striking any number of graceful poses beneath the intricately pierced, scrolled, and scalloped stone canopies. The carving is so detailed that some of the stone bangles the women wear can be moved. ✉ *Free, guide Rs. 50 for 2 people.* ⏲ *Daily 8 AM–8:30 PM; inner sanctums closed daily 1–3 and 5–6.*

South of the main temple, a smaller shrine, the **Channigaraya Temple,** is worth a good look. The other Hoysala temple, **Viranarayana,** has rows of very fine sculptures on its outer walls.

Lodging

$ **Hotel Mayura Velapuri.** This is a standard, government-run tourist hotel, low on frills but fairly clean. The big advantage is that it's literally on the edge of the temple complex, the perfect vantage point for watching the sun rise and set over this sacred site. The kitchen serves vegetarian meals, particularly South Indian thalis. ✉ *Outside temple entrance,* ☎ *8177/22209. No credit cards. Restaurant.*

Halebid

35 km (22 mi) northeast of Belur; 35 km (22 mi) north of Hassan

Halebid is a tiny rural village that was once the capital of the Hoysala ★ kingdom. Dedicated to the Hindu Lord Shiva, the **Hoysaleswara Temple** was begun by King Vishnuvardha in 1121, after the one at Belur was complete. It was left unfinished after 190 years of labor because the Delhi sultanates' attacks on it leveled its pyramid-peaked roof. Like the temple at Belur, this one has a star-shaped plan, but as a double-shrine temple, it has two of everything—one for the king and one for the queen. Moreover, the sculptors' virtuosity reached its peak here, leaving some 20,000 statues. The figures are carved in such detail that they appear to have been etched. You can see the taut fibers of the cord from which a drum hangs, feel the weight of the jewel beads dangling from a dancer's neck, almost hear the swinging of the bells around the arms of the elephant god Ganesh. At one time the temple also had 84 hanging statues, but all except 14 were eventually seized by conquerors of one stripe or another.

The breathtaking friezes wrap all the way around the temple: First comes a row of elephants for stability, then a row of lordly lions for courage, then convoluting scrolls of swift horses, then a row of people in sexual poses. Above more scrollwork are scenes from the religious epics that not only present philosophical ideas but mirror the living conditions of the time. The largest frieze is also the most exuberant: here the *apsaras* ("celestial maidens") are clothed in jewels, with bracelets on each of their several arms.

Behind the queen's shrine (the one closest to the entrance) is a giant sculpture of Nandi the bull, Shiva's vehicle, with beautifully smooth features and a polished belly that almost seems to breathe.

A small **museum** next to the temple displays various statues and brass and copper figures excavated from the surrounding area. *Free.* ⏲ *Temple, daily sunrise–sunset; museum, Sat.–Thurs. 10–5.*

A few minutes down the road, the smaller **Kedareswara Temple** bears more exquisite carving. The lovely friezes are similar to those of the main temples at Belur and Halebid, and executed with equal finesse. Here also stand two relatively unadorned early **Jain temples,** their finely polished black pillars as reflective as mirrors. Set on a low hill next to a lake, this is an attractive, peaceful spot in its own right. *Free.* ⏲ *Daily sunrise–sunset.*

Dining and Lodging

$$ ✕🏨 **Hotel Hassan Ashok.** The best lodging option in Hassan, this three-story modern hotel is about half an hour's drive from both Belur and Halebid. The rooms are reasonably priced and low on frills, with worn modern decor. Some are air-conditioned. The restaurant serves good Indian and Continental cuisine, and the staff is super-friendly. Try spicy South Indian thali or a milder Punjabi, with or without meat. *Rasam,* a typical South Indian lentil soup, is a spicy way to start your meal. ✉ *Bangalore-Mangalore Rd., Hassan 673201,* ☏ *8172/68731 or 8172/68736,* FAX *08172/67154. 45 rooms, 1 suite. Restaurant, bar, laundry service, meeting room. AE, DC, MC, V.*

$ 🏨 **Hotel Mayura Shanthala.** The rooms are plain and uninspiring, and the food is no compensation (ordinary South Indian and North Indian vegetarian fare), but this government-run tourist accommodation is near the temple and serviceable for a short stay. ✉ *Temple Rd., Halebid,* ☏ *8177/3224. Restaurant, laundry service No credit cards.*

HAMPI

★ Located in the middle of Karnataka and difficult to reach, **Hampi** (also known as Vijayanagar) is the most awesome spectacle in the state. A ruined city of vast stone temples, elephant stables, barracks, and palaces, Hampi was the center of the largest Hindu empire in South India and a major point of confluence for both Hindu and Jain worshippers.

Legend has it that the city, which is spread over 180 square km (70 square mi) in a rocky valley surrounded by rugged mountains that wouldn't look out of place in the American Southwest, was founded by two brothers, Harihara and Bukka, in 1336. Some of the buildings, however, can be dated back 1,400 years. Hampi was a large and wealthy city of about 1 million people for more than two centuries, until Muslim invaders from the north conquered the empire in 1565, and in the process destroyed the faces of the thousands of statues and sculptures that adorn the numerous temples. To see Hampi in its entirety, you should spend two full days here. Most of the ruins are open free of charge, though some, seemingly chosen at random, charge Rs. 5 or Rs. 10.

Many people choose to explore the ruins by themselves, but you'll probably get more out of them if you hire one of the official guides who wait on the road leading into the still-thriving village of Hampi Bazaar. They charge about Rs. 350 for a full day.

The ruins are spread over two main areas: In the north, near Hampi Bazaar, they center on the enormous **Virupaksha Temple,** home to hundreds of monkeys and a hangout for dozens of children intrigued by the sight of foreigners.

In the south, in what's known as the Royal Enclosure area, a vast ruined **palace** overlooks a landscape of grandiose stone buildings every bit the equal of the major Maya and Aztec monuments. Particularly spectacular are the towering elephant stables, home to the eleven elephants of the royal guard.

The fairly good **Archaeological Museum** in the southern part of the ruins takes you through the (ongoing) excavation process and displays many of the weapons and cooking utensils found at Hampi, as well as some of the larger statues taken from the erstwhile Shiva and Vishnu temples. Snakes hide in the museum's gardens, so be careful where you walk! The museum is open Saturday through Thursday from 10 to 5, and admission is free.

Dining and Lodging

Accommodations in Hampi itself are low-quality at best. There are several little rooming houses on the road leading into Hampi Bazaar, but for slightly more comfort, stay in Hospet, about 13 km (8 mi) from the ruins.

$ ✕ **Eagle Garden Restaurant.** There's a wide choice of chicken dishes at this restaurant near a canal, and the outdoor tables are fairly comfortable. ✉ *Jambunatha Rd., Hospet,* ☏ *8394/28107. No credit cards.*

$ ✕ **Manasa/Naivedyam.** This pair of restaurants at the Hotel Priyadarshini covers a few bases: Manasa has cool outdoor tables, good chicken dishes, and a bar, while Naivedyam offers indoor dining and spicy vegetarian food. The background music (which emanates from Manasa but is audible in both) is an eclectic mix of Sanskrit incantations and Céline Dion. ✉ *Hotel Priyadarshini, 45 Station Rd., Hospet,* ☏ *8394/28838 AE, DC, MC, V..*

$ 🏨 **Malligi Tourist Home.** This is the best accommodation in Hospet, considering it's the only one with facilities like currency exchange and travel assistance. It's fairly clean for a small-town Indian hotel, and the vividly colored furnishings lift the spirits. A multicuisine restaurant and a bar add to the on-site perks. ✉ *Jambunatha Rd., Hospet,* ☏ *8394/28101. 116 rooms. Restaurant, bar, pool, exercise room, coin laundry, travel services. AE, DC, MC, V.*

$ 🏨 **Priyadarshini.** This hotel has fairly large rooms, several of which have air-conditioning. Some of them have a spacious balcony. There are, however, signs of bedbugs. ✉ *45 Station Rd., Hospet 583201,* ☏ *8394/28838. 82 rooms. Restaurant, coin laundry. AE, DC, MC, V.*

KARNATAKA A TO Z

Arriving and Departing

By Bus

HASSAN (BELUR AND HALEBID)

There is no easy way to reach Hassan, the gateway to Belur and Halebid. If you don't mind the crowds, take the KSTDC-run bus from the Mysore Bus Station: The ride takes three hours, costs Rs. 40, and leaves every half hour throughout the day. Once in Hassan, hire a driver for the day and expect to pay more than Rs. 400. The KSTDC and various private companies also run tours of Belur and Halebid, and you can arrange a private car through Seagull Travels (☞ Tour Operators and Travel Agencies, *below*).

By Car

National highways connect Bangalore to Madras, the Kerala coast, Hyderabad, Bombay, and Goa.

By Plane

All flights to Karnataka land in **Bangalore,** which is 140 km (90 mi) northeast of Mysore and 240 km (150 mi) from Nagarhole National Park (Kabini River Lodge). Bangalore has domestic flights to Bombay, Madras, Mangalore, Hyderabad, Delhi, Calcutta, Pune, Goa, and Ahmedabad, and international flights to Singapore, Sharjah (UAE), and Muscat (Oman). Connecting flights from Bombay serve New York, London, and Paris. **Indian Airlines** (✉ Cauvery Bhavan, K. G. Rd., ☏ 80/526–6333; at airport, general inquiries 140, reservations 141). **Jet Airways** (✉ 1–4, M Block, Unity Buildings, J. C. Rd., ☏ 80/227–6620; at airport, ☏ ☏ 80/526–1926 or 552–1898).

In **Mangalore,** the airport can be reached at ☎ 824/752433. **Indian Airlines** (✉ Lalbagh, ☎ 824/455669 or 824/442309). **Jet Airways** (✉ Ram Bhavan Complex, ☎ 824/440694 or 824/440596).

FROM THE AIRPORT

Two pre-paid **taxi** counters compete in Bangalore's arrivals hall. Rates offered by the state government outfit are slightly lower than those of its neighbor, but either one will charge you about Rs. 150 for the ride to a major hotel. There is a fleet of metered taxis in the parking lot at the arrivals-hall exit, and the same journey with one of them should cost about Rs. 100, but it's still best to agree on a price before you begin. An **auto-rickshaw** ride into the city costs about Rs. 80, but it only works well if you have very little luggage and are not in a hurry.

If you're skipping Bangalore altogether, you can book a **car and driver** at the KSTDC counter in Bangalore's airport (☞ Visitor Information, *below*) and be straight off to Mysore or beyond. Taxis and car services will also take you long distances, but you're likely to be significantly overcharged.

By Train

BANGALORE

The reservations office at the **Bangalore City Railway Station** (☎ 131, general inquiries; ☎ 132, reservations; ☎ 133, recorded information; ☎ 134, after-hours arrivals and departures information) is open Monday through Saturday 8 to 2 and 2:15 to 8, Sunday 8 to 2. Counter 14 on the ground floor is reserved exclusively for foreign tourists, senior citizens, and people with disabilities.

HAMPI

Trains to Hospet (the jumping-off point for Hampi) run overnight from Bangalore, departing at 9:30 PM and arriving the next morning at 7:40. The KSTDC (☞ Visitor Information, *below*) also runs three-day bus tours from Bangalore. You can also reach Hospet directly from the north; trains run from Bombay to Guntakal, in Andhra Pradesh, and from there local connections run to Hospet. Note that trains in this part of the country are very slow.

MANGALORE

Mangalore is linked by train to Bombay, Delhi, Kerala (Trivandrum and Ernakulam), and Madras.

MYSORE

The reservations office at **Mysore Railway Station** (☎ 821/520100 or 821/37300) is open Monday through Saturday 8 to 2 and 2:15 to 8 and Sunday 8 to 2. The super-fast, air-conditioned, relatively expensive *Shatabdi Express* runs between Mysore and Madras via Bangalore (Rs. 400 round trip) every afternoon except Tuesday. There is also a 24-hour train to Bombay.

Getting Around

By Auto-Rickshaw

In congested cities, the "three-wheeler" is a convenient, quick, and cheap way to travel short distances. Note that the rides are bumpy, and these open vehicles expose you to a certain amount of air pollution. Figure about Rs. 7 for the first km, Rs. 4 per additional km. Between 10 PM and 5 AM, the fare is one-and-a-half times the meter reading. Meters are sometimes faulty. Very often, you can also hire an auto-rickshaw for the entire day (eight hours) for around Rs. 400; bargain with the driver, and don't pay until the day is done.

By Bus

Local buses are frequent and cheap, but decidedly not comfortable. Mornings and evenings especially are crowded, with as many as eighty people stuffed into one bus.

By Car

The best way to see beautiful Karnataka is to hire a car and driver. For journeys outside city limits, figure about Rs. 3.50 per km (the minimum distance is 250 km/155 mi), and for overnight trips a halt charge of Rs. 100 per night to feed and shelter the driver. Flat rates to get around within Bangalore or Mysore run approximately Rs. 450 for an eight-hour day, Rs. 30 for each additional hour. Hire a car from an agency listed under Visitor Information, *below*; KSTDC's rates are slightly lower than those of private companies. Driving on your own is not recommended for most foreign travelers, as traffic and road conditions can be hazardous if you're unfamiliar with the terrain and the protocol.

By Taxi

In the major cities, regular taxis charge more or less according to their meters (usually more), with an initial charge of about Rs. 70 for the first 5 km. As a tourist, you're vulnerable to being overcharged, so try to agree on a price with the driver before setting out.

There aren't many metered taxis on the streets in **Bangalore**—you'll find them mainly at the train and bus stations and the airport. Have your hotel call one, or call a radio taxi from wherever you are (☎ 80/332–0152 or 80/332–7589).

In **Mysore,** you can often flag down vacant taxis on the street. If that doesn't work, pick one up at one of the taxi stands throughout the city, or ask your hotel to get one for you. The meter rate is approximately Rs. 70 for the first 5 km (3 mi).

By Train

The scenic **Konkan Railway** leaves early in the morning for its north-bound trip along the Karnataka coast, reaching Karwar after 6 hours (Rs. 80), Margao (Goa) after 7 hours (Rs. 100). For general inquiries in Mangalore, call ☎ 824/423137; for reservations, call ☎ 824/424002.Several (air-conditioned) trains run between Bangalore and Mysore daily; the trip takes about 3 hours and the fare is Rs. 185.

Contacts and Resources

Currency Exchange

Most Western-style hotels will change money for their guests. The main branches of the **State Bank of India,** generally open weekdays 10–1, change currency and usually cash traveler's checks as well.

BANGALORE

Thomas Cook (✉ 70 M. G. Rd., ☎ 80/558–6742). **Marco Polo Travel and Tours** (✉ Janardhan Towers, 2 Residency Rd., Bangalore, ☎ 80/223–6671). **Synergy Financial Exchange LTD** (✉ 107 Raheja Plaza, 17 Commissariat Rd., D'Souza Circle, ☎ 80/558793). Most banks also exchange foreign currency and cash traveler's checks; try **ANZ Grindlays Bank** (✉ Raheja Towers 26/27, 1 M. G. Rd., ☎ 80/558–7684). The **State Bank of Mysore** has a branch in the airport arrivals area.

Late-Night Pharmacies

Al-Siddique Pharma Center (✉ K. R. Rd., opposite Jamia Masjid, near City Market, Bangalore, ☎ 80/605491) is open 24 hours. **Janata Bazaar** (✉ in Victoria Hospital, Bangalore, ☎ 80/627471) is also open 24 hours.

Travel visas can be extended at the **Office of the Commissioner of Police** (⊠ 1 Infantry Rd., Bangalore, ☎ 80/225–6242).

Tour Operators and Travel Agencies

The transport wing of the **Karnataka State Tourism Development Corporation** (☞ Visitor Information, *below*) is widely used for its car-hire service and sightseeing tours: It offers several full- and half-day bus tours of major sights in Karnataka. Most of these tours are inexpensive and low on frills—the buses are aging—but they provide a concise, well-rounded look at what's important.

The **Government of India Tourist Office** (☞ Visitor Information, *below*) trains and approves all official tour guides. Rates are low by Western standards (about Rs. 450 per eight-hour day, Rs. 900 for a trip outside the city), and the guides are informative and helpful. You can hire one directly or through most travel agents and tour operators.

Jungle Lodges & Resorts Ltd. (⊠ Shrungar Shopping Centre, 2nd floor, M. G. Rd., Bangalore, ☎ 80/559–7021 or 559–7025, FAX 80/558–6163), the outdoor-activity branch of the Karnataka Department of Tourism, has rustic facilities in the state's protected wild areas. Professional guides can take you on Jeep tours to wildlife-viewing spots or fish-rich rivers. The office is open weekdays 10 to 5:30 and Saturday 10 to 1:30 (closed 2nd Saturday of month).

BANGALORE

Ambassador Travel Services (⊠ 76 Mission Rd., Kasturi Complex, 2nd floor, Bangalore, ☎ 80/224–1516 or 80/222–1342) has reliable cars and drivers at moderate rates. **Clipper Holidays** (⊠ Suite 406, Regency Enclave, Magrath Rd., Bangalore 560025, ☎ 80/559–9032, FAX 80/227–7052) runs general-interest tours, special-interest tours, and treks of various lengths. The American Express Travel Services representative in Bangalore is **Marco Polo Travel and Tours** (☞ Changing Money, *above*). **Sri Sathya Sai Tourists** (⊠ 433/30/1, 10th Main 28th A Cross, 4th Block, Jayanagar, Bangalore 560011, ☎ 80/664–1140 or 80/646340, FAX 80/664–9940), out in a residential neighborhood, is open 24 hours a day, 365 days a year. The staff arranges general-interest tours, taxi and bus service, and currency exchange.

MYSORE

Clipper Holidays (☞ Bangalore, *above*) will arrange for a minimum of 15 people at a time to have dinner with the former prince of Mysore at his own palace. **Siddharta Tours & Travels** (⊠ Hotel Siddharta, 73/1 Guest House Rd., Nazarbad, Mysore, ☎ 821/34155 or 821/30555; ⊠ Lalitha Mahal Palace Hotel, Mysore, ☎ 821/35702) arranges tours within Karnataka. **Seagull Travels** (⊠ Hotel Metropole, Mysore, ☎ 821/439732, FAX 821/34653) also changes money.

Visitor Information

BANGALORE AND MYSORE

The **Karnataka Department of Tourism** (KDT) provides brochures, maps, and general information on Karnataka through two branches in Bangalore (⊠ K. G. Rd., Cauvery Bhavan, F Block, 1st floor, ☎ 80/221–5489; ⊠ 9 St. Marks Rd., ☎ 80/223–6854) and one in Mysore (⊠ Old Exhibition Bldgs., Irwin Rd., ☎ 821/22096 or 821/31061). The offices are open Monday through Saturday (closed 2nd Saturday of month) 10 to 1:30 and 2:15 to 5:30. In Mysore, **Skyway International Travels** makes reservations, including tour arrangements (⊠ 10 Madhu Nivas, Gandhi Square, ☎ 81/426642 or 81/426823).

The transport wing of the **Karnataka State Tourism Development Corporation** (KSTDC) is based in Bangalore (⊠ Yathrinivas Bldg., 10/4

Kasturba Rd., ☎ 80/221–2901 or 221–2902; **airport,** ☎ 80/526–8012; **railway station,** ☎ 80/287–0068). The office provides information and reservations for its state-run hotels, tours, and car-and-driver hire. Hours at the main office are Monday through Saturday 10 to 5:30 (closed 2nd Saturday of month).

The **Government of India Tourist Office** (✉ KFC Bldg., 48 Church St., Bangalore, ☎ 80/558–5417) has useful information on the region and arranges private guides. The office is open weekdays 10 to 5 and Saturday 10 to 1:30 (closed 2nd Saturday of month).

The Explorer's Sourcebook: Bangalore is a privately published insider's guide to the city sold in many hotel bookstores. The most complete map of Bangalore is the red "Road Guide to Bangalore," available in most Indian bookstores.

BELUR

The small **reception center** (☎ 8177/22218) inside the temple-yard entrance is open Monday through Saturday from 8:30 to 5:30, and sometimes on Sunday. The **Tourist Information Center** (✉ Hotel Mayura Velapuri, Temple Rd., Belur, ☎ 8233/2209) is a three-minute walk from the temple entrance and keeps the same hours as the reception center. Government-approved guides, available at the temple entrance, will take one or two people through the sights for about Rs. 50.

The **Karnataka Department of Tourism** (KDT, ✉ Vartha Bhavan, B. M. Rd., Hassan, ☎ 8172/68862) maintains an information office Monday through Saturday from 10 to 5:30 (closed the second Saturday of each month) with advice on Belur and Halebid.

HAMPI

The tourist office in Hampi Bazaar is pretty much empty, though it does have a few basic maps. There is, however, a Neha travel office on the one road through the village, as well as a sister bureau next door to Hotel Priyadarshini in Hospet. Theoretically, both are open Monday through Saturday 9 to 8, and both change money. There is also a State Bank in Hampi.

10 KERALA

Sea breezes brush coconut palms on India's southwestern shores, and ancient waterways wend their way inland to traditional fishing villages. Ayurvedic health programs invite you to unwind completely. The age-old spice-trading city of Cochin is a pungent center of commerce and cosmopolitanism; and Kerala's elaborate dance form, Kathakali, is one of India's most colorful performing arts. Between its laid-back towns and the creatures in Lake Periyar Wildlife Sanctuary, Kerala might be called elemental India.

By Vikram Singh

Updated by Shanti Menon

A CHARMING MYTH EXPLAINS the creation of Kerala, the narrow strip of a state running 560 km (350 mi) along India's western coast. Parashurama, an avatar of Vishnu, performed a series of penances to atone for a grievous sin, and the great god rewarded his devotion by reclaiming Kerala from the sea.

In 1956 the Malayalam-speaking states of Cochin and Travancore joined with the district of Malabar to form Kerala. The new Indian state wasted no time achieving a name for itself, becoming the first place in the world to adopt a communist government in a free election, a political event that caused global discussion and speculation. The fiercely pro-labor government has kept industry to a minimum in the state, leaving its rural beauty largely intact.

A tropical paradise in the south between the Western Ghats and the Arabian Sea, Kerala is one of India's most progressive states, with a literacy rate of well over 90%. Even in the shabbiest backwater toddy shop, where locals come to knock back a few glasses of potent coconut liquor, you'll find a copy of the day's newspaper. Malayalees are the most highly educated population in India, many conversant in English, Hindi, and Tamil in addition to their native Malayalam. In the nearly three millennia before the 1795 establishment of British rule, Phoenicians, Arabs, Jews, Chinese, and Europeans came in droves, attracted by the region's valuable cash crops: tea, rubber, cashews, teak, and spices—most notably black pepper and cardamom. Kerala's natural wealth and a heritage of 3,000 years of commerce with the rest of the world has made it remarkably cosmopolitan, yet the pace of life remains easy and slow.

Since Independence, many places have been renamed to reflect their names prior to British colonization. Since the British had a strong presence in Kerala, name changes are particularly germane here; hence Alleppey/Alappuzha, Calicut/Kozhikode, Cochin/Kochi, Palghat/Palakaad, Quilon/Kollam, Trichur/Thrissur, and Trivandrum/Thiruvananthapuram. Official maps and tourist brochures reflect these changes but the new (old) names are not yet in general use, as the British names had been in place for more than 200 years.

Pleasures and Pastimes

Beaches

Pristine beaches studded with coconut palms are Kerala's main attraction, and even though vacationers from all over the globe have heard the word, there are still quiet places to relax. For serious pampering, wind down in a secluded cove on the Arabian Sea near Kovalam, where many of the beach resorts offer ayurvedic health treatments (a holistic approach based on traditional Hindu medicine), massage, yoga, and meditation for a physically relaxing and mentally soothing vacation.

Cruises

A backwater cruise through Kerala's inland waterways, known locally as *kayals,* can be a two- or three-hour journey through sheltered and shady villages or a week-long adventure that runs the length of the state. Getting to the backwaters is easiest by car from Cochin, where travel agents and the tourist office can help you arrange private boat trips. If either of the resorts in Kumarakom is on your itinerary, their sister hotels in Cochin, the Casino and the Taj, will help you set things up before you arrive. The Casino Hotel Group can also arrange romantic river and lake trips on houseboats; they work with Spice Coast Cruises, based in the town of Puthenangadi, on Vembanad Lake.

Dining

The abundance of both locally grown spices and various foreign influences in Kerala's history have resulted in a savory, adventuresome cuisine. Rice is the staple, coconut milk and coconut oil are the two most important ingredients, and seafood—plentiful, fresh, and delicious—is the star. In Cochin you can buy a fresh-caught fish from the Chinese nets in Mattancherry and have it fried at a nearby stall to enjoy al fresco. Different kinds of bananas show up both cooked and raw, in entrées as well as desserts; and a type of sugar called jaggery—extracted from a native palm and not fully refined—is used in the preparation of sweets.

Kerala is known particularly for *iddi appa,* or "string hoppers"—thin strands of dough formed into little nests that are steamed and served with coconut milk and sugar for breakfast or as an accompaniment to soup, stew, or curry. Another native specialty is *puttu,* a puddinglike dish made from fresh-grated coconut and rice flour, molded and steamed.

Lodging

Nearly all the hotels in Kerala's larger cities have air-conditioning, but many in the less populated areas do not. In addition, some buildings have no window screens, so if a cool and/or bug-free sleep is part of your plan, ask about both. Most lodging places charge an additional 10 percent service fee, and the Indian government tacks on another 6–16 percent, depending on the facilities. For luxury hotels, count on paying a total of 25 percent in taxes.

Most Kerala hotels have significant off-season discounts—often up to 75 percent.

Performing Arts

The Kathakali dance-drama, performed by many companies in Cochin and at Kumarakom's Vijnana Kala Vedi Cultural Center (where it's also taught), will introduce you to a vital aspect of South Indian heritage. In addition, some 50 classical, folk, and tribal dance forms survive throughout Kerala, many unique to a particular caste, some even to a particular temple. Mohiniyattam is a beautiful dance that lies somewhere between Kathakali and classical Bharata Natyam. Padayani, performed during festivals at many South Indian temples, is a colorful re-creation of the goddess Kali's victory march after vanquishing the demon Darika. Pulikali (or Kaduvakali) brings men, brightly painted as green-, yellow-, orange-, and red-striped tigers, into the streets in the Trichur and Palghat districts. For details on which dances might be performed while you're in a certain town, inquire at the town's tourist office or the Tourist Desk in Cochin.

Shopping

Native Keralite crafts include cups, vases and teapots carved from coconut shells; baskets, floor and table mats, and carpets hand-woven from coir, the fiber made from the husk of coconut fruit; and sleeping mats and handbags made from the resilient and pliable kova grass.

Exploring Kerala

With the exception of bustling Cochin, Kerala's attractions are rustic: quiet beaches spiked with fringed coconut palms, fishing boats laden with bountiful catch, exotic wildlife, and tea and spice plantations in a tranquil and gorgeous rural landscape. Kerala is home to 12 wildlife sanctuaries and two national parks, including the renowned Lake Periyar Wildlife Sanctuary near Thekkady; at Periyar you can observe native animals and birds in their natural habitat from the comfort of a riverboat. Keralite temples are both more modest in scale and more restricted than elsewhere in India: Non-Hindus cannot enter even the courtyards of most Keralan temples.

Great Itineraries

Numbers in the margin correspond to points of interest on the Kerala map.

IF YOU HAVE 4 DAYS

Spend your first day and night in **Cochin.** The next day, charter a boat for the four-and-a-half-hour trip through the backwaters of Vembanad Lake to the resort town of **Kumarakom** for a two-day stay, or embark on a backwater cruise through the region's inland waterways. (The eight-hour journey from Quilon to Alleppey is popular.)

IF YOU HAVE 6 DAYS

Follow the four-day itinerary above, and add a side trip from Kumarakom to **Kottayam,** which has a number of old Christian churches. Move on to **Thekkady** for two nights and a full day at Lake Periyar Wildlife Sanctuary. Some travelers arrive in Kerala by car from Madurai, in Tamil Nadu (☞ Chapter 11); if that's your plan, visit Thekkady on your way west toward the coast.

IF YOU HAVE 9 DAYS

Follow the six-day itinerary, and travel south from Thekkady to **Trivandrum,** Kerala's capital. Explore its sights and quiet lanes before heading for the mellow beaches, palm-fringed lagoons, and rocky coves of **Kovalam.** Many hotels in this area have complete health and revitalization programs, including ayurvedic treatments, massage, yoga, and meditation.

Another option from Thekkady is to swing back through Cochin to **Lakshadweep,** a group of atolls off the coast of Kerala, only about a third of which are inhabited.

When to Tour Kerala

For the best weather, come to Kerala during the relatively cool, dry season: between October and February. March, April, and May are hot and quite humid

In September, the week-long harvest festival of Onam brings feasting, folk dancing, huge floral displays, and snake-boat races to various coastal areas. The Tiruvatira, in January, is a celebration of folk dancing and singing by young Malayalee women. In March, the Great Elephant March lasts four days; and late in April, just before the monsoons begin, is the festival of Vishu, a tribute to the new fruits of the season and a family gift-giving holiday.

COCHIN

1 Cochin is one of the largest and oldest ports on India's west coast, and the streets behind the docks are still lined with old merchant houses, godowns (warehouses), and open courtyards heaped with betel nuts, ginger, and peppercorns. Throughout the second millennium this ancient city exported spices, coffee, and coir, and imported culture and religion from Europe, China, and the Middle East, creating a cosmopolitan and prosperous local culture: Cochin has a synagogue, several mosques, Portuguese Catholic churches, Hindu temples, and the United Church of South India (a collection of Protestant churches), mak-

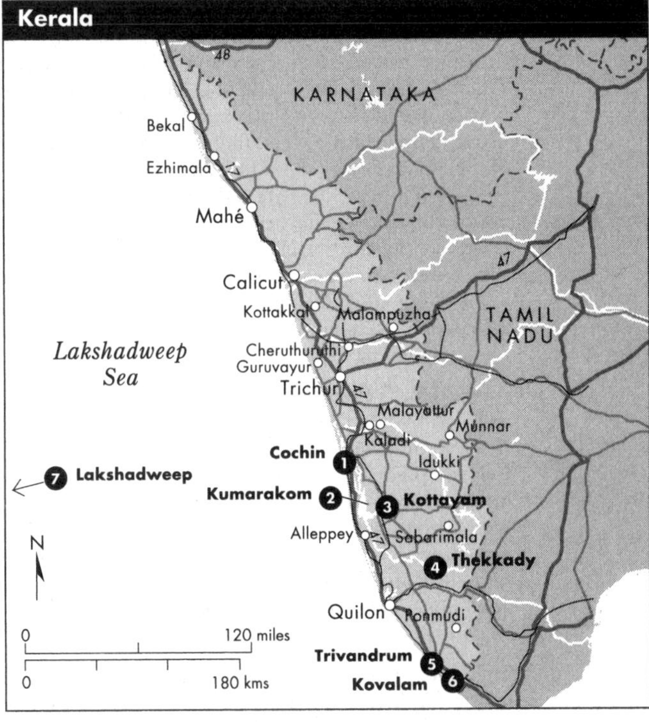

ing it South India's most ecumenical city. Salman Rushdie's novel *The Moor's Last Sigh* paints a heady, unforgettable picture of this unique place; you can pretty much smell the pepper from your armchair.

Modern Cochin incorporates the Ernakulam area on the mainland, several islands (including Willingdon, created by dredging the harbor), and the tip of the Mattancherry peninsula, all connected by a series of bridges and ferries. Private launches for hire and fleets of ferries zip through Cochin's waterways, where the journey is often as enjoyable as its objective. Ernakulam, 2 km (3 mi) from the harbor, is the commercial center; it was once the capital of the former state of Cochin. Many of the coir magnates with businesses on Gundu Island live in the residential quarter of Fort Cochin, where their faux-Tudor houses recall manor homes in Britain. Bolghatty Island, north of Ernakulam, is the most beautiful of the islands; its colonial mansion was formerly used by the Dutch governor and later by the British Resident. Mattancherry, southwest of the harbor, is home to Cochin's dwindling Jewish community and is, along with Fort Cochin, the city's historic center.

A Good Tour

In Ernakulam, visit the **Parishith Thampuran Museum** for some Cochin cultural history; then, walk north on Park Avenue (which parallels the waterfront park) to catch the ferry to Cochin. Boats depart the main jetty near the tourist office at the northern end of the park. Take a few hours to explore **Fort Cochin,** then break for lunch before continuing south to Mattancherry to see its **Dutch Palace** and **synagogue.**

TIMING

This tour will take a full day. Remember that the museum and all houses of worship close for a few hours around lunchtime. The Dutch Palace is closed on Friday, the synagogue is closed to visitors on Saturday, and the museum is closed on Monday.

Sights to See

Dutch Palace. Built by the Portuguese in the middle of the 16th century, this structure was taken over in 1663 by the Dutch, who made some additions before presenting it to the rajas of Cochin. The rajas, in turn, added some of the best **mythological murals** in India, particularly in the bedchambers. In one room, you can see the entire story of the *Ramayana* on the walls. The ladies' bedchamber features some mildly erotic depictions of Lord Krishna with his female devotees. The palace also contains a rare example of traditional Keralite flooring, which looks like polished black marble but is actually a mix of burned coconut shells, charcoal, lime, plant juices, and egg whites. On display in the coronation hall are many of the Cochin rajas' artifacts, including a fantastic palanquin made of ivory. ✉ *Palace Rd., Mattancherry,* ☎ *no phone.* 🎫 *Free.* ⏲ *Sat.–Thurs. 10–5.*

★ **Fort Cochin.** The northern tip of the Mattancherry peninsula is believed to hold the oldest European settlement in India. The Portuguese flag first appeared here in 1500, and Vasco da Gama arrived in 1502. The following year, Alfonso de Albuquerque came with half a dozen ships full of settlers—he built the fort, and the five friars in the crowd built India's first European church, **St. Francis,** here in 1510. Da Gama returned in 1524 as Portuguese viceroy of the Indies, he died here that same year, and was buried in St. Francis Church. You can still visit his gravestone, but he's buried in Lisbon; his remains were shipped back to Portugal in 1538.

The history of the church reflects European powers' struggle for colonial turf in India. The church alone was Dutch Reform from 1664 to 1804 and Anglican from 1804 to 1947; it's now part of the Church of South India. The church contains Dutch tombstones and the *Doep Boek,* a register of baptisms and marriages between 1751 and 1894 that you can view in photographic reproduction (the original is too fragile). St. Francis is a sedate church in the Portuguese style, not nearly as flamboyant as the **Santa Cruz Cathedral,** also in Fort Cochin, which verges on the gaudy. Santa Cruz was completed in 1904. ✉ *Parade Rd. and Rampath Rd.* ⏲ *Churches open sunrise-sunset.*

Parishith Thampuran Museum. Also known as the Cochin Museum, this museum holds artifacts from the former royal family, many 19th-century paintings and sculptures, and some beautiful old murals. The adjoining art gallery holds contemporary works by local Indian artists. ✉ *D. H. Rd., Ernakulam,* ☎ *484/36907.* 🎫 *Rs. 5.* ⏲ *Tues.–Sun. 9:30–12:30 and 3–5.*

★ **Synagogue.** The first migration of Jews to Kerala is thought to have taken place in the 6th century BC, followed by a much larger wave in the 1st century AD, when Jews fleeing Roman persecution in Jerusalem came and settled at Cranganore (on the coast about 26 km north of Cochin). In the 4th century, the local king promised the Jews perpetual protection and the Jewish colony flourished, serving as a haven for Jews from the Middle East and, in later centuries, Europe. When the Portuguese leader Albuquerque discovered the Jews near Cochin in the 16th century, however, he destroyed their community, having received permission from his king to "exterminate them one by one." Muslim anti-Semitism flared up as well. The Jews rebuilt in Mattancherry but were able to live without fear only after the less-belligerent Dutch had taken control in 1663. Only two or three families of the so called "white Jews" of Cochin remain today, many having left India for Israel.

This synagogue was built in 1568, when the Jews settled in Mattancherry after their expulsion from Cranganore. It was considerably embellished in the mid-18th century by a wealthy trader, Ezekiel Rahabi, who built a clock tower and paved the floor of the synagogue with hand-painted willow-pattern tiles—each one different—from China. The synagogue's most important relics are the impressive copper plates recording the 4th-century decree in which King Bhaskara Ravi Varma guaranteed the Jewish settlers domain over Cranganore. You must remove your shoes before entering. ✉ *Jew Town, Mattancherry.* 🎫 *Rs. 2.* ⏲ *Sun.–Fri. 10–noon and 3–5. Closed to visitors on Jewish holidays.*

Dining and Lodging

For a taste of delicious Keralite cuisine, seek out regional Malayalee restaurants or hotel restaurants that specialize in native fare. Many independent restaurants have grown so popular that it's advisable to call ahead for a table.

Lodging in crowded Ernakulam gives you access to most travel services and transport connections, while accommodations on the islands are quieter and more scenic.

$$$ ✕ **Jade Pavilion.** An interior pavilion, a Chinese mural, and brass lanterns create an elegant, romantic atmosphere. From the extensive menu, try lobster *sing-tu* (spicy lobster cooked in chili and oyster sauce), tiger prawns in garlic sauce, or the tasty steamed fish. ✉ *Taj Malabar Hotel, Willingdon Island,* ☎ *484/666811. AE, DC, MC, V.*

$$$ ✕ **Rice Boats.** Here, you eat inside a traditional wooden Keralite boat under a woven bamboo awning. The lighting is subdued, and oars and bamboo hats adorn the walls. The chef specializes in seafood, including *karimeen grandeur* (fresh local fish marinated in subtle spices then fried) and various lobster and prawn dishes. ✉ *Taj Malabar Hotel, Willingdon Island,* ☎ *484/666811. AE, DC, MC, V. No lunch.*

$$ ★ ✕ **Fort Cochin.** Bamboo and traditional furnishings give this outdoor restaurant the feel of a Keralite cottage. The day's catch is wheeled before you in a wooden cart, and your choice is cooked specially for you—simply grilled or exquisitely curried. ✉ *Casino Hotel, Willingdon Island,* ☎ *484/668221. AE, DC, MC, V. No lunch.*

$ ✕ **Fry's Village Restaurant.** This simple restaurant—four plain pavilions with bamboo curtains—screens out the city's bustle. At lunchtime it serves typical Kerala *thalis* (set combination meals), which incorporate such specialties as *molly* (fish fillet in a sweet green curry with coconuts) and the inexpensive *kadala* (Kerala plain curry) with *puttu* (steamed rice and coconut) for under Rs. 10. Fry's is very popular with locals, so expect a crowd. ✉ *Chittoor Rd., next to Mymoon Cinema,* ☎ *484/353983. No credit cards.*

$ ✕ **Pandhal.** Amid rough white stucco walls, a pine ceiling, and quiet waterfall, this modern, multicuisine restaurant serves a variety of seafood and Indian dishes, but it's the Chinese entrés and steaks that make the place so popular. It gets crowded in the evening. ✉ *M. G. Rd., opposite Grand Hotel,* ☎ *484/367759. Reservations essential for dinner. AE, DC, MC, V.*

$$$–$$$$ ★ 🏨 **Brunton Boat Yard.** All rooms face Cochin Harbor in this stately, exclusive hotel, built in a combination Dutch/Portuguese colonial style on the site of a former boatyard. *Pankhas,* manually operated wooden fans, dangle from the lofty ceiling of the spacious, open-air lobby. The grassy courtyard, shaded by a gracefully bowing ancient raintree, is surrounded by four sparse, almost churchlike, whitewashed corridors lined with terra-cotta tile. The rooms—dominated by huge four-poster beds so high you need a footstool to climb in—create a similar atmosphere of understated grandeur; the fixtures and furnishings are an-

tique, right down to the ceiling fans and light switches. Most rooms have private balconies, from which you can watch ships of all sizes gliding past, as well as the gleaming bodies of dolphins cavorting in the harbor. Breakfast is included in the room rate. ✉ *Fort Cochin, 682001,* ☎ *484/222557, 221461-68,* FAX *484/222562. 22 rooms, 4 suites. Restaurant, coffee shop, pool, travel services. AE, DC, MC, V.*

$$–$$$ ★ **Taj Malabar.** This luxury resort on the tip of Willingdon Island offers elegance, privacy, and fantastic sea views. The decor blends carved dark wood and Kerala-style furnishings with more modern tiles and brass. If you're inclined toward antiquity, ask for a wood-floored room in the old wing. Rooms in the new wing have modern decor and spectacular views from the higher floors. All rooms have sea or garden views. ✉ *Willingdon Island, 682009,* ☎ *484/666811,* FAX *484/668297. 99 rooms, 9 suites. 3 restaurants, bar, pool, travel services. AE, DC, MC, V.*

$$ **Casino.** This handsome Western-style hotel is an excellent value. The lobby is cozy, with cane furnishings, and the spacious rooms have elegant, modern decor. The best rooms overlook the lawn and pool. All bathrooms have showers, but not all have tubs. ✉ *Willingdon Island, 682003,* ☎ *484/668221,* FAX *484/668001. 70 rooms, 1 suite. 2 restaurants, bar, travel services. AE, DC, MC, V.*

$$ **Malabar House Residency** Luxurious yet homey, this striking 300-year-old colonial villa used to house wealthy European traders and bankers. The graceful courtyard features a lush garden and dramatically integrated swimming pool. Room decor is a curious meeting of traditional Keralite and Pottery Barn; somehow it works. The spa offers ayurvedic treatments, and the room rate includes breakfast. ✉ *1/268, 1/269 Parade Rd., Fort Cochin, 682001,* ☎ FAX *484/221199. 17 rooms. 2 restaurants, bar, spa, travel services. AE.*

$$ **The Trident.** Tasteful, stylish, and thoroughly modern, this new member of the Oberoi chain caters to business travelers. Light wooden floors brighten the rooms, which all face either the pool or the garden. The staff is pleasant and helpful, and the lobby positively gleams. ✉ *C-46-452 (II) Bristow Rd., Willingdon Island, 682003,* ☎ *484/666816,* FAX *484/668017. 96 rooms. Restaurant, bar, pool, beauty salon, exercise room, business services, travel services. AE, DC, MC, V.*

$$ **Taj Residency.** This downtown hotel caters to Cochin's ever-growing population of business travelers. Rooms in the beautifully maintained building are small, and the bathrooms have showers rather than bathtubs, but the harbor and sea views are spectacular. ✉ *Marine Dr., Ernakulam, 682031,* ☎ *484/371471,* FAX *484/371481. 108 rooms, 12 suites. Restaurant, bar, coffee shop, business services. AE, DC, MC, V.*

$ **Avenue Regent.** The lobby of this high-rise in the heart of town has art-deco red bands around the ceiling molding and in the floor pattern. Rooms are spacious, with contemporary decor. ✉ *M. G. Rd., Cochin 682016,* ☎ FAX *484/372660. 53 rooms. Restaurant, bar, business services, travel services. AE, DC, MC, V.*

Nightlife and the Arts

The Arts

Kerala's unique dance form is the 400-year-old **Kathakali** (*Katha* means "story," and *kali* means "play"), in which a story is told through dancing, pantomime, and music. Originally intended to begin at sundown and last all night (the costuming and makeup alone take five hours), Kathakali performances are now sometimes shortened to one or two hours. Many centers offer a two-hour session that includes an opportunity to watch the application of the dancers' elaborate makeup. The best performances are at the **See India Foundation** (✉ Kalthil Parambil La., ☎ 484/369471), where the director provides clear and lively explanations of the art before every 6:45 PM show. Performances at the **Cochin Cultural Center** (✉ Manikath Rd., ☎ 484/380366) are also clearly explained; they start at 6:30. Arrive an hour before the show to watch the makeup application.

Kerala's dramatic, high-flying martial art, **Kalarippayattu,** may be the oldest in Asia. Some scholars believe that Buddhist monks from India introduced Kalarippayattu to China along with Buddhism. Traditionally practiced by warrior families, participants learn both armed and unarmed combat techniques. One of the more unusual skills involves defending oneself against a knife-wielding attacker using only a piece of cloth. You can watch practitioners at **Arjuna Kalari Sangham** (✉ Puthiya Rd. Junction, ☎ 484/360980) daily 5–9 AM and 5–9 PM. The **E. N. S. Kalari Centre** (✉ Nettoor, Ernakulam, ☎ 484/700810) welcomes visitors Monday–Saturday 6 PM–7 PM and Sunday 3 PM–7 PM.

Nightlife

Most of the larger hotels have bars. After dinner, nightlife in Kerala is limited to performances of Kathakali.

Shopping

The **Cochin Gallery** (✉ C. C. 6/116 Jew Town Rd.) has various collectibles. **Indian Arts and Curios** (✉ Jew Town Rd.) is the oldest and most reliable shop on this curios- and antiques-laden street; its two outlets are filled with brass and wood items and Tanjore glass paintings. Local hotels get many of their antiques from **Crafter's** (✉ Jew Town Rd.). **Kairali** (✉ M. G. Rd., Ernakulam, ☎ 484/354507) is a government shop with a good collection of Keralite handicrafts and curios. **Surabhi** (✉ M. G. Rd., Ernakulam), run by the state's Handicrafts Cooperative Society, has an impressive selection of local products. Be suspicious of the word "antique" in all stores.

CENTRAL AND SOUTHERN KERALA

Between Cochin and Quilon, to the south, is the immense labyrinth of waterways called *kayals,* through which much of the life of the Malayalee (the people of Kerala) has historically flowed. From the vastness of Vembanad Lake to quiet streams just large enough for a canoe, the backwaters have carried Kerala's largely coconut-based products from the village to the market for centuries.

A backwater cruise through some of these inland waterways provides a window into the Malayalees' unique traditional life. You can take a two- or three-hour journey through shady and sheltered villages or devote a day to a more rugged (potentially hot) adventure like the eight-hour trip between Quilon and Alleppey. Private travel agents and the Kerala Tourism Development Corporation (KTDC) are eager to hook people up with private boats; *see* Travel Agencies *and* Visitor Information *in* Kerala A to Z, *below.*

Trivandrum is Kerala's capital. Kovalam, just south of Trivandrum, is known for its beaches and ayurvedic health treatments; and 260 km (160 mi) off the coast are the fantastical Lakshadweep Islands.

Kumarakom

❷ *80 km/50 mi south of Cochin*

A trip to this tiny, rapidly developing paradise on the shores of Vembanad Lake generally centers on a stay at the historic Taj Garden Retreat or the secluded Coconut Lagoon. The waterways are fascinating to explore by canoe. Arundhati Roy's birthplace, Ayemenem, featured in her novel *The God of Small Things,* is close by. Fans of this book might consider a trip down the river—"gray-green, with fish in it"—in a houseboat, an unforgettable opportunity to see life in Kerala at a truly Keralite pace. Shaded by a woven bamboo canopy and fanned by cool breezes, you'll drift past simple, tile-roof houses with canoes moored outside, tiny waterfront churches, and people washing themselves, their clothes, their dishes, and their children in the river. Women in bright pink and blue stroll past blindingly green paddy fields, their waist-length hair unbound and smelling of coconut oil. Graceful coconut palms are everywhere, as are political slogans painted on walls, featuring the communist hammer and sickle in colors Lenin never intended. Birds abound in the backwaters, as well as in the sanctuary on the eastern shore of Vembanad Lake. The lake also offers plenty of aquamarine recreation, and, happily, motor sports have been limited so far.

About 50 km (32 mi) north of Trivandrum, **Vijnana Kala Vedi Cultural Center** (✉ Tarayil Mukku Junction, Aranmula 689533, ☎ 4731/2552, FAX 4731/2783), established by a French woman in 1971, is dedicated to preserving the arts and heritage of Kerala. People from all over the world come to study everything from singing to cooking to language with experienced masters in a simple, village atmosphere. Space permitting, you can enroll for as little as one week.

Lodging

$$$ **Coconut Lagoon.** Accessible only by boat, this resort is one of the best in South India. You're ferried between the secluded lagoon on the shores of Vembanad Lake and two pickup points along a nearby river. The grounds are crisscrossed with canals and footbridges, and the cottages are a mixture of rustic and modern elements. The large, curving pool is a masterpiece, set near the lake under swaying palm trees. The open-air restaurant, reassambled from parts of a 300-year-old traditional Keralite home, overlooks the water and serves delicious, dramatic buffets. ✉ *Kumarakom, Kottayam 686563,* ☎ *481/525834. 42 cottages. Restaurant, pool, massage, spa, travel services. AE, DC, MC, V.*

$$$ **Taj Garden Retreat.** Completed in 1891, the main building of this verdant resort is an old colonial mansion, full of large rooms with high ceilings that open onto broad verandas. Built by the son of an English missionary, the house overlooks a lake and reflects the elegant life of plantation owners. (It opened as a Taj hotel in 1994.) Geese live next to the small private lake on the property, where you can canoe or pedalboat; and you have easy access to Vembanad Lake. ✉ *1/404 Kumarakom, Kottayam 686563,* ☎ *481/524377,* FAX *481/524371. 22 rooms. Restaurant, pool, massage, travel services. AE, DC, MC, V.*

OFF THE BEATEN PATH

ALLEPPEY – The canals of this waterborne industrial city teem with country boats. If you stop by on or around the second Saturday in August, you're in for a special treat: Throngs of supporters line the shore to watch the annual Nehru Cup snake-boat race, which starts with a water procession and concludes dramatically as the boats (propelled by as many as 100 rowers) vie for the trophy. The Alleppey Tourism Development Cooperative (ATDC; ☞ Kerala A to Z, *below*) runs daily trips between Alleppey and Quilon (8 hr, Rs. 100); after Quilon, boats continue south to Trivandrum and Kovalam. Boats leave both Alleppy and Quilon at 10:30 AM. Boats also link Alleppey with Kottayam and Changanacherry (Changanassery).

Kottayam

3 *16 km (10 mi) east of Kumarakom*

Just inland from Alleppey, this pleasant town has several Christian churches, established in the 1500s by missionaries who put down roots here. Today Kottayam is a center for rubber production and transportation: Catch bus service to the Lake Periyar Wildlife Sanctuary (☞ Thekkady, *below*), ferries to Alleppey (two-and-a-half hours), and trains plying the Cochin–Trivandrum route.

Thekkady

4 *116 km (72 mi) east of Kottayam*

Due east of Kumarakom and Kottayam, this mountain town sits at 3,000 ft above sea level in the Cardamom Hills, midway between Cochin and the temple city of Madurai in Tamil Nadu. This village is the nearest ★ population center to the **Lake Periyar Wildlife Sanctuary,** one of the best animal parks in India for spotting and photographing elephants, bison, wild boar and oxen (gaur), large Asiatic deer (sambar), and many species of birds in their natural habitat.

Lake Periyar, its many fingers winding around low-lying hills, is the heart of the 300-square-mi sanctuary. Periyar offers one of the world's most sybaritic ways of seeing big game. Forget exhausting treks or long safaris: Here, you lounge in a motor launch as it drifts around bends and comes upon elephants, deer, or bison drinking at the shores of the lake. During the dry season, when water holes in the forest are empty, leopards and tigers also pad up to the water. One word of advice: Indian children love to scream and shout at a sighting. To avoid losing the whole experience, either bribe the kids to be quiet or hire a private launch (about Rs. 500). Elephant herds are so accustomed to *quiet* visitors that they hardly notice the intrusion, although the younger pachyderms will peer at you out of curiosity and then run squealing back to their elders when your boat comes too close. The best viewing time is October through May. Brave-hearted travelers can spend a night in a jungle guest house, while the less adventurous commune with nature from the safety of a moated watchtower. If you go on a forest trek, look out for leeches. For information, contact the KTDC (☞ Visitor Information *in* Kerala A to Z, *below*). *Rs. 50; video cameras Rs. 100.*

Lodging

$$–$$$$ **Hotel Lake Palace.** Situated on an island inside the sanctuary, this idyllic former maharaja's hunting lodge is run by the state government. Eight simply appointed rooms look out through the palm-lined pathway over the lake to the wildlife preserve beyond. Meals at the multicuisine, fixed-menu restaurant are included. ✉ *Thekkady 685536,* ☎ *4869/2023; reserve through KTDC (☞ Visitor Information in Kerala A to Z, below). 8 rooms. Restaurant, refrigerators, boating, travel services. AE, DC. MC, V.*

$$$ **Shalimar Spice Village.** Twenty bone-jarring minutes off the main road to Thekkady, this rustic, intensely private retreat is for those who truly want to get away. A wooden bridge over a duck pond leads to the main building, a whitewashed, thatch-roof affair that houses a restaurant specializing in authentic Italian and Keralite food. The small, spotlessly white cottages are spread out over a hillside and vary in style. Decor is largely minimalist and perfectly executed, with only a colorful Rajasthani bedspread, a stained-glass window, or an ancient, darkwood oar adding a striking contrast to each room. Bathrooms are lavish and large. Most guests come for the special ayurvedic-treatment packages and yoga classes; the emphasis is on serenity and total relaxation.

✉ *Murikkady P.O., Kummily 685535,* ☎ FAX *486/322132. 12 cottages. Restaurant, pool, travel services. MC, V.*

$$$ **Spice Village.** Just outside the sanctuary, this charming resort features tiers of well-maintained thatch-roof cottages built into the side of a hill. The interiors are modern country-style: lots of knotty pine furnishings and trim, white walls, red-tile floors, and plaid upholstery and bedspreads. Lush plantings, including a landscaped spice garden, add fragrance and privacy. The restaurant, furnished with antique rosewood, serves delicious Indian and Continental set meals. Boating, jungle treks, and South Indian cooking classes are available. ✉ *Kummily Rd., Thekkady, 685536,* ☎ *4869/22315,* FAX *4869/22317. 47 cottages, 5 housekeeping cottages with twin beds. Restaurant, bar, pool, massage, meeting rooms, travel services. AE, DC, MC, V.*

$$$ **Taj Garden Retreat.** Built on a former coffee plantation, this woodsy Taj property offers balconied concrete cottages raised on stilts, with thatch piled on the roofs for cosmetic effect. Guest rooms are modern and reliable, and the multicuisine restaurant is excellent. ✉ *Ambalambika Rd., Thekkady 685536,* ☎ *4869/22273,* FAX *4869/22106. 32 rooms. Restaurant, bar, pool, massage, travel services. AE, DC, MC, V.*

Trivandrum

5 *222 km (138 mi) south of Cochin, 253 km (157 mi) southwest of Thekkady*

Built on seven low hills and cleansed by ocean breezes, the state capital is surprisingly calm and pleasant. Trivandrum's few sights and quiet lanes outside the town center make it an enjoyable place to stop.

The town's main architectural landmark is the **Padmanabhaswamy Temple.** Dedicated to Vishnu, it's a handsome example of South Indian temple architecture, with an impressive seven-story *gopuram* (entrance tower). The date of its construction is uncertain, although one legend traces it to 3000 BC. What *is* known is that it was built by 4,000 masons, 6,000 laborers, and 100 elephants over the course of six months. In the main courtyard, known as the **Kulasekhar Mandapam,** there is some intricate granite sculpture, supplemented by more stonework on the nearly 400 pillars supporting the temple corridors. The complex is technically open only to Hindus and keeps erratic hours, so call ahead to be assured of at least a glimpse. ✉ *M. G. Rd. at Chali Bazaar,* ☎ *471/450233.* ⏲ *Sunrise–12:30 and 4:30–9:30.*

A beautiful 80-acre park at the north end of M. G. Road packs a number of attractions in the **Museum and Art Gallery Complex.** The **Napier Museum,** with its Cubist pattern of gables, has a marvelous collection of local arts and crafts. The **Sri Chitra Art Gallery** has an eclectic collection of paintings, including works of the Rajput, Mogul, and Tanjore schools; copies of the Ajanta and Sigirya frescoes; and works from China, Japan, Tibet, and Bali, along with canvases by modern Indian painters. There's also a **zoo** on the grounds. ✉ *Museum Rd.,* ☎ *471/436275.* 🎟 *Museum and gallery Rs. 5, zoo Rs. 5.* ⏲ *Museum and gallery Thurs.–Tues. 10–5, Wed. 1–4:45; Zoo Tues.–Sun. 9–4:45.*

Shopping

Gifts Corner (✉ M. G. Rd., ☎ 471/73196) has both new and antique treasures. **Natesan's** (✉ M. G. Rd., ☎ 471/331594) is a respected art and antiques dealer. For Kerala handicrafts and souvenirs, hit the government emporium **SMSM** (✉ Statue Junction, off M. G. Rd.).

Kovalam

6 *16 km (10 mi) south of Trivandrum*

Kovalam's sandy beaches are lined with palm-fringed lagoons and rocky coves. Fishermen in *lungis* (colorful cloth wraps) drag in nets filled with the day's catch, then push their slender wooden fishing boats out again with a Malayalam "Heave ho." Here you can spend the day loafing on warm sand or rocky outcroppings, watch the sun set, then sit back as the dim lights of distant fishing boats come on.

Kovalam's irresistible beaches have given rise to tremendous development, yet the town retains a mellow atmosphere. Moreover, the international crowd has inspired a number of restaurants, most of which serve fresh, delicious seafood. In peak season, outdoor eateries spring up right on the beach—you can point to the fish of your choice from the day's catch and specify how you'd like it prepared. Kovalam is also a center for ayurvedic treatment, with many hotels offering complete health and revitalization packages (lasting anywhere from two days to two weeks) in which ayurvedic doctors, masseurs, and yoga and meditation instructors team up to optimize your physical and spiritual well-being. If you don't want to commit to extended treatment, try an ayurvedic oil massage: a vigorous rubdown involving copious amounts of oil, performed on a hard wooden table by a masseur with hands like driftwood. A post-session application of an herbal powder removes most of the unguent, leaving your skin feeling healthy and fresh. It's invigorating and relaxing, but those who prefer the delicate touch of the breeze might be better off lazing around on the sand with a good book and a cool drink.

Dining and Lodging

$ ✕ **Hotel Rockholm Restaurant.** You can eat indoors, but the best ambience here is on the delightful terrace on the bluff, with the ocean pounding below. Kovalam's best chef prepares excellent international dishes, including the daily catch. Try the seasonal fish and seafood dishes, such as grilled pomfret, fried mussels, or prawns Kerala-style. ✉ *Light House Rd.,* ☏ *471/480607. AE, DC, MC, V.*

$$$ **Kovalam Ashok Beach Resort.** Built in tiers into a bluff overlooking the Arabian Sea, this resort resembles a government housing project more than anything else, but it has a good beach and a terrific location. Rooms in the main block and the newer, sea-facing block have modern furnishings and private verandas; ask for an unobstructed sea view. The cottages, with tile floors and a cozier feel, have sea views and privacy. ✉ *Kovalam, Vizhinjam, Trivandrum 695527,* ☏ *471/480101,* FAX *471/481522. 191 rooms, 8 suites. 3 restaurants, bar, 3 pools, massage, health club, tennis court, travel services. AE, DC, MC, V.*

$$–$$$ ★ **Surya Samudra Beach Garden.** Overlooking the sea 10 km (6 mi) south of Kovalam, this gorgeous, rambling, slightly overgrown resort has an exquisite beach. Most lodgings are in stunningly restored Keralite wooden homes called *nalakettus,* each with an intricately carved facade, domed wooden ceilings, spacious open-air bathrooms, and understated decor. Rooms in simple cottages, with shared baths and interiors that blend modern and folk touches, are also available. All cottages offer privacy and ocean views, and four have air-conditioning; but they lack the beauty of the nalakettus. Loud noise is not permitted. Full ayurvedic treatments, complete with two doctors and several masseurs, are available. Meals, prepared without preservatives, are served in a delightful open-air restaurant. Reserve a room well in advance. ✉ *Pulinkudi, Mullur, Trivandrum 695521,* ☏ *471/480413,* FAX *471/481124. 18 rooms. Restaurant, bar, pool, beach, travel services. MC, V.*

$$ **Somatheeram.** Stressed-out Westerners flock to this beach resort, equipped as it is with a fully staffed ayurvedic hospital and a resident master. Various traditional treatment programs (normally two weeks in length) are available, as well as one-time treatments such as massage or medicated steam bath. Lodging is in traditional houses or simple cottages along twisting paths on 18 lush acres above the sea. The newer cottages are clustered somewhat close together, but the setting is still pleasant. None of the rooms is air-conditioned. ✉ *Chowara (near Kovalam), Trivandrum 695501,* ☎ FAX *471/481600. 45 rooms. Restaurant, beach, travel services. AE, DC, MC, V.*

$ **Hotel Rockholm.** This small seaside hotel in the thick of things overlooks a pretty, horseshoe-shape beach. The exterior is a bit dilapidated, but the rooms are spacious and clean, with modest contemporary furnishings and verandas. All rooms have overhead fans. Four of the newer rooms have air-conditioning, but their views are not as spectacular. ✉ *Light House Rd., Kovalam, Trivandrum 695521,* ☎ *471/480306,* FAX *471/480607. 22 rooms. Restaurant, travel services, massage, beach. AE, DC, MC, V.*

OFF THE BEATEN PATH

PADMANABHAPURAM Though it belongs to Kerala, this fantastic, 18th-century carved-teak palace is actually across the border in neighboring Tamil Nadu, about a 2-hr drive from Kovalam. Once home of the Travancore rajas, it's a rare—and arguably the finest—example of wooden architecture in India.

Lakshadweep

❼ *250 km (160 mi) off the coast of Kerala*

Of the 36 or so coral atolls that make up the isolated offshore paradise of Lakshadweep, only about 10 are inhabited, and their population is devoutly Sunni Muslim. Tourism here is severely restricted to protect the fragile islands and their traditional people from an onslaught of outsiders; only one island, Bangaram, is open to foreigners, and Casino Hotels operates its own resorts. Flights leave Cochin six times a week; make arrangements well in advance.

Lodging

$$$$ ★ **Bangaram Island Resort.** This resort is a true Eden of simple thatched cottages (two or four guest rooms each) with terra-cotta floors and Western furnishings. Construction is minimal; the general emphasis is on preservation of the environment. The water sports are an embarrassment of riches: snorkeling, kayaking, scuba diving, windsurfing. Book well in advance. Meals are included in the room rate. ✉ *Lakshadweep; reservations, Casino Hotel, Willingdon Island, Cochin 682003,* ☎ *484/668221,* FAX *484/668001. 27 rooms, 3 bungalows. Restaurant, bar, snorkeling, windsurfing, fishing. AE, DC, MC, V.*

KERALA A TO Z

Arriving and Departing

By Car

Not all roads are well maintained, but Kerala is a beautiful state to drive through. If you're coming from Tamil Nadu, the drive from Madurai along the Madurai–Kottayam Road is stunningly scenic. National Highway (NH) 47 runs from Salem, in central Tamil Nadu, to Cochin through some lovely country before heading down the coast to Cape Comorin in Kanya Kumari. NH 17 runs along the coast from

Mangalore to Cochin. The towns themselves are not congested. Getting to the backwaters is easiest from Cochin, where travel agents and the tourist office can help you plan your itinerary.

By Plane

All flights to Kerala land at either Cochin or Trivandrum, both of which are served by **Air India** (☏ 484/351295) and **Singapore Airlines** (☏ 484/367911). **Indian Airlines** (☏ 484/370242) serves domestic routes, as does **Jet Airways** (☏ 484/369423).

The new international airport in **Cochin** is about 40 km (25 mi) east of the city, but abominable traffic can make it a two-hour trip. Some hotels offer free airport pickup; otherwise, a taxi will cost Rs. 150–200. The small, confusing airport in **Trivandrum** is 6 km (4 mi) from the city center; taxis charge about Rs. 50. Traffic can be heavy.

Getting Around

By Auto- and Cycle-Rickshaw

Auto-rickshaws are a convenient and quick way to travel in Cochin. Figure Rs. 6 for the first kilometer and Rs. 2 per additional kilometer, or, if there's no meter, agree on a fare in advance. **Cycle-rickshaws** are not allowed in Cochin, but you might still see them in smaller towns. They should be cheaper than auto-rickshaws; just remember that the driver works hard for his money, and distances can be considerable. Set your fare in advance.

By Boat

The backwaters of Kerala are like those of Venice, on an immense scale. Planes, trains, and automobiles notwithstanding, these ancient waterways are still used for some long-distance transport and commuting. In Cochin, ferries and private boats ply between the fort, Willingdon Island, and Ernakulam throughout the day. Ferry rides cost only a few rupees; on private boats, be sure to set the rate in advance.

By Car

Bearing in mind that road conditions can range from halfway decent to deplorable, your most convenient way to get around Kerala is still via hired car with driver. Figure about Rs. 6–Rs. 8 per kilometer and a halt charge of Rs. 100 per night, and remember that an air-conditioned vehicle can make the difference between a pleasant journey and an exhausting one. Shop around, and hire a car from a government-approved travel agency (☞ Guided Tours, *below*). The coastal highway (NH 47 south of Trichur, NH 17 north) will serve most of your needs. Roads to the interior ghats (mountains) are often breathtaking, as the landscape changes from the brilliant lime green of the paddy fields to the rich, dark green of the tea plantations and the mountain jungle. The journey from Trivandrum to Cochin takes about six hours.

By Taxi

Cabs are a good option for destinations in and around **Cochin.** Fares will run about Rs. 7 for the first kilometer and Rs. 4 for each additional kilometer, and most cabs have a Rs. 60 minimum. Ask either tourist office for the latest legal rates.

By Train

Rail journeys in Kerala can be spectacularly scenic, and more comfortable (if less private) than traveling by car. The *KK Express*—which travels from Kanya Kumari, at India's southern tip, all the way up to New Delhi—is a good train to take between Trivandrum and Cochin. Check with the KTDC (☞ Visitor Information, *below*) for the latest schedules and fares.

Contacts and Resources

Currency Exchange

Most major hotels have exchange services. **Thomas Cook** (✉ M. G. Rd., Ernakulam, Cochin, ☎ 484/369729) offers good rates. The **Bank of India** (✉ Shanmugham Rd. and Willingdon Island, Cochin) and **ANZ Grindlays** (✉ Willingdon Island, Cochin) cash traveler's checks and change money, as does any branch of the **State Bank of India.**

Guided Tours

CENTRAL AND SOUTHERN KERALA

The **ATDC** conducts several backwater tours in addition to the Quilon–Alleppey run. Private companies, the KTDC, and the Tourist Desk operate half-day backwater tours for around Rs. 100– Rs. 400 (☞ Visitor Information, *below*).

The **KTDC** (☞ Visitor Information, *below*) has a series of one- to two-week specialty tours that follow a pilgrim trail through Kerala's sacred shrines. Other tours include wildlife-spotting in the Lake Periyar Wildlife Sanctuary.

COCHIN

The **KTDC** (☞ Visitor Information, *below*) conducts two inexpensive boat sightseeing tours of Cochin each day; the three-and-a-half-hour trips depart at 9 AM and 2 PM from the Sealord Jetty. The KTDC also conducts village backwater tours.

Travel Agencies

Sita Travels (✉ Tharakan Building, M. G. Rd., Ravipuram, Ernakulam, Cochin, ☎ 484/361101) can help with bookings and arrange a car and driver. The best travel agency in Kerala is the **Great India Tour Company** (main office: ✉ Mullassery Towers, Vanross Junction, Trivandrum, ☎ 471/331516, FAX 471/330579), which also leads a good health tour. Great India has offices in Cochin (✉ 1st floor, Pithuru Smarana, Srikandath Rd., Ravipuram, ☎ 484/374109, FAX 484/351328) and throughout South India. **SATM Tours and Travel** (✉ Warriam Rd., Cochin, ☎ 484/365765) designs affordable packages around your personal interests.

Visitor Information

In **Cochin,** the best source of information on Kerala is the Tourist Desk (✉ Main Boat Jetty, Ernakulam, Cochin, ☎ no phone), a private, nonprofit organization that conducts boat tours and provides clear, straightforward information on the whole state. The Kerala Tourism Development Corporation (KTDC) (✉ Tourist Reception Center, Shanmugham Rd., Ernakulam, ☎ 484/353234) is open daily 8–7. The Government of India Tourist Office (Willingdon Island, ☎ 484/668352), open weekdays 9–5:30 and Sat. 9–1, handles bookings for its own vehicles, boats, lodgings, and tours. The Kerala State Tourist Information Center (✉ Old Collectorate, Park Ave., Ernakulam, ☎ no phone), open weekdays 10–5 and alternating Saturdays 10–5, closed Sun., has statewide information. **Trivandrum** has two KTDC offices (✉ Station Rd., ☎ 471/330031; and the airport), both open weekdays 10–5. Trivandrum's Tourist Information Center (✉ Park View, across from museum, ☎ 471/62574) is also a good source. The **Alleppey Tourism Development Cooperative (ATDC)** (✉ Komala Rd., ☎ 477/243462) has information on Central Kerala.

Festivals of Kerala, an invaluable book sold at the Tourist Desk (☞ *above*), not only details festivals, but also describes all of Kerala's dance forms, boat races, temples, and regions of Kerala. Also look for the pamphlet "Kerala A to Z."

11 TAMIL NADU

Madras, the capital of Tamil Nadu, encapsulates the spirit and culture of India's southernmost state. From the Bay of Bengal to the Nilgiri Hills, Tamil Nadu resonates with the powerful Hinduism of the ancient Dravidians. The soaring, brilliantly carved, sometimes painted towers of magnificent South Indian temples dominate the landscape, just as faith permeates Tamil life.

By Molly Sholes and Vikram Singh

Updated by R. Edwin Sudhir

MORE THAN A FEW DEGREES of latitude and temperature separate India's Aryan north from its Dravidian south. Encompassing numerous cultures within them, North and South India have completely different climates, crops, cuisines, languages, architecture, and social customs.The state of Tamil Nadu—running about 500 mi along the Bay of Bengal to India's southernmost tip, Cape Comorin—is the heartland of South India. From the Tamil coast, with its rice fields and coconut and banana trees, the land rises through the low-lying Eastern Ghats (mountains) up to tea, coffee, and spice plantations in the Nilgiri Hills, and finally to the higher Western Ghats.

Hinduism pervades the Tamils' lives, beliefs, philosophy, and behavior. A rich oral tradition, 2,000-year-old religious texts and literature, and Jain and Buddhist influences have made South Indian Hinduism a distinct, vibrant, growing religion. The Tamils have survived incursions from North Indians and foreigners alike, but neither the Portuguese nor the French nor the British, who ruled Madras for 300 years, made more than a superficial dent in the soul of Tamil culture. Majestic South Indian temples with massive *gopurams* (entrance towers) and *vimanas* (towers over inner sanctums) dominate the Tamil landscape just as faith permeates Tamil life. A visit to at least one major temple is key to understanding this part of India.

About a third of Tamil Nadu is urban; many of the cities have more than 50,000 people. Even the smaller villages are not far from a city or town. A good bus system, frequent pilgrimages, a 70% literacy rate, and expanding and improving communications keep the Tamil villager reasonably well informed, far from isolated. Almost every village has a small temple, and shrines to Ganesh, the elephant-headed god of wisdom and prosperity, abound. A continuing custom for Tamil women is making designs of rice powder outside the household's front door every morning. The designs tell passersby that all is well within, and have a practical aspect as well: Ants and birds eat the rice flour and are distracted from entering the house.

Pleasures and Pastimes

Dining

A traditional Tamil meal is a balance of the six tastes of Indian cuisine: sweet, sour, pungent, astringent, salty, and bitter. Rice is a basic ingredient, whether cooked or ground into flour. Tamil dishes can be hot or bland; those that are usually mild include *idlis,* cakes made of steamed rice and blackgram, a type of lentil; plain *dosas,* crepes of rice and blackgram; *upma,* semolina and spices, often with vegetables; and curd-rice, yogurt mixed with rice at room temperature. The *thali,* available vegetarian or nonvegetarian, is essentially a multi-course feast on one platter, a chance to sample various Indian dishes at once. Decoction, or "coffee by the yard," is strong filter coffee mixed with hot milk and poured back and forth between two tumblers until it has reached the proper drinking temperature and is white with froth. It's delicious—the best cup of coffee you'll have in India.

Until recently, Tamils preferred to eat only in their homes for reasons of personal and religious purity. The best restaurants were confined to the larger hotels, which catered to foreign travelers. But as Madras becomes increasingly cosmopolitan, more locals are eating out, and a growing number of very good restaurants serve a variety of cuisines. Hotel restaurants especially have replaced the formerly ubiquitous Mughlai menus with authentic ethnic food, including Chinese and South Indian. An 8% sales tax is often levied on food and drink.

Lodging

Many of the best hotels have plush decor, rife with chintz. Unless otherwise noted, the hotels we list have air-conditioning. The state government runs "Tamilnadu" hotels, which are modest, usually clean hotels with simple restaurants—modern versions of the *dak* bungalow, or rest house, of the British Raj. Some hotels in Madras have conference rooms, dedicated business-traveler floors and suites, secretarial services, and in-room fax machines. Due to increasing commercial travel, reservations for rooms in Madras are essential, especially between December and February. Tamil Nadu levies a 20% luxury tax on room rates, and a 10% hotel-expenditure tax on the total bill.

Performing Arts

Bharatanatyam, a feminine dance form (though some men have also begun to achieve proficiency in it), and Carnatic music are the best known of the traditional South Indian performing arts. Similar in composition to North Indian music, the Carnatic art is nonetheless distinguished by its instruments and its vocal style. Many Tamil film scores are written in the Carnatic style.

Shopping

Look for silver tribal jewelry, jute placemats, copies of Chola bronzes, Kanchipuram silks, Khadi (hand-woven) shirts, carved wooden temple friezes, inlaid wooden boxes, contemporary artwork, and Thanjavur paintings. Bargaining isn't as prevalent as it once was, but almost everything here is a bargain anyway. Madras and Madurai have excellent shops, and nearly all major hotels have boutiques, most of which have fixed prices and take credit cards. Hotel stores tend to be expensive: shop around if you're buying a big-ticket item. Government-run craft emporiums have excellent selections, and surrounding most large temples are four streets of bazaars where bargaining is expected. In the past, bazaars were the *only* places to shop for groceries, household goods, jewelry, fruit, electronics, and paper products; over time, though, people have grown more accustomed to shopping in stores.

Temples

With their lofty gopurams, vimanas, and majestic *mandapams* (pillared halls), temples are integral parts of Tamil culture. The gopurams are often brilliantly polychrome, and the mandapam friezes inside depict myths and legends of Hindu gods and goddesses, and sometimes tales of the temple's benefactor. South Indian temples throng daily with pilgrims and visitors; the larger, better-known temples are pilgrimage shrines or are visited mainly on special occasions such as Pongal (harvest festival) and birthdays, while the smaller temples are part of daily life.

South Indian Hinduism is a personal, ritualistic religion. Almost anything—a tree, a rock, a sculpture—can be an object of veneration. Hindus worship at their temples in a variety of ways. Some devotees withdraw to the inner sanctum for *puja,* which consists of *darshan* ("spiritual seeing" or visual communication with the image of the deity), making a donation, and receiving blessings. Others worship a specific carved image in the mandapam frieze, and still others go to the sacred peepul tree and tie a ribbon around it. After puja, worshipers sit outside in the mandapam for a few minutes absorbing the temple ambience. In a temple courtyard, you might even see priests blessing a brand-new car. Non-Hindus are usually free to explore these houses of worship, barring only the inner sanctum.

Exploring Tamil Nadu

Great Itineraries

Any doubling back on these routes is necessitated by heavy traffic and bad road conditions. On Tamil Nadu's main north-south artery, NH 45, speeds average 35 mph (58 kph) in the middle of the day. Thanjavur and Swamimalai are on secondary roads that can also be maddeningly slow.

Numbers in the text correspond to numbers in the margin and on the Tamil Nadu, Madras, and Mamallapuram maps.

IF YOU HAVE 4 DAYS

Spend two days in historic **Madras** to see its colorful bazaars and Hindu temples. On the third day drive south via the Shore Road to **Mamallapuram,** on the Bay of Bengal, to see the cave temples. The next morning leave early to explore **Kanchipuram,** a pilgrimage town with 200 temples and a thriving silk industry, on your way back to Madras.

IF YOU HAVE 7 DAYS

Spend two days and nights in **Madras.** On your third day, visit **Kanchipuram;** continue south to **Mamallapuram** for nights three and four. On day five, move on to **Pondicherry** to explore its French heritage and unwind a bit. On day six, drive to **Tiruchirapalli,** then proceed late in the evening to **Madurai.** Devote day seven to the astonishing Meenakshi Temple before returning to Madras.

IF YOU HAVE 10 DAYS

After spending two days in **Madras,** travel to **Mamallapuram** via the Shore Road, stopping at the **Crocodile Bank** or **DakshinaChitra** en route. Day-trip to **Kanchipuram** and check out the migratory life in the **Vedanthangal Bird Sanctuary** on the way back to Mamallapuram. Spend your fifth day in Mamallapuram, exploring the cave temples and perhaps hitting the beach, before heading back to Madras. On day six, fly or take the train to **Tiruchirappalli.** Proceed to **Thanjavur** and Swamimalai on day seven to see the bronze foundry and the temples. On day eight, drive to **Madurai** and spend the night and the next day there before returning to Madras by plane or train.

When to Tour Tamil Nadu

The best time to visit is between November and February. True, the roads are in disrepair after the torrential rains of the monsoon season (which ends in September), but the sun is moderate in the winter months. This is the season for temple festivals and dance and music programs, and it's also the best time to observe migratory birds. Advance hotel and transport reservations are strongly recommended for this time of year. Note that Hindu temples close in the afternoon (noon–4). Most stores and museums are open all day.

MADRAS

Chennai is the new name for the old city of Madras, the garden gateway to South India. (The British named it after a fishing hamlet called Madraspatnam, supposedly offered to Francis Day, an East India Company trader, in 1639 by the Raja of Chandragiri, the last Vijayanagar ruler.) The fourth-largest city in India, Madras still has room to expand. From the time the British first established Fort St. George on a sliver of beach, the city has grown by absorbing the surrounding villages—thus the baffling array of neighborhood names like Nungambakkam, T. Nagar, Adyar, Mylapore, and George Town. Each area has developed distinctly, often along caste lines, from the Chettiars (a South Indian caste of traders) of George Town to the civil servants and

Tamil Nadu

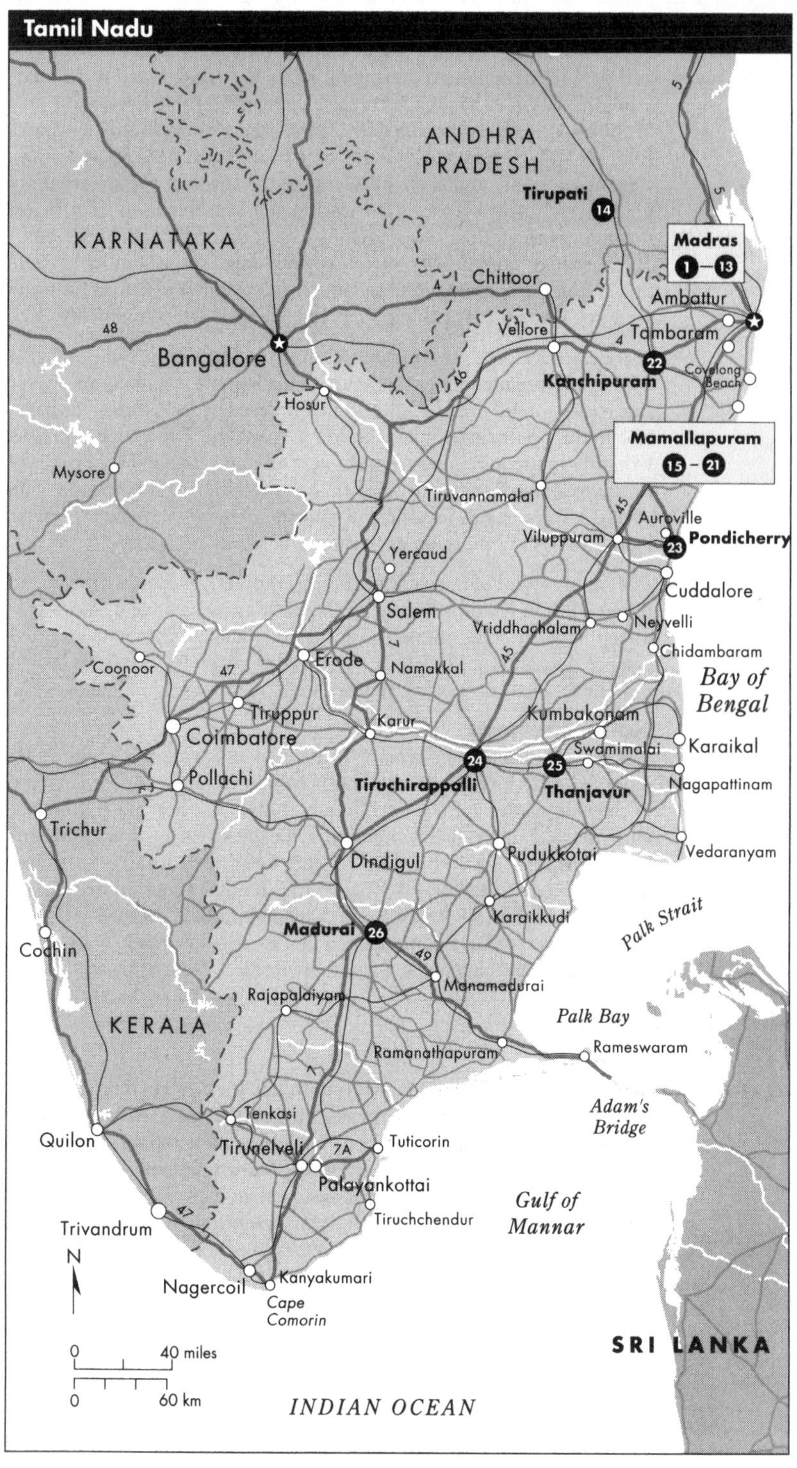

ANDHRA PRADESH
KARNATAKA
Tirupati
14
Madras
1–13
Chittoor
Ambattur
Vellore
Tambaram
Bangalore
Kanchipuram
22
Covelong Beach
Hosur
Mamallapuram
15–21
Mysore
Tiruvannamalai
Auroville
Viluppuram
Pondicherry
23
Yercaud
Cuddalore
Salem
Vriddhachalam
Neyvelli
Chidambaram
Coonoor
Erode
Namakkal
Bay of Bengal
Tiruppur
Kumbakonam
Coimbatore
Karur
Swamimalai
Karaikal
24
25
Pollachi
Tiruchirappalli
Thanjavur
Nagapattinam
Trichur
Dindigul
Pudukkotai
Vedaranyam
Karaikkudi
Palk Strait
Madurai
26
Cochin
Manamadurai
Rajapalaiyam
Palk Bay
KERALA
Ramanathapuram
Rameswaram
Adam's Bridge
Tenkasi
Quilon
Tirunelveli
Tuticorin
Palayankottai
Gulf of Mannar
Tiruchchendur
Trivandrum
N
Nagercoil
Kanyakumari
Cape Comorin
SRI LANKA
0
40 miles
0
60 km
INDIAN OCEAN
48
4
46
45
47
7
49
7A
5

industrialists of Nungambakkam. Even today, municipal boundaries expand, multistory apartment and office buildings replace bungalows, and new residential areas spring up along the Shore Road to Mamallapuram. Growth has made traffic nearly unbearable here, with pollution and noise levels rising daily. Cars, buses, trucks, auto-rickshaws (or "autos," as they're popularly called), mopeds, bicycles, motorcycles, pedestrians, and cows all compete for space in the streets; only yogic detachment keeps the frustration at a bearable level. (Traffic on the main avenues, like Anna Salai, is well regulated and moves along.) To ease congestion, the city is presently building a large number of overpasses, but the construction itself has reduced traffic to a crawl in some sections. Generally speaking, be prepared for detours and delays.

In the early 1990s, a government committee called Vision 2000 launched a program intended to reverse years of inadequate urban planning; yet side roads are still full of potholes and bordered by picked-over garbage, and many destitute people camp on city streets. The water supply is woefully inadequate, even nonexistent in some areas. Tanker trucks bringing water into the city add to the congestion and pollution. The phone system is still insufficient, and the demand for electric power increases with population growth and business expansion.

The rapid arrival of multinational corporations has changed the placid pace of life in Madras, which in the old days was alive at 5 AM and asleep by 9 PM. Still, nothing seems to have shaken the city's spiritual essence. Expanding Madras is a fascinating place, its increasingly cosmopolitan face contrasting sharply with its resolutely religious soul.

Name Changes

Just as Madras has been renamed Chennai, so have many of the street names changed, very often to honor contemporary politicians. Some of the new names are not in colloquial usage, but here's a partial list, with the old name listed first (*salai* means street or road): Mount Road—Anna ("Elder Brother") Salai; Chamier's Road—Muthuramalinga Road; Mowbray's Road—T. T. K. (Krishnamachari) Road; North Beach Road—Rajaji Salai; Nungambakkam High Road—Uttamar Gandhi Salai; Poonamallee High Road—Periyar E. V. R. High Road; South Beach Road—Kamarajar Road.

Northern Madras

A Good Tour

The best way to explore Madras is to follow the city's expansion south from Fort St. George. Some distances are short, but if the temperature is 100°F and the humidity 80%, you won't feel like walking; if oppressive heat threatens, hire a car. Start at **St. Mary's Church** ① in **Fort St. George.** Move on to the **Fort Museum** ②; then walk by the **Tamil Nadu State Legislature** ③. Return to St. Mary's Church, taking in the mixture of historic buildings and bureaucratic offices. Drive the ¼ mi to the **High Court** ④ via the road that tunnels through the fort's massive walls; park and walk to Armenian Street. Alternately, take a taxi or auto-rickshaw to N. S. C. Bose Road and get out at the junction of Armenian Street for a stroll through **George Town.** Walk down Armenian Street to the beautiful Armenian Church, which was built in 1629 and is no longer used for worship. As you wander on, look up and you'll see evidence of second-story residence—many merchants still live in George Town. On your way back to the High Court, pass the **Flower Bazaar** (✉ N. S. C. Bose Rd.), a riot of color and fragrance, on your right. Just south of N. S. C. Bose Road and before Prakasam Road (formerly Popams Broadway), check out the **Fruit Market,** where bananas ripen in enormous warehouses. Complete your tour of George Town back at the High Court.

TIMING

The ideal time to cover this route is Sunday morning, when the traffic and parking are most benign. The full tour should take 5 or 6 hours, including thorough tours of George Town and Fort St. George (2 hours each) and half an hour in the High Court.

Sights to See

★ **Fort St. George.** The first British fort in India was founded by Francis Day on a thin strip of sand leased from the Raja of Chandragiri. Christened on St. George Day in 1640, Fort St. George, complete with walls 20 ft thick, has remained the symbol of the Raj, its history intertwined with that of the rest of British India. The Indian army and civil service, Colin Mackenzie's land survey, and the British archaeological, botanical, and zoological surveys of India were all conceived on this site. Now the home of the Tamil Nadu State Legislature, it's quietest on Sunday. ✉ *Entrance on Kamarajar Rd.,* ☎ *no phone.*

2 **Fort Museum.** Once an exchange used by East India Company merchants, this building is now a museum of Indian history. Everything from old uniforms and coins to palanquins and padlocks is on display, including some wonderful old prints. Study the exhibits closely, as they're not always well labeled. ✉ *Fort St. George,* ☎ *no phone.* 🎟 *Free.* ⏲ *Sat.–Thurs. 9–5. No cameras, either still or video.*

George Town. If you tend toward agoraphobia, George Town is not the place for you, as walking—the only way to explore this teeming warren of congested streets—is often hard going. Pedestrians weave in and around vendors, carts, and cows while others conduct business on the sidewalk or in the street. Before you venture into George Town, make sure you have a detailed map of this area so you can wander with confidence; many streets have similar names. For the full experience, come in the morning, when the bustle is at its peak.

Originally called Black Town, this 1½-by-2-mi area was first settled by lower-caste artisans who provided textiles to the British traders. After Black Town was burned in the British–French wars, the new town was laid out in a perfect grid pattern, each section housing a different group or caste with its own place of worship. The street names echo George Town's mercantile history, as each area bears the cultural characteristics of the group who migrated there in the course of doing business with (or for) the East India Company: Not only Indians but Portuguese, Scots, Armenians, and Jews settled here. Another prominent group are the Chettiars; you'll notice that many of the street names end in "chetti." Two competitive subcastes of the Chettiars, who speak different languages and observe different religious traditions, live in their own areas, divided only by Prakasam Road. The Chettiar factions long vied for mercantile power, first with the East India Company and then with the merchants of the Raj. ✉ *Bordered by Basin Bridge Rd., Old Jail St., Ebrahim Sabib St., and Rajaji Rd.*

★ 4 **High Court.** This large judicial complex is a magnificent example of Indo-Saracenic architecture, built of red sandstone with intricate ornamentation on the walls and minarets. (The tallest minaret was used as a lighthouse until the 1970s.) Inside is a labyrinth of corridors and courts, most of which you can visit; court number 13 has the finest decorations inside. Within the compound is a tomb in the shape of pyramid; one of its two inscriptions is to the only son of Elihu Yale, governor of Fort St. George from 1687 to 1691. The child died in infancy and was buried in the High Court compound. ✉ *Just north of fort off N. S. C.*

Basilica of San Thome Cathedral, **13**
Church of Our Lady of Expectation, **9**
Fort Museum, **2**
High Court, **4**
Kapalishvara Temple, **12**
Madras Snake Park, **10**
Marina Beach, **5**
National Museum and Art Gallery, **8**
Parthasarathi Temple, **6**
St. George's Cathedral, **7**
St. Mary's Church, **1**
The Study, **11**
Tamil Nadu State Legislature, **3**

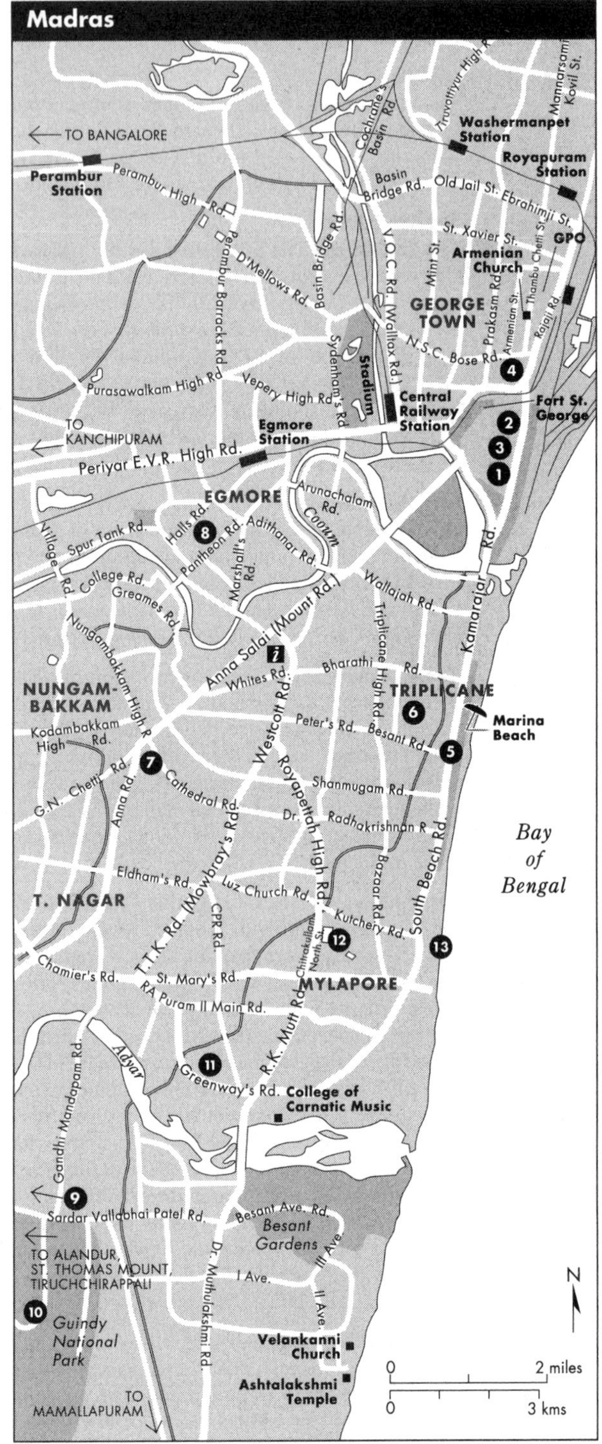

Bose Rd., near intersection with Rajaji Salai. 🎫 *Tour Rs. 10.* ⏲ *Mon.–Sat. 10–5. Guided tours, Mon.–Sat. 10:30–1:45 and 2:30–4:30.*

★ ❶ **St. Mary's Church.** Consecrated in 1680, this church is the oldest masonry structure in Fort St. George. The punkahs and some flags are gone, and the steeple has been replaced, but otherwise the building with its three-arched aisles and bomb-proof roof has not changed. The marriage of governor Elihu Yale (of Yale University fame) was the first one performed here. Job Charnock, founder of Calcutta, had his three daughters baptized here before the family moved to Bengal, and St. Mary's congregation included, at one time or another, Thomas Pitt, Warren Hastings (later the first governor general of British India), Lord Cornwallis, and Arthur Wellesley, later the Duke of Wellington. ✉ *Fort St. George.* 🎫 *Free.*

❸ **Tamil Nadu State Legislature.** This crowded, active seat of the state government occupies most of the area between St. Mary's Church and the Fort Museum. The former house of Robert Clive (of the Battle of Plassey fame) is the "Pay Accounts" office. Other sections of the fort are under military control. ✉ *Muthuswamy Iyer Rd.*

Central Madras

As Madras grew, the city moved south, expanding along the beach and inland to Egmore and Nungambakkam. The Chepauk district, home of Madras University and Chepauk Palace (now government offices), has some of India's best Indo-Saracenic buildings—a combination of Hindu, Muslim, and Victorian Gothic styles that makes a fitting display for a city with roots in all three cultures. Farther south along the beach is the Triplicane neighborhood, with the Parthasarathi Temple. Inland, toward the center of Madras is Anna Salai, a major shopping and business district. North of Anna Salai is Egmore, bordered by the curves of the Cooum River and home to the National Museum and Art Gallery. Farther south across the Cooum is Nungambakkam, traditionally a posh residential area of garden homes. It's now a mixture of expensive boutiques, hotels, and offices, but a few of the massive old houses with walled gardens remain. A new wave of small fast-food joints (as in hot dogs and pizza) and restaurants has hit Anna Salai, Egmore, and Nungambakkam.

A Good Tour

It's easiest to cover this ground by hiring a car and driver for the day, but you can also take auto-rickshaws from point to point. Early in the morning, drive south on Kamarajar Road from Fort St. George along the magnificent **Marina Beach** ⑤ and passing the Indo-Saracenic buildings of the government and university on your right. Note the brick Ice House at Presidency College: Clipper ships from New England, which used ice as ballast, used to unload it here before it found its way into the nawabs' drinks. Beyond the contemporary political structures and the public swimming pool on the ocean side is the marina promenade: Have your driver stop at its north end (just south of the pool), and take a stroll. Rejoin your driver back in the promenade parking lot and drive to the **Parthasarathi Temple** ⑥. After this burst of South Indian temple architecture, **St. George's Cathedral** ⑦ provides a striking contrast. The **National Museum and Art Gallery** ⑧ completes your tour with a superb collection of South Indian bronzes.

TIMING

The marina walk and the temple will each take an hour, the cathedral about 45 minutes, and the museum two to three hours, for a total of between five and six hours.

Sights to See

★ ❺ **Marina Beach.** This beach is a favorite early morning promenade and exercise spot. At 6 AM you can see fishing boats casting off and fit folks jogging and performing calisthenics or yoga. In the evening, strollers mix with women haggling with fishermen. During holidays the beach turns into a carnival, complete with vendors and hand-driven carousels, and everyone turns out to mingle and enjoy themselves. The undertow is strong here, so the beach is not used for swimming. ✉ *Kamarajar Rd. between Edward Eliot's Rd. and Cathedral Rd.*

★ ❽ **National Museum and Art Gallery.** This museum is known for its superb collection of Pallava and Chola (8th- to 11th-century) bronze sculptures. The best-known work is probably the Chola Nataraj—a detailed 2-ft statue of the dancing Shiva, surrounded by the cosmic fire, that appears to be in constant motion. Many of the less spectacular bronzes are still worth studying for their detail and facial expressions. Other artworks from all over South India, including ancient Buddhist statues and Jain sculptures, are well represented. The museum also has an arms gallery that's strong on weapons of the Raj period. ✉ *Pantheon Rd., Egmore,* ☎ *44/826–9638.* 🎫 *Rs. 3, still cameras Rs. 20, video cameras Rs. 100.* ⏲ *Sat.–Tues. 9:30–4:30.*

★ ❻ **Parthasarathi Temple.** Built by the Pallavas in the 8th century and rebuilt by the Vijayanagar kings in the 11th century, this Vishnu temple is dedicated to Krishna, the *sarathi* (charioteer) of Partha (Arjuna), and is probably the oldest temple in Madras. Legend has it that on the eve of the great battle in the Pandava-Kaurava War, Krishna imparted to Arjuna the *Bhagavad Gita.* After passing under the colorful gopuram, you'll enter the courtyard, which has several carved shrines. The four streets surrounding the temple have stalls selling flowers, small idols, and other puja articles; musical instruments; and jewelry. ✉ *Peter's Rd., Triplicane.* 🎫 *Free.* ⏲ *Daily 6:30–noon and 4–8.*

★ ❼ **St. George's Cathedral.** Set back from Cathedral Road in pleasant gardens, this white colonial church has a 130-ft spire. It was originally Anglican, but it became part of the Church of South India when the Diocese of Madras was constituted in 1835, and is now the Church headquarters. The interior is light and airy, with fascinating tablets and tombs. ✉ *222 Cathedral Rd.* ⏲ *Daily 8–6.*

Southern Madras

In the process of expanding ever southward, Madras incorporated old areas like Mylapore ("Town of Peacocks"), which has a 13th-century temple, and in the 1930s developed some new areas like Thyagaraja Nagar (T. Nagar). More recently, Besant Nagar and Kalakshetra Colony were incorporated, both residential areas with broad, tree-lined streets and excellent shopping areas where it's relatively easy to get around except at rush hour. (At one busy intersection in T. Nagar there's an eatery called Hotel Traffic Jam.)

A Good Drive

In the morning, hire a car and go to the cantonment, a military base and officers' training academy, to see the **Church of Our Lady of Expectation** ⑨. Drive back east to visit **Madras Snake Park** ⑩, in Guindy Park, and then **The Study** ⑪. Follow R. K. Mutt Road north to the **Kapalishvara Temple** ⑫, then turn right and continue to the end of Kutcher Road to see the **Basilica of San Thome Cathedral** ⑬, noting the Portuguese architecture in contrast to that of St. George's Cathedral.

TIMING

Allow five or six hours for this tour, as there's a lot of driving involved.

Sights to Se

★ ⓭ **Basilica of San Thome Cathedral.** It's commonly held that Thomas the Apostle ("Doubting Thomas") lived his last years in South India, walking daily from his cave at Little Mount to the beach at Mylapore to preach. Before being captured by the French, Dutch, and English, San Thome was a Portuguese enclave, its name dating from the cathedral's inception in 1504. In the 1890s the cathedral was reconstructed as a neo-Gothic structure with a 180-ft basilica. St. Thomas is thought to be entombed inside. ✉ *End of Kutchery Rd., Mylapore.*

★ ❾ **Church of Our Lady of Expectation.** Drive to the cantonment, take the brick road to the top of St. Thomas' Mount (or climb the roughly 130 granite steps from the base below), and prepare to be dazzled by a breathtaking 360-degree view that includes the entire city of Madras, with the Bay of Bengal beyond and a countryside full of green rice fields rolling away to the western horizon. After the deafening noise of city traffic and the crush of crowded streets, this peaceful and serene oasis offers a spiritual aerie nearly 300 ft above sea level. Legend has it that Thomas the Apostle was martyred while praying in front of a cross engraved in the church's natural stone base. The church was built in 1547. ✉ *St. Thomas' Mount, Alandur.* 🎟 *Free.*

★ ⓬ **Kapalishvara Temple.** Dating from the 13th century, this crowded Shiva temple is one of the best examples of Dravidian architecture in India. During the Arupathumoovar festival (commemorating the 63 Saivite saints) in March, the temple streets are closed for 10 days to make room for processions of carts and idols around the complex. Kapalishvara Temple is not a rarefied pilgrimage site but a community gathering place for worship, very much a part of daily life.

Just inside the south entrance, under the gopuram, stands the shrine to Ganesh, a smooth black image that's grown shiny from so many offerings. Worshipers break coconuts in front of and on Ganesh to ask his blessing for a new venture or just for a good day. Sometimes in the late afternoon, a priest talks to groups of widows in the courtyard or mandapam. Farther on around the temple, to the left, you may see a man prostrate himself before the Nandi (bull that is Shiva's vehicle) that guards the entrance to the inner sanctum. Continue around the building until you come to a mandapam with statues of the nine planets. It's auspicious to walk clockwise around these planets nine times, so join the procession. Several of the shrines set into the courtyard wall are accessible to non-Hindus. ✉ *Between Chitrukullan North St. and Kutchery Rd., Mylapore.* ⏲ *Daily 4 AM–noon and 4 PM–8 PM.*

★ ❿ **Madras Snake Park.** At the edge of the Raj Bhavan (Government House), the snake park gives you a chance to see and photograph the common snakes of India (more than 40 species) as well as crocodiles, monitor lizards, chameleons, and tortoises. ✉ *Raj Bhavan main post, Sardar Vallabbai Patel Rd.,* ☎ *44/235–0821.* 🎟 *Rs. 2, parking Rs. 2, cameras Rs. 5, video cameras Rs. 100.* ⏲ *Wed.–Mon. 8:30–5:30.*

★ ⓫ **The Study.** Shortly before his death in 1986, the thinker J. Krishnamurti directed that his home and gardens become a place of learning and contemplation, open to anyone who wished to study his teachings in quiet and tranquil surroundings. Called simply "The Study," the center contains a complete library of Krishnamurti's writings in addition to others' books on religion, philosophy, psychology, literature, and the arts. ✉ *Vasant Vihar, 64 Greenways Rd.,* ☎ *44/493–7803.* 🎟 *Free; donations accepted.* ⏲ *Tues.–Sun. 10–1 and 2–7.*

Dining and Lodging

$$$ ✕ **Dahlia.** The large number of expatriate Japanese who frequent this restaurant is a good sign of its authenticity. Fresh, razor-thin slices of fish come to the table with honest sauces, courtesy of a Japanese chef who's also a fish exporter. ✉ *Kaveri Complex, Nungambakkam High Rd.,* ☎ *44/826–5240. AE, MC, V.*

$$$ ✕ **Dakshin.** Decorated with Thanjavur paintings, South Indian statues, and brass lanterns shaped like temple bells, this handsome restaurant focuses on South Indian cuisine. Meals are served on banana leaves set in silver thali trays, and an Indian flutist plays nightly. For a single entrée, try Tamil Nadu's *daskshin yera* (fried prawns marinated in ginger, chili, and garlic) or the spicy *mirupakaikodi* (sautéed chili chicken) from Andhra Pradesh. ✉ *Welcomgroup Park Sheraton Hotel & Towers, 132 T. T. K. Rd.,* ☎ *44/499–4101. AE, DC, MC, V.*

$$$ ✕ **Golden Dragon.** Far Eastern elegance sets the tone in this intimate Chinese restaurant: Brass lanterns hang from the ceiling, and dragon murals surround you. Try the fish in hot tomato sauce, stir-fried lobster with garlic and scallions, or Cantonese stir-fried shredded lamb. ✉ *Taj Coromandel Hotel, 17 Nungambakkam High Rd.,* ☎ *44/827–2827. AE, DC, MC, V.*

$$$ ✕ **The Other Room.** Thousands of seashells hang from the ceiling above you, and mirrors embellish the walls. Every night but Wednesday, a Western rock band entertains and the dance floor fills up. At lunchtime, enjoy a good buffet or order à la carte from the Continental and Indian menu. Try the lobster thermidor, chateaubriand, or *sikandri raan* (spicy leg of lamb cooked in a tandoor). ✉ *Ambassador Pallava, 53 Montieth Rd.,* ☎ *44/855–4476. AE, DC, MC, V.*

$$$ ✕ **Peshawari.** This place has an attractive Pathan (Indo-Iranian) decor, with rough stone walls, copper plates, and soft lighting. The Northwest Frontier Province cuisine emphasizes tandoori dishes. Try the tasty *murgh malai kabab* (boneless chicken kebabs marinated in cheese, cream, and lime juice) or *kadak seekh reshmi* (crisp rolled chicken cooked over a grill). ✉ *Welcomgroup Chola Sheraton, 10 Cathedral Rd.,* ☎ *44/828–0101. AE, DC, MC, V.*

$$$ ✕ **Rain Tree.** Set in a garden, this restaurant offers a Bharatanatyam dance recital and/or an Indian flute performance with dinner (inquire about times). Along with the show you'll enjoy Chettinad cuisine served on a banana leaf set in a copper plate. The *vathal kozhambu* (sun-ripened berries cooked in a spicy gravy) or *yera varuwal* (prawns marinated in masala, then deep-fried) are good choices. ✉ *Taj Hotel Connemara, Binny Rd.,* ☎ *44/826–0123. AE, DC, MC, V.*

$$ ✕ **Cascade.** Quiet Chinese music accompanies tasty Chinese, Malaysian, Japanese, and Thai cuisine here. Come hungry—portions are large—and opt for Phuket fish (fried sailfish fillet with garlic and chili paste), chili crab, or Szechuan *sapo* (prawns, chicken, fish, or lamb marinated in five-spice powder, then cooked and served in a sapo dish). ✉ *Kakani Towers, K. N. K. Rd., near Taj Coromandel Hotel,* ☎ *44/825–3836. AE, DC, MC, V.*

$$ ✕ **Residency.** Wrought-iron gates welcome you to this elegant restaurant; inside are a mirrored ceiling, lace curtains bordered by heavy drapes, and rich decor. The chef prepares tasty Chinese, Indian, and Continental dishes. At lunch, there's a buffet; at night, expect a Western dance band and an à la carte menu. Try the butter chicken, spicy chili chicken, or pepper steak. ✉ *Welcomgroup Park Sheraton Hotel & Towers, 132 T. T. K. Rd.,* ☎ *44/499–4101. AE, DC, MC, V.*

$–$$ ✕ **AVM Dasa.** Spacious and informal, this place is also chic and cosmopolitan. The tasty vegetarian food is both Indian and Continental. The dining room has a high ceiling, cedar gazebo, lattice screens, and

Tiffany-style lamps, and at lunchtime a rusty but charming pianist plays Western standards. ✉ *806 Anna Salai,* ☎ *no phone. AE, DC, MC, V.*

$ ✕ **Cakes and Bakes.** This cake shop is also a Western-style café serving pizzas, sandwiches, milk shakes, and pastries. You can hunker down in the small, crowded eating area or take your food on the road. ✉ *Nungambakkam High Rd.,* ☎ *no phone. No credit cards.*

$ ✕ **Saravana Bhavan.** This chain has several clean, South Indian vegetarian eateries around Madras. Some serve fast-food thalis, while others offer good vegetarian entrées. Count on immaculate surroundings and exemplary service in any case. ✉ *Air-Conditioned Hall, Usman Rd., T. Nagar,* ☎ *44/434–5577. Thali: Dr. Radhakrishnan Salai,* ☎ *44/825–5977. MC, V.*

$ ✕ **Upper Krust.** Near the National Museum and Art Gallery, this coffee shop serves baked goods in a pleasant atmosphere. It's great value for the money. ✉ *149 Montieth Rd.,* ☎ *44/855–4332. No credit cards.*

$ ✕ **Woodlands Drive-In.** Here the cuisine hails from Udupi, a Karnataka town famous for its vegetarian food. The drive-in is also known for filling snacks like *channa bhatura* (lentils in a huge, fried puff pastry) as well as idlis and dosas. Eat in your car or in one of the dining halls in the gardens. ✉ *29-30 Cathedral Rd.,* ☎ *44/827–1981. Reservations not accepted. No credit cards.*

$$$$ ★ **Taj Coromandel Hotel.** This centrally located hotel emphasizes luxury and business amenities. The large lobby has a central marble fountain, teak accents, Thanjavur paintings, and some wonderful British prints by Edward Orme. The elegant rooms have pleasant city views, particularly those on the upper floors. Most have in-room safes, minibars, and refrigerators. ✉ *17 Nungambakkam High Rd., 600034,* ☎ *44/827–3223 or 800/458–8825.* FAX *44/827–4099. 195 rooms. 3 restaurants, bar, coffee shop, no-smoking floor, pool, barbershop, health club, business services, travel services. AE, DC, MC, V.*

$$$–$$$$ ★ **Welcomgroup Park Sheraton Hotel & Towers.** This modern hotel in central Madras has everything the business traveler could possibly need. The 16th-floor Sheraton Towers suites are the ultimate in corporate luxury, with a conference room and such amenities as voice mail, in-room fax machines, and 24-hour business centers with Internet access. The Gatsby 2000 disco, with a DJ and dancing, is one of the city's few nighttime entertainment venues. ✉ *132 T. T. K. Rd., Alwarpet 600018,* ☎ *44/499–4101,* FAX *44/499–7101. 283 rooms, 42 suites. 3 restaurants, bar, coffee shop, pool, sauna, health club, exercise room, dance club, business services, travel services. AE, DC, MC, V.*

$$$ **Ambassador Pallava.** This older hotel looks its age, but it has grand halls and a large lobby, and each guest room is decorated differently. Breakfast is included in the room rate. ✉ *53 Montieth Rd., 600008,* ☎ *44/855–4476 or 855–4068,* FAX *44/855–4492. 103 rooms, 12 suites. Restaurant, bar, coffee shop, pool, health club, dance club, business services, travel services. AE, DC, MC, V.*

$$$ **Fisherman's Cove.** Water sports are the specialty of this Taj resort hotel in Kovalam, 39 km (25 mi) south of Madras on the Shore Road to Mamallapuram. Most of the rooms in the cottages and high-rise hotel overlook the sea, so if you're not up to waterskiing and jet skiing, you can watch the action from home. ✉ *Shore Rd., Kovalam Beach, Kanchipuram district 603112,* ☎ *4113/44304,* FAX *4113/44303. 70 rooms. 2 restaurants, 2 bars, pool, tennis court, jet skiing, water skiing, baby-sitting, travel services. AE, DC, MC, V.*

$$$ **Taj Hotel Connemara.** Situated well back from the road, with pleasant garden areas, this hotel maintains a quiet Old World ambience in the heart of the commercial district. The lobby is bedecked with Hindu statues and temple friezes, and the old wing has deluxe rooms with high ceilings. The 24-hour coffee shop has live music in the evenings;

the open-air restaurant serves ethnic Chettinad cuisine and offers classical Indian dance performances at dinner. ✉ *Binny Rd., 600008,* ☎ *44/852–0123,* FAX *44/852–3361. 148 rooms, 12 suites. Restaurant, bar, pool, barbershop, beauty salon, business and travel services, meeting rooms. AE, DC, MC, V.*

$$$ **The Trident.** This modern hotel near the airport, 10 km (6 mi) outside the city, has an attractive lobby with an interior garden and water cascade. Indian fabrics adorn the spacious and elegant rooms, the best of which overlook the pool. ✉ *1/24 G. S. T. Rd., 600024,* ☎ *44/234–4747,* FAX *44/234–6699. 165 rooms. 2 restaurants, bar, pool, health club, business services, travel services, airport shuttle. AE, DC, MC, V.*

$$ **GRT Grand Days.** Soaring 100 ft high, an atrium lobby sets the scene at this excellent hotel in the heart of Madras. Glass elevators take you up to rooms equipped with all the modern conveniences, such as minibars, coffeemakers, and personalized stationery. No-smoking rooms are available, and business travelers can make use of interview and meeting rooms as well as Internet access and secretarial services. ✉ *120 Sir Thyagaraja Rd., T. Nagar, 600017,* ☎ *44/820–0500,* FAX *44/823–0778. 100 rooms, 20 suites. 2 restaurants, bar, coffee shop, pool, exercise room, business services, meeting rooms, travel services. AE, DC, MC, V.*

$$ **Radisson.** This brand-new hotel (1999) is a stone's throw from the airport. The white, colonial-style building is preceded by a charming garden and a wide porch, and the spacious rooms are furnished with glowing wooden furniture to elegant and soothing effect. Service is extremely efficient. Golf can be arranged. ✉ *355 G. S. T. Rd., St. Thomas Mount, 600016,* ☎ *44/231–0101,* FAX *44/231–0202. 94 rooms, 8 suites. Restaurant, bar, coffee shop, pool, golf privileges, meeting rooms, health club, travel services. AE, DC, MC, V.*

$$ **Welcomgroup Chola Sheraton.** The location is central, the rooms are comfortable and cozy, and guests on the Club floors get such perks as free airport transfers and champagne check-in. Light-colored furnishing gives the rooms a touch of class, and muted lighting options allow you to turn yours into a nice retreat from the heat and dust outside. ✉ *10 Cathedral Rd., 600086,* ☎ *44/828–0101,* FAX *44/827–8779. 100 rooms, 68 suites. 2 restaurants, bar, coffee shop, pool, business services, meeting rooms, travel services. AE, DC, MC, V.*

$–$$ **Quality Inn Aruna.** All of these guest rooms are large and tastefully decorated. The best overlook the pool and have nice views of Madras. The restaurant, a Jewel in the Crown, serves excellent Indian meals at reasonable prices, and live classical Indian music accompanies dinner. Breakfast is included in the room rate. ✉ *144 Sterling Rd., 600034,* ☎ *44/825–9090,* FAX *44/825–8282. 82 rooms, 6 suites. Restaurant, bar, pool, health club. AE, DC, MC, V.*

$ **The Residency.** This nine-story hotel in T. Nagar makes no pretense to maharaja elegance. But while the decor is standard, service is courteous and prompt, and it combines with the hotel's location and prices to make it very popular with Indian businessmen. Upper-floor corner rooms on two sides have nice views of Madras. The 24-hour coffee shop serves both Indian and Continental food. ✉ *49 G. N. Chetty Rd., T. Nagar, 600017.* ☎ *44/825–3434,* FAX *44/825–0085. 87 rooms, 25 suites. Restaurant, bar, coffee shop, business services. AE, DC, MC, V.*

Nightlife and the Arts

Madras's nightlife is mainly cultural. A national center of classical Indian dance and Carnatic music, Madras has been called the cultural capital of India. December is the peak month for recitals, though there are performances throughout the cooler months. For bars (normally open only until 11 PM) and discos, your best bets are large hotels.

Dance

Partially through the efforts of Western scholars, Tamil Nadu's folk music and dance have gotten renewed attention in recent years. Dances from all over India are performed at DakshinaChitra (☞ Side Trips, *below*). Bharatanatyam, long-performed only by temple dancers, was revived in the 20th century by Rukmini Devi. Widely performed in December, this is a highly stylized, dramatic dance featuring many of the *mudra* (meaningful hand gestures) that you see in Hindu statues. Other dance styles include Kathak from North India, Kathakali from Kerala, Kuchipudi from Andhra, Manipur from Manipur, and Odissi from Orissa.

Kuchipudi Art Academy (✉ 105 Greenways Rd., ☎ 44/493–7260, FAX 44/493–8473) has classes in Kuchipudi dance. The **Kalakshetra School** (✉ Tiruvanmiyur, ☎ 44/491–1169), founded by Rukmini Devi and now a government-run university, has music and dance classes that you can drop in and watch.

Music

The period from mid-December to mid-January brings hundreds of Carnatic music concerts and lectures to Madras. Concerts usually follow a set pattern: An initial melodic raga is followed by variations and improvisation by both the soloist and the accompanying instrumentalists. See the morning newspaper, *The Hindu,* for performance listings.

Outdoor Activities and Sports

Golf

The Madras Gymkhana Club has a 9-hole golf course in the center of the track at the **Madras Race Club** (☞ Horse Racing, *below*).

Horse Racing

The **Madras Race Club** (✉ Guindy Rd., Guindy, ☎ 44/345–1171) is a wonderful patch of greenery in industrial Guindy. Races are held two or more afternoons a week from November through March.

Shopping

Bazaars

Pondy Bazaar (✉ T. Nagar; bounded by Anna Salai, South Usman Rd., and Kodambakkam High Rd.) is a quintessential mixture of old- and new-style bazaars, with more than 30 stalls and stores selling everything from vegetables to silk saris and jewelry. The **Mylapore Temple Bazaar** (✉ Off Bazaar Rd. near Kapalishvara Temple) specializes in silver jewelry. **Spencer's Arcade** (✉ 768–769 Anna Salai) has three floors of shops featuring leather goods, books, clothing, groceries, crockery, and handicrafts; a Toys R Us; a Spencer's Super Store; and a good fast-food place. A central fountain is surrounded by places to sit and rest your feet. The first floor has an American Express office with travel services. All of these bazaars are open daily.

Clothing

Alison's Exports (✉ 43 College Rd., ☎ 44/826–2500) has an excellent collection of silks and cottons and an in-house tailor. **Nalli Chinnasami Chetty (Nalli's)** (✉ 9 Nageswaram Rd., opposite Panagal Park, T. Nagar, ☎ 44/434–4115) is famous for its Kanchipuram silk saris and two floors of silk fabrics. **Radha Silks** (✉ 1 Sannadhi St., Mylapore, ☎ 44/494–1906, –9) has fine Kanchipuram silks. **Shilpi** (✉ 29 Sir C. P. Ramaswamy Rd., Alwarpet, ☎ 44/499–0918 or 44/497–0503) is a very popular, chic boutique with well-designed ready-made clothes like *salwars* (tunics) and *kurtas* (shirts), skirts, and vests, as well as hand-loomed fabrics and household furnishings. **Shreenivas Silks**

and Saris (✉ 77 Sri Thyagaraya Rd., Pondy Bazaar, T. Nagar, ☎ 44/828–4758) has fabulous Kanchipuram silks.

Jewelry

G. R. Thanga Maligai (✉ 104 Usman Rd., T. Nagar, ☎ 44/434–5052) has fine gold and silver jewelry.

Souvenirs

Aparna Art Gallery (✉ 5 Bawa Rowther Rd.; Rayala Bldg., 781 Anna Salai) has old and new curios in wood and bronze, Thanjavur and Mysore paintings, and miniatures. The government-run **Central Cottage Industries Emporium** (✉ Temple Tower, 476 Anna Salai, ☎ 44/433–0809) stocks clothes, handicrafts, bronzes, hand-loomed fabrics and rugs, and jewelry from all over India. **Victoria Technical Institute (VTI)** (✉ 765 Anna Salai), in business for more than 100 years, has high-quality embroidery work, children's clothing, handicrafts, bronze and sandalwood items, metal lamps, wood carvings, and table linens.

Side Trips

Crocodile Bank

★ *34 km (21 mi) south of Madras*

Founded by American conservationist Romulus Whittaker to protect India's dwindling crocodile population and preserve the Irula (snake-catching) tribe's way of life, the Crocodile Bank has produced more than 6,000 crocodiles. They're even shipped to other countries to support croc populations worldwide. The reptiles—which also include muggers, gharials, and turtles—are housed in natural pens. Daily snake-venom extractions are an attraction and have helped the Irulas maintain their culture. ✉ *Shore Rd., Vendanemeli,* ☎ *4124/332.* *Rs. 10, cameras Rs. 10, video cameras Rs. 75; snake-venom extraction Rs. 2, cameras Rs. 2, video cameras Rs. 20.* ⏲ *Wed.–Mon. daily 10–4.*

DakshinaChitra

★ *29 km (18 mi) south of Madras*

The heritage center at DakshinaChitra is an exciting encapsulation of South Indian culture. In a pretty, almost rural setting, open-air displays present original domestic Indian architecture from the 19th and 20th centuries. Many of these buildings were painstakingly moved and reconstructed here. Stunning carved doors and lintels decorate a typical old merchant house from Chettinad next door to a 150-year-old agriculturist's house from Thanjavur. Along the 19th-century streets stand tradesmen's houses, each typical of its professional group. Artisans employ traditional techniques to make exquisite pottery, baskets, and carved stone items, some of which are for sale. Authenticity and attention to detail are the rule here. The 90-minute guided tour (for 4 to 7 people at a time; prior booking required) is extraordinarily informative about Tamil history, language, and culture. Supported by a number of prominent Madras businesses, the center is expanding its displays to represent all four states of South India. The main hall of the Chettinad House hosts folk and classical dance performances for which tickets can be reserved in advance. ✉ *Muttukadu, East Coast Rd., Chingelpet district, 603112,* ☎ *4114/45303. For brochure or reservations contact the Madras Craft Foundation, G3, 6 Urur Olcott Rd., Besant Nagar, Madras 600090,* ☎ *44/491–8943,* FAX *44/434–0149.* *Rs. 175. No charge for cameras or video cameras.* ⏲ *Wed.–Mon. 10–6.*

Tirupati

14 *152 km (94 mi) northwest of Madras*

The town of Tirupati is renowned for the ancient **temple of Lord Venkateshwara** on the Tirumala Hills, 20 km (13 mi) outside town. This is one of the few temples in India that allow non-Hindus into the inner sanctum, where the holy of holies is kept—in this case, the 9-ft black idol of Balaji. Any wish made before Balaji is expected to be granted, so long as you're a true believer with a pure heart. Thousands of pilgrims from all over India flock here every day.

Of course, all of this is good business: Tirupati's temple of Lord Venkateshwara is thought to be the richest temple in the country. Locals who house and feed the daily hordes do well financially—as do barbers, since it's believed that your chances of having your wish fulfilled increase if all your hair is shaved off. There are even stalls where you can buy a wig to cover your now-bald head, though you have to sign a statement first that you have reverence for Sri Balaji.

Joining the special darshan line, for Rs. 50, will reduce your waiting time to about 90 minutes to two hours. (Most pilgrims pay Rs. 5 and wait most of the day to get in.) When the time comes to enter the gold-painted gopuram, it won't take long: Telugu-speaking guards rush you through, hardly giving you enough time to glimpse the Dravidian-style Balaji, covered with gold jewelry and precious ornaments. This may all seem like a lot of effort for such a brief glimpse, but it's one of the few opportunities you'll have to mingle with Indian pilgrims, and it should help illustrate the power of Hindu spirituality.

Two roads, one for uphill traffic and the other for downhill traffic, help ease the flow of traffic to and from the temple, but you should still avoid going on weekends or public holidays, when the crowds can be truly daunting. There's little else of interest in Tirupati unless you want to shop for wood carvings; the local craftspeople are known for their prowess in sculpting icons of various gods and goddesses.

LODGING

$$ **Guestline Hotels and Resorts.** The more affluent pilgrims choose to stay here for relative luxury and quiet: The hotel is a good 2 mi from the train station, so milling crowds of devotees and hawkers can be temporarily left behind. The restaurants serve vegetarian Indian fare. ✉ *14-3 Karakambadi, 517501,* ☎ *8574/28366,* FAX *8574/27774. 140 rooms. 2 restaurants. AE, DC, MC, V.*

$ **Hotel Mayura.** Friendly and helpful staff make this an oasis from the ordeal of being one pilgrim among the 5,000 that visit Tirupati each day. Rooms have eclectic furnishings, but the beds are large and clean. The restaurant, Surya, serves good South Indian vegetarian dishes. ✉ *209 T. P. Area, 517501,* ☎ *8574/25925,* FAX *8574/25911. 65 rooms. Restaurant. AE, DC, MC, V.*

MAMALLAPURAM, KANCHIPURAM, AND PONDICHERRY

Mamallapuram and Kanchipuram reflect the glorious pasts of three great dynasties: Pallava, Chola, and Vijayanagar. The Pallava capital, Kanchipuram, was a town of learning and became fertile ground for a vast number of temples. From the port at Mamallapuram, the Pallavas began to trade with China and Indonesia, a tradition expanded by succeeding empires. Together, the three dynasties laid the foundations of Tamil history, language, and religion, and with each dynasty the temples became larger and more elaborate. With the destruction of its port,

Mamallapuram became a deserted historical site, so that it's now largely a traveler's curiosity, while Kanchipuram is still a major pilgrimage destination. Pondicherry, with its strong French influence, is cherished for being refreshingly different from any other place in India.

Mamallapuram

59 km (37 mi) south of Madras, 64 km (40 mi) southeast of Kanchipuram

Mamallapuram (officially renamed Mahabalipuram, the name mentioned in Chola inscriptions at the nearby Five Rathas), is a friendly old port city with four kinds of rock structures: monolithic rock temples (*rathas*); cave temples; temples constructed from a conglomeration of materials; and bas-relief sculptures carved on large rocks. In the 8th century, the Pallava dynasty conducted a thriving maritime trade here, sending emissaries to China, Southeast Asia, and Indonesia; carved stone is all that now remains of these dynamic businessmen, who ultimately ruled for 300 years.

The town of Mamallapuram sits between the beach and the sacred Five Rathas. It's a wonderful place to visit, especially between December and February, as you can divide your time between exploring magnificent ancient temples and relaxing at a beach resort. In addition to the government shops and the museum, independent shops sell granite images and carvings reminiscent of the temples; many of these are remarkably well executed. The sights are open all day but the best times to visit are early morning and late afternoon.

★ 15 Standing right on the Bay of Bengal, the **Shore Temple** has been subject for centuries to the vicissitudes of sun, sea, and sand, so it's notable for the degree of detail that remains. You enter the temple from the back, through a courtyard surrounded by a massive wall topped by reclining bulls and two Shiva towers. Although ravaged by time, the calm image of Vishnu, lying in cosmic sleep on the sea with the serpent Sesha at his side, is juxtaposed with the clamor or waves pounding on the sea wall. The Shore Temple was built by the Pallava king Rajasimha in the early 8th century. ⊠ *On ocean; follow signs.* 🎟 *Temple and Five Rathas Rs. 5, video camera Rs. 25.*

16 The world's largest bas-relief—96 ft long and 43 ft high—the **Penance of Arjuna,** also called the Descent of the Ganges, is carved on two adjacent boulders. Created by the Pallava dynasty, the work dates from the 7th century. Among the many figures depicted, both mythical and real, is a figure of Shiva with an ascetic Arjuna to his left, standing on one leg. The rendering is thought to be a scene from the *Bhagavad Gita,* in which Arjuna asks Shiva for help defeating his enemies. An extensive but unfinished Pallava water canal system included a pool above the bas-relief; the idea was that water would cascade down a natural cleft in the rock from this pool, simulating the descent of the Ganges from the Himalayas. The entire, enormous project is a fascinating and vital combination of the mundane and the mythical. ⊠ *On street leading to Five Rathas.*

More than a dozen cave temples are cut into the rock hill behind the Penance of Arjuna. Some are unfinished and some have been damaged, but many are quite remarkable. Most are atop the granite hill, so you
17 have to take a short hike to reach them. The **Krishna Mandapam,** one of the later cave temples, has a naturalistic figure of a cow being milked. A sculpture on the back wall of this 12-column cave is a relief of Krishna holding up the Govardhan mountain to protect his people from floods ordered by the thunder god Indra.

Adivaraha Cave, **19**
Five Rathas, **18**
Krishna Mandapam, **17**
Lighthouse, **21**
Mahishasuramardini Cave, **20**
Penance of Arjuna, **16**
Shore Temple, **15**

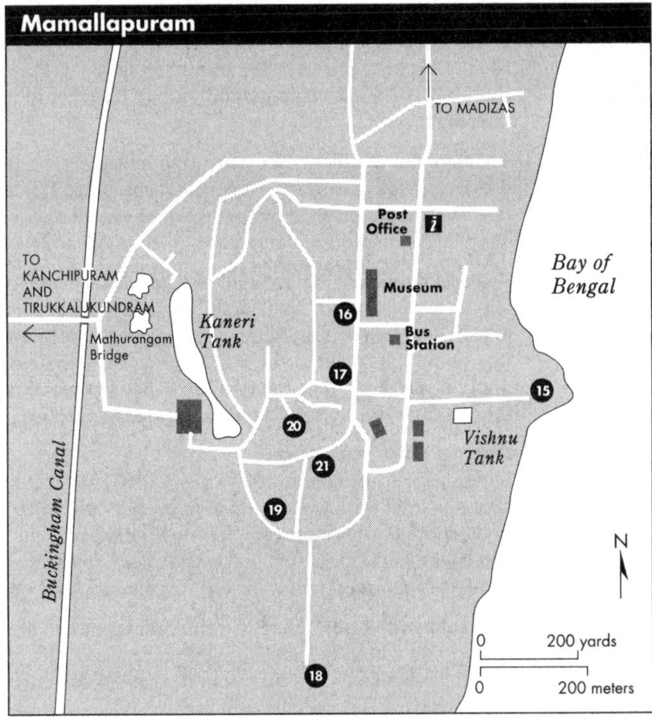

★ 18 The **Five Rathas** are also called the Pancha Pandava Rathas for the Five Pandava sons in the Hindu epic *Mahabharata.* The Rathas, probably the most famous example of Pallava architecture, are carved out of five pieces of granite, each temple distinctive, with its own elevation, plan, and exquisite detail. From north to south, the individual Rathas are the **Draupadi** (named for the wife of the Pandavas), dedicated to the goddess Durga, a warrior wife of Shiva who rides a lion; the **Arjuna** (named for the charioteer of the *Bhagavad Gita,* part of the *Mahabharata*), dedicated to the thunder god Indra; the **Bhima** (named for a Pandava son), the largest temple; the **Sahadeva** (named for a Pandava prince), part of which represents a Buddhist chapel; and the **Dharmaraja,** dedicated to Shiva. Three animal sculptures—an elephant, a lion, and the Nandi bull (the vehicles of Indra, Durga, and Shiva)—complete the display. Because all the temples are unfinished, it's assumed that the animal carvings were meant to have been moved to the appropriate Ratha. The diversity of the images and their meanings reveals the complexity of South Indian Hinduism; studying them is a minicourse in the history of South Indian temple architecture.

19 The **Adivaraha Cave** is interesting for its two portraits of two royal Pallava kings with two goddesses.

★ 20 The **Mahishasuramardini Cave,** near the lighthouse on top of the hill, is probably the most outstanding of the mandapams. On the right wall is a carved panel depicting Durga riding a prancing lion and defeating the buffalo demon Mahishasura. On the opposite wall, in sharp contrast to this battle scene, is the deeply carved relief of Vishnu reclining on the great serpent Sesha. In this position, Vishnu is usually in a cosmic sleep, epitomizing his role as preserver of the universe. At the back of the cave are three cells containing statues of Shiva, his consort Uma, and their son Skanda—collectively known as Somaskanda, a common Pallava theme.

21 Built by the British and used until just a few years ago, the **lighthouse** gives a good view and serves as a landmark in navigation. You can climb it daily between 9 and 5:30; admission is Rs. 3. Past the lighthouse, the remaining mandapams and rathas on the hill are not terribly interesting.

The **Tiger Cave,** which is actually two boulders set together, is in a shady grove near the ocean. It's a favorite picnic spot. Dedicated to Durga, the cave is distinguished by the crown of carved tiger heads around its temple. ✉ *Saluvankuppam, 5 km (3mi) north of Mamallapuram.*

Tirukkalukundram (Sacred Hill of Kites) is the name of both a village and its temple, which has Dutch, English, and ancient Indian inscriptions. The ride here from Mamallapuram takes you through paddy fields. Pilgrims come to climb the 500 steps to the temple on the hilltop at noon, in the hope that the two kites (hawks) will come to be fed by the Brahmin priests. ✉ *15 km (9 mi) west of Mamallapuram.*

Dining and Lodging

Lodging in Mamallapuram varies widely, from inexpensive guest houses in town with weekly and monthly rates (that often include meals), to the more costly resorts overlooking the ocean. The "lodges" (small hotels) are fairly clean, ordinary, and cheap. There's an abundance of good, inexpensive, restaurants serving mainly seafood.

$–$$ ✕ **Ideal Beach Resort.** Here you can eat in a garden or a simple indoor restaurant, where the murals, sculptures, and recommended dishes are all Sri Lankan. Try the rice and curry or fish curry; follow either one with *vatil appam* (custard). Indian and Continental food are also available. ✉ *Shore Rd.,* ☎ *4114/42240 or 4114/424430. MC, V.*

$ ✕ **German Bakery.** This friendly rooftop café is one of two run by a German-Nepali partnership (the other is in Ladakh). Simple, good bread, Western-style health foods, and cappuccino are offered, and breakfast is served all day. It's a great favorite with foreign travelers. ✉ *Rooftop, Uma Lodge, Post Office Rd.,* ☎ *no phone. No credit cards.*

$ ✕ **Seafront Restaurant and Whispering Woods.** Set under a thatched roof on the beach, near a small outdoor dance floor, the Seafront has a lively atmosphere. Open flames light the romantic Whispering Woods, which has tables in a pine grove out of sight—but not sound—of the beach. Both places, part of the Silver Sands hotel, serve Chinese, Continental, and Indian dishes, including fresh seafood. Try the Gujarati and Rajasthani thali if you're in the mood for sweet-and-spicy fare. ✉ *Silver Sands, Kovalam Rd.,* ☎ *4114/42283. AE, DC, MC, V.*

$ ✕ **Sunrise Restaurant.** In a cozy thatched hut, with no ocean view but good tropical breezes, this restaurant serves Indian, Continental, and Chinese cuisine. Try the fish steak steamed with tomato, garlic, and butter; grilled lobster; or jumbo prawns. ✉ *Beach Rd.,* ☎ *4114/42336. No credit cards.*

$$ 🏨 **Temple Bay Ashok Beach Resort.** Overlooking the ocean, this government-owned complex has rooms in a main building and in cottages with two doubles per unit. The rooms and cottages vary widely in quality and character: The newer cottages are more sterile but have nicer facilities. Some rooms are quite elegant, even luxurious. The restaurant serves a variety of cuisines. ✉ *Kovalam Rd., 603104,* ☎ *4114/42251,* FAX *4114/42255. 36 rooms, 29 cottages. Restaurant, bar, pool, tennis court, beach, travel services. AE, DC, MC, V.*

$ 🏨 **Ideal Beach Resort.** Run by Tamils from Sri Lanka, this relaxing resort has a tropical atmosphere, with lots of shrubs, trees, and sculptures. The best upstairs rooms have ocean views. The restaurant serves good Sri Lankan food as well as Indian and Continental dishes. Musicians and dancers perform on a stage near the large swimming pool.

A tennis court is under construction. ✉ *Mamallapuram 603104,* ☎ *4114/42240 or 4114/42443,* FAX *4114/42243. 32 rooms, 5 cottages. Restaurant, bar, pool, massage.*

En Route From October to March, thousands of waterbirds, egrets, pelicans, storks, and herons come to nest in the **Vedanthangal Bird Sanctuary,** the oldest bird haven in India. The best times to see them are late afternoon and early morning in December and January. A total of 115 species have been spotted here. ✉ *35 km (22 mi) south of Chengalpattu, off NH 45 on road to Uttiramerur; for information contact the Wild Life Warden, DMS Compound, Anna Salai, Madras 600026,* ☎ *44/432–1471.* ⏲ *Daily 8–6.* 🎫 *Rs. 2.*

Kanchipuram

22 *76 km (47 mi) southwest of Madras, 45 km (28 mi) north of Mamallapuram*

Former capital of the ancient Pallavas, Kanchipuram holds the remains of three great dynasties—Pallava, Chola, and Vijayanagar—that for centuries weathered internal conflict and external trade but never northern invasion. The dynasties merely jostled each other, building ever greater shrines to their developing and intertwining sets of deities. Today, Kanchipuram, nicknamed the Golden City of 1,000 Temples (as well as "Kanchi"), is one of the seven holy pilgrimage sites for Hindus, with temples to both Shiva and Vishnu. Through the diversity of building styles here, you can trace the development of Dravidian temple architecture from the 8th century right up to the present.

Through temple construction and patronage of the arts, the dynastic kings made Kanchipuram a great center of learning, not only for Hindus but also for Buddhists and Jains. Many Tamil religious and literary works were written between the Pallava and Vijayanagar periods. Today the tradition of spiritual study and teaching founded by an *acharya* (spiritual teacher) is carried on by the Sankaracharya Math, which runs several schools and a library in this area. The Math headquarters are in the center of Kanchipuram.

The temples we cover below are some of the more famous, but there are plenty of others to explore. When you visit the pilgrimage temples, be prepared for rows of beggars and children beseeching you for candy and/or pens. Kanchipuram temples close from 12:30 to 4 PM, so do your sightseeing in the morning or early evening. Many of the temples have their own elephants (relating to the elephant-headed god Ganesh), who patiently stand by the main gopuram to bless anyone who makes a contribution. The elephants take the money in their trunks. It's an intriguing way to participate in a Hindu ritual.

The **Ekambareswara Temple** was originally built before the mid-9th century by the Pallavas, but its most significant feature, a massive, 200-ft gopuram with more than 10 stories of intricate sculptures, was a 16th-century addition by the Vijayanagar kings. The temple is dedicated to Shiva, who appears in the form of earth, one of Hinduism's five sacred elements. Inside the courtyard is a mango tree thought to be 2,500 years old; each of its four main branches is said to bear fruit with a different taste, representing the four Hindu Vedas (sacred texts). Of the original 1,000 pillars that once stood in the mandapam, fewer than 600 remain. The Ekambareswara Temple is in the Saivite Brahmin section of Kanchipuram: On your way to the main entrance, notice the houses on either side of the rather dusty road. Uniformly white, they have open porches with raised sitting platforms. Some have *kolams* (rice-flour designs) in front of the entrance. These Brahmin houses epitomize the religious and cultural ambience of the temples; until fairly recently, Kanchipuram was a town segregated residentially by caste. ✉ *Between W. and N. Mada Sts., northwest part of town.*

Built mainly during the reign of King Rajasimha (700–728), **Kailasanatha Temple**—named for Kailasa, Shiva's Himalayan paradise—carried the development of Pallava temple architecture one step beyond the monolithic Dharmaraja Ratha and Shore Temple at Mamallapuram. From the dressed rock of the Shore Temple, the construction of Kailasanatha progressed to granite foundations and the more easily carved sandstone for the superstructure. The sculpted tower over the sanctum can trace its lineage in shape, design, and ornamentation to both the Shore Temple and the Dharmaraja Ratha. The cell-like structures surrounding the sanctum are similar in design to the Five Rathas; all have extensive sculptures of Shiva in various poses, symbolizing different aspects of his mythology. On one side of the inner courtyard are small cells with remnants of colored paintings on the wall. Attempts to repair the sandstone artwork have been unsuccessful, detracting from the original imagery; moreover, the mandapam and the sanctuary were later connected by an intermediary structure that damaged the symmetry of the whole temple; still, removed from teeming hordes of pilgrims, this quiet temple is an excellent place to observe the heraldic lions standing on their hind feet and contemplate the oral Hindu tradition preserved in stone. ✉ *Putleri St., 1½ km (1 mi) west of town center.*

In the heart of the old town, topped by a brilliant, gold-plated gopuram, **Sri Kamakshi Temple** hosts a famous winter car festival each February or March: Deities from a number of temples are placed on wooden temple carts and pulled in a procession through the surrounding streets. Kamakshi is the respectful, loving-eyed wife of Shiva. ✉ *Odai St.*

Built in the 8th century, **Vaikunthaperumal Temple** (Vishnu's paradise) is a single structure whose principal parts make an integrated whole. The four-story vimana is square, with three shrines, each depicting Vishnu in a different pose. The Vaikunthaperumal Temple is unusual for two components: its corridor for circumambulation of the shrines on the second and third floors, and its cloisters, with a colonnade of lion pillars and extensive sculptures bearing Pallava inscriptions. ✉ *1 km (1//2 mi) southwest of train station.*

Also known as the Devarajaswamy Temple, **Varadaraja Temple** (Bestower of Boons) is dedicated to Vishnu and is a favorite pilgrimage destination. Its exquisitely carved 100-pillar mandapam (with, in fact, 96 pillars) is one of the finest in India, and its decoration includes a massive chain carved from one stone. The temple was originally built in the 11th century, but the 100-ft gopuram was restored by the Vijayanagar kings 500 years later. ✉ *3 km (2 mi) southeast of town; follow Gandhi Rd. until you see the temple.* 🎫 *Rs. 5, camera Rs. 5, video camera Rs. 50.*

Dining and Lodging

Accommodations in Kanchipuram are more for pilgrims than leisure travelers, and there are no restaurants in the Western sense.

$ ✕ **Hotel Saravana Bhavan.** Service is excellent in this hotel's immaculate, high-quality vegetarian restaurant that serves a basic thali, *puri* (deep-fried bread), and snacks like masala dosas. It's a good place for a cup of South Indian coffee. One room is air-conditioned. ✉ *Center of town,* ☎ *4112/22505. MC, V.*

Shopping

Kanchipuram's silks and saris are famous throughout India for their brilliant colors and rich brocades of real gold or silver. Over 20,000 people work with silk alone in this city of weavers, whole families crafting fabric in or near their homes using age-old techniques. If you're curious about the process, stop into the **Weavers' Service Centre** (20 Railway Station Rd.) and ask if you can visit some weavers at work. Alas, silk is often more expensive in Kanchi than in Madras; buy from government-approved shops, many of which are on T. K. Nambi Street. **Shreenivas Silk House** (✉ 17-A, T. K. Nambi St.) is one of the best.

Pondicherry

23 *134 km (83 mi) south of Mamallapuram, 160 km (100 mi) south of Madras*

Small and quiet, Pondicherry is a lovely and unusual place to take the pace of life down a few notches. A former French holding, Pondicherry still retains the flavor of its colonizers, who left only in 1954. From the red *kepis* (caps) of the policemen to street names like Rue Romain Rolland, the French influence is deep-rooted and pervasive.

A stroll down coastal **Goubert Avenue** (also known as Beach Road) is quiet and pleasant, with minimal traffic. To prolong your proximity to the roar of crashing waves, kick back at the 24-hour restaurant **Le Café,** perched on the oceanfront. Close by are a **statue of Mahatma Gandhi** encircled by eight monolithic pillars; a **War Memorial** honoring those who died in World War II; and the **Hôtel de Ville** (Town Hall). This Union Territory, now also known as Puducheri, is a slice of France on Indian soil.

About 10 km (6 mi) north of Pondicherry is **Auroville,** an international village conceived by The Mother, a companion of Sri Aurobindo. Once a freedom fighter, Sri Aurobindo moved to Pondicherry from Calcutta and founded the Ashram to propagate his ideas, a synthesis of yoga and modern science. Inaugurated in 1968, Auroville attracts those in search of enlightenment without the trappings of traditional religion. With over 1,300 residents from all over the world, Auroville is meant to reflect the unity of the human spirit. Parts of the village are still under construction, including its central meditation hall, Matrimandir.

Dining and Lodging

There are many hotels near the bus stand, with limited facilities but attractively low prices. Dining options include Indian, Chinese, French, and Italian cuisine; good restaurants are clustered on and around Goubert Avenue.

$–$$ **Hotel Anandha Inn.** This imposing structure is one of Pondy's newest hotels. The rooms in the back, away from the main road, are the quietest. The restaurant serves Indian, Chinese, and Continental cuisine. ✉ *S. V. Salai, 605003,* ☎ *413/330711,* FAX *413/331241. 65 rooms. Restaurant, bar, business services, travel services. AE, DC, MC, V.*

$–$$ **Hotel Mass.** The Hotel Mass is popular with business travelers, and its bar is frequented by locals as well as guests. At press time the rooms were being renovated. ✉ *M. M. Adigal Salai, 605001,* ☎ *413/337221,* FAX *413/333654. 35 rooms. Restaurant, bar, pool, business services, travel services. AE, DC, MC, V.*

Shopping

Shopping is concentrated near the shore. Jawaharlal Nehru Street is particularly chockablock with stores selling everything from clothing to sweets. **La Boutique d'Auroville** (✉ 38 J. N. St., ☎ 413/337264) is the official sales outlet for products from Auroville, which range from fine pottery to leather goods.

TIRUCHIRAPPALLI, THANJAVUR, AND MADURAI

Stretching toward the south end of Tamil Nadu, these three cities were centers of dynastic activity for almost a thousand years. Between them, the Pallavas, Pandyas, Cholas, Vijayanagars, Nayaks, and Marathas left an architectural legacy of forts, palaces, and, of course, fantastic temples.

Tiruchirappalli

24 *325 km (202 mi) southwest of Madras*

Tiruchirappalli (City of the Three-Headed Demon) was a pawn in the feudal wars of the Pallavas, Pandyas, and Cholas, which continued until the 10th century, and from which point the Vijayanagar Empire reigned supreme. In the 18th century, Tiruchirappalli was at the center of the Carnatic wars between the British and French; and between these two violent periods, there were periodic Muslim incursions. All of this international activity had an influence on South India temple architecture, which reached its zenith in the Vijayanagar period under the Nayaks of Madurai (who built most of Tiruchirappalli) with the construction of one of the largest temples in South India: the Ranganathaswamy, on the island of Srirangam. Like Kanchipuram, Srirangam was at one time a center of religious philosophy and learning.

Tiruchirappalli—also known as Trichy—is spread-out, with hotels centered in the southern cantonment (the old Raj military area). If you don't hire a car, auto-rickshaws are probably the best transportation here. The flat landscape to the north is dominated by the Rock Fort, near the bridge to Srirangam, which lies between the Cauvery River and its tributary, the Kolidam.

The military and architectural heart of Tiruchirappalli is its startling ★ **Rock Fort,** rising 272 ft above the city on the banks of the Cauvery River. Cut into the rock, 437 steps lead up to a temple dedicated to Lord Vinayaka (the mythical half-man, half-bird Garuda who is Vishnu's vehicle; he's prominent in *The Mahabharata*), then on to the summit. Along the way are various landings and shrines: an ancient temple dedicated to the elephant-headed god Ganesh, a Shiva temple, and cave temples cut into the rock. Finally, at the top, you're rewarded with a breathtaking view of Tiruchirappalli and the fertile countryside around it. To the north, the Srirangam temples rise dramatically out of fields and riverbeds.

At the base of the Rock Fort are two excellent temple bazaars, Chinna and the Big Bazaar, plus interesting narrow side streets that lead to the heart of the old city. Both bazaars sell almost everything, but they specialize in articles of worship. You'll also find wood and clay toys, traditional Trichy crafts.

Covering more than 1 square km (¼ square mi) and dedicated to ★ Vishnu, Srirangam's **Sri Ranganathaswamy Temple** (also known as the Great Temple), was built by various rulers of the Vijayanagar Empire between the 13th and 18th centuries, with a few 20th-century additions. The single-sanctum temple has seven concentric walls, 22 gopurams, and a north-to-south orientation rather than the usual east-to-west. The outer three courtyards are essentially bazaars.

Just as the Pallavas had rampant lions, the Vijayanagar dynasty had rearing horses, magnificently displayed here in the Horse Court, the fourth courtyard of the Seshadgiri mandapam. At the time of the Festival of Vaikuntha Ekadasi (in honor of Vishnu's paradise), pilgrims can see the idol of Ranganatha brought into the mandapam from the inner sanctum under the golden dome; and during the January Car Festival, Srirangam's magnificent temple carts—exceptional in their artisanship—are taken out for a series of processions. The temple's extensive and beautiful collection of precious gems is included in the cart display. An island of temples, Srirangam was also a center of religious philosophy and learning. The great Vaishnava Acharya Ramanuja taught and wrote in the Srirangam school at the end of the 11th century. ✉ *Srirangam Island.* 🎫 *Rs. 3 to climb wall for panoramic view, camera Rs. 20, video camera Rs. 75.*

About 2½ km (1½ mi) east of the Great Temple, **Sri Jambukeswara Temple** (Shiva, Lord of India) is smaller, but its large central court is an excellent example of the Dravidian architecture from the final phase of the Madeira period (around 1600). The courtyard pillars are remarkable for their rampant dragons, elaborate foliated brackets, and royal Nayak portraits. ✉ *Srirangam Island.* 🎫 *Free, camera Rs. 10, video camera Rs. 125.* ⏲ *Daily 6–12 and 4–9.*

Another shrine to Shiva is **Thiruvanaikkaval,** named for a legendary elephant that worshipped the linga (the phallic stone that is Shiva's primary abstract symbol). In the Mambukeswaram pagoda the linga is submerged in water—one of the five elements that Shiva represents. The architecture of this temple, with five walls and seven gopurams, is among the finest Dravidian work still in existence. ✉ *3 km (2 mi) east of Srirangam.*

Dining and Lodging

Trichy's hotels are concentrated in the cantonment area, also called Junction (for the Tiruchirappalli Junction Railway Station).

$ ✕ **Amaravathi.** Chinese and Indian cuisine is served here in a dimly lit tropical setting of green-and-white lattice work. ✉ *13-D Williams Rd., Cantonment,* ☎ *431/460936, 411127. No credit cards.*

$ ✕ **Woodlands.** Both Indian and Continental vegetarian cuisines go for reasonable prices here. Your best bet is the thali. ✉ *Femina Hotel, 14-C Williams Rd., Cantonment,* ☎ *431/461551. AE, DC, MC, V.*

$$ 🏨 **Femina Hotel.** This central hotel has a bright, open marble lobby and clean and attractive rooms. The best rooms have little verandas and stunning views of the Great Temple and St. Joseph's Church, with its new steeple. Beer is available through room service for consumption only in your room. ✉ *14-C Williams Rd., Cantonment, 620001,* ☎ *431/414501,* FAX *431/410615. 157 rooms. Restaurant, room service, travel services. AE, DC, MC, V.*

$$ 🏨 **Hotel Sangam.** This modern (in the '70s sense), Western-style hotel is surrounded by a lawn. The best rooms overlook the pool. At press time the lobby and restaurant were undergoing renovation. ✉ *Collectors Office Rd., 620001,* ☎ *431/414700, 414480,* FAX *431/415779. 56 rooms. Restaurant, bar, coffee shop, pool, health club, travel services. AE, DC, MC, V.*

$$ 🏨 **Jenneys Residency.** The best rooms in this high-rise hotel are spacious and well furnished. ✉ *3/14 McDonald's Rd., 620001,* ☎ *431/414414,* FAX *431/461451. 110 rooms, 13 suites. Restaurant, bar, coffee shop, pool, health club, travel services. AE, DC, MC, V.*

Thanjavur

25 *55 km (34 mi) east of Tiruchirappalli*

Nestled in the highly fertile delta of the Cauvery River, Thanjavur was the capital of the Cholas during their supremacy (907–1310). A fortuitous combination of flourishing agriculture, competent monarchs (who established a highly centralized administrative system, yet gave autonomy to village assemblies), and a long religious revival, begun under the Pallavas in Kanchi, culminated in the building of the Thanjavur's Brihadiswara Temple. The two greatest Chola monarchs, Rajaraja I (985–1016) and his son Rajendra I (1012–1044), consolidated their South Indian empire from coast to coast, including Kerala, and added Ceylon, the Maldives, and Srivijaya, in what is now Indonesia, to their holdings. As a result, active trade developed with Southeast Asia and China, fostering a two-way cultural exchange: Thanjavur painting of the period shows some Chinese influence, and in Java, Indian influence led to universal appreciation of the epic poem *The Ramayana.* The length and economic prosperity of the Chola reign served as a foundation for religious development: Tamil hymns were written down and codified, religious thinkers wrote commentaries on ancient texts, and new schools of Hindu philosophy developed.

★ Although this soaring monument to Rajaraja's spirituality is dedicated to Shiva, the sculptures on the gopuram of the **Brihadiswara Temple,** or Great Temple, depict Vishnu, and those inside are Buddhist. Until they were uncovered in 1970s, the more interesting Chola frescos on the walls of the inner courtyard had been obscured by later Nayak paintings. Within a single courtyard, a giant Nandi bull (second-largest in India, next to the one in Mysore) and pillared halls point toward the 190-ft vimana, a pyramidal tower capped by a single 80-ton block of granite. This massive capstone was pulled to the top along an inclined plane that began in a village 6 km (4 mi) away. The delicate carving on the round granite cupola minimizes the capstone's size and provides a visual break from the massive pyramid. The temple's carefully planned and executed architecture make it a fine example of Dravidian artisanship; in fact, it's a UNESCO World Heritage Site. ✉ *West Main Rd. at S. Rampart St.,* ☎ *no phone.* ⏲ *6 AM–12:30 PM and 4–8:30.*

Thanjavur Palace is the central building in the great fort built by Nayak and Maratha kings. It's hard to find your way around this rabbit warren, but visits to the **Art Gallery** (in Nayak Durbar Hall) and the **Royal Museum** are worth the effort. The art gallery has a magnificent collection of Chola bronzes with different interpretations of the same figure from early and late in the Chola dynasty and from the 18th century. The Royal Museum displays clothing, arms, and other regal memorabilia. Near the art gallery is the **Saraswati Mahal Library,** a scholars' paradise with 46,000 rare palm-leaf and paper manuscripts in many languages. The library is open Thursday–Tuesday 10–1 and 1:30–5:30, admission is free, and cameras and video cameras are forbidden. ✉ *Entrance on east wall, off East Main St.* ⏲ *Daily, except national holidays; museum 9–6, art gallery 9–1 and 3–6.* 🎫 *Art Gallery Rs. 3, camera Rs. 30, video camera Rs. 200; Royal Museum Rs. 1, camera Rs. 15, video camera Rs. 100.*

Dining and Lodging

Small vegetarian restaurants are easy to find in Thanjavur, especially along Gandhiji Road.

$–$$ 🏨 **Hotel Parisutham.** This modern hotel within walking distance of the Great Temple has a marvelous pool, pleasant canal views, and comfortable, well-equipped rooms. The attentive service includes a hot towel (cold in summer) when you arrive. In the evening, cultural performances take place around the pool. ✉ *55 G. A. Canal Rd., 613001,* ☎ *4362/31801 or 31844,* FAX *4362/30318. 50 rooms. Restaurant, bar, pool, business services, travel services. AE, DC, MC, V.*

$ **Ideal River View Resort.** Amid 45 acres of paddy fields and semi-jungle, the Ideal River View Resort offers air-conditioned cottages with balconies facing the river. Connected by road to Thanjavur, 4 km (2½ mi) away, it's a quiet, scenic place to unwind after sightseeing. The restaurant serves a mixture of Indian, Continental, Chinese, and Sri Lankan cuisine. ✉ *Vennar Bank, Palli Agraharam, 613003.* ☎ *4362/50533 or 4362/50633,* FAX *4362/51113. Restaurant, travel services.*

Shopping

R. Govindarajan (✉ 31 Kuthiraikatti St., Karantha, ☎ 4362/51282) has a large selection of Thanjavur paintings, brass and copper artifacts, wood carvings, and glass.

OFF THE BEATEN PATH

KUMBAKONAM – This village is noted for the 12th-century **Dharasuram** or **Airataesvara Temple,** a well-preserved, little-used temple modeled after the one in Thanjavur. There are large statues and slender columns with interesting miniature sculptures. The priest speaks English (not always the case). ✉ *37 km (23 mi) northeast of Thanjavur.*

SWAMIMALAI – This village, whose name translates as "Hill of Swamis," has an interesting Murgan temple (dedicated to the Tamil god of war). Its real claim to fame, however, is its tradition of casting bronzes using the ancient wax process. Many of the Chola bronzes were made here, and today there's a brisk export trade in Chola replicas and contemporary bronzes. **Rajan Industries** (✉ 107 Main Rd., Thinmakudi,, ☎ FAX 435/22886) has created major bronze works for European and American museums; the store sells classic and modern bronzes, Thanjavur paintings, and wood carvings. ✉ *30 km (18 mi) northeast of Thanjavur.*

Madurai

26 *191 km (118 mi) southwest of Thanjavur, 142 km (88 mi) south of Tiruchirappalli.*

Once the capital of the Pandya dynasty, the second-largest city in Tamil Nadu supposedly got its name from the Tamil word for honey. According to legend, when King Kulasekhara Pandya first built Madurai over 2,500 years ago, Shiva shook nectar from his locks to purify and bless the new city. Known as the Temple City, Madurai's old city, south of the Vaigai River, was laid out in accordance with ancient temple custom, with the great Meenakshi Temple at the center. Shops and stalls surround the Meenakshi on three concentric squares of streets that are used for religious processions almost every day.

★ The **Meenakshi Temple,** also called the Great Temple, has two sanctuaries, one to Meenakshi (the fish-eyed goddess, consort of Shiva) and the other to Shiva in the form of Sundareswar. Legend has it that Shiva married the daughter of a Pandya chief in this form, and the temple's car festival celebrates this event each spring.

The gopurams are painted in bright—almost garish—polychrome. Enter through the eastern gopuram, where vendors at stall after stall sell puja items and flowers. On summer afternoons, when the temple is closed, the entrance is full of sleeping shopkeepers who enjoy the cool drafts created by the temple corridors.

The temple's high point is the Hall of a Thousand Pillars, built around 1560 and adorned with 985 elaborately carved pillars. The **Temple Art**

Museum, also in the Hall of a Thousand Pillars, has beautiful paintings and sculptures, not all of which are accurately labeled. Among the many mandapams, the Kambattadi Mandapam is outstanding for its excellent sculptures depicting the manifestations of Shiva.

An excellent way to appreciate this awesome site is to wander slowly around the various crowded mandapams, observing the devotees. At 9:30 PM, return to the main temple to watch Shiva being carried to Meenakshi's bedroom, a procession that begins at the eastern gopuram. Around the temple's Tank of the Golden Lilies are hundreds of shops: a miniature city, almost impossible to walk through. ✉ *Between N., S., E., and W. Chithirai Sts.,* ☎ *452/744360.* 🎫 *Temple free; museum Rs. 3, camera Rs. 25, video camera not allowed.* ⏲ *Temple, daily 4:30 AM–12:30 PM and 4 PM–9:30 PM; museum, daily 9–6.*

Tirumala Nayak Mahal, an Indo-Saracenic palace, was built by Tirumala Nayak in 1636 and partially restored by Lord Napier, governor of Madras from 1866 to 1872. The palace is now largely in ruins, but its excellent sound-and-light show, nightly at 6:45 in English, dramatizes Madurai's past. ✉ *1½ km (1 mi) north of Meenakshi Temple,* ☎ *452/732945.* 🎫 *Palace Rs. 2, sound-and-light show Rs. 2–Rs. 5.* ⏲ *Daily 9–1 and 2–5.*

Dining and Lodging

It's not hard to find a decent restaurant in sprawling Madurai, especially around the temple. There are plenty of places to stay on the west side of town, but the nicer hotels lie across the river to the north.

$ ✕ **New Arya Bhavan.** At this popular eatery a few blocks west of the temple, you can have delicious North and South Indian vegetarian fare in the garden or head next door to the air-conditioned Arya Bhavan by Night, which serves South Indian specialties from 4 PM to 2 AM. ✉ *241-A W. Masi St.,* ☎ *452/740577 and 452/740345. No credit cards.*

$$$ 🏨 **Taj Garden Retreat.** Aptly named, this hilltop hotel with a verdant setting offers a view of Madurai from 6 km (4 mi) away. The rooms in the period bungalow retain a British colonial atmosphere, with vintage etchings on the walls, hardwood floors, and airy verandas with beautiful views. The restaurant serves Indian and Continental cuisine. ✉ *Pasumalai, 7 T. P. K. Rd., 625004,* ☎ *452/601020,* FAX *452/604004. 50 rooms. Restaurant, bar, pool, tennis court. AE, DC, MC, V.*

$$ 🏨 **Germanus Days Inn.** Opened in 1999, this brand-new member of the Days Inn chain offers warm and efficient service. The luxurious rooms have an international appeal, particularly to business travelers. ✉ *28 Bypass Rd., 625010,* ☎ *452/610011 and 452/700426,* FAX *452/603478. 59 rooms, 4 suites. Restaurant, bar, laundry service, travel services. AE, DC, MC, V.*

$$ 🏨 **Hotel Madurai Ashok.** The spacious, luxurious rooms look out over well-kept lawns and a garden with a swimming pool. The restaurant serves Continental, Indian, and Chinese cuisines both à la carte and buffet-style. Four rooms have refrigerators. ✉ *Alagarkoil Rd., 625002,* ☎ *452/537531,* FAX *452/537530. 43 rooms. Restaurant, bar, pool. AE, DC, MC, V.*

$$ 🏨 **Pandyan Hotel.** This unpretentious hotel is centrally located, 20 minutes from the airport and 10 minutes from the train station and shops. The Queen's Room, which has large sliding doors, has a view of the Meenakshi Temple. The restaurant serves South Indian, Chinese, and Continental fare. ✉ *Race Course Rd., 625002,* ☎ *452/537090,* FAX *452/533424. 57 rooms. Restaurant, bar. AE, DC, MC, V.*

Shopping

Shops full of carvings, textiles, and brasswork line the streets near Meenakshi Temple, particularly Town Hall Road and Masi Street. The **Handloom House** (✉ East Veli St.) has great hand-loomed cottons.

TAMIL NADU A TO Z

Arriving and Departing

By Car

Madras is linked to the north by National Highway 5 (NH 5), to the west by NH 4, and to the south by NH 45. Generally speaking, road and traffic conditions can make driving more time-consuming than the distance suggests; driving to Madras is most feasible from Bangalore, 334 km (207 mi) to the west. Car travel by night is not recommended—too many wild truck drivers.

By Plane

Madras's Meenambakkam Airport is served by several international carriers (☞ Air Travel *in* Smart Travel Tips A to Z). Within India, **Indian Airlines** (✉ 19 Rukmani Laksmipathi Rd./Marshalls Rd., Madras, ☎ 44/855–5200, 44/855–5204, or 44/140) and **Jet Airways** (✉ Thapar House, 43/44 Montieth Rd., Egmore, Madras, ☎ 44/855–5353) connect Madras with Bombay, Delhi, Calcutta, Bangalore, Cochin, and Trivandrum as well as Tiruchirappalli and Madurai (☞ Getting Around, *below*).

The airport is about 16 km (10 mi) from the center of Madras. A shuttle to any of the major hotels costs Rs. 50. Hired cars are available through prepaid booths just past the baggage claim areas; the ride will cost around Rs. 300.

By Train

See "Smart Travel Tips A to Z" for information on Indrail Passes and descriptions of trains. The Indian Railways booking service in Madras is in Besant Nagar on the ground floor of Rajaji Bhavan Complex. It's a bit more expensive than the Indrail office on the second floor of the Central Station (open 10 to 5), but it's much more convenient and efficient. Railway booking offices are open Monday through Saturday 8 to noon and 12:15 to 2, Sunay 8 to noon. There's also good train service to Bangalore both day and night. See the monthly *Hallo! Madras* for train schedules.

Getting Around

By Auto-Rickshaw

In congested towns and cities this is the fastest and most economical way to get around. Often the meters don't work, so agree on a price before departure. The set rate is about Rs. 7 for the first kilometer and Rs. 2.25 for each additional kilometer.

By Hired Car

Many travelers fly or take a train to Madurai or Tiruchirappalli, then hire a car and driver for the rest of their stay in Tamil Nadu. Drivers know the major routes, and as long as you're satisfied with your driver it can be both convenient and pleasant to have him with you for several days. Rates change, so get a price in advance and be sure it includes a halt charge if you're traveling overnight. Distances within Tamil Nadu are measured from mile 0 at Fort St. George. Hire a car from a government-licensed operator (☞ Travel Agencies, *below*) and figure about Rs. 3 to Rs. 7 per km, with a halt charge of Rs. 100 per night.

NH 7 (from Bangalore) and NH 45 (from Madras) are the state's major north–south arteries. East–west roads include NH 4 (Madras–Bangalore), NH 46 (Vellore–Bangalore), NH 47 (Salem–Coimbatore), and NH 49 (Madurai east to the coast and west into Kerala). From Madras, the drives south to Kanchipuram, Mamallapuram, and Pondicherry are short and simple. The Shore Road is more scenic than the NH 45, and gets you to Mamallapuram in one hour. The drive from Tiruchirappalli to Thanjavur goes through beautiful, lush green paddy fields interspersed with canals. The day-long drive from Madras to Madurai on NH 5 takes you through several villages.

By Cycle-Rickshaw

In temple cities and villages, this is a leisurely, pleasant, and cheap way to travel. Just remember that pedaling in the heat is strenuous: These people work hard. Set the fare in advance and be generous. Cycle-rickshaws in Kanchipuram cost about Rs. 70–Rs. 100 for the day.

By Plane

Indian Airlines (✉ Dindigul Rd., ☎ 431/462233) has regular flights from Tiruchirappalli to Madras and Madurai. Trichy's airport is 8 km (5 mi) from the city center.

By Taxi

Taxis can be expensive, and are normally found only outside the big hotels, but they're a good way to see sights within major cities. A taxi should cost about Rs. 7 for the first km and Rs. 2 per additional km. Make sure the driver uses his meter, or agree on the fare in advance.

With any kind of metered transit, it's wise to use a map to familiarize yourself with the shortest route to your destination. This is best done *before* you get into the taxi (or auto-rickshaw), but even with your driver staring at you in the rearview mirror, a little map work helps keep you from being taken advantage of. In smaller towns, which often have unmetered vehicles, *always* set the fare in advance.

By Train

The air-conditioned chair-car service from Madras to Tiruchirappalli (6 hours) and Madurai (7½ hours) is a relaxing way to see the countryside. The trains going south leave on the meter-gauge track from **Egmore Station** (first-class inquires and reservations, ☎ 44/535–3545). See the monthly *Hallo! Madras* for schedules.

There are two daily trains from Madras to Tirupati, the *Tirupati–Madras Express* and the *Saptagiri Express*. Both take three hours. You can book a bus tour of Tirupati at the bus stand on Esplanade Road or at Central Station or Egmore Station.

Contacts and Resources

Consulates

The **United Kingdom** consulate (✉ 24 Anderson Rd., Madras 600006, ☎ 44/827–3136) is open weekdays 8:30–4. Its Consular Section (☎ 44/827–0658), for visa and passport services, is on the same premises. The **United States** consulate (✉ 220 Anna Salai, Madras 600006, ☎ 44/827–3040, FAX 44/825–0240) is open weekdays 8:15–5.

Currency Exchange

In Madras, **American Express** (✉ G-17 Spencer Plaza, Anna Salai, ☎ 44/852–3638, FAX 44/852–3573) is open 9:30–6:30; **Thomas Cook** (✉ Ceebros Centre, 45 Uttamar Gandhi Salai, ☎ 44/855–4600, FAX 44/858–8532) has a foreign-exchange office that is open daily 9:30–6. In other cities it's best to cash travelers checks at your hotel. The State Bank will cash them but it's a laborious process.

Travel Agencies

American Express (✉ G-17 Spencer Plaza, Anna Salai, Madras, ☎ 44/852–3592 or 44/852–3596) shares an office with their money-changing services. **Ashok Travel and Tours** (✉ 46 Pantheon Rd., Madras, ☎ 44/855–3203) is open Monday through Saturday 10 to 5:30. The sales office of the **Tamil Nadu Tourism Development Corporation** (✉ 3 Periyar E. V. R. High Rd., Madras, ☎ 44/56–0294) is open weekdays 9:45 to 6. **Welcome Tours and Travels** (✉ 150 Mount Rd., Madras, ☎ 44/852–1614, FAX 44/858–6655) provides extremely efficient service and is open 24 hours a day throughout the year. The **Thomas Cook** (✉ Ceebros Centre, 45 Uttamal Gandhi Salai, Madras, ☎ 44/855–4600, FAX 44/855–5090) travel agency shares an office with its currency-exchange service and is open Monday through Saturday 9:30 to 6. Most major hotels also have travel desks where you can easily arrange a car and driver.

Visitor Information

IN MADRAS

The **Government of India Tourist Office** has offices opposite Spencer's (154 Anna Salai, Madras 600002, ☎ 44/852–4295) and at the airport's domestic terminal (☎ 44/234–0386), with knowledgeable staff and an astoundingly comprehensive computer database. The offices are open weekdays 9 to 5:45 and Saturday 9 to 1, closed Sunday. *Hallo! Madras,* an informative monthly for the promotion of tourism, lists tours, music halls, cinemas, events, and airline and train schedules. It's available free at the Government of India Tourist Office and for Rs. 10 at bookstores. The "In the City" section of the Friday edition of *The Hindu* lists cultural events for the coming week.

Near the Government of India Tourist Office in town, the **Tamil Nadu Tourism Development Corporation** (✉ 25 Dr. Radhakrishnan Salai, ☎ 44/854–6843) provides information and reserves cars and guided tours. The **India Tourist Development Corporation** (ITDC, ✉ 29 Victoria Crescent at Commander in Chief [C-in-C] Rd., ☎ 44/827–8884) arranges excursions throughout the state. If you plan to visit any restricted areas or need your visa extended, you should head for the **Foreigners' Regional Registration Office** (✉ Shastri Bhavan Annexe Bldg., Haddows Rd., ☎ 44/827–8210).

OUTSIDE MADRAS

There's no tourist office in **Kanchipuram:** Contact the Tamil Nadu Tourism Development Corporation (☞ *above*) in Madras before your trip. The main tourist office (✉ W. Veli St., ☎ 452/734757) in **Madurai** is open weekdays 10 to 5:45 There are branches at the airport and the train station. The **Thanjavur** tourist office (✉ Hotel Tamilnadu complex, Gandhi Rd., ☎ 4362/21421) is open Tuesday through Sunday from 10 to 1 and 2 to 5. In **Tiruchirappalli,** the tourist office (✉ Hotel Tamilnadu complex, 1 Williams Rd., ☎ 431/460136; counters at train station and airport) is open every day from 10 to 5:45. In **Pondicherry,** the staff at the Tourist Information Bureau of the Directorate of Tourism (✉ 40 Goubert Ave., ☎ 431/334575) is very helpful; the office is open Monday through Saturday from 10 to 5:30.

12 HYDERABAD

Capital of the southeastern state of Andhra Pradesh, Hyderabad is relatively undiscovered as a cultural destination, but its rich Muslim heritage combines intriguingly with its dynamic software industry. The city is known for its fiery cuisine, its shopping—especially for pearls—and, increasingly, its success in the global business of information technology.

By Nigel Fisher

Updated by R. Edwin Sudhir

THE VAST MAJORITY of visitors to Hyderabad are here on business. Modern software and telecommunications industries, as well as traditional textile and jewelry trades, thrive here, and the clutch of multinational companies—including Microsoft—who chose Hyderabad for their research and development centers in the late 1990s have given the city a much-needed fillip and new international status. Hyderabad is now making a strong bid to steal the limelight from Bangalore in the information-technology sector; some young telemarketers in Hyderabad work nighttime-only schedules to accommodate U.S. business hours.

It's too bad more leisure travelers don't visit, as they're missing an Indian treasure. Hyderabad is the capital of the southeastern state of Andhra Pradesh, a state full of influences as varied as Buddhism in Ashoka's time and the Mogul influx of the 16th century. Only 400 years old, Hyderabad reflects most dramatically its Mogul and Telugu heritage. Set on rolling hills around the beautiful Hussain Sagar Lake, the city's minarets pierce the clear blue sky. Here you can shop for pearls and bangles, enjoy terrific food, and watch the colorful city go by.

A teeming metropolis, Hyderabad is home to approximately 5 million people who sometimes appear to be on the streets en masse. Traffic can be horrendous: if it's moving, be prepared to hear the crunch of an accident; if it's gridlocked, be prepared to cover your nose, as exhaust fumes can make breathing difficult. The city administration is racing to construct overpasses (a few are already in use) to ease the congestion, and its army of cleaners, who toil through the night, ensures that Hyderabadis wake up to a spanking clean city.

Andhra Pradesh has a long stretch of coastline along the Bay of Bengal, and inland is the Deccan Plateau. The plateau tends to be very dry, even arid at higher elevations, and the coastline, dotted with fishing villages, is prone to flooding by monsoons, especially around the deltas of the Krishna and Godavari rivers. The size of France, this huge state comprises speakers of 16 languages (headed by Telugu and Urdu), and except for Hyderabad and Secunderabad, it has few cities. Indeed, Andhra Pradesh has remained a relative backwater in terms of infrastructure; but it's one of the few states in India where Muslims and Hindus, who make up 87 percent of the population, live together in relative harmony.

Hyderabad began with the establishment of the Qutab Shahi dynasty. Quli Qutab Shah wrestled Hyderabad from the Bahamani kingdom in 1512 and established the fortress city of Golconda. Lack of sufficient water and epidemics of plague and cholera convinced the fifth Quli to venture beyond his fortress and create a new city 10 km (6 mi) away on the Musi River, with Charminar, an arch, as its center. Four great roads fanned out from Charminar toward the four points of the compass.

The grandness of the city and the wealth of the Qutab Shahi kingdom attracted the interest of Aurangzeb, the last great Mogul ruler. His armies lay siege to Golconda and captured it in 1687. For the next half century Hyderabad wallowed, but when the Mogul empire began to fragment, the viceroy, Asaf Jah I, seized the opportunity to proclaim himself *nizam* (ruler). From 1923 to 1948, with the assistance of British protection, the Muslim nizams ruled, hoarding wealth while the vast majority of the population was kept in poverty. The wealth of the nizams went beyond imagination and stories of the last nizam abound: He used a 260-carat diamond as a paperweight and during World War II he presented Britain's Royal Air Force with a squadron of Hurricane fighters. When India was granted independence from Great Britain, the nizam Usman Ali refused to join the Union. He held out for a year until India marched in its army and annexed the territory.

Note that everyone uses the city name Hyderabad even when they are referring to its twin city, Secunderabad, across the lake on its north side. Secunderabad is of little interest to travelers, except that its railway station receives many of Hyderabad's long-distance trains.

Pleasures and Pastimes

Dining

Hyderabad is famous for food, including *haleem* (a slow-cooked treat of pounded wheat, mutton, and spices), Hyderabadi *biriani* (a baked meat and rice dish), and *bagare baingan* (eggplant in a spicy poppy- and sesame-seed sauce). Some of the best haleem is found in the Old Town around the Mecca Masjid, though it's also available in classy restaurants. Chilies are grown on the plateau and among locals it's a point of pride to shock the taste buds with fiery pain. The main hotels usually have a couple of restaurants, one Indian and one European, and, except for one or two exceptions, these are the best (and safest) places to dine.

In 1994 the Andhra Pradesh government brought in prohibition. Only in leading hotels could alcohol be served and only then to out-of-state visitors who had to purchase a "drinking license" that permitted a couple of drinks a night at the hotel bar. In 1997 legislation was passed to end prohibition while imposing many restrictions on what, where, when, and to whom alcohol may be sold. Implementation will take time, but hotel restaurants have been the first to capitalize on the more liberal spirit of the drinking laws.

Lodging

Hyderabad has more hotel rooms than it can fill, and new construction is everywhere. New business hotels offer services and amenities of international caliber at prices half those of Delhi. These range from opulent to utilitarian. The Taj Group has a contract to transform the nizam's Falaknuma Palace into a luxury boutique hotel, but until that happens (the process is held up by litigation), Hyderabad will have no hotels of real charm. Inexpensive hotels with fairly primitive amenities are found around the train station in Secunderabad and in the center of Hyderabad.

Shopping

Hyderabad is a gathering center for the many handicrafts of Andhra Pradesh. Look for *nirmal* toys (delightfully colorful, lightweight wooden toys), *bidri* ware (a gunmetal-like alloy used for bangles, cufflinks, bowls, and other items), and ikat textiles (tie-dyed before they're woven). You'll also find silk, wool, and cotton carpets from the Warangal district. Hyderabad is the center of India's pearl trade: Pearls from southeast Asia are sent here for polishing, sorting, and piercing. For pearls, the most exciting place is the Charminar Market, particularly just north of Charminar itself. The market bustles with everything you're likely to want, from textiles and handicrafts to bangles (west of Charminar). The omnipresent glass bangles worn throughout the country are produced in great quantities here.

EXPLORING HYDERABAD

Concentrate on Hyderabad if you're passing through Andhra Pradesh. Most of the city's interesting sights are in the Old Town, making it easy to walk around or take short auto-rickshaw trips. Don't bother with Hyderabad's twin city, Secunderabad, which, aside from its railway station, has little to offer the traveler. If you have the stamina and will be heading south to Madras, consider a detour to the temple town of Tirupati.

Great Itineraries

Numbers in the text correspond to numbers in the margin and on the Hyderabad map.

IF YOU HAVE 1 DAY

You could actually cover all of Hyderabad's major sights in one day, but it would be a tiring day indeed. Try to spend at least two nights here. If you do only have one day, take an auto-rickshaw to the **Golconda Fort,** the original defensive settlement of Hyderabad, and the palatial tombs of the Muslim rulers, the **Qutab Shahi Tombs,** both several miles west of the city. Back in the Old Town, spend the rest of the day exploring **Charminar,** a four-story arched, minaret-topped gateway, and the area around it, which has good shopping.

IF YOU HAVE 2 DAYS

Follow the one-day itinerary your first day. The next day, visit the **Mecca Masjid,** India's second-largest mosque. Then head to the **Falaknuma Palace,** if it's open, and the eclectic **Salar Jung Museum.**

IF YOU HAVE 3 DAYS

Spend at least one day covering the sights mentioned above, then look outside the city. The most compelling attraction in Andhra Pradesh outside Hyderabad is the temple town of **Tirupati** (☞ Chapter 10), 732 km (454 mi) southeast of Hyderabad and accessible by tour bus in 12 hours. From there you can continue on by bus or train to Madras, four hours away.

When to Tour Hyderabad

Winter—mid-October through March—is the ideal time to visit, as the weather is dry and the temperature rarely climbs higher than 72°F (22°C). Evenings can even be chilly, requiring a sweater. In summer the temperature soars up to 104°F (40°C), cooling down just a little during the monsoon rains that fall from June through September.

A Good Tour

Make your first stop **Golconda Fort** ①, the original defensive settlement of Hyderabad. You can take an auto-rickshaw there, but to see it properly requires walking up a steep hill to its summer palace, and that is better done before the noonday sun beats down. From the fort go over to the nearby **Qutab Shahi Tombs** ②, the palatial tombs of the Muslim rulers, which are also better seen and photographed before the sun is overhead. From here it's a 7-km (4½-mi) auto-rickshaw ride to the center of the Old Town, whose landmark is **Charminar** ③, with its magnificent minarets. All around Charminar are bustling bazaars and close by is Laad Bazaar with rows of shops selling glass bangles, perfume, and lacquer. About 330 ft south of Charminar is India's second-largest mosque, the **Mecca Masjid** ④. The **Falaknuma Palace** ⑤ is another 2 km (1 mi) south. The **Salar Jung Museum** ⑥ is north of Charminar but still on the south side of the Musi River. In the evening, you may want to return to Golconda Fort to attend the sound-and-light show, especially if you're here on a Wednesday or Sunday, when the show is in English.

TIMING

This route can be covered in one extremely full day, but it's best split into two days. On account of Hyderabad's strong Muslim influence, the museums and some shops may be closed on Fridays. Non-Muslims are discouraged from visiting mosques on Fridays.

Sights to See

3 **Charminar.** South of the Musi River, near the impressive Osmania Hospital and High Court buildings, you enter the Charkaman area in the heart of the Old City between four (*char*) great gates (*kaman*). Within these gates you'll find not only Hyderabad's famed pearl and bangle markets, but also the striking Charminar, an imposing granite edifice built by Mohammed Quli Qutab Shah in 1591 to appease the forces of evil and protect this new city from plague and epidemic. The arches, domes, and minarets show Islamic influence, while much of the ornamentation is Hindu in style. ⊠ *Charkaman center.* 🎟 *Free; 50 paise to ascend minarets.* ⏲ *Daily sunrise–sunset.*

5 **Falaknuma Palace.** This stunning late-19th-century palace built by a Paigah noble is not open to the public, but it may one day be transformed into a luxury hotel by the Taj Group, along with its peaceful Japanese gardens. People do often walk the 20 minutes south of Charminar, however, on the off chance that they'll be allowed to marvel at the stained-glass windows, carved ceilings, fine Italian marble staircases, and general 19th-century opulence that took nine years to create. Acquired by the sixth nizam in 1897, the palace has hosted both Indian and European royalty. Inquire at the tourist office (☞ Visitor Information *in* Hyderabad A to Z, *below*) or your hotel for more information. ⊠ *Tank Bund Rd.*

1 **Golconda Fort.** A clap at the gate of this fort echos clearly up to its summer palace, high on the hill just outside the city. These are the ruins of what was once the state capital: It often sheltered whole communities under siege for months, and though tremendously worn by time and war, it tells stories in crumbling stone. The fort only fell to one siege, but that siege was disastrous. After eight months of bottling up the fort, Aurangzeb—with the assistance of a traitor who opened what is now called the Victory Gate—sent his troops storming in. In the belief that there was hidden gold here, Aurangzeb ordered the roofs of all palaces ripped off; so, 300 years later, only the walls stand amid the weeds and moss. The excellent, nightly sound-and-light show is performed in English every Wednesday and Sunday. ⊠ *6 km (4 mi) west of the city (contact Andhra Pradesh Travel & Tourism Development Corporation in Hyderabad,* ☎ *40/351–2401).* 🎟 *Rs. 20 for admission and light show.* ⏲ *Tues.–Sun. sunrise–end of light show; light show, Nov.–Feb., daily 6:30; Mar.–Oct., daily 7.*

4 **Mecca Masjid.** India's second-largest mosque, located in the Charkaman area in the center of the old part of town (south of Charminar), can hold 10,000 worshipers. Non-Muslims are welcome except at prayer time, which includes, of course, all day Friday. Some bricks here were made with earth brought from Mecca in 1618. The nizams' tombs line the left side of the courtyard. ⊠ *Kishan Prasad Rd., southwest of Charminar,* ☎ *no phone.* 🎟 *Free.* ⏲ *Sat.–Thurs. except during services, which take place early morning.*

2 **Qutab Shahi Tombs.** Each of the seven distinctive tombs of the Qutab Shahi dynasty has a square base surrounded by pointed arches. The seventh is unfinished because Shah Abdul Hassan was rudely interrupted in the building of his tomb by Aurangzeb, who defeated him and captured the Golconda Fort. ⊠ *2 km (1 mi) north of Golconda Fort,* ☎ *no phone.* 🎟 *Rs. 20.* ⏲ *Sat.–Thurs., 9:30–5.*

Charminar, **3**
Falaknuma Palace, **5**
Golconda Fort, **1**
Mecca Masjid, **4**
Qutab Shahi Tombs, **2**
Salar Jung Museum, **6**

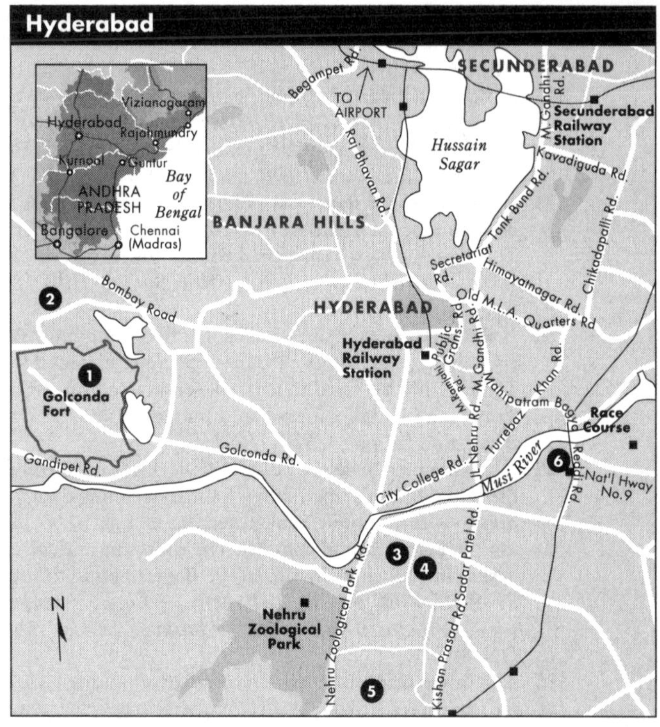

❻ **Salar Jung Museum.** When you see the wealth of this collection, you might be astonished to learn that it all belonged to one man: Mir Yusuf Ali Khan Salar Jung III, who for a short time was prime minister. Thirty-five thousand items are crammed into 35 rooms. The fantastic Chola sculptures, European glass, Chinese jade, jeweled weapons, and modern Indian paintings are displayed with little information, but they're well worth a look anyway. ✉ *C. L. Badari Malakpet (south of Musi River),* ☎ *040/523211.* 🎫 *Rs. 5.* ⏲ *Sat.–Thurs., 10–5.*

Tank Bund Road. A showpiece of Hyderabad, Tank Bund is a promenade across the top of the dam that holds back the waters of Hussain Sagar Lake (4 mi by ½ mi), a dominant feature of the city. Many hotels are positioned so that their rooms overlook the lake, which is often used as a venue for sporting events. The road is lined with statues of the state's native sons, and a stunning sight from here is the 52-ft-high, 350-ton monolithic statue of Lord Buddha in the middle of the lake. ✉ *East side of Hussain Sagar Lake.*

DINING AND LODGING

$$$ ✕ **Dakhni.** White walls hung with handsome paintings, dark wood pillars, and upholstered chairs and settees intimately placed around the room create an elegant atmosphere. The chef serves good Andhra Pradesh and Deccan regional specialties. This is a good place to order haleem. ✉ *Taj Residency, Rd. No. 1, Banjara Hills,* ☎ *40/339–9999. AE, DC, MC, V.*

$$$ ✕ **Firdaus.** This restaurant evokes the elegance of the nizams, with waiters dressed in *sherwanis* (long Nehru-style jackets), *punka* (fans) gently swaying from the ceiling, and live *ghazal* (classical Indian vocal music) performances nightly, except Tuesday. The chef serves regal Hyderabadi cuisine. Try the *achar gosht* (lamb cooked in pickled tomato masala paste) and *nizami handi* (vegetable and cottage-cheese curry) or bagare baingan. ✉ *Krishna Oberoi, Rd. No. 1, Banjara Hills,* ☎ *40/339323. AE, DC, MC, V.*

$$$ ✕ **Kabab-E-Bahar.** Outdoors on the edge of the lake, set on a lovely lawn, this restaurant serves excellent Hyderabadi cuisine buffet-style or à la carte. Try the very good kebabs and barbecue items. ✉ *Taj Residency, Rd. No. 1, Banjara Hills,* ☎ *40/339–9999. DC, MC, V. No lunch.*

$$$ ✕ **Szechwan Garden.** Overlooking beautiful waterfalls and surrounded by a Chinese rock garden, this restaurant offers tasty Szechuan cuisine. Try the honey spareribs, chicken in lotus leaves, or prawns in oyster sauce. ✉ *Krishna Oberoi, Rd. No. 1, Banjara Hills,* ☎ *40/339–3079. AE, DC, MC, V.*

$$ ✕ **Palace Heights.** This tasteful upper-floor restaurant in a modern high-rise has a great city view. Pictures of former nizams decorate the walls; antiques add a refined touch. Ask for a table by a window and choose from Continental, Chinese, and Indian cuisine. ✉ *Triveni Complex, Abids Rd.,* ☎ *40/242520. DC, MC, V.*

$$$ **Holiday Inn Krishna.** Bold relief work adorns the high walls around the Holiday Inn's open lobby lounge, which is designed more to impress—with rambling sunken seating in a garishly colored pattern—than to enfold you in comfort. The rooms have thick carpets, writing desks, and couches. ✉ *Rd. No. 1, Banjara Hills, 500034,* ☎ *40/339–3939,* FAX *40/339–2684. 141 rooms, 5 suites. 2 restaurants, bar, no-smoking rooms, pool, health club, business services, travel services. AE, DC, MC, V.*

$$$ ★ **Krishna Oberoi.** Set on nine acres overlooking Hussain Sagar Lake, the Oberoi is a striking blend of modern architecture tempered by strong Mogul elements. Beautiful fountains and formal gardens ornament the front lawn, though a water shortage prevents the fountains from being turned on. Rooms have soft pastel decor and TVs with several international channels. Those facing the gardens and lake are the choicest; Room 434 is ideal. Service is exemplary. ✉ *Rd. No. 1, Banjara Hills, 500034, Andhra Pradesh,* ☎ *40/339–2323,* FAX *40/339–3079. 262 rooms, 14 suites. 3 restaurants, bar, pool, health club, nightclub, business services, travel services. AE, DC, MC, V.*

$$ **Ramada Hotel Manohar.** Located just outside the airport—with soundproof rooms to eliminate aircraft noise—the Ramada is a good option for business travelers. It's got all the trappings of an international hotel, with service to match. ✉ *Near Airport Exit Rd., Begumpet, 500016,* ☎ *40/781–9917,* FAX *781–9801. 110 rooms, 25 suites. 2 restaurants, bar, coffee shop, pool, health club, business services, travel services. AE, DC, MC, V.*

$$ **Taj Residency.** This modern high-rise on Banjara Hills overlooks its own small lake. The spacious lobby is bedecked with marble, and the contemporary rooms are comfortable. The best rooms are those with lake views from upper floors. ✉ *Rd. No. 1, Banjara Hills, 500034,* ☎ *40/339–9999,* FAX *40/339–2218. 118 rooms, 9 suites. 3 restaurants, bar, coffee shop, no-smoking floor, tennis court, pool, business meeting rooms, travel services. AE, DC, MC, V.*

$ **Green Park.** Located near the airport, in the Greenlands area, this hotel has a marble lobby and comfortable rooms with modern decor. The best rooms overlook the garden. It's an excellent value for business travelers. ✉ *Begumpet Rd., 500016,* ☎ *40/375–7575,* FAX *40/375–7677. 148 rooms, 15 suites. Restaurant, bar, coffee shop, concierge floor, business services. AE, DC, MC, V.*

$ **Viceroy.** This new hotel stands conveniently between Hyderabad and Secunderabad and has stunning views over Hussain Sagar Lake. Glass elevators and terraced balconies overlook the open lobby; all the facilities are modern. The best rooms have lake views, complete with spectacular sunsets. Note that some rooms have just a shower, no bathtub. ✉ *Tank Bund Rd., 500380,* ☎ *40/753–8383,* FAX *40/753–8797. 137 rooms. Restaurant, coffee shop, pool, health club, business services, travel services. AE, DC, MC, V.*

SHOPPING

Mangatrai Pearls (✉ 5-9-46, Basheerbagh, opposite Hotel Shanbagh, ☎ 40/235728; ✉ 22-6-191 Pathergatti, near Charminar, ☎ 040/457–7339) offers both high-quality pearls and good service. **Sanchay** (✉ Shops 21 and 22, Babukhan Estate, Basheerbagh; ☎ 40/329–9738) has a fine selection of high-quality hand-loomed silks. The **Lepakshi Handicrafts Emporium** (✉ 94 Minerva Complex, Gunfoundry, ☎ 40/781–4729) has a good variety of bidri ware, hand-loomed garments, and saris.

HYDERABAD A TO Z

Arriving and Departing

By Plane

Hyderabad is served by frequent flights from all over India. **Indian Airlines** (☎ 40/236902 for reservations, 329–9333 for inquiries) has flights between Hyderabad and Bangalore, Bombay, Calcutta, Delhi, and Madras. **Air India** (☎ 40/211804) has service to Bombay and Singapore. Privately owned **Jet Airways** (☎ 40/380–1222) and **Sahara India Airlines** (☎ 40/781–7940) also serve Hyderabad; check with travel agents for current schedules of other domestic airlines.

The airport is just north of Hussain Sagar Lake, on Sardar Patel Road in Secunderabad. You can get a prepaid taxi from the airport terminal; depending on your destination, the fare can range from Rs. 50 to Rs. 300.

By Train

Hyderabad and Secunderabad are major rail centers. Some trains use either or both stations, but most long-distance trains use only Secunderabad. An auto-rickshaw to the center of Hyderabad costs Rs. 35. From Delhi, the *Rajdhani Express* takes 23 hours, while the less-expensive *A.P. Express* takes 26 hours, when it's running on time. From Bombay, the *Hyderabad–Bombay Express* takes 14 hours; from Madras, the *Charminar Express* takes 15 hours; and from Bhubaneswar, the *Falaknuma* takes 19 hours.

Getting Around

By Car

Traffic is a nightmare, so we don't recommend renting a car. Both **Airtravels** (✉ 1005 Babukhan Estate, 10th floor, Basheerbagh, ☎ 40/241024, FAX 40/831247) and **Cosy Cabs** (✉ Karan Apartments, Begumpet, ☎ 40/776–2023 or 40/776–0409, FAX 40/776–7146) provide cars and drivers 24 hours a day.

By Rickshaw and Taxi

Hyderabad is manageable on foot once you reach the district you want to explore; to do that, metered auto-rickshaws or cycle rickshaws are your best bet. Auto-rickshaws have a tendency to go the long way to your destination unless you know—or pretend to know—where you're going. Unmetered taxis are overpriced and get you into more trouble in traffic, which becomes unbearable at rush hour. Only a cryptologist can understand most addresses here, so landmarks and patience will serve you well.

By Bus (Tirupati)

For a trip to Tirupati en route to Madras, you can either take the 15-hour train to Madras and connect from there, or take the direct bus from Hyderabad, which leaves 4 times a day and takes 12 hours. **Darsham Hill Transport** (✉ M. J. Road, Hyderabad, ☎ 40/501519) runs weekend tours that leave Hyderabad for Tirupati on Friday at 3:30 PM and return on Monday at 7 AM.

Contacts and Resources

Business Services

The major hotels have business facilities for their guests, but these can be a bit pricey. Wherever you see large yellow-and-black signs reading S.T.D., I.S.D., FAX, you're likely to get a better deal. Translation services are available from **Hyderabad Translation Bureau** (✉ 1-7-143 Kancharla Towers, 409 Rama Krishna Land, Golconda Cross Rd., ☎ FAX 40/761–3355, 760–4654) and **Alliance Française de Hyderabad** (✉ Adarshnagar, ☎ 40/236646).

Currency Exchange

All of the major hotels will change money for their guests. You can also visit **Thomas Cook** (✉ 6-1-57 Nasir Arcade, Saifabad, ☎ 40/231988), open Monday through Saturday from 9:30 to 6. Near the clock tower, **Synery Forexpress** (✉ Navketan 62, 5th floor, Sarojini Devi Rd., ☎ 40/780–6552) is open seven days a week.

Express Mail and Courier Services

Blue Dart Express (✉ 1-2-61/62 Siddam Shetty Complex, Park Lane, ☎ 40/812746 or 40/812907) is associated with Federal Express and can get packages just about anywhere.

Tours

Ashok Travels (✉ Lal Bahadur Stadium, ☎ 40/230766) runs deluxe buses to attractions within Andhra Pradesh.

Travel Agencies

In addition to tourist offices and hotel-based travel agents, you can always consult the following for assistance with travel plans: **Jubilee Travels and Tours** (✉ 6-3-1090/B/A Somajiguda Raj Bhavan Rd., ☎ 40/331–2379). **Sita World Travels** (✉ Sita House, 3-5-874, Hyderguda, ☎ 40/233628). **Mercury Travels** (✉ 92–93 Suryakiran Bldg., S. D. Rd., ☎ 40/781–2678).

Visitor Information

The **Andhra Pradesh Travel & Tourism Development Corporation Ltd** (APTTDC; ✉ Yatri Nivas, Sardar Patel Rd., ☎ 40/781–6375) is open daily from 9:30 to 5:30 and has counters in both train stations. Its Tourism Information Centre (Yatri Nivas, Sardar Patel Rd., Secunderabad, ☎ 40/781–6375) is open daily from 6:30 AM to 7 PM. The **Government of India Tourist Office** (✉ Sandozi Bldg., Himayat Nagar, ☎ 40/763–0037) is hard to find, has very little information on the region, and tends to be behind the times anyway. The monthly pamphlet **"Channel 6"** lists the latest urban goings-on; pick it up in a bookshop or major hotel.

13 BHUBANESWAR

Capital of the eastern coastal state of Orissa, Bhubaneswar is an easy-going temple city with 500 ancient shrines. Small and reasonably peaceful, it's also a town of artisans, as are the villages of Raghurajpur and Pipli. Closer to the water, Konark is famous for its half-ruined Sun Temple—once a complete horse-drawn chariot in stone, 225 feet tall—while Puri still draws intense crowds of pilgrims to its towering Jagganath Temple.

By Nigel Fisher

Updated by R. Edwin Sudhir

ORISSA IS A TANGIBLY religious place. The state was once a center of Buddhist learning, but changes in ruling dynasties brought changes in faith, moving away from Buddhism first to Jainism (circa 1st century BC) and then to Hinduism. It's now one of Hinduism's most active pilgrimage areas. The temple cities of Bhubaneswar, Puri, and Konark are showcases for Orissa's distinctive sacred architecture, with its unusual shapes and fabulous, often erotic, sculptures; particularly in Bhubaneswar, the temples represent a coherent development of the Nagara style of Indo-Aryan design. Even beyond the hundreds of temples, you'll see signs of devotion everywhere: From village huts to taxis to hotels, the smiling face of Lord Jagannath, an avatar of Krishna and Orissa's main god, looks back at you.

Orissa is also known as Utkala—"Land of Arts and Crafts." Striking crafts pop up everywhere, from the gaily colored appliqué umbrellas of Pipli to brass *dhokra,* animal and human figures of twisted wire. On palm-sheltered side streets, sculptors chisel statues from stone, and weavers create silk and cotton fabrics by hand.

Whether you're walking through Bhubaneswar's airport or a path in a tiny village, keep in mind that Orissa's infrastructure and facilities are very basic. Be patient, and prepare to settle into a slower pace.

Pleasures and Pastimes

Architecture

The temples of Bhubaneswar, Konark, and Puri, built between the 7th and 15th centuries, bear elaborate and fascinating detail. Canonical texts governed their creation, dictating structural forms and proportions derived from religious principles. The Orissan temple consists almost entirely of a vaulting spire thrusting upward from among much-lower turrets. Supporting the tower is the cube-shaped *deul* (shrine for the deity); next to the deul stands the *jagamohan* (porch), a meeting place for worshipers, usually square with a pyramidal roof. Sometimes one or two more halls—a *natmandir* (dancing hall) and a *bhogmandir* (hall of offerings)—are set in front of the porch.

The architecture may seem heavy, but the sculpture on these temples is graceful, animated, often exuberantly erotic, and steeped in mythology. Most temples have a sacred tank in their yards, in which worshipers bathe themselves for religious cleansing.

Dining

In Bhubaneswar and Orissa's other towns and resort areas, expect good food at low prices in decidedly unassuming restaurants. You'll find fresh seafood—lobster, prawns, and fish called *bekti* and *rui*—and a profusion of excellent vegetables, which benefit from Orissa's mineral-rich soils. Unfortunately, not many restaurants have long menus of traditional Orissan food, but most places we review serve a few Orissan specialties. Look for curries prepared with coconut milk, creamy gravies made with yogurt, and delicious *baigan* (eggplant) and *bhindi* (okra) dishes.

Lodging

You don't come to Orissa for the hotels. As a general rule, they're mainly utilitarian. Rates, however, are significantly lower than in more heavily traveled parts of India, and discounts are readily available. The pricier hotels offer air-conditioning and currency exchange, and their rooms have bathrooms with tubs.

Shopping

Orissa is renowned for its ancient handicraft traditions. Look for *pata chitra* (exquisitely detailed, fine-lined religious paintings on cloth prepared specially for this purpose, using only vegetable and other natural dyes); *tala patra* (palm-leaf art); dhokra; *tarkashi* (exquisite silver-filigree jewelry and other items, created mostly in Cuttack, north of Bhubaneswar); and appliqué work from Pipli. Serious shopping entails side trips to the beautiful, largely hidden Orissan villages that are home to master craftspeople.

As in most of India, travelers are subject to grossly inflated prices, even in remote artisan hamlets. Start bargaining at half the original price and you may end up with a 30% to 40% "discount." While it may seem inappropriate, even rude, to haggle over unique pieces of art that venerable old artisans display for you in their huts, don't worry; it's expected. In Pipli, competition drops the rate of initial inflation; here you'll only need to bargain down 5% to 10%. If you shy away from dickering, you can always buy good artifacts at fixed prices at the government emporiums.

EXPLORING BHUBANESWAR

Bhubaneswar's main temples are clustered in the Old Town within about 3 km (2 mi) of one another. It's entirely feasible to walk from one to the next, or you can hire a car and driver or a cycle-rickshaw.

The city is divided in two by the rail line. On the southeastern side is Old Town, with higgledy-piggedly streets, most of them unpaved, winding between residential areas and the temples. On the northwestern side is New Town, with wider streets and buildings spread out over a large area. There is no downtown, but the Station Square, just to the west of the railway station, is a gathering spot for auto-rickshaws and taxis. Two main streets, Janpath and Sachivalaya Marg, run north–south through New Town; these are crossed by the east-west road Raj Path, which goes west from Station Square out to National Highway 5, the trunk road heading north to Calcutta and south to Hyderabad.

Great Itineraries

Orissa's main destinations are Bhubaneswar, Konark, and Puri. If you're short on time, you can see this trio in two days, one devoted to Bhubaneswar and the other to Konark and Puri, with a possible stop at Pipli. With more time, you can spend another two or more days idling at Gopalpur-on-Sea, three hours south of Bhubaneswar by train.

Numbers in the margin correspond to points of interest on the Bhubaneswar and Environs map.

IF YOU HAVE 1 DAY

If you're on a flying visit, spend it exploring the ancient Hindu temples of **Bhubaneswar.** Head directly to the Old Town to see Bindusagar; the Vaital, Parasurameswara, Mukteswar, Kedareswar, and Rajarani temples; and Brahmeswar. Hire transport to reach the Lingaraj Temple Complex and get back from there to the New Town. You'll also probably have time to visit the Tribal Museum, near the Baramunda Bus Station, west of New Town, to see the folk crafts of Orissa.

IF YOU HAVE 2 DAYS

Explore **Bhubaneswar**'s Old Town on your first day. The next morning, leave early for the 90-minute journey to **Konark** and spend an hour or more at the Sun Temple. Have breakfast in Konark village and perhaps a swim at Konark's beach, Chandrabhapa, before going on to **Puri.** Spend an hour or two among the milling pilgrims and souvenir stalls; have lunch at the Mayfair; then head back for Bhubaneswar, stopping along the way at **Raghurajpur** to see the artisans, **Pipli** to inspect the appliqués, and **Dhauli,** the hill where Ashoka the Great slaughtered his enemies and then, in disgust, embraced Buddhism.

IF YOU HAVE 3 DAYS

Follow the two-day itinerary above. On your third day, take a three-hour train journey south to Berhampur and hop an auto-rickshaw to **Gopalpur-on-Sea.** From here you can return to Bhubaneswar or continue south to Andhra Pradesh.

When to Tour Bhubaneswar

The ideal time to visit is from October to March, when the temperature is around 77°F (25°C) during the day and the air is relatively dry. After March the heat starts building up to 95°F (35°C) until the monsoon rains come in late May or early June. This cools things down a bit, but the rain can come down in buckets until mid-September.

Old Town and New Town

1 **Bhubaneswar** is known as India's city of temples, and once had some 7,000 religious shrines. Today only a fraction survive, but they still total around 500, in various stages of preservation. Unfortunately, the greatest Bhubaneswar temple, the Lingaraj, is off-limits to non-Hindus; you can see its huge tower from miles away, but the closest most foreign travelers will get to it is a viewing stand erected during the British Raj, when Lord Curzon, the British Viceroy, paid a visit.

Admission is technically free at all of Bhubaneswar's lovely temples. Upon entering any one of them, however, you may be harassed for money by the priest, who will follow you around, grumbling, with a dog-eared notebook (a phony donation register) scribbled with the names of foreign tourists and the amounts they've allegedly donated—with an extra zero tacked onto the end of each figure. The money is usually pocketed for the priest's own use rather than the preservation of the temple, but it's sometimes worth giving Rs. 10 or so just to avoid being tailed by a cranky priest.

The temples are open daily, from sunrise to sunset. Entrance into the inner sanctums of active temples may be restricted for half an hour or so during offering times (early morning, around noon, and late afternoon).

A Good Tour

Most of the sights—the ancient Hindu temples—are in the Old Town. All of the major temples are within an area of less than 3 mi by 1 mi, so you can walk among them if it's not too hot. If it is, make an arrangement with a taxi or auto-rickshaw; just negotiate the price first or you'll be taken for a ride. Start with **Bindusagar,** where early-morning bathers seek blessings. From here a walk west brings you to the 8th-century **Vaital Temple.** On the opposite (east) side of Bindusagar is the 7th-century **Parasurameswara Temple.** About 1 km (½ mi) to the west is the 10th-century **Mukteswar Temple;** on the same grounds is the whitewashed **Kedareswar Temple.** Continue east for 700 yards to see the 11th-century **Rajarani Temple,** standing pristine on manicured grounds. A little farther along the road going east are crossroads; turn right (south) and you'll come to wonderfully carved **Brahmeswar.** You might want transport to travel the 3 km (2 mi) to the **Lingaraj Temple Complex;** to walk here, retrace your steps to the crossroads and turn left onto Tankapai Road, back down the way you came, but before Rajarani take another left that will bring you down to Puri Road. Cross over and head up the small busy road lined with stalls to the temple.

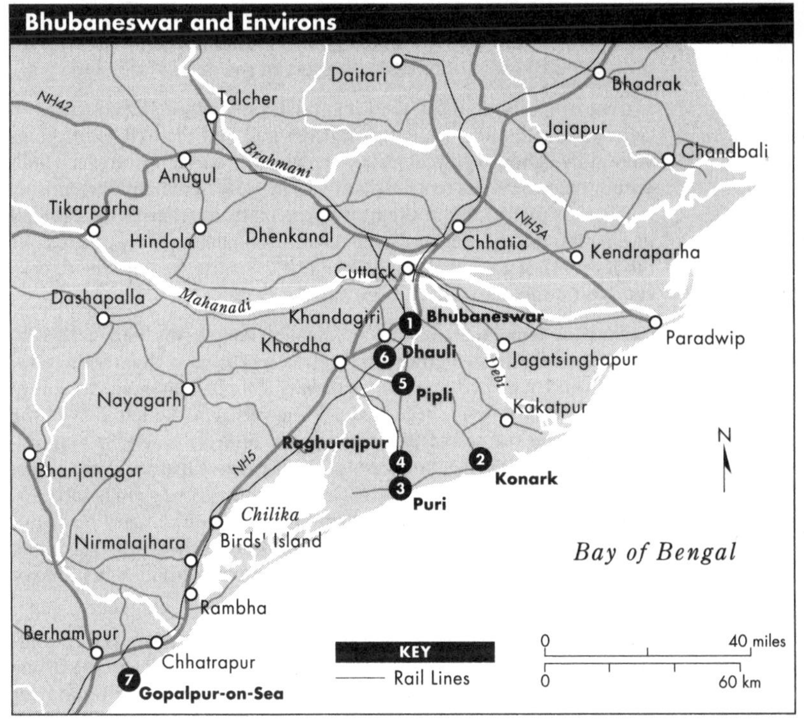

If there's still time left in the day, visit the **Tribal Museum** to learn about Orissa's various cultures and crafts.

TIMING

It takes a full morning to see all the temples. It's best to start early, around 8 AM, so as not to be hiking around in the midday sun. Most of the temples will take 15–20 minutes to explore, though you might want to spend more time browsing the stalls and soaking up the pilgrimage atmosphere around the Lingaraj Temple Complex. If you go on to the Tribal Museum, allow 15 minutes to get there and another 45 minutes inside.

Sights to See

All of these temples are in Old Town.

Bindusagar. Surrounded by a stone embankment, the largest sacred tank in Bhubaneswar was the central point around which Bhubaneswar's multitude of temples was originally built. Believing that this tank is filled with water from every sacred stream and tank in India, and can therefore wash away sins, pilgrims come here to cleanse themselves.

Brahmeswar Temple. The outside of this 11th-century temple is sumptuously carved with scrolls of monkeys, swans, and deer, figures of gods and goddesses, and religious scenes. Over the entrance is a row of similar figures representing the nine planets. If you're lucky, you'll be shown around by a squat priest who will hold forth on the temple's carvings and their complicated symbolic significance. (He'll expect a tip.)

Lingaraj Temple Complex. This giant 11th-century shrine is considered the ultimate in Orissan temple architecture by Hindu devotees and art historians alike. A world in itself, with some 100 smaller votive shrines, the temple sits in a huge walled compound that teems with activity. The closest non-Hindus will get to this temple is the small, raised platform 100 yards away, from which you can strain to see the buildings' profuse exterior carvings, a high point of Hindu decorative art. Alas, unless you've brought binoculars, most of the details will elude you.

Dating from about 1050, the Lingaraj Temple originally consisted of only the porch and shrine; the dancing hall and the hall of offerings were added about 100 years later. The *vimana* (curvilinear tower), built without mortar, soars to a height of 147 ft. Note that many enterprising locals post themselves at the foot of the platform stairs with a phony guest register and demand a donation for climbing the stairs. The money will not go to the temple, let alone the stairs, but into their pockets. Non-donors are likely to be harassed.

★ **Mukteswar Temple.** Bhubaneswar's smallest temple was built in the 10th century. Its earthy-red sandstone body is encrusted with intricate carvings, from emaciated, crouching *sadhus* (Hindu holy men) to voluptuous, buxom women bedecked with jewels. On the left side of the entrance, the statues of bearers grimace under the temple's monumental weight. The Mukteswar's most distinctive feature is its *torana,* a thick-pillared, arched gateway draped with carved strings of beads and ornamented with statues of smiling women in languorous positions. Buddhist influence is visible here. Beyond the torana, set back in a shady yard, stands the **Kedareswar Temple,** with its 8-ft statue of Hanuman, the monkey god.

Parasurameswara Temple. Built in AD 650, this small temple is the oldest of those remaining in Bhubaneswar. It's a perfect example of the pre-10th-century Orissan style: A high spire curves up to a point over the sanctum, which houses the deity, and the pyramid-covered jagamohan, where people sit and pray. The facade is covered with carvings of Ganesh, the elephant god of wisdom and prosperity, and other deities and ornamentation.

★ **Rajarani Temple.** Standing by itself in green rice fields, far back from the road, this 11th-century structure is perhaps the most harmoniously proportioned temple in the city, and is definitely the most peaceful. The Orissan king who created the Rajarani died before its finishing touch—a deity—was installed, leaving its sanctum sanctorum eternally godless, yet filled with a lingering calm. There are no aggressive priests here. The temple's carvings are lovely, with dragons tucked into cracks, enchanting couples in erotic poses, and beautiful women smiling with a distinctly non-stony warmth. A small tip to the gardener-caretaker will get you inside.

Tribal Museum. This small, informal museum, run by the state's tribal-research institute, provides a glimpse of the traditions and daily lives of many of Orissa's 62 tribes. Set back in a garden, several thatched-roof huts in various styles house jewelry, ornaments, weapons, figurines, dresses, and other everyday objects. Many of the items are still in use, but some are being phased out as the modern world seeps in. ✉ *Tribal Research and Training Institute, National Hwy. No. 5, CRPF Sq.,* ☎ *674/403649.* 🎫 *Free.* 🕙 *Mon.–Sat. 10–5; closed 2nd Sat. of month.*

Vaital Temple. This 8th-century structure near the Bindusagar tank is one of the area's earlier temples. Unlike others in Bhubaneswar, it's devoted to tantric goddesses, and its two-story, barrel-shaped roof shows the influence of South Indian architecture. Bring a flashlight, if possible, to see the macabre carvings inside.

DINING AND LODGING

$$ ✕ **Chandini.** The name means canopy, and in this elegant restaurant an
★ antique *chandini* is suspended from the center of the ceiling. Paintings of Rajput heroes adorn the walls, along with old daggers and *jharokahs,* bay-window frames of carved stone. The kitchen serves delicious, somewhat small portions of Indian cuisine, from tangy, light tandoori dishes to richly gravied meats. Try the traditional Orissan *dahi machli,* Bay of Bengal fish cooked in creamy yogurt sauce. ✉ *The Oberoi, C.B. 1, Nayapalli,* ☎ *674/440890. AE, DC, MC, V. Closed Mon.; no lunch.*

$$ ✕ **Executive-Swosti.** This cozy restaurant is a great place to sample traditional Orissan fare. With a few hours' advance notice, the chef will prepare specialties such as *santula* (mixed vegetables in coconut sauce) and dahi machli. For dessert, a rich square of *gajar ka halwa* (carrot halvah) is buttery, sweet, and divine. Brown leather and mirrors create a dark, 1980s ambience, but it's brightened by green-and-white gingham linens and friendly service. The kitchen also serves Chinese and Continental food. ✉ *Hotel Swosti, 103 Janpath,* ☎ *674/404395. AE, DC, MC, V.*

$ ✕ **Cooks' Kitchen.** Two young locals decided to open this very simple upstairs eatery based on the tremendous popularity of their tiny fast-food stand downstairs. The good selection of Indian and Chinese food includes *paneer pasanda,* chunks of curdled cheese with a zesty stuffing and a thick tomato sauce. ✉ *260 Bapuji Nagar,* ☎ *674/530025. No credit cards.*

$ ✕ **Dawat.** Once your eyes adjust to the darkness, you'll find yourself in a small dining room with white stucco walls and royal-blue tablecloths. Locals and travelers both like Dawat for its slightly more upscale (by Bhubaneswar standards) atmosphere and for its Chinese and good, reasonably priced Indian fare. Try the vegetable *dopiaza,* a spicy mix of fresh vegetables cooked *al dente.* ✉ *620 Sahid Nagar,* ☎ *674/507027. No credit cards.*

$ ✕ **Govinda.** After your temple tour, take a taxi or auto-rickshaw to the massively popular International Hare Krishna temple's in-house eatery, known for its simple, hygienic, strictly vegetarian meals served on metal thali trays that allow you to sample several dishes at once. Remember that this is a religious place, not a bona fide restaurant: Leave your shoes at the entrance gate and prepare to eat with your hands. ✉ *Iskon Temple, National Hwy. No. 5, near The Oberoi,* ☎ *674/554283. No credit cards.*

$ ✕ **Hare Krishna.** You won't find any onions, garlic, or oil in the tasty fare at this popular upstairs restaurant; it observes the strictest culinary rules of the Hare Krishna sect. Cool (it's known for its air-conditioning) and decidedly dark, the dining room has mirrored walls and barely lit lamps. A single green bulb spotlights the charming fountain at the front of the room—a sculpture of Shiva emerging from rocky Mt. Kailas with the Ganges River flowing out of his hair. Try the vegetables sautéed in spicy tomato gravy or "*Makhan chor* delight" (grated cheese and carrots simmered in a mild tomato gravy). Finish with *kheer* (sweet rice and milk pudding). ✉ *Lalchand Market Complex, Station Sq.,* ☎ *674/503188. MC, V.*

$ ✕ **Venus Inn.** The menu in this age-old popular upstairs dining hall offers an endless variety of *dosas* (South Indian stuffed crepes) and *uttappams* (South Indian–style pizzas). Try the *rawa masala sada* dosa, stuffed with a slightly salty-and-sweet grain mixture, or the butter coconut uttappam, an Orissan specialty. A small, dark room filled with blue Formica-topped tables, this place is best suited for a quick, hearty lunch or snack rather than a lingering dinner. ✉ *217 Bapuji Nagar,* ☎ *674/531738. No credit cards.*

$$$ **Garden Inn.** This centrally located hotel is among the best in Bhubaneswar. Impressively designed to feel like an elegant garden, the three-story beige stucco building is fronted by stately pillars and a large terrace topped with a profusion of magenta bougainvillea. The window-lined lobby and hallways are sunny, and filled with leafy plants in terra-cotta pots. The rooms, contemporary in style, are decorated with Orissan-print bedspreads in dark greens and maroons; deluxe rooms look out over the central courtyard. Friendly service ensures a comfortable stay. ✉ *112 Kharvel Nagar, Janpath, Bhubaneswar 751001,* ☎ *674/514120,* FAX *674/504254. 61 rooms, 6 suites. Restaurant, bar, coffee shop, pool, beauty salon, 2 tennis courts, sauna, exercise room, dry cleaning, laundry service, business services, meeting rooms, travel services. AE, DC, MC, V.*

$$$ ★ **The Oberoi.** At this handsome two-story hotel, the most expensive in town, the lobby's lights are tucked inside huge, brass temple bells, and the balcony is mounted on sandstone pillars and guarded by stone lions. Even at full occupancy, the common areas have a peaceful air. The rooms, overlooking either the pool or extensive landscaped gardens, have attractive, modern teak furnishings complemented by Orissan hand-loomed fabrics, brass lamps, and framed prints of Bhubaneswar's temples. The only drawback is that the hotel is 10 km (6 mi) from the central part of New Town and even farther from the temples. ✉ *C.B. 1, Nayapalli, Bhubaneswar 751013,* ☎ *674/440890,* FAX *674/440898. 64 rooms, 6 suites. 2 restaurants, bar, pool, 2 tennis courts, jogging, baby-sitting, dry cleaning, laundry service, business services, meeting rooms, travel services. AE, DC, MC, V.*

$$ **Sishmo.** A giant replica of the wheel at the Sun Temple, Konark, reminds you that you're in the city of temples. Rooms have all the conveniences, from cable TV to minibar; ask for one on a higher floor so you get at least a glimpse of the many temples dotting the skyline. The large lobby is quiet and comfortable, setting the tone for a relaxing stay. ✉ *86/A-1 Gautam Nagar, Bhubaneswar 751014,* ☎ *674/433600 or 674/433601,* FAX *674/433351. 64 rooms, 8 suites. 2 restaurants, bar, coffee shop, laundry service, business services, travel services. AE, MC, V.*

$ **Swosti.** Friendly and well run, the Swosti offers efficient, courteous service and reasonable rates. The cozy lobby is decorated with Orissan pata chitra (highly detailed temple paintings). The building is on one of Bhubaneswar's main thoroughfares, close to the train station; for maximum quiet, ask for a room in the back. All of the good-sized rooms are clean, with plain, contemporary decor; most have bathtubs. ✉ *103 Janpath, Bhubaneswar 751001,* ☎ *674/404178 or 674/404397,* FAX *674/407524. 53 rooms, 3 suites. 2 restaurants, bar, laundry service, meeting rooms, travel services. AE, DC, MC, V.*

$ **Bhubaneswar.** Many of the budget hotels on Cuttack Road rent rooms for around Rs. 120. This one is clean and friendly, offering fan-cooled rooms with private baths. The small dining room serves reasonable Indian fare and some European dishes. To get here from the train station, exit on the side opposite the town center (east) and walk south. Bhubaneswar Hotel is about 200 yards south on the right side. ✉ *Cuttack Rd., Bhubaneswar 751001,* ☎ *674/416977. 15 rooms. Restaurant. No credit cards.*

$ **Kalinga Ashok.** The lobby of this government-operated hotel is full of Orissan touches, including a miniature replica of Konark's chariot temple tucked in the corner. Room furnishings are slightly worn but comfortable, with dark carpeting and coordinating drapes and bedspreads with large floral designs. ✉ *Gautam Nagar, Bhubaneswar 751014,* ☎ *674/431055 or 674/431056,* FAX *674/432001. 58 rooms, 6 suites. 2 restaurants, bar, laundry service, meeting rooms, travel services. AE, DC, MC, V.*

$ ☐ **Prachi.** The modest rooms in this boxy, three-story hotel lack its lobby's Orissan touches, bearing instead a simple, slightly worn Western decor of dark-wood furniture and plain carpeting in pea green or orange-brown. The standard rooms tend to be stuffy; ask for a deluxe room overlooking the pool and for a bathroom with a tub. ✉ *6 Janpath, Bhubaneswar 751001,* ☎ *674/502689,* FAX *674/503287. 55 rooms, 6 suites. 2 restaurants, pool, beauty salon, health club, laundry service, meeting rooms, travel services. AE, DC, MC, V.*

NIGHTLIFE AND THE ARTS

The Arts

Odissi, the classical dance form native to Orissa, is perhaps the most lyrical style of Indian dance, flowing with graceful gestures and postures. Watching a performance is like seeing the sculpted dancers on the Sun Temple at Konark (☞ South to the Bay of Bengal, *below*) spring suddenly to life. In addition to classical Odissi, folk and tribal dances are still performed during festivals throughout the state; the **Konark Dance Festival,** in December, features the best of Odissi and other dance forms. Other than festivals, there are no regular cultural programs here. For information, contact the Orissa Department of Tourism (☞ Bhubaneswar A to Z, *below*) or the College of Dance, Drama, and Music, near Rabindra Mandap.

Nightlife

Most people congregate in hotel bars for a nightcap or a post-sightseeing beer. The bar at the **Oberoi** (☞ *above*) is a smart place to relax. The **Hotel Swosti** (☞ *above*) is a good informal option if you're in the center of town. For a local place with a mixed clientele in the evening, try the dimly lit bar in the **Hotel Pushpak** (✉ Cuttack Rd., ☎ 675/408371).

SHOPPING

Bhubaneswar's main shopping area is **Capital Market,** along the central stretch of Raj Path. Several good fabric and handicrafts shops, including the two government emporiums, are in the Tower Market shopping complex off the eastern side of Raj Path. All along Raj Path are stalls selling everything from bananas to bedcovers, mostly wares for locals; most are open daily from around 6 AM to 10 PM.

Kalamandir (✉ 3 Western Tower Market Bldg., ☎ 674/530596) is one of the largest fabric and clothing shops in eastern India; it stocks traditional Orissan textiles as well as styles from all over India. **Kalinga Art Palace** (✉ Plot 2132/4323, Nageswar Tangi, ☎ 674/51454) specializes in tribal artwork, with a notably large and high-quality collection of brass-wire dhokra, both new and antique. **Odissika** (✉ 265 Lewis Rd., ☎ 674/433314) has a host of stone carvings, terra-cotta objects, dhokra, and other authentic Orissan handicrafts. **Orissan State Handloom Weaver's Cooperative Society (Boyanika)** (✉ Western Tower Market Bldg., Hall 2, Ashok Nagar, ☎ no phone) has lovely saris, bedcovers, and fabrics in various Orissan styles and textures. **Sudarshan Arts and Crafts Village** (✉ CB-5, Nayapalli, ☎ 674/402052) is a teaching center for stone-carving, where you can stroll through the small yard and watch young artisans squatting in the shade chiseling away at 10 different kinds of stone. **Utkalika** (✉ Orissa State Handicrafts Emporium, 1 Eastern Tower Market Bldg., Ashok Nagar, ☎ 674/530187), the government's fixed-price emporium, has a great selection of every type of Orissan handicraft.

SOUTH TO THE BAY OF BENGAL

The countryside around Bhubaneswar is lush with rice paddies so green they seem to glow, as well as coconut, mango, banana, and cashew trees. These verdant stretches are punctuated with tiny villages of mud huts with thatched roofs, their dry brown walls decorated with traditional white paintings. Konark, near the coast, is renowned for its extraordinary, half-ruined Sun Temple, and Puri's Jagannath Temple is one of Hinduism's holiest shrines. The villages of Raghurajpur and Pipli are known for their craftwork. Dhauli, the hill associated with Ashoka the Great, has a gentle Buddhist pagoda; and Gopalpur-on-Sea is a beach destination.

Konark

❷ *64 km (40 mi) southeast of Bhubaneswar*

The sleepy town of Konark is home to one of India's most fabulous temples. The village exists for the temple, earning its income entirely from tourism via souvenir shops, food stalls, and basic restaurants.

★ Legend shrouds the **Sun Temple,** or "Black Pagoda," so called because of the dark patina that has covered it over the centuries. Built by King Narasimha in the 13th century in the shape of the sun god Surya's chariot—probably as much as a monument to Narasimha and his victory over the Muslims as to Surya—it is a wonder of architecture and engineering. Today, only half the main temple and the audience hall remain to suggest the Sun Temple's original shape, but the complex once had a dancing hall, an audience hall, and a tremendous tower that soared to 227 ft; by 1869 the tower had fallen to ruin, and the audience hall had to be filled with stone slabs and sealed off to prevent its collapse. The temple's location on coastal sand (it's not quite coastal; the sea has since receded 3 km [2 mi] from here) is majestic, but the briny air and the softness of the underlying dunes have taken their toll.

The Sun Temple was designed in the form of a chariot, with 24 wheels pulled by seven straining horses. Every last one of its surfaces is intricately carved with some of the most fantastic sculpture in India: platforms, horses, colossal mythical animals, whimsical depictions of daily life, images of war, erotic pairings. Every structural feature is significant; the chariot's seven horses represent the seven days of the week, the 24 wheels are the 24 fortnights of the Indian year, and the eight spokes of each wheel are the eight *pahars* into which the ancients divided day and night.

Try to arrive between 7 and 8 AM, before the busloads of pilgrims and other tourists show up. The Archaeological Survey of India provides guides, but ask to see an identification badge, as many less-informed freelance guides are also eager to take you around. The going rate is Rs. 20 per person. A tourist-information officer at the **Yatri Nivas** (☎ 6758/35820 and 6758/35821), an Orissa Tourism Development Corporation (OTDC) guest house just before the temple, is on duty Monday through Saturday from 10 to 5 (except the second Saturday of each month), and the guest-house staff can help travelers 24 hours a day.

Any of the tour operators and travel agencies in Bhubaneswar (☞ Bhubaneswar A to Z, *below*) can arrange a day trip to Konark for you, but you can usually get a better price by simply cutting a deal with a local taxi driver. The trip takes about an hour and a half. ✉ *Off Puri Rd.* 🎟 *Rs. 5.* ⏲ *Daily sunrise–sunset.*

Puri

❸ *60 km (36 mi) south of Bhubaneswar, 35 km (21 mi) south west of Konark*

The coastal town of Puri is heavily visited, containing as it does one of Hinduism's most sacred sites, the **Jagannath Temple.** Vast and beautiful, the temple is strictly off-limits to non-Hindus, who can glimpse it only from a distance; even the late Prime Minister Indira Gandhi was denied entrance, as she had married a non-Hindu. Still, it's fascinating to watch the pilgrims thrust their way to the temple through the crowds of vendors and vehicles that jam Puri's main street. Puri attracts even more crushing hordes during Rath Yatra (the midsummer "car" festival, involving processions of deities on carts), one of the most spectacular of India's temple fairs.

Although Puri is touted as a beach getaway, it's gotten rather seedy. Locals sometimes use the beach as a cat does a sandbox. If you're looking for some clean, uncrowded sand in Orissa, hold out for Gopalpur-on-Sea.

Lodging

$$–$$$ 🏨 **Mayfair Beach Resort.** This vaguely New Mexico–style building with burnt-orange stucco walls is softened by lots of green vegetation. Most of the rooms have balconies that look over rooftops to the sea, just 300 ft away, and are cozily furnished with bric-a-brac. Meals are served on a patio, which is also a pleasant place to relax and have a beer. ✉ *Chakratirtha Rd., Puri 752002,* ☎ *6752/24041 or 6752/27800,* FAX *6752/24242. 34 rooms. 2 restaurants, pool, travel services. AE, MC, V.*

$ 🏨 **South Eastern Railway Hotel.** Sometimes called the BNR Hotel, this is the only designated Heritage Hotel in Orissa. With its Raj ambience and relaxed pace (the SILENCE BETWEEN 2 AND 4 PM sign ensures you an undisturbed siesta), it harks back to an age gone by. High ceilings and sea breezes keep the place pleasantly cool; here, as at the Mayfair, you're about 300 ft from the beach. There's even a billiards room where you can shoot a few frames at leisure. Inquire about off-season discounts. ✉ *Chakratirtha Rd., Puri 752002,* ☎ *6752/22063 and 6752/23006,* FAX *6752/23005. 34 rooms. Restaurant, billiards, laundry service, travel services. MC, V.*

Raghurajpur

★ ❹ *16 km (10 mi) north of Puri, 44 km (27 mi) south of Bhubaneswar*

Less than two hours' drive from Bhubaneswar, the **artisans' village** of Raghurajpur is a must-see. Every dwelling in this idyllic village set back from the main road is owned by a skilled artisan, and the art they produce—stone and wood carvings, pata chitra, tala patra (intricately etched and painted palm leaves)—is worth a trip in itself. If you're interested, the craftspeople will demonstrate their processes. The pata chitra artists, for example, do everything the old-fashioned way, from the preparatory rubbing of cloth with tamarind-seed gum and stones to executing razor-fine strokes of color with dyes made from plants and crushed stones. True, the prices are raised for travelers, but you can bargain them down to lower than you'd pay anywhere else; just expect to pay in rupees. Most artisans welcome customers daily from around 9 to 1 and 3 to 6.

Pipli

❺ *16 km (10 mi) southeast of Bhubaneswar, 28 km (17 mi) north of Puri*

The little village of Pipli is famous throughout India for its brightly colored **appliqué work.** Dozens of shops line both sides of the main street, each crammed with piles of cheery wall hangings, bedspreads, lamp shades, bags, beach umbrellas, and more in patchworks of bright greens, yellows, blues, and reds. You can watch the artisans sew in some of the shops.

Dhauli

★ ❻ *6 km (4 mi) southwest of Bhubaneswar*

It was from the top of this hill that India's legendary king, Ashoka the Great, looked down, in 272 BC, over the verdant countryside littered with bodies after his armies invaded what was then Kalinga. Overcome with horror, Ashoka underwent a transformation: He abandoned his drive to conquer, began to practice Buddhism, and went on to incite a moral and spiritual revolution throughout Orissa and the rest of India. The spot of **Ashoka's vantage point and conversion** is marked by the carving of an elephant emerging from a rock—said to be the oldest rock-cut sculpture in India (3rd century BC)—symbolizing the birth of Buddha and the emergence of Buddhism. Also carved into the stone are the Ashokan edicts in which the once-ruthless warrior declared that all men are his children.

A bit farther up the hill is the **Shanti Stupa,** a Buddhist peace pagoda built jointly by Japanese and Indian groups in 1972. Visible from most points in Bhubaneswar, this striking, white-domed building, topped with several umbrella-like protrusions, resembles a massive alien crustacean from below; moving closer, you can sense how beautiful and peaceful it is. The view from here is lovely: the Daya River curving through the green rice paddies and cashew trees. ✉ *Puri Rd.*

Gopalpur-on-Sea

❼ *178 km (110 mi) southwest of Bhubaneswar*

Gopalpur-on-Sea, Orissa's most popular beach resort is actually just a small fishing village with a few hotels scattered along the shore. The town itself has one street, which in turn has a few shops to satisfy the locals. The beach is long; you don't have to walk far to find solitude.

To get here, take a three-hour train ride from Bhubaneswar to Berhampur (164 km, or 102 mi, south of the city), then transfer to an auto-rickshaw (Rs. 80) for the 14-km (9-mi) ride southeast.

Lodging

$$$ 🏨 **Oberoi Palm Beach.** While the Oberoi is the best hotel in Gopalpur-on-Sea, don't expect the kind of Oberoi you experienced in Calcutta or Hyderabad. All is a bit worn here, and the staff may not be lickety-split. Rooms in this U-shaped building face the courtyard; those on the ground floor are susceptible to looks from passers-by. The dining room serves good Indian and Continental fare, but tends to smell like curry. A lawn, with games for children, separates the hotel from the beach. ✉ *Jagmohan Singh Rd., Gopalpur-on-Sea 761002,* ☎ *680/282021,* FAX *680/282300. 18 rooms. Restaurant, pool. AE, DC, MC, V.*

$ 🏨 **Holiday Home.** The location is excellent—just across the road from the beach and minutes from the center of town (such as it is). Rooms offer no more pampering than a bed and a table and chairs, but they're mopped down every day and—despite gaping holes, exposed pipes, and falling plaster—the bathrooms are functional. The overhead fans are hardly necessary with the constant sea breeze cooling the rooms. The staff is helpful and friendly. Meals can be served on request. ✉ *Gopalpur-on-Sea 761002,* ☎ *680/282049. 18 rooms. No credit cards. Restaurant.*

BHUBANESWAR A TO Z

Arriving and Departing

By Plane

Bhubaneswar Airport is about 5 km (3 mi) from the center of town. **Indian Airlines** (☎ 674/406472 or 674/530593; airport, ☎ 674/401084 or 141) flies to Bhubaneswar from Delhi, Calcutta, Madras, and Hyderabad.

The trip between the airport and city center takes about 15 to 20 minutes. Most hotels provide free **shuttle service** if you give them your flight information in advance. White Ambassador tourist **taxis** wait outside the terminal; fares are theoretically fixed, but be sure to agree on one before setting out. The fare to a central hotel should be around Rs. 75; to the Oberoi, slightly farther, about Rs. 110.

By Train

Bhubaneswar is on the Calcutta-to-Hyderabad/Madras line. The trip takes about eight hours from Calcutta on the overnight train, 20 hours from Hyderabad, and 25 hours from Madras. Suggestions from the staff at the train station's tourist-information center should be taken with a grain of salt; they'll push high-priced hotels from which they get commissions. Auto-rickshaws stand ready to meet all trains. The main exit, where the reservation office is located, is on the west side (on your right, coming from Calcutta). If you want to go directly to Cuttack Road, where the cheaper hotels are, take the east exit.

Getting Around

Hiring a car and driver for a half or full day is not expensive, and is the most convenient way to get around the city—you avoid having to haggle over fares with taxi or auto-rickshaw drivers.

By Auto-Rickshaw

Auto-rickshaws are cheaper and slower than taxis, but quicker through heavy traffic. Apply the same fare rules as you would for taxis.

By Cycle-Rickshaw

For short distances, cycle-rickshaws are easiest. A horde of them will await you at the train station; negotiate a fare with your pedaler before he pushes off.

By Hired Car with Driver

You can hire a car and driver from a travel agency (☞ *below*), but taxis willingly rent themselves out for half or a full day. When negotiating with the driver, specify which places you plan to visit, as your itinerary, plus the length of time, will determine the fare. Four hours of local sightseeing should cost about Rs. 250 in a non-air-conditioned Ambassador car and around Rs. 700 with air-conditioning. For shorter excursions covering more than 10 km (6 mi) per hour, figure about Rs. 3 per km (Rs. 7 for a car with A/C), with a halt charge of Rs. 10 per hour.

By Taxi

Taxis in Orissa don't have meters, so you have to dicker for every ride. Ask your hotel for the appropriate taxi fare and then negotiate.

Contacts and Resources

Currency Exchange

Most Western-style hotels will change money for their guests. You can also cash traveler's checks at the various national banks in Bhubaneswar; try the main branch of the **State Bank of India** (✉ near Market Building, Raj Path). Banking hours are weekdays, 10 to 2, and sometimes Saturday 10 to noon.

Guided Tours

A private tour guide can seriously enhance your sightseeing, especially with such artistically rich and potentially foreign monuments as Orissa's temples. The most knowledgeable and English-proficient guides are those trained by the Government of India Tourist Office; you can hire one through the OTDC or the Government of India Tourist Office (☞ *below*) for around Rs. 250 per half-day and Rs. 500 for a full day (eight hours). Overnight stays cost an additional Rs. 800 for the guide's food and accommodation.

Travel Agencies

The **Orissa Tourism Development Corporation (OTDC)** (✉ Panthanivas, Old Block, Lewis Rd., Bhubaneswar, ☎ 674/431515), has reliable cars and drivers and conducts several good tours of Bhubaneswar and the whole region, all at reasonable rates. **Swosti Travels** (✉ 103 Janpath, ☎ 674/518257, FAX 674/407524) is a well-established local company with strong experience in the region. You can also try **Mercury Travels** (✉ The Oberoi, Nayapalli, ☎ 674/440890), which has cars and drivers at decent rates. **Sita World Travels** (✉ 14A Bapuji Nagar, Janpath, ☎ 674/531408) arranges trips in and around Bhubaneswar. **Nabagunjara Travels Pvt. Ltd.** (✉ Balighar, 10, Rathandandra Rd., Bhubaneswar, ☎ 674/431659/759; ✉ 9, S. N. Banerjee Rd., Calcutta, ☎ 33/244-0802), in business since 1982, leads tours in Orissa.

Visitor Information

The **Orissa Department of Tourism** (✉ 5 Jayadev Marg, near Panthanivas, Bhubaneswar 751002, ☎ 674/431299; Bhubaneswar airport, ☎ 674/404006; Bhubaneswar train station, ☎ 674/530715) is the best source of information on the state. The main office is open Monday through Saturday from 10 to 5 (closed second Sat. of month). The **Government of India Tourist Office** (✉ B-21, B. J. B. Nagar, Kalpana Area, Bhubaneswar 751014, ☎ 674/432203; Bhubaneswar airport, ☎ no phone) is also helpful; they're available weekdays from 10 to 5.

14 CALCULTTA

Calcutta is India's best city for walkers, with streets that tell stories. Old mansions dripping with moss and spotted with mildew recall a rich mixture of foreign influence, particularly that of the founding British, and local affluence. Known at once for its Bengali heritage and cosmopolitan outlook, Calcutta is the creative capital of India, promoting art, music, and drama and drawing the best from performers and their fans. More than its louder urban counterparts, Calcutta will surprise you with its warmth and hospitality.

NOTHING CAN PREPARE A YOU for Calcutta. As the birthplace of an empire and the home of the late Mother Teresa, as a playground for the rich and a haven for the destitute, as a wellspring of creative energy and a center for Marxist agitation, Calcutta almost dares people to make sense of it. Whether it repels you or seduces you, Calcutta will impress itself upon you. To understand India today and learn from it, a trip to Calcutta is vital.

By Nigel Fisher

Updated by Modhurima Sinha

In 1690, Job Charnock, an agent for the British East India Company, leased the villages of Sutanati, Gobindpur, and Kalikutta and formed a trading post to supply his firm. Legend has it that Charnock had won the hearts of Bengalis when he married a local widow, thus saving her from *sati* (the custom that calls for a widow to throw herself on her husband's funeral pyre). Through Charnock's venture, the British gained a foothold in what had been the Sultanate of Delhi under the Moguls, and the directors of the East India Company became Indian *zamindars* (landowners) for the first time. It was here, as traders and landowners, that British entrepreneurs and adventurers began what would amount to the conquest of India and the establishment of the British Raj. More than any other city in India, Calcutta is tied to the evolution and disintegration of the British presence.

Calcutta is the capital of the state of West Bengal, which borders Bangladesh (formerly East Bengal). The Bengali people—animated, laconic, intellectual, spirited, argumentative, anarchic, imaginative, and creative—have dominated this city and made it the soul of India for more than 150 years. Among the first to react to the intellectual and political stimuli of the West, they have produced many of India's most respected filmmakers, writers, scientists, musicians, dancers, and philosophers. Having embraced 19th-century European humanism, such Bengalis as the poet Rabindranath Tagore and others revived their indigenous culture and made the first organized efforts to oust the British. Emotions here ran high early on, and agitation in Bengal broke away from what would later be called Gandhian politics to choose terrorism—one reason the British moved their capital from Calcutta to Delhi in 1911.

Calcutta remained cosmopolitan and prosperous throughout the British period. But after Independence and Partition, in 1947, trouble began when the world's center of jute processing and distribution (Calcutta) was separated from its actual production center (the eastern Bengali hinterland). For Calcutta and the new East Pakistan, Partition was equivalent to separating the fingers of an industry from the thumb. Natural disasters—commonly cyclones and droughts but also, as in 1937, earthquakes—had long sent millions to Calcutta in search of shelter and sustenance; after Partition a wave of 4 million political refugees compounded and complicated the pressure. Conflict with China and Pakistan created millions more throughout the 1960s, and Pakistan's 1971 military crackdown alone sent 10 million temporary refugees into the city from what would soon become Bangladesh. By the mid-1970s, Calcutta was widely seen as the ultimate urban disaster. Riddled with disease and squalor, plagued by garbage and decay, the heart of the British Raj, the Paris of Asia, had quickly and dramatically collapsed.

Or had it? Calcutta's entire metropolitan district covers over 426 square km (264 square mi) and is home to over 12 million people. It comprises two municipal corporation areas (Calcutta and Howrah), 32 municipalities, 62 nonmunicipal urban centers, and more than 500 villages, and it has not collapsed. As one local put it, "Calcutta is full of challenges, but there is hope and even fun in meeting those challenges." Today's traveler may actually notice more poverty in Bombay than in the city more often associated with human strife. Calcutta remains open, smiling, and thoughtful: Amid the difficulties there is dignity, and amid the crises there are ideas.

Name Changes

Many streets in Calcutta have been renamed in a rather haphazard way. Though some maps and street signs have only the new names, you're more likely to see just the old or both. Taxis and rickshaws use the names interchangeably, but old names are still favored, as most of the new names are ridiculously long and obscure. The most important name changes: Chowringhee Road is now Jawaharlal Nehru (J. L. Nehru) Road; Ballygunge Circular is now Pramathesh Barua Sarani; Bowbazar is now B. B. Ganguly Street; Harington Street is now Ho Chi Minh Sarani; Lansdowne Road is now Sarat Bose Road; Lower Circular Road is now A. J. C. Bose Road; Rippon Street is now Muzaffar Ahmed Street; and Theater Road is now Shakespeare Sarani. A complete list is available at the Government of India Tourist Office or in *Calcutta: Gateway to the East.*

Pleasures and Pastimes

Dining

Like no other city in India, Calcutta has a tradition of dining out. Ironically, Bengali food itself was long noticeably absent from the city's restaurants, but this has changed in recent years. Bengali cuisine is highly varied in flavor and has both vegetarian and nonvegetarian strands, with fish and seafood, particularly prawns, figuring heavily. Two popular Bengali dishes are *macher jhol* (fish stew) and *chingri malai* curry (prawns cooked in coconut milk and spices). Note that Thursday in Calcutta is dry and meatless—no alcohol or red meat is served in most establishments. The unique cuisine that has developed in Calcutta since the influx of the Moguls in the 16th century is called Calcutta-Mughlai and remains the most common food in Calcutta today—it's what you'll see in carts and stalls throughout the city. Staples include *champ* (chicken or mutton cooked slowly in large, thick-cast open pans), *birianis* (rice-and-meat dishes), and tandoori items, none of which resembles its namesake in places such as Oudh or Hyderabad. From roadside vendors, the most popular item is the Calcutta roll, in which seasoned meats and chutneys are wrapped in thick *parathas* (rich Indian breads) with onions and sometimes even eggs. Not to be missed are Bengali sweets, which fill the life of every native: Sweet shops are everywhere, and the variety of their fare—from *payash* (fine-quality rice cooked in thickened milk) to *gokul pitha* (coconut and solidified milk balls, fried and dipped in sugar syrup) is beyond tempting. Two unsurpassed goodies are *rosogollas* (balls of cottage cheese soaked in sugar syrup), associated specifically with Calcutta, and the classic Bengali *misti doi* (sweetened yogurt).

Lodging

Calcutta's top few hotels are luxury establishments that meet international standards and then some. A luxury tax of 22% is added to your bill.

Shopping

All of India tempts the shopper here: a vast array of goods arrive in Calcutta from around the subcontinent, including crafts from Bangladesh and Assam. Prices are tantalizingly inexpensive. The irritants are touts, hustlers, and the instant friends who approach you claiming they have nothing to sell and later getting openly ticked off if you don't buy their goods. Learn to dicker: Everything purchased from a roadside vendor is negotiable, even new paperbacks at a sidewalk bookstall.

Some of the most interesting crafts in West Bengal are brightly painted terra-cotta figurines and bas-reliefs, as well as other pottery items. *Dhokra* are cast figures made of clay and metal. Shells, bell metal, and soapstone are other media used in popular Bengali trinkets and figurines. Calcutta's bazaars and shops sell all kinds of textiles, including embroideries. With its longtime traditions of literacy and cosmopolitanism, Calcutta is also a good place to restock your English-language reading material.

Street Life

The vibrant interplay between survival and extinction is unusually manifest in Calcutta: The city throbs with a tenacious grasping for life. You feel it in the barrage on your senses, especially those of sound, smell, and sight. It is exhilarating, exhausting, and occasionally disquieting. Calcutta imposes culture shock—pedestrians scurry out of the way of horn-blaring vehicles swerving to avoid another beat-up vehicle and scraping past the rib-cage of a rickshaw-wallah (person who pulls a rickshaw). The frequent political processions can get old, but a walk through the old bookstalls on College Street will leave you rejuvenated. You will have a sense of achievement at having survived Calcutta. There is no city like it in the world.

EXPLORING CALCUTTA

Calcutta and Howrah (also written as Haora) straddle the Hooghly River with Calcutta on the east side, Howrah on the west. Across the Hooghly from Calcutta's old quarter, the Howrah district—which holds Calcutta's massive train station—is a constantly expanding suburb. On the eastern side of town is Salt Lake City, a planned, spotlessly clean residential community.

In Calcutta itself, the Howrah Bridge spills into Bara Bazaar, the vibrant wholesale market area that anchors the city's commerce. North Calcutta includes Bara Bazaar and Calcutta University and extends to the distant neighborhood of Chitpur and the Jain Temple in Tala. The heart of Central Calcutta remains B.B.D. Bagh (Binoy-Badel-Dinesh Bagh, formerly Dalhousie Square), where commerce and government have been concentrated since British times. Central Calcutta also holds the expansive Maidan park, the crowded bazaar at New Market, and the upmarket shops and restaurants on Park Street. At the south end of the Maidan are the Victoria Memorial and Calcutta's racecourse. South Calcutta has the Kali Temple and the late Mother Teresa's hospice in Kalighat and the National Library and zoo in Alipore. To the east is the Science City complex, comprising a huge auditorium and museum with scientific and educational exhibits.

Great Itineraries

At just over 300 years of age, Calcutta is a relatively new Indian city. You can breeze through its monuments, buildings, and temples in two or three days. Calcutta does offer something other than buildings, though—its teeming life and ambience. This can wear you down in two days or entice you to stay much longer than your schedule allows.

Numbers in the text correspond to numbers in the margin and on the Calcutta map.

IF YOU HAVE 2 DAYS

If you have only one day in Calcutta, you'll have to be very selective. With two days, start by taking the pulse of the city's heart, **B.B.D. Bagh.**

Take a taxi to the as the Jain **Paresnath Temple,** and from there continue to the eclectic **Marble Palace,** nearby **Nakhoda Mosque,** and **Rabindra Bharati University Museum.** At day's end, cross the **Howrah Bridge** by cab and drive south along the bank of the Hooghly River for a good look back at the city. (Cross back on the Second Hooghly Bridge, or Vivekananda Setu.) The next day, enter the **Maidan** and visit the **Victoria Memorial** and **St. Paul's Cathedral.** Back out on **Chowringhee** (J. L. Nehru Road), amble up to the **Indian Museum.** This plan should leave you time enough for shopping in the late afternoon and early evening in the fabulous, century-old New Market, where everything under the sun is for sale under one roof.

IF YOU HAVE 3 DAYS

You can see most of Calcutta's major sights comfortably in three days. Start by exploring **B.B.D. Bagh,** then take a taxi to **College Street** and walk around for a sense of the city's intellectual energy. Walk from College Street to the **Nakhoda Mosque,** European-style **Marble Palace,** and **Rabindra Bharati University Museum,** with its Bengali-school paintings and Tagore memorabilia. From here it's a short cab ride to the **Paresnath Temple.** Continue on to **Kumartuli** to see artists create clay icons by the river.

The next day, taxi up to the **Belur Math Shrine,** then cross back to the **Dakshineshwar Kali Temple** for a quick overview of Hinduism. Driving south on the east side of the river, cross the **Howrah Bridge** and drive south on Foreshore Road for the best view of Calcutta over the Hooghly. Cross back on the Second Hooghly Bridge. You can now enter the **Maidan** and breathe some fresh air before before visiting the **Victoria Memorial, Fort William,** and the **Eden Gardens.** Finish by treating yourself to some shopping in **New Market.**

On day three, taxi down to **Nirmal Hirday** to visit the late Mother Teresa's first charitable home, then walk over to the famous **Kalighat Kali Temple.** You'll need a cab from here to **St. Paul's Cathedral,** but from the cathedral you can walk to **Chowringhee** and up to the **Indian Museum,** detouring a few blocks to Park Street to read colonial history from the headstones in **South Street Park Cemetery.**

When to Tour Calcutta

The hottest weather arrives in April and grows increasingly stifling through June, when the monsoon season begins. Monsoons run through mid-September and cool Calcutta down, though the occasional downpour means you can expect a soaking or two. Try to come between October and March, when the weather is most temperate. For an extraordinary visit, see Calcutta during the greatest Bengali festival of the year, the Durga Puja (Durga is an incarnation of Kali, Calcutta's patron goddess). Colorful, handmade Hindu idols, sometimes in excess of 20 ft tall, are ceremoniously moved in large processions through the streets for several hours before reaching the river and being immersed in the Hooghly. The pujas (homage; literally, "worship") take place over several days in September and October; confirm the dates beforehand with the tourist office or an Indian travel agent. The rites and processions have an amazing vibrancy, often blending tradition with innovation; some idols even honor contemporary themes such as recent flood victims or the film star of the moment.

North Calcutta

The streets in northern Calcutta are more crowded and narrower than those elsewhere in the city. This—the old village of Sutanuti—is where the Indians lived while the British spread their estates east and south

B.B.D. Bagh, **10**
Belur Math Shrine, **9**
College Street, **1**
Dakshineshwar Kali Temple, **8**
Eden Gardens, **14**
Fort William, **15**
General Post Office, **12**
Howrah Bridge, **5**
Indian Botanical Gardens, **23**
Indian Museum, **19**
Kalighat Kali Temple, **20**
Kumartuli, **7**
Marble Palace, **3**
Nakhoda Mosque, **2**
National Library, **22**
Nirmal Hirday, **21**
Ochterlony Monument, **13**
Paresnath Temple, **6**
Rabindra Bharati University Museum, **4**
St. Paul's Cathedral, **17**
South Park Street Cemetery, **18**
Victoria Memorial, **16**
Writers' Building, **11**

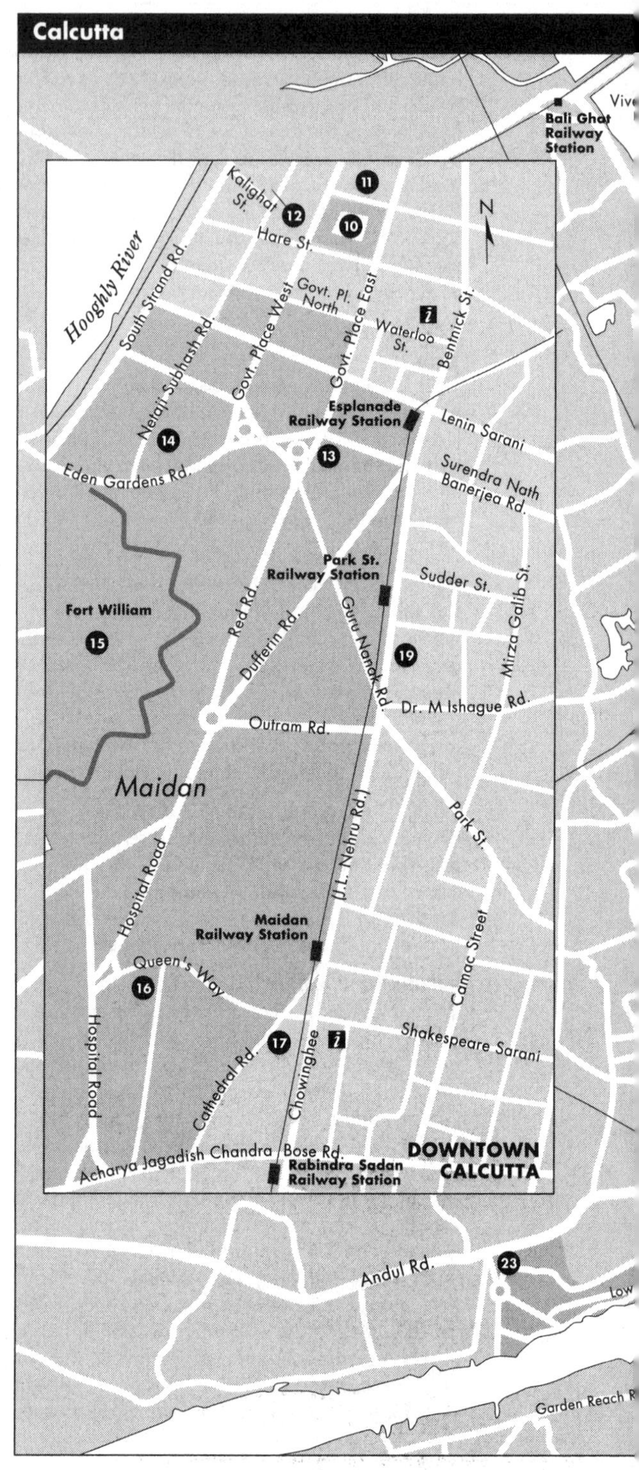

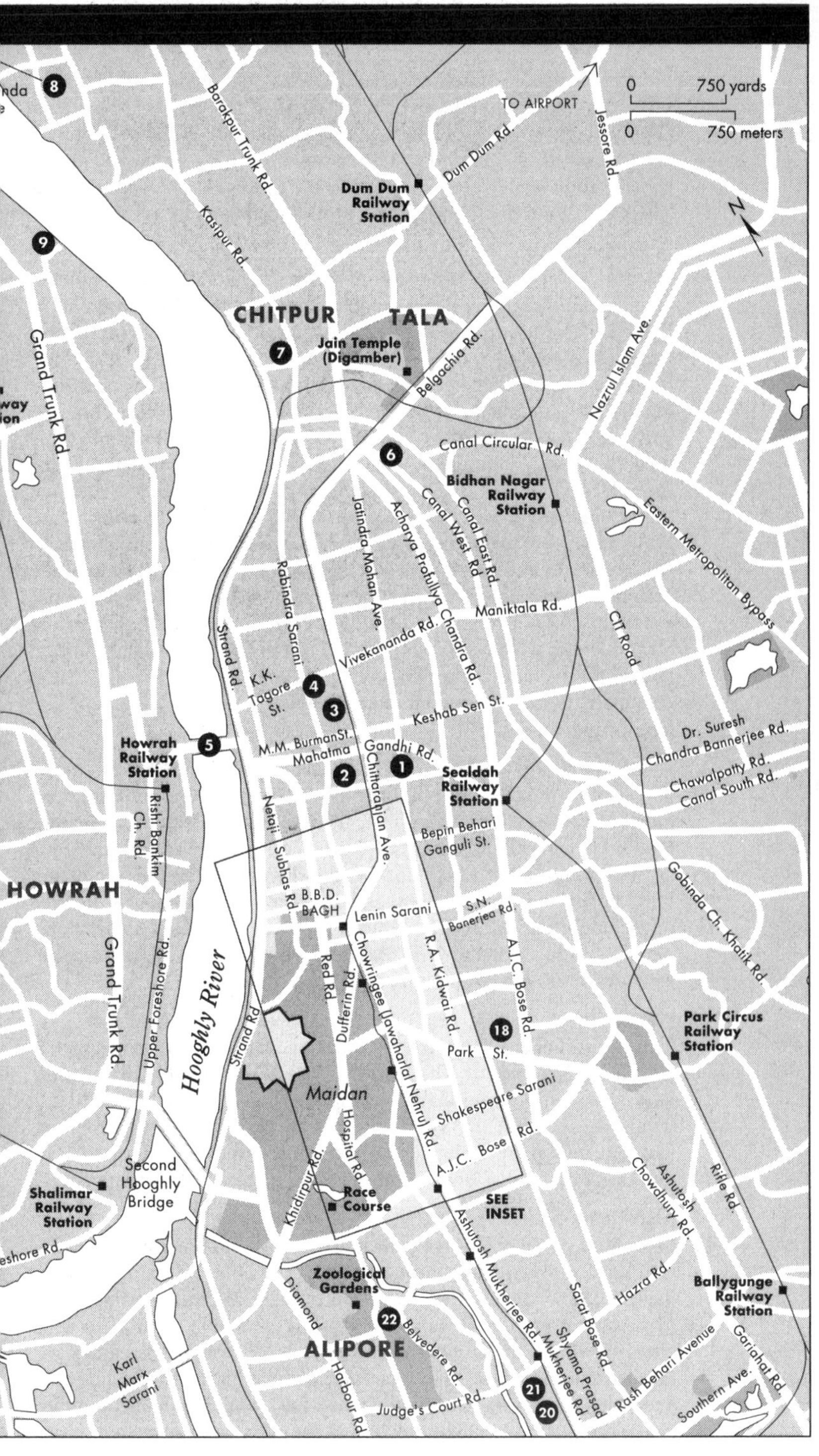

TO AIRPORT
0 750 yards
0 750 meters
Barakpur Trunk Rd.
Kasipur Rd.
Dum Dum Rd.
Dum Dum Railway Station
Jessore Rd.
CHITPUR
TALA
Jain Temple (Digamber)
Belgachia Rd.
Grand Trunk Rd.
Nazrul Islam Ave.
Canal Circular Rd.
Bidhan Nagar Railway Station
Jatindra Mohan Ave.
Acharya Profullya Chandra Rd.
Canal West Rd.
Canal East Rd.
Eastern Metropolitan Bypass
Rabindra Sarani
Maniktala Rd.
CIT Road
Strand Rd.
Vivekananda Rd.
K.K. Tagore St.
Keshab Sen St.
Dr. Suresh Chandra Bannerjee Rd.
Howrah Railway Station
M.M. BurmanSt.
Mahatma Gandhi Rd.
Chittaranjan Ave.
Sealdah Railway Station
Chawalpatty Rd.
Canal South Rd.
Rishi Bankim Ch. Rd.
Netaji Subhas Rd.
Bepin Behari Ganguli St.
HOWRAH
B.B.D. BAGH
Lenin Sarani
S.N. Banerjea Rd.
Gobinda Ch. Khatik Rd.
Grand Trunk Rd.
Upper Foreshore Rd.
Hooghly River
Strand Rd.
Red Rd.
Dufferin Rd.
Chowringee (Jawaharlal Nehru) Rd.
R.A. Kidwai Rd.
A.J.C. Bose Rd.
Park St.
Park Circus Railway Station
Maidan
Hospital Rd.
Shakespeare Sarani
A.J.C. Bose Rd.
Second Hooghly Bridge
Shalimar Railway Station
Khidirpur Rd.
Race Course
SEE INSET
Ashutosh Chowdhury Rd.
Rifle Rd.
eshore Rd.
Zoological Gardens
Ashutosh Mukherjee Rd.
Hazra Rd.
Ballygunge Railway Station
Diamond Harbour Rd.
Belvedere Rd.
Sarat Bose Rd.
ALIPORE
Shyama Prasad Mukherjee Rd.
Rash Behari Avenue
Gariahat Rd.
Karl Marx Sarani
Judge's Court Rd.
Southern Ave.

of Fort William and Dalhousie Square (B.B.D. Bagh). The architecture is charming, reflecting some Italian and Dutch influence.

North Calcutta's attractions are somewhat scattered. You'll need to take taxis at least sporadically. The bazaar areas surrounding Mahatama Gandhi Road are at once intensely commercial and residential; tourists are thin on the ground here, despite the fascinating sights and atmosphere. You may attract some curious stares, but anyone you stop and speak to is bound to be friendly and welcoming.

A Good Tour

Start with a morning coffee at the Indian Coffee House (☞ College Street, *below*), then browse through the bookstalls on **College Street** ①. Walk west, crossing Chittaranjan Avenue, to the huge, sandstone **Nakhoda Mosque** ②, and climb to the top floor for a great view of the bustle in the streets below. Walk back to Chittaranjan Avenue, turn left (north), then left after a few blocks on Muktaram Basu Street—halfway down the block on the left you'll see the **Marble Palace** ③, a melange of international architecture, statues, and furnishings. From the palace it's a short walk north to Tagore Street, where you turn left for the **Rabindra Bharati University Museum** ④ in the poet's former home. Walking further west on Tagore Street brings you to the Hooghly River, with the **Howrah Bridge** ⑤ a block to the south. North and south of the Howrah Bridge along the waterfront is the **wholesale flower market** (☞ Off the Beaten Path, *below*)—before 7 AM. Also in this area is Strand Road, which heads south toward the Second Hooghly Bridge and, in the evening, makes for a delightful riverside stroll in that area. At sunset, both river and city look magical; Calcutta becomes a different town altogether.

A short taxi ride will bring you to the Jain **Paresnath Temple** ⑥, perhaps one of the cleanest buildings in Calcutta. A 30-minute walk or quick cab ride farther north, near the river, is an area called **Kumartuli** ⑦, where thousands of potters fashion clay images of gods and goddesses for Hindu festivals. The **Dakshineshwar Kali Temple** ⑧, a major Hindu pilgrimage site, requires another taxi ride north. Cross the Second Hooghly Bridge to the suburb of Howrah and head south along Belur Road to the **Belur Math Shrine** ⑨, headquarters of the Ramakrishna Mission. Return downtown by taxi.

TIMING

This tour takes the better part of a day and can be very tiring; pack a lunch before you set off. The Marble Palace, Rabindra Bharati museum, Paresnath Temple, and Dakshineshwar Kali Temple each take 30–60 minutes to absorb. Try to sandwich your touring between the rush hours, and remember that the Belur Math Shrine is closed from noon to 3:30 and the Nakhoda Mosque is off-limits for a spell on Friday morning.

Sights to See

❾ **Belur Math Shrine.** This is the headquarters of the Ramakrishna Mission, a reform movement inspired by Ramakrishna Paramahansa, who died in 1886. Having forsaken his privileged Brahmin heritage, Ramakrishna preached the unity of religious faiths and an adherence to altruistic values for all people. His disciple, Swami Vivekananda, established the mission in 1898. The Belur Math Shrine resembles a church, a temple, or a mosque, depending on where you're standing. Somber *aarti* (chants and hymns) are sung in the immense prayer hall every evening; visitors are more than welcome. ✉ *Belur Rd., Howrah (2 km/1 mi south of Second Hooghly Bridge [Vivekananda Setu]).* ⏲ Daily 6:30–noon and 3:30–7:30.

❶ **College Street.** Part of the animated area around Calcutta University, the sidewalks of College Street are stuffed with bookstalls where you just might discover a treasure. The neighborhood establishments here, like the classic **Indian Coffee House** (⊠ 15 Bankin Chatterjee St.), are crowded every night with students and intellectuals. Opposite the coffee house, a huge colonial building houses the university's **Presidency College,** arguably the most prestigious seat of learning in India.

★ ❽ **Dakshineshwar Kali Temple.** Far north along the Hooghly, this 19th-century complex with 13 temples is a major pilgrimage site for devotees of Shiva, Kali, Radha, and Krishna. The variety of temples makes this site a good introduction to the Hindu deities for the uninitiated. It was here that the 19th-century mystic Ramakrishna had the vision that led him to renounce his Brahmin caste and propound altruism and religious unity. His most famous disciple, Swami Vivekananda, went on to be a major force in the intellectual and spiritual growth of Calcutta and founded the Ramakrishna Mission, headquartered in the **Belur Math Shrine** (☞ *above*). Ramakrishna's room here is a museum. ⊠ *P. W. D. Rd., near Second Hooghly Bridge (Vivekananda Setu).* ⊙ *Dawn–10 PM.* 🎫 *Free.*

❺ **Howrah Bridge.** The Howrah train station almost dumps you onto this structure, and the bridge in turn dumps you just north of Bara Bazaar in the heart of old Calcutta. Indeed, it seems more like a bazaar itself than a simple transport link between Howrah and Calcutta. Bordered by thin walkways, the bridge's eight lanes of chaotic traffic bear 2 million people each day in rickshaws, cars, scooters, bicycles, pushcarts, and animal-drawn carts. The web of girders stretches 1,500 ft over the Hooghly.

❼ **Kumartuli.** In this area, countless potters create the millions of clay images that serve as idols during Calcutta's Hindu festival season. ⊠ *Chitpur Rd., between Bidhan Sarani and Jatindra Mohan.*

★ ❸ **Marble Palace.** One of the strangest buildings in Calcutta was the inspiration of Raja Rajendra Mullick Bahadur, a member of Bengal's landed gentry. Mullick built the palace in 1855, making lavish use of Italian marble. It's set behind a lawn cluttered with sculptures of lions, the Buddha, Christopher Columbus, Jesus, the Virgin Mary, and Hindu gods. Near a small granite bungalow (where Mullick's descendants still live), a large pool is home to some exotic birds with large headdresses. The palace has an interior courtyard, complete with a throne room where a peacock often struts around the seat of honor. The upstairs rooms are downright Baroque: Enormous mirrors and paintings cover the walls (including works by Reynolds, Rubens, and Murillo), gigantic chandeliers hang from the ceilings, and hundreds of statues and Far Eastern urns populate the rooms. The floors bear multicolored marble inlay on a giant scale, with a calico effect. Even the lamps are detailed creations, especially those on the staircases, where metal women are entwined in trees with a light bulb on each branch. Movie producers use the palace for Hindi films. ⊠ *46 Muktaram Basu St., off Chittaranjan Ave.* 🎫 *Free (technically you must obtain a pass from the West Bengal Tourist Office 24 hours in advance); tip your guide.* ⊙ *Tues., Wed., and Fri.–Sun. 10–4.*

★ ❷ **Nakhoda Mosque.** This massive red sandstone mosque, which can hold 10,000 worshipers, was built in 1926 as a copy of Akbar's tomb in Agra. Each floor has a prayer hall. The top floor has nice views of the streets below, which are crowded with stalls selling everything from paperback editions of the Koran to greasy kebabs. ⊠ *Mahatma Gandhi Rd. and Rabindra Sarani.* 🎫 *Free.* ⊙ *Daily sunrise–8 PM.*

★ ❻ **Paresnath Temple.** Built in 1867 and dedicated to Sitalnathji, the 10th of the 24 *tirthankaras* (perfect souls), this Jain temple is a flamboyant one, filled with inlaid-mirror pillars, stained-glass windows, floral-pattern marble floors, a gilded dome, and chandeliers from 19th-century Paris and Brussels. The garden holds blocks of glass mosaics depicting European figures, and statues covered with silver paint. Paresnath is an unusual place of honor for the typically ascetic Jains. ✉ *Badridas Temple St., near Raja Dinendra St.* ⏲ *Daily sunrise–noon and 3–7.*

★ ❹ **Rabindra Bharati University Museum.** Within the walls of Rabindranath Tagore's cheerful, lemon-yellow home (which opens onto tree-lined galleries on the second floor), the university fosters cultural activities and maintains a display of paintings by artists of the Bengali school. The nerve center of Calcutta's intellectual activity around the turn of the 20th century, Tagore's abode now holds a wealth of memorabilia, including beautiful sepia photographs of the poet (quite fetching as a young man), his family, and his contemporaries. ✉ *6/4 Dwarkanath Tagore La.,* ☎ *33/239–6601.* 🎫 *Free.* ⏲ *Weekdays 10–5, Sat. 10–1:30.*

OFF THE BEATEN PATH

WHOLESALE FLOWER MARKET – If you're an early riser, historic northern Calcutta offers a few unusual morning activities. Above a soft, green-and-brown carpet formed by years of discarded vegetation, rickety stalls rise and colorful, fragrant merchandise flows at Calcutta's wholesale flower market. Blossoms are everywhere: on the ground, on people's heads, in carts and trucks, and on display. A tremendous bouquet goes for a few rupees. But get here early, while the bridge is still shrouded in mist and the representatives of florists and hotels, along with people in charge of weddings and funerals, are carting away the fragrant stock. By 7 AM things start winding down, and by 8 you may as well sleep in. If you managed the flower market early enough, there may still be time to visit what's left of the old Chinatown, north of Lal Bazaar—the **Chinese market** is alive between 6 AM and 8 AM, supplying the city's Chinese restaurants for the day. People doing business here enjoy breakfast at this hour: hot soup, noodles, and dumplings (often filled with pork). Breakfast on the street is a unique and tasty adventure; just think twice about the pork, especially if your stomach's not hardened yet. ✉ *Below and south of Howrah Bridge along the waterfront.*

Central Calcutta and the Maidan

The British first built Fort William in the middle of a dense jungle. When disagreements led the local Bengali ruler, Siraj ud-Daula, to attack and destroy it, the British response was a quick and decisive battle led by Robert Clive. Following the Battle of Plassey (some 160 km/100 mi north of town), which transformed the British from traders into a ruling presence in 1757, the forest was cut down in order to provide a clear line for cannon fire in case of attack. It is really from the year 1757 that modern Calcutta traces its history, and from the new, impenetrable Fort William (completed in 1773) that the city began its explosive growth.

Starting just north of the fort, central Calcutta became the commercial and political heart of the city. It was here that the British conducted business, and here that they built their stately homes. The immense area cleared for British cannons is now Calcutta's 3-square-km (2-square-mi) park, the Maidan, and central Calcutta now goes beyond the Maidan to B.B.D. Bagh square and most of the commercial and residential areas to the east of the giant park.

A Good Walk

Around **B.B.D. Bagh** ⑩ are some of the finest examples of Victorian architecture in Calcutta. Most of the buildings are still offices (government or otherwise) and are most interesting from the outside, even when admission is permitted. On the north side of the square is the **Writers' Building** ⑪; in the southeast corner is St. Andrew's Church, built in 1818. West and one block north is the **General Post Office** ⑫, and to its left is the redbrick Collectorate, Calcutta's oldest public building. Two blocks south is St. John's Church, which holds Job Charnock's mausoleum. (If the church is locked, you can call the vicar, ☎ 33/248–3439.) The High Court Building is on the next block south. Head east two blocks (until you're due south of B.B.D. Bagh) to see Raj Bhavan, home of the governor of West Bengal.

Cross Lenin Sarani and you're in the **Maidan,** a place to escape street traffic and diesel fumes and to enjoy green grass. Walk down Government Place East and you'll come to a traffic circle dominated by the **Ochterlony Monument** ⑬. Veer southwest and go down Eden Gardens Road to the **Eden Gardens** ⑭, which have a photogenic Burmese pagoda. If you walk along Strand Road toward the Hooghly from here, it's easy to arrange a brief, refreshing boat ride—boatmen are bound to approach you with offers of a "romantic" turn on the waters. Be careful, as the boats are often quite rickety; the going rate is about Rs. 50 for half an hour.

Continue a mile directly south of Eden Gardens to **Fort William** ⑮, the East India Company's main strategic defense in Calcutta. Red Road cuts south through the Maidan to the **Victoria Memorial** ⑯, which serves (somewhat ironically) as a postcard image of Calcutta and houses a compelling museum of the city's history as well as some Raj memorabilia. Two hundred yards to the east along Queen's Way is **St. Paul's Cathedral** ⑰.

Queen's Way hits J. L. Nehru Road, colloquially known by its old name—**Chowringhee.** This is Calcutta's main drag—a wide boulevard bustling with pedestrians by day and a place for the homeless to stretch out by night. On the other side of Chowringhee, Queen's Road becomes Shakespeare Sarani, and after another 100 ft you'll see Calcutta's government tourist office on the right. Further north on Chowringhee, Park Street comes in at an angle. Park Street shares with Chowringhee the prestige of having high rents for shops, hotels, and restaurants, and, in fact, if you're wandering around hungry in the evening, this is the best street to prowl for a good restaurant. About a mile down the street to the east is the **South Park Street Cemetery** ⑱, with the graves of many British who changed the course of India and never made it back to old Blighty. Back on Chowringhee, shortly after the intersection with Park Street is the **Indian Museum** ⑲, well worth dropping into for its collection of Indian antiquities. By now you will be in need of a little sophistication, which you can find at the Oberoi Grand hotel, an Victorian oasis just 200 yards farther up the thoroughfare.

TIMING

Two of the most interesting attractions on this route are the Victoria Memorial and the Indian Museum, for which you should allow 40 minutes apiece; the whole walk should take approximately four hours. If you are touring in the hot season, April–July, avoid walking during high noon.

Sights to See

★ ⑩ **B.B.D. Bagh.** The hub of all Calcutta, this square is still often referred to by its former name, Dalhousie Square. Once the administrative home of the East India Company, it later gave way to late-Victorian buildings used by the Colonial Civil Service and now houses the Indian government bureaucracy. Foot traffic is thick here. ✉ *East of Hooghly River, just south of Howrah Bridge.*

★ **Chowringhee.** North Calcutta may be Calcutta's intellectual heart, but in an age of business-friendly communist governments, the slick commercial area east of the Maidan is the city's spinal cord. Now technically called Jawaharlal (or J. L.) Nehru Road, Chowringhee runs along the east side of the Maidan, with shops, hotels, and old Victorian buildings lining the other side of the wide pavement. In the evening, hawkers do their best with potential shoppers, and at night, the homeless bed down.

14 **Eden Gardens.** These flower-speckled gardens in the northwest corner of the Maidan are often crowded, but you can still find relief from the busy streets. Don't miss the picturesque Burmese pagoda. ✉ *Eden Gardens Rd.* 🎫 *Free.* ⏲ *24 hours.*

15 **Fort William.** The irregular septagon south of the Eden Gardens is surrounded by a moat almost 50 ft wide. Begun in 1757 after Robert Clive's victory over Siraj ud-Daula at Plassey, Fort William was designed to prevent any future attacks. The fort's walls, as well as its barracks, stables, and Church of St. Peter, have survived to this day chiefly because the fort has, in fact, never been attacked. The Indian government still uses the fort, but it's closed to the public. ✉ *Strand Rd.*

12 **General Post Office** (GPO). This building's massive white Corinthian columns rest on the site of the original Fort William, where the British were attacked in 1756 and many officers were imprisoned by Siraj ud-Daula in the infamous "Black Hole of Calcutta," a tiny space that caused most of the group to suffocate. ✉ *Netaji Subhash Rd.*

19 **Indian Museum.** India's oldest museum has one of the largest and most comprehensive collections in Asia, including one of the best natural-history collections in the world. It's known locally as *Jadu Ghar,* the "House of Magic." The archaeology section has representative antiquities from prehistoric times to the Mogul period, including relics from Mohenjodaro and Harappa, the oldest excavated Indus Valley civilizations. The southern wing includes the Bharhut and Gandhara rooms (Indian art from the 2nd century BC to the 5th century AD), the Gupta and medieval galleries, and the Mogul gallery.

The Indian Museum also houses the world's largest collection of Indian coins; ask at the information desk for permission to see it. Gems and jewelry are on display. The art section on the first floor has a good collection of textiles, carpets, wood carving, papier-mâché figures, and terra-cotta pottery. A gallery on the third floor contains exquisite Persian and Indian miniature paintings, and banners from Tibetan monasteries. The anthropology section on the first floor is devoted to cultural anthropology, though the museum plans to establish India's first comprehensive exhibit on physical anthropology; some interesting specimens are an Egyptian mummy donated in 1880 by an English seaman, a fossilized 200-million-year-old tree trunk, the lower jaw of a 26-m (84-ft) whale, and meteorites dating back 50,000 years. ✉ *27 J. L. Nehru Rd.,* ☎ *33/249–9853.* 🎫 *R. 1 (free Fri.).* ⏲ *Sept.–Apr., Tues.–Sun. 10–4:30; May–Aug., Tues.–Sun. 11–5.*

★ **Maidan.** Known as Calcutta's "green lung," the city's expansive park is dotted with some of the its most significant attractions and is highly prized by its citizens, who turn out in the morning for sports and pony rides, in the evening for snacks and carriage rides. The area came into existence when forests were cleared to give Fort William a clear line of fire. ✉ *Just south of B.B.D. Bagh to just north of Alipore, and from the Hooghly River to J. L. Nehru Rd. and the shops of Park St.*

⓭ **Ochterlony Monument.** On the north end of the Maidan stands a 148-ft pillar commemorating Sir David Ochterlony's military victories over the Nepalese in the border war of 1814–16. Built in 1828, the impressive monument has a curious design: the base is Egyptian, the column is Syrian, and the cupola is Turkish. Now officially called the Shahid Minar (Martyr's Tower), it's been the site of many a political rally and student demonstration during Calcutta's turbulent post-Independence history. ✉ *J. L. Nehru Rd.*

⓱ **St. Paul's Cathedral.** Completed in 1847, the cathedral now has a steeple modeled after the one at Canterbury; previous steeples were destroyed by earthquakes in 1897 and 1934. Florentine frescoes, the stained-glass western window, and a gold communion plate presented by Queen Victoria are prize possessions. Interestingly, birds congregate in the interior eaves. ✉ *Cathedral Rd., east of Victoria Memorial,* ☎ *33/244–5756.* ⏲ *Daily 9–noon and 3–6.*

⓲ **South Park Street Cemetery.** The graves and memorials here form a repository of British imperial history. People who lived within the Raj from 1767 on are buried here, and in the records of their lives you can see the trials and triumphs of the building of an empire. ✉ *Park St. at Rawdon St.,* ☎ *no phone.* ⏲ *Sunrise–sunset.*

★ ⓰ **Victoria Memorial.** This massive, white marble monument was conceived in 1901 by Lord Curzon and built over a 20-year period. Designed in a mixture of Italian Renaissance and Saracenic styles, surrounded by extensive, carefully manicured gardens, and preceded by a typically sober statue of Victoria herself, it remains the single greatest symbol of the British Raj. Inside the building is an excellent museum of the history of Calcutta (there's a lot to read, but it will really sharpen your sense of the British-Bengali relationship) and various Raj-related exhibits including Queen Victoria's writing desk and piano, Indian miniature paintings, watercolors, and Persian books. Cameras and electronic equipment must be left at the entrance. ✉ *Queen's Way,* ☎ *33/248–5142.* 🎫 *Rs. 2.* ⏲ *Tues.–Sun. 10–4:30; sound-and-light show Tues.–Sun. 7:15 and 8:15.*

⓫ **Writers' Building.** The original "writers" were the clerks of the British East India Company. Now a government office building, this dramatically Baroque edifice is closed to the public. ✉ *North side of B.B.D. Bagh.*

Southern Calcutta

Calcutta's rich and powerful moved consistently south as the city grew more and more crowded and unpleasant. Here you'll see an interesting mix of large colonial homes, modern hotels and businesses, open space, and crowded temple areas.

A Good Tour

You can reach **Kalighat Kali Temple** ⑳ by metro, getting off at Kalighat Station and walking north on Murkaharji Road for 10 minutes; or you can take a taxi, an interesting ride through a variety of neighborhoods. **Nirmal Hirday** ㉑, where Mother Teresa lived, work, and is buried, is just around the corner. The **National Library** ㉒ is a short taxi ride from either and puts you near the Taj Bengal hotel, a restful place for a coffee break. To reach the **Indian Botanical Gardens** ㉓, across the Hooghly River in southern Howrah, take another taxi (about 15 minutes) across the Second Hooghly Bridge (Vivekananda Setu).

TIMING

Give yourself a full morning to cover this ground. Allow an hour and a half to arrive at and see Kalighat Kali Temple, another hour if you want to visit Nirmal Hirday. You many want to skip the National Library unless you want to bundle it with a high-class rest stop (or a stay) at the Taj Bengal, and go straight to the Indian Botanical Gardens.

Sights to See

★ 23 **Indian Botanical Gardens.** Across the Second Hooghly Bridge (Vivekananda Setu) in Howrah are the massive botanical gardens, first opened in 1786. Darjeeling and Assam teas were developed here. The gardens' banyan tree has one of the largest canopies in the world, covering a mind-boggling 1,300 square ft. The gardens are so huge that you can even find a place to relax on Sunday, when locals turn out in droves to enjoy their day off. ✉ *Between Andul Rd. and Kurz Ave., Shibpur, Howrah,* ☎ *33/660–3235.* 🎫 *Free.* ⏲ *Daily, 1 hr after sunrise–1 hr before sunset.*

★ 20 **Kalighat Kali Temple.** Built in 1809, the Kali is one of the most significant pilgrimage sites in India, with shrines to Shiva, Krishna, and Kali, the patron goddess of Calcutta. Human sacrifices were reputed to be common here during the 19th century, but only goats are slaughtered now, then offered to Kali with Ganges water and *bhang* (uncultivated hemp). The building, though surrounded by others, repays a close look with thin, multicolored layers of painted trim and swaths of tilework. Only Hindus are allowed in the inner sanctum, but the lanes and brilliant flower markets surrounding the temple have a lovely atmosphere in themselves. ✉ *Kalighat Rd.* ⏲ *Daily sunrise–sunset.*

22 **National Library.** Once home to the lieutenant governor of Calcutta, this hefty neo-Renaissance building houses miles of books and pleasant reading rooms. The rare-book section holds some particularly significant works, adding to the importance of this 2-million-volume facility. There are no displays as such, but the grounds make for a pleasant short walk in scholarly company. ✉ *Belvedere Rd. (near Taj Bengal hotel), Alipore,* ☎ *33/223–5381.* ⏲ *Weekdays 9–8, weekends 10–6.*

21 **Nirmal Hirday** (Pure Heart). Mother Teresa's first home for the dying is now one of 300 affiliated organizations worldwide that care for people in the most dire need. Learn more about Mother Teresa's work at the headquarters of the **Missionaries of Charity** (✉ 54A A. J. C. Bose Rd., ☎ 33/244–7115). It can be inspiring to see the joy among the people in one of the missionaries' homes or refuges. Mother Teresa is buried in this building—her home for 44 years—in what was formerly the cafeteria. ✉ *Next to Kali Temple.*

DINING

Many locals insist that Calcutta's best Chinese food is found in the leather-tanning area called Tangra (Chinatown), about half an hour's drive from the city center. Try the China Haus (☎ 33/244–2273), Lily's Kitchen (☎ 33/329–1783), Kim Ling (no phone), Kafulok (☎ 33/329–4130), or China Pearl (☎ 33/328–3238).

For breakfast or tea with sandwiches, try **Flury's** (✉ 18 Park St.), Calcutta's first Swiss confectioner and now an institution.

Bengali

$$$ ✕ **Aheli.** This was Calcutta's first upscale Bengali restaurant, and it still draws a crowd. Traditional Bengali delicacies such as *macher sorse paturi* (fish cooked with mustard paste) and chingri malai curry are

served in an intimate terra-cotta dining room. ✉ *Peerless Inn, 12 J. L. Nehru Rd.,* ☎ *33/228–0301 or 33/228–0302. AE, DC, MC, V.*

$$$ ★ ✕ **Kewpies.** Quaint and exclusive, this restaurant is in high demand at the moment. The delicious *thalis* (combination platters) are available both vegetarian and nonvegetarian, the latter with assorted meats or fish only, are served in a typically Bengali style: on cut banana leaves. You can also order the thali's vegetable or meat portions à la carte. ✉ *2 Elgin La.,* ☎ *33/475–9880. Reservations essential. No credit cards.*

$$ ★ ✕ **Suruchi.** Popular and informal, Suruchi ("Good Taste") serves a Bengali menu of fish and prawns. For years it was the only real restaurant to do so. Diners sit at rows of tables under overhead fans, and the menu changes daily according to the fresh catch. This is a simple, unpretentious Bengali meal at a reasonable price. ✉ *89 Elliot Rd.,* ☎ *33/475–9880. Reservations not accepted. No credit cards.*

Chinese and Southeast Asian

$$$$ ✕ **China Valley.** Enormous statues of male and female Chinese figures dominate the decor, surrounded by a stunning array of vases and urns, and large aquariums filled with iridescent tropical fish spur the imagination. China Valley's food is top-grade; a popular dish is the hot, spicy prawn Shanghai with rice. ✉ *Ideal Plaza, 11/1 Sarat Bose Rd.,* ☎ *33/247–0294. Reservations essential. AE, DC, MC.*

$$$ ✕ **Bar-B-Q.** This local favorite serves Cantonese and Szechuan dishes in a setting that innovatively mixes Chinese and German-chalet decor under a name that, of course, conjures neither of the two. Try the crisp fried chicken served with a mild "surprise" sauce or the boneless chili chicken. ✉ *43 Park St.,* ☎ *33/299916. Reservations essential on weekends. AE, DC, MC, V.*

$$$ ★ ✕ **Chinoiserie.** Consistently rated one of the best Chinese restaurants in India (no mean honor these days), this specialty restaurant boasts delicacies such as Peking duck and a highly unusual selection of corn dishes. One crunchy appetizer consists of deep-fried kernels of American corn; another dish features corn delicately flavored with garlic. Unsurpassed food, a calm green-and-beige color scheme accented by old-world mirrors and paintings, and excellent Taj service make dining here an experience. ✉ *Taj Bengal, 34B Belvedere Rd., Alipore,* ☎ *33/223–3939. AE, DC, MC, V.*

$$$ ✕ **Eau Chew.** Off the beaten track in Central Calcutta, this simple joint serves exotic Chinese cuisine that must be ordered a day in advance. (Phone to announce the number in your party and propose a time.) The Chimney Soup—for which you throw raw ingredients into a boiling broth—is highly recommended, as are Josephine's Noodles and whole fish. ✉ *P-32 Mission Row Extension, Ganesh Chandra Ave.,* ☎ *33/237–8260. Reservations essential. No credit cards.*

$$$ ✕ **Zen.** Art Deco meets postmodern in the sleek lines of this Southeast Asian restaurant, which serves cuisines from all over the region. The Thai green curry and Indonesian specialties, such as *soto ayam* (glass noodles) and *nasi gorang* (mixed fried rice) are rare finds in India. ✉ *Park Hotel, 17 Park St.,* ☎ *33/249–7336. Reservations essential for dinner. AE, DC, MC, V.*

Indian and Eclectic

$$$$ ★ ✕ **Sonargaon.** The name means "golden village," and this North Indian restaurant is a tasteful replica of a rural home, complete with a courtyard, a well, dark wood on taupe stone, copper curios, and metal light fixtures. Popular dishes include *kakori* kebab (minced lamb kebab), *murg Wajid Ali* (stuffed, pounded chicken breast marinated

in saffron and cooked in a mildly spicy sauce), and chingri malai. On weekends you can lunch like a royal zamindar with a Bengali thali, a sparkling silver platter holding delectable *hilsa* fish in mustard, *luchi* (delicate Bengali bread puffs), and other regional specialties. Whatever your main course, don't pass up the misti doi for dessert. ✉ *Taj Bengal, 34B Belvedere Rd., Alipore,* ☎ *33/223–3939. Reservations essential. AE, DC, MC, V.*

$$$ ★ ✕ **Charnock City.** Rich in ambience, this exclusive restaurant has a superb ninth-floor, glass-wall view of Salt Lake City and the Calcutta skyline. It's also right above one of Calcutta's best bookstores, and attracts an upmarket, mostly local crowd. The kitchen serves both Indian and Continental fare, with more Indian dishes on offer. ✉ *KB-26 Salt Lake City, Sector III,* ☎ *33/358–1349 or 33/358–1086, ext. 44. V.*

$$$ ✕ **Zaranj.** Choose a vegetarian or nonvegetarian prix-fixe menu and tuck into a succession of dishes for less than Rs. 200. You can also choose from a large à la carte menu, but the fixed meal is an excellent opportunity to try several Mughlai preparations. Dinners here are very relaxing: the furnishings are plush and comfortable, and the staff doesn't rush you. ✉ *26 J. L. Nehru Rd.,* ☎ *33/249–5572. Reservations essential. AE, DC, V.*

$$ ✕ **Blue Fox.** Located right in the thick of things and popular with a young, hip contingent, the large and spacious Blue Fox has high ceilings, an overhead loft with additional tables, and quiet modern-Indian decor. Among the various Indian and Continental dishes, the sizzlers and crab or lobster thermidor are good bets. ✉ *55 Park St.,* ☎ *33/249–7948. DC.*

$$ ★ ✕ **Taaja.** Taaja ("Fresh") is one of the best Continental restaurants in Calcutta, serving Greek, French, Italian, Spanish, and Hungarian food, but it goes beyond this classification to offer dishes from the Caribbean and Far East as well. The menu gives new meaning to the word "eclectic." Paella, Cajun crab cakes, Thai chicken, *khau suey* (Burmese noodles with meat), moussaka, cannelloni, and lasagna are all memorable choices. ✉ *29/1A Ballygunge Circular Rd.,* ☎ *33/476–7334. Reservations essential. MC, V.*

$ ✕ **The Sheriff.** Yes, it's Calcutta's only Wild West joint, and it's very popular with the smart crowd. The walls of this small space are bedecked with Stetsons, Colt revolvers, and lassos, and the waiters are dressed as cowboys. The Mexican food is fair enough if you need a little variety. ✉ *Sarat Bose Rd. at Elgin Rd.,* ☎ *33/280—6761 or 33/280–6444. Reservations essential. AE.*

$ ★ ✕ **Peter Cat.** Peter Cat's so-called cello kebab—biriani-style rice with egg, butter, two mutton kebabs, and one chicken kebab—is the most popular dish in Calcutta. The dining room is intimate, with white stucco walls, Tiffany-style lamps, and soft lighting, and the menu is a mixture of good Continental and Indian dishes, especially tandoori fare. ✉ *18 Park St.,* ☎ *33/229–8841. DC, V.*

Tibetan

$ ✕ **Momo Plaza.** Calcuttans love Tibetan food, and Momo Plaza is an ideal place for a Tibetan snack if you can forego physical ambience for the duration. The pork-stuffed *momos*—dumplings which are also popular in Nepal—come steamed or fried, served with a very hot red-chili paste and accompanied by a light, watery spring-onion soup called *thukpa.* ✉ *2A Suburban Hospital Rd.,* ☎ *33/247–8250. No credit cards.*

LODGING

Unless otherwise noted, hotels have central air-conditioning and foreign-exchange facilities, and rooms have bathrooms with tubs. Some luxury hotels have exclusive floors with special privileges or facilities for the business traveler.

$$$$ ★ **Oberoi Grand.** The height of elegance, this impeccably maintained Victorian landmark in the center of town has a glowing white facade and a rich marble and dark-wood interior. The heritage is rich, service is top-notch, and the restaurants are excellent. Guest rooms lack any sense of antiquity, but they're spacious, with wall-to-wall carpeting and modern bathrooms. The best rooms overlook the interior courtyard and pool. ✉ *15 J. L. Nehru Rd., 700013,* ☎ *33/249–2323,* FAX *33/249–1217. 221 rooms, 11 suites. 3 restaurants, bar, pool, sauna, health club, business center, travel services. AE, DC, MC, V.*

$$$$ ★ **Taj Bengal.** A mere 10 years old, Calcutta's Taj is a fusion of modern India and the nation's cultural heritage. On the fringe of the city center, the hotel overlooks the Maidan and Victoria Memorial. The cavernous lobby is stylish and inviting, colored in tawny taupes and ice green, with running water and palm trees creating a sense of total calm. Modern Indian art, artifacts (including terra-cotta reliefs), and antiques are showcased throughout the building. Decor in the rooms, which you access via quiet triangular atriums, is essentially Western, with Eastern accents and Indian prints. Some rooms have window seats, and all frame their views with cheery flower boxes. The showers are fabulous. Service is truly outstanding here—familiar, smooth, and detail-oriented. ✉ *34B Belvedere Rd., Alipore, 700027,* ☎ *33/223–3939,* FAX *33/223–1766. 217 rooms, 12 suites. 3 restaurants, bar, pool, health club, nightclub, business center, travel services. AE, DC, MC, V.*

$$$ **Ashok—Airport.** This modern high-rise with pleasant rooms is primarily for those whizzing through Calcutta in one night only. It's clean and fresh, but offers little excitement and is far from Calcutta's attractions. ✉ *Calcutta Airport, 700052,* ☎ *33/552–9111,* FAX *33/552–9137. 149 rooms, 9 suites. 2 restaurants, bar, pool, beauty salon, business center, travel services. AE, DC, MC, V.*

$$$ **Hotel Hindustan International.** The HHI provides modern rooms within its plain white walls. Decor is neat and trim throughout, if not particularly inspiring. The best rooms overlook the pool, but many others have good views of Calcutta. ✉ *235/1 A. J. C. Bose Rd., 700020,* ☎ *33/247–2394,* FAX *33/247–2824. 212 rooms, 12 suites. 3 restaurants, bar, pool, spa, health club, nightclub, business center, travel services. AE, DC, MC, V.*

$$$ ★ **Park Hotel.** Inspired decoration has turned the Park into one of the best hotels in Calcutta. Everything in this long, white building in the thick of things on Park Street has been designed with care: The lobby sparkles with mirrors and cut-glass chandeliers amid rich wood and marble; the restaurants and café are creative in everything from daring decor (black Art Deco meets Zen) to such simple touches as serving cappuccino. The rooms are comfortable, if small, and the staff is cheerful and helpful: the bar and nightclub are very popular with both Indians and expats. ✉ *17 Park St., 700016,* ☎ *33/249–7336,* FAX *33/249–7343. 155 rooms, 10 suites. 2 restaurants, bar, pool, nightclub, business center, travel services. AE, DC, MC, V.*

$$ **Astor.** In this price category, the Astor is the least expensive and quite possibly the best in Calcutta. The staff is laid-back and friendly; the rooms are clean if somewhat small; and there are three restaurants, including a casual beer garden, ideal for whiling away a balmy evening. ✉ *15 Shakespeare Sarani, 700071,* ☎ *33/282–9957,* FAX *33/287–7430. 35 rooms. 3 restaurants. AE, MC, V.*

$$ **Kenilworth.** Popular with repeat visitors to Calcutta, this Best Western hotel has two attractive wings and pretty gardens. The common rooms are filled with marble and cheerfully furnished; guest rooms are comfortable and spacious, with standard, anonymous decor. Continental breakfast is included. ✉ *1–2 Little Russell St., 700071,* ☎ *33/242–8394,* FAX *33/242–5136. 110 rooms. 2 restaurants, bar, bookstore, business center, travel services. AE, DC, MC, V.*

$$ **Peerless Inn.** Situated on a crowded street near the Oberoi Grand and New Market, the Peerless has somewhat cramped rooms and decor in need of a facelift, but its location and price make it popular. The presence of the Bengali restaurant Aheli (☞ Dining, *above*) is a bonus. ✉ *15 J. L. Nehru Rd., 700013,* ☎ *33/243–0301,* FAX *33/248–6650. 123 rooms. 3 restaurants, bar, health club, business center. AE, DC, MC, V.*

$ ★ **Fairlawn.** If you want old-fashioned charm and a taste of life in the Raj, stay in this Calcutta landmark, built in 1801. A small hotel, the Fairlawn has memorabilia-cluttered walls and a great general ambience. Rooms have chintz bedspreads and old-fashioned bathtubs. Ask for an air-conditioned room in the summer. All meals are included. ✉ *13A Sudder St., 700013,* ☎ *33/245–1510,* FAX *33/244–1835. 20 rooms. Restaurant. AE, MC, V.*

NIGHTLIFE AND THE ARTS

The Arts

Calcutta is India's deepest well of creative energy. Artists here live in the inspiring shadow of such pillars as Rabindranath Tagore and Satyajit Ray; and, happily, the anxiety of influence has not intimidated contemporary artists. To find out what's happening, check *Calcutta This Fortnight,* available from the West Bengal Tourist Office (☞ Visitor Information *in* Calcutta A to Z, *below*) and *CalCalling,* available in hotels. Other sources include "City Watch," on page 3 of the *Statesman,* and the *Sunday Telegraph*'s magazine section. *Calcutta: Gateway to the East* has comprehensive listings.

English-language plays are regularly staged by the **British Council** (☎ 33/242–5478). Many auditoriums host regular performances of music, dance, and theater—the most Bengali of the performing arts. Be sure to see what's happening at the **Academy of Fine Arts** (✉ Cathedral Rd., ☎ 33/242–1205), and don't be intimidated if the offerings are in Bengali—you can still see some fascinating dramatizations of familiar stories by the likes of Shakespeare and Goethe. Another venue for Bengali stage productions is **Kalamandir** (✉ 48 Shakespeare Sarani, ☎ 33/247–9086). Bengali dance and theater are often performed at **Rabindra Sadan** (✉ Cathedral Rd., ☎ 33/248–9936). Many movie theaters around **New Market** (☞ Shopping, *below*) feature English-language films. Ask your hotel or the tourist office for information on current events; if they don't know what's on, they'll help you find out.

Art galleries worth visiting include the **Academy of Fine Arts,** which has a permanent collection of paintings (and manuscripts) by Rabindranath Tagore. The **Birla Academy of Art and Culture** (✉ 108–109 Southern Ave., ☎ 33/762843) has interesting displays of art old and new. Modern Indian art is frequently shown at **Galerie 88** (✉ 28B Shakespeare Sarani, ☎ 33/247–2274).

Nightlife

Nightlife became a Calcutta phenomenon in the 1990s—with the advent of discotheques, affluent young people began to hit the floors. Eating out, however, remains the nocturnal activity of choice, with 24-hour coffee shops at the top hotels doing a brisk business.

Bars and Lounges

The most attractive places to have a nightcap are the Oberoi Grand and the Taj Bengal. The pub at the Park Hotel is one of the few places with decent beer on tap, making it a pleasant afternoon watering hole. The bar at the Fairlawn Hotel draws an interesting group and is much more social than the others. Bars stay open until 11 PM or midnight and are closed on Thursday.

Discos

Calcutta's clubs are technically open only to members and hotel guests, but you can get in for either a cover charge or a smile, depending on the doorman. All clubs retain good DJs for a mixture of Indian pop and Western dance music. **Anticlock** (✉ Hotel Hindustan International, ☎ 33/247–2394) is a good all-around choice. **Someplace Else,** at the Park Hotel (☎ 33/249–7336), is quite glitzy, drawing some real talent and going Latin on Thursday. Breathe freely at the spacious **Incognito** (✉ Taj Bengal, ☎ 33/248–3939), where an upmarket crowd relaxes around a glass-enclosed dance floor.

SPORTS AND OUTDOOR ACTIVITIES

Calcutta still puts class first when it comes to sports, with the result that you need to be a member's guest to enter the golf and racing clubs. The **Royal Calcutta Golf Club** (✉ 120 Deshpran Sahmal Rd., ☎ 33/473–2316) caters to the elite. For horse-racing enthusiasts, the **Royal Calcutta Turf Club** (RCTC, ✉ 11 Russell St., ☎ 33/249–1109) has an old-world air of sophistication. Whether you want to watch or play, get cricket information from the **Calcutta Cricket and Football Club** (✉ 19/1 Gurusaday Rd., ☎ 33/475–8721). The **Calcutta Polo Club** (✉ 51 J. L. Nehru Rd., ☎ 33/242–2031) has the polo schedules.

SHOPPING

Shopping in Calcutta bazaars is an adventure, and a test of your ability to shake off touts. Part of the century-old **New Market** (officially Sir Stuart Hogg Market, ✉ 19 Lindsay St., off J. L. Nehru Rd., behind Oberoi Grand) houses about 2,500 stores under one roof, selling cotton saris, Bankura clay horses, Malda brassware, leather from Shantiniketan, silk from Murshidabad, *khadi* cloth (handmade cotton), poultry, cheeses, nuts, and other foods.

Head up **Rabindra Sarani** from Lal Bazaar Road (near the West Bengal Tourist Office) and you'll soon enter an Islamic world. Women walk by in *burqas* (long, black, tent-shape robes), their eyes barely visible behind spiderlike veils. Men sit on elevated platforms selling Bengali *kurtas* (shirts) and pants, and colorful *lungis* and white *dhotis* (both wraps) for men. Other vendors sell vials of perfume created from flowers. Rabindra Sarani is interesting all the way to Chitpur Road.

On and around **Chitpur Road** you'll see a mixture of potters and shops that make musical instruments. East of Chitpur Road is **Bowbazar,** home to Calcutta's jewelers and an amazing array of good-quality gold and silver plus beautifully designed and crafted stone settings. Prices are reasonable, and each shop has an astrologer to help you find the most auspicious stone for your stars.

Auctions

Calcutta's Sunday auctions take place along Russell Street. A trip to the oldest auction house, the **Russell Exchange** (✉ 12C Russell St., ☎

33/249–8974), or any of its neighbors is invariably entertaining. Goods auctioned range from antiques and period furniture to crockery and cutlery.

Bookstores

The eighth-floor **Charnock City Book Store** (✉ KB-26, Salt Lake City, Sector III, ☎ 33/358–1349 or 33/358–1086) has the most spacious, attractive book displays in town and carries CDs as well. Its rooftop restaurant (☞ Dining, *above*) has a unique and stunning view of Calcutta. **Oxford Bookstore-Gallery** (✉ 17 Park St., ☎ 33/297–8509) is strong on magazines and technical books, has a small art gallery, and hosts a lecture series. **Seagull** has the widest range of titles, including Calcutta's largest selection of English-language fiction by both Indian and non-Indian authors. Exhibitions and seminars add to the mix.

Clothing and Textiles

Monapali and **Silk Route** (✉ 15 Loudon St., ☎ 33/406103) are co-managed designer boutiques with lovely collections of women's saris and *salwar-kameez* (a two-piece outfit of long, loose-fitting tunic over loose pants tapered at the ankle) in cotton, satin, and silk. Designs are inspired by the Far East and enhanced with Indian motifs and artwork: batik, embroidery, and *zardozi* (gold threading).

Try the **Handloom House** (✉ 2 Lindsay St.) for crafted textiles, mostly cottons. **Manjusha** (✉ 7/1D Lindsay St.) sells all manner of textiles. **Dakshinapan** (✉ near Dhakuria Bridge) houses government emporiums from all the states of India, making it an excellent place to eyeball a wide range of styles. The innovative **Weavers Studio** (✉ 5/1 Anil Moitra Rd., 2nd floor, Ballygunj Pl., ☎ 440–8937) sells high quality natural-dyed and embroidered textiles.

Crafts

For curios in a hurry, head to **Central Cottage Industries** (✉ 7 J. L. Nehru Rd.). Quaint little **Konark Collectables** (✉ Humayun Court, 20 Lindsay St., ☎ 33/247–7657) is stuffed with handicrafts.

SIDE TRIPS

Escape Calcutta's traffic and enrich your Bengali experience with a trip to either of two peaceful havens to the west. Vishnupur is characterized by its centuries-old terra-cotta temples, built from the local red clay and all but alive with the epic scenes carved into their panels. Shantiniketan is home to the university founded by Rabindranath Tagore, a center for art, music, and Bengali heritage. Nearby Sriniketan is a center of batik, embroidery, and terra-cotta craftsmanship.

Vishnupur

152 km (94 mi) west of Calcutta (8–10 hrs by road, overnight by train)

Set in a land of rich red soil, Vishnupur was the capital of the Hindu Malla kings from the 16th to 19th centuries, and saw fit to convert its surroundings into some mind-blowing terra-cotta temples. Between its intricate, lifelike temple panels and Old World charm, Vishnupur is exquisite, an integral part of Bengal. The clay pottery created here—particularly the Bankura horse, named for the district—attracts thousands for its sheer beauty and color. It's a long trip from Calcutta, but Vishnupur is worth a detour for its exceptional carvings and figurines, immortalizing old Bengal at its artistic best.

Built out of the local red laterite soil, the temple town is scattered with monuments to the Malla rulers. Sights are spread out, so the easiest way to explore is to hire a cycle-rickshaw and ride through the maze of narrow streets. Be sure to see the **Madan Gopal, Madan Mohan, Radhagobinda, Rasmancha,** and **Shyamrai** temples, all built around the 16th century; each has a story to tell through its intricately carved figurines. **Dalmadol** is a cannon of pure iron. **Pathar Darwaza** ("Doorway of Stone") marked the entrance to the Malla fort. Vishnupur is a great place to buy souvenirs, especially terra-cotta toys, conch-shell handicrafts, jewelry, and silk. In August or September, local snake charmers demonstrate their age-old prowess at a snake festival called the *jhapan,* at which, among other activities, men throw cobras at each other to test their respective mettle.

The only decent place to stay here is **Vishnupur Tourist Lodge** (✉ P.O. Vishnupur, Bankura, ☏ 03244/52013), which is simple and comfortable but definitely nothing fancy. Reserve a room through the West Bengal Tourist Office in Calcutta (☞ Calcutta A to Z, *below*).

Shantiniketan

★ *210 km (130 mi) northwest of Calcutta (four hours by train)*

Nobel Laureate Rabindranath Tagore's dream became reality here: a university dedicated to the liberal arts. Today the art and music schools at **Vishvabharati** are some of the best in the country. Designed in 1901 as a group of cottages in a green, idyllic setting, Shantiniketan embodies the Bengali artistic heritage. In accordance with Tagore's vision, some classes are still held outside, under the shade of huge trees, and stunning abstract sculptures reach toward the sky. A weekend retreat for many, Shantiniketan is almost a pilgrimage to Bengalis.

Within the university, **Rabindra Bhavan** is a museum full of photographs, Tagore's personal belongings, and the poet's much-coveted Nobel Prize. The art school, **Kala Bhavan,** is decorated with frescoes and murals outside, and you can watch students at work inside. **Sangeet Bhavan** is the music school. **Uttarayan,** where Tagore lived, is a charming complex of five houses, ranging from mud hut to mansion, in a variety of architectural styles.

A few minutes' drive outside Shantiniketan, **Sriniketan** is a rural-development center helping locals fend for themselves by creating stunning handicrafts—colorful batiks; intricate embroidery on saris, scarves, and bags; and terra-cotta items, including jewelry. This is a hidden shopper's paradise, with some of the most beautiful and exclusive craft items in Bengal.

Dining and Lodging

$ 🏨 **Chhuti.** This sprawling hotel is the best in the vicinity, with a resort-like ambience and good food. Built with an eye for detail, it has all the amenities of a high-rise back in the metropolis. Guest rooms are spacious, clean, and refreshing, and the caring, experienced staff looks after weary travelers' needs. ✉ *248 Charupally, Jamboni, Bolpur,* ☏ *3463/52692. Restaurant.*

$ 🏨 **Marks and Meadows.** More a resort than a mere rest stop, this is an ideal place to unwind. Surrounded by greenery, it comprises clean, tidy, nicely decorated rooms and some cottages as well. ✉ *Sriniketan,* ☏ *33/245–8831 (or –0179) or 33/244–8254,* FAX *33/245–8831. Restaurant, pool, badminton, table tennis, recreation room, meeting room.*

CALCUTTA A TO Z

Arriving and Departing

By Car

You enter Calcutta from the southwest by National Highway (NH) 6, from the northwest by NH 2, or from the north along NH 34, which stretches into Sikkim and Darjeeling. NH 36 reaches Calcutta from Bangladesh.

By Plane

All international and domestic airlines use Dum Dum Airport, 15 km (9 mi) north of the city. **Indian Airlines** (☎ 33/236–0810 or –0730). **Jet Airways** (33/229–2737 or –2660).

BETWEEN THE AIRPORT AND CITY CENTER

When you leave the baggage claim, you'll see counters where you can arrange free **shuttle** service if your hotel offers it. Outside the baggage claim/customs area, you can hire a **taxi** through the prepaid-taxi counter; the ride downtown takes about 40 minutes and costs around Rs. 100. Hire a taxi on your own through one of the hustlers outside the terminal and it will cost about Rs. 350. The **airport coach** (Rs. 50) goes to most of the upscale hotels and to the city center; its counter is also near the baggage-claim area.

By Train

Every day an incredible number of trains roll into and out of **Howrah Junction** (✉ 1 block south of the west end of Howrah Bridge, ☎ 33/220–3545 [–54] or 131), which is divided into the neighboring Old and New Howrah stations. A permanent population resides on the platforms among the ferocious crowds of travelers, vendors, and other locals; indeed, "platform children" attend school between the tracks here, taught to read and write by volunteers. The **main reservation office** (✉ 6 Failie Pl., ☎ 33/220–6811) has a foreign-tourist section upstairs, open daily 9–1 and 1:30–4; buying tickets here is a breeze with either foreign currency or a valid encashment certificate for rupees. There are also **ticket offices** on the first floor of Old Howrah Station, the second floor of New Howrah Station, and in Kalighat (for first-class bookings; ✉ 14 Strand Rd., ☎ 33/220–3496) and Rabindra Sadan (✉ 61 J. L. Nehru Rd., ☎ 33/247–2143).

Sealdah Station (✉ east end of Bepin Behari Ganguly St., ☎ 33/350–3535 or 33/350–3496) is used exclusively by trains to and from northern destinations such as Darjeeling. Tickets are sold on the platform level.

Getting Around

Despite its congestion, Calcutta is a fairly manageable city. Most Calcuttans rely on buses, trams, and the spotless metro. You will probably rely mostly on taxis, rickshaws, and your feet (the bus system is indecipherable, the rickety trams are good only for an early-morning ride, and the metro is somewhat limited). Calcutta is not a good city for driving. Take a cab to or from the area you're visiting, then rely on your feet or a sturdy rickshaw. In response to the painful traffic situation, authorities have made many roads in Calcutta one-way, then the other way, then two ways at various times throughout the day and week.

By Auto-Rickshaw

Auto-rickshaws are cheaper than taxis, but they're not as easy to find in the city center. At rush hour they can be more-efficient (albeit dirtier) alternatives; taxis are liable to get stuck in traffic.

By Hired Car with Driver

You can hire a car and driver through one of the travel agencies listed below, or through the following rental agencies: **Europcar Shaw Distributors** (✉ 8/1 Sarat Bose Rd., ☎ 33/475–8916), **Hertz** (✉ New Kenilworth Hotel, ½ Little Russel St., ☎ 33/242–8394), or **Wenz** (✉ Oberoi Grand, ☎ 33/249–2323, ext. 6247). Expect to pay Rs. 700 for half a day (four hours) and 80 km (50 mi), with an hourly and per-km rate beyond that. If you plan to do a lot in very little time, hiring a car can be useful, but hailing plain old taxis can be cheaper, and saves you from having to find parking or remember where you left your car and driver.

By Rickshaw

Calcutta is the last city on earth to use enormous Chinese-style rickshaws pulled by men on foot. At least 1 million people depend on the hard-earned wages of these men for what little daily sustenance and shelter they get. Many pullers say they wouldn't trade positions with cycle-rickshaw wallahs for anything. If you ever get the chance to pull a rickshaw, you will be horrified at how difficult it is, even when the rickshaw is empty. With that in mind, don't rush your driver, and tip generously—the driver deserves it. Rickshaw fares fluctuate depending on the distance to be traveled and the amount of traffic congestion; negotiate ahead of time, using Rs. 15 per 10 minutes as a guide.

By Subway

Calcutta's metro system, which has been evolving over the past few decades, is clean and efficient. Only the central part of the system is complete, from Tollygunge to Central Station in Tiretta; eventually (though not in the foreseeable future) it will connect Dum Dum Airport with downtown. Tickets cost Rs. 2–Rs. 3 and are available from machines and windows in every station. The metro runs daily until 9 PM and is crowded only at rush hour. Metro stations are marked on the government's tourist map, available free from tourist offices and most hotels.

By Taxi

The base fare in Calcutta is Rs. 10, and the meter should read about Rs. 25 after 3 km. The legal inflation factor, however, is 100%, and it changes periodically; so ask your hotel for the current inflation factor. If a driver refuses to turn the meter on, find another taxi. Traffic, unfortunately, plagues Calcutta, possibly bringing your cab to a full stop amid humid air and diesel exhaust, so at rush hour you may just want to find a sweet shop and wait until it's over.

Contacts and Resources

Currency Exchange

American Express (✉ 21 Old Court House St., ☎ 33/248–6281). **ANZ Grindlays Bank** (✉ 19 Netaji Subhash Rd., ☎ 33/220–8346). **Bank of America** (✉ 8 India Exchange Pl., ☎ 33/242–2042). **Citibank** (✉ Tata Center, 43 J. L. Nehru Rd., ☎ 33/292–9220). **State Bank of India** (✉ 33 J. L. Nehru Rd., ☎ 33/402430). **Thomas Cook** (✉ Chitrakoot Bldg., 230A A. J. C. Bose Rd., ☎ 33/247–5378).

Consulates

United Kingdom: ✉ 1 Ho Chi Minh Sarani, 700071, ☎ 33/242–5171, FAX 33/242–3435. **United States:** ✉ 5/1 Ho Chi Minh Sarani, 700071, ☎ 33/242–3611, FAX 33/242–2335.

Guided Tours

The most interesting tours in Calcutta are the walks through various neighborhoods led by the **Foundation for Conservation and Research of Urban Traditional Architecture** (CRUTA; ✉ 67B Beadon St., 700006, ☎ 33/554–6127).

Travel Agencies

These agencies can help with reservations and arrange cars with drivers: **American Express** (✉ 21 Old Court House St., ☎ 33/248–4464), **Ashok Travel and Tours** (✉ Government of India Tourist Office, 4 Shakespeare Sarani, ☎ 33/440901; Ashok Hotel, ☎ 33/552–9111), **Mercury Travels** (✉ 46C J. L. Nehru Rd., ☎ 33/443555; Oberoi Grand, ☎ 33/249–2323), and **Thomas Cook** (✉ Chitrakoot Bldg., 230A A. J. C. Bose Rd., ☎ 33/247–5378).

Visitor Information

The **West Bengal Tourist Office** (✉ 3/2 B.B.D. Bagh E, 700001, ☎ 33/248–8271, 33/248–5917, or 33/248–5168; also at the airport and the Howrah Junction train station) is open Monday through Saturday from 10 to 5. The regional **Government of India Tourist Office** (✉ 4 Shakespeare Sarani, ☎ 33/242–1472 or 33/242–5813) is well equipped to help baffled travelers; it's open Monday through Saturday from 9 to 6. The **Calcutta Information Centre** (✉ 1/1 A. J. C. Bose Rd., ☎ 33/248–1451) is also helpful.

15 PORTRAITS OF INDIA

India's Religions

Books and Films

Vocabulary

Dining Glossary

INDIA'S RELIGIONS

HINDUISM, BUDDHISM, JAINISM, and Sikhism all came into being in India, even though Buddhism is now largely practiced elsewhere in Asia. Islam came from outside the country, yet India's large Muslim minority comprises the second-largest Muslim population in the world, after Indonesia's. India's calendar is crowded with festivals, and religion is evident everywhere in Indian life—from politics to art and architecture and the daily activities of millions of devotees.

Hinduism

Hinduism, with its literally countless gods and goddesses, extends back at least three millennia, to the hymns and ritual mantras of the ancient Sanskrit *Vedas.* It's almost impossible to define Hindu tradition in a way that would include all its major variants; the tradition's hallmark, perhaps, is its ability to adapt disparate elements—from local deities to rival philosophical systems—into a recognizably Hindu context. Perhaps the best way to start is with the *Bhagavad Gita,* a marvelous work of religious synthesis set in the midst of battle in the epic *Mahabharata.* Arjuna, one of five brothers who are the epic's heroes, falters on the battlefield, concerned that no good will come of defeating his enemies, who are also his cousins. Arjuna's charioteer, Krishna, an incarnation of the great god Vishnu, reminds him that Hindus believe in reincarnation and their ultimate goal is *moksha,* liberation from the endless cycle of rebirth. There are reasons, Krishna says, for the rivalry that led to the battle, and as a young warrior Arjuna must fulfill his particular duty (*dharma*) through action (*karma*) that is unconcerned with benefits or reward. Fulfilling one's assigned duty and moral obligation to society is a necessary step toward attaining higher religious knowledge (*jnana*) and the ultimate goal of union with God through devotion (*bhakti*). The *Gita,* as it is called, has a place in the homes of almost all modern Hindus. It does not have canonical authority above that of many other texts, yet it gives in outline a basic set of beliefs that are held in common.

Sacrifice is an essential part of dharma, and central to the practice of the earliest stage of Hinduism embodied in the *Vedas.* An offering to a god blesses the worshiper in return. Beginning with the *Upanishads,* appendixes to the *Vedas,* sacrifice has also been seen in metaphorical terms, as the sacrifice of the baser aspect of one's individuality, so that the individual soul, or spirit (*atman*), can merge with *brahman* (universal consciousness) and allow the realization of moksha.

Some Hindus also practice yoga, a combination of physical culture and meditation practice that is exemplified by the ascetics and sadhus in such places as Varanasi. Yoga (which literally means "yoke" or "union") uses mental and physical discipline to purify the body and rid the practitioner of conscious thought, so he or she can experience a sense of detachment from the realities of the physical world and a higher knowledge (jnana) similar in some ways to gnosis in the Western tradition. In the *Bhagavad Gita* many other forms of dedicated behavior, such as devotion or disinterested action, are described as forms of yoga.

Strictures underlying dharma and karma also help explain the thousands of castes that divide Hindus, which have been conceptualized in a framework of four segregated rankings: Brahmins (priests), Kshatriyas (nobles and warriors), Vaishyas (tradesmen), and Shudras (menial laborers). A fifth grouping, Panchama, falls outside this framework: the lowest rung of society. Once commonly known as "untouchables," the people in this class were named Harijans, or "Children of God," by Mahatma Gandhi and now prefer to be called Dalits, or the "oppressed."

To most Westerners, the caste system seems like cause for revolution, but it was also a complex and even flexible way of ordering society. In ancient India, unlike many other places, there was no all-powerful priestly class, and slavery was rare. There is evidence of considerable shifting in the status of various castes (though not of individuals) in Indian history. Still, for those in the lowest categories, the system was doubtless cruel. While it is said that they accepted their fate, understanding it as a direct result of their karma in previous births, poetry by lower-caste Hindus from as early as the 12th century explicitly rejects caste. Centuries passed before the untouchables found their way out of exclusion; the catalysts were Mahatma Gandhi and Bhimrao Ramji Ambedkar, a Dalit leader who was one of the principle authors of the Indian Constitution. Despite their frequent disagreements, Gandhi's and Ambedkar's efforts changed the way modern India thinks about caste, and saw to it that discrimination based on caste was legally abolished in 1947. In practice, caste still regulates many aspects of Hindu behavior, such as marriage practices; and caste is emerging as a dominant element of Indian politics, much as ethnicity has done in the United States and other Western political systems.

Hindu Temples

The Hindu temple is filled with symbols. Before the structure is built, a priest traces a *mandala,* which represents the cosmos and determines the placement of all rooms and icons. The center of the temple, called the inner sanctum, represents the egg or womb from which all life originates; this is where the sacred deity resides. The *vimana* (spire) is directly over the inner sanctum, drawing devotees' attention to the heavenly realm and its connection with the sacred deity.

Many festivals take place in the temple's *mandapam,* a front porch that may be an elaborate pillared pavilion or a simple overhang. Water is the agent of purification. Ideally, a temple is constructed near a river or lake, but if no natural water source is available, a large tank is often built, with steps around it for ease of ablutions. Before the devout Hindu worships, he takes a ritual dip to rid himself of impurities. Daily *darshan,* or viewing of the idol—usually performed at sunrise, noon, sunset, and midnight—is imbued with sacred traditions. Ancient rituals combine in an elaborate pageantry that can include such personalized acts as feeding the deity or brushing its teeth, performed with a touching gentleness toward the god's idol. These rituals are often paralleled in worship at home shrines.

Before the priest enters the temple, he takes his sacred dip. The actual darshan takes place during a ceremony known as *arati* (moving flame), which begins with the clanging of a bell to ward off any evil presence and awaken the sleeping deity. Burning camphor sweetens the air as the priest recites mantras and blesses the idol with oils and sandalwood paste. The deity receives offerings of incense (an aroma favored by the gods), vermilion powder, flowers, and decorative platters of food. Lamps of *ghee* (clarified butter) and more camphor are waved before the idol; then the priest blesses the devotees, and often the door to the inner sanctum is closed to let the deity return to its sleeping state. Worshipers are given sweets and other food that has been offered to the deity; this food is known as *prasada* (translated by one scholar as "the edible form of God's grace"), and can be taken home for distribution to friends and family members.

The Hindu Pantheon

It has been said that there are 330,000,000 gods in the Hindu pantheon. For the worshiper, this bewildering profusion can be simplified by dedication to a single god or goddess, or by the idea that many gods and goddesses are forms of a few great gods and goddesses. The celebrated German Indianist Max Muller has said that Hindus are not so much pantheists as xenotheists: Supreme divinity can be invested serially in the deity being worshiped at any one moment by a particular person.

Through the mythology, iconography, and devotional song that surrounds them, Hindu gods and goddesses are remarkably personalized. This is in striking contrast to the abstract notion of ultimate reality, or brahman, found in the *Upanishads* and subscribed to by many Hindus even as they worship one or more specific anthropomorphized gods and goddesses. A well-known story about Krishna and the *gopis* (the pastoral maidens of Braj, near Agra) illustrates the delight Hindus take in the incarnation of their gods. Visited by a philosopher who expounded the higher truths of atman and brahman, which cannot be seen or described, one gopi said: "It's all very well to know brahman, but can the ultimate reality put its arms around you?"

Most important deities are clustered around the incarnations, families, and mythological associates of two great gods, Vishnu and Shiva, and their female consorts.

Brahma, creator of the world and progenitor of all living things, is the third member of the Hindu trinity. He is the keeper of cosmic time and a sort of master-of-ceremonies advancing story lines in myths, but he is not actively worshiped. In sculpture and painting, Brahma has four heads and four arms, each holding sway over a quarter of the universe and signifying one of the four *Vedas*. The rosary that he counts in one hand represents time, and his lotus seat represents the earth. Brahma's vehicle is the swan, symbol of the freedom that comes with knowledge. His consort is Saraswati, the goddess of learning.

Shiva is most famously depicted dancing the *tandava* dance of destruction, with which cosmic epochs come to an end so that new ones can be born. Shiva is the yogic ascetic par excellence, wearing snakes as garlands, ashes as ointment, and an animal-skin loincloth, and meditating in the Himalayas from one eon to the next. Paradoxically, however, he is married to Parvati, and his family and love life are celebrated in myth and art. Shiva's non-anthropomorphic form is the linga, a phallic symbol that rests in a *yoni,* which represents the womb. Worship of the linga is not explicitly phallic worship; the icon is as much an abstract representation of the axis mundi, the axis on which the world spins, or of how divine presence manifests itself on earth to Hindus.

Shiva's consorts take many forms, and are often considered aspects of one general goddess (Devi) or a female divine principle (*shakti*). Principle among these is Parvati, the daughter of Himalaya with whom Shiva had two sons: Ganesh, the elephant-headed god of wisdom and prosperity, and Kartikeya, known as Murugan in South India. Other shaktis include Durga, slayer of the buffalo demon, and Kali, sometimes called the goddess of death and depicted in terrible aspect, wearing a garland of skulls and dancing on Shiva's dead body. Shiva's mount, Nandi, the sacred bull, usually guards the entrance to a Shiva temple. Priests who pray to Shiva have three horizontal stripes painted on their foreheads.

The preserver of the universe, Vishnu, has nine known avatars, and a 10th is prophesied. Each successive avatar reflects a step up the evolutionary cycle, beginning with the fish and moving up to the ninth, Buddha, accepted by the all-embracing Hindus as a figure in their own pantheon. Vishnu's most popular incarnations are Rama and Krishna (the sixth and seventh, respectively), the two gods that embody humanity. Vishnu priests have three vertical stripes painted on their foreheads.

Vishnu appears with four arms to signify the four cardinal directions and his command over the realms they encompass. In one hand, he carries the lotus, symbol of the universe; in the other, a conch shell, which represents the evolutionary nature of all existence. The wheel in Vishnu's third hand refers to the rotation of the earth, with each spoke honoring a specific season of the year. In his fourth hand, Vishnu often holds a weapon to protect him from demons. A common image of Vishnu has him lying on a bed of coils formed by his serpent, Ananta, who symbolizes time; creation will begin when Vishnu wakes up. Vishnu has two consorts: Bhudevi, the goddess of Earth, and Lakshmi, the goddess of wealth and prosperity, who rose from the foam of the ocean like Venus. Lakshmi assumes a different name with each of Vishnu's avatars. When Vishnu is Rama, she's Sita; when he's Krishna, she's Radha.

Rama is the ideal king. As the hero of the Hindu epic *Ramayana,* he slew the 10-headed demon, Ravana, who had kidnapped Sita. This episode, including Sita's rescue by Hanuman, the monkey god and Rama's faithful servant, is celebrated during Dussehra, one of India's most festive holidays. There are three distinct phases in Krishna's mythology. (Some 19th-century Europeans saw this as the conflation of three different pre-Hindu gods into one Hindu one, but this concept is laughable to Krishna's devotees.) In the first phase, Krishna is a playful boy god, stealing butter from his mother's pantry. In the next, he is an amorous, flute-playing cowherd and the focus of a huge body of love poetry. Finally, he is the charioteer of the *Mahabharata,* interceding on behalf of the heroes and offering the wisdom of the *Bhagavad Gita.*

In addition to these major gods, there are countless village and regional gods, sometimes affiliated in myth with the great pan-Indian Hindu gods or goddesses. There are also many goddesses not paired off with male gods or celebrated in Sanskrit texts, such as Shitala Mata, the smallpox goddess (whose worship continues despite the eradication of smallpox). Since medieval times at least, great devotees from a wide range of castes and communities have also been venerated, religious communities organized around their teachings.

Jainism

The origins of Jainism (the name comes from the word *jina,* or victor) go back more than 2,500 years. Jainism became a powerful sect during the time of Parsvanatha, who lived in the 8th century BC. At this time Hindu Brahmins dominated much of Indian religious life; like Buddhism, Jainism developed under the patronage of prosperous non-Brahmin communities. Jains revere 24 *tirthankaras* (perfect souls), men believed to have achieved spiritual victory and attained moksha.

Parsvanatha, the 23rd tirthankara, was a prince who renounced his wealth to become an ascetic. He advocated honesty, respect for all life (in the belief that every creature has a soul), and *ahimsa* (nonviolence); and he abhorred any form of theft and the ownership of property. The 24th tirthankara was Mahavira (Great Hero), who lived in the 6th century BC, around the time of the historic Buddha. Mahavira also became a monk, and eventually shed his clothes as a sign of devotion and absolute self-denial. He advocated a life of poverty, even though he realized his example would be difficult to follow.

In 300 BC, the original Jain scriptures were finally committed to writing. Jainism also split into two sects: Svetambaras, who wear white clothes, and Digambaras, who practice nudity and believe that women cannot achieve moksha until they are reborn as men. Women, according to Digambaras, are the greatest source of earthly temptation.

Rejecting the existence of a supreme being, Jains follow the model of the 24 tirthankaras. They divide the universe into three worlds, which are divided in turn into numerous levels—devotees want to cross the metaphorical river of existence and obtain freedom for the soul from all three realms. The Jain cosmology is a common motif in religious paintings: The lower world, which normally looks like truncated pyramids, represents various infernos occupied by mortals who have sinned. The middle world, which resembles a disc, contains all nonliving matter and life forms, including human beings who are struggling through the cycle of rebirth and striving for liberation. The upper world, often drum-shape with a bulging middle, is the realm of the gods and spirits. Some paintings also take the shape of the Cosmic Man: the truncated pyramids are turned into legs, the disc becomes the waist, and the upper world extends up from the abdomen. When gods are depicted in the cosmos, their visible serenity increases as they move up each level within the upper world.

The restrictions of Jainism are extensive. Because Jains are supposed to avoid all occupations that involve the destruction of any life form, many Jains are members of the trading community. Few are farmers. Jains are not permitted to eat meat or eggs, and many even shun vegetables and edible roots for fear of ingesting microscopic creatures in the process. They must also take 12 vows that include the practice of ahimsa and meditation, restrictions on the acquisition of wealth and unnecessary belongings, and the commitment to spend some time as a monk or nun.

An important Jain symbol is the swastika, with each appendage representing the four possible stages of birth: life in hell, life as an insect, human life, and life as a god or demon. The three dots on top of the swastika stand for right faith, right knowledge, and right conduct. The half moon above the dots stands for moksha: the ultimate Jain goal.

Because one vow instructs devotees to contribute generously to the construction and maintenance of temples and animal hospitals, Jain temples are often exquisitely adorned. (The Charity Birds Hospital in Delhi is another remarkable response to this instruction.) Images of the 24 tirthankaras, depicted as ascetics with or without clothes, embellish most Jain temples. Parsvanatha is blue and usually appears with a snake; Mahavira is golden, and usually appears with a lion.

Islam

"There is no God but Allah, and Mohammed is His Prophet"—this is the *shahadah* (religious creed) and most important pillar of the Islamic faith. Islam originated with Mohammed (whose name means "highly praised"), who was born around AD 571 in the Arabian town of Mecca. A series of revelations from Allah, passed on through the Angel Gabriel, instructed Mohammed to preach against the paganism practiced by the Meccans. Mohammed saw himself as a social reformer, advocating a virtuous life in a city where virtue had vanished; but the Meccans saw him as a menace and a threat, and forced him to flee to Yathrib (now Medina).

This flight, in AD 622—which Muslims now call *hijra*—marks the beginning of the era in which Mohammed established the concept of Islam (which means "submission" and "peace") as a way of life. By the time Mohammed died in AD 632, the inhabitants of an expanse stretching from Samarkand (in Uzbekistan) to the Sahara had converted.

With the death of Mohammed, his father-in-law, Abu Bakr, one of the first converts to Islam, became the next ruler and was called caliph—"successor of the Prophet." In AD 656, during the reign of the fourth caliph, Ali (the Prophet's nephew and the husband of his daughter Fatima), civil war broke out. Ali moved his capital to Mesopotamia, where he was murdered by Muslim dissidents.

Ali's death signaled the beginning of a period of dissension between the traditionalists, Sunnis, who followed the orthodox teaching and example of the Prophet, and Ali's supporters, who claimed Ali's right to the caliphate based on his descent from the Prophet. In time, Ali's supporters broke away from the Sunnis and formed a sect known as the Shia, or Shiites.

Originally political in nature, the differences between the Sunnis and Shiites took on theological overtones. The Sunnis retained the doctrine of leadership by consensus. After Syrians massacred Hussain, Ali's son, at Karbala, in Iraq, the Shiites strengthened their resolution that only Mohammed's rightful heirs should rule. They modified the *shahadah:* "There is no god but Allah; Mohammed is the Prophet of God, and Ali is the Saint of God."

Islam demands submission to Allah—a God who is invisible yet omnipresent. To represent Allah in any form is a sin, thus the absence of icons in mosques and tombs. Every bit of decoration—often fashioned out of myriad tiny gems—is limited to inscriptions of the Koran, Muslims' holy scripture, and the names of Mohammed and his important followers.

Muslims believe that Allah has existed throughout time, but that humans had strayed from his true teaching until Mohammed set them straight. Islam has concepts similar to those of Judaism or Christianity: guardian angels, the day of judgment, the general resurrection, heaven and hell, and the eternal life of the soul. Muslims also follow a strict code of ethical conduct that encourages generosity, tolerance, and respect and forbids adultery, gambling, usury, and the consumption of pork and alcohol. Other Muslim duties are known as the five pillars of the faith: the recitation of the shahadah; *salat* (daily prayer); *zakat* (alms); *siyam* (fasting); and *haj* (pilgrimage). The believer must pray to Allah five times daily, preceding each occasion by a ritual washing of the hands, feet, neck, and head. Men pray at a mosque under a prayer leader whenever possible, and are obliged to do so on Friday. Women may also attend public worship but are segregated from men.

The ninth month of the Muslim calendar, Ramadan—in which Mohammed received his revelations—is a month of required fasting from sunrise to sunset for all but the weak, pregnant women, and young children. In addition to food, drinking, smoking, and sexual intercourse are prohibited during daylight hours.

A Muslim is supposed to make the haj to the Great Mosque in Mecca once in his life to participate in 10 days of special rites, held during the 12th month of the lunar calendar. While on the haj, the pilgrim wears an *ihram* (seamless white robe) to symbolize equality and devotion to Allah and abstains from sexual relations, shaving, and cutting his hair and nails. The returning pilgrim is entitled to the honorific "hajji" before his name and a turban carved on his tombstone.

The word mosque, or *masjid,* means "a place of prostration." Mosques are generally square in shape; built of stone, clay, or brick; and centered on an open courtyard surrounded with *madrasas* (cloisters) for students of the Koran. After the *muezzin* (crier) sings the call for prayer from the minaret (tower), the faithful line up in rows behind the *imam* (one who has studied the Koran). The imam stands in the sacred part of the masjid facing the *mihrab,* a niche in the wall that indicates the direction of Mecca. When the imam prays, the mihrab—an ingenious amplifier—bounces the imam's voice back to the devotees. Only prayers are heard and prostrations are made in the mosque; ceremonies connected with birth, marriage, and death occur elsewhere.

Popular Islam in India involves not only prayer at home and in the mosque, but worship at the graves of great religious teachers of the past. On the anniversaries of the saints' deaths—the *urs,* or time of ascent to heaven—great fairs attract pilgrims, sometimes of many faiths, from all over the country.

Sikhism

The founder of Sikhism, Guru Nanak, was born into a Hindu family in 1469, at a time when the Lodi sultanate—a Muslim dynasty from Afghanistan—ruled his North Indian homeland. From an early age, he railed against the caste system, the corruption of Hindu priests, their superstitious beliefs, and their unwieldy family of gods. In his poems and teachings, Guru Nanak urged egalitarianism based on love and devotion to a single, non-incarnate divinity called the Wahi Guru, conceived as the embodiment of truth, goodness, and uniqueness. (These three words form the common Sikh greeting "Sat Sri Akal.")

Nanak's view of Sikhism, recorded in the *Adi Granth,* upheld the Islamic idea that the goal of religion was union with God, who dwelled within the soul. He believed that, through meditation and dharma (Hindu concepts), devotees could rid themselves of impurities, free themselves from the endless cycle of rebirth, and attain eternal bliss. For Hindus at the bottom of society, Sikhism offered equality and tolerance; they gladly converted, becoming Sikhs—disciples.

During the early years of the Mogul Empire, Sikhism flourished without interference until Emperor Jahangir assumed the throne. Resenting the Sikhs' rejection of Islam, Jahangir ultimately tortured and murdered the fifth guru. When Aurangzeb, the next emperor, revealed his own ruthless intolerance, Gobind Singh, the 10th and final guru, forged the Sikhs into a martial community that he called the *khalsa* ("pure"). Gobind Singh instructed every Sikh man to observe and wear the five *kakkari* (visible symbols): *kesh* (uncut hair and beard), *kachh* (boxer shorts), *kara* (a steel bangle), *kanga* (a wooden comb), and *kirpan* (a dagger). All Sikh men also assumed the surname Singh, meaning "lion" (though not all Singhs are Sikhs), and Sikh women adopted the name Kaur, meaning "lioness" or "princess." Members of the khalsa were to follow a strict code of conduct that forbade the use of alcohol and tobacco and advocated a life of meditation and courage.

Buddhism

Siddhartha Gautama was born into a princely family in Lumbini, near the India–Nepal border, around 563 BC. Upon encountering suffering during his first venture outside the palace as a young man, he renounced his privileged status—an act called the Great Renunciation—to live as an ascetic. He then entered a lengthy meditation that led to his Great Enlightenment, or nirvana.

Transformed, Siddhartha went to Sarnath, India (near Varanasi), and preached his revolutionary sermon on the *dharma* (truth), also called "The Setting in Motion of the Wheel of Truth or Law." His discourse set forth his Four Noble Truths, which define the essence of Buddhism: (1) Life is connected to suffering, (2) a suffering that arises from greed, insatiable desires, and man's self-centered nature; (3) once man understands the cause of his suffering, he can overcome it by following (4) the Eightfold Path.

The Eightfold Path includes right views and right aspirations, which lead to wisdom. Right speech, right behavior, right means of livelihood, and right efforts to follow the path to salvation relate to proper and intelligent conduct. Right meditation and right contemplation bring nirvana (supreme bliss).

Siddhartha Gautama became the Buddha (Enlightened One), or Sakyamunni (Sage of the Sakya clan), and his faith became Theravada Buddhism, a religion of compassion and reason in which images were not worshiped, the existence of a permanent soul (*atman* to Hindus) was denied, and the authority of the Hindu *Vedas* was rejected. In the 1st century AD a second school, Mahayana Buddhism, was formed and introduced the concept of the *bod-*

hisattva, the enlightened being who postpones his own nirvana to help others. Unlike Theravadans—who prayed only before symbols, such as the Buddha's empty throne or his footprints—Mahayanists also worshiped before depictions of the various Buddhas, other gods and goddesses, and revered bodhisattvas. Over time, Mahayana Buddhism divided into subsects, based on differences in philosophical systems or ritual practices.

Ironically, Buddhism did not survive as a popular religion in India after its classical period. This is partly because of Hindu thinkers' response to the Buddhist challenge, embodied in works like the *Bhagavad Gita;* partly because increasingly sophisticated philosophy and esoteric ritual held little attraction for lay followers; and partly because major Buddhist institutions were destroyed by Muslim iconoclasts. While Indian teachers brought Buddhism to Tibet and China—and it spread from there—Buddhist remnants in India are limited mainly to such monuments as the Great Stupa at Sanchi (Madhya Pradesh), the Ajanta caves, and sculptures in major museums. Nevertheless, Buddhist artworks are among India's great treasures, evolving over time from stupas holding relics of the Buddha to elaborate temple structures depicting scenes from the life of the Buddha and episodes in his past lives. Later tantric Buddhist art, which continued to flourish in Nepal and Tibet, includes a large pantheon of past and future Buddhas, goddesses, Bodhisattvas, and historical teachers of the faith.

Two major communities still practice Buddhism in India. Tibetans in India include those in Himalayan areas such as Ladakh, which were closely connected to Tibet, and some 100,000 refugees who fled Tibet after the Chinese took over in 1951 and are now dispersed in various parts of India. The Dalai Lama, head of the Gelugpas, the largest Tibetan Buddhist sect, now lives in Dharamsala, Himachal Pradesh, where a sizable Tibetan community works to preserve their traditions and the welfare of the refugee community. The other main Buddhist group, sometimes called neo-Buddhist, was founded by the Dalit leader Bhimrao Ramji Ambedkar, who urged fellow untouchables to abandon Hinduism in favor of Buddhism because the latter does not recognize caste.

—By Kathleen Cox and Andy McCord

BOOKS AND FILMS

The classic work on early Indian history is A. L. Basham's *The Wonder that Was India*. Stanley Wolpert's *New History of India* (6th ed.) is a good survey. In *The Discovery of India*, Jawaharlal Nehru's sense of his country's history is passionate and poetic. *India Britannica*, by Geoffrey Moorhouse, is an entertaining and informative history of the British Raj. *Freedom at Midnight*, by Larry Collins and Dominique Lapierre, is a spellbinding account of India's break from Britain; *City of Joy*, by the same authors, is a powerful portrait of Calcutta. *India: A Million Mutinies Now*, by V. S. Naipaul, is an optimistic sequel to the author's brilliant but infuriating earlier books on India. Diana Eck's *Banaras: City of Light* is an engaging profile of the religious life of Varanasi, including an account of Hinduism as it has been lived over the centuries. Elisabeth Bumiller's balanced presentation of the lives of Indian women, *May You Be the Mother of a Hundred Sons*, stands out. Sunil Khilnani's *The Idea of India* is a brilliant essay on India's post-Nehru efforts to build an entity out of its challenging size, diversity, and economy. K. Ilaiah's *Why I am not a Hindu* stirred a far-reaching debate on caste in contemporary India. Nirad Chaudhuri's *Autobiography of an Unknown Indian* is a memoir of the Bengali author's early days in colonial India, including lively, insightful descriptions of Indian customs, castes, and relations with the British. *In Light of India* is a collection of learned essays by the Nobel Laureate and former Mexican ambassador Octavio Paz; in it, "Feasts and Fasts" compares Indian and Mexican cuisines in such a way that both take on greater significance. Gita Mehta's *Snakes and Ladders* is a collection of short pieces on the state of modern India. James Cameron's *An Indian Summer* is a glib but loving memoir by a British journalist who lived in India both during and after the Raj.

Barbara Stoler Miller's *The Bhagavad-Gita: Krishna's Council in Time of War* is the best translation of the classic Hindu text. To understand the great Sanskrit epic *Mahabharata*, the most readable place to start is the screenplay to Peter Brook's film and stage version. Classical Hindu myths are retold in prose form in *Gods, Demons, and Others*, by the master writer R. K. Narayan, and more recently in the acclaimed volume *Ka*, by Roberto Calasso. A. K. Ramanujan's *Speaking of Shiva* is a stunningly beautiful translation of devotional poems from South India. *Myths and Symbols in Indian Art and Civilization*, by Heinrich Zimmer (completed and edited by Joseph Campbell), is essential for the art or mythology buff, and Stuart Cary Welch's *India: Art and Culture, 1300–1900* is a lavishly illustrated volume by a great connoisseur. The colorful minibook *India and the Mughal Dynasty*, by Valérie Berinstain, makes a great pocket companion in much of North India. For ravishing photographs see *A Day in the Life of India*, people going about their business; *India Modern*, a contemporary treatment of traditional buildings and crafts; and the oversize retrospective *River of Colour: The India of Raghubir Singh*.

Rudyard Kipling's *Kim* is still the most intimate fictional account of India by a Westerner. In E. M. Forster's *A Passage to India*, the conflict between Indians and their British rulers is played out in the story of a man accused of rape. *Midnight's Children*, by Salman Rushdie, is the epic tale of a boy who was born the moment India gained independence. Rushdie's *The Moor's Last Sigh*, woven around a young man of mixed heritage, paints incomparably sensual portraits of Bombay and Cochin. Vikram Seth's mesmerizing *A Suitable Boy* portrays middle-class life in the 1950s through a timeless story of young love. Rohinton Mistry's *A Fine Balance* is an extraordinary study of the human condition, as experienced by a motley group of characters in 1970s Bombay; Mistry's *Such a Long Journey* weaves the poignant tale of a Parsi householder caught in a sudden whirl of tragedy. Arundhati Roy's *The God of Small Things*, set in 1960s Kerala, tells a disturbing story of brother-and-sister twins raised by a single mother. Bapsi Sidhwa's *Cracking India* sees the bloody partition of India and Pakistan through the eyes of a young girl in Lahore. Amit Chaudhuri's short novel *A Strange and Sublime Address* (published in the U.S. with Chaudhuri's *Freedom Song*) is a gorgeous story about a 10-year-old boy's stay with relatives in Calcutta. Anita Desai's *Fasting, Feasting* concerns a contemporary Indian family whose son goes off to college in the United States. *Hullabaloo in the Guava Orchard,* by Anita Desai's daughter Kiran Desai, is a hilarious look at family life in small-town India, centering on a young man's decision to go live in a guava tree. *Love and Longing in Bombay,* by Vikram Chandra, is a collection of short stories with a single narrator. Upamanyu Chatterji's *English August* is a funny account of a contemporary rookie in the Indian Civil Service. Ahmed Ali's *Twilight in Delhi* gives a poignant account of Muslim urban society early in the 20th century. Khushwant Singh's *Delhi* is a bawdy and ultimately moving romp through Delhi's tumultuous history.

Not all good Indian writing has been published in the West. Once you're in India, look for English translations of Intizar Hussain's *Basti* and A. R. Ananthamurthy's *Samskara,* as well as new translated fiction from Macmillan India. Bengali poet and Nobel Laureate Rabindranath Tagore can be read in translation in such volumes as *Gitanjali* (1911) and *The Crescent Moon* (1913). Tagore's novels *Gora* and *The Home and the World* are classics.

Traveler's India is a magazine designed to get your creative juices flowing as you plan your trip, with features on destinations, activities (horseback-riding in Rajasthan, say), people (a short interview with Vikram Chandra; a profile of an American curator of Indian art), and history. For an issue or a subscription contact Zeno Marketing Communications, Inc. (✉ 599 Edison Dr., East Windsor, NJ 08520, 609/426–0016, zenocom@aol.com).

The prolific Indian film industry has produced a wealth of historical and adventure movies, as well as some of the great international art films. India's premier filmmaker, Satyajit Ray, wrote and directed *Pather Panchali* (1955), *Aparajito* (1956), and *The World of Apu* (1959), a powerful trilogy depicting poverty and tragedy in the life of a Bengali boy. A prime example of Indian costume melodrama is *Aan* (1952), directed by Mehboob, a story of royalty tamed by peasants. *Shakespeare Wallah* (1965), written by Ruth Prawer Jhabvala and James Ivory and directed by Ivory, features a group of English actors on tour in India. *Heat and Dust* (1982), also written by Prawer Jhabvala and directed by Ivory, re-creates India's past through the discovery of a series of old letters. Deepa Mehta has made two major films: *Fire* (1996), in which two beautiful but neglected sisters-in-law turn to each other for affection, and *Earth* (1999), an adaptation of Bapsi Sidhwa's novel *Cracking India.* Both were highly controversial in India, as is Mehta's latest film, *Water,* set in Varanasi.

Films set in India by Western directors are numerous. *Phantom India* (1969), directed by Louis Malle, is an epic documentary of Indian life. The award-winning *Gandhi* (1982), directed by Richard Attenborough, traces the adult life of the leader of India's independence movement. Based on E. M. Forster's novel, *A Passage to India* (1984) was directed by David Lean. *The Jewel in the Crown* (1984), a TV series based on part of Paul Scott's *Raj Quartet,* is an epic portrayal of Britain's last years of power in India, involving a romance between a British woman and an Indian man. *Salaam Bombay* (1988), directed by Mira Nair, is a heartbreaking fictionalized exposé of Bombay's homeless and slum children. *City of Joy* (1992), starring Patrick Swayze, is based on Collins' and Lapierre's book about Calcutta.

VOCABULARY

Ashram: religious retreat
Auto-rickshaw: three-wheeled motorized vehicle
Avatar: incarnation of a deity
Ayurvedic medicine: Indian herbal medicine
Bagh: garden
Baoli: step well
Bhagavad Gita: Hindu religious text containing Krishna's lessons on faith; part of the *Mahabharata* (☞ *below*)
Cantonment: military area
Dharma: divine law; religious duty
Ghat: stepped area leading down to a river
Ghazal: Urdu song
Gompa: Tibetan-Buddhist monastery
Guru: teacher
Haveli: mansion with interior courtyard
Hill station: mountain town developed as a Raj-era retreat
Mahabharata: epic poem written in Sanskrit
Maidan: urban park
Marg: major road
Prayer wheel: prayer-inscribed cylinder containing paper or cloth strips, each inscribed with "Om Mani Padme Hum." When the prayer wheel is rotated—always clockwise—the mantra is sent to heaven
Raj: the former British rule on the Indian subcontinent
Rajput: onetime martial warrior in northwest India
Sadhu: mendicant ascetic; holy person
Stupa: tall hemisphere made of stone or clay, used as a receptacle for offerings
Tank: an artificial body of water, often adjoining a temple for ablutions
Wallah: person associated with a particular duty, such as a rickshaw-wallah

DINING GLOSSARY

Aloo: potato
Aloo tikki: fried potato patties
Baigan: eggplant
Barfi: milk-based sweetmeats
Bhaji: vegetable fritters
Bhindi: okra
Biriani: rice cooked with meat or vegetables
Chaat: cold, spicy fruit or vegetable salad
Chai: tea
Chapati: unleavened bread cooked in an iron pan
Chawal: rice
Chenna: chickpeas
Chutney: pickled relishes
Curd: yogurt
Dal: cooked lentils
Dosa: fried, crepe-style pancake
Dum pukht: sealed, slow-cooked aromatic dishes
Falooda: cellophane vermicelli that often comes with *kulfi* (☞ *below*)
Feni: Goan cashew-nut liquor
Firni: sweet ground-rice pudding with pistachios
Ghee: clarified butter
Gobi: cauliflower
Gosht: lamb or mutton

Gulab jamun: fried, doughy milk balls in syrup
Idli: steamed rice cakes
Jhingha: prawn; also called *chingra*
Kadhai: foods prepared in an iron pot similar to a wok
Katoris: small metal bowls placed on the *thali* (☞ *below*)
Kheer: thick, creamy rice pudding with almonds
Kofta: spicy meat or vegetable balls
Kulcha: *naan* (☞ *below*) stuffed with herbs and onion
Kulfi: Indian ice cream
Lassi: cold yogurt-and-milk drink
Masala: spicy gravy
Masala chai: spicy tea with whole cardamom, clove, and cinnamon
Masala dosa: potato-stuffed dosa
Mattar: peas
Muchli: fish
Murg: chicken
Murg reshmi: spicy minced chicken roll
Naan: slightly leavened bread prepared in a tandoori
Nimbu pani: lemonade
Paan: a digestive (and sometimes a narcotic) consisting of betel leaf filled with lime paste, crushed betel nut, and sweet and aromatic spices
Paan liqueur: Sikkimese betel-nut liqueur
Pakora: deep-fried vegetable fritter
Paneer: Indian-style cottage cheese
Pappad: fried, thin wafer made with bread and pepper; also called *pappadam*
Paratha: shallow-fried unleavened bread made with ghee
Piaz: onion
Pillau: spiced rice with meat or vegetables
Pudina paratha: paratha with mint
Puri: deep-fried puffed bread
Raan: roast lamb or mutton with spices
Raita: chopped vegetables mixed with yogurt
Rasgullah: syrupy-sweet cream-cheese balls
Rogan gosht: lamb with yogurt
Saag: spinach; also called *palak*
Sambhar: spicy sauce served with dosa and idli
Samosa: deep-fried pastry stuffed with meat or vegetables
Shaan-e-murgh: chicken breast stuffed with paneer
Shami kebab: deep-fried ground meat patty
Subzi: vegetables
Tandoori: foods cooked in a clay oven fired by charcoal
Thali: traditional all-you-can-eat meal of assorted dishes, often served on a steel plate
Tikka: skewered and barbequed chunks of meat, vegetables, or cheese

INDEX

Icons and Symbols

★ Our special recommendations
✕ Restaurant
🏨 Lodging establishment
✕🏨 Lodging establishment whose restaurant warrants a special trip
Good for kids (rubber duck)
☞ Sends you to another section of the guide for more information
✉ Address
☎ Telephone number
⏲ Opening and closing times
🎟 Admission prices

Numbers in white and black circles ③❸ that appear on the maps, in the margins, and within the tours correspond to one another.

A

Adinath Temple, *119*
Adivaraha Cave, *333*
Adventures
Himachal Pradesh, 30–33
Ladakh, 37–39
permits for, 56–57
Sikkim, 50, 52
Uttar Pradesh, 46–48
Afghan Memorial Church of St. John the Baptist, *221*
Agra and environs, *10, 11, 13, 101, 102, 104–116.* ☞ *Also* North Central India
Agra Fort, *104–106*
Ahmed Shah's Tomb, *194*
Ahmedabad and environs, *12, 13, 192–200.* ☞ *Also* Gujarat
Aina Mahal, *201*
Air travel. ☞ Plane travel
Airataesvara Temple, *341*
Airports, *xi*
Ajanta and Ellora Caves, *11, 215, 243–251*
currency exchange, 251
dining, 244–245, 250
festivals and seasonal events, 13, 250
guided tours, 251
lodging, 244, 254–246
nightlife and the arts, 250
transportation, 250–251
travel agencies, 251
visitor information, 251
Ajmer, *161*
Akal Takht, *18*
Akali Mata, *204*
Akbar's private chambers, *112*
Akbar's Tomb, *102, 104, 106*
Alakananda River, *47*
Alamgir Mosque, *127, 128*
Albert Hall Museum, *149*
Alchi Choskor, *34–35*
Allahabad, *13*
Alleppey, *14, 308*
Aloobari monastery, *49*
Amer Fort and Palace, *149–151*
Amritsar, *16–20.* ☞ *Also* the Himalayas
Anguri Bagh, *105*
Anjuna, *262*
Ankh Michauli, *112*
Appliqué work, *366*
Arambol Beach, *260*
Aranmula, *14*
Archaeological Faculty (Vadodara), *209*
Archaeological Museum (Bodhgaya), *134*
Archaeological Museum (Hampi), *293*
Archaeological Museum (Khajuraho), *120*
Archaeological Museum (Lothal), *208*
Arjuna, *333*
Armory (Jaipur), *151*
Art galleries and museums. ☞ *Also* Museums
Bombay, 217, 221–222
Calcutta, 373, 376, 378, 386, 389
Delhi, 73, 74, 89
Goa, 262, 263
Guajarat, 194, 198, 201, 209
Hyderabad, 349, 351
Himalayas, 19, 26, 29
Karnataka, 281, 285, 286
Kerala, 303, 304, 310
North Central India, 113, 127, 128
Rajasthan, 149, 152, 166, 167, 173, 182
Tamil Nadu, 323, 324, 340, 341–342
Arts-and-crafts villages, *149, 152, 157, 174, 180, 192, 202–203, 365, 366, 389*
Ashoka Pillar, *132*
Ashoka's vantage point and conversion, *366*
Asthika Samaj Temple, *224*
ATMs, *xxiii*
Aurangabad, *243–246*
Auraville, *337*

B

Baba Bangla Sahib Gurdwara, *70–71*
Babulnath Temple, *223*
Backwater cruises, *11–12, 300-301*
Bada Bagh, *182*
Badal Mahal (Jaisalmer), *182*
Badal Mahal (Kumbhalgarh), *180*
Baga Beach, *260–271*
Bagru, *158*
Bahai Temple, *70, 71*
Baijanth temple, *45*
Bailie Guard Gate, *135*
Bakrid (holiday), *14*
Balsamand Lake and Garden, *166*
Banana boats, *266*
Bangalore, *273, 274–283.* ☞ *Also* Karnataka
Banganga (temple complex), *223*
Banquet Hall, *135*
Baoli, *199*
Bara Darwaza (Western Gate), *75*
Bara Imanbara, *135*
Bars and lounges
Bhubaneswar, 363
Bombay, 237–238
Calcutta, 387
Delhi, 90
Jodhpur, 169
Karnataka, 281–282, 288
Kerala, 307
Basilica of Bom Jesus, *262–263*
Basilica of San Thome Cathedral, *324, 325*
Bay of Bengal, *364–367*
Beaches, *7*
Bombay, 12, 216, 223, 251–252
Bhubaneswar, 366
Goa, 260–262
Gujarat, 190, 206–207
Karnataka, 14, 290
Kerala, 300, 311
Tamil Nadu, 323, 324
Begging, *xi*
Belur, *273, 291–292.* ☞ *Also* Karnataka
Belur Math Shrine, *373, 376, 377*
Bengal Natural History Museum, *49*
Bhageshwar temple, *45*
Bhagirathi River, *47*
Bharat Kala Bhavan Museum, *127, 128*
Bharati Sanskruti Darshan, *201*
Bharatpur, *102, 148, 160–161*
Bharatya Lok Kala Mandal, *173*
Bhavnagar, *192*
Bhilangana Valley, *48*

Bhima, *333*
Bhiwali, *44*
Bhubaneswar, *7, 356–368*
architecture, 356
Bay of Bengal, 364–367
currency exchange, 368
dining, 356, 361
festivals and seasonal events, 13–14, 363
guided tours, 368
itineraries, 357–358
lodging, 356, 362–363, 365, 366–367
nightlife and the arts, 363
shopping, 356, 363
transportation, 367
travel agencies, 368
visitor information, 368
when to tour Bhubaneswar, 358
Bhuj, *192, 201–202*
Bhuri Singh Museum, *29*
Bhutia Busti monastery, *49*
Bibi-ka-Maqbara, *244*
Bicycling, *31, 186*
Big Foot Museum, *262, 263*
Bikaner House, *73*
Billiards, *238*
Bindusagar, *358, 359*
Binsar, *45*
Bir, *32*
Birbal's Palace, *112*
Bird hospital, *64, 65*
Boat race, *308*
Boat travel
Goa, 267
Kerala, 313
North Central India, 139
Bodhgaya, *14, 102, 133–134*
Bodhi tree, *133–134*
Bogmalo Beach, *261*
Bombay, *6, 10, 214–243, 253–256*
bazaars, 217, 220, 221, 222, 240
climate, xxxii
consulates, 255
currency exchange, 255
dining, 12, 215, 221, 224–225, 228–231
emergencies, 256
festivals and seasonal events, 15
Fort District and environs, 216–217, 220–222
guided tours, 256
itineraries, 216
lodging, 12, 215, 231–236
Malabar Hill and environs, 216, 223–225
nightlife and the arts, 236–238
outdoor activities and sports, 238–239
pharmacies, 256
shopping, 239–243
transportation, 253–255
travel agencies, 256
visitor information, 256
when to tour Bombay, 216
Bowling, *238, 282*
Brahma Kumaris Spiritual University, *179*
Brahma Temple, *118*
Brahmeswar Temple, *358, 359*
Brihadiswara Temple, *340*
Brindavan Gardens, *285–286*
Buddha Jayanti (festival), *14*
Buddhist complex (Khajuraho), *120*
Buland Darwaza, *113*
Bull Temple, *275*
Bus travel, *xi*
Ajanta and Ellora Caves, 250
Goa, 267, 268
Himalayas, 53–54
Hyderabad, 354
Karnataka, 294, 296
Business hours, *xi*

C

Calaba, *216*
Calangute Beach, *260, 261*
Calcutta, *7, 12, 370–392*
B.B.D. Bagh, 372, 373, 379–380
Central Calcutta, 378–381
Chowringhee, 373, 379, 380
climate, xxxii
College Street, 373, 376, 377
consulates, 391
currency exchange, 391
dining, 371, 382–384, 389
excursions, 388–389
festivals and seasonal events, 14
guided tours, 391
itineraries, 372–373
Kumartuli, 373, 376, 377
lodging, 371, 385–386, 389
Maidan, 373, 378–381
name changes, 371
nightlife and the arts, 386–387
North Calcutta, 12, 373, 376–378
outdoor activities and sports, 387
shopping, 371–372, 387–388
Southern Calcutta, 381–382
street life, 372
transportation, 390–391
travel agencies, 392
visitor information, 392
when to tour Calcutta, 373
wholesale flower market, 376, 378
Calico Museum of Textiles, *194*
Camel Festival, *13, 162*
Camel safaris, *37, 169, 184*
Cameras and photography, *xi*
Car rentals, *xii*
Car travel, *xv–xvi*
Bhubaneswar, 367
Bombay, 253, 255
Calcutta, 390, 391
Gujarat, 211
Himalayas, 53–54
Hyderabad, 353
Karnataka, 294, 296
Kerala, 312–313
North Central India, 137, 139–140
Rajasthan, 185, 187
Tamil Nadu, 343–344
Carnival, *13, 258*
Catamaran travel, *254*
Cattle fair, *13, 171*
Cauvery River, *289*
Caves
Ajanta and Ellora Caves, 11, 215, 243–251
Bombay, 216, 225
Tamil Nadu, 332, 333–334
Cenotaphs, *115*
Central Sikh Museum, *19*
Chamba, *29*
Champaner, *209*
Chamundi Hill, *284*
Chandan Yatra (festival), *13–14*
Chandigarh, *22*
Chandra Mahal, *151*
Changing money, *xxiii.* ☞ *Also* Currency exchange *under cities and areas*
Channigaraya Temple, *292*
Char Bagh (garden), *150*
Charity Birds Hospital, *64, 65*
Charminar, *349, 350*
Chaturbhuj Temple (Khajuraho), *120*
Chaturbhuj Temple (Orchha), *115*
Chaubatia Orchards, *45*
Chaukhandi Stupa, *132*
Chausath Yogini Temple, *120, 127, 128*
Chenna Peak, *43*
Chhatrapati Shivaji Terminus, *217, 220*
Children and travel, *xii–xiii*
Chilling, *39*
Chitra Festival, *14*
Chitragupta Temple, *121–122*
Chittaurgarh, *179–180*
Chor Bazaar, *217, 220*
Chowpatty Beach and Marine Drive, *12, 223*
Church of Our Lady of Expectation, *324, 325*
Church of Our Lady of Immaculate Conception, *262, 263*
Churches
Bombay, 221
Calcutta, 373, 379, 381
Goa, 262–263
Gujarat, 206
Himalayas, 26, 28
Kerala, 304
Tamil Nadu, 320, 323, 324, 325
Churi Ajitgarh, *163*
City Palace (Jaipur), *149, 151*

City Palace Museum (Udaipur), *173*
Climate, *xxxii–xxxiii*
Clock tower, *135*
Cochin, *11, 12, 302–307*. ☞ *Also* Kerala
Colaba, *220*
College of Fine Arts, *209*
Colossal monolithic statue, *290*
Colva Beach, *260, 261*
Computers, *xiii*
Consulates. ☞ Embassies and consulates
Corbett National Park, *41–42, 63*
Crafts Museum, *70, 71*
Crafts Villages. ☞ Arts-and-crafts villages
Credit cards, *xxiii*
Crematoriums, *125, 166*
Cricket, *91, 238–239, 387*
Crocodile Bank, *318, 330*
Crocodiles, *123, 266, 318, 330*
Cruises, *11–12, 266, 300–301*
Currency exchange, *xxiii*. ☞ *Also under cities and areas*
Customs, *xiii–xv*

D

Dabhoi Fort, *209*
DakshinaChitra, *318, 330*
Dakshineshwar Kali Temple, *373, 376, 377*
Dalai Lama's private residence, *26*
Dalhousie, *28*
Dalmadol cannon, *389*
Dance, *8*
Bhubaneswar, 363
Bombay, 236
Delhi, 62, 89
Ellora Dance Festival, 250
Ellora Festival of Classical Music and Dance, 13
Elephanta Festival of Music and Dance, 13
Gujarat, 198
Himalayas, 26
Karnataka, 272, 280–281, 288, 290–291
Kerala, 306–307
Khajuraho Dance Festival, 13, 118
Konark Dance Festival, 14, 363
North Central India, 13, 118, 137
Rajasthan, 156
Tamil Nadu, 328–329
Darga Sharif, *161*
Darjeeling, *48–50*. ☞ *Also* the Himalayas
Darshani Deorhi, *19*
Dashashvamedh Ghat, *127, 128*
Daulatabad Fort, *244*
Deeg, *161*
Deer Park, *133*
Delhi, *5–6, 10, 60–97*
bookstores, 97
Chandni Chowk, 64, 65
climate, xxxiii
Connaught Place, 92
currency exchange, 96
dining, 12, 61, 76–77, 80–84
Diplomatic Enclave, 92
emergencies, 96
festivals and seasonal events, 13
Gali Parante Wali, 64, 65
itineraries, 63
lodging, 62, 85–88
New Delhi, 63, 69–76
nightlife and the arts, 62, 88–91
Old Delhi, 63, 64–65, 68–69, 91–92
outdoor activities and sports, 91
pharmacies, 96
post offices, 97
price charts, 61, 62
shopping, 62, 91–93
South Delhi, 93
transportation, 94–96
travel agencies, 97
visitor information, 97
when to tour Delhi, 63–64
Desert Fair, *13*
Desert National Park, *184*
Devaraja Market, *284*
Devi Jagdamba Temple, *121*
Dhamekh Stupa, *132*
Dharamsala, *25–27*
Dharasuram Temple, *341*
Dharmaraja, *333*
Dhauladhar, *32*
Dhauli, *358, 366*
Dhirdham Temple, *49*
Dhobi Ghat (Bombay), *221*
Dhobi Ghat (Varanasi), *127, 128*
Dhola Vira, *192, 203–204*
Dilwara Temples, *179*
Dining, *xv, 7–8, 12*. ☞ *Also under cities and areas*
Dinman Hardaul's Palace, *115*
Disabilities and accessibility, *xv*
Discos
Bombay, 238
Calcutta, 387
Delhi, 89–90
Karnataka, 282
Diu, *192, 206–207*
Diwali (festival), *14*
Diwan-i-Am (Agra), *106*
Diwan-i-Am (Fatehpur Sikri), *12*
Diwan-i-Am (Jaipur), *150, 151*
Diwan-i-Khas (Agra), *106*
Diwan-i-Khas (Delhi), *69*
Diwan-i-Khas (Fatehpur Sikri), *112*
Dolphin-spotting tours, *266*
Draupadi, *333*
Driving. ☞ Car travel
Drogpa Villages, *36–37*
Dudhsagar Waterfalls, *262, 263*
Duladeo Temple, *119–120*
Durbar Hall (Gwalior), *114*
Durbar Hall (Mysore), *14, 284–285*
Durbar Hall (Varanasi), *130*
Durga Puja (festival), *14*
Durga Temple, *127, 128–129*
Durgiana Temple, *20*
Dussehra (festival), *14, 285*
Dutch Palace, *303, 304*
Duties, *xiii–xv*

E

Eastern Group of Temples (Khajuraho), *118–119*
Ecology Centre, *34*
Eden Gardens, *373, 379, 380*
Ekambareswara Temple, *335–336*
Electricity, *xvi*
Elephant Festival, *13*
Elephanta Caves, *216, 225*
Elephanta Festival of Music and Dance, *13*
Ellora Caves. ☞ Ajanta and Ellora Caves
Ellora Dance Festival, *250*
Ellora Festival of Classical Music and Dance, *13*
Embassies and consulates, *xvi*
Bombay, 255
Calcutta, 391
Tamil Nadu, 344
Emergencies, *xvi–xvii*
Bombay, 256
Delhi, 96
Himalayas, 56
Etiquette and behavior, *xvii*

F

Falaknuma Palace, *349, 350*
Fateh Prakash Mahal, *180*
Fatehpur Sikri, *10, 101, 102, 104, 111–113*. ☞ *Also* North Central India
Festivals and seasonal events, *13–14*. ☞ *Also under cities and areas*
Film industry, *236*
Fishing
Himachal Pradesh, 30
Himalayas, 30, 46–47
Karnataka, 289
Uttar Pradesh, 46–47
Five Rathas, *333*
Flora Fountain, *217, 220*
Flower Bazaar (Madras), *320*
Folklore Museum, *182*

Fort Cochin, *303, 304*
Fort Museum, *320, 321*
Fort St. George, *320, 321*
Fort William, *373, 379, 380*
Forts
Ajanta and Ellora Caves, 244
Calcutta, 373, 379, 380, 389
Delhi, 64, 68–69, 70, 75
Gujarat, 209
Hyderabad, 349, 350
Kerala, 303, 304
North Central India, 104–106, 113–114, 115, 127, 130
Rajasthan, 12, 149–151, 152, 159, 161, 165, 166–167, 170, 173, 174, 179–180, 181–182
Tamil Nadu, 320, 321, 338
Fruit Market (Madras), *320–321*

G

Gadsisar Lake, *182*
Gandhi Jayanti (festival), *14*
Gandhi Smriti, *71–72*
Gandhi statue, *337*
Ganesh Pole, *150*
Ganesha Chaturthi (festival), *14*
Gangasagar Mela (festival), *13*
Gangaur Festival, *13*
Ganges River, *12, 13, 47*
Gangotri, *47–48*
Gangtok, *xxxiii, 52–53*
Gardens
Bombay, 224
Calcutta, 373, 379, 380, 381, 382
Delhi, 70, 73
Himalayas, 20
Karnataka, 275, 276, 285–286
North Central India, 115
Rajasthan, 149, 150, 152, 166, 173, 174, 179, 182
Garjia Temple, *42*
Gateway of India, *217, 220*
Gay and lesbian travel, *xvii*
General Post Office (Calcutta), *379, 380*
George Town (Madras), *320, 321*
Ghantai Temple, *119*
Gharial Sanctuary, *123*
Gir National Park and Wildlife Sanctuary, *192, 205–206*
Goa, *6, 258–269*
architecture, 258
communications, 268
currency exchange, 261, 268
dining, 259, 261, 264
festivals and seasonal events, 13, 258
itineraries, 260
lodging, 259, 264–265
nightlife and the arts, 266
outdoor activities and sports, 261, 266
pharmacies, 268
shopping, 267
tour operators and travel agencies, 268
transportation, 267–268
visitor information, 261, 269
when to tour Goa, 260
Godly Museum, *284*
Golconda Fort, *349, 350*
Golden Temple, *18–19*
Golf
Bombay, 239
Calcutta, 387
Delhi, 91
Karnataka, 282
Rajasthan, 156
Tamil Nadu, 329
Gomateshwara statue, *290*
Gopalpur-on-Sea, *358, 366*
Goubert Avenue (Pondicherry), *337*
Government lodging, *xxi*
Government Silk Weaving Factory, *285, 286*
Great Elephant March, *13*
Guamukh, *47–48*
Guda Vishnoi, *166, 170*
Gujarat, *6, 190–212*
Ahmedabad and environs, 12, 13, 192–200
currency exchange, 209, 211
dining, 190–191, 195–196, 200, 202
festivals and seasonal events, 13, 191
itineraries, 192
Kathiawar Peninsula, 204–210
Kutch, 200–204
lodging, 191, 196–198, 200, 202–203, 205–206, 207, 208, 209–210
nightlife and the arts, 198
permits, 211–212
shopping, 191, 198–199, 202
transportation, 210–211
travel agencies, 209, 212
visitor information, 212
visual arts and architecture, 191
when to tour Gujarat, 192
wildlife, 191–192, 200, 205–206, 208
Gugari Mahal, *113–114*
Gulistan Tourist Complex, *113*
Gurdwara, *43*
Guru Ram Das Langar, *18*
Guru Shikhar, *179*
Gwalior, *10, 102, 113–114*
Gwalior Fort, *113–114*
Gyan Bhandar, *182*
Gyanvapi Mosque, *125, 129*

H

Haji Ali Shrine, *216, 223–224*
Halebid, *273, 274, 291, 292–293*. ☞ *Also* Karnataka
Hampi, *11, 273, 274, 293–294*. ☞ *Also* Karnataka
Handicraft Centre, *26*
Hanging Gardens, *224*
Happy Valley Tea Estate, *49*
Haridwar, *13*
Harmandir Sahib, *19*
Hatheesing Jain Temple, *194*
Hauz Khas, *72*
Havelis, *163, 182–183*
Hawa Mahal (Fatehpur Sikri), *112*
Hawa Mahal (Jaipur), *149, 151*
Hazrat Nizamuddin Darga, *70, 72–73*
Health clubs, *282, 288*
Health concerns, *xvii–xix*. ☞ *Also* Emergencies
Hemis Festival, *14*
Heritage Hotels, *xxii*
High Court, *320, 321, 323*
Himachal Emporium, *29*
Himachal Pradesh, *20, 22–33*. ☞ *Also* the Himalayas
Himalayas, *5, 16–58*
adventures, 30–33, 37–39, 46–48, 50, 52
Amritsar, 16–20
climate, xxxiii
currency exchange, 56
Darjeeling, 48–50
dining, 20, 23, 24, 25, 26–27, 28, 29, 30, 35, 41–42, 44, 45–46, 49, 52–53
emergencies, 56
festivals and seasonal events, 13, 14
Himachal Pradesh, 20, 22–33
Ladakh, 14, 33–39
lodging, 20, 22–23, 24, 25, 27, 28, 29, 30, 35–36, 40, 41–42, 44, 45–46, 49–50, 53
permits, 56–57
Sikkim, 13, 14, 50, 52–53
tour operators, 29, 57
transportation, 53–56
Uttar Pradesh, 39–48
visitor information, 57–58
Himalayan Mountaineering Institute, *49*
Hindu Temples (Himalayas), *45–46*
Holi (festival), *13*
Holidays, *xx, 13*
Home stays, *187*
Horse and buggy rides, *239*
Horse racing
Bombay, 239
Calcutta, 387
Karnataka, 282, 288
Tamil Nadu, 329
Horseback riding, *31*
Hostels, *xxii*
Hôtel de Ville (Town Hall; Pondicherry), *337*

Hotels, *xxii.* ☞ *Also* Lodging *under cities and areas*
House of Maryam, *112*
Howrah Bridge, *373, 376, 377*
Hoysaleswara Temple, *292*
Humayun's Tomb, *70, 73*
Hussainabad Imambara, *135*
Hyderabad, *6–7, 347–354*
business services, 354
currency exchange, 354
dining, 348, 351–352
express mail and courier services, 354
itineraries, 349
lodging, 348, 352–353
shopping, 348, 353
Tank Bund Road, 351
tours, 354
transportation, 353–354
travel agencies, 354
visitor information, 354
when to tour Hyderabad, 349
Hydrofoil travel, *255*

I

Id-ul-Fitr (holiday), *13*
Id-ul-Zuha (holiday), *14*
Independence Day, *14*
Indian Botanical Gardens, *381, 382*
Indian Museum, *373, 379, 380*
Indus River, *38*
Insurance, *xx*
International Seafood Festival, *14*
Itineraries, *10–11.* ☞ *Also under cities and areas*
Itmad-ud-Daulat's Tomb, *101, 102, 104, 106–107*

J

Jag Mandir palace, *173–174*
Jagannath Temple, *365*
Jagat Shiromani Temple, *151*
Jageshwar temple, *45*
Jahangir Mahal, *115*
Jahangiri Mahal, *105*
Jai Vilas Palace, *114*
Jaigarh Fort, *150*
Jain Temple (Bombay), *223, 224*
Jain Temple (Ranakpur), *178*
Jain Temples (Halebid), *292*
Jain Temples (Jaisalmer), *182*
Jain Temples (Osian), *170*
Jaipur and environs, *10, 13, 14, 146, 148–162.* ☞ *Also* Rajasthan
Jaipur House, *73*
Jaisalmer and environs, *12, 13, 146, 148, 181–184.* ☞ *Also* Rajasthan
Jaleb Chowk, *150*
Jallianwala Bagh, *19–20*
Jami Masjid (Ahmedabad), *194*
Jama Masjid (Delhi), *65, 68*
Jama Masjid (Fatehpur Sikri), *113*
Janapada Loka Folk Arts Museum, *281*
Jantar Mantar, *149, 151–152*
Jas Mandir, *150*
Jaswant Thada, *166*
Javari Temple, *118*
Jawahar Kala Kendra, *149, 152*
Jeep safaris, *30–31, 37–38*
Jehangir Art Gallery, *217, 221*
Jet skiing, *266*
Jhula Devi Temple, *45*
Jhunjhunu, *163*
Jodh Bai's Palace, *112*
Jodhpur and environs, *146, 148, 165–171.* ☞ *Also* Rajasthan
Juna Mahal, *182*

K

Kailasanatha Temple, *336*
Kala Bhavan, *389*
Kala Raksha, *202*
Kalatope Wildlife Sanctuary, *28*
Kali River, *47*
Kali Temple, *209*
Kalighat Kali Temple, *373, 381, 382*
Kalika Mata, *180*
Kalyana Mandap, *284*
Kamala Nehru Park, *223, 224*
Kanak Vrindavan Gardens, *149, 152*
Kanchenjunga, *52*
Kanchipuram, *318, 331–332, 335–337.* ☞ *Also* Tamil Nadu
Kandariya Mahadev, *121*
Kangra Valley, *24–25, 31*
Kapalishvara Temple, *324, 325*
Karnataka, *6, 11, 271–298*
architecture, 271
Bangalore, 273, 274–283
Belur, 273, 291–292
currency exchange, 296
dining, 271, 277–279, 286–287, 293, 294
festivals and seasonal events, 13, 14, 285
Halebid, 273, 274, 291, 292–293
Hampi, 11, 273, 274, 293–294
itineraries, 273–274
lodging, 272, 279–280, 287–288, 289, 290, 291, 292, 293, 294
Mangalore, 274, 290–291
Mysore, 14, 273, 283–290
nightlife and the arts, 272, 280–281, 288
outdoor activities and sports, 282, 288
pharmacies, 296
safaris, 272
shopping, 272–273, 282–283, 288–289
tour operators and travel agencies, 297
transportation, 272, 274, 294–296
visitor information, 297–298
when to tour Karnataka, 274
Kashi Vishvanath Temple, *125, 129*
Kathiawar Peninsula, *204–210.* ☞ *Also* Gujarat
Kedareshvara Temple, *127, 129*
Kedareswar Temple, *358*
Kedareswara Temple, *292*
Keneseth Eliyahoo Synagogue, *222*
Keoladeo National Park, *160–161*
Kerala, *6, 10, 300–314*
Central and Southern Kerala, 307–312
Cochin, 11, 12, 302–307
cruises, 11–12, 300–301
currency exchange, 314
dining, 301, 305, 311
festivals and seasonal events, 13, 14, 301
guided tours, 314
itineraries, 302
lodging, 301, 305–306, 308, 309–310, 311–312
nightlife and the arts, 301, 306–307
shopping, 301, 307, 310
transportation, 312–312
travel agencies, 314
visitor information, 314
when to tour Kerala, 302
Khajiar, *28*
Khajuraho, *10, 11, 13, 102, 116–124.* ☞ *Also* North Central India
Khajuraho Dance Festival, *13, 118*
Khajuraho Village, *123*
Khas Mahal (Agra), *105–106*
Khas Mahal (Delhi), *69*
Khimsar, *170–171*
Kinnaur, *29–30, 31, 32*
Kirti Mandir, *209*
Kirti Stambh, *180*
Konark, *11, 14, 357–358, 363, 364*
Konark Dance Festival, *14, 363*
Konkan Railway, *272, 274*
Kothi Building, *209*
Kottayam, *14, 302, 309*
Kovalam, *11, 12, 302, 311–312*

Krishna Mandapam, *332*
Kulasekkhar Mandapam, *310*
Kullu, *30–31*
Kumaon Circle, *40–41, 46*
Kumarakom, *302, 307–308*
Kumbakonam, *341*
Kumbh Mela (festival), *13*
Kumbha Shyam, *180*
Kumbhalgarh, *180*
Kumbhalgarh Sanctuary, *180*
Kutch, *200–204*. ☞ *Also* Gujarat
Kutch Museum, *201*

L

La Martinière College, *136*
Lachhmangarh, *163*
Ladakh, *14, 33–39*. ☞ *Also* the Himalayas
Lahaul, *29–30, 32*
Lake Palace, *173–174*
Lake Periyar Wildlife Sanctuary, *10, 11, 309*
Lake Pichola, *173–174*
Lakhpat, *203*
Lakshadweep, *302, 312*
Lakshmana Temple, *121*
Lakshmi Marayan temple complex, *29*
Lakshmi Vilas Palace, *203*
Lal Bagh Botanical Gardens, *275, 276*
Lalguan Mahadeva, *120*
Lal Qila (Red Fort), *64, 68–69*
Lamayuru, *38*
Language, *xx*
Laxminarayan Temple, *115*
Leh, *30, 31, 32–33, 34–36, 37, 38*
Libraries
Calcutta, 381, 382
Delhi, 75
Rajasthan, 174, 182
Tamil Nadu, 324, 325, 340
Lighthouse, *334*
Lingaraj Temple Complex, *358, 359–360*
Little Rann of Kutch, *200*
Lodging, *xx–xxii, 12*. ☞ *Also under cities and areas*
taxes, xxvii
Lodi Gardens, *70, 73, 92–93*
Lohagarh Fort, *161*
Lolark Kund, *127*
Lord Krishna Temple, *290*
Losar (festival), *13*
Losel Doll Museum, *26*
Lothal, *192, 208*
Lower Mall Road (Ranikhet), *45*
Lucknow, *102, 124, 134–137*. ☞ *Also* North Central India
Ludarva Temples, *182, 183*
Lutyens's Imperial City, *70, 73–74*

M

Machhi Bhavan, *106*
Madan Gopal temple, *389*
Madan Mohan temple, *389*
Madras, *xxxiii, 11, 318, 320–321, 323–331*. ☞ *Also* Tamil Nadu
Madras Snake Park, *324, 325*
Madurai, *11, 14, 318, 338, 341–343*. ☞ *Also* Tamil Nadu
Magen Hassidim Synagogue, *222*
Mahabodhi Society, *134*
Mahabodhi Temple, *133*
Mahadeva Temple, *121*
Mahamandir monastery, *166*
Maharaja Fateh Singh Museum, *209*
Maharao's complex, *201*
Maharashtra Beaches, *216, 251–252*
Mahatma Jyotiba Phule Market, *217, 221*
Mahishasura statue, *284*
Mahishasuramardini Cave, *333*
Maidan, *373, 378–381*
Mail and shipping, *xxii*
Makar Sankranti (festival), *13*
Makarpura Palace, *209*
Malpe Beach, *290*
Mamallapuram, *11, 318, 331–335*. ☞ *Also* Tamil Nadu
Man Mandir, *113*
Manali, *23–24, 30, 31–33, 37, 38*. ☞ *Also* the Himalayas
Mandore Gardens, *166*
Mandvi, *192, 203*
Mangaladas Market, *221*
Mangalore, *274, 290–291*. ☞ *Also* Karnataka
Mani Bhavan, *223, 224*
Manikarnika Ghat, *125, 129–130*
Marble Palace, *373, 376, 377*
Margao, *260*
Marina Beach, *323, 324*
Martial arts, *307*
Marwar Festival, *14*
Matangesvara Temple, *120*
Matunga, *216, 223, 224–225*
Mecca Masjid, *349, 350*
Meenakshi Temple, *14, 341–342*
Meherangarh Fort, *165, 166–167*
Mint (Fatehpur Sikri), *111*
Missionaries of Charity, *382*
MLV Tribal Research Institute, *174*
Modhera, *192, 199–200*
Molela, *180*
Money, *xxii–xxiii*
Moriri Lake, *36–37, 38*
Mosques
Bombay, 216, 223–224
Calcutta, 373, 376, 377
Delhi, 65, 68, 69, 75–76
Gujarat, 194, 195
Himalayas, 43
Hyderabad, 349, 350
North Central India, 106, 112, 113, 125, 127, 128, 129
Moti Masjid (Pearl Mosque; Agra), *106*
Moti Masjid (Pearl Mosque; Delhi), *69*
Mount Abu, *148, 179*
Mt. Kanchenjunga, *14*
Mountain biking. ☞ Bicycling
Mubarak Mahal, *151*
Muharram (holiday), *14*
Mukandgarh, *163*
Mukteswar Temple, *358, 360*
Mulagandha Kuti Vilhari Temple, *132*
Mumbadevi Temple, *222*
Mumtaz Mahal, *69*
Museum and Art Gallery Complex, *310*
Museum of Christian Art, *262, 263*
Museums. ☞ *Also* Art galleries and museums
Bhubaneswar, 359, 360
Bombay, 217, 221–222
Calcutta, 373, 376, 378, 379, 380, 389
Delhi, 69, 70, 71–72, 73, 74–75, 76
Goa, 262, 263
Guajarat, 194, 201, 206, 208, 209
Himalayas, 19, 20, 26, 29, 34, 49
Hyderabad, 349, 351
Karnataka, 281, 284, 285, 286, 293
Kerala, 303, 304, 310
North Central India, 109, 113, 114, 120, 127, 128, 130, 132, 134
Rajasthan, 149, 152, 166, 167, 173, 174, 182
Tamil Nadu, 320, 321, 323, 324, 330, 340, 341–342
Music, *8*
Bombay, 236–237
Delhi, 62, 89
Gujarat, 198
Himalayas, 26
Karnataka, 272, 280–281, 288
Kerala, 306–307
North Central India, 132, 137
Tamil Nadu, 328–329
Mussaman Burj, *106*
Mussoorie, *39–40*
Mysore, *14, 273, 283–290*. ☞ *Also* Karnataka

Mysore Palace, *284–285*
Mythological murals, *304*

N

Nagarhole National Park, *273, 274, 289–290*
Nagaur, *13, 171*
Nagina Masjid (Agra), *106*
Nagina Mosque (Fatehpur Sikri), *112*
Nahar Garh Fort, *149, 152*
Nainital, *43–44*
Nakhoda Mosque, *373, 376, 377*
Nakki Lake, *179*
Nalanda, *134*
Nandi (Shiva's holy bull), *284*
Nandi Temple, *122*
Napier Museum, *310*
Narayan Sarovar, *203*
Nasik, *13*
Nathamal Ki Haveli, *183*
Nathdwara, *148, 180*
National Gallery of Modern Art (Bombay), *217, 221–222*
National Gallery of Modern Art (Delhi), *73, 74*
National Gandhi Museum, *76*
National Library, *381, 382*
National Museum (Delhi), *74*
National Museum and Art Gallery (Madras), *323, 324*
Naubat Khana, *111*
Nauchowki (Nine Pavilions), *180*
Nawab Asaf-ud-Daulah, *135*
Nawalgarh, *163*
Naya Mandir, *209*
Nazar Arts Gallery, *209*
Neelkanth Mahadev, *160*
Neemach Mata, *173, 175*
Nehru Cup snake-boat race, *308*
Nehru Memorial Museum, *74–75*
New Market (Calcutta), *373*
Nirmal Hirday, *373, 381, 382*
Nirona, *202*
Norbulingka Institute for Tibetan Culture, *26*
North and South Secretariats, *73*
North Central India, *6, 99–141*
Agra and environs, 10, 11, 13, 101, 102, 104–116
currency exchange, 140
dining, 100, 109, 113, 122, 129, 130, 134, 136
festivals and seasonal events, 13, 99–100, 118, 132, 137
guided tours, 140
itineraries, 101–102
Khajuraho, 10, 11, 13, 102, 116–124
lodging, 100–101, 109–110, 114, 116, 122–123, 130–131, 134, 136–137
nightlife and the arts, 99–100, 132, 137
shopping, 101, 110–111, 116, 123, 131–132, 137
transportation, 137–140
travel agencies, 140
Varanasi and Lucknow, 10, 12, 102, 124–125, 127–137
visitor information, 140–141
when to tour North Central India, 102
Nubra Valley, *36–37, 38–39*

O

Observatory Hill, *49*
Ochterlony Monument, *379, 381*
Old Goa, *260*
Old Satyanarayan Temple, *201*
Onam (festival), *14*
Orchha, *10, 102, 114–116*
Orissa, *14*
Osian, *166, 170*

P

Packages and tours, *xxix*
Packing for India, *xxiv–xxv*
Padam, *36*
Padmaja Naidu Zoo, *49*
Padmanabhapuram temple, *212*
Padmanabhaswamy Temple, *310*
Pagoda, *366*
Palace of Akbar's Turkish wife, *112*
Palaces
Ajanta and Ellora Caves, 244
Calcutta, 373, 376, 377
Delhi, 64, 65
Gujarat, 201, 203, 209
Himalayas, 34, 49
Hyderabad, 349, 350
Karnataka, 11, 14, 275, 276, 284–285, 293
Kerala, 303, 304
North Central India, 11, 104, 105–106, 107–109, 111–114, 115, 127, 130
Rajasthan, 12, 149–151, 152, 166, 167, 173–174, 180, 182
Tamil Nadu, 342
Palitana, *192, 207*
Palolem Beach, *260, 262*
Panaji, *14, 260*
Panch Mahal, *112*
Panchmukhi Mahadeva, *115*
Pandupol, *160*
Pang Lhabsol (festival), *14*
Pangong Tso, *36–38*
Panna National Park, *123–124*
Parasurasameswara Temple, *358, 360*
Paresnath Temple, *373, 376, 378*
Parishith Thampuran Museum, *303*
Parks, national, *41–42, 63, 123–124, 148, 159–161, 184, 191–192, 205–206, 273, 274, 289–290.* ☞ *Also* Wildlife sanctuaries
Parsvanath Temple, *119*
Parthasarathi Temple, *323, 324*
Parvati Temple, *122*
Passports, *xxv*
Patan, *199–200*
Pathar Darwaza, *389*
Patola saris, *199*
Patwon Ki Haveli, *183*
Pawagadh Fort, *209*
Peace Park, *179*
Pemayangtse, *53*
Penance of Arjuna (bas-relief), *332*
Phool Mahal (gardens), *115*
Phool Mahal (flower palace), *167*
Photography, *xi*
Pipli, *358, 366*
Plane travel, *x–xi*
Ajanta and Ellora Caves, 251
Bhubaneswar, 367
Bombay, 254
Calcutta, 390
with children, xii
Delhi, 94–95
Goa, 267
Gujarat, 210
Himalayas, 54–55
Hyderabad, 353
Karnataka, 294–295
Kerala, 313
North Central India, 138
Rajasthan, 185–186
Tamil Nadu, 343, 344
taxes, xxvii
Polo, *91, 156, 387*
Pondicherry, *318, 331–332, 337–338.* ☞ *Also* Tamil Nadu
Pongal (festival), *13*
Pony treks, *31*
Presidency College, *377*
Price charts
in Delhi, 61, 62
for dining, xv
for lodging, xxi
Prince of Wales Museum, *217, 222*
Pubs, *90–91, 281–282*
Punjab Government Museum, *20*
Pune, *14*
Puram (festival), *14*
Purana Qila (Old Fort), *70, 75*
Puri, *14, 358, 365*
Pushkar, *14, 162*
Pushkar Festival, *14*

Q

Qila-i-Kunha Masjid, *75*
Qutab Minar, *75–76*
Qutab Shahi Tombs, *349, 350*
Quwwat-ul-Islam Masjid, *75–76*

R

Rabindra Bharati University Museum, *373, 376, 378*
Rabindra Bhavan, *389*
Radhagobinda temple, *389*
Rafting
Himachal Pradesh, 31
Ladakh, 38
Sikkim, 52
Uttar Pradesh, 47
Raghurajpur, *358, 365*
Rai Praveen Mahal, *115*
Rail travel. ☞ Train travel
Raj Bhavan, *49*
Raj Ghat, *14, 76*
Raj Mahal, *115*
Rajarani Temple, *358, 360*
Rajasthan, *6, 143–188*
camel safaris, 169, 184
currency exchange, 187
dining, 144–145, 152–154, 161, 163–164, 167–168, 174–175, 178–179, 180, 1183
festivals and seasonal events, 13, 14, 162, 169, 171, 174
itineraries, 146, 148
Jaipur and environs, 10, 13, 14, 146, 148–162
Jaisalmer and environs, 12, 13, 146, 148, 181–184
Jodhpur and environs, 146, 148, 165–171
lodging, 145, 154–156, 159, 160, 161, 162, 163–165, 168–169, 170–171, 175–177, 178–179, 180, 183–184, 187
nightlife and the arts, 156, 169
outdoor activities and sports, 156, 169
Shekhavati, 12, 13, 63, 146, 148, 162–165
shopping, 145–146, 156–158, 170, 177–178, 184
tour operators, 187
transportation, 185–187
travel agencies, 188
Udaipur and environs, 12, 13, 146, 148, 171–180
visitor information, 188
when to tour Rajasthan, 148
Rajgir, *134*
Rajsamand Lake, *180*
Ram Bagh (gardens), *20*
Ram Nagar Fort and Palace, *127, 130*
Ram Raja Temple, *115*
Ramganga River, *46–47*
Ranakpur, *146, 148, 178*
Rang Mahal (Painted Palace), *69*
Rangeet River, *52*
Rani-ka-Vav, *199*
Ranikhet, *44–45*
Ranikhet Tweed and Shawl Factory, *45*
Ranthambhore Fort, *159*
Ranthambhore National Park, *148, 159*
Rashtrapati Bhavan, *74*
Rasmancha temple, *289*
Rath Yatra (festival), *14*
Ravechi, *204*
Red Fort Museum of Archaeology, *69*
Religion, *xxv–xxvi*
Republic Day, *13*
Residency, *135*
Residential Museum, *285*
Resorts, *252*
Restaurants. ☞ Dining
Rhododendron trek, *52*
Rock Fort, *338*
Royal Hammams, *69*
Royal Museum (Thanjavur), *340*
Royal Museum (Varanasi), *130*
Royal Stables, *113*
Rumi Darwaza, *135*

S

Sabarmati Ashram, *194–195*
Safaris, *30–31, 37–38, 169, 184, 272*
Safety, *xxvi*
Sahadeva, *333*
Sahasra Linga Tank, *199*
Sahasratal, *48*
Sahelion Ki Bari (Garden of the Maidens), *173, 174*
Sailing, *239, 266*
St. Francis Church (Cochin), *304*
St. Francis Church (Dalhousie), *28*
St. Francis of Assisi (Diu), *206*
St. George's Cathedral, *323, 324*
St. John's Church in the Wilderness, *26*
St. Mary's Church, *320, 323*
St. Mary's Island, *290*
St. Paul (church; Diu), *206*
St. Paul's Cathedral (Calcutta), *373, 379, 381*
Sajjan Garh, *173, 174*
Salar Jung Museum, *349, 351*
Salawas, *170*
Salim Chisti's tomb, *113*
Salim Singh Ki Haveli, *183*
Salim's Paper, *158*
Sam Sand Dunes, *184*
Sanganer, *158*
Sangeet Bhavan, *389*
Sangla, *33*
Sankat Mochan Temple, *127, 130*
Sansad Bhavan, *74*
Santa Cruz Cathedral, *304*
Saraswati Mahal Library, *340*
Saris, *199*
Sariska National Park, *63, 148, 159–160*
Sarnath, *14, 102, 132–133*
Sarnath Archaeological Museum, *132*
Sarod Ghar, *114*
Sas-Bahu Temple, *113*
Sassoon Dock, *220*
Satiyon ka Pagthiya, *182*
Sé (St. Catherine's Cathedral), *263*
Senior-citizen travel, *xxvi*
Shaare Rahamin, *222*
Shanti Stupa (Dhauli), *366*
Shanti Stupa (Leh), *34*
Shantinath, *119*
Shantiniketan, *389*
Shatrunjaya, *207*
Sheesh Mahal (Agra), *106*
Sheesh Mahal (Jaipur), *150*
Sheesh Mahal (Jodhpur), *167*
Sheesh Mahal (Orchha), *115*
Shekhavati, *12, 13, 63, 146, 148, 162–165.* ☞ *Also* Rajasthan
Shekhavati Festival, *13*
Sher Mandal, *75*
Shiladevi Temple, *151*
Shilp Darshan Mela (festival), *13*
Shilpgram, *174*
Shilpgram Utsav, *174*
Shimla, *xxxiii, 22–23, 30–31*
Shitala Temple, *127, 130*
Shiva Temple, *206*
Shivam Zari Palace, *64*
Shopping, *xxvi–xxvii, 8–9.* ☞ *Also under cities and areas*
Shore Temple, *332*
Shri Digamber Jain Temple, *158*
Shrinathji Temple, *180*
Shyamrai temple, *389*
Sidi Saiyad Mosque, *194, 195*
Sikar, *163*
Sikkim, *13, 14, 50, 52–53.* ☞ *Also* the Himalayas
Singh Pole, *150*
Sinquerim Beach, *260, 262*
Sisadia Rani ka Bagh, *149, 152*
Sisganj Gurdwara, *64, 69*
Skiing, *31–32*
Snake-boat race, *308*
Snow View, *43*
Soccer, *91, 387*
Somnath, *206*
South Park Street Cemetery, *373, 379, 381*

Southern Group of Temples (Khajuraho), *119–120*
Spiti, *29–30, 31, 32, 38.* ☞ *Also* the Himalayas
Sravanabelagola, *290*
Sri Chamundeswari Temple, *284*
Sri Chitra Art Gallery, *310*
Sri Jambukeswara Temple, *339*
Sri Jayachamarajendra Art Gallery, *285, 286*
Sri Kamakshi Temple, *336*
Sri Ma Naini Temple, *43*
Sri Ranganathaswamy Temple, *338–339*
Sriniketan, *389*
Study, *324, 325*
Sumrasar, *202*
Sun Temple, *11, 14, 364*
Sunset Point, *179*
Surajkund Crafts Mela (festival), *13*
Swamimalai, *341*
Sweitana Temple, *64, 69*
Swimming, *91, 266*
Synagogues, *216, 222, 303, 304–305*

T

Tabo Gompa monastery, *29*
Taj Mahal, *11, 104, 107–109*
Taj Mahal Museum, *109*
Taj Mahotsav (festival), *13*
Tamil Nadu, *6, 10, 316–345*
climate, xxxiii
consulates, 344
currency exchange, 344
dining, 316–317, 326–327, 334, 336, 337, 339, 340, 342
festivals and seasonal events, 13, 14
itineraries, 318
Kanchipuram, 318, 331–332, 335–337
lodging, 317, 327–328, 331, 334–335, 336, 337, 339, 340–341, 242
Madras, xxxiii, 11, 318, 320–321, 323–331
Madurai, 11, 14, 318, 338, 341–343
Mamallapuram, 11, 318, 331–335
name changes, 320
nightlife and the arts, 317, 328–329
outdoor activities and sports, 329
Pondicherry, 318, 331–332, 337–338
shopping, 317, 329–330, 337–338, 341, 343
Thanjavur, 318, 338, 340–341
Tiruchirapalli, 318, 338–339
transportation, 343–344
travel agencies, 345
visitor information, 345
when to tour Tamil Nadu, 318
Tamil Nadu State Legislature, *320, 323*
Tazia Tower, *182*
Taxes, *xxvii*
Teej (festival), *14*
Teesta River, *52*
Telephones, *xxvii–xxviii*
Teli ka Mandir Temple, *113*
Temple Art Museum, *341–342*
Temple of Lord Channakeshava, *291–292*
Temple of Lord Venkateshwara, *331*
Temple of the Guardian Deities, *34*
Temples
Bhubaneswar, 11, 14, 358, 359–360, 364, 365
Bombay, 11, 222, 223, 224
Calcutta, 373, 376, 377, 378, 381, 382, 388–389
Delhi, 64, 69, 70–71
Gujarat, 194, 199–200, 201, 204, 206, 207, 209
Himalayas, 18–19, 20, 25, 26, 29, 34–35, 42, 43, 45–46, 49
Karnataka, 11, 275, 284, 290, 291–292, 293
Kerala, 310, 312
North Central India, 11, 113, 115, 118–122, 125, 127, 128–129, 130, 132, 133
Rajasthan, 151, 158, 160, 163, 170, 173, 174, 178, 179, 180, 182, 183
Tamil Nadu, 14, 317, 323, 324, 325, 331, 332, 333, 334, 335–336, 338–339, 340, 341–342, 349
Tennis, *91*
Thai Monastery, *134*
Thanjavur, *318, 338, 340–341.* ☞ *Also* Tamil Nadu
Theater
Bombay, 236–237
Calcutta, 386
Delhi, 89
Karnataka, 290–291
Thekchen Choling temple, *26*
Thekkady, *302, 309–310*
Thiruvanaikkaval, *339*
Tibetan Children's Village, *26*
Tibetan Handicraft Center, *28*
Tibetan Institute of Performing Arts (TIPA), *26*
Tibetan Monastery, *134*
Tibetan Refugee Handicraft Center, *34*
Tiger Cave, *334*
Time, *xxviii*
Tiphaereth Israel Synagogue, *222*
Tipping, *xxviii*
Tipu's Palace, *275, 276*
Tirthan River, *30*
Tiruchirapalli, *318, 338–339.* ☞ *Also* Tamil Nadu
Tirukkalukundram, *334*
Tirumala Nayak Mahal, *342*
Tirupati, *331, 349, 354*
Tombs
Delhi, 70, 72–73
Guajarat, 194
Hyderabad, 349, 350
North Central India, 101, 102, 104, 106–107, 113, 135
Rajasthan, 161
Tour operators. ☞ *Under cities and areas*
Tours and packages, *xxix*
Towers
Bombay, 224
Delhi, 75–76
North Central India, 106
Rajasthan, 180, 182
Towers of Silence, *224*
Train travel, *xxix–xxxi*
Ajanta and Ellora Caves, 251
Bhubaneswar, 367
Bombay, 254
Calcutta, 390, 391
Delhi, 95
Goa, 267–268
Gujarat, 210, 211
Himalayas, 55–56
Hyderabad, 353
Karnataka, 272, 274, 295, 296
Kerala, 313
North Central India, 138–139
Rajasthan, 186
Tamil Nadu, 343, 344
Travel agencies, *xxxi.* ☞ *Also under cities and areas*
Traveler's checks, *xxiii*
Treasury (Fatehpur Sikri), *111*
Treasury (Lucknow), *135*
Trekking
Himachal Pradesh, 32–33
Ladakh, 38–39
pony, 31
Sikkim, 52
Uttar Pradesh, 47–48
Tribal Museum, *359, 360*
Trichur, *14*
Trichy. ☞ Tiruchirappalli
Trivandrum, *xxxiii, 302, 310*
Tso Moriri, *36–37*
Tunda Vandh, *203*

U

Udaipur and environs, *12, 13, 146, 148, 171–180.* ☞ *Also* Rajasthan
Udupi, *274, 290*
Ujjain, *13*
Umaid Bhawan Palace Museum, *166, 167*

Upper Mall Road (Ranikhet), *44*
Uttar Pradesh, *39–48.* ☞ *Also* the Himalayas
Uttarayan, *389*

V

Vadodara, *192, 208–210*
Vadodara Museum and Art Gallery, *209*
Vagator Beach, *262*
Vaidyanath Temple, *25*
Vaikunthaperumal Temple, *336*
Vaital Temple, *358, 360*
Vajrasan, *134*
Vamana Temple, *118*
Varadaraja Temple, *336*
Varah Temple, *120–121*
Varanasi, *10, 12, 102, 124–125, 127–137.* ☞ *Also* North Central India
Vedanthangal Bird Sanctuary, *318, 335*
Vegetable market (Bhuj), *201*
Velavadar Wildlife Sanctuary, *192, 208*
Victoria Memorial, *373, 379, 381*
Victoria Terminus. ☞ Chhatrapati Shivaji Terminus
Vidhana Soudha, *275, 276–277*
Vijay Stambh, *180*
Vijnana Kala Vedi Cultural Center, *308*
Viranarayana temple, *292*
Virupaksha Temple, *293*
Visas, *xxv*
Vishnupur, *388–389*
Vishabharati, *389*
Vishvanath Temple, *122*
Visitor information, *xxxi.* ☞ *Also under cities and areas*

W

War Memorial, *337*
Waterskiing, *266*
Weather, *xxii–xxxiii*
Web sites, *xxxi*
Western Group of Temples (Khajuraho), *120–122*
When to go, *xxxii–xxxiii*
Wildlife sanctuaries, *9–10, 11, 28, 41–42, 63, 123–124, 133, 148, 159–161, 180, 184, 191–192, 200, 205–206, 208, 273, 274, 289–290, 309, 318, 324, 325, 330, 335*
Windsurfing, *266*
Writers' Building, *379, 381*

Y

Yakshagana, *290–291*
Yiga-Choling monastery, *49*
Yoga, *91, 163*

Z

Zanskar, *38*
Zaveri Bazaar, *217, 222*
Zoological Garden (Mysore), *284, 285*
Zoos
Himalayas, 49
Karnataka, 284, 285